sendmail

sendmail

Bryan Costales
with Eric Allman & Neil Rickert

O'Reilly & Associates, Inc.
103 Morris Street, Suite A
Sebastopol, CA 95472

sendmail

by Bryan Costales with Eric Allman and Neil Rickert

Copyright © 1993 O'Reilly & Associates, Inc. All rights reserved.
Printed in the United States of America.

Editor: Tim O'Reilly

Production Editor: Ellen Siever

Printing History:

November 1993:	First Edition.
February 1994:	Minor corrections.
September 1994:	Minor corrections.

ISBN: 1-56592-056-2

[12/95]

Table of Contents

27: Defined Macros 413

28: Class Macros 447

Figures

Tables

Preface

King Gordias of Phrygia created a knot so complex that it spawned the myth that only the future ruler of Asia could untie it. Called the Gordian Knot, it defied all attempts to unravel it, until Alexander the Great eventually came along and cut it with his sword. For many years, system administrators world wide have been awaiting just such a sword with which to cut the Gordian Knot that is *sendmail*. Unfortunately, no such sword has ever materialized. So, as an alternative, two years ago I began the laborious process of untying that knot the hard way with this book.

But, you may ask, "why the effort?" Like the dinosaur, *sendmail* predates the dawn of computing time. Isn't it time to replace *sendmail* with something new, something better, something modern? Not so. Age has not brought *sendmail* retirement; rather, age has brought it maturity and reliability. The *sendmail* program has withstood the tests of time because it is more than just a program, it is a facility and a philosophy. The *sendmail* program is a general-purpose, internetwork mail-routing facility with a high degree of flexibility and configurablity. The philosophy is that one configurable program, *sendmail*, can solve the mail-routing needs of sites from large to small, and from complex to simple.

These strengths of *sendmail* are also its chief weaknesses. The price of configurability has been complexity. The *sendmail* program is difficult to configure and even more difficult to understand completely. Its configuration file, for example, can be positively frightening. But don't despair. With this book in hand, you should be able to configure *sendmail* to meet any need. I hope to bring the days of the *sendmail* guru to an end.

History

The *sendmail* program was originally written by Eric Allman while a student and staff member at the University of California at Berkeley. At the time, one campus machine (*Ingres*) was connected to the ARPAnet, and was home to the INGRES project for which Eric was working. Another machine (*Ernie CoVax*) was home to the Berkeley UNIX project and had recently started using UUCP. These machines (as well as several others on campus) were connected by a low-cost network built by Eric Schmidt, called Berk-Net. Software existed to move mail within ARPAnet, within UUCP, and within BerkNet, but none yet existed to move mail between these three networks.

The sudden increase in protocol types, coupled with the anticipation of an eventual explosion in the number of networks, motivated Eric to write *delivermail*—the precursor to *sendmail*. The *delivermail* program shipped in 1979 with 4.0 and 4.1 BSD UNIX. Unfortunately, *delivermail* was not flexible enough to handle the changes in mail transport requirements that actually occurred. Perhaps its greatest weakness was that its configuration was compiled-in.

In 1980, ARPAnet began converting from NCP (Network Control Protocol) to TCP (Transport Control Protocol). This change increased the number of possible hosts from 256 to over one billion. It also converted from a "flat" hostname space (like MIT-XX) into a hierarchical name space (like XX.MIT.EDU). Prior to this change, mail was transported using the *ftp* protocol (File Transfer Protocol). Afterward, a new protocol was developed for transporting mail called SMTP (for Simple Mail Transfer Protocol). These developments were not instantaneous. Some networks continued to run NCP years after most others switched to TCP. SMTP itself underwent many revisions before finally settling into its present form.

Responding to these and other changes, Eric converted *delivermail* into *sendmail*. To ensure that messages transferred between networks would obey the conventions required by those networks, Eric took a "liberal" approach—modifying messages to conform, rather than rejecting them. At the time, for example, UUCP messages often had no headers at all, so *sendmail* had to create them from scratch.

The first *sendmail* program was shipped with 4.1c BSD (the first version of Berkeley UNIX to include TCP/IP). From that first release to the present,*

---

*With one long gap between 1982 and 1990.

Eric has continued to modify and enhance *sendmail*, first at UC Berkeley, then at Britton Lee, and now back at UC Berkeley. The current version of *sendmail* is 8.x (or V8 for short). V8 is a major rewrite that includes many bug fixes and significant enhancements.

But Eric hasn't been the only one working on *sendmail*. In 1987, Lennart Lovstrand of the University of Linköping, Sweden, developed the IDA enhancements to BSD *sendmail* Version 5. IDA (which stands for "Institutionen för Datavetenskap") injected a number of improvements into *sendmail* (such as support of *dbm* files and separate rewriting of headers and envelope) and fixed a number of bugs. As the 90s approached, two offspring of IDA appeared.

Neil Rickert (Northern Illinois University) and Paul Pomes (The University of Illinois) took over maintenance of IDA *sendmail*. With contributions from around the world, their version (UIUC IDA) represents a continuation of the work begun by Lennart Lovstrand. Neil has focused on fixing and enhancing the configuration files into their current *m4*-based form. Paul has maintained the code, continually adding enhancements and fixing bugs. In general, their version is large, ambitious, and highly portable, and has succeeded in solving many complex mail transport problems.

A variation on IDA *sendmail* has also been developed by Paul Vixie (while at Digital Equipment Corporation). Called KJS (for King James) *sendmail*, it is a more conservative outgrowth of Lennart Lovstrand's last IDA release. The focus of KJS has been on code improvement rather than changes to configuration files.

In addition to these major offshoots, many vendors have modified *sendmail* to suit their particular needs. In general, many vendor versions are broken and should be avoided.

This explosion of *sendmail* versions has led to a great deal of confusion. Solutions to problems that work for one version of *sendmail* fail miserably with others. Beyond this, configuration files are not portable, and some features cannot be shared. Add to this the complexity of *sendmail*, and it becomes obvious that a book like this is needed.

Eric Allman Speaks

I have to admit that I'm surprised by how well *sendmail* has succeeded. It's not because of a large marketing organization or a deep-pockets budget. I think there are three reasons.

First, *sendmail* took the approach that it should try to accept, clean up, and deliver even very "crufty" messages instead of rejecting them because they didn't meet some protocol. I felt this was important because I was trying to gateway UUCP to the ARPAnet. At the time, the ARPAnet was small, UUCP was an anarchy (some say it still is), and UNIX mail programs generally didn't even understand headers. It was harder to do, but after all, the goal was to communicate, not to be pedantic.

Second, I limited myself to the routing function—I wouldn't write user agents or delivery backends. This was a departure from the dominant thought of the time, where routing logic, local delivery, and often the network code was incorporated directly into the user agents. But it did let people incorporate their new networks quickly.

Third, the *sendmail* configuration file was flexible enough to adapt to a rapidly changing world: the 1980s saw new protocols, networks, and user agents proliferate.

And, of course, it didn't hurt that it was free, available at the right time, and did what needed to be done.

Configuring *sendmail* is complex because the world is complex. It is dynamic because the world is dynamic. Someday *sendmail*, like X11, will die—but I'm not holding my breath. In the meantime, perhaps this book will help.

When I started reviewing Bryan's manuscript, I had been avoiding any major work on *sendmail*. But then I started reading about various petty bugs and annoyances that all seemed easy to fix. So I started making small fixes, then larger ones; then I went through RFC1123 to bring the specs up-to-date, cleaned up a bunch of eight-bit problems, and added ESMTP. It would be fair to say that the book and *sendmail* Version 8 fed on each other—each has improved the presence of the other.

Neil Rickert Speaks

I got into *sendmail* by necessity. We had a 4.2 BSD system which did not understand name servers, and we had just been connected to the Internet. If we were to have e-mail service, I had to master *sendmail* and DNS (Domain Naming System) in a hurry. I looked into IDA *sendmail* and, while I appreciated its flexibility, I quickly found things that I didn't like. Before long I was heavily involved in *sendmail*.

The most obvious feature of *sendmail* is its complex configuration, which has caused grief to many a system administrator. The *sendmail* program is often criticized for the way it is configured. That indeed is its weak point. But at the same time, it is also *sendmail*'s strong point, for it provides flexibility to set policy at run time. This flexibility has solved many problems in the complex world of UUCP mail, SMTP mail, BITNET gateways, MX forwarding, and gatewaying for PC networks.

We might hope for a simpler world where this extra flexibility is unnecessary. Doubtless we will someday reach such a wonderful state. But with the current rapid pace of technological change, I expect the flexibility of *sendmail* to be a valuable asset for quite a few years. I hope that this book will be an equally valuable asset.

Organization

We've divided this book into three parts, each addressing a particular aspect of *sendmail* as a whole.

Part I

Part One is a tutorial—a hands-on, step-by-step introduction to *sendmail* for the beginner and a succinct review for the more experienced user. Chapters 1 through 4 form an overview of e-mail in general, then the roles, behavior, and parts of *sendmail*. Chapters 5 through 14 examine the configuration file in detail. Along the way, we develop a mini-configuration file, suitable for use on some client workstations. Chapter 15 concludes the tutorial, appropriately tying up loose ends.

Part II

Part Two covers general administration of *sendmail* for the more experienced user. Chapter 16 shows how to obtain the source, and how to compile and install *sendmail*. It includes tips showing how to tune header behavior and illustrates the *checkcompat()* routine. Chapter 17 covers DNS in general and MX records specifically. Chapter 18 shows how to protect your site from intrusion. And Chapters 19 through 22 round out the picture with details about the queue, aliases, mailing lists, logging, and statistics.

Part III

Part Three is the nitty-gritty—a reference section that provides more detail about *sendmail* than you may ever need. Each chapter is dedicated to a specific aspect of *sendmail* or its configuration file. Chapter 27, for example, details defined macros, including an alphabetized reference. And Chapter 33 shows all the debugging switches, never before documented at all.

Audience

This book is primarily intended for system administrators who have been granted the dubious distinction of administering e-mail. But not all UNIX systems are managed by administrators. Many are managed by programmers, network engineers, and even by inexperienced users. It is our hope that this book speaks to all of you, no matter what your level of experience.

UNIX gurus (even those specializing in *sendmail*) should find Part Three to be of value. Even Eric keeps a copy on his desk. In it, every tiny detail of *sendmail* is listed alphabetically. There is, for example, a single chapter dedicated to options, with every option listed and explained.

The experienced system administrator who wants to install and manage either IDA or V8 *sendmail* should read Parts Two and Three first to gain the needed background. Then read Chapter 16, *Compile and Install sendmail*.

The nascent system administrator probably wants to use the vendor-supplied *sendmail* and simply make it work. Here, the tutorial in Part One will be of value. Then read Part Two for help in understanding how to administer *sendmail*. Finally, Part Three will reveal answers to those many nagging questions that seem to be otherwise undocumented.

The true beginner should begin with Part One, skipping ahead as needed for more detail in the other parts.

UNIX and sendmail Versions

For the most part, we illustrate *sendmail* under BSD UNIX and its variants (like SunOS 4.x). Where AT&T System V (SysV) differs, we show appropriate, alternative procedures.

Our primary focus throughout this book is on two different versions of *sendmail*:

- UIUC IDA Version 5.65c, from *ftp.uu.net*. This version has been pretty much stable since 1991.

- BSD V8 *sendmail*, from *ftp.cs.berkeley.edu*. This version continues to be developed. Our coverage of it ends with Version 8.6.

For completeness, and where necessary, we also discuss V5 and earlier* BSD *sendmail*, as well as the SunOS, Ultrix, and NeXT versions.

Conventions Used in This Handbook

The following typographic conventions are used in this book:

Italic   is used for names, including pathnames, filenames, program and command names, usernames, hostnames, machine names, and mailing-list names, as well as for mail addresses. It is also used to emphasize new terms and concepts when they are introduced. Finally, italic is used for program-produced variable output and to highlight comments. In the example `Too many trusted users` (*maxtrust* max), *maxtrust* is an integer showing the maximum.

---

*The versions jump from 5 to 8 because the managers of the BSD 4.4 UNIX distribution wanted all software to be released as version 8. Prior to that decision, the new BSD *sendmail* was designated Version 6. V6 survived only the alpha and beta releases before being bumped to V8.

Constant Width	is used in examples to show the contents of files or the output from commands. This includes examples from the configuration file or other files such as message files, shell scripts, or C language program source. Constant-width text is quoted only when necessary to show enclosed space; for example, the five-character "From " header.

Single characters, symbolic expressions, and command-line switches are always shown in constant-width font. For instance, the o option illustrates a single character, the rule $-$ illustrates a symbolic expression, and -d illustrates a command-line switch.

Constant Bold	is used in examples of interactive sessions to show commands or other text that would be typed literally by the user. For example, **cat /etc/sendmail.pid** means to type "cat /etc/sendmail.pid" exactly as it appears in the text or example.

Constant Italic	is used in examples to show variables for which a context-specific substitution should be made. In the string $num, for example, *num* will be a user-assigned integer.

%	denotes an ordinary user shell.

#	indicates a *root* shell.

Every example should be viewed as though it is text on a whiteboard. The surrounding paragraphs will reference text within the example. Such referenced text will match the font used in the example (sans bold), despite any other font conventions. For example:

```
# The name of the central mail hub
DHhub.us.edu
```

When we reference hub.us.edu in the example, we use constant width. But when we speak of *hub.us.edu* in the abstract, we use an italic font.

Acknowledgments

First and foremost, I must thank George Jansen, who literally spent months turning my first horrendous, stream of consciousness words into a form suitable for publication. He is truly the unsung hero of this work, and an editor extraordinaire.

Jon Forrest and Evi Nemeth both beat the tutorial chapters to death. Their feedback was extremely valuable in helping to trim and focus those chapters into a more useful form. Never let it be said that too many cooks spoil the broth—in this case they helped flavor it toward perfection.

Bruce Mah volunteered to be the guinea pig. In addition to learning *sendmail* from the (woefully unorganized) early drafts, he caught many grammatical errors that somehow slipped by all the others. Despite a heavy workload of his own, he somehow managed to stick with this project throughout.

Needless to say, this book would not have been possible at all if Eric Allman had not written *sendmail* in the first place. Every draft has passed through his hands, and he has spent many hours ensuring technical correctness, providing valuable insight, and suggesting interesting solutions to *sendmail* problems.

Equal praise must go to Neil Rickert. He too has seen every draft and provided enlightening feedback about IDA and, indeed, about all versions of *sendmail*. His insight into configuring *sendmail* has enriched both this book and the V8 configuration files.

Thanks and praise must go to Tim O'Reilly for wanting to do this book in the first place. His experience has shaped this book into the form it has today. He was aware of the "big picture" throughout and kept his hands on the pulse of the reader, and without his advice, a book this complex and massive would have been impossible.

Additional thanks must go to Lenny Muellner for tuning *troff* macros to satisfy the needs of this somewhat unique manuscript, and to Edie Freedman for gracefully accepting my unhappiness with so many cover designs until the current one, which I consider perfect.

The production folks at ORA did a yeoman's job of achieving an outstanding finished book. So a special thank you to Ellen Siever for copyediting the book and managing the project, Kismet McDonough for her help in each phase of the production, Chris Reilly for the figures, Jennifer Niederst for design help, Ellie Cutler for doing the index, and Gigi Estabrook for proofreading.

Just as some are thanked for what they did, others should be thanked for what they didn't. A thank you to Frederick M. Avolio for not spilling the beans until the last moment. And a thank you to Bill Carter for not being around during the last big push.

Finally, thanks to a list of folks, each of whom helped in small but notable ways: Kristin Jerger, Paul Pomes, Nelson Morgan, all the folks at the International Computer Science Institute, and to many of those who posted interesting questions to *comp.mail.sendmail.*

We'd Like to Hear From You

We have tested and verified all of the information in this book to the best of our ability, but you may find that features have changed (or even that we have made mistakes!). Please let us know about any errors you find, as well as your suggestions for future editions, by writing:

```
O'Reilly & Associates, Inc.
103 Morris Street, Suite A
Sebastopol, CA 95472
1-800-998-9938 (in the US or Canada)
1-707-829-0515 (international/local)
1-707-829-0104 (FAX)
```

You can also send us messages electronically. To be put on the mailing list or request a catalog, send email to:

```
info@ora.com      (via the Internet)
uunet!ora!info    (via UUCP)
```

To ask technical questions or comment on the book, send email to:

```
bookquestions@ora.com   (via the Internet)
```

I

Tutorial

The first part of this book is a tutorial mainly intended for those with a limited understanding of *sendmail*. Its aim is to provide the novice with an introduction to *sendmail* so that its more complex aspects may be readily comprehended and applied.

Chapter 1,   *Introduction*, covers MTA versus MUA, why *sendmail* is so complex, and gives an overview of some of *sendmail*'s parts.

Chapter 2,   *The E-Mail Message*, describes the differences between the header, body, and envelope of a mail message.

Chapter 3,   *The Roles of sendmail*, shows that *sendmail* can process aliases, queue messages for later transmission, deliver locally and remotely, and run in the background listening for incoming mail.

Chapter 4,   *How To Run sendmail*, illustrates use of the -b (become), -v (verbose), and -d (debugging) command-line switches.

Chapter 5,   *The sendmail.cf File*, provides a quick overview of all the commands found in the *sendmail.cf* file.

Chapter 6,   *Mail Delivery Agents*, describes the hub approach and shows how M (delivery agent) commands can be used to forward mail to a central hub machine.

Chapter 7,   *Macros*, shows how one text expression can be automatically propagated throughout the configuration file.

1

Introduction

Imagine yourself with pen and paper, writing a letter to a friend far away. You finish the letter and sign it, reflect for a while on what you've written, then tuck it into an envelope. You put your friend's address on the front of the envelope, your return address in the left-hand corner, a stamp in the right-hand corner, and the letter is ready for mailing. Electronic mail (e-mail for short) is similar, but instead of pen and paper, a computer is used.

The post office transports physical envelopes, whereas *sendmail* transports electronic envelopes. If the recipient (your friend) is local (in the same neighborhood or on the same machine) only a single *sendmail* or post office is involved. If the recipient is distant, the mail message will be forwarded from the local post office (local *sendmail*) to a distant one (remote *sendmail*) for delivery. Although the *sendmail* program is similar to the post office in many ways, it is superior in others:

- Delivery typically takes seconds rather than days. As a consequence, post office mail has come to be called "snail mail."

- Change of address (forwarding) is immediate. Making a change to the *aliases*(5) database (or a user's ~/.forward file) can cause mail to be forwarded anywhere in the world immediately.

- Other post office hosts are looked up dynamically. The *sendmail* program uses the Domain Naming System (DNS) to find where it should forward mail. Mail Exchanger (MX) records under DNS allow mail delivery to be easily switched from one machine to another. (DNS and MX records are discussed in Chapter 17, *DNS and sendmail*.)

- Electronic mail can be routed to or from other services. The *sendmail* program can deliver mail through programs that access other networks (like UUCP and BITNET). This would be like the post office delivering a package from United Parcel Service.

This analogy between the post office and *sendmail* will break down as we explore *sendmail* in more detail. But it serves a role in this introductory material, and we will continue to use it to illuminate a few of the *sendmail* program's more obscure points.

MUA Versus MTA

The acronym MUA stands for *mail user agent.* MUAs are any of the many programs users run to read, reply to, compose, and dispose of e-mail. Examples of MUAs include the original UNIX mail program, */bin/mail,* the Berkeley *Mail*(1) program, its System V equivalent *mailx*(1), free software programs like *mush*(1), *elm*(1), and *mh*(1), and commercial programs like *zmail.* (We won't be covering MUAs in this book.)

The acronym MTA stands for *mail transport agent.* MTAs are programs that handle mail delivery for many users and forward e-mail between machines. Other MTAs include *MMDF, Smail 2.x,* and *Zmailer.* (We'll only be covering *sendmail* in this book.)

An MUA is like the pen and paper with which you compose a letter. There may be many MUAs. An MTA is like the post office. There is usually only one MTA on a given machine.

The *sendmail* program (an MTA) is necessary because mail delivery is seldom simple. Some sites, for example, arrange for all e-mail to be forwarded to a central mail server. To discover this, an MUA would need to find, read, and understand the *sendmail* program's configuration file. It would also have to look up network information to see if mail should be forwarded to a different machine. And it would have to know if user information is stored in local or networked database files and how to access those files.

As the job of transporting mail extends beyond the local machine, the need for an MTA separate from the MUAs increases. The *sendmail* program can forward mail from one machine to another on the same network and can route mail from the current network to a totally different network.

Why Is sendmail So Complex?

In its simplest role, that of transporting mail from one local user to another, *sendmail* is almost trivial. All vendors supply a *sendmail* (and configuration file) that will accomplish this. But the job of *sendmail* becomes progressively more complicated, and the configuration file more difficult to modify (*tune*), as the need to provide a wider range of services increases. Hosts connected to the Internet, for example, need to make *sendmail* aware of the DNS. Hosts with UUCP connections, on the other hand, need to have *sendmail* run the *uux* program.

The *sendmail* program needs to route mail between a wide variety of networks. Consequently, its configuration file is designed to be very flexible. This allows a single binary to be distributed to many machines, while still allowing each machine to customize *sendmail* for its own particular needs. It is this configurability that makes *sendmail* complex.

Consider, for example, the need to deliver mail to a particular user. The *sendmail* program decides on the appropriate method based on its configuration file. One such decision process might include the following steps:

- If the user receives mail on the local machine, deliver the mail using the */bin/mail* program.
- If the receiving user's machine is connected to the sending machine using UUCP, the sending machine uses *uux* to send the message.
- If the receiving user's machine is on the Internet, the sending machine transfers the mail over the Internet.
- Otherwise, the message may need to be transferred to another network (like BITNET), or possibly rejected.

Some Parts of sendmail

The *sendmail* program is more than just a single program. It is a collection of programs, files, directories, and services. The key to *sendmail* is a configuration file that defines the location and behavior of all its other parts and includes rules for *rewriting* addresses. A queue directory holds mail until it can be delivered. An *aliases* file allows alternate names for users and enables development of mailing lists.

The Configuration File

The configuration file contains all the information *sendmail* needs to do its job correctly. The configuration file is a text file, with one piece of information per line.

One type of line provides a way to represent addresses and other text symbolically. Those symbols can later be used in place of the original text. Another type of line allows multiple items of text to be represented by a single symbol. Another provides necessary information to *sendmail*, such as file locations, permissions, and modes of operation.

Rewriting rules and rule sets are lines used to transform one address into another which may be required for delivery. They are perhaps the single most confusing aspect of the configuration file. Because the configuration file is designed to be fast for *sendmail* to read and parse, rules often can look cryptic to humans:

```
R$+@$+          $:$1<@$2>       focus on domain
R$+<$+@$+>       $1$2<@$3>       move gaze right
```

But, what appears to be complex is really just succinct. The R to the left of each line, for example, stands for *rewrite*, and the $+ expressions mean match one or more parts of an address. With experience, such expressions (and indeed the configuration file as a whole) soon become clear.

The Queue

Not all mail messages can be delivered immediately. Local resources, for example, may be temporarily unavailable (such as adequate disk space), or remote resources may be inaccessible (such as a remote host being down). When a message's delivery is delayed, *sendmail* must be able to save that message until the needed resource becomes available. The *sendmail* queue is a directory that holds mail until it can be delivered. A message may be queued because:

- The destination machine may be unreachable or down.
- When a message has many recipients, some messages may be successfully delivered and others may fail. Those that fail are queued for a later attempt.
- *Expensive* mail (such as mail to be sent over a low-speed line) can be queued for later delivery.
- For safety, *sendmail* can be configured to queue all mail messages.

Aliases and Mailing Lists

Aliases allow mail sent to one address to be redirected to another address. They also allow mail to be appended to files or piped through programs, and they form the basis of mailing lists. The heart of aliasing is the *aliases*(5) file (often stored in database format for swifter lookups). Aliasing is also available to the individual user via a file called *.forward* in the user's home directory.

Additional Information Sources

The *sendmail* program (in source form) comes with two documents by Eric Allman that are required reading. *Sendmail—An Internetwork Mail Router* provides an overview of *sendmail,* including its underlying theory. *Sendmail Installation and Operations Guide* provides installation instructions and a succinct description of the configuration file. Many vendors also provide online manuals when *sendmail* is supplied as a precompiled program. These documents may reveal vendor-specific customizations that may not be documented in this book.

The RFCs

A complete understanding of *sendmail* is not possible without at least some exposure to a series of documents issued by the Internet Engineering Task Force (IETF) at the Network Information Center (NIC). These numbered documents are traditionally called *Requests for Comments,* but are usually referred to by a kind of shorthand. Document number 822, for example, is usually called *RFC822.* RFCs are available via anonymous FTP from many sites, like *ftp.uu.net.* The RFCs of importance to *sendmail* are included with the *sendmail* source distribution.

RFC822

The division of mail messages into header and body portions, and the syntax and order of header lines are all defined in RFC822, titled *Standard for the Format of ARPA Internet Text Messages.* It also describes the form of addresses.

RFC821

When *sendmail* transports mail from one machine to another over a TCP/IP network, it does so using a protocol called the *Simple Mail Transfer Protocol*, or SMTP for short. SMTP is documented in RFC821. (SMTP messages are shown when *sendmail* is run with the –v (verbose) switch.)

RFC1123

RFC1123 is an extension to RFC821 and RFC822. It makes several amendments to the original documents and cleans up some previously ambiguous information.

RFC819

RFC819 is entitled *Domain Naming Convention for Internet User Applications* and describes the hierarchical form of machine naming used today. This document defines the form an address must take.

RFC976

RFC976 is entitled *UUCP Mail Interchange Format Standard* and describes the format for the transmission of messages between machines using UUCP.

Other Books

There are two areas of complexity that are only touched on in this book: The Domain Naming System (DNS), and the details of TCP/IP network communications. At a typical site, a significant number of mail-related problems turn out not to be problems with *sendmail*, but rather with one of these other areas.

The Domain Naming System is well documented in the book *DNS and BIND* by Paul Albitz and Cricket Liu (O'Reilly & Associates, Inc., 1992).

The protocols used to communicate over the Internet are called the TCP/IP system (for Transport Control Protocol/Internet Protocol). It is well documented in the book *TCP/IP Network Administration* by Craig Hunt (O'Reilly & Associates, Inc., 1992).

Finally, many mail problems only have solutions at the system administration level. The *sendmail* program is a *root*-owned process that can only be installed and managed by *root*. The art of functioning effectively as *root* is superbly covered in the *UNIX System Administration Handbook* by Evi Nemeth, Garth Snyder, and Scott Seebass (Prentice Hall, 1989).

2

The E-mail Message

Most users do not run the *sendmail* program directly. Instead they use any one of many mail user interfaces (MUAs) to compose and send e-mail. Those user interfaces invisibly pass that e-mail to *sendmail,* creating the appearance of instantaneous transmission. The *sendmail* program then takes care of delivery in its own mysterious fashion.

Run sendmail by Hand

Although most users don't run *sendmail* directly, it is perfectly legal to do so. You, like many system managers, will often need to do so as a means of tracking down and solving mail problems.

Here's a demonstration of one way to run *sendmail.* First, in a directory where you have write permission, like your home directory, create a file named *sendstuff* with the following contents:

```
This is a one line message.
```

Second, transmit this file to yourself by running *sendmail* directly with the following command line:

```
% /usr/lib/sendmail you <sendstuff
```

Here you have run *sendmail* directly by specifying its full pathname.* The *you* is your login name. It is supplied to *sendmail* as the single command-line argument. When you run *sendmail,* any command-line arguments that

---

*That path may be different on your system. If so, substitute the correct path in all the examples that follow.

do not begin with a – character are considered to be the names of recipients (the names of the people to whom you are sending the e-mail message).

The <sendstuff causes the contents of the file you created (*sendstuff*) to be fed (redirected) into the *sendmail* program. The *sendmail* program reads from its standard input and treats everything it reads (up to the end of the file) as the contents of the mail message that it should transmit.

Now view the mail message you just sent. How you view mail will vary. Many users just type *mail* to view their mail. Others use the *mh*(1) programs and must type *inc* to receive and *show* to view their mail. No matter how you normally view your mail, save the message you just sent to yourself in a file. That file ought to look something like this:

```
From you@Here.US.EDU  Sat Feb  7 08:11:44 1993
Delivery-Date: Sat, 07 Feb 93 08:11:45 PST
Return-Path: you@Here.US.EDU
Received: from Here.US.EDU by Here.US.EDU (4.1/1.11)
        id AA04599; Sat, 7 Feb 93 08:11:44 PST
Date: Sat, 7 Feb 93 08:11:43 PST
From: you@Here.US.EDU (Your Full Name)
Message-Id: <9102071611.AA02124@Here.US.EDU>
To: you

This is a one line message.
```

The first thing to note is that this file begins with nine lines of information that were not in your original message. Those lines were added by *sendmail* and your local delivery program. (The *sendmail* program does not deliver mail itself. Instead, it uses local programs like */bin/mail* to do the actual delivery. We'll cover this in more detail soon.) Those nine lines (which appear at the beginning of the message) are called the *header.*

The last line of the file is the original line from your *sendstuff* file. That line is separated from the header by one blank line. The contents of the mail message, everything following the first blank line that follows the header, is considered the *body* of the message (see Figure 2-1).

Ordinarily, when you send mail with your MUA, the MUA adds a header and feeds both a header and body to *sendmail.* This time, however, you ran *sendmail* directly and only gave it a message body.

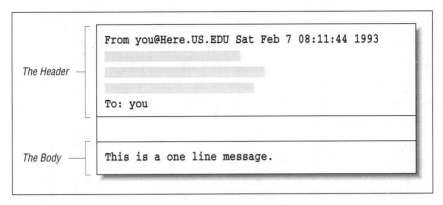

Figure 2-1: Every mail message is composed of a header and a body

The Header

All mail messages are composed of two parts, a header and a body. The header consists of all the lines of text from the first line until a blank line. The body is everything following that first blank line up to the end of the file. The first blank line is a part of neither.

There are many header lines that can appear in a mail message. Some are mandatory, some are optional, and some may appear multiple times. Those that appeared in the message you mailed to yourself were all mandatory. That's why they were added to your message. Let's examine that header in more detail.

```
From you@Here.US.EDU  Sat Feb  7 08:11:44 1993
Delivery-Date: Sat, 07 Feb 93 08:11:45 PST
Return-Path: you@Here.US.EDU
Received: from Here.US.EDU by Here.US.EDU (4.1/1.11)
        id AA04599; Sat, 7 Feb 93 08:11:44 PST
Date: Sat, 7 Feb 93 08:11:43 PST
From: you@Here.US.EDU (Your Full Name)
Message-Id: <9102071611.AA02124@Here.US.EDU>
To: you
```

The five character "From " line is only required by some programs (like */bin/mail)* and is not required by others (like *mh)*. In our example, it was added by */bin/mail*—the program that performed the actual delivery. (We show how to set up the actual delivery in Chapter 6, *Mail Delivery Agents.)*

The `Delivery-Date:` line shows the date and time that the message was delivered into your system mailbox. That line is usually added by the program that performs final delivery (usually */bin/mail)* rather than by *sendmail.* The *sendmail* program does not actually deliver mail to the user's mailbox. Instead it runs other programs to perform that delivery.

The `Return-Path:` line is added by *sendmail.* This line should contain the precise address that can be used by the recipient to reply to the sender. It should only be added on the host that performs final delivery, otherwise it could be misleading.

One `Received:` line appears for each machine that handled the message on its way from the sender to the recipient. Each machine that handles a mail message adds one of these lines. Each line constitutes a *hop.* If there are too many such lines (too many hops), the mail message will *bounce*—be returned to the sender as failed mail. Note that this header line actually occupies two lines in the file. The indented line below it is a continuation of the one above.

The `Date:` line gives the date and time that the message was originally sent. Depending on the vagaries of network connections and machines being up or down, that date can differ from the `Delivery-Date:` by several days. If the clocks on two machines are not synchronized, the `Delivery-Date:` may precede the `Date:`.

The `From:` line lists the e-mail address and the full name of the sender. The order of the two can legally be reversed, and, if so, would look like this:

```
From: Your Full Name <you@Here.US.EDU>
```

Note that the five-character "`From `" line is added by some delivery software and is not an official header like `From:`.

The `Message-Id:` line is like a serial number. It is constructed from the date, the time, a unique filename, and the originating machine name to form a string that is guaranteed to be unique worldwide.

The `To:` line shows a list of one or more recipients. Multiple recipients are separated from each other with commas:

```
To: name1,name2,name3
```

A complete list of all header lines of importance to *sendmail* is presented in Chapter 31, *Headers.* The important concept here is that the header precedes, and is separate from, the body in all mail messages.

The Body

The body of a mail message is comprised of everything following the first blank line to the end of the file. When *sendmail* reads a mail message from its standard input, it presumes that the message is composed of a header and a body. When you sent your *sendstuff* file it contained only a body.

Now edit the file *sendstuff* and add a small header so that it can be sent with *sendmail* once again.

```
Subject: a test                              ← add
                                             ← add
    This is a one line message.
```

The Subject: header line is an optional one. The *sendmail* program passes it through as-is. Here, the Subject: line is followed by a blank line and then the message text, forming a header and a body.

Send this file to yourself again, running *sendmail* by hand as you did before:

```
% /usr/lib/sendmail you <sendstuff
```

Notice that our Subject: header line was carried through without change:

```
From you@Here.US.EDU  Sat Feb  7 08:11:44 1993
Delivery-Date: Sat, 07 Feb 93 08:11:45 PST
Return-Path: you@Here.US.EDU
Received: from Here.US.EDU by Here.US.EDU (4.1/1.11)
        id AA04599; Sat, 7 Feb 93 08:11:44 PST
Date: Sat, 7 Feb 93 08:11:43 PST
From: you@Here.US.EDU (Your Full Name)
Message-Id: <9102071611.AA02124@Here.US.EDU>
Subject: a test                              ← note
To: you

    This is a one line message.
```

The Envelope

Any given mail message can have more than one recipient. Each recipient gets a copy of the mail message. For example, consider sending mail to yourself and to a user on another machine. You each get a copy of the mail message, but each copy is delivered on a different machine, and each takes a different route. (See Figure 2-2).

As we've mentioned, *sendmail* doesn't do the actual delivery. Instead it runs other programs, like */bin/mail,* to perform that delivery. However, when mail is being forwarded to another machine over a TCP/IP network, like Ethernet, *sendmail* itself can forward a mail message.

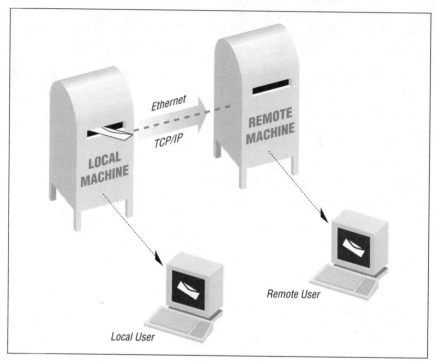

Figure 2-2: Local versus remote delivery

To handle delivery to diverse recipients, the *sendmail* program uses the concept of an *envelope.* This envelope is analogous to the physical envelopes used for post office mail. Imagine that you want to send two copies of a document, one to your friend in the office next to yours and one to a friend across the country:

```
To: friend1, friend2@remote
```

After you photocopy the document, you stuff each copy into a separate envelope. You hand one envelope to a clerk, who carries it next door and hands it to `friend1` in the next office. This is like */bin/mail* delivering the mail on your local machine. The clerk drops the other copy in the slot at the corner mailbox, and the post office forwards that envelope across the country to `friend2@remote`. This is like *sendmail* forwarding a mail message to a remote machine.

To illustrate the envelope, consider one way that *sendmail* might run the */bin/mail* program to perform local delivery:

```
          deliver to local mailbox
               ↓
/bin/mail -d friend1
              ↑
          the envelope recipient
```

Here the −d tells */bin/mail* to append the mail message to the system mailbox for the user friend1.

Information that describes the sender or recipient, but is not part of the message header, is considered envelope information. The two may or may not contain the same information. In the case of */bin/mail*, the e-mail message showed two recipients in its header:

```
To: friend1, friend2@remote
```

But the envelope information given to */bin/mail* only showed one (the one appropriate to local delivery):

```
-d friend1
```

To further illustrate the envelope, consider *sendmail* forwarding a mail message over the network. It too uses the concept of the envelope, as Figure 2-3 shows in this greatly simplified conversation between the local *sendmail* and the remote machine's *sendmail*.

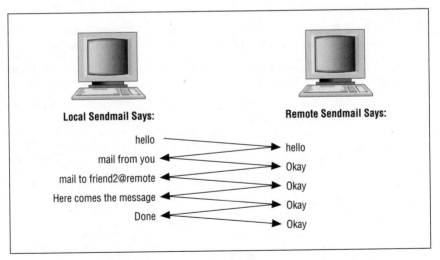

Figure 2-3: A simplified conversation

The local *sendmail* tells the remote machine's *sendmail* that there is mail from you and to `friend2@remote`. It conveys this sender and recipient information before it transmits the mail message that contains the header. Because this information is conveyed separately from the message header, it is called the envelope. There is only one recipient listed in the envelope, whereas there were two listed in the message header:

```
To: friend1, friend2@remote
```

The remote machine does not need to know about the local user, `friend1`, so that bit of recipient information is excluded from the envelope.

A given mail message can have many envelopes (like the two here), and the header will be common to them all. Clearly it is neither appropriate nor possible for the header to describe specific delivery in all cases. Envelopes are necessary to customize delivery to each recipient.

Things to Try

- Some files, like this chapter, contain lines that begin with the five characters "`From `" (the fifth character is a space). What UNIX utilities are available to aid in sending such a file with those lines intact?

- In the file *sendstuff*, we created a one-line header that began with `Subject:`. What would the effect be of making that header all lowercase? What does RFC822 have to say about this?

- How does *sendmail* behave when it is given a message that only contains a header? Does it add a blank line to create an empty body?

- If your MUA supports a `-v` (verbose) command-line switch, send mail to someone at a remote machine using that switch. You should be able to observe the actual conversation between the local *sendmail* and the remote machine's *sendmail*.

3

The Roles of sendmail

The *sendmail* program listens to the network for incoming network mail, and forwards mail messages to other machines. It hands local mail to a local program for local delivery and can deliver mail by *appending* to files and *piping* through other programs. It can queue mail for later delivery, and it understands the aliasing of one recipient name to another.

These are the roles of *sendmail*. On systems where *sendmail* is running properly, these roles are central to the flow of all electronic mail.

The File System Hierarchy

The *sendmail* program's position in the local file system hierarchy can be viewed as an inverted tree. When *sendmail* is run, it first reads its */etc/sendmail.cf* configuration file. Among the many items contained in that file are the locations of all the other files and directories that *sendmail* needs (Figure 3-1).

Usually the locations listed in the configuration file are specified as full pathnames (like */var/spool/mqueue* as opposed to *mqueue*). As the first step in our tour of those files, run the following command to gather a convenient list of them:

```
% grep "/[^0-9].*/" /etc/sendmail.cf
```

The output produced by the *grep*(1) command looks something like the following:

```
OA/etc/aliases
OQ/var/spool/mqueue
OS/etc/sendmail.st
OH/usr/lib/sendmail.hf
Mlocal,    P=/bin/mail, F=rlsDFMmnP, S=10, R=20, A=mail -d $u
Mprog,     P=/bin/sh,   F=lsDFMeuP,  S=10, R=20, A=sh -c $u
Muucp,     P=/bin/uux,  F=msDFMhuU,  S=13, R=23,
```

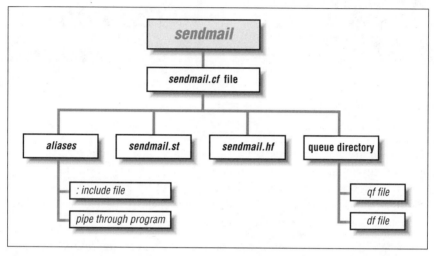

Figure 3-1: The sendmail.cf file leads to everything else

Notice that some lines begin with an O character, and others with an M character. The O marks a line as a configuration option. The options in the above describe the location of the files *sendmail* uses. The letter following the O is the name of the option. A, for example, defines the location of the *aliases*(5) file. The lines that begin with M define *delivery agents*. A delivery agent is a program that handles final local delivery to a user's mailbox (the `Mlocal`), handles delivery through a program (the `Mprog`), or forwards over a UUCP connection (the `Muucp`).

First we will examine the files in the O option lines. Then we will discuss local delivery and the files in the M delivery agent lines.

The Aliases File: /etc/aliases

Aliasing is the process of converting one recipient name to another. One use is to convert generic names (like *root*) to real usernames. Another is to convert one name into a list of many names (for mailing lists).

Take a few moments to examine your *aliases* file. The location of that file is determined by the OA option line in your *sendmail.cf* file. For example:

```
OA/etc/aliases
```

Compare what you find in your *aliases* file to the small example *aliases* file listed below:

```
# Mandatory aliases.
postmaster: root
MAILER-DAEMON: postmaster

# The five forms of aliases
John_Adams:     adamj
xpres:          nixon,ford,carter,reagan
oldlist:        :include: /usr/local/oldguys
nobody:         /dev/null
ftphelp:        |/usr/local/bin/sendhelp
```

Your *aliases* file is probably far more complex than this example. In reality, however, the few simple forms shown above are all it can contain.

Lines that begin with a # are comments. Empty lines are ignored. As the first comment indicates, there are two aliases that are mandatory in every *aliases* file. Both are the simplest form of alias: a name and what to change that name into. The name on the left of the : is changed into the name on the right. Names are not case sensitive. For example, POSTMASTER, Postmaster, and postmaster are all the same.

For every envelope that lists a local user as a recipient, *sendmail* looks up that recipient's name in the *aliases* file. (A local user is any address which would normally be delivered on the local machine. That is, *postmaster* is local, whereas *postmaster@remote* may not be.) When *sendmail* matches the recipient to one of the names on the left of the *aliases* file, it replaces that recipient name with the text to the right of the : character. For example, postmaster is replaced with root.

After a name is substituted, the new name is then looked up, and the process is repeated until no more matches are found. The name MAILER-DAEMON is first changed to postmaster. Then postmaster is looked up again and changed to root. Since there is no entry for root in the *aliases* file, the mail message is delivered into *root's* mailbox.

Every *aliases* file must have an alias for postmaster that will expand to the name of a real user. Mail about mail problems is always sent to postmaster.

When mail is bounced (returned because it could not be delivered for any of a number of reasons), it is always sent from MAILER-DAEMON. That alias is needed to handle the situation of users replying to bounced mail.

There are five forms that an *aliases* file line can take:

```
# The five forms of aliases
John_Adams:     adamj
xpres:          nixon,ford,carter,reagan
oldlist:        :include: /usr/local/oldguys
nobody:         /dev/null
ftphelp:        |/usr/local/bin/sendhelp
```

You have already seen the first (it was the form used to convert post-master to root). In the above example, mail sent to John_Adams is delivered to the user whose login name is adamj.

The xpres: line illustrates that one name can be expanded into a list of many names. Each of those new names is given a copy of the mail message, and each becomes a new name for further alias processing.

The oldlist: line illustrates that a mailing list can be read from a file. The expression :include: causes *sendmail* to read a file and to use the names in that file as the list of recipients.

The nobody: line illustrates that a name can have a file as an alias. The mail message is appended to the file. The */dev/null* file listed here is a special one. That file is an empty hole into which the mail message simply vanishes.

The ftphelp: line illustrates that a name can change into the name of a program. The | character causes *sendmail* to pipe the mail message through the program whose full pathname follows (in this case, the full pathname is */usr/local/bin/sendhelp*).

The *aliases* file has the potential of becoming very complex. It can be used to solve many special mail problems. The *aliases* file is covered in greater detail in Chapter 20, *Aliases.*

The Queue Directory: /var/spool/mqueue

A mail message can be temporarily undeliverable for a wide variety of reasons, such as a remote machine being down or a temporary disk problem. To ensure that such messages are eventually delivered, *sendmail* stores them in its queue directory until they can be delivered successfully.

The OQ line in your configuration file tells *sendmail* where to find its queue directory:

```
OQ/var/spool/mqueue
```

The location of that directory is a full pathname. Its exact location varies from vendor to vendor, but you can always find it by looking for the OQ line in your configuration file.

If you have permission, take a look at the queue directory. It may be empty if there is no mail waiting to be sent. If it is not empty, a listing of its contents will look something like this:

```
dfAA07038 dfAA08000 lfAA08000 qfAA07038 qfAA08000
```

When a mail message is queued, it is split into two parts, with each part saved in a separate file. The header information is saved in a file whose name begins with the characters qf. The body of the mail message is saved in a file whose name begins with the characters df.

In the above listing, there are two mail messages queued. One is identified by the unique string AA07038 and the other by AA08000.

The *sendmail* program periodically goes through the queue and attempts to deliver each message. While it is attempting delivery, it locks the message (to prevent simultaneous processing) by creating another file whose name begins with the characters lf.* In the above listing, the message identified as AA08000 is locked because *sendmail* is currently attempting delivery.

The internals of the queue files, and the processing of those files, is covered in Chapter 19, *The Queue*.

Local Delivery

Another role of the *sendmail* program is to deliver mail messages to local users on the local file system. That role can be accomplished by appending a message to a user's system mailbox, by feeding the mail message to a program, or by appending the message to a file other than the user's mailbox.

In general, *sendmail* does not deliver mail directly into files. You saw the exception in the *aliases* file, where you could specifically tell sendmail to append mail to a file. This is the exception, not the rule.

---

*Newer versions of *sendmail* don't use lf files.

In your *sendmail.cf* file are two lines that define local delivery agents, the ones that *sendmail* uses to deliver mail to the local file system:

```
Mlocal,    P=/bin/mail, F=rlsDFMmnP, S=10, R=20, A=mail -d $u
Mprog,     P=/bin/sh,   F=lsDFMeuP,  S=10, R=20, A=sh -c $u
```

The */bin/mail* program is used to append mail to the user's system mailbox. The */bin/sh* program is used to run other programs that handle delivery.

Delivery to a Mailbox: /bin/mail

The configuration file line that begins with `Mlocal` defines how mail is appended to a user's mailbox file. That program is usually */bin/mail*, but can easily be a program like *deliver*(1) or *mail-local*(8).

Under UNIX, a user's system mailbox is a single file that contains a series of mail messages. The usual UNIX convention (but not the only possibility) is that each message in that file begins with the five characters "`From `" and ends with a blank line.

The *sendmail* program neither knows nor cares what a user's system mailbox looks like. All it cares about is the name of the program it must run in order to add mail to that mailbox. In the example, that program is */bin/mail*. The `M` configuration lines that define delivery agents are introduced in Chapter 6, and covered in detail in Chapter 26.

Delivery Through a Program: /bin/sh

Mail addresses that begin with a `|` character are the names of programs to run. You saw one such address in the example *aliases* file:

```
ftphelp:     "|/usr/local/bin/sendhelp"
```

Here, mail sent to the address `ftphelp` is transformed via an alias into the new address `|/usr/local/bin/sendhelp`. The `|` character at the start of this new address tells *sendmail* that this is a program to run, rather than a file to append to. The intention here is that the program will receive the mail and do something useful with it.

The *sendmail* program doesn't run mail delivery programs directly. Instead it runs a shell and tells that shell to run the program. The name of the shell is listed in the configuration file in a line that begins with `Mprog`:

```
Mprog,     P=/bin/sh,   F=lsDFMeuP,  S=10, R=20, A=sh -c $u
```

In this example, the shell is the */bin/sh*(1). Other programs can appear in this line. A somewhat uncommon alternative is */bin/ksh*(1), the Korn Shell.

Network Forwarding

Another role of *sendmail* is that of forwarding mail to other machines. A message is forwarded when *sendmail* determines that the recipient is not local. The following lines from a typical configuration file define delivery agents for forwarding mail to other machines:

```
Mether,     P=[TCP], F=msDFMuCX, S=11, R=21, A=TCP $h
Muucp,      P=/bin/uux, F=msDFMhuU, S=13, R=23, A=uux - -r $h!rmail ($u)
```

The actual lines in your file may differ. The name `ether` in the above example may appear in your file as `tcpld` or `ddn` or something else. The name `uucp` may appear as `uucp-l` or `uucp-d`. There may be more such lines than we've shown here. The important point for now is that some `M` lines deal with local delivery, while others deal with network forwarding.

TCP/IP

The *sendmail* program has the *internal* ability to forward mail over only one kind of network, one that uses TCP/IP. The line that instructs *sendmail* to do this is:

```
Mether,     P=[TCP], F=msDFMuCX, S=11, R=21, A=TCP $h
```

The `[TCP]` may appear as `[IPC]`. The two are equivalent.

When *sendmail* forwards mail on a TCP/IP network, it first sends the envelope sender address to the other site. If the other site accepts the sender name as legal, the local *sendmail* then sends the envelope recipient list. The other site accepts or rejects each recipient one by one. If any recipients are accepted, the local *sendmail* sends the message (header and body together).

UUCP

The line in the configuration file that tells *sendmail* how to forward over UUCP looks like this:

```
Muucp, P=/bin/uux, F=msDFMhuU, S=13, R=23, A=uux - -r $h!rmail ($u)
```

This line tells *sendmail* to send UUCP network mail by running the */bin/uux* program. The *uux*(1) program (for *UNIX to UNIX eXecute*) is only given the list of recipient names from the envelope. It reads the mail message, header and body, from its standard input.

Other Protocols

There are many other kinds of network protocols that *sendmail* can use to forward e-mail. Some of them may have shown up when you ran *grep* earlier. Other common possibilities are:

```
MFAX,  P=/usr/lib/phquery,  F=DFMhnmur,     A=phquery -x fax $u
MDmail,      P=/usr/bin/mail11v3, F=CmnXNH, S=10, R=14, A=mail11 $g $x $h
Mmac,  P=/usr/bin/macmail,  F=CDFMmpsu, R=16, S=16, A=macmail -t $u
```

The MFAX line defines one of the many possible ways to send a FAX using *sendmail*. FAX (for *facsimile transmission*) is a kind of office-to-office network. In it, images of documents are transmitted over telephone lines. In the configuration line above, the */usr/lib/phquery* program is run, and a mail message is fed to it for conversion to and transmission as a FAX image.

The MDmail line defines a way of using the *mail11*(1) program to forward e-mail over DECnet. A DECnet network is mostly used by DEC (Digital Equipment Corporation) machines that run the VMS operating system.

The Mmac line defines a way to forward mail to Macintosh machines that are connected together on an AppleTalk network.

In all of these examples, note that *sendmail* forwards e-mail over other networks by running programs tailored specifically to that use. Remember that the only network that *sendmail* can forward over directly is a TCP/IP-based network. (Actually we're fudging for simplicity. V8 *sendmail* can also send messages over an ISO network.)

The sendmail Daemon

Just as *sendmail* can forward over a TCP/IP-based network, it can also receive mail that is forwarded to it over that network. To do this, it must be run in *daemon* mode. A daemon is a program that runs in the background and is independent of control from all terminals.

As a daemon, *sendmail* is run once, usually when your machine is booted. It runs in the background and *listens* to the TCP/IP network. Whenever an e-mail message is sent to your machine, the sending machine talks to the *sendmail* daemon listening on your machine.

To see how your system runs *sendmail* in daemon mode, run one of the following two commands:

```
% grep sendmail /etc/rc*
% grep sendmail /etc/init.d/*
```

The first line is for most BSD-based UNIX systems. The second line is for most System V-based UNIX systems. One typical example of what you will find is:

```
/etc/rc.local:if [ -f /usr/lib/sendmail -a -f /etc/sendmail.cf ]; then
/etc/rc.local:    /usr/lib/sendmail -bd -q1h; echo -n ' sendmail'
```

This shows that *sendmail* is run at boot time with a command line of:

```
/usr/lib/sendmail -bd -q1h
```

The `-bd` command-line switch tells *sendmail* to run in daemon mode. The `-q1h` command-line switch tells *sendmail* to wake up once per hour and process the queue.

Things to Try

- When your machine boots, it executes the commands in one or more Bourne shell scripts. Examine the script that runs the *sendmail* program in daemon mode. Write a small Bourne shell script that checks for the existence of the *echo*(1) program and then executes that program. Model it around the way *sendmail* is run.

- For each program that is mentioned in your configuration file's M lines (like */bin/mail* and */bin/uux*) read the appropriate online manual. Examine the possible command-line arguments to determine how envelope information is passed. Compare what you discover to the A= part of each corresponding M line.

- Locate all the files mentioned in O lines in your configuration file. For any that exist, what kind of file is it, data or text? If it is text, read it. What purpose do you suppose it has?

4

How to Run sendmail

As you saw in the last chapter, one way to run *sendmail* is simply to give it the name of a recipient as its single command-line argument. Multiple recipient addresses can also be given. For example, the following will send the mail message to george, truman, and teddy.

```
% /usr/lib/sendmail george,truman,teddy
```

In general, the *sendmail* program understands two different kinds of command-line arguments. Arguments that *do not* begin with a − character (like george) are assumed to be recipient addresses. Arguments that *do* begin with a − character are taken as switches that modify the behavior of *sendmail*. The switch-style command-line arguments we will cover in this chapter are shown in Table 4-1.

Table 4-1: Some Command-line Switches

Flag	Description
−b	Set operating mode
−v	Run in verbose mode
−d	Run in debugging mode

The complete list of switch-style command-line line arguments, along with an explanation of each, is presented in the reference part of this book in Chapter 32, *The Command Line*.

Become Mode (−b)

The *sendmail* program can function in a number of different ways (*become something else*) depending on the form of the −b argument you give to it. One form, for example, causes it to print the contents of the queue and exit. Another causes it to rebuild the *aliases* database and exit. The complete list of all of the −b command-line mode-setting switches is shown in Table 4-2.

Table 4-2: Forms of the −b Command-line Switch

Flag	Description
−ba	Use old-style ARPAnet protocols (obsolete)
−bd	Run as a daemon
−bi	Initialize alias database
−bm	Be a mail sender
−bp	Print the queue
−bs	Run SMTP on standard input
−bt	Test mode: resolve addresses only
−bv	Verify: don't collect or deliver
−bz	Freeze the configuration file

We will only cover a few forms in this chapter. Others will make appearances as this tutorial proceeds. The complete list is discussed in Chapter 32, *The Command Line*.

A few of the options shown in Table 4-2 are available by running *sendmail* under different names. Those names, and a description of their functions, are shown in Table 4-3.

Table 4-3: Other Names for sendmail

Name	Flag	Description
smtpd	−bd	Run as a daemon
newaliases	−bi	Initialize alias database
mailq	−bp	Print the queue
bsmtpd	−bs	Single-connect SMTP

The fact that a program can have different names requires a brief explanation. Under UNIX, a program is a file on disk, and that file is only known to the system by its *inode* number. We won't go into the details of inodes, except to mention that each disk file has a unique inode number associated with it.

Program names are really just entries in directories. Each directory entry is composed of a name (so that users can identify that disk file with a human-understandable name), and an inode number (so that the disk file can be located by the system). Thus, it is perfectly legal for two different filenames, in the same or different directories, to each point to the same inode or disk file (see Figure 4-1).

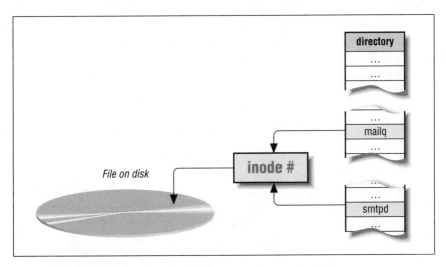

Figure 4-1: Disk files may have multiple names

When a program is run, it is given its command line as an array of strings. The zeroth argument (`argv[0]` in the C language) is always the name that is used to run the program. When *sendmail* is run, it looks at its `argv` and checks to see what name was used to run it. If that name is *smtpd*, it functions in exactly the same way it would if it had been given the -bd command-line switch. If that name is *mailq*, it functions in exactly the same way it would if it had been given the -bp command-line switch, and so on.

Daemon Mode (–bd)

The *sendmail* program can become a daemon, running in the background and listening for incoming mail from other machines.

As an administrator of your site's mail system, you will occasionally need to kill the currently running *sendmail* daemon and start a new one. This is necessary because *sendmail* only reads its configuration file once, when it first starts. When it starts as a daemon, it reads its configuration file and then continues to run forever, never reading the configuration file again. As a consequence, it will never know of any changes in that configuration file.

When you, as an administrator, change something in the *sendmail.cf* configuration file, you *always* need to kill and restart the *sendmail* daemon. But, before you can kill the daemon, you need to know how to correctly restart it. This information is in one of your system *rc* files.

On a Berkeley UNIX-based system, the daemon is usually started like this:

```
/usr/lib/sendmail -bd -q1h
```

On an AT&T System V-based system, it is often started like this:

```
/usr/lib/sendmail -bd -q15m &
```

Both use the `-bd` command-line switch to specify daemon mode. The `-q` switch tells *sendmail* how often to look in its queue for pending mail and to process any that it finds. The `-q1h` switch says to process the queue once per hour (the `1h`), and the `-q15m` switch says to process the queue once per quarter hour (fifteen minutes, the `15m`).

The actual command to start the *sendmail* daemon on your system may be more or less complex than we've shown. If you manage many different brands of systems, you'll need to be familiar with starting the daemon on all of them.

Before you can start the *sendmail* daemon, you need to make sure there is not already a daemon running. This is done by using the *ps*(1) program. How you run *ps* is different on BSD UNIX and System V UNIX. For BSD UNIX, the command you use and the output it produces resemble the following:

```
% ps ax | grep sendmail | grep -v grep
   99   ?   IW    0:07 /usr/lib/sendmail -bd -q1h
```

For System V-based systems, you use a slight variation on the *ps* command, and the look of the output differs:

```
% ps -ae | grep sendmail
   165 ?          0:01 sendmail
```

In either case, the *pid* (process identification number) of the currently-running *sendmail* daemon is the leftmost number printed. Once you have that *pid*, you can kill the currently running *sendmail* daemon using the *kill*(1) command. The complete process of killing and starting a new *sendmail* daemon on a System V machine looks similar to the following:

```
% grep "sendmail.*-bd" /etc/init.d/*
/etc/init.d/mail:     /usr/lib/sendmail -bd -q15m &
% ps -ae | grep sendmail
   165 ?          0:01 sendmail
% kill 165
% /usr/lib/sendmail -bd -q15m
```

The process of killing *sendmail* on BSD systems is similar.

Under IDA and V8 *sendmail*, the *pid* of the currently running daemon can be found in the file */etc/sendmail.pid.* If you are running either of those versions, the processes of killing the daemon will look like this:

```
% kill `cat /etc/sendmail.pid`      ← IDA
% kill `head -1 /etc/sendmail.pid`  ← V8
```

Take the time to learn the particulars of how to kill and start a new *sendmail* daemon on your machine. Whenever you change your *sendmail.cf* configuration file, you need to kill and start a new daemon because the old daemon has no way of knowing about the changes in that file.

If you forget to kill the daemon first, you may see the following message, and the attempt to run a second daemon will fail:

```
getrequest: cannot bind: Address already in use
```

Unfortunately, we must now introduce complexity into what you have just learned. The way *sendmail* performs most of its jobs is using *fork*(2). When *sendmail* forks, it creates an exact copy of itself. That copy is called the *child* process. The original is called the *parent* process. The child process handles one specific task on behalf of the parent. The parent, in the meantime, continues to run doing other important tasks. This multiplicity is necessary if *sendmail* is to perform its job most efficiently.

For example, suppose that the *sendmail* daemon is listening for incoming mail. Once each quarter hour, that daemon looks in the queue for any pending outgoing mail, and, if it finds any, processes the queued messages.

If *sendmail* didn't fork, it would be unable to listen for incoming mail while it was processing the queue.

But because *sendmail* forks, and because it can fork many times and produce many children, you should avoid killing the daemon while any of its offspring are alive. The way you detect children is exactly the same as finding the *pid* to kill the daemon. That is, with the *ps* program.

The following example illustrates *ps* on a BSD UNIX-based machine. The output shows that there are two *sendmail* programs running. The one in the parentheses is the child. Before you kill the *sendmail* daemon, you should rerun *ps* periodically until there are no children listed.

```
% ps ax | grep sendmail | grep -v grep
   99    ?  IW    0:07 /usr/lib/sendmail -bd -q1h
 16858 ?  S     0:00 -AA16803 (sendmail)
```

Show Queue Mode (–bp)

Another function of *sendmail* is its ability to display the contents of the queue directory. It can do that in two ways, as a program named *mailq* or under its own name with the -bp command-line switch. Whichever way you run it, it prints the contents of the queue directory and exits. If the queue is empty, *sendmail* prints the following:

```
Mail queue is empty
```

If, on the other hand, there is mail waiting in the queue, the output is far more verbose, possibly containing lines similar to these:

```
                Mail Queue (1 requests)
--QID-- -Size- ----Q-Time----- ------------Sender/Recipient------------
AA29775   702 Thu Mar 12 16:51 <you@here.us.edu>
          Deferred: Host fbi.dc.gov is down
                             <george@fbi.dc.gov>
```

Here the output produced by the -bp switch shows that there is only one mail message in the queue. If there were more, each entry would look pretty much the same as this. Each is composed of at least two lines.

The first line always shows details about the message and the sender. The AA29775 is the identification part for the qf (header) and df (body) queue files. That identifier is followed by the size of the message body (the size in bytes of the df file), and the date that this message was originally queued. This line ends with the name of the sender.

A second line may appear giving a reason for failure (if there was one). A message may be queued intentionally or because it couldn't be delivered.

The third line shows the addresses of the recipients.

The output produced by the -bp switch is covered in Chapter 19, *The Queue.*

Rebuild Aliases Mode (–bi)

Because *sendmail* may have to search through thousands of names in the *aliases* file, that file is usually stored on disk in *dbm*(3) database format.* The use of a database significantly improves lookup speed.

Although *sendmail* is able to automatically update that database whenever the *aliases* file is changed, there will be times when you will need to rebuild it yourself. You do this by either running *sendmail* under the name *newaliases* or with the -bi command-line switch. Both of the following command lines accomplish the same thing:

```
% /usr/lib/sendmail -bi
% newaliases
```

When you enter either command, there is a delay while *sendmail* rebuilds the *aliases* database. After it is rebuilt, *sendmail* prints a summary of what it did:

```
859 aliases, longest 615 bytes, 28096 bytes total
```

This line shows four things. First it shows that the database was successfully rebuilt. Then it shows the number of aliases processed, the size of the biggest entry to the right of the : in the *aliases* file, and the total number of bytes entered into the database.

The *aliases* file and the ways to manipulate that file are covered in Chapter 20, *Aliases.*

Verify Mode (–bv)

A handy tool for checking aliases is the -bv command-line switch. That switch causes *sendmail* to recursively look up a name in the *aliases*(5) file and report the ultimate real name that it found.

---

*V8 *sendmail* uses the faster *hash*(3) format.

To illustrate, consider the following abstract from a complex *aliases* file:

```
animals:        farmanimals,wildanimals
bill-eats:      redmeat
birds:          farmbirds,wildbirds
bob-eats:       seafood,whitemeat
farmanimals:    pig,cow
farmbirds:      chicken,turkey
fish:           cod,tuna
redmeat:        animals
seafood:        fish,shellfish
shellfish:      crab,lobster
ted-eats:       bob-eats,bill-eats
whitemeat:      birds
wildanimals:    deer,boar
wildbirds:      quail
```

Although you can figure out what the name `ted-eats` ultimately expands to, it is far easier to have *sendmail* perform that task for you. By using *sendmail*, you have the added advantage of being assured accuracy, which is especially important in large and complex *aliases* files.

In addition to expanding aliases, the `-bv` switch performs another important function. It verifies whether or not the expanded aliases are in fact deliverable. Consider the following one-line abstract from an *aliases* file:

```
root:       fred,larry
```

In this example, the user `fred` is the system administrator and has an account on the local machine. The user `larry`, however, has left, and his account has been removed. You can run *sendmail* with the `-bv` switch to see if both names are valid:

```
% /usr/lib/sendmail -bv root
```

This tells *sendmail* to verify the name `root` from the *aliases* file. Since `larry` (one of `root`'s aliases) doesn't exist, the output produced looks like this:

```
larry... User unknown
fred... deliverable
```

Verbose Mode (–v)

The `-v` command-line switch tells *sendmail* to run in *verbose* mode. In that mode, *sendmail* prints a blow-by-blow description of all the steps it is taking in delivering a mail message. To watch *sendmail* run in verbose mode, send mail to yourself as you did in the Chapter 2, *The E-mail Message*:

```
% /usr/lib/sendmail -v you < sendstuff
```

The *-v* switch causes *sendmail* to run in verbose mode. The output produced shows that *sendmail* delivers your mail locally:

```
you... Connecting to  via local...
you... Sent
```

When *sendmail* forwards mail to another machine over a TCP/IP-based network, it communicates with that other machine using a language called SMTP (Simple Mail Transfer Protocol). To see what SMTP looks like, run *sendmail* once again, but this time, instead of using *you* to make yourself the recipient, give *sendmail* your address on another machine.

```
% /usr/lib/sendmail -v you@remote.domain < sendstuff
```

In place of the *you@remote.domain*, put your e-mail address at some other machine on which you have an account. The output produced by this command line will look similar to the following:

```
you@remote.domain... Connecting to remote.domain via ether...
Trying 123.45.123.4... connected.
220 remote.Domain Sendmail 4.1/1.11 ready at Fri, 13 Mar 92 06:36:12 PST
>>> HELO here.us.edu
250 remote.domain Hello here.us.edu, pleased to meet you
>>> MAIL From:<you@here.us.edu>
250 <you@here.us.edu>... Sender ok
>>> RCPT To:<you@remote.domain>
250 <you@remote.domain>... Recipient ok
>>> DATA
354 Enter mail, end with "." on a line by itself
>>> .
250 Mail accepted
>>> QUIT
221 remote.domain delivering mail
you@remote.domain... Sent
```

The lines that begin with numbers and the lines that begin with >>> characters constitute the SMTP conversation. We'll discuss those shortly. The first two lines, and the last line, are *sendmail* on your local machine telling you what it is trying to do and what it has successfully done:

```
you@remote.domain... Connecting to remote.domain via ether...
Trying 123.45.123.4... connected.
...
you@remote.domain... Sent
```

The first line shows to whom the mail is addressed and that the machine `remote.domain` is on the network. The second line shows the Internet address of the machine named `remote.domain`. The last line simply confirms that the mail message was successfully sent.

The middle thirteen lines constitute the SMTP conversation:

```
220 remote.Domain Sendmail 4.1/1.11 ready at Fri, 13 Mar 92 06:36:12 PST
>>> HELO here.us.edu
250 remote.domain Hello here.us.edu, pleased to meet you
>>> MAIL From:<you@here.us.edu>
250 <you@here.us.edu>... Sender ok
>>> RCPT To:<you@remote.domain>
250 <you@remote.domain>... Recipient ok
>>> DATA
354 Enter mail, end with "." on a line by itself
>>> .
250 Mail accepted
>>> QUIT
221 remote.domain delivering mail
```

In the above conversation, your local machine displays what it is saying to the remote host by preceding each line with `>>>` characters. The messages (replies) from the remote machine are displayed with leading numbers. We now explain that conversation.

```
220 remote.Domain Sendmail 4.1/1.11 ready at Fri, 13 Mar 92 06:36:12 PST
```

Once your *sendmail* has connected to the remote machine, your *sendmail* waits for the other machine to initiate the conversation. The other machine says it is ready by sending the number 220 followed by its name (the only required information); the program name (usually, but not always, *sendmail*); and the version of that program. It also states that it is ready and gives its idea of the local date and time.

If your sendmail waits too long for a connection without receiving this initial message, it prints "Connection timed out" and queues the mail message for later delivery.

```
>>> HELO here.us.edu
250 remote.domain Hello here.us.edu, pleased to meet you
```

Next the local *sendmail* sends (the `>>>`) the word HELO, for hello, and its own hostname. The remote machine replies with `250` and the acknowledgment that your hostname is acceptable. One problem would occur here if your machine sent its short name in the HELO message to a Sun system. The remote Sun would think that the short name was part of its domain and reply with an error, that it never heard of `here` in the domain `remote.domain`. This is one reason why it is important for your *sendmail* to always use your machine's fully-qualified domain name. A fully-qualified name is one that begins with the host's name, followed by a dot, then the entire DNS domain.

```
>>> MAIL From:<you@here.us.edu>
250 <you@here.us.edu>... Sender ok
```

If all has gone well so far, the local machine sends the name of the sender from the envelope of the mail message. Here that sender address is accepted by the remote machine.

```
>>> RCPT To:<you@remote.domain>
250 <you@remote.domain>... Recipient ok
```

Next the local machine sends the name of the recipient from the envelope for the mail message. If the user you were not known to the remote machine, it would reply with an error of "User unknown."

```
>>> DATA
354 Enter mail, end with "." on a line by itself
>>> .
```

After the envelope information has been sent, your *sendmail* then attempts to send the mail message (header and body combined). The DATA essentially tells the remote "get ready." (The message data is not printed as it is sent.) A dot on a line by itself is used to mark the end of a mail message. This is a convention of the SMTP language. Because mail messages may contain lines that begin with dots as a valid part of the message, *sendmail* doubles each such beginning dot before it is sent. For example, consider sending the following explanatory text through the mail:

```
My results matched yours at first:
126.71
126.72
.
.
...
126.79
But then the numbers suddenly jumped high, looking like
noise saturated the line.
```

To prevent any of these lines from being wrongly interpreted as the end of the mail message, *sendmail* inserts an extra dot at the beginning of any line that begins with a dot.

```
My results matched yours at first:
126.71
126.72
..
..
....
126.79
```

```
But then the numbers suddenly jumped high, looking like
noise saturated the line.
```

The program running at the receiving end (for example, another *sendmail*) strips those extra dots when it receives the message:

```
250 Mail accepted
>>> QUIT
221 remote.domain delivering mail
```

After the mail message has been successfully sent, the local *sendmail* sends QUIT to say it is all done. The remote machine acknowledges that it is delivering the mail that was sent to it.

The -v (verbose) switch for *sendmail* is most useful with mail sent to other machines. It allows you to watch the SMTP conversation as it occurs and can help in tracking down the reasons why some mail messages fail to reach their destinations.

Debugging Mode (–d)

The *sendmail* program has a mode of operating called the *debugging* mode. The *sendmail* program is placed in debugging mode by using the -d command-line switch. That switch produces far more information than -v. To see for yourself, enter the following command line, but substitute your own login name in place of the *you*:

```
% /usr/lib/sendmail -d you < /dev/null
```

This command line produces many screens of output. We won't explain this output, because it is explained in Chapter 33, *Debugging With –d*. For now it is sufficient to observe that the *sendmail* program's debugging output can produce a great deal of information.

In addition to producing lots of debugging information, the -d switch can be modified to display specific debugging information. By adding a numeric *category* to the -d switch, output can be limited to one specific aspect of the *sendmail* program's behavior.

Type in this command line, but change *you* to your own login name.

```
% /usr/lib/sendmail -d40 you < /dev/null
```

Here, the -d40 is the debugging switch with a category of 40. That category limits *sendmail*'s program output to information about the queue. The following output shows you some information about how your mail message was queued. An explanation of this output is covered in Chapter 33.

```
Version 8.1
queueing AA11403
queueing 5c4e8="you":
        mailer 0 (local), host `', user `you',
        ruser `<null>'
        next=4cbec, flags=10, alias 5b8a8
        home="/n/yourhost/you", fullname="Your FullName"
```

In addition to a category, a *level* may also be specified. The level adjusts the amount of output produced. A low level produces little output, a high level produces greater and more complex output. The level follows the category in the form:

```
category.level
```

For example, enter the following command line:

```
% /usr/lib/sendmail -d0.1 -bp
```

The -d0 instructs *sendmail* to produce general debugging information. The level of .1 limits *sendmail* to its minimal output. That level could have been omitted, because a level of .1 is the default. Recall that -bp causes *sendmail* to print the contents of its queue.

The output produced looks something like the following:

```
Version 8.1
Mail queue is empty
```

Here, the -d0.1 switch causes *sendmail* to print its version. Now, run the same command line again, but this time change the level from .1 to .5:

```
% /usr/lib/sendmail -d0.5 -bp
```

The increase in the level causes *sendmail* to print a little more information:

```
Version 8.1
canonical name: here.us.edu
Mail queue is empty
```

This time, *sendmail* printed its version as before, but it also printed another line of information, because the level of debugging was increased. That new line shows you what *sendmail* thinks your host's *canonical* name is. A canonical hostname is a fully-qualified domain name. That is, it contains a hostname, a dot, and a full domain specification.

All categories and levels are described in Chapter 33. That chapter explains all the variations in the form of the -d switch, the default values for category and level, and how debugging alters the way the *sendmail* program runs.

Things to Try

- If you have access to two machines, kill the *sendmail* daemon on one, then send mail to that machine from the other using the −v (verbose) switch. What does this tell you about why it is important to always re-start the daemon after you have killed it? How can you tell that a remote *sendmail* daemon has died?

- Using the −v switch, send mail to yourself. In the message body, include nothing but lines that begin with dots. Does the message get through intact?

- Begin forming the habit of routinely running *mailq* several times per day. Start to learn the many reasons that mail is queued rather than sent.

- Write a shell script that runs *sendmail* with the −bv (verify) switch to determine if every alias in the *aliases*(5) file is good and print those that aren't. Be sure to filter the output so that good addresses (those marked as `deliverable`) are not printed.

- Read the online manuals for all the MUAs on your system, such as that for */usr/ucb/Mail.* For which MUAs is it possible to indirectly run *sendmail* in verbose mode? That is, which will pass a −v command-line switch through to *sendmail*?

5

*The
sendmail.cf File*

The lines of text that form the *sendmail.cf* file have been described by some as resembling modem noise, and by others as resembling Mr. Dithers swearing in the comic strip "Blondie."

```
R$+@$=W      ← sendmail.cf file
{$/{{.+      ← modem noise
!@#!@@!      ← Mr. Dithers swearing
```

Certainly, constructs like the following can be intimidating to the newcomer:

```
R$+@$=W       $@$1@$H       user@thishost -> user@hub
R$=W!$+       $@$2@$H       thishost!user -> user@hub
R@$=W:$+      $@@$H:$2      @thishost:something
R$+%$=W       $@$>3$1@$2    user%thishost
```

But think back to your early days of C programming. Did you feel any more comfortable with an expression like this?

```
#define getc(p)   (--(p)->_cnt>=0? ((int)*(p)->_ptr++):_filbuf(p))
```

Like any new language, learning the *sendmail.cf* "mail-routing" language requires time and practice. In the chapters that follow, we will introduce you to the *sendmail.cf* language. We begin with the *sendmail.cf* file.

Overview of the sendmail.cf File

The *sendmail.cf* configuration file is read and parsed by *sendmail* every time *sendmail* starts up. Because *sendmail* is run every time electronic mail is sent, its configuration file is designed to be easy for *sendmail* to parse, rather than easy for humans to read.

The *sendmail.cf* file contains information necessary for *sendmail* to run. It lists the locations of important files and specifies the default permissions for those files. It contains options that modify *sendmail's* behavior. And, most importantly, it contains rules and rule sets for rewriting addresses.

The *sendmail.cf* configuration file is line-oriented. A configuration command, composed of a single *letter*, begins each line:

```
Troot                    ← good
 Troot                   ← bad, does not begin a line
Troot OQ/var/mqueue      ← bad, two on one line
OQ/tmp/mqueue            ← good
```

Each configuration command is followed by certain parameters that are required for each type of command. For example, the T command is followed by usernames (like *root*). The O command is followed by the letter Q, then the full pathname of a directory. The complete list of configuration commands is shown in Table 5-1.

Table 5-1: The sendmail.cf File Configuration Commands

Command	Description
V	Define configuration file version (V8 only)
M	Define a mail delivery agent
D	Define a macro
R	Define a rewriting rule
S	Declare a rule-set start
C	Define a class macro
F	Define a class macro from a file or a pipe
O	Define an option
H	Define a header
P	Define delivery priorities
T	Declare trusted users
K	Declared a keyed database (V8 only)

Some commands, like V and T, only appear once in your *sendmail.cf* file. Others, like R, appear often.

Blank lines and lines that begin with the # character are considered comments and ignored. A line that begins with either a tab or a space character is considered a continuation of the preceding line.

```
# a comment
Troot
     postmaster   ← continuation of T line above
  ↑
  tab
```

Anything other than one of the commands in the table, a blank line, a space, a tab, or a # character that begins a line is an error. If the *sendmail* program finds such a character when reading the configuration file, it prints a warning like the following, ignores that line, and continues to read the configuration file:

```
sendmail.cf: line 15: unknown control line "A"
```

Here, *sendmail* found a line in its *sendmail.cf* file that began with the letter A. Since A is not a legal command, *sendmail* printed a warning. The line number is that of the line in the *sendmail.cf* file that began with the illegal character.

An example of each kind of command is illustrated in the following sections. They are actual commands that you will see developed throughout this tutorial. Don't be concerned if you don't understand the details at this time. All that is now mysterious will eventually become clear.

Comments

Comments are necessary if others are to understand your *sendmail.cf* file. They can also remind you of what you did months ago. They only slow down *sendmail* the tiniest amount, so don't be afraid of over-commenting. When the # character begins a line in the *sendmail.cf* file, that entire line is treated as a comment and ignored. For example, the entire following line is ignored by the *sendmail* program:

```
# The default form for the sender's address.
```

Besides beginning a line, comments can also follow commands. Under pre-V8 *sendmail*, comments can *only* follow three commands: S (rule set), P (priority), and R (rewriting rule). That is:

```
Pjunk=100         # this is a comment
S3                # this is a comment
CWlocalhost mailhost # but this won't work!
```

But, under version 8 (V8) *sendmail*, comments may follow *any* command. That is, the third line above would be valid. The new form of comments for V8 *sendmail* only works if you use the new V (version) command shown in the next section.

Note that for both the old and the new versions, comments that follow commands cannot go beyond the end of the line.

Version (V8 Only)

Many new features have been introduced in V8 *sendmail*. To prevent older versions from breaking when reading new style *sendmail.cf* files, a new V, for *version*, command has been introduced. If you are running V8 *sendmail*, you should use the V command to take advantage of the new features.

The form for the version command looks like this:

```
V5
```

The V must begin a line. The version number that follows must be 3 or higher for the new features of the V8 *sendmail.cf* file to become effective. The number 5 is appropriate for *sendmail* Version 8.6. The 5 indicates that the look of the *sendmail.cf* file has undergone five major changes over the years, with the fifth being the current and most recent. The meaning of each version is detailed in Chapter 23, *The Configuration File*.

Mail Delivery Agents

Recall that the *sendmail* program does not itself deliver mail. Instead, it calls other programs to perform that delivery. The M *sendmail.cf* command defines a mail delivery agent (a program that delivers the mail). For example, as previously shown:

```
Mlocal, P=/bin/mail, F=lsDFMmnP, S=7, R=7, A=mail -d $u
```

This tells *sendmail* that `local` mail is to be delivered using the */bin/mail* program. The other parameters in this line are introduced in the next chapter and detailed in Chapter 26, *Delivery Agents*.

Macros

The ability to define a value once and then use it in many places makes maintaining your *sendmail.cf* file easier. The D *sendmail.cf* command defines a macro. A macro is a single letter that has text as its value. Once defined, that text can be referenced symbolically elsewhere:

```
DRmail.us.edu
```

Here, R is the name of a macro that has the string `mail.us.edu` as its value. That value is accessed elsewhere in the *sendmail.cf* file with an expression like $R. Macros are introduced in Chapter 7, *Macros*, and detailed in Chapter 27, *Defined Macros*.

Rules

At the heart of the *sendmail.cf* file are sequences of rules that transform mail addresses from one form to another. This is chiefly necessary because addresses must conform to many differing standards and forms. The R *sendmail.cf* command is used to define a transformation (rewriting) rule:

```
R$-             $@$1@$H        user -> user@hub
```

Mail addresses are compared to the rule on the left ($-). If they match that rule, they are transformed based on the middle rule ($@$1$@$H). The text at the right is a comment. The details of rules like this are more fully explained beginning in Chapter 8, *Addresses and Rules*, and detailed in Chapter 25, *Rules*.

Rule Sets

Because transformations may require several steps, rules are organized into sets, which can be thought of as subroutines. The S *sendmail.cf* command begins a rule set:

```
S3
```

This particular S command begins a rule set named rule set 3. All the R commands (rules) that follow it belong to this set. A set ends when another S command appears to define another set. Rule sets are introduced in Chapter 8, *Addresses and Rules*, and detailed in Chapter 24, *Rule Sets*.

Class Macros

There are times when the single text value of a D command (macro definition) is not sufficient. Often you will want to define multiple values for a macro and view those values as elements in an array. The C *sendmail.cf* command defines a class macro. A class macro is like an array, in that it can hold many items:

```
CW localhost fontserver
```

The name of the class (here W) is a single letter. This class macro contains two items: localhost and fontserver. A class macro has its values "fetched" elsewhere in the *sendmail.cf* file with an expression like $=W. Class macros are introduced in Chapter 12, *Class*, and detailed in Chapter 28, *Class Macros*.

File Class Macros

To make administration easier, it is often convenient to maintain long or volatile lists of text values in a disk file. The F *sendmail.cf* command defines a file class macro. It is just like the C command above, except that the array values are taken from a file:

```
FW/etc/local/ournames
```

Here, the file class macro W obtains its text values from the disk file indicated (/etc/local/ournames).

The file class macro can also take its list of text items from the output of a program. That form looks like this:

```
FW|/usr/local/bin/shownames
```

Here, *sendmail* runs the program /usr/local/bin/shownames. The output of that program is appended to the class macro W. Both forms of file class macro are introduced in Chapter 12, *Class Macros*, and detailed in Chapter 28, *Class Macros*.

Options

Options tell the *sendmail* program many useful and necessary things. They specify the location of key files, define how *sendmail* will act and how it will dispose of errors, set timeouts, and tune *sendmail* to your particular needs.

The O command is used to set *sendmail* options. One example of the option command looks like this:

```
OQ/var/spool/mqueue
```

Here, option Q (the name of the directory where mail will be queued) is set to be /var/spool/mqueue. Options are introduced in Chapter 13, *Setting Options*, and detailed in Chapter 30, *Options*.

Headers

Mail messages are composed of two parts, a header followed (after a blank line) by the body. The body may contain virtually anything. The header, on the other hand, must contain very specific lines of information that must conform to certain standards. The H command is used to specify which mail headers must be included in a mail message and how each will look:

```
HReceived: $?sfrom $s $.by $j ($v/$V)
```

This particular H command tells *sendmail* that a `Received:` header line will be added to the header of every mail message. Headers are introduced in Chapter 14, *Header, Priority, Trusted* and detailed in Chapter 31, *Headers.*

Priority

Not all mail has the same priority. Mass mailings (to a mailing list for example) should be transmitted after mail to individual users. The P command sets the beginning priority for any given mail message. That priority is used to determine a message's order when the mail queue is processed.

```
Pjunk=-100
```

This particular P command tells *sendmail* that mail with a `Precedence:` header line of `junk` should be processed last. Priority commands are introduced in Chapter 14 and detailed in Chapter 31.

Trusted Users

For some software (like UUCP) to function correctly, it must be able to tell *sendmail* whom a mail message is from. This is necessary when that software runs under a different user identity (*uid*) than that specified in the `From:` line in the message header. The T *sendmail.cf* command lists those users of programs that are *trusted* to override the `From:` address in a mail message.

```
Troot daemon uucp
```

This particular T *sendmail.cf* command declares that there are three users who are to be considered trusted. They are *root* (who is a god under UNIX), *daemon* (*sendmail* usually runs as the pseudo-user *daemon*), and *uucp* (necessary for UUCP software to work properly). Trusted users are introduced in Chapter 14, *Header, Priority, Trusted* and detailed in Chapter 18, *Security.*

Keyed Databases (V8 Only)

Certain information, such as a list of UUCP hosts, is better maintained outside of the *sendmail.cf* file. V8 *sendmail* offers external databases (called *keyed* databases) for faster access to such information. Keyed databases come in several forms, the nature and location of which are declared with the K configuration command:

```
Kuucp hash /etc/mail/uucphosts
```

This particular K command declares a database with the symbolic name uucp, of the type hash, the location of which is /etc/mail/uucp-hosts. The K command is detailed, and the types of databases are explained, in Chapter 29, *Database Macros.*

Things to Try

- Run your *sendmail* with a -d0 debugging switch as you learned in the last chapter. What version of *sendmail* are you running on your system? Does it support the new V (version) command?

- Examine the *sendmail.cf* file on your system. Although you don't yet know what any of it does, you should be delightfully surprised to discover that you already know what most of the 12 configuration commands are generally meant to do.

- Determine how your site is organized. Is it arranged to be convenient for users or for the administrator? Are the two necessarily exclusive?

6

Mail Delivery Agents

Rather than having each individual workstation in a network handle its own mail, one alternative is to have a powerful central machine handle all mail. Such a machine is called a *mail hub* and is analogous to the way Federal Express originally handled package delivery. In the old days, when you sent a package with Federal Express from, say, San Francisco to Los Angeles, that package was first sent to Memphis, Tennessee (see Figure 6-1). The Memphis location was the Federal Express hub. All packages went there first and were then delivered from that hub.

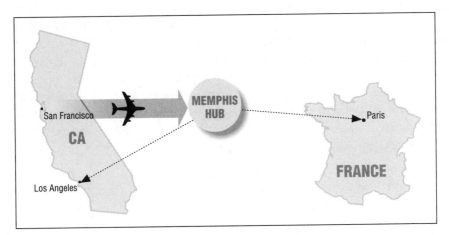

Figure 6-1: The Federal Express hub approach

The advantage to this approach is that the Memphis hub was the only Federal Express office that needed the special knowledge of how to deliver packages anywhere in the world. Local offices only needed to know how to deliver to the hub.*

In a similar way, your workstations can be thought of as the outlying offices (client machines), and your central mail handling machine as the hub. For mail, the hubperforms the following functions for the entire site:

- All incoming mail is sent to the hub, meaning that no mail is ever sent directly to a client machine. This hub approach has several advantages. No client needs to run a *sendmail* daemon to listen for mail. No client's name needs to be known to the outside world, thus insulating client machines for easier security.

- Rather than having each client send its mail directly to the outside world, all outgoing mail from clients is sent to the hub, and the hub then forwards that mail to its ultimate destination. The advantages here are that clients do not need to be continually aware of changes in the Internet; that deferred mail queues on the hub, not on the client machine, making management simpler; and that, using *rdist*(1), a single, simple *sendmail.cf* file may be distributed to all the clients.

- All outgoing mail is modified so that it appears to have come from the hub. The alternative is to have *reply* mail returned directly to each client. The advantages of the hub approach are that all mail appears to come from a single, giant machine (making replying to mail easier); that the client does not need to be able to receive mail; and that insulating clients for security becomes easier.

- All mail to local users is delivered to, and spooled on, the hub. The alternative is to have one or more separate mail spool directories on separate client machines. The advantages of the hub approach are that all local delivery is handled by one machine; that no client needs to accept mail for local delivery; and that management is easier with a single spool.

There are disadvantages to the hub approach when the site network is composed of differing machine architectures, and when machines are spread over many networks:

- At sites where there is a huge amount of mail constantly flowing, the load on the hub can become excessive. This can cause client mail to be queued rather than sent, even when mail is destined for local delivery.

---

*Federal Express now has several regional hubs.

- For the hub to work, it needs to know of all users on the system. Either it must have a master */etc/passwd* file that is the union of all systems' *passwd* files, or it must use NIS to access such a master file.* In the absence of universal user *passwd* knowledge, it must have an *aliases* file entry for every local user.

- Because all mail passes through the hub, rather than being sent to a recipient directly, there are unavoidable delays. Those delays are negligible at small sites (a couple of hundred or so users), but can become significant at sites with a huge number of users.

- If a client machine has direct UUCP connections, or is connected to multiple networks, a more complex configuration file is needed.

The client.cf File

The purpose of this tutorial is to develop a small *sendmail.cf* file for the clients of a hub scheme. It will perform only two tasks: instructing *sendmail* to send all mail to the hub and making all mail appear as though it originally came from the hub.

In creating this client file, care must be taken to avoid overwriting the system file with a file of that same name. For safety's sake, we will call our file *client.cf.* The complete text for that *client.cf* file shown in Appendix D, *The client.cf File*, but don't take the time to type it in just yet. We will be developing it in pieces and examining those pieces individually in the chapters that follow.

In this chapter, we will begin the process of developing a *client.cf* file from scratch. It needs to perform two tasks:

- It will instruct *sendmail* to send all mail to another machine that serves as a mail hub. Recall that in the hub design, no workstation receives mail, and all mail from clients is sent first to the hub and from there to the outside world.

- It will make all outgoing mail appear as though it originally came from that hub. Thus, replies to mail will be delivered to the hub, rather than to the client.

In this chapter we tackle the first task—how to get mail from the client machine to the hub.

---

*See *Managing NFS and NIS* by Hal Stern (O'Reilly & Associates, 1992).

Define a Mail Delivery Agent

Other than forwarding mail messages over a TCP/IP network, *sendmail* does not handle mail delivery itself. Instead, it runs other programs that perform delivery (see Figure 6-2). The programs it runs are called *delivery agents*. Information about which agent performs which kind of delivery is defined in the *sendmail.cf* file.

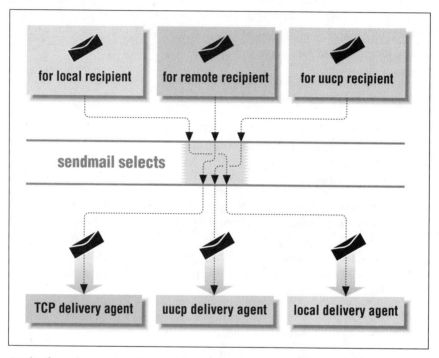

Figure 6-2: The nature of the recipient determines the delivery agent

The first item to create in the *client.cf* file is a definition of the program (delivery agent) that forwards mail to the hub machine. That definition provides *sendmail* with the information it needs to deliver mail using that delivery agent. Initially, the information *sendmail* needs will only include the name and location of that program. Thus, in its preliminary form, the definition for the mail delivery program, looks like this:

```
# Mailer to forward all mail to the hub machine
Mhub,    P=[IPC], A=IPC $h
```

This is a minimal (and still useless) two-line configuration file. Go ahead and type it in. Be sure to call this new file *client.cf*. The first line is a comment. The second is a configuration command that defines a delivery agent. It contains three parts, each separated from the others by commas—a symbolic name and two equates.

Mhub
:   The M that begins the line defines a mail delivery agent. The hub immediately following is the symbolic name for the delivery agent. This symbolic name is the part of this definition that will be referenced by other parts of the configuration file when you write them.

P=[IPC]
:   The P= equate stands for Path. This says that the full pathname of the program used to handle the delivery is called [IPC]. ([IPC] is a special name used internally by *sendmail* to represent its *internal ability* to communicate over TCP/IP networks. It stands for inter-processor communications). For other mail delivery agent definitions, the name following the = would be the full pathname of a program, like */bin/mail.*

A=IPC $h
:   The A= equate stands for Argument vector (list). It is used to specify the command-line arguments that will be given to the P= program when it is run. The zeroth argument is the name of the program (here IPC without brackets). The rest of the arguments, of which there is only one here, the $h, are the actual command-line arguments. The $h is a macro that contains the recipient's hostname. We'll describe macros in the next chapter. The A= equate must always be the last item in a delivery agent definition.

Testing the client.cf File

You can actually get *sendmail* to successfully parse this two-line *client.cf* configuration file. To run *sendmail* in rule-testing mode, enter this command line:

```
% /usr/lib/sendmail -oQ/tmp -Cclient.cf -bt
```

For now, you need to include -oQ/tmp in the command line to prevent *sendmail* from trying to change to the *mqueue* directory (which probably doesn't exist under the current directory). If you leave out the -oQ/tmp switch, *sendmail* exits with this confusing error:

```
cannot chdir(mqueue): No such file or directory
```

The -Cclient.cf tells *sendmail* to use the file *client.cf* in the current directory as its configuration file, rather than the system */etc/sendmail.cf* file. The `-bt` tells *sendmail* to run in interactive rule-testing mode, which we'll use often throughout this tutorial. The above command line produces output like the following:

```
No local mailer defined
No prog mailer defined
ADDRESS TEST MODE
[Note: No initial ruleset 3 call]
Enter <ruleset> <address>
>
```

The notifications of no `local` or `prog` mailer definitions are not important yet. The *sendmail* program prints them and continues to run. The ADDRESS TEST MODE is a result of the `-bt` command-line argument. This mode allows you to test address rewriting rules and will be very useful when you begin writing them in Chapter 8, *Addresses and Rules*. The [Note: No initial ruleset 3 call] appears for the IDA *sendmail* programs, but not for earlier versions.* This message lets you know that rule set 3 is no longer called first in rule-set testing mode, a point we'll cover later.

You exit *sendmail* by typing CTRL-D† at the > prompt:

```
> ^D
%                        ← your UNIX prompt returns
```

The local and prog Delivery Agents

When you ran *sendmail* in rule-testing mode, *sendmail* complained that two delivery agent definitions were missing:

```
No local mailer defined
No prog mailer defined
```

To keep *sendmail* happy, those two mail delivery agent definitions will now be added to the *client.cf* file. As it happens, these are already in your system *sendmail.cf* file, and you can copy them by typing the following command:‡

```
% egrep "^Mlocal|^Mprog" /etc/sendmail.cf >> client.cf
```

---

*It also appears for V8 *sendmail*, but in a slightly different form.
†The traditional end-of-file indicator for the UNIX keyboard is CTRL-D. Yours may vary.
‡If you lack *egrep*(1) on your system, you'll need to *grep*(1) for `local` and `prog` separately.

Note that the ^M above is actually two characters ^ and M, not a CTRL-M. This command line causes the *egrep*(1) program to search the file */etc/sendmail.cf* for any lines that begin (the ^) with either Mlocal or Mprog. The >> appends the result (the lines found) onto the end of the *client.cf* file.

Now load the *client.cf* file into your editor. It will look something like this:*

```
# Mailer to forward all mail to the hub machine
Mhub,   P=[IPC], A=IPC $h
Mlocal, P=/bin/mail, F=lsDFMmnP, S=10, R=20, A=mail -d $u
Mprog,  P=/bin/sh,   F=lsDFMeuP,  S=10, R=20, A=sh -c $u
```

Right off the bat, you'll notice two new definitions that are a bit more complicated than the hub definition. Each of the new M configuration commands declares a symbolic name, like hub. Here those names are local and prog—the two names *sendmail* complained were missing. Although these local and prog definitions are important and heavily used in a full-fledged *sendmail.cf* file, the *client.cf* file only uses them to keep *sendmail* from complaining.

Both of these new delivery agent definitions are composed of six parts (each separated from the others by commas), a symbolic name and five equates. The F=, S=, and R= equates are new. You've seen the M, P=, and A= before in the hub definition.

M   All mail delivery agent definitions begin with the M configuration-file command. Like all configuration commands, that M must begin a line.

```
Mhub,   P=[IPC], A=IPC $h
Mlocal, P=/bin/mail, F=lsDFMmnP, S=10, R=20, A=mail -d $u
Mprog,  P=/bin/sh,   F=lsDFMeuP,  S=10, R=20, A=sh -c $u
↑
```
define a delivery agent

The symbolic name for each delivery agent follows the M, with no intervening space. The symbolic names here are hub, local, and prog. The delivery agent called hub forwards mail to the central hub machine. The local delivery agent delivers mail to users on the local machine. The prog delivery agent provides a way for mail to be delivered by piping it through a program (more on this later).

---

*If any of the equates shown here are missing, you need to type them in by hand.

P=   The P= equate (for Path) specifies the full pathname of the pro-
      gram that performs the delivery.

```
Mhub,    P=[IPC], A=IPC $h
Mlocal,  P=/bin/mail, F=lsDFMmnP, S=10, R=20, A=mail -d $u
Mprog,   P=/bin/sh,   F=lsDFMeuP,  S=10, R=20, A=sh -c $u
         ↑
         full pathname of program
```

Your program names may differ, but, in general, the program for
local places a mail message into the local user's mail spool file,
and the program for **prog** sends a mail message through a program.

A=   The A= equate (for Argv) specifies the command-line arguments to
      be supplied to each corresponding program.

```
Mhub,    P=[IPC], A=IPC $h
Mlocal,  P=/bin/mail, F=lsDFMmnP, S=10, R=20, A=mail -d $u
Mprog,   P=/bin/sh,   F=lsDFMeuP,  S=10, R=20, A=sh -c $u
                                                ↑
                                    command line (argv)
```

Notice that these use the $u macro, whereas the hub definition
uses the $h macro. The $u macro contains the name of the recipient. That name can be either a username, like *bob*, or a program
name, like */u/bob/bin/sortmail*—depending on the nature of the
delivery definition. Macros are explained in the next chapter. The
A= equate must always be last.

Three parts in the new definitions were not used in the hub definition.
They are:

F=   The F= equate (for Flags) specifies certain flags that tell *sendmail*
      more about the delivery agent definition. Each flag is a single letter
      and each is boolean—either set or not set by being correspond-
      ingly present or absent.

```
Mhub,    P=[IPC], A=IPC $h
Mlocal,  P=/bin/mail, F=lsDFMmnP, S=10, R=20, A=mail -d $u
Mprog,   P=/bin/sh,   F=lsDFMeuP,  S=10, R=20, A=sh -c $u
                      ↑
                      flags for delivery agent
```

There are many flags to choose from. They are all described in
Chapter 26, *Delivery Agents*, but we will describe a few of them
later in this chapter.

S=   The S= equate (for Sender) specifies which rule set to use when
      rewriting the sender's address.

```
Mhub,    P=[IPC], A=IPC $h
Mlocal,  P=/bin/mail, F=lsDFMmnP, S=10, R=20, A=mail -d $u
Mprog,   P=/bin/sh,   F=lsDFMeuP,  S=10, R=20, A=sh -c $u
                                   ↑
                            sender rule set
```

Addresses need to be rewritten because different delivery agents require addresses to be in different forms. For example, the [IPC] agent requires the form *user@host.domain*, while the uucp agent (if you had need for one) requires the form *host!user.* Here, the S= says that addresses should be rewritten using rule set 10. We will cover rule sets in Chapter 8, *Addresses and Rules.*

R=   The R= equate (for Recipient) specifies which rule set to use when rewriting the recipient's address.

```
Mhub,    P=[IPC], A=IPC $h
Mlocal,  P=/bin/mail, F=lsDFMmnP, S=10, R=20, A=mail -d $u
Mprog,   P=/bin/sh,   F=lsDFMeuP,  S=10, R=20, A=sh -c $u
                                        ↑
                              recipient rule set
```

Again, those addresses need to be rewritten because different delivery agents require different forms of addresses. Here, the R= says to use rule set 20.

Skipping Rule Sets

Because we won't be covering rule sets for a while, and in order to simplify things for now, edit the *client.cf* file once again and change the S= and R= equates in the new prog and local definitions:

```
# Mailer to forward all mail to the hub machine
Mhub,    P=[IPC], A=IPC $h
Mlocal,  P=/bin/mail, F=lsDFMmnP, S=0, R=0, A=mail -d $u
Mprog,   P=/bin/sh,   F=lsDFMeuP,  S=0, R=0, A=sh -c $u
                                   ↑    ↑
                                  new  new
```

All four equates are changed to zero because there are no rule sets yet. When an S= or an R= equate in a delivery agent definition is zero or missing, *sendmail* skips the delivery agent-specific part of rule-set processing.

Adding Comments

Now add some informative comments to the *client.cf* file. Comments are an important part of every configuration file. They remind you of what you are trying to do now and what you have done in the past.

```
### Mailer Delivery Agent Definitions                    ← new
# Mailer to forward all mail to the hub machine
Mhub,    P=[IPC], A=IPC $h
# Sendmail requires these, but we won't use them.       ← new
Mlocal, P=/bin/mail, F=lsDFMmnP, S=0, R0, A=mail -d $u
Mprog,  P=/bin/sh,   F=lsDFMeuP,  S=0, R=0, A=sh -c $u
```

The kind of comments used here are whole-line comments. That is, the line begins with a # character, so the whole line is ignored by *sendmail*. We use ### in front of the first line to set it off as a heading.

After you write this latest form of the *client.cf* file, run *sendmail* in rule-testing mode once again.

Testing the New Delivery Agent Definitions

This time, when you run *sendmail,* add a special debugging command-line argument that shows how *sendmail* interpreted the delivery agent definitions:

```
% /usr/lib/sendmail -d0.15 -oQ/tmp -Cclient.cf -bt
```

This is the same command line you have run all along with one addition. The -d0.15 debugging argument tells *sendmail* (among other things) to show you how it interpreted your delivery agent definitions. Running the above command line produces output* like the following:

```
← assorted other information here and above
mailer 0 (hub):  P=[IPC] S=0 R=0 M=0 F= E=\n A=IPC $h
mailer 1 (local): P=/bin/mail S=0 R=0 M=0 F=DFMPlmns E=\n A=mail -d $u
mailer 2 (prog): P=/bin/sh S=0 R=0 M=0 F=DFMPelsu E=\n A=sh -c $u
ADDRESS TEST MODE
[Note: No initial ruleset 3 call]
Enter <ruleset> <address>
>
```

This output, in addition to verifying that *sendmail* properly interpreted the *client.cf* file, reveals two equates you haven't seen before: the M= and the E=. We won't explain them here, because you don't need them for the *client.cf* file. They are explained in detail in Chapter 26, *Delivery Agents.*

---

*This is the most complete output, as produced by V8 *sendmail.* Other versions produce less and/or somewhat different output.

In the above output, also notice that there are several equates that were not included in the original Mhub delivery agent definition. The hub definition only included the P= and A= equates:

```
Mhub,    P=[IPC], A=IPC $h
```

When *sendmail* interpreted this definition, it did not find specifications for the S=, R=, M=, F=, or E= equates. Rather than complaining about those missing equates, it gave all but E= a value of zero (the default), and it gave E= the value of the newline character, \n:

```
mailer 0 (hub): P=[IPC] S=0 R=0 M=0 F=  E=\n A=IPC $h
                        ↑   ↑   ↑  ↑    ↑
                     zero zero zero empty newline
```

Note that when the F= equate has a zero value, it is displayed as an empty list of flags.

Add the Missing Parts to Mhub

The final step in creating the hub mail delivery agent definition is to fill in its missing elements. That is, to add to that definition the F=, S=, and R= equates that the prog and local definitions already have.

Edit the *client.cf* file again and add the new parts shown below to the Mhub definition.

```
# Mailer to forward all mail to the hub machine
Mhub,    P=[IPC], S=0, R=0, F=mDFMuCX, A=IPC $h
                  ↑    ↑    ↑
                 new  new  new
```

Here the S= and R= equates are given a value of zero. The S= equate specifies the sender rewriting rule set. The R= equate specifies the recipient rewriting rule set. Because there are no rule sets yet, these equates are set to zero. You will be giving them real rule-set numbers when we begin to cover rule sets in Chapter 8, *Addresses and Rules.*

The flags listed in the F=mDFMuCX equate of the hub definition are typical of those generally used in [IPC] delivery agent definitions. You may want to change these depending on your needs. All the available flags are listed in Chapter 26, *Delivery Agents.* The ones we selected are summarized in Table 6-1.

Table 6-1: The hub Delivery Agent's F= Flags

Flag	Description
m	This agent can deliver to more than one user at a time.
D	Include date information in the header.
F	Include a From: line in the header.
M	Include a Message-ID in the header.
u	Preserve the case of the recipient name.
C	Append our hostname if missing from a user's address, and if we are a recipient agent.
X	Pass lone dots on a line by doubling them.

The mailer delivery agent definitions are now roughed out. Remember that the symbolic name (the hub, local, or prog) is the only part of each that will be referenced in later rule sets. Also notice that the last equate of each definition, the A= command-line equate, ends with a macro ($h or $u). We cover macros in the next chapter.

Things to Try

- Create a mail delivery agent definition that has no symbolic name, or one that has what you suspect is an illegal name. What happens when you run *sendmail* with the -d0.15 command-line argument?

- Define two different mail delivery agents that have the same symbolic name. Does *sendmail* catch the error, or does it replace the first with the second?

- Make a typo in one of the equates. For example, instead of S=6 enter s=6. What happens?

- The P= equate is used to state the full pathname of the program that delivers the mail message. Since the parts are separated from each other by commas, is it possible to include a comma in that pathname? If so, how?

- The P= equate is used to state the full pathname of the program that delivers the mail message. What happens if that program does not exist, or if that program is not executable? Is this detected by *sendmail* when the *sendmail.cf* file is read?

- The A= equate specifies the command-line arguments that are given to the P= program when it is run. Can you include commas in those command-line arguments?

- When a line in the *sendmail.cf* file begins with a space or tab character it is joined (appended) to the line above it. Can you split delivery agents over multiple lines for readability using this mechanism?

- Gather all of the lines in your system's current *sendmail.cf* file that define mail delivery agents. In each of the lines printed, you will see one field that declares the full path of a mail delivery program. For each of those P= fields, locate and read the online manual for the program specified. Do the arguments in the A= field make sense to you?

7

Macros

One of the major strengths of the *sendmail.cf* file is that it allows arbitrary text to be referenced symbolically. This is very similar to the use of variables by the Bourne and C shells:

```
R=mailhost          ← Bourne shell
set R=mailhost      ← C shell
DRmailhost          ← sendmail.cf file
```

The above commands all cause a variable with the single-letter name R to be assigned the value `mailhost`.

The expression for later using the value stored is the same for all three:

```
$R                  ← Bourne shell
$R                  ← C shell
$R                  ← sendmail.cf file
```

That is, all of the above expressions yield the value stored in $R, in this case the text `mailhost`. Once you define the value of R as `mailhost`, you can thereafter use the expression $R anywhere you need to use the text `mailhost`.

Overview of Macros

Macros can greatly simplify your work. They allow you to represent text symbolically and in one central place. Changes in that text are automatically propagated to the rest of the file. That is, consider the following definition in your *sendmail.cf* file:

```
DRmailhost
```

If you use the expression $R anywhere in that file, a single change to the definition of DRmailhost changes the value of $R throughout the file.

The format for defining macros is somewhat limited:

```
DXtext
```

The letter D must begin the line. The name of the macro, here X, immediately follows with no intervening space. That name is immediately followed (again with no intervening space) by the text (value) for the macro's definition. The value is all the text up to the end of the line.

Macros may only have single-character names, whereas shell variables may have arbitrarily long names.

```
ALONGNAME=first      ← shell names may be long
DAfirst              ← sendmail.cf names are a single letter
```

Although this restriction to a single letter makes a configuration file less readable, it has the advantage of making that file faster for *sendmail* to parse.

Macros are not expanded (replaced with their values) when the configuration file is read. They are expanded as needed while *sendmail* is running and processing mail, except in rule sets. Macros in rule sets *are* expanded when the configuration file is read.

Defining Macros

In the previous chapter, you roughed out delivery agent definitions for the hub, local, and prog delivery agents. Notice that the last part of each, the A= command-line part, ends with a macro:

```
### Mailer Delivery Agent Definitions
# Mailer to forward all mail to the hub machine
Mhub,   P=[IPC], F=mDFMuCX, S=0, R=0, A=IPC $h
# Sendmail requires these, but we won't use them.
Mlocal, P=/bin/mail, F=lsDFMmnP, S=0, R=0, A=mail -d $u
Mprog,  P=/bin/sh,   F=lsDFMeuP,  S=0, R=0, A=sh -c $u
                                                      ↑
                                                   macros
```

There are two kinds of macros: those that you define and those that *sendmail* defines. Macros that have uppercase names, such as $R, are ones that you optionally define. Those that have lowercase names, such as $h and

$u, are either ones that *sendmail* defines or ones that *sendmail* requires you to define.

You have already seen an example of an uppercase macro:

```
DRmailhost
```

This gives the macro named R the value `mailhost`.

Somewhere on your network, there may be a machine whose alias is *mailhost,* or something similar, like *mailrelay.* This is the alias of the machine that serves as the mail hub for your site. If no such alias exists, you have to use an actual machine name (like *mail.us.edu*). Now load the *client.cf* file into your editor, and add your first macro, R.

```
### Defined macros                                    ← new
# The name of the mail hub                            ← new
DRmailhost                                            ← new
                                                      ← new
### Mailer Delivery Agent Definitions
# Mailer to forward all mail to the hub machine
Mhub,   P=[IPC], F=mDFMuCX, S=0, R=0, A=IPC $h
# Sendmail requires these, but we won't use them.
Mlocal, P=/bin/mail, F=lsDFMmnP, S=0, R=0, A=mail -d $u
Mprog,  P=/bin/sh,   F=lsDFMeuP,  S=0, R=0, A=sh -c $u
```

Here four new lines have been added to the *client.cf* file. The first two are comments, and the fourth is a blank line to visually separate macro definitions from delivery agent definitions. The third line is the new macro definition. As the comment says, this R macro will contain as its value the name of the host to which all mail will be forwarded.

Take a moment to test this new version of the *client.cf* file. The following command is similar to the one you've been using all along, but this time we introduce a new trick for exiting *sendmail:*

```
% /usr/lib/sendmail -oQ/tmp -Cclient.cf -bt </dev/null
```

The `</dev/null` we've added to the end of the command line causes *sendmail* to read from the device */dev/null* instead of from your keyboard. That device is a special one in that it always returns EOF (end-of-file) and here acts like typing CTRL-D at your keyboard. The output of that command will look something like this:

```
ADDRESS TEST MODE
Enter <ruleset> <address>
[Note: No initial ruleset 3 call]
>
```

This is just what you've seen all along. The *sendmail* program reads and parses the *client.cf* file, then enters rule-testing mode. There are no errors in the *client.cf* file, so *sendmail* prints no error messages. The only difference between this and previous runs is that this time you did not have to press CTRL-D to exit *sendmail*.

Predefined Macros

The *sendmail* program internally defines many macros for you. You have already seen $u (which contains the recipient's username) and $h (which contains the recipient's hostname) in our delivery agent definitions. They are given values by *sendmail* instead of being given values with D macro definitions in your configuration file.

A short list of some of the more common predefined macros is shown in Table 7-1. As you can see, the limitation of macro names to a single letter can make it difficult to remember what they do.

Table 7-1: Some Predefined Macros

Macro	Description
$w	Local hostname
$m	Local NIS domain name (SunOS)
$m	Internet domain name (BSD)
$v	Version of the currently-running *sendmail*
$b	Date in RFC822 format

To watch the processing of all the macro definitions, run *sendmail* once again. This time add a -d35.9 command-line switch, which tells *sendmail* to print each macro as it is defined:

```
% /usr/lib/sendmail -d35.9 -Cclient.cf -oQ/tmp -bt < /dev/null
```

The output produced is surprisingly long, considering the small size of the *client.cf* file:

```
Version 8.1
define(* as $*)
define(+ as $+)
define(- as $-)
define(= as $=)
define(~ as $~)
define(# as $#)
define(@ as $@)
define(: as $:)
define(> as $>)
define(? as $?)
```

```
define(| as $|)
define(. as $.)
define([ as $[)
define(] as $])
define(0 as $0)
define(1 as $1)
define(2 as $2)
define(3 as $3)
define(4 as $4)
define(5 as $5)
define(6 as $6)
define(7 as $7)
define(8 as $8)
define(9 as $9)
define(w as "here.us.edu")            ← note
define(m as "us.edu")                 ← note
define(v as "8.1")                    ← note
define(b as "Fri, 13 Jan 93 05:51:39 -0800")   ← note
define(R as "mailhost")               ← note
ADDRESS TEST MODE
Enter <ruleset> <address>
[Note: No initial ruleset 3 call]
>
```

The first 25 lines of this output show *sendmail* reserving macro names that will be used as operators. (Operators are introduced in Chapter 8, *Addresses and Rules.*) The last five definitions are the only ones we are interested in for now. The first four of those show *sendmail* internally defining four macros for your use. The last definition shows *sendmail* processing the DRmailhost line in the *client.cf* file.

This output demonstrates another concept. Some internal definitions are always made before the configuration file is read. You can change them from inside your *client.cf* file. To change $w for example, you might place the following into your configuration file:

```
Dwmyhost.my.domain
```

Doing this would cause the text myhost.my.domain to replace the text here.us.edu as the value of the macro named w.

Finally, note that in the preceding output there are no definitions for the $h and $u macros that were used in the delivery agent definitions. They are macros that, although internally defined, are not actually given values until mail is sent. That is, they are not defined until after the configuration file is read, and, as a consequence, you cannot change their values from within your configuration file.

Required Macros

The *sendmail* program requires that certain macros be defined in every *sendmail.cf* file for *sendmail* to work properly. Although there are many such required macros for a full *sendmail.cf* file, only five are required for *client.cf*, as shown in Table 7-2.

Table 7-2: Some Required Macros

Macro	Description
$j	Official domain name for the local machine
$n	Identity of the error message sender
$l	Look of the UNIX From line
$o	The characters that separate address components
$q	Default form for the sender's address

This section explains each as we add it to the *client.cf* file.

```
# The local official domain name
Dj$w
```

This defines the official (fully-qualified) domain name to be the same as the local hostname ($w). At some sites, that hostname is the short name of the machine, like *here*, instead of the full name, like *here.us.edu*. To find out if your machine is one of those, run:

```
% /usr/lib/sendmail -d0.4 -bt < /dev/null
```

If your short hostname is printed as the canonical name, you will need to change this definition of $j into two new definitions:

```
DDus.edu
Dj$w.$D
```

Here, your local domain is added to your hostname when it lacks one. The first line defines D to have the domain name us.edu as its value. The second line then defines j to be the value of $w (your short hostname), a dot, and then the value of $D (your domain name). You should of course use your own domain name for $D.

Identity of the error message sender
DnMailer-Daemon

When an error occurs and a mail message is sent back to the original sender (bounced), $n is used to show the identity of the error message sender. The name `Mailer-Daemon` is traditional, but not otherwise defined in any standards. You should not change that name arbitrarily, however, because many people filter their mail based on that exact name.

Look of the UNIX From line
DlFrom $g $d

The five-character "From " line* (four letters and a space) is the line that marks the beginning of a mail message in a file of many such messages under UNIX. Each line begins with the five characters "From ". The $g that follows contains the address of the sender relative to the recipient. The $d is the current date in UNIX C language library *ctime*(3) format. The $g and $d are internally defined by *sendmail* when mail is actually sent.

The format of this "From " line is very important. Until you are more of an expert at *sendmail* you should use this line as we have shown it.

The characters that separate address components
Do.:%@!^=/[]

The *sendmail* program needs to be told which characters separate the various parts of an address. In addition to those, *sendmail* internally appends several other characters to that list. They are:

    ( ) < > , ; \ " \r \n

In this list, the \r and \n are the carriage return and newline characters respectively.

When an address is parsed by *sendmail*, it is divided into parts, or *tokens*, using the above lists of separators to form the divisions. For example:

gw@here.us.edu	*becomes* → gw @ here . us . edu
here!there!him	*becomes* → here ! there ! him
adam&eve+apple	*becomes* → adam&eve+apple

---

*This style of line is also required by the UUCP suite of software. This is a UNIX peculiarity which is not shared by all UNIX programs. The *mh*(1) programs discard that line.

In the above, the first is divided into seven distinct tokens and the second into five distinct tokens. Both are divided based on the separation characters. The third, however, is not divided at all, because neither & nor + appears in either list.

The characters in the $o definition are crucial to the proper working of *sendmail*. Until you are more of an expert with the workings of *sendmail*, you should use the characters as we've shown them.

```
# Default form for the sender's address
Dq<$g>
```

The $q macro defines the form for the sender's address. That is, it determines the appearance of the From: header line. It is made from the $g macro surrounded by < and > brackets. At the time $q is expanded in the From: header, the $g macro contains the sender's address relative to the recipient. For domain-based mail, that is simply the sender's full domain address. For UUCP mail, it is the full path back to the sender. For any kind of mail, it is the exact address to use to get mail back to the sender. This definition can vary, but it will do for our modest needs.

Putting It All Together

After adding these required definitions to our *client.cf* file, that file now looks like this:

```
### Defined macros
# The name of the mail hub
DRmailhost
# The Local official domain name.        ← new
Dj$w                                      ← new
# Whom errors should appear to be from.   ← new
DnMailer-Daemon                           ← new
# The look of the UNIX From line.         ← new
DlFrom $g    $d                           ← new
# The characters that separate address components.  ← new
Do.:%@!^=/[]                              ← new
# The default form for the sender's address.        ← new
Dq<$g>                                    ← new

### Mailer Delivery Agent Definitions
# Mailer to forward all mail to the hub machine
Mhub,    P=[IPC], F=mDFMuCX, S=0, R=0, A=IPC $h
# Sendmail requires these, but we won't use them.
Mlocal, P=/bin/mail, F=lsDFMmnP, S=0, R=0, A=mail -d $u
Mprog,  P=/bin/sh,   F=lsDFMeuP, S=0, R=0, A=sh -c $u
```

The *client.cf* file can be tested once again. It still does nothing and still produces no errors:

```
% /usr/lib/sendmail -d35.9 -Cclient.cf -oQ/tmp -bt < /dev/null
```

Again, the `-d35.9` command-line switch tells *sendmail* to print each macro as it is defined. The output produced, with the first 25 lines (the operators) omitted, looks like this:

```
← 25 lines omitted
define(w as "here.us.edu")
define(m as "us.edu")
define(v as "8.1")
define(b as "Fri, 13 Jan 92 05:51:39 -0800")
define(R as "mailhost")
define(j as "$w")                                    ← note
define(n as "Mailer-Daemon")                         ← note
define(l as "From $g  $d")                           ← note
define(o as ".:%@!^=/[]")                            ← note
define(q as "<$g>")                                  ← note
ADDRESS TEST MODE
Enter <ruleset> <address>
[Note: No initial ruleset 3 call]
>
```

Things to Try

- Uppercase macro names are for your use. Lowercase names are reserved for *sendmail*'s use. Twenty-five special characters are also reserved by *sendmail* for use as operators. What happens if you try to define a macro whose name is another character, like a tab or an underscore?

- What happens if you try to define a macro whose name is one of the operator characters, like +?

- Using the `-d35.9` command-line switch, determine what happens if you define two macros, each with the same name.

- Any *sendmail.cf* command may be continued and extended by beginning the next line with a tab or a space. Using the `-d35.9` command-line switch, determine the effect of continuing a macro definition. For example:

  ```
  DAsomething
  tab    somethingmore
  ```

- The text value of a macro must immediately follow the character name of that macro, with no intervening space. Can the text itself contain arbitrary spaces or tabs?

- Using *grep*(1), find all the D commands in your site's actual *sendmail.cf* file. For those that are common to both that file and the *client.cf* file, how do those definitions differ? If you can, explain any differences you find.

8

Addresses and Rules

Before delving into the inner workings of rules, we need to create a fictional network to provide a common ground for discussing mail addresses.

A Fictional Network

Consider the network shown Figure 8-1, which consists of three sites (the circles) each interconnected by high-speed networks (the solid lines). Each site is a DNS *domain* composed of many individual computers. Each domain is set up differently, as we will show, but from the user's point of view, the process of sending mail from a machine in one domain to a machine in another is the same in all cases.

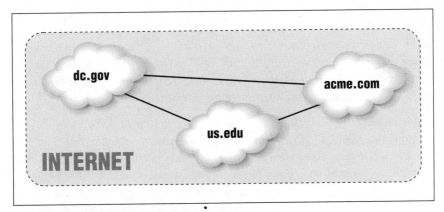

Figure 8-1: Domains in our fictional network

A domain name is interpreted right to left. The *com* in *.acme.com*, for example, means that *acme* is a part of the top-level domain *com* (for *commercial*). There are many commercial sites in the *com* top-level domain, but only one *acme* among them. Similarly, *edu* is the top-level domain for educational institutions, like universities, and *gov* is the top-level domain for United States government organizations.

A domain includes many machines. Each machine inside a domain is a host with a name. A *fully-qualified domain name* is one that includes the name of a host, a dot, and then the domain name. For example, *sec.acme.com* is a fully-qualified domain name because it is a machine with the hostname *sec*, a dot, then the domain name *acme.com*.

The dc.gov Domain

Figure 8-2 shows what the *.dc.gov* domain looks like on the inside. It is composed of three machines (although in the real world it might be composed of many more). These three machines are connected together on a private network for security (the solid lines). Only one machine, *fbi.dc.gov*, has a connection to the outside world. Mail from the outside world always goes to *fbi.dc.gov* first; from there it is forwarded to the appropriate machine on the internal network. For example, the user *george* eventually receives his mail on his own machine (*wash.dc.gov*), even though that mail is first received by *fbi.dc.gov*. The *fbi.dc.gov* machine is called a *gateway* because it forms a gate between the internal and external networks through which all network traffic (like mail) must flow. It is also called a *forwarder*, because it accepts mail for another machine, then forwards that mail to the other machine.

Despite the presence of a gateway, users in *.dc.gov* still receive mail on their individual machines. Inside *.dc.gov*, mail from one machine to another goes directly over the internal network. The gateway is not involved. But mail destined for the outside world must always first go to the gateway, which then forwards that mail over the outside network.

Mail addressed to the domain (*dc.gov* rather than a specific machine like *wash.dc.gov*) will be delivered to the gateway machine. Unfortunately, under our fiction, the gateway does not know about any of the users at other machines in the domain. As a consequence, mail to a user at the domain (*user@dc.gov*) will fail and bounce.

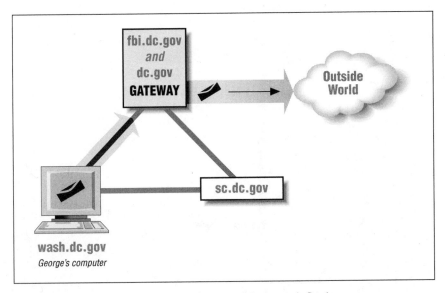

Figure 8-2: The dc.gov domain is only accessible through fbi.dc.gov

The acme.com Domain

Figure 8-3 shows the *.acme.com* domain. It is different from *.dc.gov* because all machines are connected directly to the outside world and to each other. All machines can directly receive mail from the outside world. For example, the user *tim* receives and reads his mail on the machine *boss.acme.com*, but unlike the previous network, there is no gateway.

Like *fbi.dc.gov*, the machine *sec.acme.com* will receive all mail addressed to the domain *acme.com*. But unlike the gateway *fbi.dc.gov*, *sec.acme.com* knows about all the users in its domain.* So mail to *tim@acme.com* will be correctly forwarded to *tim* at *boss.acme.com*.

---

* It runs NIS (formerly Yellow Pages) and can mount the home directories of all users.

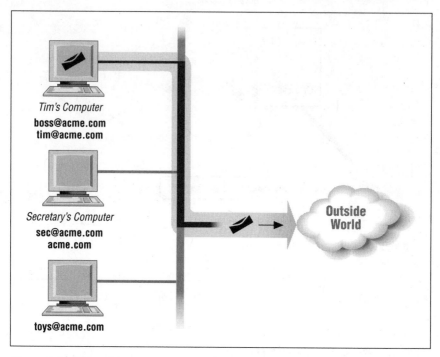

Figure 8-3: All machines in acme.com connect to the outside world

The us.edu Domain

Figure 8-4 shows a third way to set up a domain. In this domain, all mail (both inside and outside) is delivered to the machine *mail.us.edu*. Unlike the previous two examples, no mail is ever delivered to the other machines. Instead, it is delivered into the master spool directory on *mail.us.edu*. The other machines then network *mount* that directory so users can read their mail from any machine. Under this system, mail only needs to be addressed using the name of the local recipient, an @, and the name of the domain (like *user@us.edu*). This arrangement eliminates the need for users elsewhere in the world to know any specific machine's name.

All three forms of domains have their advantages and disadvantages. We don't favor any one above another. In this and the chapters to follow, we consider our machine to be in the *.us.edu* domain. We selected it only because it allows the simplest *sendmail* configuration file to be used.

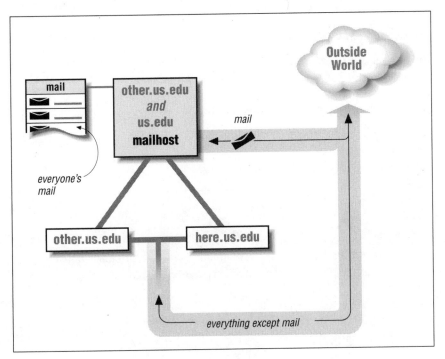

Figure 8-4: Only mail.us.edu receives mail in the domain us.edu

UUCP and Host Paths

In addition to our fictional network, consider two hosts that are connected to *acme.com* using dial-up lines (Figure 8.5). Under UUCP, one needs to know exactly how hosts are connected in order to send mail to any one of them. To get mail from *sec.acme.com* to *sonya*, for example, you need to send that mail to *lady* first.

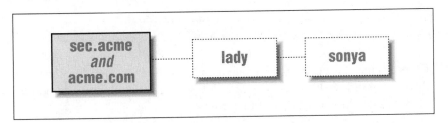

Figure 8-5: UUCP connections to sec.acme.com

Why Rules?

Rules in a *sendmail.cf* file are used to modify mail addresses, to detect errors in addressing, and to select mail delivery agents. Addresses need to be modified because they can be specified in many ways, yet are required to be in particular forms by delivery agents. To illustrate, consider Figure 8.6, and mail sent with the address:

```
friend@uuhost
```

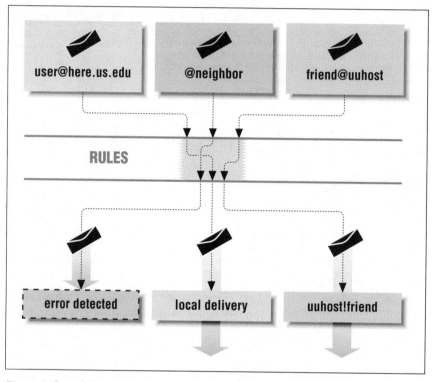

Figure 8-6: Rules modify addresses, detect errors, and select delivery agents

If the machine uuhost were connected to yours over a dial-up line, the message would likely be sent using UUCP software. That software requires addresses to be expressed in UUCP form:

```
uuhost!friend
```

Another of the roles of *sendmail.cf* rules is to detect (and reject) errors locally. This prevents them from propagating over the network. Mail to an address without a username is one such error:

```
@neighbor
```

It is better to detect this kind of error locally, rather than having the host `neighbor` reject it.

Delivery agents are the means used by *sendmail* to actually transmit or deliver mail messages. Rules examine the address of each envelope recipient and select the appropriate delivery agent. For example:

```
user@here.us.edu
```

Here, rules detect that `here.us.edu` is the name of the local machine and select the `local` delivery agent to perform final delivery to the user `user`'s system mailbox.

In the previous two chapters, you were introduced to delivery agent and macro definitions. In this chapter we will begin our coverage of rule sets— the means for tying those definitions to addresses.

Rule Sets

Sequences of rules are grouped together into rule sets. Each set is similar to a subroutine. A rule set is declared with the S command, which must begin a line in *sendmail.cf.* For example:

```
S0
```

This begins the declaration of the rules that forms rule set number 0. Rule sets are numbered starting from 0. The sets 0 through 6 are internally defined by *sendmail* to have very specific purposes, as shown in Table 8-1. We'll expand on most of these throughout the rest of the tutorial. Rule-set definitions may appear in any order in the configuration file. For example, rule set S5 may be defined first, followed by S2, and then S7. The rule sets are gathered when the *sendmail.cf* file is read, and they are sorted internally by *sendmail.*

If a rule set is undefined, the result is the same as if it were defined but had no rules associated with it. It is like a subroutine that contains nothing but a *return* statement. It does nothing and produces no errors.

Table 8-1: The Purposes of Rule Sets

Rule Set	Purpose
0	Resolve a mail delivery agent
1	Process sender address
2	Process recipient address
3	Preprocess all addresses
4	Postprocess all addresses
5	Process sender headers (IDA only)
5	Rewrite unaliased local users (V8 only)
6	Process recipient headers (IDA only)

The *client.cf* file contains no rule-set definitions yet. To observe the effect of rules that do nothing, rerun *sendmail* on that file:

```
% /usr/lib/sendmail  -oQ/tmp -Cclient.cf -bt
ADDRESS TEST MODE
[Note: No initial ruleset 3 call]
Enter <ruleset> <address>
>
```

The −bt command-line switch causes *sendmail* to run in address-testing mode. In this mode, *sendmail* waits for you to type a rule set and an address. It then shows you how the rule set *rewrites* the address. As the prompt requests, you can now enter an address by specifying a rule-set number, and then a space and a mail address.

```
> 0 gw@wash.dc.gov
rewrite: ruleset  0   input: "gw" "@" "wash" "." "dc" "." "gov"
rewrite: ruleset  0 returns: "gw" "@" "wash" "." "dc" "." "gov"
>
```

The rule set specified is 0, but you can specify any number. If you are running an old version of *sendmail,* two things will be different than what you see above. First, the initial output *will not* include a [Note: No initial ruleset 3 call], but *will* include two extra rewrite lines. Second, old versions of *sendmail* always assume you want to see the effect of rule set S3, whether you do or not.*

---

*Originally you could not specify a series of rule sets in rule-testing mode, so rule set 3 had to be artificially inserted by *sendmail.* Multiple rule sets may now be specified as a comma-separated list, so an artificial call to rule set 3 is no longer required.

The `rewrite:` word that begins each line of address-testing mode output is simply there to highlight rewriting lines when they are mixed with other kinds of debugging output. The `input` means that *sendmail* placed the address into the workspace (more about this soon). The `returns` shows the result after the rule set has rewritten that address based on its rules.

The address that is fed to *sendmail*, `gw@wash.dc.gov` is first split into parts (tokens) based on the separating characters defined by the Do macro in the last chapter and those defined internally by *sendmail*:

```
# Standard characters that separate address components.
Do.:%@!^=/[]
  ↑
```
plus internally defined: ()<>,;\"\r\n

For clarity, each token is printed within full quotation marks (but some versions of *sendmail* omit the full quotation marks):

```
"gw" "@" "wash" "." "dc" "." "gov"
```

The `input:` shows the seven tokens passed to rule set 0. The `returns:` shows, since there is no rule set 0, that undefined (empty) rule set returns those tokens unchanged.

```
rewrite: ruleset  0   input: "gw" "@" "wash" "." "dc" "." "gov"
rewrite: ruleset  0 returns: "gw" "@" "wash" "." "dc" "." "gov"
```

Rules

Each rule set may contain any number of individual rules, including none. Rules begin with the R configuration command, and each rule is composed of three parts:

```
S0
Rlhs        rhs         comment
```

The first line, the `S0`, declares the start of rule set 0. All the lines following the S line and beginning with R belong to that rule set. A new rule set begins when another S line with a different number appears.

Each R line is an individual rule in a series of rules that form a rule set. In the *sendmail.cf* files of major mail-handling sites, a given rule set can have a huge number of rules. But our hypothetical rule set 0 has only one rule, and hence only one line that begins with an R:

```
S0
Rlhs        rhs        comment
       ↑          ↑
     tab        tab
```

Each rule has three distinct parts, each divided from the others by one or more tab characters. You can use space characters inside each part, but you *must* use tabs to separate the parts.

The leftmost part of the rule is called the LHS, for *left-hand side.* The middle part is called the RHS, for *right-hand side.* These form the rule. A `comment` may optionally follow the RHS, and must be separated from the RHS by one or more tab characters.

The LHS and RHS form an *if-then* pair. If the LHS evaluates to true, the RHS is executed. If it evaluates to false, *sendmail* skips to the next rule for that rule set (if there is one).

```
  if true →          do this
     ↓                  ↓
  Rlhs               rhs                      comment
     ↓
otherwise go to next rule
```

The Workspace

Whether the LHS is true or false is determined by making comparisons. When an address is processed by a rule set for rewriting, *sendmail* first tokenizes it, then stores those tokens internally in a buffer called the *workspace.*

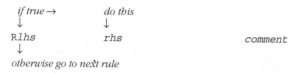

```
"gw" "@" "wash" "." "gov"   ← in the workspace
```

When the LHS of a rule is evaluated, it too is tokenized, then those tokens are compared to the tokens in the workspace. If both the workspace and the LHS contain exactly the same tokens, a match is found, and the result of the LHS comparison is true. To illustrate, temporarily add the following two lines to the end of the *client.cf* file:

```
S0
Rleft.side    new.stuff      this is a comment
```

Don't forget that the three parts of the rule are separated from each other by tab characters. This creates a demo rule that illustrates a few introductory concepts about rules.

Now run *sendmail* in rule-testing mode, just like you did before:

```
% /usr/lib/sendmail  -oQ/tmp -Cclient.cf -bt
ADDRESS TEST MODE
[Note: No initial ruleset 3 call]
Enter <ruleset> <address>
>
```

Also as before, enter rule set 0 and a typical e-mail address at the prompt:

```
> 0 gw@wash.dc.gov
rewrite: ruleset  0   input: "gw" "@" "wash" "." "dc" "." "gov"
rewrite: ruleset  0 returns: "gw" "@" "wash" "." "dc" "." "gov"
>
```

Notice that nothing is rewritten, even though there is a rule set 0 and a rule in the *client.cf* file. Remember that a rule is only rewritten if the workspace and the LHS exactly match. For the demo rule, they do not match:

```
gw@wash.dc.gov          ← the workspace
       ↑
       nothing matches
       ↓
Rleft.side      new.stuff      this is a comment
```

Now, at the prompt, enter the exact text that appears in the LHS of the demo rule:

```
> 0 left.side
rewrite: ruleset  0   input: left . side
rewrite: ruleset  0 returns: new . stuff
```

An amazing thing has happened. The rule has actually rewritten an address. The address `left.side` is given to rule set 0 and is rewritten by the rule in that rule set to become the address `new.stuff`. This transformation is possible because the workspace and the LHS exactly match each other, so the result of the LHS comparison is true:

```
left.side          ← the workspace
     ↑
     exact match, so: "true"
     ↓
Rleft.side      new.stuff      this is a comment
     ↑              ↑
     if true, then do this
```

Before leaving this demo rule set, perform one final experiment. Enter the text `left.side` again, but this time change the letters to uppercase:

```
> 0 LEFT.SIDE
rewrite: ruleset  0   input: LEFT . SIDE
rewrite: ruleset  0 returns: new . stuff
>
```

Notice that the workspace and the LHS still match, even though they now differ by case. This illustrates that all comparisons between the workspace and the LHS of rules are done in a case-insensitive manner. This property enables rules that solve complex problems to be written, without the need to distinguish between upper- and lowercase letters.

The Flow of Addresses Through Rules

When rule sets contain many rules, the flow is from the first through the last (top down), in the order they are declared in the configuration file. To illustrate, modify the two demo lines you added to the *client.cf* file, replacing them with the four new demo lines shown below:

```
S0
Rx      y
Ry      z
Rz      a
```

Here, there are only two parts to each rule (the comment is missing). Remember that the LHS of each must be separated from the RHS by tab characters.

Before you test these new rules, consider what they do. The first rule rewrites any x in the workspace into a y. The second rule rewrites any y in the workspace into a z. And the last rule rewrites any z that it finds in the workspace into an a.

Now run *sendmail* in rule-testing mode once again:

```
% /usr/lib/sendmail  -oQ/tmp -Cclient.cf -bt
ADDRESS TEST MODE
[Note: No initial ruleset 3 call]
Enter <ruleset> <address>
>
```

Next, one at a time, enter rule set 0 and one of the letters x, y, and z:

```
> 0 x
rewrite: ruleset  0    input: x
rewrite: ruleset  0 returns: a
> 0 y
rewrite: ruleset  0    input: y
rewrite: ruleset  0 returns: a
> 0 z
rewrite: ruleset  0    input: z
rewrite: ruleset  0 returns: a
>
```

Note that no matter which of x, y, or z you enter, each is rewritten into a. This illustrates the flow of addresses (the workspace) through rules.

Let's look in detail at what is going on by examining the input. When you first enter rule set 0, the first rule of that rule set tries to match its LHS to the workspace:

```
x               ← the workspace
↑
exact match, so: "true"
↓
Rx      y
```

The LHS exactly matches the workspace, so the RHS rewrites the workspace so that x is replaced by y.

Now the next rule tries to match its LHS to the workspace. But the workspace is now the workspace that was rewritten by the first rule:

```
x               ← the original workspace
↑
exact match, so: "true"
↓
Rx      y       ← first rule rewrites
y               ← workspace to be this
↑
exact match, so: "true"
↓
Ry      z       ← second rule
```

The key point here is that each rule compares its LHS to the *current* contents of the workspace—contents that may have been rewritten by earlier rules. Bearing this in mind, it should now be clear why all three letters are rewritten to a.

```
x    becomes →  y  becomes →  z  becomes →  a
y    becomes →  z  becomes →  a
z    becomes →  a
```

Now feed one more letter into *sendmail* in rule-testing mode. This time enter anything other than an x, y, or z:

```
> 0 b
rewrite: ruleset  0    input: b
rewrite: ruleset  0 returns: b
```

Here, the workspace remains unchanged because b does not match the left-hand side in any of the three rules. If the LHS of a rule fails to match the workspace, that rule is skipped, and the workspace remains unchanged.

Operators Versus the Workspace

Rules would be pretty useless if they always had to match the workspace exactly. Fortunately, that is not the case. In addition to literal text, you can also use operators. Operators are like wildcards in that they allow the LHS of rules to match arbitrary text in the workspace. To illustrate, consider this rule:

```
R$+        $@match
  ↑          ↑
 lhs        rhs
```

This LHS begins with the first character following the R. The LHS in this example is:

```
$+
```

This is an operator. The truth of this if-statement is determined by a process called *pattern matching*. The LHS $+ (a single operator) is a pattern that means "match one or more tokens." The address that is being evaluated is tokenized, placed into the workspace, and then the workspace is compared to that pattern.

```
gw@wash.dc.gov
    ↓
 tokenized into
    ↓
"gw" "@" "wash" "." "dc" "." "gov"    ← in the "workspace"
```

When matching the workspace to an LHS pattern, *sendmail* scans the workspace from left to right. Each token in the workspace is compared to the operator (the $+) in the LHS pattern. If the tokens all match the pattern, the if part of the if-then pair is true.

The $+ operator simply matches any *one or more* tokens:

```
workspace         pattern
"gw"              $+         ← match one token ("one")
"@"                          ← and optionally more ("or more")
"wash"                       ↓
"."
"dc"
"."
"gov"
```

As you can see, if there are any tokens in the address at all (the workspace is not empty) the LHS rule $+ evaluates to true.

Other Text in the LHS

A rule of $+ (match one or more tokens) is not sufficient to handle all possible addresses (especially bad addresses).

> gw@wash.dc.gov   ← $+ *should match and does*
> @wash.dc.gov   ← $+ *matches an incomplete address*

To make matching in the LHS more effective, *sendmail* allows other text to appear in the pattern. To make sure that the address in the workspace contains a user part, the @ character, and a host part, the following LHS pattern can be used:

> $+@$+

Just like the address in the workspace, this pattern is tokenized before it is compared for a match. Operators (like $+) are tokenized individually, and the @ is a token because it is a separator character defined by the o macro:

> # Standard characters that separate address components.
> Do.:%@!^=/[]

The pattern of $+@$+ is separated into three tokens:

> "$+" "@" "$+"

Text in the pattern must match text in the workspace *exactly* (token for token) if there is to be a match. A good address in the workspace (one containing a user part and a host part) will match our new LHS ($+@$+):

workspace	*pattern*	
"gw"	"$+"	← *match one or more*
"@"	"@"	← *match exactly*
"wash"	"$+"	← *match one*
"."		↓ *or more*
"dc"		
"."		
"gov"		

Here, the flow of matching begins with the first $+, which matches one token (of the one or more) in the workspace. The @ matches the identical token in the workspace. At this point, the $+@ part of the pattern has been satisfied. All that remains is for the final $+ to match its one or more of all the remaining tokens in the workspace.

But a bad address in the workspace will not match. Consider an address, for example, that lacks a username:

```
wash.dc.gov                    ← in the workspace

workspace        pattern
"@"                "$+"        ← match one
"wash"                         ←  or more
"."
"dc"
"."
"gov"
                   "@"         ← match exactly (fails!)
                   "$+"
```

Here, the first $+ incorrectly matches the @ in the workspace. Since there is no other @ in the workspace to be matched by the @ in the pattern, the first $+ matches the entire workspace. Because there is nothing left in the workspace, the attempt to match the @ fails. When any part of a pattern fails to match the workspace, the entire LHS fails (the if part of the if-then is false).

Minimal Matching

One small bit of confusion may yet remain. When an operator like $+ is used to match the workspace, *sendmail* always does a *minimal match*. That is, it only matches what it needs to for the next part of the rule to work. Consider:

```
R$+@$+
```

In this LHS, the first $+ matches everything in the workspace up to the first @ character. For example, consider the following workspace:

```
a@b@c
```

In the above, $+@ causes the $+ to match only the characters up to the first @ character, the a. This is the minimum that needs to be matched, and so it is the maximum that will be matched.

More Play With LHS Matching

Take a moment to replace the previous demo rules with the following four new demo rules in the *client.cf* file:

```
S0
R@          $@one
R@$+        $@two
R$+@$+      $@three
R$+         $@four
```

These four demo rules are for demonstration purposes only (you'll see how to declare a real one soon enough). We've given each temporary RHS a number to see if it is selected. The $@ in front of each RHS prevents any successful rewrite from being carried to any subsequent rules. (We'll cover this property in more detail soon.) Now run *sendmail* in rule-testing mode:

```
% /usr/lib/sendmail -oQ/tmp -Cclient.cf -bt
ADDRESS TEST MODE
[Note: No initial ruleset 3 call]
Enter <ruleset> <address>
>
```

The first address to specify is an @:

```
> 0 @
rewrite: ruleset   0    input: "@"
rewrite: ruleset   0 returns: "one"
>
```

The @ causes the first temporary RHS to be selected because the rule is:

```
R@        $@one
```

The LHS here (the pattern to match) contains the lone @. That pattern matches the tokenized workspace @ exactly, so the RHS for that rule is returned.

Next enter an address that just contains a host and domain part, but not a user part:

```
> 0 @your.domain
rewrite: ruleset   0    input: "@" "your" "." "domain"
rewrite: ruleset   0 returns: "two"
>
```

The first thing to notice is what was *not* printed! The workspace does not match the pattern of the first rule. But instead of returning an error, the workspace is carried down *as-is* to the next rule—where it does match:

> *@your.domain does not match, so*
> ↓
> R@ $@one
> ↓
> *try the next rule*
> ↓
> R@$+ $@two

Now enter an address that fails to match the first two rules, but successfully matches the third:

```
> 0 you@your.domain
rewrite: ruleset   0    input: "you" "@" "your" "." "domain"
rewrite: ruleset   0 returns: "three"
>
```

The flow for this address is:

your@your.domain does not match, so
↓

R@ $@one
↓

try the next rule, which doesn't match, so
↓

R@$+ $@two
↓

try the next rule, which does.
↓

R$+@$+ $@three

The fourth rule contains the original lone $+:

R$+ $@four

It is there to catch any addresses that slip past the first three. Go ahead and test it. Try addresses like your login name, or UUCP addresses like *you@host.uucp* and *host!you.* Can you predict what will happen with weird addresses like *@@* or *a@b@c?*

When you are done experimenting, exit rule-testing mode and delete the five temporary lines you added for this demonstration.

Things to Try

- Try feeding *sendmail* an extremely long address in rule-testing mode. Something like a.a.a... with 50 a and dot characters. What does this tell you about the limit on the size of the workspace? Is this a limit of tokens or of characters?

- Look through your system *sendmail.cf* file for all lines that declare rule sets (S lines). Are there any that have no rules (R lines) associated with them? Do the comments near them explain clearly why no rules are present?

- What happens if you use spaces rather than tabs to separate the LHS from the RHS of rules? Is the error message clear? What happens if the RHS is separated from the comment with spaces instead of tabs? How does this illustrate the importance of testing all new rules with rule-testing mode?

In this chapter:
- *Introducing Rule Set 0*
- *The RHS Triple*
- *Testing Rule Set 0*
- *The error Delivery Agent*
- *Things to Try*

9

Rule Set 0

The function of rule set 0 is to decide which mail delivery agent will handle delivery for a particular recipient address. Figure 9-1 shows how rule set 0 relates to the other rule sets. (We cover the other rule sets in the chapters to come.)

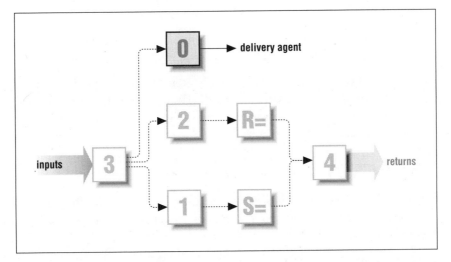

Figure 9-1: The flow of rule set 0

Rule set 0 is called once for each recipient listed in a mail message. The purpose of rule set 0 is to determine a *triple* from each address that it is given. A triple is composed of three parts: the symbolic name of the mail delivery agent, the name of the user to whom the mail is addressed, and the name of the host to which the mail will be sent. We'll expand on these soon. In the previous chapter you learned about rule sets and rules. In this chapter, we will introduce you to rule set 0 and show you how to design real rules. Rule set 0 is important because it determines which delivery agent will deliver the mail message to each recipient.

Introducing Rule Set 0

Recall that one goal of the *client.cf* file is to cause *sendmail* to forward all mail to a central hub machine for processing. To lay the groundwork for this, we designed the hub delivery agent in Chapter 6, *Mail Delivery Agents*, and declared it like this:

```
# Mailer to forward all mail to the hub machine
Mhub,    P=[IPC], S=0, R=0, F=mDFMuCX, A=IPC $h
```

As this goal implies, we don't want to design any fancy rules for rewriting the recipient's address, we simply want to send it to the hub as-is.

The rule that follows does just that. It may look complicated, but recall that it is basically just an if-then statement:

```
S0
R$+            $#hub $@$R $:$1          forward to hub
```

The first line (the S0) declares the start of rule set 0. The R line is the first of many possible rules that will form rule set 0.

You saw the LHS of this rule in the last chapter. The $+ operator is used to match *one or more* tokens in the workspace. Essentially, this LHS will match anything in the workspace, but will fail to match an empty workspace.

The RHS Triple

The job of rule set 0 is to resolve each address into a triple: the delivery agent's symbolic name, the name of the host, and the name of the user (see Figure 9-2).

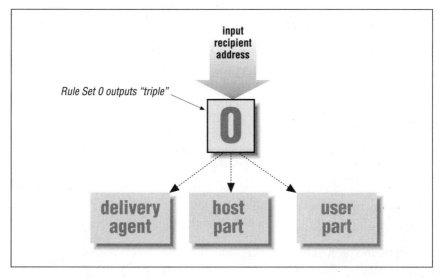

Figure 9-2: Rule set 0 resolves a triple

Recall that rules are like if-then statements. If the rule in the LHS evaluates to true, then *sendmail* evaluates the RHS.

```
if true →          do this
↓                  ↓
R$+                $#hub $@$R $:$1           forward to hub
↓
otherwise go to next rule
```

This RHS resolves all three parts of the triple. To accomplish this, the text of the RHS is *transformed* and then copied into the workspace.

```
$#hub              → copied as is (delivery agent part)
$@$R               → defined macro is expanded (host part)
$:$1               → positional macro is expanded (user part)
```

We examine these parts in order, showing how each is transformed and copied into the workspace. Operators are shown in Table 9-1.

Table 9-1: Rule 0 RHS Operators You Will See

Operator	Description
$#	The Mail delivery agent
$@	The Host
$:	The User

The Delivery Agent ($#)

The first part of the triple is the name of the delivery agent. The RHS $# operator tells *sendmail* that the text following (up to, but not including, the next operator and ignoring spaces) is the symbolic name of the delivery agent to use.

The symbolic name hub is defined in our *client.cf* file as:

```
# Mailer to forward all mail to the hub machine
Mhub,   P=[IPC], F=mDFMuCX, S=0, R=0, A=IPC $h
```

When the RHS is copied into the workspace, any operators like $# are copied as-is and become new tokens:

> "$#" ← *the workspace thus far*

As before, the quotation marks are only there to make each token easier to discern visually. They are not a part of the token.

When text, such as hub, is copied into the workspace, it is tokenized using the separation characters defined by the $o macro.* Since our symbolic name hub contains none of those characters, it is copied as a single token into the workspace:

> "$#" "hub" ← *the workspace thus far*

The Host ($@)

The second part of the triple is the hostname. The RHS $@ operator tells *sendmail* that the text following (up to, but not including, the next operator and ignoring spaces) is the address of the host to which the mail will be sent. The name of the host is in $R. Combined, they look like this:

> $@$R

Whenever *sendmail* encounters a *$letter* in the RHS, it takes that expression to be a macro's value. You previously defined $R to contain the name of the host to which all mail will be sent:

```
# The name of the mail hub
DRmailhost
```

The second part of the triple is now copied to the workspace. The $@ is copied as-is. The $R is expanded (its value taken), and then that value is

---

* As a result, the symbolic name of the mail delivery agent cannot contain any of those characters.

broken into tokens and copied into the workspace. For a $R of `mailhost`, the workspace looks like this:

"$#" "hub" "$@" "mailhost" ← *the workspace thus far*

The User ($:)

The third part of the triple is the username. The RHS $: operator tells *sendmail* that the following text (up to but not including the next operator and ignoring spaces) is the user to whom mail is being sent. Here, that username is $1. Combined, they look like this:

$:$1

When *sendmail* sees a $*digit* in the RHS, it uses that digit as a *count* into the pattern-matching operators of the LHS. In this example, the LHS has only one pattern-matching operator, $+, and the $1 indicates that operator. If there were more than one pattern-matching operator in the LHS, for example:

$+.$+
↑ ↑
$1 $2

then $1 would indicate the first $+, and $2 would indicate the second $+.

A $*digit* tells *sendmail* to copy whatever tokens the corresponding LHS pattern-matching operator matched. If the original workspace had contained:

"boss" "@" "acme" ← *in the original workspace*

Then the lone $+ (match one or more) LHS operator would match the entire workspace (all of its tokens).

All of the original workspace's tokens are then copied. The workspace will finally contain:

"$#" "hub" "$@" "mailhost" "$:" "boss" "@" "acme"

After *sendmail* has completed its writing of the workspace, the workspace (the triple) is *returned.*

Testing Rule Set 0

To see that what we describe is actually what happens, take a moment to add rule set 0 to the *client.cf* file:

```
### Mailer Delivery Agent Definitions
# Mailer to forward all mail to the hub machine
Mhub,    P=[IPC], F=mDFMuCX, S=0, R=0, A=IPC $h
Mlocal,  P=/bin/mail, F=lsDFMmnP, S=0, R=0, A=mail -d $u
Mprog,   P=/bin/sh,   F=lsDFMeuP,  S=0, R=0, A=sh -c $u

### The Rule Sets                                          ← new
S0 select delivery agent                                   ← new
R$+      $#hub $@$R $:$1           forward to hub          ← new
```

Now run *sendmail* in rule-testing mode and give it the address boss@acme:

```
% /usr/lib/sendmail -oQ/tmp -Cclient.cf -bt
ADDRESS TEST MODE
[Note: No initial ruleset 3 call]
Enter <ruleset> <address>
> 0 boss@acme
rewrite: ruleset  0   input: "boss" "@" "acme"
rewrite: ruleset  0 returns: $# "hub" $@ "mailhost" $: "boss" "@" "acme"
> ^D
%
```

The change to the workspace caused by rule set 0 is exactly as predicted:

```
$# "hub" $@ "mailhost" $: "boss" "@" "acme"
```

The symbolic delivery agent name is used by *sendmail* to select a delivery agent definition. The symbolic name is indicated by the special operator $# in the RHS of a rule:

```
Mhub,    P=[IPC], F=mDFMuCX, S=0, R=0, A=IPC $h
         ↑
     selected by $#hub in rule set 0
```

The $@ in the RHS of a rule indicates the name of the host where mail will be delivered. The text that forms that name is copied into $h for use by the delivery agent. Similarly, the $: in the RHS of a rule indicates the name of the user. The text that forms that name is copied into $u.

```
                          from $@ in rule set 0
                            ↓
Mhub,    P=[IPC], F=mDFMuCX, S=6, R=6, A=IPC $h
Mlocal,  P=/bin/mail, F=lsDFMmnP, S=0, R=0, A=mail -d $u
                                                      ↑
                          from $: in rule set 0
```

Rule set 0 is different from the other rule sets in several important ways. We'll begin explaining the other rule sets in the next chapter. For now, just be aware that there are a few exceptions to the rules in *sendmail*.

- Rule set 0 is the only one that may use $# to return the symbolic name of a delivery agent. If any other rule set returns a $#, the $# can cause unpredictable errors.

- The $@ and the $: in rule set 0, when those operators follow the $#, have different meanings than they do in all the other rule sets. They are even different than they are in rule set 0 itself when they don't follow a $#. You got a glimpse of $@ used as a prefix in the last chapter. We'll expand on it and on $: in the next chapter.

The error Delivery Agent

Although all mail, under the hub scheme, should be passed to the hub for processing, certain errors should still be handled locally. By recognizing these errors locally, the user is advised of mistakes immediately, rather than having to wait for mail to bounce.

When we discussed delivery agents, we showed you that *sendmail* requires the local and prog delivery agents. Because *sendmail* requires them, you had to define them yourself (to keep *sendmail* from complaining):

```
Mlocal, P=/bin/mail, F=lsDFMmnP, S=0, R=0, A=mail -d $u
Mprog,  P=/bin/sh,   F=lsDFMeuP,  S=0, R=0, A=sh -c $u
```

Inside *sendmail*, a third specially-defined delivery agent exists. Called error, that delivery agent is one that you don't have to define yourself.

The error delivery agent is the internal mechanism *sendmail* uses to processes errors. Whenever that delivery agent is selected, it causes *sendmail* to print the username part of the triple (the $: part) as an error message.

For example, recall the earlier experiment with four demo rules:

```
S0
R@        $@one
R@$+      $@two
R$+@$+    $@three
R$+       $@four
```

When this rule set was given an address of *@host* (note the missing user part), the RHS rewrote the workspace to be `two`.* We use a similar technique to select the *sendmail* program's built-in error handling delivery agent `error`.

Add the following new line to the *client.cf* file's rule set 0. Don't forget that the LHS, RHS, and comment must be separated from each other by tab characters, not spaces. But note that the RHS may contain space characters (not tabs) for clarity.

```
### The Rule Sets
S0 select delivery agent
R@$+     $#error $: Missing user name              ← new
R$+      $#hub $@$R $:$1                 forward to hub
```

Run *sendmail* again, this time to see which addresses are caught locally as errors and which are passed onward to the central hub.

```
% /usr/lib/sendmail -oQ/tmp -Cclient.cf -bt
ADDRESS TEST MODE
[Note: No initial ruleset 3 call]
Enter <ruleset> <address>
> 0 @acme
rewrite: ruleset  0   input: "@" "acme"
rewrite: ruleset  0 returns: $# "error" $: "Missing" "user" "name"
```

Here you are supplying an address that lacks a username. As expected, the `error` delivery agent is selected. If someone attempted to send mail to such an address, they would get the error:

```
@acme... Missing user name
```

Now feed *sendmail* a legal address:

```
> 0 boss@acme
rewrite: ruleset  0   input: "boss" "@" "acme"
rewrite: ruleset  0 returns: $# "hub" $@ "mailhost" $: "boss" "@" "acme"
```

This legal address, one with both a user and domain part, bypasses the error-handling rule and is accepted for delivery via the hub delivery agent.

Take some time to experiment. Give *sendmail* an assortment of addresses and try to predict which will produce errors and which will not.

---

*We are fudging here for the sake of a simple example. In reality, a leading @ is legal for route addresses. See Chapter 25, *Rules*.

Things to Try

- Devise an error-handling rule that will detect an address that contains a username and an @ character, but no host or domain part.

- Is it possible to have text in the LHS that is literally $+, rather than an operator with the same characters?

- The *client.cf* file uses $#error to handle errors in rule set 0. Examine your site's *sendmail.cf* file to see if it is legal to use $#error in other rule sets.

10

Rule Set 3

The job of rule sets 1 through 4* is to change recipient and sender addresses in both the header and the envelope into a form appropriate for a given delivery agent. Each kind of address takes a different path through the rule sets. The possibilities (which can be confusing) are illustrated in Figure 10-1.

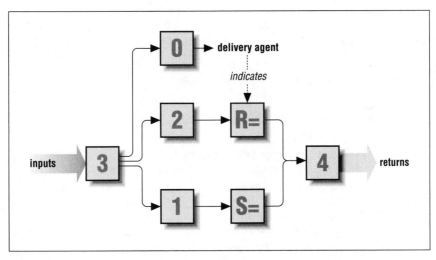

Figure 10-1: The flow of addresses through rule sets

*Rule sets 5 and 6 have purposes which differ between the BSD and IDA versions of *sendmail*. We won't be covering those differences in this tutorial.

The sender's address on the envelope, for example, is first rewritten by rule set 3, then by rule set 1, then by the rule set specified by the S= equate in the delivery agent definition, and finally by rule set 4.

All addresses, even the one used to select a delivery agent, begin with rule set 3. All sender addresses flow through rule sets 3 and then 1. All recipient addresses flow through 3 and then 2. Each then flows through the rule set that is specified by the S= or R= equate for a delivery agent. Each is then "post-processed" by rule set 4. But, because the role of rule set 0 is to select a delivery agent (and therefore the appropriate S= and R= equates) rule set 0 needs to be processed before an address can go through rule sets 1 or 2.

In the previous few chapters you began to learn about rules sets in general, and rule set 0 specifically. However, before the recipient address can be processed by rule set 0, it must first be processed by rule set 3. All addresses are pre-processed by rule set 3.

Why Preprocess?

To understand why a preprocessing rule set (rule set 3) is needed, we need to briefly examine how users specify addresses. One common way to send mail is by using the reply feature of your mail-reading program (MUA). That feature looks at the From: line in the mail message's header and uses the text that follows as the address for the reply. That text can take one of two forms:

```
From: address (Full Name and other comments)
From: Full Name <address>
```

Both forms are legal. The first is an e-mail address followed by arbitrary text in parentheses, usually the user's full name. The parentheses form a comment. Your mail reading program often strips that comment before sending the mail, so *sendmail* sees only address. But even if the comment isn't stripped, *sendmail* removes (and saves) it before entering rule set 3.

The second form has the user's full name first, followed by the e-mail address in angle brackets. When your MUA sends e-mail using this form of return address, it hands *sendmail* the entire text: full name, and address in angle brackets.

In both cases, what *sendmail* needs is the address part. But, as in the second case, *sendmail* can get more than just the address. Thus *sendmail* needs a way to discard everything else.

```
Full Name <address>
        ↓
```
needs to be transformed into
```
        ↓
address
```

The *sendmail* program handles this initial transformation of all addresses by pre-processing them using rule set 3.

Rule Set 3

In its initial form, rule set 3 looks like this:

```
S3 # preprocessing for all rule sets
R$*<$*>$*    $2              basic RFC822 parsing
```

As with rule set 0, the definition of rule set 3 begins with the S configuration command. The S must begin a line, and the 3 must immediately follow with no intervening spaces.

The only rule in rule set 3 is composed of three parts, each separated from the others by tab characters.

```
R$*<$*>$*    $2              basic RFC822 parsing
   ↑          ↑  ↑             ↑
  LHS       tabs RHS  tabs    comment
```

The LHS

The operator in this LHS, the $*, is different than the $+ operator you saw in rule set 0. Recall that the $+ operator matches one or more tokens in the workspace. To review, consider the LHS rule:

```
$+@$+
```

This LHS easily matches an address like *you@here.us.edu* in the workspace:

workspace	LHS	
"you"	$+	← *match one or more*
"@"	"@"	← *match exactly*
"here"	$+	← *match one*
"."		↓ *or more*
"us"		
"."		
"edu"		

This same LHS, however, does not match an address like *@here.us.edu.*

```
workspace        LHS
"@"              $+        ← match one
"here"           ↓    or more
"."
"us"
"."
"edu"
                 "@"       ← match exactly, fails!
                 $+
```

Because the $+ operator needs to match one or more tokens, it fails when there is nothing in front of the @.

The $* operator is just like the $+ operator, except that it *will* match nothing. If the LHS had used $* instead of $+, an address like *@here.us.edu* would be matched:

```
workspace        LHS
                 $*        ← match zero or more
"@"              "@"       ← match exactly
"here"           $*        ← match zero
"."              ↓    or more
"us"
"."
"edu"
```

The LHS in rule set 3 matches anything or nothing, provided there is a pair of angle brackets in the workspace somewhere:

```
R$*<$*>$*    $2                    basic RFC822 parsing
```

For example, consider an address that might be given to *sendmail* by your MUA:

```
Your Fullname <you@here.us.edu>
```

This address is tokenized and placed into the workspace. That workspace is then compared to the LHS:

```
workspace        LHS
"Your"           $*        ← match zero
"Fullname"       ↓    or more
"<"              "<"       ← match exactly
"you"            $*        ← match zero
"@"              ↓    or more
"here"
"."
"us"
"."
"edu"
">"              ">"       ← match exactly
                 $*        ← match zero or more
```

The RHS

Recall that the objective of rule set 3 is to strip everything but the address part (the text between the angle brackets). That stripping is accomplished by rewriting the workspace using the rule in the RHS:

```
R$*<$*>$*    $2              basic RFC822 parsing
             ↑
```
strip all but the address

Remember, when a $digit appears in the RHS, that digit is used as a count into the pattern-matching operators of the LHS.

```
$*<$*>$*
↑  ↑  ↑
```
$1 $2 $3

A $1 indicates the first $*, a $2 indicates the second $*, and a $3 indicates the third $*. Comparing this ordering of operators to the test address, you see:

workspace	LHS		RHS
"Your"	$*	← *match zero*	$1
"Fullname"		↓ *or more*	
"<"	"<"	← *match exactly*	
"you"	$*	← *match zero*	$2
"@"		↓ *or more*	
"here"			
"."			
"us"			
"."			
"edu"			
">"	">"	← *match exactly*	
	$*	← *match zero or more*	$3

This illustrates that the middle (second) $* matches the *you@here.us.edu* part of the workspace. When the RHS rewrites the workspace, it does so by copying the tokens matched by that second operator (specified in the RHS with the $2 positional operator).

The Comment

The rule contains this comment:

```
basic RFC822 parsing
```

RFC822 defines many aspects of e-mail headers and e-mail addresses. Among its many definitions is the standard that an e-mail address in angle brackets may be surrounded by optional non-address material. This comment both reflects the reasoning behind our rule and is phrased identically to similar comments in many *sendmail.cf* files.

Test Rule Set 3

Take a few moments to experiment and to observe the transformation from a user-specified address into one that *sendmail* can use. Add the following new rule set 3 to the rule sets in the *client.cf* file.

```
### The Rule Sets
S0 # select delivery agent
R@$+     $#error $: Missing user name       bounce bad address
R$+      $#hub $@$R $:$1                     punt to hub

S3 # preprocessing for all rule sets                     ← new
R$*<$*>$*    $2                  basic RFC822 parsing     ← new
```

Now run *sendmail* again. Up to now you have been testing rule set 0, so you have specified a 0 following the > prompt. Instead, you will now specify a 3 because you are testing rule set 3.

```
% /usr/lib/sendmail -oQ/tmp -Cclient.cf -bt
ADDRESS TEST MODE
[Note: No initial ruleset 3 call]
Enter <ruleset> <address>
> 3 Your Fullname <you@here>
rewrite: ruleset  3   input: "Your" "Fullname" "<" "you" "@" "here" ">"
rewrite: ruleset  3 returns: "you" "@" "here"
```

As expected, the new rule causes everything except the "good" e-mail address, the address between the angle brackets, to be thrown away.

Before we improve rule set 3, take a few moments to experiment. Try putting the fullname last. Try omitting the e-mail address between the angle brackets. Try nesting angle brackets in an address, like <a<b>c>.

As a closing note, recall that *sendmail* does minimum matching when comparing operators to the workspace. Although $*, for example, can match zero or more, it prefers to match zero if possible, and if not, then to match the fewest tokens possible. A LHS of $*@$+, for example, will match as shown in Table 10-1.

Table 10-1: What $\$$ in $\$*@\$+$ Matches for Different Addresses*

Address	$* matches	@	$+
a.b.c@d.e	a.b.c	@	d.e
a@b@c	a	@	b@c
@b@c		@	b@c

Expecting operators to over-match can cause you to misunderstand what a rule will do.

Missing Addresses

The current, and only, rule in rule set 3 accepts anything or nothing (the $*) between the angle brackets:

```
R$*<$*>$*    $2              basic RFC822 parsing
```

But, "nothing" can be a legal address. The expression <> is a legal sender address that is used when sending bounced mail to prevent further bouncing. To catch such addresses, a new rule needs to be written preceding the first. That new rule looks like this:

```
R$*<>$*      $n              handle <> error address
```

Here, the LHS matches any address that has nothing between the angle brackets. Observe how this new LHS catches such an address:

workspace	LHS	
	$*	← *match zero or more*
"<"	"<"	← *match exactly*
">"	">"	← *match exactly*
	$*	← *match zero or more*

When such an empty address is matched by the LHS of the new rule, the workspace is rewritten by the RHS of that rule to contain only the single macro $n. Recall from Chapter 7, *Defined Macros*, that $n was defined to be the name of the user from whom all bounced mail is sent:

```
DnMailer-Daemon
```

To observe the effect of this new rule in action, add it to the *client.cf* file. This new rule should precede the existing rule in rule set 3.

```
.  S3 # preprocessing for all rule sets
   R$*<>$*     $n     handle <> error address              ← new
   R$*<$*>$*   $2     basic RFC822 parsing
```

Now run *sendmail* in rule-testing mode once again:

```
% /usr/lib/sendmail -oQ/tmp -Cclient.cf -bt
ADDRESS TEST MODE
[Note: No initial ruleset 3 call]
Enter <ruleset> <address>
>
> 3,0 Your Fullname <you@here>
rewrite: ruleset   3    input: "Your" "Fullname" "<" "you" "@" "here" ">"
rewrite: ruleset   3 returns: "you" "@" "here"
rewrite: ruleset   0    input: "you" "@" "here"
rewrite: ruleset   0 returns: $# "hub" $@ "mailhost" $: "you"  "@"  "here"
```

Here two rule sets (3 and 0) are specified instead of one as you have been doing all along. Rule set 3 is called first; it throws away everything but the address between the angle brackets. The rewritten workspace is then given to rule set 0, which selects the hub delivery agent. This is as it should be, with a good address being forwarded to the mail hub.

But now give *sendmail* an empty address, one with nothing between the angle brackets:

```
> 3,0 <>
rewrite: ruleset  3   input: "<" ">"
rewrite: ruleset  3 returns: "Mailer-Daemon"
rewrite: ruleset  0   input: "Mailer-Daemon"
rewrite: ruleset  0 returns: $# "hub" $@ "mailhost" $: "Mailer-Daemon"
"@"   "here" "." "us" "." "edu"
```

Just as you may have expected, the empty address is caught by the new rule in rule set 3 and converted (in the workspace) to the value of $n. Rule set 0 then recognizes `Mailer-Daemon` as a lone user address and tacks on the domain of the hub. Note that the last line in the above example wraps to occupy two lines because of the narrow margins.

Nested Angle Brackets

Another kind of address that can cause problems is one containing nested angle brackets. These occur because of bugs in MUAs.* For example, consider the following address:

```
<a<b>c>
```

Run sendmail in rule-testing mode, using the current *client.cf* file.

```
% /usr/lib/sendmail -oQ/tmp -Cclient.cf -bt
```

Now give the nested address shown above to rule set 3.

```
3 <a<b>c>
rewrite: ruleset  3   input: "<" "a" "<" "b" ">" "c" ">"
rewrite: ruleset  3 returns: "a" "<" "b"
```

Clearly this is wrong. The correct address would have been b, the address inside the innermost of the nested angle brackets. The rule that made the mistake is this one:

```
R$*<$*>$*    $2                   basic RFC822 parsing
```

---

*Also because RFC733 misspecified angle bracket use.

And here is why:

workspace	LHS	
	$*	← *match zero or more*
"<"	"<"	← *match exactly*
"a"	$*	← *match zero*
"<"		↓ *or more*
"b"		
">"	">"	← *match exactly*
"c"	$*	← *match zero*
">"		↓ *or more*

Because the workspace is scanned left to right, the second < is not seen as anything special. That is, there is no concept in this rule of innermost and outermost angle brackets pairs.

To handle nested angle brackets, another rule needs to be designed.* That new rule looks like this:

```
R$*<$*<$*>$*>$*    $2<$3>$4                de-nest brackets
```

This new rule matches any address in the workspace that contains nested brackets. Using the count of LHS operators, the RHS strips away the outermost layer.

```
R$*<$*<$*>$*>$*    $2<$3>$4                de-nest brackets
  ↑  ↑  ↑  ↑  ↑
  $1 $2 $3 $4 $5
```

To test this new rule, add it to the *client.cf* file:

```
S3 # preprocessing for all rule sets
R$*<>$*            $n             handle <> error address
R$*<$*<$*>$*>$*    $2<$3>$4       de-nest brackets         ← new
R$*<$*>$*          $2             basic RFC822 parsing
```

Run *sendmail* again to test this new rule:

```
> 3 <a<b>c>
rewrite: ruleset  3  input: "<" "a" "<" "b" ">" "c" ">"
rewrite: ruleset  3 returns: "b"
```

As predicted, the second rule de-nested, thus allowing the third rule to isolate the address part.

---

*In Chapter 24, *Rule Sets*, we show a single rule that de-nests a nearly unlimited number of angle brackets.

Using what you have learned so far, predict how *sendmail* will handle this address:

```
<<<a>>>
```

Feed it to *sendmail* in rule-testing mode to see if you are correct. Remember that *sendmail* performs minimum matching.

As a general motto when designing your own rule sets, be liberal in what you accept (including addresses like `<<<a>>>`), but conservative in what you generate (never send out such ugly addresses).*

Details of Rule Flow

To better see what is happening inside each rule, you need to rerun *sendmail* with a `-d21.12` debugging command-line switch.

```
% /usr/lib/sendmail -oQ/tmp -Cclient.cf -d21.12 -bt
```

The `-d21.12` switch tells *sendmail* to print each rule as it is processed. Run *sendmail* again, with this new switch. This time, when you feed in a nested address, you get considerably more output:

```
> 3 <a<b>c>
rewrite: ruleset  3   input: "<" "a" "<" "b" ">" "c" ">"
-----trying rule: $* "<" ">" $*
----- rule fails
-----trying rule: $* "<" $* "<" $* ">" $* ">" $*
-----rule matches: $2<$3>$4
rewritten as: "a" "<" "b" ">" "c"
-----trying rule: $* "<" $* "<" $* ">" $* ">" $*
----- rule fails
-----trying rule: $* "<" $* ">" $*
-----rule matches: $2
rewritten as: "b"
-----trying rule: $* "<" $* ">" $*
----- rule fails
rewrite: ruleset  3 returns: "b"
>
```

This output may appear complicated, but it is really fairly straightforward. The first two lines and last two lines are what you have been seeing all along (when you *didn't* use the `-d21.12` switch):

---

*Paraphrased from *The Robustness Principle*, RFC793, TCP specification. Jon Postel, Ed.

```
> 3 <a<b>c>
rewrite: ruleset  3   input: "<" "a" "<" "b" ">" "c" ">"
rewrite: ruleset  3 returns: "b"
>
```

Everything in between those lines is new output caused by the −d21.12 switch. That new output shows each rule in rule set 3 being called and processed in turn. The first rule looks for empty angle brackets:

```
R$*<>$*        $n                     handle <> error address
```

The workspace (tokenized from the input of <a<b>c>) is compared to the LHS of this rule:

```
-----trying rule: $* "<" ">" $*
----- rule fails
```

The LHS doesn't match (the rule fails) because the angle brackets of the workspace are not empty. Consequently, the RHS of the first rule is not called, and the workspace is unchanged.

The second rule is the de-nesting one:

```
R$*<$*<$*>$*>$*    $2<$3>$4                de-nest brackets
```

The workspace (still <a<b>c>) is compared to the LHS of this rule.

```
-----trying rule: $* "<" $* "<" $* ">" $* ">" $*
```

The LHS matches the workspace, so the workspace is rewritten based on the RHS of that rule, and the extra angle brackets are stripped away:

```
-----rule matches: $2<$3>$4
rewritten as: "a" "<" "b" ">" "c"
```

The new workspace is then compared to the LHS of the same rule *once again*—that is, to the rule that just did the rewriting. If it were to match again, it would be rewritten again. This property can continue forever and can be useful in solving many configuration problems. We'll cover this property more fully in the next chapter.

So the rewritten workspace is compared once again to the first rule. The workspace (having been rewritten by the second rule) now contains:

```
"a" "<" "b" ">" "c"
```

This time the comparison fails:

```
-----trying rule: $* "<" $* "<" $* ">" $* ">" $*
----- rule fails
```

The last of the three rules then gets a crack at the workspace. That rule is:

```
R$*<$*>$*    $2                        basic RFC822 parsing
```

That workspace is still:

```
"a" "<" "b" ">" "c"
```

The workspace is once again matched, so it is rewritten again based on the RHS of the third rule:

```
-----trying rule: $* "<" $* ">" $*
-----rule matches: $2
rewritten as: "b"
```

After the third rule rewrites the workspace, it again tries to match that rewritten workspace and fails:

```
-----trying rule: $* "<" $* ">" $*
----- rule fails
```

As you can see, the `-d21.12` debugging switch can be very useful. It shows you exactly what each rule is trying to do. It shows you each rewrite of the workspace, and it shows you the order in which rules are being applied. (Note that in real rule sets, this output can easily run to many screens.)

Things to Try

- Design a rule whose LHS always matches anything in the workspace, and whose RHS always rewrites so as to leave the workspace unchanged. What happens when you test this rule?
- Design a rule whose LHS will match *name* in the workspace, but will not match *name@host*. Is this possible with just $+ and $*?
- What happens if you arrange rules in a different order? Try reversing the first two rules in our rule set 3.
- Design and test two rules that remove unbalanced angle brackets. That is, one that rewrites <a<b>c into a<b>c, and another that rewrites a<b>c> into a<b>c.

11

Rule Sets 1 and S=

Recall that the purpose of the *client.cf* file we have been developing is two-fold: to forward all mail to a central mail hub for processing, and to make all mail appear as though it is sent from the hub. The first purpose is fulfilled with a rule set 0 that always selects the hub delivery agent. This chapter begins the process of satisfying the second purpose. By designing appropriate rule sets 1 and S=, the sender's address may be rewritten so that it always appears to be from the hub.

Also recall that the recipient's address is first processed by rule set 3 and then by rule set 0. Rule set 3 finds an address among other text and cleans it up by removing nested angle brackets. After that, rule set 0 selects a delivery agent appropriate for the recipient's address. If the address is a bad one, rule set 0 selects the error delivery agent. For a valid address, it selects the hub delivery agent. Once the delivery agent is selected, the processing of other addresses, like the sender's address, may proceed.

Flow of the Sender's Address

When *sendmail* begins processing a mail message for delivery, it first looks for all the envelope recipients. Each recipient address found is processed first by rule set 3, then by rule set 0, which selects a delivery agent.

After all the recipients have had appropriate delivery agents selected for them, *sendmail* processes the sender's address. There is usually only a single sender* for any given mail message. The sender's address (or

---

*The envelope sender and the header sender are not necessarily the same.

addresses) may appear in the envelope, or in a From: header line, or it may be derived from the *uid* of the process that ran *sendmail.*

As shown in Figure 11-1, each sender's address is processed by rule set 3 first and then by rule set 1. Then, for each recipient in the list of recipients, each sender's address is custom processed by the rule set specified in the recipient delivery agent's S= equate. This custom processing is necessary because different delivery agents may want the sender's address to have a different appearance. One example is the difference between a domain-based delivery agent (needing an address like *gw@wash.dc.gov*) and a UUCP-based delivery agent (needing a routing path like *fbi!wash!gw*).

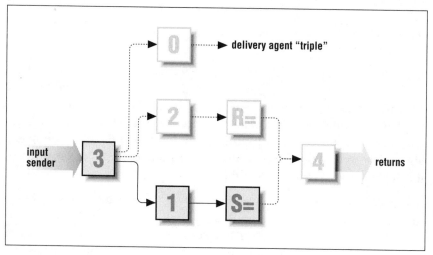

Figure 11-1: The flow of the sender's address

In general, all addresses are preprocessed by rule set 3. After that, the sender's address is always processed by rule set 1, no matter what the delivery agent. Then the sender's address is custom processed by the rule set specified by the S= equate of each delivery agent for each recipient.

We will examine the custom S= processing first, then discuss why a generic rule set 1 is not needed in the *client.cf* file.

Rule Set S=

In the original hub delivery agent definition, the S= equate was set to zero:

```
Mhub,    P=[IPC], F=mDFMuCX, S=0, R=0, A=IPC $h
                                  ↑
                         no custom processing
```

The S= equate is used to specify the number of the rule set that will perform delivery agent-specific custom processing of the sender's address.
When that equate specifies a rule set of 0, *sendmail* is told that no custom
processing will be done. Now that we intend to do custom sender address
processing, we will change the 0 to the number of a real rule set and write
that rule set.

Recall that rule sets 0 through 6 have special internal meaning to various
versions of *sendmail*. When selecting a rule number for use in a delivery
agent's S= equate, you need to be careful to select one that does not
already have internal meaning for *sendmail*. For the purposes of the *cli-
ent.cf* file we suggest rule set 10.*

As the first step in creating rule set 10, edit the *client.cf* file and change the
S=0 to S=10 in the hub delivery agent definition.

```
Mhub,    P=[IPC], F=mDFMuCX, S=10, R=0, A=IPC $h
                                   ↑
                          change 0 to a 10
```

This change tells *sendmail* that rule set 10 will custom rewrite the sender's
address for this (the hub) delivery agent. But before you can create a rule
set 10, we need to review why that rule set is necessary.

All Mail From the hub

Recall that one purpose of *client.cf* is to make all messages appear to be
from the hub. The purpose of a custom rule set 10 is to rewrite the sender's
address in such a way that the mail message always appears to have originated at the hub machine.

```
From: user@client
        ↓
     becomes
        ↓
From: user@hub
```

---

*A good convention is to number all S= rule sets in the range of 10 through 19 and all R= rule
sets in the range of 20 through 29.

This could be done by rule set 3, but that would affect all addresses, both recipient and sender, which is not appropriate. Mail should not appear to be both *to and from* the hub, but should appear to be only *from* the hub. This could also be in rule set 1 (which we will cover soon), but that would affect all sender addresses. You don't want to rewrite all sender addresses, just those that are being sent through the hub. You may someday want to use `prog` or `local` delivery agents, and the sender's address should be left unchanged for them.

Rule Set 10

The first step in creating any new rule set is to make sure it is not already in use. You do that by editing your configuration file (here, the *client.cf* file) and searching for that rule-set number. In this case, search for S10, to see if it has been declared. If it hasn't been declared, search for =10, to see if it has been reserved. In the *client.cf* file, you'll find that it has been reserved by the hub delivery agent, but that is only because you reserved it earlier.

```
Mhub,    P=[IPC], F=mDFMuCX, S=10, R=0, A=IPC $h
                                  ↑
                              reserved
```

In large, complex configuration files you will often find that rule sets are reserved by delivery agents, but never declared.*

Now that you are sure there are no misreserved rule sets in any delivery agent S= equates, you can design a rule set 10. Place the following new rule after rule set 3 in the *client.cf* file:

```
S3 # preprocessing for all rule sets
R$*<>$*          $n              empty brackets
R$*<$*<$*>$*>$*  $2<$3>$4        de-nest brackets
R$*<$*>$*        $2              basic RFC822 parsing
S10 # Rewrite the sender for the hub                      ← new
```

Here rule set 3 is defined, and followed by three rules. The S10 both ends rule set 3 and begins rule set 10. All that remains to be done is to create some rules for this new rule set.

---

*Rule sets can also be reserved in the RHS of rules. We'll cover that later in this tutorial.

Rewrite the Lone User Name

The sender's address can take several forms. It can be a user's login name, like *gw* or *ben*. It can be a user at a host, like *gw@wash* or *ben@fbi*. It can be a user at a fully-qualified name like *gw@wash.dc.gov* or *ben@fbi.dc.gov*.

Rule set 10 first looks for an address that is just a simple user's name, like *gw*, and makes it appear as though it is from the mail hub. To do this, you need a new LHS operator, $-. The $- operator matches *exactly one* token in the workspace. The first rule in rule set 10 uses the $- operator like this:

```
S10 # Rewrite the sender for the hub
R$-          $@$1@$H              user -> user@hub          ← new
```

Because $- is the only operator in the LHS, a match occurs only if the workspace contains a single token:

```
$-                matches     "you"
$-                does not match   "you" "@" "localhost"
```

This LHS is used to look for an address that contains only a user's login name. When such a match is found, the RHS ($@$1@$H) rewrites that address by appending an @ and the name of the mail hub machine, which was stored in the $H macro.

The RHS contains two operators that you have seen before and one that you haven't. The two you are familiar with are:

```
$@                return immediately
$1                positional operator
```

When $@ begins the RHS of any rule, it tells *sendmail* to return (exit the current rule set) immediately after it has rewritten the workspace. If the $@ operator did not appear at the start of the RHS, *sendmail* would rewrite the workspace and then evaluate the LHS again. The $@ also prevents the workspace from being carried down to any additional rules in the current rule set. An immediate return from this rule is desirable because it makes the user address appear to be that of the hub machine, which is exactly what is wanted.

The actual rewriting is done by the $1@$H. The $1, which you have seen before, takes the username matched by the LHS of $- (the first and only operator, thus $1). Then an @ character is appended. Lastly, the macro $H is appended to the workspace.

The macro $H contains the address of the mail hub machine as it is known to the outside world. This is different from the $R that you defined earlier, which contains the address of the mail hub machine as it is known to the

internal network. Before you can use the value of $H, you need to define it
in the *client.cf* file:

```
# The name of the mail hub
DRmailhost
# The hub as it is known to the outside world          ← new
DHmail.us.edu                                           ← new
```

This new macro definition places the text `mail.us.edu` into the macro
named H. Now the RHS of `$1@$H` will rewrite the workspace into:

```
"you"  "@"  "mail"  "."  "us"  "."  "edu"
  ↑     ↑     ↑
  $1    @    $H
```

This is exactly what is wanted. Any sender address (remember that `S=10`
handles only sender addresses) consisting of nothing more than the name
of a user will be rewritten so that it appears to come from the mail hub.
Table 11-1 shows the three LHS operators you now know.

Table 11-1: Three LHS Operators You Now Know

Operator	Description
$+	Match one or more tokens
$*	Match zero or more tokens
$-	Match exactly one token

A Word About $H

In the *client.cf* file, $R is defined to be the name of the hub machine as it is
known internally to your network. $H is defined to be the name of that
same machine as it is known to the outside world. Note that both names
could be the same at your site.

The important point about $R is that it contains a symbolic name, like
mailhost. That allows the machine that is used as the hub to be easily
changed should the need arise. As your site becomes larger and more complex, you may want to have several hubs for routing messages to the outside world. Or you might want to have one machine handle all outgoing
mail and another handle all incoming mail. Making $R internally symbolic
makes such changes easy.

The important point about $H, on the other hand, is that it contains a fully-
qualified domain name that is listed with the Domain Naming System or the

UUCP maps and is known to all other sites in the world. This is the machine part of the address that other sites will use when they reply to mail sent from the hub.

Remember that a name like *you* with an @ and the value of $H added, makes the address of the local sender (*you*) look as though it is from the hub (*mail.us.edu*). When someone at another site replies to this address, the reply will go to the *hub*, rather than to the local (client) machine. This is an important distinction, because later we will show that the client machine will (by design) be unable to receive mail.

Testing So Far

If you haven't already done so, add the new macro and the new rule set 10 to the *client.cf* file.

```
# The name of the mail hub
DRmailhost
# The hub as it is known to the outside world    ← new
DHmail.us.edu                                     ← new
```

Remember to replace `mail.us.edu` with a real machine name—the name of the hub machine at your site.

The new rule set looks like this:

```
S10 # Rewrite the sender for the hub
R$-          $@$1@$H              user -> user@hub    ← new
```

Now test the new rule by running *sendmail* in rule-testing mode:

```
% /usr/lib/sendmail -oQ/tmp -Cclient.cf -bt
ADDRESS TEST MODE
Enter <ruleset> <address>
[Note: No initial ruleset 3 call]
>
```

At the prompt, specify rule set 3 first because all addresses are preprocessed by that rule. Then specify rule set 10, because the hub delivery agent definition specifies that rule in its S= equate.

```
> 3,10 you
```

Following the list of rule sets, give the sender's address. Remember that the lone login name should be rewritten to appear as though it is from the hub. The output produced by *sendmail* looks like this:

```
rewrite: ruleset  3    input: "you"
rewrite: ruleset  3 returns: "you"
rewrite: ruleset 10    input: "you"
rewrite: ruleset 10 returns: "you" "@" "mail" "." "us" "." "edu"
```

Success!

Handling user@this.host

Rule set 10 next needs a rule that will take a user with the hostname of the client and change only the host part. Consider an address of the form:

```
user@this.host
```

Here the user part is what you just dealt with, a user's login name like *you*. That name is followed by an @ character and then the local host's name. One method of matching this form of address in the LHS would be to match the user, the @ character, and *any* hostname (recall that the $+ matches one or more tokens in the workspace):

```
R$-@$+
```

This form is easy to use, because the $+ would match any hostname at all and wouldn't require that you know all the possible names for the local host ahead of time. Unfortunately, you shouldn't use this approach, because you only want to rewrite the sender's address if it is that of the local machine. Using $+ would cause it to be rewritten whether or not it is the address of the local machine.

But how could the sender's address not be from the local machine? Recall that *sendmail* gets its sender address from one of four places: from the envelope, from the From: header, from the -f switch (see below), or from the *uid* of the process that ran *sendmail.*

Consider, for example, a USENET news-posting program that posts news by sending mail. It may be desirable to have all such posted news appear to be from the news program on the news server machine. One way to achieve this is by running *sendmail* with the -f switch:

```
-f news@news.server
```

Here the -f switch causes *sendmail* to use the address specified in the command line as the address of the sender.

But in this news example, you would not want to change the address of the sender to appear as though it were from the hub. That would undo what news tried to do with the −f switch.

A better approach is to match the user, the @ character, and the specific, local hostname:

```
R$-@$w
```

Recall that $w was defined to be the fully-qualified canonical name of the local host. This LHS matches only a workspace (sender's address) that begins with a single user's login name (the $-), followed by an @, and then by the name of the local host (the $w).

Add this new rule to the *client.cf* file.

```
S10 # Rewrite the sender for the hub
R$-     $@$1@$H        user -> user@hub
R$-@$w      $@$1@$H         user@local -> user@hub       ← new
```

Notice how, other than their comments, the two rules differ only in their LHS. The flow through these rules is that the first tries to match a lone user-name in the workspace. If that match fails, the second rule tries to match the workspace. It only matches a workspace that contains the name of a user at the local machine. To observe this rule in action, run *sendmail* in rule-testing mode again:

```
% /usr/lib/sendmail -d35.9 -oQ/tmp -Cclient.cf -bt
```

This time we added the −d35.9 debugging command-line switch, which tells *sendmail* to print each macro as it is defined.

```
← 25 lines omitted
define(w as "here.us.edu")                                    ← note
define(m as "us.edu")
define(v as "8.1")
define(b as "Fri, 13 Jan 92 05:51:39 -0800")
define(R as "mailhost")
define(H as "mail.us.edu")
define(j as "$w")
define(n as "Mailer-Daemon")
define(l as "From $g  $d")
define(o as ".:%@!^=/[]")
define(q as "<$g>")
ADDRESS TEST MODE
Enter <ruleset> <address>
[Note: No initial ruleset 3 call]
>
```

Note that *sendmail*, in this example, defines $w as here.us.edu, the name of the local machine. Your local machine name will, of course, differ.

Fortunately, you don't have to know what that name is in order to design a new rule. Simply use $w, and let *sendmail* do all the work.

Now, give *sendmail* rule sets 3 and 10 as you did before, but this time specify a sender's address that contains a user and a host part.

```
> 3,10 you@here.us.edu
          ↑
        the same as appeared in $w
```

The user part can be any login name. The host part must be the text that is stored in the $w macro (displayed when you just ran *sendmail* with the -d35.9 debugging command-line switch above).

```
rewrite: ruleset  3    input: "you" "@" "here" "." "us" "." "edu"
rewrite: ruleset  3 returns: "you" "@" "here" "." "us" "." "edu"
rewrite: ruleset 10    input: "you" "@" "here" "." "us" "." "edu"
rewrite: ruleset 10 returns: "you" "@" "mail" "." "us" "." "edu"
>
```

As intended, rule set 10, the custom rule set for rewriting the sender's address for the hub delivery agent, made the local address appear to be from the hub.

Note, however, that you cannot specify macros when testing addresses; that is, the following does not work:

```
> 3,10 you@$w
```

The *sendmail* program does not recognize macros in addresses. They aren't recognized because macros in rule sets are expanded when the configuration file is read, not when addresses are given to it. The command above results in the following erroneous output:

```
rewrite: ruleset  3    input: "you" "@" $w
rewrite: ruleset  3 returns: "you" "@" $w
rewrite: ruleset 10    input: "you" "@" $w
rewrite: ruleset 10 returns: "you" "@" $w
>
```

Rule Set 1

When we began this chapter, we explained that the sender's address was processed by a series of three rules: rule set 3, rule set 1, and the custom rule set specified by the S= delivery agent equate. We've described rule set 3 and S=, but haven't yet described rule set 1. In the scheme of sending all mail to a central hub, we don't really need a rule set 1. That's because there is nothing we need to do to *all* sender addresses. In fact, most configuration files, even at large sites, have no need for a rule set 1.*

---

*Eric says, "given it to do over, rule sets 1 and 2 wouldn't exist."

Still, it is wise to add a dummy rule set 1 (one that does nothing) to the *client.cf* file. For one thing, this makes it clear that you haven't simply omitted rule set 1 by oversight. It also allows us to illustrate some points about rule sets in general.

```
S10 # Rewrite the sender for the hub
R$-          $@$1@$H              user -> user@hub
R$-@$w       $@$1@$H              user@local -> user@hub
S1 # Generic sender rewrite (unused)                              ← new
```

We place rule set 1 last in the *client.cf* file, as we will continue to do with any other unused rules. This declaration of rule set 1 illustrates three points about rule sets in general:

- Rule sets do not have to be in numeric order in the configuration file. The *sendmail* program reads the entire file and sorts the rule sets internally.

- A rule set that has no rules following it is a "do-nothing" rule set. The workspace passed to it is returned unchanged.

- Rule sets that are declared but unused should have a comment included which indicates your intention.

The positioning of rule sets in the configuration file is largely a matter of individual taste. Some administrators like to keep custom rule sets (like rule set 10) next to the delivery agent definition rather than with the general rules. We favor no approach over another. The overriding concern in any configuration file—which tend to be complex—should be for clarity and organization.

Things to Try

- All machines can be known by two names: the normal hostname (as defined by $w) and the generic name *localhost*. Design and test a rule for rule set 10 that tests for and rewrites a sender address like *you@localhost*.

- When we speak of the sender, we have lumped together the envelope and header senders into one. Try to think of examples where the sender header address should be rewritten in a different way than the sender envelope address.

- At a site that has more than one hub, it would be necessary to route mail from some clients to one hub and mail from other clients to another. Think of a basis for such a division (like subnets or NIS domains) and design a set of rules (in a single configuration file) to rewrite the sender address appropriately for a selected hub.

- Consider the need to match subsets of a subdomain. For example, assume that the local hostname is *here* and the local domain is *my.sub.domain*. At such a site, all of the following are legal addresses: *you@here*, *you@here.my*, and *you@here.my.sub.domain*. But the following is illegal: *you@here.my.sub*. Modify rule set 10 in the *client.cf* file so that it recognizes all the legal forms of addressing in a subdomain.

12

Class

In rule sets, it is often advantageous to compare individual tokens to multiple strings when determining a match. For example, consider the rules developed in the last chapter, the custom sender rewriting rules from the hub delivery agent's S=10 equate:

```
S10 # Rewrite the sender for the hub
R$-        $@$1@$H            user -> user@hub
R$-@$w     $@$1@$H            user@local -> user@hub
```

The second rule's LHS looks for a sender's address that is composed of a single user's name, followed by an @ character and the name of the local machine (the value of $w). Any such address is rewritten by the RHS to appear as though it is from the central forwarding machine as defined by the $H macro.

Now suppose the local machine is known by several names, in addition to the name in $w. All machines, for example, can refer to themselves as *localhost*. Some machines can play special roles at a site (such as having a printer or containing a central directory of fonts), and it is perfectly normal for such machines to have more than the two usual names, $w and *localhost*.

To convert the sender's address so that it appears to come from the central forwarder, no matter what the local host's name, you may employ *sendmail* classes. In this chapter, we will cover the class configuration command and its cousin, the file configuration command. Proper use of the class and file commands allows you to replace many rules with a single rule.

The Class Command

The class command declares a macro whose value is a list of strings. Rule sets may then compare the workspace to that list of strings. One such list could be a list of names by which the local machine is known. The class command is like the declaration of an array of strings.

A class is referenced in the LHS with the $= prefix:

```
$=X
```

Here, X is the class name. The workspace is tokenized as usual, then the appropriate token is *looked up* to see if it was defined as belonging to the class X. If it was, the workspace at that point is considered matched. We'll cover this in more detail shortly.

Declaring a Class

The words that form the list of words in a class are put there by using the C configuration command. The form for the class configuration command is:

```
CXlist
```

The class configuration command starts with the letter C, which must begin a line. That C is immediately followed (with no intervening white space) by the name of that class (the X above). A class name can be any single ASCII character. A white space-separated *list* of word elements follows on the same line. Space between the X and the *list* is optional.*

For example, the following declaration places the three possible names for the local machine into the class named w:

```
Cw localhost printer1 fontserver
```

Multiple declarations of the same class macro may coexist. Each appends its word elements to the preceding list. That is, the following example produces the same result as the one above.

```
Cw localhost
Cw printer1 fontserver
```

Both examples define a class named w, and both assign to that class the same list (array) of three words.

---

*Note that this is different from the D command, where there must not be any space between the D and the macro name.

Two caveats

First, class names (like w) and macro names (like Dw) are completely independent. To illustrate, consider the following two configuration commands:

```
Dwlocalhost
Cwlocalhost
```

Both assign the word `localhost` to macros named w. The first assigns that name to a macro, the second to a class. Internally, *sendmail* stores the word `localhost` twice, first as type "macro" and second as type "class." Although both share the same value (the word `localhost`), macros and classes are completely independent of each other.

Second, the words that make up a class list of words should not contain any of the separation characters used in tokenizing the workspace. Not all versions of *sendmail* will work properly if class words contain those characters.

```
Cw localhost localhost.us.edu
```

The second of the two words above contains the dot separation character. That form is *multitokened,* because it is composed of five tokens. Such multitokened words should not be used in class definitions, because they will not work as expected for all versions of *sendmail.*

Multiple Known Names for the Local Host

As an example of one common use of the class macro, consider that machines are often known by multiple names. In addition to `localhost` and the value of $w, a machine might also serve a printer, or have another name which indicates it serves all fonts.

One way to account for all such possibilities is with a series of rules like those below:

```
R$-@$w          $@$1@$H          user@local -> user@hub
R$-@localhost   $@$1@$H          user@localalias -> user@hub
R$-@printhost1  $@$1@$H          user@localalias -> user@hub
R$-@fontserver  $@$1@$H          user@localalias -> user@hub
```

Fortunately, the class configuration command provides an alternative. In place of the last three lines above, a class may be used instead.

The class definition looks like this:

```
# All the possible names by which I might be known
Cw localhost printer1 fontserver
```

This configuration file C command declares that the class macro named **w** contains as its list the three words shown.

Use of a class list allows two rules to be written that do exactly the same thing as the four rules above:

```
R$-@$w          $@$1@$H          user@local -> user@hub
R$-@$=w         $@$1@$H          user@othernames -> user@hub
```

But why two rules instead of one? A separate rule like the first is necessary because macro values (such as $w) won't work as expected when used as part of a class list of words. That is, the following might not work:

```
Cw $w localhost printer1 fontserver
   ↑
   unwise
```

Since you are generally not allowed to use macro values in class lists,* you need to test for $w in a separate rule.†

Class Macros in the LHS

The list of words in a class are referenced in the LHS of rules by prefixing the class name (a letter) with the characters $=. For the class named **w**, the expression in the LHS looks like this:

```
$=w
```

To understand how this expression is evaluated, we need to look at how the words in the original C command were stored.

```
Cw localhost printer1 fontserver
```

Each word in this list is stored internally by *sendmail* in its *symbol table*. The symbol table holds all the words that appear in the configuration file. It holds the values of macro definitions and the symbolic names of delivery agents. It also holds the words that form a class list.

Next, we need to review how the workspace is tokenized and compared to the LHS of a rule. Just before the LHS is compared to the workspace, the

---

*IDA 5.65c, V8, and a few other vendors, allow this.

†Actually, we are fudging for the sake of an example. Most versions of *sendmail* automatically include the value of $w in the class w for you, along with any other host aliases they can find.

workspace is tokenized. The address of a local user in the workspace might look like, and be tokenized, like the following:

```
you@localhost    becomes →    "you" "@" "localhost"
```

When the $=w expression appears in the LHS of a rule, it is compared to the workspace at the point that corresponds to its position in the LHS.

```
R$-@$=w          $@$1@$H          user@othernames -> user@hub
    ↑
   here
```

When performing its minimum match of the workspace to the LHS, *send-mail* performs the following:

```
$-      match george
@       match @
$=w     does localhost match any token in class w?
```

When *sendmail* encounters a class-matching expression in the LHS, it looks up the corresponding token from the workspace in its symbol table. Here it looks up localhost. Because localhost is listed in the symbol table as belonging to the class w, *sendmail* finds a match. If there were no localhost in the symbol table, the match would fail. If there were one or more localhost entries in the symbol table, but none marked as belonging to class w, the match would also fail.

Class Macros in the RHS

When a match in the LHS allows the RHS to rewrite the workspace, the token matched by the $= prefix can be referenced with a $*digit* positional operator. This differs from the $ macro prefix you learned about earlier. Macros are expanded when the configuration file is read (so $*digit* doesn't work), but classes are given values only when a rule is matched (so $*digit* does work).

We don't use the positional operator in the RHS because we don't need to know what word matched. Instead, we take the username from the LHS with $1, add an @ character and the name of the forwarding hub machine (the $H):

```
R$-@$=w          $@$1@$H          user@othernames -> user@hub
  ↑ ↑              ↑
  1 2              $2 not needed
```

Testing Class

Add the new rule just developed to the *client.cf* file.

```
S10 # Rewrite the sender for the hub
R$-        $@$1@$H          user -> user@hub
R$-@$w     $@$1@$H          user@local -> user@hub
R$-@$=w     $@$1@$H          user@othernames -> user@hub  ← new
```

And add a class definition for w that is appropriate for your machine:

```
# All the possible names by which I might be known     ← new
Cw localhost printer1 fontserver                        ← new
```

Now run *sendmail* in rule-testing mode once again:

```
% /usr/lib/sendmail -oQ/tmp -Cclient.cf -bt
ADDRESS TEST MODE
Enter <ruleset> <address>
[Note: No initial ruleset 3 call]
>
```

To test the new rule, specify rule set 10 and give *sendmail* an address with a user and @localhost part:

```
> 10 user@localhost
rewrite: ruleset 10   input: "user" "@" "localhost"
rewrite: ruleset 10 returns: "user" "@" "mail" "." "us" "." "edu"
```

This is just as expected. After all, the value in $H is mail.us.edu. Now give *sendmail* another address, only this time add your domain to the host part:

```
> 10 user@localhost.us.edu
rewrite: ruleset 10   input: "user" "@" "localhost" "." "us" "." "edu"
rewrite: ruleset 10 returns: "user" "@" "localhost" "." "us" "." "edu"
```

This time there is no match, and the workspace remains unchanged. Although there is a localhost in the class w, the rule we created does not account for any trailing domain part:

```
$-      matches user
@       matches @
$=w     matches localhost
          . us . edu   ← is unmatched.
```

Adding the Domain

There are three approaches to writing a rule that matches any of the local hostnames with a domain added.

1. Use a $* operator to match anything after the local hostname. This is unwise because it assumes that anything that follows the host is a domain, which might not always be true.

2. Use your domain name directly in the rule. Although this will work, it is better to use a macro in case you change your domain at a later date or port this file to a machine on another domain.

3. Use a macro that has your domain name as its value.

We will use the third approach because it is the cleanest. Begin by adding a macro definition for your local domain to the *client.cf* file. Use the D macro to hold that value:

```
### Defined macros
# The name of the mail hub
DRmailhost
# Our official fully qualified hostname.
Dj$w
# Our domain name.                               ← new
DDus.edu                                         ← new
# Whom errors should appear to be from.
```

You should replace the *us.edu* with the name of your own local domain and use your own domain in the examples that follow.

Next add another rule to rule set 10. This new rule looks for any of your local names (in $=w) that are followed by the local domain name just defined for $D:

```
S10 # Rewrite the sender for the hub
R$-          $@$1@$H      user -> user@hub
R$-@$w       $@$1@$H      user@local -> user@hub
R$-@$=w      $@$1@$H      user@othernames -> user@hub
R$-@$=w.$D   $@$1@$H      user@domain -> user@hub        ← new
```

Note that the value in $D can contain multiple tokens, whereas none of the words in the $=w list can. This is because the $D is expanded when the configuration file is read. Internally, *sendmail* stores the new LHS of the line something like this:

```
$- @ $=w . us . edu
```

Each of the multiple tokens in $D is compared to corresponding tokens in the workspace. Only one token in the workspace is compared to the $=w, so $=w may not be multitokened.

Now run *sendmail* once again and feed it the address that failed in the last test (but use your local domain):

```
% /usr/lib/sendmail -oQ/tmp -Cclient.cf -bt
ADDRESS TEST MODE
Enter <ruleset> <address>
[Note: No initial ruleset 3 call]
> 10 user@localhost.us.edu
rewrite: ruleset 10   input: "user" "@" "localhost" "." "us" "." "edu"
rewrite: ruleset 10 returns: "user" "@" "mail" "." "us" "." "edu"
```

As expected, the new rule in rule set 10 does its job. It finds that the `localhost.us.edu` part of the address matches the `$=w.$D` part of the rule and rewrites the workspace to make the sender's address appear as though it is from the `hub`.

Internally Defined Class ($=w)

Before the *sendmail* program reads its configuration file, it tries to find the name of the local host. It does that by first finding the official name and making that the value of the macro w. It then strips off the domain part and adds the remaining hostname to the class w.

To see what name *sendmail* finds for $w, run *sendmail* with the `-d0.4` debugging switch:

```
% /usr/lib/sendmail -d0.4 -bp
```

The output produced looks like this:

```
Version 8.1
    ← possibly other stuff here
canonical name: here.us.edu
Mail queue is empty
```

The canonical (official) name of the local host, as *sendmail* understands it, is printed. This is the value that *sendmail* gives to the macro w. Then everything from the first dot to the end is stripped off the canonical name, and the result (`here`) is added to the class w before the configuration file is read.

The File Form of Class

It is not always possible or convenient to list the values for a class directly in the configuration file. Information that might be better stored in other files would include:

- The names of hosts that are connected to the local machine via UUCP. At some sites, such connections are created and discontinued often, and it is undesirable to be constantly changing the configuration file.

- The names of hosts that are being moved from one location to another. During a move, it is better to modify an external file while each hostname is changed and then to modify the configuration file after all the moves are done.

- The alternative names for a machine may vary from machine to machine, yet a single configuration file may be shared among them. When such a *boilerplate* configuration file is centrally maintained (and distributed with *rdist*(1), for example) names that indicate the specialty roles of a machine should be external to that file.

The *client.cf* file lists all the known names for the local host in the class w:

```
# All the possible names by which I might be known
Cw localhost printer1 fontserver
```

To make this configuration file more universal and general in purpose, it would be better to store the two host-specific names (`printer1` and `fontserver`) in a separate file. To externalize words for a class list, you use the F configuration command. That command looks like this:

```
Fw/path
```

Here the F must begin a line. It tells *sendmail* that this is a class definition, just like the C command we just illustrated. The name of the class (here w) must immediately follow the F with no intervening space. Optional space may separate the classname from the */path*. With the C command, a list of words follows the name on the same line, but with the F command the name of a *file* follows. The */path* is the full pathname of a file. For demonstration purposes, we will name that file */etc/mynames*.

Edit the *client.cf* file and make the following two changes:

```
# All the possible names by which I might be known
Cw localhost                                        ← new
Fw /etc/mynames                                     ← new
```

The first class definition starts with the letter C and tells *sendmail* to add the name `localhost` to the list of words in the class w. The second line tells *sendmail* to read the file named */etc/mynames* and to add the words in that file to the class w. Note that the name w is the same for each line. The C and F commands differ only in where the words are taken from.

Now run *sendmail* and notice what happens when the file */etc/mynames* doesn't exist:

```
% /usr/lib/sendmail -oQ/tmp -Cclient.cf -bp
client.cf: line 22: cannot open /etc/mynames: No such file or directory
Mail queue is empty
```

As you would expect, *sendmail* prints an error message when it fails to find the file. But as you might not expect, *sendmail* prints the error warning and continues to run.

Now create an empty file */etc/mynames*. If you lack write permission, create a file you are permitted to write to (like */usr/tmp/mynames*) and use it in the following examples and in the *client.cf* file:

```
% cp -i /dev/null /etc/mynames
% chmod 644 /etc/mynames
```

In the above example, the `-i` switch for *cp*(1) prevents accidently overwriting the file */etc/mynames* if it already exists. The second line gives that file safe permissions. The */etc/mynames* file now exists but is empty.

Run *sendmail* again and notice that the warning is no longer printed:

```
% /usr/lib/sendmail -oQ/tmp -Cclient.cf -bp
Mail queue is empty
```

The *sendmail* program doesn't care if the file in an F configuration command is empty; it cares only that the file exists.

Now to complete the transition from a *client.cf* containing only a C command to one that contains C and F commands, put the following two hostnames into the file */etc/mynames*, one word per line:

```
printer1
fontserver
```

The *sendmail* program reads this file, takes each word, and adds it to the class **w**.

But why one per line? To answer this question, we need to examine how *sendmail* reads the files specified in the F configuration command.

The scanf(3) Pattern

The *sendmail* program reads lines of text from an F configuration-command file in two steps. First it reads the whole line by calling the *fgets*(3) function. Then it *extracts* a word from that line using the *scanf*(3) function.

The *scanf*(3) function extracts selected text from a line using a conversion specification. The default conversion specifier used by *sendmail* is:

```
%s
```

This tells *scanf*(3) to select the first *space-delimited* word in the line. That is, if the line contains multiple words like the following, *scanf*(3) only selects the first:

```
word1 word2 word3
   ↑
  space
```

Because *scanf*(3) selects only the first word in a line (here `word1`), you need to place each word for a class on a separate line in the file.

Occasionally, one word per line will not be convenient. To support such circumstances, *sendmail* offers a variation on the F command that looks like this:

```
Fw/path pat
```

When the name of the file (*/path*) is followed by a space and then a pattern (*pat*), *sendmail* uses that pattern in place of the default `%s` with *scanf*(3). Consider the following example, in which all the words for a class are placed on a single line:

```
printer1 fontserver
```

Ordinarily this would cause the second word `fontserver` to be missed. But giving the F command the appropriate *scanf*(3) pattern causes *sendmail* to accept both words:

```
Fw/etc/mynames %[^\n]
```

This somewhat cryptic-looking pattern tells *sendmail* to select all words on a line. Specifically, it causes *scanf*(3) to accept all characters up to, but excluding, the newline character (see the online manual for *scanf*(3)). Each word in that line of text is then added to the class w.

This illustrates two points. First, the limitation that you can have only one word per line in the file */etc/mynames* is due to the default `%s` pattern. Second, if a line in an F file has multiple words per line, and if an appropriate pattern is used to select them, *sendmail* happily adds each to a class.

Things to Try

- Design a *scanf*(3) pattern that will create a class from the */etc/hosts* file. The object is to skip the leading IP address of each line.

- Design a *scanf*(3) pattern that will create a class from your UUCP *Systems* file (or *L.sys* for old UUCP). The object is to select just the host-name from each uncommented line.

- Design a *scanf*(3) pattern that will create a class from the */etc/passwd* file. The object is to create a list of user login names.

- In an F command, rather than specifying the name of a file, specify the name of a directory or a device like */dev/null*. Does *sendmail* care? How does it handle (or not) nonfiles?

- Use */usr/dict/words* as a class file. Does reading a huge file slow *sendmail* down noticeably?

13

Setting Options

The *client.cf* file is now roughed out enough so that it can almost be used to send mail. All that remains are two important loose ends: options, which we will cover in this chapter, and headers, which we will cover in the next.

Thus far, whenever you've run *sendmail*, you've had to run it with a command-line switch of -oQ/tmp.

```
% /usr/lib/sendmail -oQ/tmp -Cclient.cf -bt
```

That switch tells sendmail to set the option (-o) whose name is Q to have a value of /tmp. The Q option tells *sendmail* where to find its queue directory. Recall that the queue is used by *sendmail* to temporarily store mail messages (usually because they cannot immediately be delivered).

Although you may assign values to options from the command line, it is more efficient to declare them in the configuration file. If you had used an option to declare the location of the queue file in the configuration file, the above command line would have been simplified to the one below:

```
% /usr/lib/sendmail  -Cclient.cf -bt
```

Options: An Overview

Options are declared in the configuration file by beginning a line with the letter O:

```
OQ/tmp
```

The name of the option (here Q) immediately follows the O with no intervening space. An option name is always a single letter. The value to be assigned to the option immediately follows the option letter, again with no intervening space. The values for some options are strings (like /tmp), while the values for others can be numbers (like 3), times (like 3d for three days), or a boolean (like True). There are no hard rules for which type of value belongs with which option. Instead, you will need to look up each option in Chapter 30, *Options*, and use the type indicated there.

Before adding an option to the *client.cf* file, run *sendmail* once again, but this time omit the -oQ/tmp:

```
% /usr/lib/sendmail  -Cclient.cf -bt < /dev/null
                      ↑
                      note -oQ/tmp missing
```

This time, instead of entering rule-testing mode, *sendmail* prints the following error and exits:

```
cannot chdir(mqueue): No such file or directory
```

This error illustrates two things. First, it shows that if you fail to tell *send-mail* where to find its queue directory, it uses the relative name (mqueue) as the pathname of that directory. And second, it shows that *sendmail* always does a *chdir*(2) to change directory into its queue when it first starts up.

Now add a declaration for option Q to the *client.cf* file. Traditionally, option declarations follow the macro definitions, so place your first option there:

```
# The location of the queue directory          ← new
OQ/tmp                                          ← new
```

Now run *sendmail* in rule-testing mode again, and again omit the -oQ/tmp command-line switch. This time *sendmail* runs successfully.

Required Options

The *sendmail* program offers over 50 options for you to choose from. We will cover only a few here. Recall that the purpose of our configuration file is to forward all mail to a central mail hub. In keeping with the simplicity of this task, you need to declare only those few options that are required for most configuration files, and then only a subset of those. The options you will declare in the *client.cf* file are shown in Table 13-1.

Table 13-1: Some Required Options

Option	Description
Q	Location of the queue directory
T	Limit the life of queued messages
d	Default delivery mode
F	Default file permissions
g	Default group identity
u	Default user identity
L	Default logging level
r	Timeout for SMTP reads
o	Accept old-style lists of addresses
B	Unquoted space replacement character

We'll describe each of these required options briefly; then you can add them to the *client.cf* file for testing.

The Location of the Queue Directory (OQ)

You have already learned about the Q option, but before going on to other options, we need to clarify the meaning of the queue and this option.

Queued mail always looks like *authentic* mail to *sendmail*. That is, the *sendmail* program *trusts* the mail it finds there, believing that only *sendmail* placed it there. If the queue directory is world-writable (as */tmp* is), anyone can create queued mail and thereby create forged mail messages. To help prevent forged mail, the queue directory should be writable only by *root*. Unfortunately, for the purpose of our exercises, such a directory (were you to use it) would prevent you from testing the *client.cf* file. You would need to be *root* while testing, which isn't desirable and may not be possible.

To help you to remember to change the *client.cf* file later, add a comment now showing the need to make the change and the correct path to use:

```
# The location of the queue directory"
# Change to this for release: OQ/var/spool/mqueue        ← new
OQ/tmp
```

Note that on some systems, the /var needs to be replaced with /usr.

Limit the Life of Queued Messages (OT)

Mail is usually placed into the queue because it could not be transmitted immediately. Periodically, *sendmail* attempts to retransmit each queued message. After a certain amount of time, messages that have not been successfully transmitted are bounced. The T option specifies the amount of time to wait before bouncing a message.

```
# return queued mail after this long
OT5d
```

The T option is one that takes time as its argument. Here, the 5d represents five days. The letter following the number specifies the units. The above, for example, could have been represented like this:

```
OT120h
```

This tells *sendmail* to bounce queued mail after 120 hours, which is the same amount of time as five days.

Five days may seem like a long time. After all, the mail hub should always be up and always be accepting mail. But suppose the hub crashed on Friday evening and replacement parts weren't available until Tuesday morning. In this situation, queued mail on all the clients would start bouncing before the server was repaired.

When choosing a value for the T option, take into account the worst-case scenario you can imagine. If the hub has "same day" service, a value of 1d might be enough. If the hub has to be shipped out for repair, you may want to consider a value like 14d (two weeks).*

The Default Delivery Mode (Od)

There are several modes in which the *sendmail* program can run. Each determines how *sendmail* interacts with the program that ran it. For the *client.cf* file, you want the user's MUA to connect to *sendmail* for message transmission, but to arrange for the appearance that the message was sent almost instantaneously. This is best for users, because they won't want to wait a long time for their prompt to return whenever the mail hub is busy.

---

*You should also consider including MX records for the hub, so mail will be sent to another server if the hub is down. (We cover MX records in Chapter 17, *DNS and sendmail*.)

The delivery mode to use is called *background* because it causes *sendmail* to accept a message and then run in the background (thus allowing the MUA to continue at once). The delivery mode is set with the d option:

```
# default delivery mode (deliver in background).
Odbackground
```

Note that only the b of background is recognized by *sendmail*. So you will often find this same declaration in other configuration files more succinctly expressed like this:

```
Odb
```

Other possible values for the d option are documented in Chapter 30, *Options*.

The Default File Permissions (OF)

The *sendmail* program frequently needs to create new files (like files in its queue). The file permissions given to each created file are determined by the value of the F option. That value can range from 0600 (readable and writable only by *sendmail*) to 0666 (readable and writable by anyone in the world). For the sake of security, we'll select the first value—the most restrictive.

```
# temporary file permissions -- 0600 for secure mail
OF0600
```

Note that the value must be expressed in octal notation. (See *chmod*(1) for details.)

The Default User Identities (Ou and Og)

Again, for security, *sendmail* tries to avoid running as *root* whenever possible. When delivering failed mail to your `~/dead.letter` file, for example, it runs as you. If it finds itself in a situation where it must not be *root*, but cannot otherwise decide on a real user's identity, *sendmail* assumes the identity of the user defined by the u and g options.

```
# default UID and GID.
Ou1
Og1
```

The u option defines the *uid* under which to run, and is here defined to be 1 (for the user *daemon*). The g option defines the *gid* under which to run, and is here defined as 1 (for the group *daemon*). The values given to these options must be numeric—using names won't work.*

---

*Except in V8 *sendmail*, where names will work.

At security-conscious sites, these are often set to the numbers for the user *nobody* and the group *nogroup* (65534 for both, under SunOS).

The Default Logging Level (OL)

Recall that option b told *sendmail* to run in the background. Because it is in the background, *sendmail* should not print information about its activities to your screen. On the other hand, you do want to record information about its activities to help solve future problems.

The method used by *sendmail* to invisibly record its activities is called *logging.** The setting of the L option allows you to turn logging completely off or to specify a logging level. The higher the logging level, the more detailed the information logged. That is, low levels log only serious problems, middle levels also log statistical information, and high levels include debugging information.

```
# Level at which to syslog errors.
OL9
```

Here, we've chosen a level of 9. This is a middle level, which, in addition to causing serious problems to be logged, also causes statistics such as message size to be logged.

Typically, logged information is written by the system into a file called *syslog*. The location of that file can vary from version to version of UNIX, but is generally specified in the file */etc/syslog.conf* and documented in the online manuals for *syslog*(3) and *syslogd*(8).

Timeout for SMTP Reads (Or)

The local client *sendmail* talks to *sendmail* on the hub using a language called the Simple Mail Transfer Protocol (SMTP). You saw a glimpse of that language earlier (Chapter 4, *How to Run sendmail*) when you ran *sendmail* in verbose mode with the −v switch.

---

*The actual mechanism used is called *syslog*(3), and is described in Chapter 22, *Logging and Statistics*.

SMTP is a dialogue between the two *sendmail* programs. Your *sendmail* sends a line of text telling the other what it wants to do:

```
RCPT To:<friend@hub.us.edu>
```

Here, your *sendmail* is saying that the recipient of the e-mail message is the user `friend` at the hub. Your *sendmail* then waits for a reply. One such reply might be:

```
250 <friend@hub.us.edu>... Recipient ok
```

Here, the other *sendmail* is telling yours that the recipient address is acceptable. The amount of time that your *sendmail* will wait for a reply in its SMTP dialogue is set using the r option.

```
# Wait for SMTP replies. Give the hub a break.
Or1h
```

Here the amount of time to wait is specified as one hour (1h). Like the timeout in the queue option (T) you saw above, the r option takes time as its value. If you accidently leave off the h for hours (or m for minutes), the units default to days.*

We selected a value of one hour to allow plenty of time for the hub to reply. This is necessary because the hub will not always be able to respond quickly. If, for example, the recipient is the address of a huge mailing list, the hub (if otherwise busy) could easily take nearly an hour to verify all the addresses. This value might be as large as four hours if the hub is talking to machines all over the world (some of them old and slow and connected over slow and busy networks).

Accept Old-style Lists of Addresses (Oo)

The current standard for specifying multiple recipients is to separate each address from the others with commas. Unfortunately, this has not always been the standard; old software may still exist which separates addresses with spaces.

```
abe,george,andrew      ← new style
abe george andrew      ← old style
```

To prevent old software from breaking, you need to tell *sendmail* that the use of spaces is acceptable and that, if it finds such old-style lists, it should

---

*The default is minutes for V8 *sendmail*.

replace the spaces with commas. You tell *sendmail* this by specifying the o option.

```
# default messages to old style.
OoTrue
```

The o option is ether true (accept and convert) or false (don't accept). The True makes it true. In actual practice, only the T is recognized, and either T or t will work. To turn it off, use F or f (for false) or omit the entire declaration. If you omit the true or false, but include the option, it defaults to true.

The Unquoted Space Replacement Character (OB)

Recall from Chapter 8, *Addresses and Rules,* that any address can be split up into tokens in the workspace. The address is then rewritten according to rules specified in rule sets. After all the tokens have been (possibly) rewritten, they are rejoined to form an address again.

The B option exists for those times when two adjoining tokens are just words (rather than a word and a separating character). For example, suppose the workspace began by containing the following tokens:

```
a @ b . c
```

Then suppose some rule always changed the last two tokens into the single word LOCAL. The result of rewriting would look like this:

```
a @ b LOCAL
```

Here we have four tokens, the last two of which are text. The question becomes, what do we insert between them? Unless you tell *sendmail* to do otherwise, it always sticks a space between them. Thus, the default is to join these tokens together into this:

```
a@b LOCAL
```

Because we set the o option above to true, this single (but odd) address wrongly becomes two:

```
a@b, LOCAL
```

To prevent this kind of mishap, we use the B option to change the replacement character from a space to a dot:

```
# Replace unquoted spaces with a dot.
OB.
```

With this declaration in the configuration file, the previous tokens are joined together like this:

```
a@b.LOCAL
```

This forms a single address, which is what is wanted. But what does the "unquoted" in the comment mean?

When parts of an address are surrounded in full quotation marks, those parts are viewed by *sendmail* as a single token. Thus, an address like this:

```
"abe lincoln"@wash.dc.gov
```

is tokenized like this:*

```
"abe lincoln"  @  wash  .  dc  .  gov
```

When these tokens are joined back together, the abe and lincoln are viewed by *sendmail* as one token (with a space included), rather than two (with need of a space replacement character).†

Testing the Options

Now that the necessary options have been described, add them to the *client.cf* file. As the name "option" implies, the values you give them are somewhat optional. You are free to change timeouts and the like to values you consider more appropriate.

```
# The location of the queue directory
# ---> Change to this for release: OQ/var/spool/mqueue
OQ/tmp
# default delivery mode (deliver in background).
Odbackground
# temporary file permissions -- 0600 for secure mail
OF0600
# default UID and GID.
Ou1
Og1
# Level at which to syslog errors.
OL9
# Wait for SMTP replies. Give the hub a break.
Or1h
# default messages to old style.
OoTrue
# Replace unquoted spaces with a dot.
OB.
```

---

*We have omitted the usual quotation marks around tokens so that the quotation marks around the name will be more visible.

†Actually, the address is sent as-is to another site. The B option there causes the confusion.

Take a moment to test these new option declarations. Run *sendmail* in rule-testing mode just to see if it complains about anything.

```
% /usr/lib/sendmail -Cclient.cf -bt < /dev/null
ADDRESS TEST MODE
Enter <ruleset> <address>
[Note: No initial ruleset 3 call]
>
```

Here there are no problems. The things to watch out for are mostly typos, like setting option O when you meant o.

Sending Mail

The *client.cf* file is now at a point in its development where it can be used for sending mail. The mail it generates will be illegal in a few ways, but we will gloss over those illegalities for now and deal with them in the next chapter. In case you've forgotten, you send mail to yourself with *sendmail* like this:

```
% /usr/lib/sendmail -Cclient.cf you
```

After your enter this command, *sendmail* pauses and waits for you to enter the e-mail message you want to send. Enter a subject header line, a blank line (to separate the header from the body), a brief message to yourself, and conclude by entering a dot on a line by itself.

```
Subject: testing

testing
.
```

Your message is now forwarded to the mail hub machine, where (if all has gone well) it is delivered. Using your favorite MUA, read the message you just sent and save it to a file. That file will look something like this:

```
From you@us.edu Sun Feb 21 07:29:30 1993
Return-Path: <you@us.edu>
Received: from here.us.edu by mail.us.edu (8.1)
        id AA11850; Sun, 21 Feb 93 07:29:27 PST
Date: Sun, 21 Feb 93 07:29:27 PST
From: you@us.edu (Your Full Name)
Message-Id: <9302211529.AA11850@mail.us.edu>
Subject: test
To: you

testing
```

The first thing to notice in this saved message is that header lines have been added. You gave *sendmail* only a Subject: header line when you ran it, but now there are eight header lines.

These header lines were added by the mail hub machine. Because they were added by the hub and not by your local machine, a few of them are illegal. The Received: header, for example, shows only that the hub received the message from the local machine. There is no indication (other than by implication) that the local machine received it in the first place.

Another problem is the Message-Id: header. Every e-mail message is supposed to have a message identifier that is guaranteed unique world-wide. Part of that identifier is supposed to be the name of the originating machine (your local machine). In the above header, however, it contains the name of the mail hub.

We cover headers in the next chapter.

Things to Try

- What problem would you foresee with declaring the location of the queue directory using a relative pathname? Suppose you used "OQ." (for the current directory)? What if you were *root* when you tried this?

- The OL logging-level option uses *syslog*(3) to record messages. Read the online manual for *syslog*(3) on your system, and determine where *sendmail* logging information is stored. Does the logging level we specified (9) produce too much or too little information? Use tail -f to watch that information, while at the same time sending mail with the *client.cf* file.

- The Or option sets the timeout for SMTP replies. Would it be courteous to your hub for you to make that timeout very small? What happens if you make it 0? Use the -v switch to watch the SMTP conversation with various small settings of Or.

14

Header, Priority, Trusted

In the previous chapter, you sent mail to yourself and saw that several header lines were added by *sendmail* when the original message had only one. In the message you received, some unsuitable header lines were added by the hub machine. We begin this chapter by looking at the header configuration command, then we will add that command to the *client.cf* file so that legal headers can be produced.

Headers

The header configuration command begins with the letter H. Like all configuration commands, it begins a line. The H is then followed by the text of a header.

    Hname: field

The *name* is the name of a header, like Subject. The list of all header names of interest to *sendmail* can be found in Chapter 31, *Headers*. The name is followed by a colon and then text appropriate to the nature of the name (the *field*). Optional white space can surround the colon.

RFC822 (modified by RFC1123) specifies that certain header lines must appear in all e-mail messages. Of those, the two you will first add to the *client.cf* file are shown in Table 14-1.

Table 14-1: Two Required Headers

Name	Description	When Added
From:	Address of the sender	If missing
Received:	Record of receipt	Always

Unless otherwise specified (as you will see later), headers declared in the configuration file are only added to a mail message if that particular *name* is missing. The exception to this rule is the `Received:` header. It is special in that it is always added to a mail message, even if there is already one there.

The From: Header

The `From:` header contains the official address of the sender. Declaring the `From:` header is simplicity itself, because it uses as its *field* a macro you've already declared:

```
HFrom: $q
```

Recall that the $q was declared earlier as:

```
Dq<$g>
```

Here, $q is defined as the value of the $g macro surrounded by angle brackets. Also recall that $g is the address of the sender (generated by *sendmail*) as it appears in the envelope. That address, when you are the sender, was generated by rule set 10:

```
S10 # Rewrite the sender for the hub
R$-          $@$1@$H                user -> user@hub
```

The sender address (*you*) is rewritten by this rule so that it becomes *you@mail.us.edu.* That is, the hostname and domain of the hub machine are appended so that the mail appears to come from the hub. This is the envelope address of the sender and the address placed into $g. For e-mail sent by you, the value given to $q and thus to the `From:` header is:

```
From: <you@mail.us.edu>
```

The `From:` header is only added to an outgoing mail message if there is not already one there. It is placed into the *client.cf* file to ensure that no mail leaves the local machine without this required header.

The Received: Header

The `Received:` header is a special one. It is always added to the header portion of every mail message, even if there is already one there.

The `Received:` header is used to make a record of each machine that mail has passed through. When *sendmail* calculates a hop count (to bounce mail with too many hops) it does so by counting the `Received:` header lines. The declaration of the `Received:` header is a bit complicated. A minimal `Received:` header declaration looks like this:

```
HReceived: by $j id $i; $b
```

The word `by` is mandatory. It must be followed by the fully-qualified, official name of the local machine. That name was declared earlier by giving the appropriate value to `$j`:

```
Dj$w
```

Here the value given to `$j` is taken from `$w`. Recall that `$w` is given its value by *sendmail* when that program first starts up, and it should contain the fully-qualified name of the local host.

The next item in the `Received:` header is the word `id` followed by `$i`. The `$i` macro is another that is given its value by *sendmail*. It contains the identifier portion of the filenames used (or that would be used) to store the message in the queue. It typically looks like AA*digits*. This value is useful for locating a record of the mail message in the log file created by *syslog*(3) and the L option (see Chapter 22, *Logging and Statistics*).

The `Received:` header definition concludes with a semicolon, followed by the current date and time as stored in `$b`. The `$b` macro contains the current date in ARPAnet format. That is: the day of the week, the month, the day, the time, the year, and the time zone.

These three items in the `Received:` header, when viewed together, create a unique identification of the current message. They form the minimum information required in this header.

Testing So Far

Add the `From:` and `Received:` headers to the *client.cf* file. The new lines in *client.cf* will look like this:

```
# default messages to old style.
OoTrue
# Replace unquoted spaces with a dot.
OB.

#### Header Declarations                           ← new
HFrom: $q                                           ← new
HReceived: by $j id $i; $b                          ← new
```

Here they follow the options that were added in the last chapter. As usual, a comment has been included to clarify your intent. You may want to review Chapter 7, *Macros*, for an explanation of the $j, $i, and $b macros.

Now send mail to yourself just like you did at the end of the last chapter:

```
% /usr/lib/sendmail -Cclient.cf you
Subject: testing

testing
.
```

Receive the mail you just sent, save it to a file, and look at what you saved. It will look something like this:

```
From you@us.edu Sun Feb 21 07:29:30 1993
Return-Path: <you@us.edu>
Received: from here.us.edu by mail.us.edu (8.1)
        id AA11850; Sun, 21 Feb 93 07:29:27 PST
Received: by here.us.edu id AA02315; Sun, 21 Feb 93 07:28:00 PST
Date: Sun, 21 Feb 93 07:29:27 PST
From: you@mail.us.edu (Your Full Name)
Message-Id: <9302211529.AA11850@mail.us.edu>
Subject: test
To: you

testing
```

Notice that a new `Received:` header was added. This is the one just declared in the *client.cf* file. Notice that the two `Received:` headers form a trail of who first received the message and how it was passed from one machine to the other.

Also notice that the contents of the From: header has changed. Something has removed the angle brackets and added your full name. What happened was this:

1. On the hub machine, the address in the envelope for the sender is taken from the RCPT message that the local machine sends during the SMTP conversation. That address is the value of $g with angle brackets added.

2. On the hub machine, the address in the From: header is compared to the sender envelope address. The address in the From: header that *client.cf* supplied was the value of $g surrounded in angle brackets.

3. Whenever the address in the envelope for the sender and the address in the From: header are identical, *sendmail* removes the From: header and creates a new one. Thus *sendmail* on the hub machine removed the From: header and created a new one that included your full name.

The definition of $q on the hub machine is more complex then that in the *client.cf* file. One possible definition might look like this:

```
Dq$g$?x ($x)$.
```

This is just like the local definition, but it has a macro *conditional* added to the end. A macro conditional is simply an if-endif construction, where $? is the if, and $. is the endif. The above definition, then, can be broken down like this:

Dq	*define macro q*
$g	*as: the value of $g*
$?	*if*
x	*the macro $x contains a value*
($x)	*add this to the definition*
$.	*endif*

The macro $x contains as its value the full name of the sender. If that full name is not known, $x has no value and $q is defined as $g. If $x does contain a value, $q is defined as $g ($x). Macro conditionals are described in Chapter 27, *Defined Macros*.

Headers Versus Delivery Agent Flags

Some headers should only be inserted into a mail message if one delivery agent is selected, but not if another is selected. For example, one traditionally should include the Full-Name: header when mail is being delivered with UUCP, but should not include it for most other delivery agents.

The mechanism that governs inclusion versus exclusion is a list of flags that prefix the header definition in the configuration file. Those flags are composed of a series of one or more letters, all of which are surrounded with a pair of ? characters.

```
H?flags?name: value
```

When *sendmail* decides if a header is to be added to the mail message, it compares the `flags` listed with the flags of the delivery agent's F= equate.

```
Mhub,    P=[IPC], F=mDFMuCX, S=0, R=0, A=IPC $h
                     ↑
                   flags
```

If a given *flag* (letter) appears in both, the header is added to the mail message. Otherwise it is not.

Traditionally, for example, the x flag is used to indicate the need for a Full-Name: header. But our hub delivery agent does not have an x in its F= flags. Since that is the only delivery agent we use, we need to add a Full-Name: header to the *client.cf* file.

The Full-Name: Header

The Full-Name: header is used to display the full name of the sender, as taken from the *gecos* field of the *passwd*(5) file. You saw above how the hub machine tries to add the sender's full name to the From: header. But since you don't necessarily have control over the hub, you should add a Full-Name: header locally, so that the full name is displayed even if the hub fails to add it.

The way to declare the Full-Name: header is like this:

```
H?x?Full-Name: $?x$x$.
```

First prefix it with the ?x? flag. This means that the Full-Name: header is only added if the delivery agent also contains that flag.

The value given to the Full-Name: header is just like the conditional you saw earlier. If ($?) the macro x contains a value, use that value ($x), endif ($.). We use this conditional test so that the full name is added only if it is known.

Next, to make the `Full-Name:` effective, you need to add an **x** flag to the hub delivery agent declaration:

```
Mhub,    P=[IPC], F=xmDFMuCX, S=0, R=0, A=IPC $h
                     ↑
                    add
```

Now any mail that uses the hub delivery agent for a recipient (all mail) will add a `Full-Name:` header to the message if there is not already one there. If the full name is known (`$x` has a value), that name follows the `Full-Name:` header on the same line; otherwise the header contains only the header name.

The Date: Header

The `Date:` header is required in all messages to show the time and day that the message originated. It is a good idea to include `?`*flags*`?` in its definition, so that custom delivery agents that do not need the `Date:` can be designed later.

```
H?D?Date: $a
```

The `$a` is the *origin date* of the mail message in RFC822 format. That date is set internally by *sendmail* to be correct for inclusion in the `Date:` header.

An `F=D` flag already exists in the hub delivery agent:

```
Mhub,    P=[IPC], F=xmDFMuCX, S=0, R=0, A=IPC $h
                     ↑
                  add the date
```

That D was originally put in this delivery agent definition with the `Date:` header in mind.

The Message-Id: Header

The `Message-Id:` header is used to uniquely identify each mail message. It must be inserted into the message when it is first created (first handled by *sendmail*). The form of the `Message-Id:` header is very specific:

```
H?M?Message-Id: <$t.$i@$j>
```

Here a ?M? prefix is included. The hub delivery agent definition already has the F=M flag listed:

```
Mhub,    P=[IPC], F=xmDFMuCX, S=0, R=0, A=IPC $h
                      ↑
             add the message identifier
```

The field following the `Message-Id:` must follow particular rules. First, it must be surrounded by angle brackets. Then, what appears between the angle brackets must look like a legal address:

<address>

The address must be composed of pieces of information that uniquely identify the mail message world-wide. We create that address in a way that is commonly used in most configuration files:

```
<$t.$i@$j>
```

The $t is the current date and time represented by an integer. The $i is the local unique identifier for the queue file for this message (even if the message isn't queued), and $j is your host's fully-qualified domain name. Other information may be used, provided the result looks like a legal address and provided no two identical identifiers ever go out.

Headers Learned So Far

Now add all the headers so far described to the *client.cf* file.

```
# default messages to old style.
OoTrue
# Replace unquoted spaces with a dot.
OB.

### Headers
HFrom: $q
HReceived: by $j id $i; $b
H?x?Full-Name: $?x$x$.
H?D?Date: $a
H?M?Message-Id: <$t.$i@$j>
```

Note that the `Full-Name:` header uses the ?x? flag, so you need to add that same flag to our hub delivery agent definition:

```
Mhub,    P=[IPC], F=xmDFMuCX, S=0, R=0, A=IPC $h
                      ↑
                     new
```

With these few additions, the *client.cf* file is almost ready to use, but we won't test it yet. First we need to discuss priorities.

Priorities

The priority of a mail message determines its position among other messages in the queue when the queue is processed. Priority, as a header line, also defines whether or not a bounced message should be returned to the sender. Priorities are not hardcoded into *sendmail*. Instead they need to be declared in the configuration file. The typical declaration, and the one we will use, looks like this:

```
Pspecial-delivery=100
Pfirst-class=0
Plist=-30
Pbulk=-60
Pjunk=-100
```

These lines use the P (priority) configuration command. Like all configuration commands, the P must begin the line. It is followed by a name, an equal sign, and a value. The general form looks like this:

```
Pname=value
```

There are only five possibilities for *name* that are legal:

special-delivery

> This mail message needs to be processed before any others. This priority is only effective when the message is being delivered from the queue.

first-class

> Unless otherwise declared with a Precedence: header, the message is first-class by default.

list   The message originated as part of a mailing list. It should be deferred until other more important mail has been processed from the queue.

bulk   The message is a broadcast, like a mailing list, but less important. If the message can't be delivered, throw it away instead of bouncing it.

junk   Absolutely worthless mail. Test messages and mail from some programs fall into this category. Like bulk, it is discarded rather than bounced.

The *value* assigned to each *name* is somewhat arbitrary. The ones we use are common. As you gain familiarity with the queue and mailing lists, you may want to adjust these values. In general, the higher the number, the higher the priority. By convention, formal first-class mail has a priority of zero, with positive numbers used for high-priority mail and negative numbers used for various kinds of bulk mail.

The P configuration command only tells *sendmail* the *value* to assign to a given *name*. It has no other effect. The values are only used when a mail message is processed that has a `Precedence:` header line in it. The inclusion of `Precedence:` header lines is left to MUAs.

To illustrate, imagine that a user on your machine is managing a mailing list. The software used to create each mailing for the list arranges to include a `Precedence:` header in each outgoing message. That header looks like this:

```
Precedence: list
```

The mailing-list message is given to *sendmail* on the local machine. The local *sendmail* sees the `Precedence:` header in the message and extracts the field of that header, the `list`. It then compares `list` to each of the *name* parts of its P configuration lines. It finds a match with the line:

```
Plist=-30
```

Because it finds a match, it uses the *value* from this configuration command as the initial priority of the mail message. If there is no match (or if the original message lacks a `Precedence:` header) the initial priority of the mail message defaults to zero.

Now add P configuration commands to the *client.cf* file. Traditionally, they are placed after the header commands:

```
H?D?Date: $a
H?M?Message-Id: <$t.$i@$j>

### Priority
Pspecial-delivery=100
Pfirst-class=0
Plist=-30
Pbulk=-60
Pjunk=-100
```

Sending Real Mail

The *client.cf* file is now complete and ready to use for sending all kinds of user mail. As you did before, send mail to yourself using *sendmail* directly:

```
% /usr/lib/sendmail -Cclient.cf you
Subject: testing

testing
.
```

Receive this message as you usually receive mail and save it to a file. The contents of that file should look something like this:

```
From you@us.edu Sun Feb 21 07:29:30 1993
Return-Path: <you@us.edu>
Received: from here.us.edu by mail.us.edu (8.1)
        id AA11850; Sun, 21 Feb 93 07:29:27 PST
Received: by here.us.edu id AA02315; Sun, 21 Feb 93 07:28:00 PST
Date: Sun, 21 Feb 93 07:29:27 PST
From: you@mail.us.edu (Your Full Name)
Message-Id: <9302211529.AA11850@here.us.edu>          ← note
Subject: test
To: you

testing
```

Note the change between this message's header and that of the previous message you sent. Instead of the hub machine adding a `Message-Id:` header, the local machine added that header. You can tell, because the local machine's name appears there instead of the hub's name.

Actually, the `Date:` was also added locally, but there is nothing to indicate that fact. A `Date:` should be added locally to accurately reflect the posting date of the message. If you didn't supply a `Date:`, instead allowing the hub to supply it, and the hub were down for a while, that header would be inaccurate by the amount of time the hub was down.

Trusted User

A trusted user is one who can use the `-f` switch to specify the name of the sender in the command line.* This switch is necessary to make certain kinds of mail work. UUCP, for example, requires this switch because UUCP mail is always given to *sendmail* by a program running as the pseudo-user

---

*Trusted users as a concept, and the T command, have been eliminated from V8 *sendmail*. See Chapter 18, *Security*, for more details.

uucp. If *uucp* could not change the identity of the sender, all UUCP mail would wrongly appear to come from *uucp.* When UUCP runs *sendmail,* it uses the -f command-line switch as shown below to change the identity of the sender:

```
-f newsender
```

Here, `newsender` is the address of the sender that *sendmail* should use in place of *uucp.* This is the envelope sender, and it is the address that will appear in various sender headers like `From:`.

For security reasons, *sendmail* does not let just anyone use the -f switch. Instead, it expects a list of approved users to appear in the configuration file. The T configuration command is used to list those users who are allowed to use the -f switch:

```
T user1 user2 ....
```

The T begins the line (as do all configuration commands) and is followed by a list of approved user login names. Each name is separated from the others (and optionally from the T) with white space.

The T command to use in the *client.cf* file looks like this:

```
T root daemon
```

We list *root* because some root-run programs need to send mail under the identity of other users. We list *daemon* for the same reasons, and because most long-running background processes are owned by the user *daemon.* If your local machine is set up to receive UUCP mail, you need to add *uucp* to this list.

Once you add the T command to the *client.cf* file, you are almost ready to use that file as the official configuration file.

Things to Try

- Everything to the left of the colon is taken as the name of the header. What error message do you get if you omit the colon? Is it possible to include a colon in the name?
- Gather all your system configuration file's header definitions. For each that is not in the *client.cf* file, why do you suppose it is necessary?
- In the *client.cf* file, only one delivery agent is doing anything (the hub). Does it make sense to include ?*flags*? in the headers in this situation? Can you safely remove those flags and the corresponding flags from the F= flags of the hub to make *client.cf* smaller?

- Priority configuration commands specify the beginning order for processing mail from the queue. Since mail is always sent to the hub
machine at once, does it make sense to set those priorities in the *cli-
ent.cf* file? Would there be any harm in omitting them and letting the
hub assume that responsibility?

- The trusted configuration command defines a small list of users who
can change the identity of the sender. It is intended to limit the ability of
other users to forge mail. The trusted configuration command has been
completely eliminated from V8 *sendmail*. Suggest reasons why its elimination is a good idea, and what impact its elimination has on forged
mail.

15

Loose Ends

In this chapter, we will complete our tutorial by tying up a few loose ends and installing a *client.cf* file as the system configuration file.

Test the Configuration File

Clearly you won't want to install the *client.cf* file as the main *sendmail.cf* file until you've made sure it does what it was intended to do. One of the better ways to test a new configuration file is to create a file of addresses for which you already know the correct outcome, then feed the contents of that file to *sendmail* in rule-testing mode. We will use a list that is short, but sufficient, for your initial needs.

```
3,0 user@here
3,0 user@here.us.edu
3,0 user@foo
3,0 foo!user
3,0 user
```

Each line begins with a list of rule-set numbers through which to pass each address. We use 3,0 because ours is a newer version of *sendmail* which does not automatically call rule set 3 first. If yours is an older version, you should delete the 3, from the start of each line. The addresses listed are humbly few, but will suffice for the needs of the *client.cf* file. No matter the form of the address, each should be forwarded to the hub as-is. The way to test the *client.cf* file with this list looks like this:

```
% /usr/lib/sendmail -Cclient.cf -bt < list \
        | grep "0 returns" \
        | sed -e "s/^.*returns://"
```

Here, `list` is the name of the file into which you saved the above list of rule sets and addresses. The output produced contains indications that each will be passed as-is to the hub.

```
$# "hub" $@ "mail" "." "us" "." "edu" $: "user" "@" "here"
$# "hub" $@ "mail" "." "us" "." "edu" $: "user" "@" "here" "." "us"
"." "edu"
$# "hub" $@ "mail" "." "us" "." "edu" $: "user" "@" "foo"
$# "hub" $@ "mail" "." "us" "." "edu" $: "foo" "!" "user"
$# "hub" $@ "mail" "." "us" "." "edu" $: "user" "@" "mail" "." "us"
"." "edu"
```

Notice that all will be delivered using ($#) the hub delivery agent. Also notice that each will be forwarded ($@) to the hub machine (mail.us.edu) for delivery. Finally, note that the user part ($:) will be the original address, unchanged for all but the last. As intended, any lone recipient name has the address of the hub machine appended to it.

Further testing would be suggested if the output varied in unexpected ways. It might be necessary to run *sendmail* in rule-testing mode by hand, testing each rule and sequence of rules individually to find any mistakes in the *client.cf* file. If the *client.cf* file tests okay, you are now (but for a few loose ends) ready to install it as the official *sendmail.cf* file.

The Real Queue and OQ

In the current *client.cf* file, the queue is defined as the */tmp* directory. Because of its nature, the */tmp* directory is always world-readable, -writable, and -searchable. Any file placed in */tmp* can be accessed by any user on the system to copy or remove. The use of */tmp* clearly violates the need for confidentiality.

Another drawback to using */tmp* is that */etc/rc* files, executed when the system boots, often remove everything from */tmp*. You certainly would not want queued mail messages removed just because the machine rebooted.

Instead of */tmp*, you should use the existing mail queue directory to store queued messages. If you haven't already done so, find that location by looking for the Q option declaration in your existing *sendmail.cf* file:

```
% grep ^OQ /etc/sendmail.cf
OQ/usr/spool/mqueue
```

Here, we are looking for lines in the */etc/sendmail.cf* file that begin with the letters OQ. Remember that your *sendmail.cf* file may not be in */etc*. Replace the location used above with one suitable for your situation.

Edit the *client.cf* file and replace OQ/tmp with the result you found. At the same time, remove the comment that was left there reminding you to do just that:

```
# The location of the queue directory
# Change to this for release: OQ/var/spool/mqueue     ← remove
OQ/usr/spool/mqueue                                   ← change
```

This change causes *sendmail* to use the correct queue, but it has an unfortunate side effect. Recall that *sendmail* runs as the *root* unless an unsafe command-line switch causes it to give up that privilege. The −C switch you've been using all along to run *sendmail* is just such an unsafe switch. Consequently, if you were to now run *sendmail* as:

```
% /usr/lib/sendmail -Cclient.cf you
```

the −C would cause *sendmail* to run as an ordinary user. For confidentiality, the *queue* directory is usually protected by making it only accessible by *root*. Ordinary users, such as we've been assuming you are, lack permission to access the *queue* directory. Running the above command now will likely result in the error:

```
cannot chdir(/usr/spool/mqueue): Permission denied
```

You need to install the *client.cf* file in place of the system *sendmail.cf* file so that you can successfully run *sendmail*. With the *client.cf* file installed, you no longer need to use the −C switch to tell *sendmail* where to find its configuration file. Unfortunately, before you can perform that replacement, you need to first make sure other machines know about it.

MX Records

Recall that in the hub/client setup, all mail goes to the hub machine and none is ever delivered directly to the client. This requires two things: that all mail to the client be automatically sent to the hub machine instead of to the client; and that the hub machine accept mail addressed to the client as though that mail were addressed to the hub machine instead. Forcing all mail to go to the hub machine requires that you create Mail Exchanger (MX) records.

If you already administer the DNS maps, the changes we will make are simple. If you don't, you will have to ask your DNS administrator to make the changes for you. How DNS interacts with *sendmail* is described in greater detail in Chapter 17, *DNS and sendmail.* You may want to jump ahead to that section, then return here, to better understand the changes we are making.

To arrange for all mail to go to the hub machine, first find the primary file for your DNS zone. We won't tell you where to find it, because you either know where it is or you probably lack permission to edit it. Somewhere in the primary file for your DNS zone is an entry for the local client. It looks something like this:

```
here            IN    A       123.45.67.8
                IN    HINFO   Sun4/75 unix
```

Remember that the local machine is *here.us.edu.* The entry for this machine begins with its hostname (with the domain part omitted). The IN says that this is an Internet-type entry—the only type currently supported. The A says that this is an *address* record, one that associates an IP address with a hostname. The IP address is the *dotted quad* that follows (the 123.45.67.8).

Other lines may follow the A record. Here we show an HINFO (host information) record that describes the hardware and the operating system for the local machine.

Immediately below the A record for the local machine, add a new MX record:

```
here            IN    A       123.45.67.8
                IN    MX      13 mail            ← add
                IN    HINFO   Sun4/75 unix
```

Two pieces of information are necessary for an MX record. The first is a relative preference (the 13), which must be a number. The preference is only used when there is more than one MX record for a host. If there were two, the host with the lowest preference would be tried first, and then the host with the higher preference, if the first failed. The number selected doesn't matter, because there is only one MX record for this host.

The second item (the one following the preference) is the name of the hub machine to which mail will be sent in place of sending it to the client. If the domain part for both the hub machine and the client machine is the same, only the hostname of the hub machine needs to appear in this record. The hostname of the hub in all our examples has been `mail`, so that is what we used:

```
IN      MX      13 mail
                   ↑
                host name of our mail hub
```

You should, of course, replace `mail` with the actual name of your central mail-handling machine.

If the hub machine is in a different domain than the client, a fully-qualified domain name needs to be specified in place of `mail`. For example, consider that all local mail is being sent offsite to the central server at *wash.dc.gov*:

```
IN      MX      13 wash.dc.gov.
                             ↑
                 note the dot at the end
```

If you place a fully-qualified name in an `MX` record, be sure to terminate that name with a dot. That dot tells DNS that this name is complete. Without it, DNS automatically adds your local domain to the name, resulting in an unknown address. For `mail` above, the dot was omitted because the local domain should be added.

After you've made this change, you need to wait for the old record to time out. How long you wait depends on the value of the Time To Live (TTL) defined for the record. A TTL can appear in two places. It can appear in the A record, or it can appear elsewhere as a default TTL. If it appears in the A record, it will be a number between the hostname and the `IN`:

```
here    28800       IN      A       123.45.67.8
         ↑
        Time to Live (TTL) for this record
```

TTL values are always in seconds. Here the A record will time out and any new information will be updated after eight hours have elapsed. Depending on when it was last updated, you may have to wait up to eight hours for the new `MX` record to be recognized.

If the A record has a TTL, you should duplicate that TTL in the new `MX` record so they both time out together:

```
here    28800       IN      A       123.45.67.8
        28800       IN      MX      13 mail
```

At most sites, the TTL for A and MX records are not stored with them, but are defined by a default TTL elsewhere. To find the default TTL, look at the top of the same file for a Site Of Authority (SOA) record:

```
@       IN      SOA     us.edu. postmaster.us.edu. (
                                1.43      ; serial number
                                7200      ; secondary refresh
                                1800      ; secondary retry
                                3600000 ; secondary expire
                                86400 )  ; minimum default ttl
```

The details of your SOA record will differ, but the desired information can still be found. The SOA record includes a parenthetical list of five numbers. The last is the default TTL that will be used for all records that don't specify one. Here, that default is 86400 seconds, or 24 hours.

If your MX records lack individual TTLs (because the A record lacks them), you will need to wait the default TTL period of time for the new MX record to become known.

We've omitted a few wrinkles, like *reloading* the name server, for a simpler description of the process. If you have permission to change the zone map file, you have doubtless changed it before and are familiar with the missing steps. If you haven't, a short section like this one can't begin to give you the information you need to manage DNS. Instead, we refer you to *DNS and BIND* by Paul Albitz and Cricket Liu (O'Reilly & Associates, Inc., 1992).

Hub Accepts Mail for Client

Recall that mail to your machine will be delivered to the hub instead, because of the MX record you just created. Unless you change the configuration of the hub, that mail will bounce, because the hub doesn't yet know it should accept it.

Again, you may lack permission to make the required changes. But for the sake of illustration, we'll assume you can.

You need to modify the hub's configuration file so that the hub thinks mail to your local machine is instead mail to itself. The first step is to edit the hub's configuration file and search for the rule which allows it to recognize itself. Because every machine needs to recognize itself under the name localhost, you should search for that string first:

```
# We always want localhost to be considered local.
Cwlocalhost
```

Here is the portion of one example configuration file that declares
localhost as equivalent to the hub's hostname. Recall that class w is special because it is initialized internally by *sendmail* to contain all the possible names of a machine. All, that is, except localhost, which always
needs to be added to class w in the configuration file.

We searched for localhost instead of Cw because some configuration
files use a letter other than w to list alternative names. The following illustrates one of those other letters:

```
# Other name for our machine
CO localhost printserver faxhost
```

If your hub's configuration file is like this, you need to use the letter O (or
whatever letter appeared) in place of the more standard letter w in the
examples to follow.

Now that you have the name (letter) of the class of other names, you need
to add the local workstation's name to that list. This can be done in either
of two ways. If the local machine is the only one that will be using the *cli-
ent.cf* file, you can add its name to the existing class definition:

```
# Other name for our machine
CO localhost printserver faxhost here
                                   ↑
              add the local machine's name here
```

If, on the other hand, yours is just the first of many machines that will be
using the *client.cf* file, you should create an external file now, so that the
hub's configuration file only needs to be edited once:

```
# Other name for our machine
CO localhost printserver faxhost
# Clients for which we receive mail        ← new
FO/etc/mail/clientlist                     ← new
```

If you use the external file approach, make certain to create that file and
add the local machine's name to it before continuing.

After modifying the hub's *sendmail.cf* file, you should test it. Run *sendmail*
in rule-testing mode and give it the local machine's name as part of each
address.

```
% /usr/lib/sendmail -bt
ADDRESS TEST MODE
Enter <ruleset> <address>
>
```

This example shows that the hub is running an old version of *sendmail*, one that always calls rule set 3 first. Bear that in mind as you feed it addresses.

To test whether or not the hub's *sendmail* recognizes the local machine as local to the hub, you need to see if rule set 0 selects the `local` delivery agent. Since rule set 3 is automatically called first, don't specify it. In its absence, the rules called for this version of *sendmail* will be 3, then 0.

```
> 0 user@here
rewrite: ruleset  3    input: "user" "@" "here"
rewrite: ruleset  6    input: "user" "<" "@" "here" ">"
rewrite: ruleset  6 returns: "user" "<" "@" "LOCAL" ">"
rewrite: ruleset  3 returns: "user" "<" "@" "LOCAL" ">"
rewrite: ruleset  0    input: "user" "<" "@" "LOCAL" ">"
rewrite: ruleset 30    input: "user"
rewrite: ruleset  3    input: "user"
rewrite: ruleset  3 returns: "user"
rewrite: ruleset  0    input: "user"
rewrite: ruleset  9    input: "user"
rewrite: ruleset  9 returns: "user"
rewrite: ruleset  0 returns: $# "local" $: "user"
rewrite: ruleset 30 returns: $# "local" $: "user"
rewrite: ruleset  0 returns: $# "local" $: "user"
>
```

Success! The output produced will vary depending on your hub's configuration file and version of *sendmail*, but the result you are seeking will be the same. The last line of output (what rule set 0 returns) should show that the `local` delivery agent was selected (the $# operator).

Now perform the same test, but this time include your domain as part of the hostname:

```
> 0 user@here.us.edu
rewrite: ruleset  3    input: "user" "@" "here" "." "us" "." "edu"
rewrite: ruleset  6    input: "user" "<" "@" "here" "." "us"
"." "edu" ">"
rewrite: ruleset  6 returns: "user" "<" "@" "LOCAL" ">"
rewrite: ruleset  3 returns: "user" "<" "@" "LOCAL" ">"
rewrite: ruleset  0    input: "user" "<" "@" "LOCAL" ">"
rewrite: ruleset 30    input: "user"
rewrite: ruleset  3    input: "user"
rewrite: ruleset  3 returns: "user"
rewrite: ruleset  0    input: "user"
rewrite: ruleset  9    input: "user"
rewrite: ruleset  9 returns: "user"
rewrite: ruleset  0 returns: $# "local" $: "user"
rewrite: ruleset 30 returns: $# "local" $: "user"
rewrite: ruleset  0 returns: $# "local" $: "user"
>
```

Again, your local machine is recognized as `local` by the hub's configuration file. If it isn't, there is a serious problem with the hub, because it will also be unable to recognize `localhost.us.edu`.

If all tests well, you need to kill and restart the *sendmail* daemon on the hub. Review Chapter 4, *How To Run sendmail*, if you've forgotten how to do this. Beware any frozen configuration file. If one exists, you will have to refreeze it (see the discussion of the `-bz` switch in Chapter 32, *The Command Line*).

Prevent the Daemon from Running

Once your MX record has taken effect, and once the hub has been configured to recognize your machine as local to itself, no mail will ever again be delivered to your local machine. Since there will be no incoming mail connections, you no longer need to run a *sendmail* daemon. Preventing the daemon from running involves two steps. First you need to kill the running daemon, then you need to modify your *rc* files so the daemon never runs again. We won't show you how to kill the daemon, because you already learned that. Instead we'll jump directly into preventing it from ever running again.

If you haven't already done so, search your *rc* files to see how *sendmail* is started when the machine first boots. Under SysV, for example, that command and its results might look like this:

```
grep "sendmail.*-bd" /etc/init.d/*
/etc/init.d/mail:    /usr/lib/sendmail -bd -q15m &
```

Under BSD 4.4 UNIX, however, they will look like this:

```
% grep sendmail /etc/rc*
/etc/rc:echo -n ' sendmail';          sendmail -bd -q30m
```

In the following, we will describe the BSD version. It is somewhat simpler to describe, but the underlying lessons are the same for both.

To be safe, save a copy of the *rc* file before changing it:

```
% cp /etc/rc /etc/rc.orig
```

Then edit the *rc* file and search for the shell code that runs *sendmail*. It will look something like this:

```
echo -n ' nfsd';          nfsd -u -t 6
echo -n ' nfsiod';        nfsiod 4
```

```
echo -n ' sendmail';          sendmail -bd -q30m            ← note
echo -n ' inetd';             inetd
```

Find the line that runs the daemon (*sendmail* with the **-bd** command-line switch) and comment out that line by prefixing it with a **#** character. For completeness, you should also insert an appropriate comment and **echo** command to show what you have done and why:

```
echo -n ' nfsd';              nfsd -u -t 6
echo -n ' nfsiod';            nfsiod 4

# This workstation no longer receives mail directly.  ← add
#echo -n ' sendmail';         sendmail -bd -q30m            ← comment out
echo -n ' No-sendmail'                                      ← add
echo -n ' inetd';             inetd
```

Extreme care must be taken when putting changes into any of the *rc* files. These are only executed when the system is rebooted, so errors won't show up until a very awkward moment. A mistake here can potentially keep your workstation from booting.

Arrange for Hourly Queue Runs

When your local machine had a *sendmail* daemon running, that daemon probably processed the queue periodically. You can tell, because it included a *–qperiod* command-line switch when it was started from its *rc* file:

```
echo -n ' sendmail';          sendmail -bd -q30m
```

The *period* following the **-q** (here 30 minutes) tells *sendmail* to deliver any messages in its queue once each half hour. But because *sendmail* is no longer running in daemon mode, you need another way to periodically process the queue.

The *cron*(8) facility provides just that mechanism. The *cron*(8) facility is a system-level events scheduler. It reads a file of times and dates, and executes the programs listed for each at the appropriate moments.

Unfortunately, *cron*(8) differs between new and old versions of UNIX. Under new versions, each user has a separate file. Under old versions there is one central file for all users. We will illustrate with the new version, again because it is simpler to present. If your system is an older version of UNIX, observe that the underlying principles are the same.

Edit the existing crontab entry for the user *root* (you need to be *root* to do this):

```
# crontab -e root
```

You will be presented with a *crontab*(5) sequence of lines. A Sun, for example, may present you with this:

```
15 3 * * * find / -name .nfs\* -mtime +7 -exec rm -f {} \; -o -fstype
nfs -prune
5 4 * * 6 /usr/lib/newsyslog >/dev/null 2>&1
15 4 * * * find /var/preserve/ -mtime +7 -a -exec rm -f {} \;
```

Ignore the existing entries. You will be adding a new entry to the end of the file. That new entry will look like this:

```
15 * * * * /usr/lib/sendmail -q
```

The numbers and * characters to the left define the time that each event (line) should be executed. Left to right, they are: minutes, hours (24-hour clock), month, day of month, and day of week. A * matches all possibilities. This entry, then, means to execute the command at 15 minutes after any hour, in any month, on any day, and any day of the week. Thus *sendmail* will be run at quarter past the hour, every hour of every day.

The command to be run is *sendmail* with a -q switch. That switch tells *sendmail* to process the queue once and then exit.

With *cron*(8) set up to periodically process the queue, you can now safely rely on the hub. If the hub is down, all mail is queued until the hub comes back up. Then an hourly run of *sendmail* processes that queued mail, sending all the queued mail to the hub.

Install the client.cf File

At last! All the pieces are in place, and you can install the *client.cf* file as the official system configuration file.

As we explained when we began developing the *client.cf* file, you should not type it in yourself. The pieces we developed were strictly instructional, and should not be used as-is. Instead you should see Appendix D, *The client.cf File*, for a full listing and information about how to get a copy via anonymous FTP.

Just to be safe, once you have obtained, tuned, and tested a *client.cf* file, make a backup copy of the system configuration file:

```
# cp /etc/sendmail.cf /etc/sendmail.cf.orig
```

The # prompt indicates that you are doing this as *root*. Next, overwrite the system configuration file with the new *client.cf* file.

```
# cp ./client.cf /etc/sendmail.cf
```

That's all there is to it. From now on, any mail sent from your machine will result in *sendmail* using your configuration file in place of the original.

Once again, it is important to test. Send mail to yourself and others using your favorite MUA. Examine the results of each (especially the header information), and ask others to do so too. If anything is amiss, first try to fix the new configuration file. If that fails, put the saved original back as the system configuration file until you can solve the problem.

Some problems will doubtless require expertise beyond that provided in this tutorial. For those, you will need to take on the reference chapters which follow. This will be even more necessary if you are managing a hub machine, or if you want mail delivered locally.

Things to Try

- A file of rules and addresses is valuable as a tool for testing new and revised versions of a configuration file. Develop a small shell script that feeds such a file to *sendmail* in rule-testing mode, then filters the output to display only the returns of interest. Is it possible to test rules other than those that select a delivery agent? Determine the value of such other lines in the file, add them, and tune your script to make them useful.

- Is it possible to protect the queue directory with narrow permissions (like 0700), yet still allow ordinary users to run *sendmail* in rule-testing mode?

- Is it legal to have an MX record point to itself? What about having an MX record pointing to a CNAME? What are wildcard MX records, and what pitfalls might you expect to encounter if using them?

- Consider a hub machine that is connected to two different domains. What rules might it have to include to recognize itself (or its clients as itself) in either domain? Remember that some versions of *sendmail* allow multitoken class matches, whereas other don't. What is the most portable way to recognize oneself in two domains?

- If a client is hybrid (a client in the client-hub scheme, that still needs to be able to receive mail) what changes will be required? Does anything need to be added to the *client.cf* file? Will rule set 0 need to be modified to select the `local` or `prog` delivery agents? Will a daemon still have to run?

II

Administration

The second part of this book discusses the administration of *sendmail*. It begins with three chapters more or less dedicated to one-time events and concludes with four chapters of a more ongoing nature.

Chapter 16,   *Compile and Install sendmail,* shows how to obtain, customize, and install *sendmail* from source. We also illustrate the little-known *checkcompat()* routine.

Chapter 17,   *DNS and sendmail,* covers the Domain Naming System and MX records as they relate specifically to *sendmail.*

Chapter 18,   *Security,* presents several good techniques to protect your site from unwanted intrusion. Although we focus on *sendmail,* these lessons are applicable to many other situations.

Chapter 19,   *The Queue,* explains what the queue is and where it is located. We then show (among other things) how to deal with: too many queued messages, messages that are too old, and messages that need to be dequeued individually.

Chapter 20,   *Aliases,* covers delivery through the *aliases*(5) file, to users, files, and through programs. We also cover required aliases and how to rebuild the alias databases.

Chapter 21,   *Mailing Lists and ˜/.forward,* describes the nature of mailing lists. Internal versus `:include:` lists are contrasted. We then cover the user's *.forward* file.

Chapter 22,   *Logging and Statistics,* illustrates the ins and outs of *sys-log*(3) and the *syslog.conf*(5) file. We then cover statistics with the S option, the *sendmail.st* file, and the *mailstats*(8) program. We conclude by showing how to gather statistics from *syslog*(3)'s log files.

16

Compile and Install sendmail

Vendors can be years behind the state of the art when adapting software for their own use. SunOS, for example, bases its adaptation of *sendmail* on the 4.3 BSD release. As a consequence, we can't recommend using any of the vendor-supplied versions of *sendmail* on a major mail-handling machine. If you are responsible for such a machine, we recommend that you obtain one of the latest versions of *sendmail* in source form, then build and install it yourself.

In this chapter we show you how to do just that. To minimize confusion, we limit our discussion to two major versions of *sendmail*, IDA and V8.

Decide Which Version

First, you must choose the version of *sendmail* that is best for you and for your site's needs. This is a long-term decision, because switching versions later becomes more difficult as the complexity of your site increases. To aid you in this decision we discuss the pros and cons of IDA and V8, based on typical site considerations.

Consider Heterogeneity

If your site is heterogeneous,* IDA *sendmail* may be a slightly better choice
than V8. As shown in Table 16-1, IDA *sendmail* supports a somewhat wider
spectrum of operating systems and architectures than does V8. However,
over time, V8 will be ported more and more widely.

Table 16-1: Comparison of Operating System Support

IDA	V8	Operating System
yes	yes	AIX (3)
yes	no	AIX (RT)
yes	no	AT&T 7300 (3B1)
yes	yes	BSD 4.3
yes	yes	BSD 4.4
yes	yes	Convex
no	yes	Dell SysV
yes	no	Domainos
yes	no	Dynix
yes	yes	HPUX
yes	yes	IRIX
yes	no	Interactive Systems SysV UNIX
no	yes	Linux
no	yes	Mach 386
yes	yes	MIPS/RISCos
yes	yes	NeXT
no	yes	OSF/1
yes	no	PTX
yes	no	Pyramid OSx
yes	yes	Sun OS 4.x (Solaris 1.x)
yes	yes	Sun OS 5.x (Solaris 2.x)
yes	no	USG platforms
yes	no	Ultrix 3.x
yes	yes	Ultrix 4.x
yes	no	Umax 4.3

---

*A site with only Suns might be considered heterogeneous if it includes sun3 and sun4 archi-
tectures and SunOS 4.x and 5.x operating systems.

Unfortunately, the ongoing development of *sendmail* means this table is likely to be out of date. For up-to-the-minute information, you should obtain and consult the source (see the next section).

Consider Security

Although neither version is 100 percent secure, V8 has the highest level of security. If your site deals in sensitive matters, or if you are particularly concerned about security, you should investigate V8 before making your decision (see Chapter 18, *Security*).

Consider Protocol Support

Both IDA and V8 *sendmail* support UUCP. IDA also supports the newer (albeit somewhat broken) "bsmtp" batched UUCP protocol.

IDA *sendmail* supports the *mail11*(1) program for exchanging mail with hosts on DECnet. V8 does not.

V8 *sendmail* supports the ISO protocol in addition to the standard TCP/IP protocol. IDA does not.

IDA is more mature than V8, in that it has fewer recent major changes.

Obtain the Source

In this section we discuss how to get the *sendmail* source via anonymous FTP. If you lack network FTP access, we will also show how to get the source using e-mail.

V8 sendmail

V8 *sendmail* is available from *ftp.cs.berkeley.edu*. It is in the *ucb/sendmail* directory. When you *cd* to that directory, instructions are displayed telling you what to *get*.

You should also read the *comp.mail.sendmail* USENET news group. Discovered bugs, bug fixes, and new releases are discussed in it.

IDA sendmail

IDA *sendmail* is widely available. You can use *archie*(1) to find a nearby site, or you can get the source from *ftp.uu.net* in the */pub/network-ing/mail/sendmail* directory under the name:

```
sendmail-5.65c+IDA-1.4.4.1.tar.Z
```

This is a compressed *tar*(1) file of release 1.4.4.1 of the IDA modifications to version 5.65 of BSD *sendmail*. The release numbers at the right change periodically as minor bugs are fixed.

IDA *sendmail* is also discussed in the newsgroup *comp.mail.sendmail*.

Via ftpmail

If you lack network FTP access, but have UUCP to Internet mail, you can still get the *sendmail* source. Just send an e-mail message to the address *ftpmail@decwrl.dec.com*. In the body of the message, give the name of the anonymous FTP host (one of those shown above) and the FTP commands you want to run. The *ftpmail* server will run anonymous FTP for you and mail the files back to you. To get a complete help file, send a message to the server with no subject and the single word help in the body. The following is an example e-mail session that should obtain the IDA *sendmail* source:

```
% mail ftpmail@decwrl.dec.com
Subject:
reply your e-mail address here
connect ftp.uu.net
chdir /networking/mail/sendmail
chdir sendmail-5.65c+IDA-1.4.4.1.tar.Z-split
binary
uuencode          ← or btoa if you have it
get README
get part01
get part02
get part03
get part04
get part05
get part06
get part07
get part08
quit
.
```

The directory shown in the fourth command contains the compressed *tar* split up into smaller, more easily mailed pieces. You get the README for instructions on how to reassemble those pieces.

What's Where in the Source

The source tree for IDA unpacks to create the directory named *sendmail* with everything inside that directory. An *ls*(1) of that directory looks like the following, where the trailing slash characters indicate directories:

```
% ls sendmail
ANNOUNCE        README-HPUX     cf/         src/
ChangeLog       README-UIUC     doc/        support/
Distfile        READ_ME         ida/        ucbMail.patch
INSTALL         S5/             mailstats/  uiuc/
Makefile        aux/            praliases/  uk.extras/
RCS/            binmail/        rmail/
```

V8 *sendmail* unpacks into the current directory. Thus you need to make a directory first, then *cd* into that directory and extract. We called the directory we created *bsd*.

```
% ls bsd
Makefile        cf/         mailstats/  rmail/
READ_ME         contrib/    makemap/    src/
RELEASE_NOTES   doc/        praliases/
```

Note that the two directory listings are very similar. The READ_ME and RELEASE_NOTES files provide the most up-to-date information about changes, new features, and bug fixes. Read the documents in the *doc* subdirectory. Also note that there are important comments in *src/Makefile*.

You will find everything you need to build *sendmail* in the *src* subdirectory. The files you'll need to edit are:

conf.h   Specifies database library support, maximum sizes, and other properties

conf.c   Specifies C language code to support specific and unusual needs

pathnames.h Specifies the location of important files

Makefile   Specifies where to install the binaries and how to compile them

Decisions in conf.h

One of the *sendmail* program's chief strengths is its configurability. The configuration file (*sendmail.cf*) provides the means to tune *sendmail* for each machine at a site. The source file *conf.h*, on the other hand, allows you to tune *sendmail* at the site, policy, or architecture level.

The *conf.h* file uses C preprocessor `#define` directives to define a number of C language macros. The complete list is given in Appendix C, *#define Macros in conf.h*. For IDA *sendmail*, some `#define` directives also appear in files in a subdirectory called *sendmail/src/config*.

The *conf.h* file is divided into three sections. The first, near the top, contains definitions you should rarely need to change:

```
/*
**  Table sizes, etc....
**      There shouldn't be much need to change these....
*/
```

The third (last) part of *conf.h* is a series of conditional expressions used to adapt *sendmail* to a variety of architectures. For IDA *sendmail* these are handled with a single `#include` directive:

```
# include "config/bsd44.h"
```

With V8 *sendmail*, everything is included inside the *conf.h* file. You only need to change this section if you intend to port V8 to a previously unsupported architecture or operating system.

The second part is the one we will focus on. It determines the properties of *sendmail*:

```
/*
** Compilation options.
**  #define these if they are available; comment them out otherwise.
*/
```

The changes we will suggest fall into four categories:

- Deciding which features to use when configuring a mail hub and which to use on a "dumb" client machine
- Deciding which database library support you need
- Deciding what protocol support you need: TCP/IP or ISO
- Other miscellaneous decisions

Knowledgeable Hub's conf.h

If you are configuring a mail hub, the *conf.h* file probably requires few changes. A mail hub, for the purpose of our discussion, is any machine that can receive mail as well as send it. The only decisions you need to make for such a machine deal with database library support and (for V8 only) the protocols used.

Note that you may also need to change *conf.h* when porting *sendmail* to a new machine or operating system. We don't cover porting here, as that is beyond the scope of this book. Other decisions are best deferred until after you've installed *sendmail* and run it for a while. An ambitious rewrite of the configuration file, for example, may require that you redefine MAXRWSETS (the maximum number of rule sets) and recompile *sendmail*. All the definitions that you may wish to change are listed in Appendix C.

Dumb Client's config.h

In the tutorial, you saw one way to set up a central mail hub machine. The focus there was on clients that do not receive mail. For such clients, you will not need all the abilities of *sendmail*. Thus, you can produce a smaller *sendmail* by undefining (commenting out) the unnecessary abilities as shown below:

```
# define LOG           1  /* enable logging */
# define SMTP          1  /* enable user and server SMTP */
# define QUEUE         1  /* enable queueing */
/*# define UGLYUUCP    1  /* output ugly UUCP From lines */
# define NETINET       1  /* include internet support */
/*# define SETPROCTITLE 1  /* munge argv to display current status */
/*# define NAMED_BIND  1  /* use Berkeley Internet Domain Server */
/*# define MATCHGECOS  1  /* match user names from gecos field */
```

Here we only leave the ability to LOG with *syslog*(3), to exchange incoming and outgoing mail with SMTP, to queue messages (QUEUE) in the event that the hub is down, and to connect to the network (NETINET). Note that for IDA *sendmail* you will define DAEMON rather than NETINET.

If the address of the hub is listed locally in each workstation's */etc/hosts* file or the like, you won't need NAMED_BIND. If, on the other hand, that hub's name is only listed in the DNS maps, you should leave NAMED_BIND defined.

For IDA *sendmail* you also need to select the appropriate operating system support. You do this by changing the line:

```
# include "config/bsd44.h"
```

Here you change bsd44.h to one of the filenames contained in the sub-directory *sendmail/config*.

Database Library Selection in conf.h (IDA)

Database libraries are required for maintenance of the *aliases*(5) database (see Chapter 20, *Aliases*). You need to decide which database library to use. IDA *sendmail* offers the widest selection:

```
# define DBM          1 /* use DBM library (may require -ldbm) */
# define NO_PADDING 1 /* don't pad dbm strings with ASCII NULL */

/*
* Define only 1 of the various {N,G,S,M,H}DBM libraries. N.B., HDBM
* assumes that ndbm.o was included in the libhash.a file.
*/
# define NDBM         1 /* new DBM library available (requires DBM) */
/*# define GDBM        1 /* gnu DBM library available (requires DBM) */
/*# define SDBM        1 /* Ozan Yigit's PD ndbm (requires DBM) */
/*# define MDBM        1 /* UMaryland's ndbm variant (requires DBM) */
/*# define HDBM        1 /* Berkeley's hashing package (requires DBM) */
```

As you can see from the comments, you need to define DBM no matter which database library you choose. DBM is sufficient all by itself, but isn't recommended. At a very minimum you should consider using NDBM, the new DBM replacement shipped with most recent versions of UNIX.

If you trust free software to remain stable, GDBM can be used with very satisfactory results. It emulates NDBM very well and is considered by many to be superior. Two other variations on NDBM—SDBM and MDBM—will also work.

HDBM requires the BSD *db*(3) package.* This package differs in several key ways from DBM and its variants. Most noticeable is its binary independence. Unlike DBM, a database built with HDBM can be shared by machines of differing architectures. It also uses a hashing algorithm that makes lookups faster. If you don't mind the effort of porting *db*(3) to your system, it is highly recommended.

The NO_PADDING definition is intended for sites that use NIS to propagate the *aliases* database. If you have *sendmail* rebuild that database, you still need to undefine NO_PADDING for the */var/yp/Makefile* to be able to create a usable map. See Chapter 29, *Database Macros*, for a discussion of padding in relation to databases you create yourself.

---

*The *db*(3) package is available via anonymous FTP from *ftp.cs.berkeley.edu* in the file */ucb/4bsd/db.x.x.tar.Z* (where the x.x is the version number).

Database Library Selection in conf.h (V8)

V8 *sendmail* supports two basic forms of databases for *aliases*(5) files. The *ndbm*(3) form is a superset of the classic *dbm*(3) library. The BSD *db*(3) library offers faster lookups and is architecture-independent. In addition to these basic forms, V8 *sendmail* can utilize NIS network maps. All three forms of database access can be used with the K (Keyed lookup) configuration file command or in alias file definitions.

Unlike IDA, the database library support for V8 is declared in the *Makefile*. We cover *Makefiles* soon.

If you elect to use *db*(3) library support, you can also take advantage of the BSD User Database.*

```
# ifdef NEWDB
# define USERDB    1    /* look in user database (requires NEWDB) */
# endif
```

If USERDB is defined in *conf.h*, the location of the user database can be declared in the configuration file with the U option (see Chapter 30, *Options*). This user database allows you to maintain centralized information about all accounts, among which is an indication of where each user prefers to have mail delivered.

Protocol Selection in conf.h (V8)

Under V8 *sendmail* you have a choice of two protocols:† either TCP/IP (defined with NETINET) or ISO (defined with NETISO). You must select one or the other, or both. If you select neither, the DAEMON automatically becomes undefined and daemon support is left out of the binary.

---

*The BSD User Database is available via anonymous FTP from *ftp.cs.berkeley.edu*.

†Actually, stubs are built in for support of NS and X.25 protocols. These might be implemented in the future, but no guarantee is made that they will in fact ever be supported. Programmers interested in implementing them should contact Eric.

Other Decisions in conf.h

Before considering yourself finished with *conf.h*, carefully read Appendix C to familiarize yourself with all the available #define macros. You will doubtless discover some that are of interest to your site. For example:

- If your site uses NIS alias maps, you may want *sendmail* to support them. IDA can support NIS maps by defining YP, and V8 can support them by defining NIS.

- If your site is acting as a gateway between a TCP/IP network and a DECnet network you may wish to use the *mail11* program. IDA can support that program by defining MAIL11V3.

- If you need to debug *sendmail* from a remote location, you may want to allow SMTP debugging. This risky setup can be enabled with the SMTPDEBUG definition.

Decisions in conf.c

The file *conf.c* contains C language functions, structures, and arrays that you may alter to better suit your *sendmail* needs. Usually, the *conf.c* file can be left untouched and *sendmail* will compile and run just fine—so many readers can comfortably skip this section. Among the items we will discuss in it are:

- Masks that determine the default behavior of all recognized headers

- The minimum degree of privacy desired site-wide

- How to filter mail inside *sendmail* with a single subroutine

Header Decisions in conf.c

The *sendmail* program has a built-in understanding of many header names. How those names are used is determined by a set of flags in *conf.c*. Site policy determines which flags are applied to which headers. But, in general, *conf.c* applies them in the way best suited for almost all Internet sites. If you desire to redefine the flags for a particular header name, look for the name's declaration in the C language structure definition HdrInfo in *conf.c*. Be sure to read the comments in that file. Changes to header flags represent a permanent site policy change and should not be undertaken lightly. (We illustrate this process after explaining the flags.)

The flags that determine header use are listed in Table 16-2. Note that each flag name is prefixed with an H_.

Table 16-2: Header flags in conf.c

Flag	Description
H_EOH	Terminates all headers
H_RCPT	Contains a recipient address
H_DEFAULT	If already in headers, don't insert
H_RESENT	A `Resent-` header
H_CHECK	Checks header flags against delivery agent flags
H_ACHECK	Ditto, but always (not just default)
H_FORCE	Insert this header (allows duplicates)
H_TRACE	Count these to get the hop count
H_FROM	Contains a sender address
H_VALID	Has a validated field value
H_ERRSTO	An `errors-to:` header (V8 and SunOS only)

Note that there no flag that always causes a particular header to be removed, nor is there a flag that always causes a particular header to be replaced (although you can trick *sendmail* with H_ACHECK as described below):

H_EOH   Headers marked with this flag cause *sendmail* to immediately stop all header processing and treat the rest of the header lines as message body. This is useful for separating RFC822-compliant header lines from headers created by a non-compliant network.

H_RCPT   Headers marked with this flag are assumed to contain valid recipient addresses in their fields. Only headers with this flag can lead to message delivery. These addresses will be rewritten. These headers are only used to determine the recipient address if the -t command switch is used.

H_DEFAULT   The *sendmail* program automatically sets this flag for all headers declared in the configuration file. Only one of each header that is marked with this flag is allowed to exist in the headers portion of a mail message. If such a header already exists, *sendmail* does not add another. The H_FORCE and H_TRACE flags override this flag. This flag must never be specified in *conf.c*—it is set automatically by H configuration commands.

H_RESENT   This flag tells *sendmail* that the header line is prefixed with the `resent-` string. Only headers marked with this flag can tell *sendmail* that this is a "forwarded" message. If no "forwarded" headers are found, *sendmail* strips any bogus resent- header lines from the message's header.

H_CHECK   If a header definition in the configuration file begins with a ?*flags*? conditional, this flag is set for that header. It tells *sendmail* to insert this header only if one of its ?*flags*? corresponds to one of the delivery agent's F= flags. This flag must never be specified in *conf.c*—it is set automatically when *sendmail* reads H lines with ?*flags*? header flags.

H_ACHECK   This flag marks a header that should normally be discarded, unless a delivery agent's F= flag calls for its inclusion. It is usually set for the Bcc: header which is discarded for the privacy of a blind carbon copy list, and the Full-Name: header, which is intended as a way for a user to add a full name (the $x macro) when there is no full name defined in the *passwd*(5) file. Note that H_ACHECK, when combined with bogus ?*flags*? of a header configuration file declaration can cause appropriate headers to always be deleted or replaced (see Chapter 31, *Headers*). Also note that under V8 *sendmail* the H_ACHECK flag alone always causes a header to be replaced.

H_FORCE   This flag causes *sendmail* to always insert a header. It is used in the *conf.c* file with selected trace headers. It can be thought of as allowing duplicates. That is, the header will be inserted even if one like it is already present.

H_TRACE   Headers marked with this flag are counted when determining a mail message's "hop" count. This flag is intended for use in the *conf.c* file.

H_FROM   Headers marked with this flag are assumed to contain a valid sender address. This flag is intended for use in the *conf.c* file.

H_VALID   This flag is set and cleared internally by *sendmail* to indicate to itself that a particular header line has been correctly processed and can now be used as-is. This flag should never be used in the *conf.c* file.

H_ERRSTO   Under SunOS and V8 *sendmail*, this flag specifies which headers can be used for returning error notification mail. Those headers take priority over all others for that notification.

To illustrate one use of these header flags, consider the `Return-Path:` header. Technically, this header should only be inserted by the site performing final delivery. Unfortunately, some mail always seems to arrive with this header already (and wrongly) in place. One way to ensure that it is replaced locally during final delivery is to add a declaration for that header to *conf.c*. Here we illustrate with IDA *sendmail*, currently lacking a `Return-Path:` declaration in *conf.c*.

```
/* trace fields */
"received",              H_TRACE|H_FORCE,
"via",                   H_TRACE|H_FORCE,
"mail-from",             H_TRACE|H_FORCE,
"x400-received",         H_TRACE,

/* Misc. added declarations */              ← new
"return-path",           H_ACHECK,          ← new
```

We added the last two lines above, which tell *sendmail* to replace this header if it is declared in the configuration file and if the ?*flags*? preceding that declaration correspond to an F= flag in the delivery agent definition.

In delivery agent definitions, the F=1 flag means that the delivery agent will perform final delivery. This allows configuration file header definitions like the following to be added:

```
?l?Return-Path: <$g>
```

Headers in general, and the ?*flags*? associated with them, are described in Chapter 31, *Headers*.

Uses of checkcompat( ) in conf.c

Inside *conf.c* is the often overlooked routine *checkcompat()*. It has existed since Version 3, and is intended to allow the site administrator to accept, reject, and log mail delivery attempts. It contains comments describing one way to code it. In this section we provide three other examples of ways it can be used.

The *checkcompat()* routine is inherently "internal" in that it must understand internal data structures that may change. Since you are modifying source code, you have to be prepared to read source code—the following descriptions are only examples.*

How checkcompat( ) works

When *sendmail* prepares to deliver mail, it first checks the size of the mail message and rejects (bounces) it if it is larger than the limit imposed by the M= (Maximum) delivery agent equate. Next, it calls the *checkcompat( )* routine. If *checkcompat( )* returns TRUE (EX_OK for V8 as defined in *<sysexits.h>*) the mail message is delivered. Otherwise the message is rejected. The *checkcompat( )* routine is called once for each recipient.

The argument given to *checkcompat( )* is:

```
checkcompat(to)
        register ADDRESS *to;
```

Here, to is a pointer to a structure of *typedef* ADDRESS which contains information about the recipient. Envelope information is available in the global variable CurEnv, a pointer to a structure (actually a linked list of structures) of *typedef* ENVELOPE. Both are defined in *sendmail.h*.

For V8 *sendmail* the *checkcompat( )* routine takes an additional argument:

```
checkcompat(to, e)
        register ADDRESS *to;
        register ENVELOPE *e;
```

Here, to is a pointer to a structure just like before. But e is a pointer to a structure (actually a linked list of structures) of *typedef* ENVELOPE which contains information about the current envelope. The argument e is used just like CurEnv. Both types are defined in *sendmail.h*.

In general you can use almost any of the global variables defined in *sendmail.h* and in *conf.c*. The most interesting and useful variables are:

to->q_host

> The host part of the recipient address as returned following the $@ part of rule set 0.

to->q_user

> The user part of the recipient address as returned following the $: part of rule set 0.

---

*Really doing this right for all versions would require hundreds of pages of text.

`to->q_mailer->m_name`

> The symbolic name of the delivery agent as returned following the $# part in rule set 0.

`RealHostAddr`

> The IP address of the sending host. For IDA *sendmail,* this is a structure of type *sockaddr_in* as described in *<netinet/in.h>*. For V8, this is a union of several *sockaddr_* types depending on your selection of protocol type. This can be zero for locally submitted mail.

`RealHostName`

> A string containing the definitive canonical name of the sending host. If it can't be resolved to a name, it will contain the host's IP number in text form, surrounded by square brackets.

`e->e_from` or `CurEnv->e_from`

> Structures of type ADDRESS, just like `to` above, but containing information about the sender.

Accept Only Mail From Our Domain

If your site lives behind a *firewall,** you may want to use *checkcompat( )* to configure the internal *sendmail* so that it only accepts mail generated locally. The external *sendmail* (outside the firewall or part of it) acts as a proxy. That is, it accepts external mail destined for internal delivery from the outside and forwards it to the internal *sendmail.* Because the external *sendmail* is part of the local domain, its envelope always appears local. Any external mail that somehow bypasses the firewall needs to be bounced. Note that this example is specific to V8 *sendmail:*

```
checkcompat(to, e)
    register ADDRESS *to;
    register ENVELOPE *e;
{
    static long ourdomain = 0x7b2d4300; /* 123.45.67.0 in hex */

    if (RealHostAddr.sa.sa_family == 0)
    {
        /* this is a locally submitted message */
        return EX_OK;
    }
    if (RealHostAddr.sa.sa_family != AF_INET ||
        (RealHostAddr.sin.sin_addr.saddr & 0xffffff00) != ourdomain)
```

---

*A firewall is a machine that lies between the local network and the outside world. It intercepts and filters all network traffic and rejects any that are considered inappropriate.

```
        {
                usrerr("553 End run mail not allowed");
                return (EX_UNAVAILABLE);
        }
        return (EX_OK);
}
```

The usrerr() routine causes a warning to be printed at the sending site, and returning EX_UNAVAILABLE causes the mail message to be bounced. Bounced mail is sent back to the originating sender, and a copy is sent to the local postmaster.

Note that V8 *checkcompat()* can return any of the values defined in <*sysexits.h*>. EX_TMPFAIL, for example, indicates that the message should be queued. Contrast this to the IDA implementation of the next example which can only return TRUE or FALSE.

Also note that this code is only a suggestion. It doesn't take into account that RealHostAddr may contain 0x7f000001 (*127.0.0.1* for *localhost*), nor does it expect RealHostAddr to be NULL.

Refuse to Act as a Mail Gateway

If you've spent many months getting your mail hub set up and running perfectly, you may not want outsiders using it as a knowledgeable mail relay. One way to prevent such unwanted use is to set up *checkcompat()* in *conf.c* so that it rejects any mail from outside your domain that is destined to another site outside your domain. As a side effect, this will prevent outsiders from directly posting into your mailing lists. The following example is for IDA *sendmail*:

```
checkcompat(to, e)
        register ADDRESS *to;
{
        static long ourdomain = 0x7b2d4300; /* 123.45.67.0 in hex */

        if (RealHostAddr.sin_family == 0)
        {
                /* this is a locally submitted message */
                return (TRUE);
        }
        do
        {
                /* only accept local delivery from outside */
                if (strcmp(to->q_mailer->m_name, "local") != 0)
                {
                        usrerr("553 External gateway use prohibited");
                        return (FALSE);
                }
```

```
        } while (to = to->q_next);
        return (TRUE);
}
```

This example illustrates that `to` is really a linked list of recipients. The `do-while` loop checks each one to be sure the `local` delivery agent is used. Note that other forms of local delivery should also be included in the check, like a check for the `prog` delivery agent. If there are many such legitimate local delivery agents, checking for an appropriate `F=` delivery agent flag may be simpler.

Limit the Size of Guest Messages

Suppose your site has reserved *uid*s from 900 to 999 for guest users. Because guests are sometimes inconsiderate, you may want to specially limit the size of their messages and the number of simultaneous recipients they may specify. One way to do this is with *checkcompat( )*. Here we demonstrate, again using V8 *sendmail*:

```
#define MAXGUESTSIZE 8000
#define MAXGUESTNRCP 4
checkcompat(to, e)
        register ADDRESS *to;
        register ENVELOPE *e;
{
        /* does q_uid contain a valid uid? -- no external */
        if (! bitset(QGOODUID, e->e_from.q_flags))
                return (EX_OK);
        if (e->e_from.q_uid < 900 || e->e_from.q_uid > 999)
                return (EX_OK);
        if (e->e_msgsize > MAXGUESTSIZE)
        {
                syslog(LOG_NOTICE,
                        "Guest %s attempted to send %d size",
                        e->e_from.q_user, e->e_msgsize);
                usrerr("553 Message too large, %d max",
                        MAXGUESTSIZE);
                return (EX_UNAVAILABLE);
        }
        if (e->e_nrcpts > MAXGUESTNRCP)
        {
                syslog(LOG_NOTICE,
                        "Guest %s attempted to send %d recipients",
                        e->e_from.q_user, e->e_nrcpts);
                usrerr("553 Too many recipients for guest, %d max",
                        MAXGUESTNRCP);
                return (EX_UNAVAILABLE);
        }
        return (EX_OK);
}
```

Note that q_uid will only have a valid *uid* if the sender is local. For external mail coming in, q_uid will be 0.

Decisions in pathnames.h (V8 Only)

Under V8, the file *pathnames.h* may also require modification before you can compile and install *sendmail*. It contains definitions for the locations of two key files.

_PATH_SENDMAIL.CF

> The location of the configuration file. The *sendmail* program needs this location to find its configuration file and the location of all its other files and directories.

_PATH_SENDMAIL.PID

> The location of the file containing the process identification number of the running daemon. That number is used by scripts and humans to kill and restart the daemon. Under V8 *sendmail*, this file contains a second line of information showing the command line used to execute the daemon.

There are two good reasons to change these definitions:

- If your existing *sendmail* setup uses different locations for these files, you may want to duplicate that setup.
- If you feel uneasy about replacing your existing *sendmail* with a new one, you can temporarily change the filenames in *pathnames.h* (say, for example, from *sendmail.cf* to *sendmail.cf.new*). You can then change them back to the originals after a comfortable transition period.

Note that the IDA version of *sendmail* contains these definitions (and the path of the freeze file) in *conf.h*. Also note that any can be overridden in the *Makefile* with a -D argument to the compiler.

Decisions in Makefile

The *make*(1) program is used to compile and install *sendmail*. The rules followed by *make* are defined in a file called *Makefile* in the *src* subdirectory.* In the *src/Makefile* of both IDA and V8 *sendmail*, you will find only

---

*Under V8 *sendmail*, there are many Makefiles to choose from. With the Sun operating system, for example, you may choose *Makefile.SunOS*.

a few items that need tuning. Most configuration has already taken place in *conf.c* and *conf.h*. The decisions you need to make in the IDA *Makefile* are:

CC=	Choice of compiler
DBMLIB=	Support for database libraries selected in *conf.h*
support	Particular settings for CFLAGS, LDFLAGS, and LIBS based on your particular architecture

The decisions you need to make in the V8 *Makefile* depend on whether you use the traditional *make*(1) program or the BSD 4.4 version of *make*( ). For the traditional *make*(1), you use *Makefile.dist* and need to define the following:

DBMDEF=	Choose which database libraries you will use
ENVDEF=	Compiler –D switches, such as –D_AIX3
INCDIRS=	Compiler –I switches, such as –I../db/include
LDOPTS=	Linker options, such as –Bstatic for SunOS
LIBDIRS=	Linker –L switches, such as –L/usr/local/lib
LIBS=	Linker –l libraries, such as –ldbm
BINDIR=	Where to install *sendmail*
STDDIR=	Where the *sendmail.st* file goes
HFDIR=	Where the *sendmail.hf* file goes
OBJADD=	Where additional object files will be found that need to be linked in.

For the new 4.4 BSD *make*(1) program, there are fewer decisions to make:

DBMDEF=	Choose which database libraries you will use
CFLAGS=	Override *conf.h* in the *Makefile*
LDADD=	List additional library support needed

IDA Makefile

The IDA *Makefile* offers a wide range of support for many operating systems and machine types. It may appear daunting at first glance, but with a little guidance, you should have few problems.

Selection of a compiler is very straightforward. Your standard system compiler should work just fine. In all likelihood it is called *cc*. Depending on your background and experience, however, you may prefer something else. The *gcc* (GNU C compiler) is one option. Sun's unbundled C compiler is another. You select a compiler with the CC= directive:

```
CC=      cc
#CC=     gcc -Dvax -ansi -fpcc-struct-return -fstrength-reduce
```

The default is to use *cc*. The second line shows a recommendation for using the *gcc* compiler. With *gcc* you need to replace the **vax** in **-Dvax** with the appropriate name for your machine's architecture. You may use any of the filenames in *src/config* with the *.h* removed. For example, if you are compiling on a Sun, you might use the following line based on *src/config/sun4.h*:

```
CC=      gcc -Dsun4 -ansi -fpcc-struct-return -fstrength-reduce
```

Next you need to decide which database library to use based on what you selected in *conf.h*. The choices offered are:

-lndbm   If you chose GDBM or NDBM

-lsdbm   If you chose SDBM

-lmdbm   If you chose MDBM

-lhash   If you chose HDBM (or possibly -ldb)

-ldbm   If you chose the simple DBM

For example, if you decide to use the University of Maryland's *ndbm* variant, called MDBM, you will set the following line in *Makefile*:

```
DBMLIB= -lmdbm
```

Finally you must choose your machine's architecture. Search through the file for the appropriate entry and uncomment the definitions you find there. For example, if your machine is a Mips running the RISC/os operating system, you will uncomment the two lines shown below:

```
# Mips running RISC/os.
CFLAGS=       -systype bsd43 -O -Olimit 600 -I. ${DEFS}
LIBS= -ldbm -lmld
#
```

V8 Makefile

V8 *sendmail* has not been as widely ported as IDA, and its approach to *Makefile* is different. In the *src* directory you must first decide which *Makefile* best suits your machine's architecture, and rename it to *Makefile*:*

```
Makefile.AIX       Makefile.HP-UX    Makefile.OSF1     Makefile.Utah
Makefile.BSD43     Makefile.HPUX     Makefile.SCO      Makefile.dist
Makefile.BSDI      Makefile.IRIX     Makefile.Solaris
Makefile.ConvexOS  Makefile.Linux    Makefile.SunOS
Makefile.Dell      Makefile.NeXT     Makefile.ULTRIX
```

For example, under Sun's operating system, you will perform the following steps:

```
% mv Makefile Makefile.orig
% mv Makefile.SunOS Makefile
```

After selecting a *Makefile*, edit it.

Your next decision is the database library support you need. Here you have four choices that depend on your decisions in *conf.h*:

NEWDB   Support for the new *db*(3) library, both hash and btree forms

NDBM   Support for the new form of *dbm*(3) called *ndbm*(3)

NIS   Support for the NIS maps

none   No support for any keyed lookup, including aliases. This will make *sendmail* crawl, and is not recommended. Note that *dbm*(3) is not supported. External databases can be extremely valuable, providing easy solutions to complex problems. We recommend you include support for them all even if you don't immediately foresee a need.

Below we illustrate the selection of two forms of database:

```
DBMDEF= -DNEWDB -DNDBM
```

When these two forms are selected, old databases are read using NDBM, but new databases are created using NEWDB.

Next the ENVDEF directive needs to be tuned. This directive in the V8 *Makefile* serves two functions. First, it is used to specify compiler-specific switches (like -Bstatic for Sun).

```
ENVDEF= -Bstatic
```

---

*You may alternatively use the -f switch with *make* and skip the renaming.

Second, it is used to define additional protocol support, such as ISO:

```
ENVDEF= -Bstatic -DNETISO
```

The last decision in *Makefile* is that of selecting which libraries to link against. This is done with the LIBS directive. The default is:

```
LIBS=   -ldbm -lcompat -lutil -lkvm
```

It is likely that you have to add or change libraries in this list depending on your architecture and operating system. To discover which you need, run *make*(1) (see the next section) and observe which routines the linker reports as missing.

Run Make

After all your decisions have been made in *conf.h*, *conf.c*, *pathnames.h*, and *Makefile*, you are ready to build *sendmail*. First (especially if you are building as *root*), run:

```
# make -n
```

This displays all the commands that *make* will generate, without actually executing them. If all looks well, run *make* again, this time without the -n.

Use libresolv.a (IDA and V8)

If your site is connected to the Internet, you will have defined NAMED_BIND in *conf.h*. To include support for DNS lookups, you need to also link with the resolver library. If, when you compiled *sendmail*, the linker reported *_res_** routines as missing, you need to specify the resolver library with -lresolv:

```
LDADD=  -ldbm -lcompat -lutil -lkvm -lresolv
```

This shows one way to include that library with the V8 *Makefile*. Another way might look like this:

```
# libraries required on your system
LIBS=   /usr/local/lib/libresolv.a
```

To make certain that *sendmail* achieves its best use of lookups, make sure your resolver library is derived from the latest BIND release: BIND 4.9.*

The tricky part is finding out which resolver library your system supports. With SunOS systems, for example, resolver support in the standard C

---

*4.8.3 is also good. 4.9 is available via anonymous FTP from *gatekeeper.dec.com*.

library uses NIS for name resolution. Although this setup *may* be good for most applications, it is inappropriate for *sendmail*. There is a *libresolv.a*, but it is based on BIND 4.3, so should probably be replaced with a newer version.

If your resolver library is not the correct one, you need to compile and install the newest version. You should do this, even if it is only used by *sendmail*.

Other Missing Library Routines

When you run *make*(1) you may find that your C library is missing needed functions. For example, some of the System V machines are missing the *rename*(2) system call.

IDA and V8 *sendmail* differ in their philosophies about how to fulfill the shortcomings of some C libraries. V8 takes the attitude that it will not support "brain dead" systems. IDA, on the other hand, attempts to remedy the situation with selected C source in *sendmail/support*. We take no stand on which approach is better. Instead, we'll list the routines offered by IDA, then examine one example, the *rename*( ) function.

IDA support

The following C language files are available in *sendmail/support* under IDA:

```
flock.c  getenv.c getopt.c getusershell.c mktemp.c
perror.c rename.c setenv.c strcasecmp.c   syslog.c
```

Each corresponds to a missing function. To include such a missing routine with the *sendmail* source, simply copy it to *sendmail/src* (along with any needed *.h* files), and add it to the list of SRCS= and OBJS= definitions. Then run *make*(1) again.

V8 *sendmail* doesn't support replacement routines for systems that lack them. There is good reason for this, especially at the system call level. Consider this description of the system call *rename*(2):

```
rename(path1, path2)
  ...
rename() guarantees that an instance of path2 will  always
exist,  even if the system should crash in the middle of the
operation.
```

If you look at the IDA replacement, *rename.c,* you will see:

```
/* get rid of any existing target file */
if (access(new, F_OK) == 0)
        unlink(new);
```
← *crash here*
```
/* link the old to the new */
if (link(old, new) < 0)
        return(-1);

/* unlink the old name */
return(unlink(old));
```

Notice that new (i.e path2) is removed before the link, thus making it possible for an instance of path2 to not exist after a crash.

The manual page for the *rename*(2) system call describes many conditions and protections that are not handled by the replacement. Although the replacement will work for much of the time, using it opens the door for possible problems that you may regret later.

Install

There are two approaches to installing a new *sendmail:*

- If you choose to run the new *sendmail* in place of the original, you will first need to create and install a new configuration file. Both V8 and IDA use *m4*(1) to automate the process of configuration file creation. V8 is described in Appendix E, *V8 m4 Configuration,* and IDA in Appendix F, *IDA m4 Configuration.*

- If you choose to keep the original and install the new *sendmail* in parallel (until you can trust it), you may proceed with the installation, and defer configuration files until later. Note that this choice presumes you customized the file locations in *pathnames.h* (or *conf.h* for IDA).

After you have compiled *sendmail* (and if the configuration file is ready and tested), you can install it as your production version. If you are already running a *sendmail* and will be overwriting that binary, you will need to kill that version first (see Chapter 4, *How To Run sendmail*).

To install *sendmail,* first type:

```
make -n install
```

You use −n to be sure the installation caused by the *Makefile* is in fact correct for your site. A typical such run for IDA, for example, might look (in part) like this:

```
install -c -s -o root -m 4511 sendmail /usr/sbin
mkdir /usr/spool/mqueue
chown root.daemon /usr/spool/mqueue
chmod 755 /usr/spool/mqueue
```

In the first line notice that the *sendmail* binary will be installed in the /usr/sbin directory. This may not be suitable for your site. You may change that location by editing the following two lines:

```
#     install -c -s -o root -m 4511 sendmail ${DESTDIR}/usr/lib
      install -c -s -o root -m 4511 sendmail ${DESTDIR}/usr/sbin
```

You can uncomment the first and comment the second to relocate *sendmail* to the more common */usr/lib* directory. The precise location will be governed by your */etc/rc* files (see Chapter 3, *The Roles of sendmail*).

Next notice that *Makefile* will try to create the queue directory even if it already exists. You may want to change this to:

```
mkdir -p /usr/spool/mqueue
```

The −p prevents *mkdir*(1) from complaining if the directory already exists. Also, the location may need to be changed if you decide to place the queue elsewhere—like on a disk by itself:

```
mkdir -p /mqueue
chown root.daemon /mqueue
chmod 755 /mqueue
```

Finally, note the permissions. For the best security, the queue directory should be mode 700.

```
chmod 700 /mqueue          ← for best security
```

Pitfalls

- Before replacing your current *sendmail* with a new version, be sure that the queue is empty. The new version may not be able to properly process old (or different) style queued files.

- If you change the location of the queue to a different disk, be sure that disk is mounted (in */etc/rc*) before the *sendmail* daemon is started. If *sendmail* starts first, there is a risk that messages will be queued in the mount point before the disk is mounted. This will result in mysteriously vanishing mail.

- Always save the old *sendmail* and configuration file. The new version may work fine for a while, then suddenly fail. If the failure is difficult to diagnose, you may need to run the old version while you fix the new version.

- Some operating systems allow disks to be mounted such that *suid* permissions are disallowed. If you relocate *sendmail*, avoid locating it on such a disk.

17

DNS and sendmail

DNS stands for the *Domain Naming System*. A domain is any logical or physical collection of related hosts or sites. A naming system is best visualized as an inverted tree of information that corresponds to fully-qualified hostnames (see Figure 17-1).

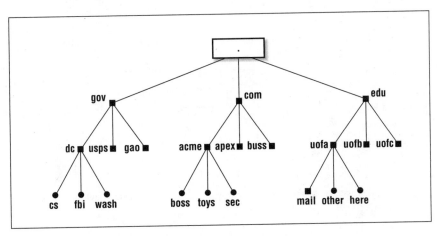

Figure 17-1: Domain names form a tree of information

The parts of a fully-qualified name are separated from each other with dots. For example:

```
here.uofa.edu
```

This name describes the machine here that is part of the uofa subdomain of the edu top-level domain. In Figure 17-1, the dot at the top is the "root" of the tree. It is implied, but never included in fully-qualified domain names:

```
here.uofa.edu.
           ↑
        implied
```

The root corresponds to actual machines (of which *ns.internic.net* is one of several). Each has knowledge of all the top-level domains (such as gov, com, etc.). Each of the top-level domains in turn has one or more machines with knowledge of the next level below. For example, edu "knows" about the subdomains uofa, uofb, and uofc, but may not know about anything below those subdomains, nor about the other domains next to itself like com.

A knowledgeable machine, one that contains and distributes information about its domain and subdomains, is called a *name server*. Each box in the figure represents a name server for a portion of a domain. Each is only required to have knowledge of what is immediately above and below it. This minimizes the amount of knowledge any given name server must store and administer.

To illustrate the way this distributed information is used, consider Figure 17-2. It shows the steps taken when a user on *here.uofa.edu* (the local host) sends an e-mail message to a user on *fbi.dc.gov* (the remote host).

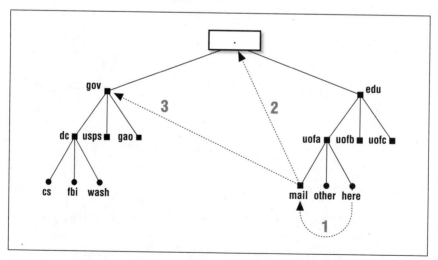

Figure 17-2: How DNS lookups are performed

1. The local *sendmail* needs the IP number of the remote host in order to initiate a network connection. The local *sendmail* asks its local name server (say *mail.uofa.edu*) for that address. The *mail.uofa.edu* name server may already know the address (having cached that information during a previous inquiry). If so, it gives the requested address to the local *sendmail*, and no further DNS requests need to be made. If the local name server doesn't have that information, it contacts other name servers for the needed informations.

2. In the case of *fbi.dc.gov*, the local name server next contacts the root server (the dot in our example). The root server will likely not have the information requested, but will indicate the best place to enquire. For our example, the root server recommends the name server for the *.gov* domain and provides our local name server with the address of that *.gov* machine.

3. The local name server then contacts the *.gov* name server. This process continues until a name server provides the needed information. As it happens, any name server can return the final answer if it happens to have it in its cache. For our example, *.gov* knows the address for *fbi.dc.gov*. It returns that address to the local name server, which in turn returns the address to the local *sendmail*.

This is a simplified description. The actual practice can be more or less complex depending on who is "authoritative" about which machines and domains, and what is cached where.

The *sendmail* program needs the IP address of the machine to which it must connect. That address can be returned by name servers in three possible forms:

- An MX (Mail Exchanger) record lists one or more machines that have agreed to receive mail for a particular site or machine. Multiple MX records are tried in order of preference. An MX record need not point to the original receiving host. MX records always take precedence over A records.

- An A (for address) record gives the IP address directly.

- A CNAME (alias) record refers *sendmail* to the real name, which may have an A record or MX records.

Which DNS: 4.8.3 or 4.9?

Before we discuss DNS in greater detail, we must first attend to an administrative detail. Every site on the Internet should run BIND software version 4.8.3 at the minimum. BIND provides the software and libraries needed to perform DNS enquiries. Version 4.8.3 was the last stable version before Paul Vixie (while at *dec.com*) started rewriting the code. The current release is 4.9.*

If you are currently running version 4.8.3, there is no pressing need to change. If, however, you are running an old version or a questionable vendor's version, you should probably get version 4.9 and install it at your site. BIND 4.9 is available via anonymous FTP from *gatekeeper.dec.com*, in the directory *pub/BSD/bind/4.9.*

We won't describe how to install BIND in this book. Instead you should refer to the book *DNS and BIND* by Paul Albitz and Cricket Liu (O'Reilly & Associates, 1992).

DNS Enquiries by sendmail

The *sendmail* program uses DNS in four different ways:

- When *sendmail* first starts, it may use DNS to get the canonical name for the local host. That name is then assigned to the $w macro ($j for V8). If DNS returns additional names for the local host, those names are assigned to the class $=w.

- When another host connects to the local host to transfer mail, the local *sendmail* looks up the other host with DNS to find the other host's canonical name.

- When delivering network SMTP mail, *sendmail* uses DNS to find the address (or addresses) to which it should connect.

- When *sendmail* expands $[and $] in the RHS of a rule, it looks up the hostname (or IP number) between them.

We discuss each of these uses individually.

---

*As of the final draft of this manuscript, release 4.9.2 was the most recent.

Determine the Local Canonical Name

All versions of *sendmail* use more or less the same logical process to obtain
the canonical name of the local host. As illustrated in the sample program
below, *sendmail* first calls *gethostname*(3) to obtain the local host's name.
That name may either be a short name or a fully-qualified one depending
on which comes first in the */etc/hosts* file. If the call to *gethostname*(3) fails,
the name of the local host is set to *localhost*.

```
#include <sys/types.h>
#include <sys/socket.h>
#include <sys/param.h>
#include <netdb.h>
#include <stdio.h>

main()
{
        char hostbuf[MAXHOSTNAMELEN];
        struct hostent *hp;

        /* Get the local hostname */
        if (gethostname(hostbuf, sizeof(hostbuf)) < 0)
                strcpy(hostbuf, "localhost");
        printf("hostname = \"%s\"\n", hostbuf);

        /* canonicalize it and get aliases */
        if((hp = gethostbyname(hostbuf)) == NULL)
                perror("gethostbyname"), exit(2);
        printf("canonical = \"%s\"\n", hp->h_name);
        while (*hp->h_aliases != NULL)
        {
                printf("alias: \"%s\"\n", *hp->h_aliases);
                ++hp->h_aliases;
        }
}
```

The local hostname is then given to the *gethostbyname* routine to obtain
the canonical name for the local host. That same routine also returns any
aliases (other names for the local host).

On some Suns and Ultrix machines that are set up to use NIS services, the
canonical name is the short name, and a fully-qualified name that should
have been the canonical name appears as an alias. For such systems, you
must link with the BIND library (*libresolv.a*) when compiling this program
or compiling *sendmail*. That library gets its information from DNS rather
than from NIS.

If a good BIND library is not available, or if it is not convenient to compile and install a new version of *sendmail*, you can circumvent the short name assigned to $w by defining $j like this:

```
Dj$w.domain
```

Here, the *domain* is your site's full domain name. This causes $j to have your host's fully-qualified (and canonical) name assigned to it.

The canonical name found by *gethostbyname*(3) is assigned as the value of the $w macro. The short name, and any aliases, are added to the class $=w.

Look Up a Remote Host's Name

When *sendmail* begins to run as a daemon, it creates a socket, binds to that socket, and listens for incoming SMTP connections. When a remote host connects to the local host, *sendmail* uses the *accept*(2) library routine to accept the connection. The *accept*(2) routine provides the IP address of the remote machine to *sendmail*. The *sendmail* program then calls *gethostbyaddr*(2) to convert that IP address to a canonical (official) hostname.

The *sendmail* program needs the canonical hostname for four reasons:

- The remote hostname is compared to the local hostname to prevent *sendmail* from connecting to itself.
- The remote hostname claimed in the HELO SMTP line is compared to the canonical name. If they differ, *sendmail* complains.
- The macro $s is assigned the canonical hostname as its value.
- The canonical name is included in many log messages produced by the setting of the L option and is available for inclusion in `Received:` header lines.

If IDENTPROTO is defined when compiling V8 *sendmail*, the local host also connects to the *identd*(8) daemon at the sending host to find who opened the connection. If available, that user and host information is assigned to the $_ macro.

Look Up Addresses for Delivery

When *sendmail* prepares to connect to a remote host for transfer of mail, it first calls the *res_search*(3) BIND library routine to find all the MX (Mail Exchanger) records for the host (we'll elaborate on MX records soon). If it finds any MX records, it sorts them in order of preference. If V8 *sendmail* finds two preferences that are the same, it randomizes the selection between the two when sorting.* It then tries to deliver the message to each

---

*This is broken in many other versions of *sendmail*.

host in that list, one at a time, until one of them succeeds, or until they all fail.

If no MX records are found, *sendmail* tries to deliver the message to the single original host.

Whether *sendmail* tries to connect to the original host or to a list of MX hosts, it calls *gethostbyname*(2) to get the network address for each. It then opens a network connection to that address and attempts to send SMTP mail.

The $[and $] Operators

The $[and $] operators are used to canonicalize a hostname. Any aliases are converted to the official hostname, and any IP addresses are converted to fully-qualified domain names. The *sendmail* program passes the name between the $[and $] operators to the *gethostbyname*(3) routine, and replaces the original expression with the result.

If the address is an IP number (like [123.45.67.8], note the surrounding square brackets), *sendmail* calls *inet_addr*(3) to convert that address to a network address. It then calls *gethostbyaddr*(2) to convert the network address into a canonical hostname.

$[and $] under V8

Under V8 *sendmail*, the preceding $[and $] lookups are more complex.*
Here is a simplified description of how they are performed.

Each lookup is actually composed of many lookups that occur in the form of a loop within a loop. In the outermost loop, the following logic is used:

- If the address has at least one dot somewhere in it, *sendmail* looks up that address unmodified first.

- If the unmodified address is not found, and if the RES_DNSRCH bit is set (see the I configuration option), *sendmail* looks up variations on the domain part of the address. The default domain is tried first (for a host in the *sub* subdomain at *dc.gov*, that would be *sub.dc.gov*, thus looking up *host.sub.dc.gov*). If that fails, *sendmail* then throws away the lowest part of the domain and tries again (looks up *host.dc.gov*).†

---

*Most of this complexity is to make wildcard MX records work properly.

†In later versions of BIND, a search attribute can be given in */etc/resolv.conf.* If present, *sendmail* uses that list of possible domains in place of this described logic.

- If the address has no dots and the RES_DEFNAMES bit is set (see the I configuration option), *sendmail* tries the SINGLE default domain (looks up *host.sub.dc.gov*). This is for compatibility with older versions of DNS.

Each lookup described above is performed using the following steps:

- Try the hostname with a T_ANY query which requests all the DNS records for that host. This tends to cause the local name server to pre-load its cache. If it succeeds, A (Address) records and/or MX (Mail Exchanger) records are among those returned. However, success is not guaranteed, because sometimes only NS (Name Server) records are returned. In that instance the following steps are also taken.

- Try the hostname with an T_A query which requests the A record for that host.

- Try the hostname with a T_MX query which requests MX records for the host.

Each query searches the data returned as follows:

- Search for a CNAME (alias) record. If one is found, replace the initial hostname (the alias) with the canonical name returned and start over.

- Search for an A record (the IP address). If one is found, the hostname just used to query is considered the canonical address.

- Search for an MX record. If one is found, and if a default domain has not been added, treat the MX record like an A record. For example, if the input hostname is *sub.dc.gov* and an MX record is found, the MX record is considered official. If, on the other hand, the input hostname has no domain added (is *sub*) and the query happens to stumble across *sub.dc.gov* as the MX record, the following searches are also tried.

- If an MX record is found, and no MX record has been previously found, the looked-up hostname is saved for future use. For example, if the query was for *sub.dc.gov* and two MX records were returned (*hostA.sub.dc.gov* and *hostB.sub.dc.gov*), *sub.dc.gov* is saved for future use.

- If no MX record is found, but one was found previously, the previous one is used. This assumes that the search is normally from most to least complex (*sub.sub.dc.gov, sub.dc.gov, dc.gov*).

As you can see, unraveling even a small part of *sendmail* can introduce more complexity than answers.

Set Up MX Records

An MX record is simply the method used by DNS to route mail bound for one machine to another instead. An MX record is created by a single line in one of your *named*(8) files:

```
hostA    IN      MX 10 hostB
```

This line says that all mail destined for hostA in your domain should be delivered to hostB instead. The IN says that this is an Internet-type record, and the 10 is the preference for the MX record.

An MX record may point to another host or to the original host.

```
hostA    IN      MX 0 hostA
```

This line says that mail for hostA will be delivered to hostA. Such records may seem redundant, but they are not. We'll cover why shortly.

A host can have multiple MX records (one pointing to itself or not).

```
hostA    IN      MX 0   hostA
         IN      MX 10  hostB
```

Here, hostA has the lowest preference number (0 versus 10 for hostB), so delivery will be attempted to itself first. If hostA is down, delivery will be attempted to hostB host instead.

Usually, MX records point to hosts inside the same domain. Thus, managing them does not require the cooperation of others. But it is legal for MX records to point to hosts in different domains:

```
hostA    IN      MX 0   hostA
         IN      MX 10  host.other.domain.
```

Here, you must contact the administrator at other.domain and obtain permission before creating this MX record. We cover this concept in more detail when we discuss disaster preparation later in this chapter.

Although MX records are usually straightforward, there can be a few problems associated with them.

MX Must Point to an A Record

The A record for a host is a line that gives the host's IP address:

```
hostC  IN     A    123.45.67.8
```

Here, hostC is the host's name. The IN says this is an Internet-type record. The A marks this as an A record. The 123.45.67.8 is the IP address for the host hostC.

An MX record must point to a hostname that has an A record. To illustrate, consider the following:

```
hostA  IN    MX  10 hostB         ← illegal
       IN    MX  20 hostC
hostB  IN    MX  10 hostC
hostC  IN    A   123.45.67.8
```

Note that hostB lacks an A record, but hostC has one. It is illegal to point an MX record at a host that lacks an A record. Thus, the first line above is illegal, whereas the second line is legal.

Although such a mistake is difficult to make when maintaining your own domain tables, it can easily happen to you if you rely on a name server in someone else's domain, as shown:

```
hostA    IN     MX  10 mail.other.domain.
```

The other administrator might, for example, retire the machine mail and replace its A record with an MX record that points to a different machine. Unless you are notified of the change, your MX record will suddenly become illegal.

Note that *sendmail* is possibly more forgiving than other MTAs. It also accepts an MX record that points to a CNAME record. The presumption is that the CNAME correctly points to an A record.

MX Records Are Non-recursive

Consider the following MX setup, which causes all mail for hostA to be sent to hostB, and all mail for hostB to be sent to hostB, or to hostC if hostB is down.*

```
hostA  IN     MX  10 hostB
hostB  IN     MX  10 hostB
       IN     MX  20 hostC
```

---

*We are fudging for the sake of simplicity. Here we assume all the hosts also have A records.

One might expect *sendmail* to be smart and deliver mail for hostA to hostC if hostB is down. But *sendmail* won't do that. It does not try to recursively look for additional MX records. If it did, it could get hopelessly entangled in MX loops. Consider the following:

```
hostA    IN     MX   10 hostB
hostB    IN     MX   10 hostB
         IN     MX   20 hostC
hostC    IN     MX   10 hostA      ← potential loop
```

If your intention is to have hostA MX to two other hosts, then you must state that explicitly:

```
hostA    IN     MX   10 hostB
         IN     MX   20 hostC
hostB    IN     MX   10 hostB
         IN     MX   20 hostC
```

Another reason *sendmail* refuses to follow MX records beyond the target host is that preferences in such a situation are undefined. Consider the example with the potential loop above. What is the preference of hostA when MX'd by hostB to hostC? Should it be the minimum of 10, the maximum of 20, the mean of 15, or the sum of 30?

Wildcard MX Records

Wildcard MX records provide a shorthand for MX'ing many hosts with a single MX record.

```
*.dc.gov.      IN  MX   10 hostB
```

This says that any host in the domain .dc.gov (where that host doesn't have any record of its own) should have its mail forwarded to hostB.

```
; domain is .dc.gov
*.dc.gov.      IN  MX   10 hostB
hostA          IN  MX   10 hostC
hostB          IN  A    123.45.67.8
```

Here, mail to hostD (no record at all) will be forwarded to hostB. But the wildcard MX record will be ignored for hostA and hostB, because they each have a record of their own.

Care must be exercised when setting up wildcard MX records. It is easy to create ambiguous situations that *sendmail* may not be be able to handle correctly. Consider, for example:

```
; domain is sub.dc.gov
*.dc.gov.       IN  MX  10 hostB.dc.gov.
*.sub.dc.gov.   IN  MX  10 hostC.dc.gov.
```

Here, an unqualified name like just plain `hostD` matches both wildcard records. This is ambiguous, so *sendmail* automatically picks the most complete one (`*.sub.dc.gov.`) and uses that MX record.

One compelling weakness of wildcard MX records is that they match any hostname at all, even for machines that don't exist.

```
; domain is sub.dc.gov
*.dc.gov.       IN  MX  10 hostB.dc.gov.
```

Here, mail to *foo.dc.gov* will be forwarded to `hostB.dc.gov`, even if there is no host *foo* in that domain.

Wildcard MX records almost never have any appropriate use on the Internet. They are often misunderstood and are often just used to save the effort of typing hundreds of MX records. They do, however, have legitimate uses behind firewall machines and on non-Internet networks.

What? They Ignore MX Records?

Many older MTAs on the network ignore MX records, and some Sun sites wrongly run the non-MX version of *sendmail* (that is, they should use */usr/lib/sendmail.mx*). Because of this, you will occasionally find some sites that insist on sending mail to a host even though that host has been explicitly MX'd to another.

To illustrate why this is bad, consider a UUCP host which only has an MX record. It has no A record, because it is not on the network:

```
uuhost  IN  MX  10 uucpserver
```

Here, mail to `uuhost` will be sent to `uucpserver`, which will forward the message to `uuhost` with UUCP software. An attempt to ignore this MX record will fail because `uuhost` has no other records. Similar problems can arise for printers with direct network connections, terminal servers, and even workstations that don't run an SMTP daemon like *sendmail*.

If you believe in DNS, and disdain sites that don't, you can simply ignore the offending sites. In this case the mail will fail if your MX'd host doesn't run a *sendmail* daemon (or another MTA). This is not as nasty as it sounds.

There is actually considerable support for this approach—failure to obey MX records is a clear violation of published network protocols. RFC1123, *Host Requirements*, section 5.3.5, notes that obeying MX records is mandatory.

On the other hand, if you want to insure that all mail is received, even on a workstation whose mail is MX'd elsewhere, you can run the *sendmail* daemon on every machine.

Caching MX Records

Although you are not required to have MX records for all hosts, there is good reason to consider doing so. To illustrate, consider the following host that only has an A record:

```
hostB          IN  A   123.45.67.8
```

When *sendmail* first looks up this host, it asks the local name server for all records. Because there is only an A record, that is all it gets.

But note that asking for all records caused the local name server to cache the information. The next time *sendmail* looks up this same host, the local name server will return the A record from its cache. This is faster and reduces Internet traffic. The cached information is "non-authoritative" (because it is a copy) and includes no MX records (because there are none).

When *sendmail* gets a non-authoritative reply that lacks MX records, it is forced to do another DNS lookup. This time it specifically asks for MX records. In this case, there are none, so it gets none.

Because `hostB` lacks an MX record, *sendmail* performs a DNS lookup each and every time mail is sent to that host. If `hostB` were a major mail receiving site, its lack of an MX record would be causing many *sendmail* programs, all over the world, to waste network bandwidth with otherwise useless DNS lookups.

We strongly recommend that every host on the Internet have at least one MX record. As a minimum, it can simply point to itself with a 0 preference:

```
hostB          IN  A   123.45.67.8
               IN  MX  0 hostB
```

This will not change how mail is routed to `hostB`, but will reduce the number of DNS lookups required.

Ambiguous MX Records

RFC974 leaves the treatment of ambiguous MX records to the implementor's discretion. This has generated much debate in *sendmail* circles. Consider:

```
foo     IN MX 10 hostA
foo     IN MX 20 hostB          ← mail from hostB to foo
foo     IN MX 30 hostC
```

When mail is sent from a host (`hostB`) that is an MX record for the receiving host (`foo`), all MX records of a preference equal to or greater than `hostB` must be discarded. The mail is then delivered to the remaining MX host with the lowest value preference (`hostA`). This is a sensible rule, because it prevents `hostB` from wrongly trying to deliver to itself.

It is possible to configure `hostB` so that it views the name `foo` as a synonym for its own name. Such a configuration results in `hostB` never looking up any MX records because it recognizes mail to `foo` as local.

But what should happen if `hostB` does not recognize `foo` as local, and if there is no `hostA`?

```
                              ← no hostA
foo     IN MX 20 hostB        ← mail from hostB to foo
foo     IN MX 30 hostC
```

Again, RFC974 says that when mail is being sent from a host (`hostB`) that is an MX record for the receiving host (`foo`), all MX records of a preference equal to or greater than `hostB` must be discarded. In this example, that leaves *zero* MX records. Three courses of action are now open to *sendmail*, but RFC974 doesn't say which it should use:

- Assume that this is an error condition. Clearly *hostB* should have been configured to recognize *foo* as local. It didn't (hence the MX lookup and discarding in the first place), so it must not have known what it was doing. V8 *sendmail* with the w option not set (undeclared or declared as false) will bounce the mail message.

- Look to see if *foo* has an A record. If it does, go ahead and try to deliver the mail message directly to *foo*. If it lacks an A record, bounce the message. This approach runs the risk that *foo* may not be configured to properly accept mail (thus causing mail to disappear down a black hole). Still, this approach may be desirable in some circumstances. V8 *sendmail* with the w option set and the UIUC version of IDA *sendmail* always try to connect to *foo*. Other versions of IDA (like KJS) do not.

- Assume (even though it has not been configured to do so) that *foo* should be treated as local to *hostB*. No version of *sendmail* makes this assumption.

This situation is not an idle exercise. Consider the MX record for uuhost presented in the previous section:

```
uuhost   IN   MX  10 uucpserver
```

Here, uuhost has no A record, because it is connected to uucpserver via a dial-up line. If uucpserver is not configured to recognize uuhost as one of its UUCP clients, and if mail is sent from uucpserver to uuhost, it will query DNS and get itself as the MX record for uuhost. As we have shown, that MX record is discarded, and an ambiguous situation has developed.

Using nslookup

If your site is connected to the Internet, you can use the *nslookup*(1) program to interactively find MX and other records. To run *nslookup*, just type its name:

```
% nslookup
```

Note that you may have to give the full pathname. Under SunOS, *nslookup* lives in the */usr/etc* directory, and under Ultrix, it lives in */usr/ucb*.

Once *nslookup* is running, it prints the name of your default name server and the IP address for that machine. It then prints a > character as a prompt and awaits input.

```
Server:  Mail.US.EDU
Address:  123.45.67.8

>
```

To tell *nslookup* to look up only MX records, use the *set* command:

```
> set type=mx
>
```

Now look up some real hosts and domains. First look up the domain *berkeley.edu** by entering its name at the prompt:

```
> berkeley.edu.
```

---

*The University of California at Berkeley.

Note the trailing dot which tells *nslookup*(1) that the local, default domain should not be appended prior to the lookup. The output produced by the above lookup looks like this:

```
> berkeley.edu.
Server:  Mail.US.EDU
Address:  123.45.67.8

berkeley.edu     preference = 5, mail exchanger = ucbvax.Berkeley.EDU
berkeley.edu     preference = 10, mail exchanger = mammoth.Berkeley.EDU
ucbvax.Berkeley.EDU      inet address = 128.32.137.3
ucbvax.Berkeley.EDU      inet address = 128.32.133.1
ucbvax.Berkeley.EDU      inet address = 128.32.130.12
ucbvax.Berkeley.EDU      inet address = 128.32.149.36
mammoth.Berkeley.EDU     inet address = 128.32.149.78
>
```

The first two lines again show the name and IP address of the local DNS server. The next two lines show that the domain `berkeley.edu` has two MX records. Mail addressed to that domain is sent to the machine with the lowest preference, which happens to be `ucbvax.berkeley.edu`.* If that machine is down (or not accepting mail), the message is sent to the machine with the next higher preference, `mammoth.berkeley.edu`. The last five lines show the IP addresses (A records) for those two machines. The machine `ucbvax.berkeley.edu` has four addresses because it has four network interfaces.

Now look up a real UUCP host, *lady*. Enter its name as if it were a part of the *berkeley.edu* domain.

```
> lady.berkeley.edu.
```

The output produced shows that *lady* has an MX record:

```
lady.berkeley.edu         preference = 5, mail exchanger = icsib.ICSI.Ber
keley.EDU
icsib.ICSI.Berkeley.EDU inet address = 128.32.201.15
>
```

Mail sent to `lady.berkeley.edu` is instead delivered to the machine `icsib.ICSI.Berkeley.EDU`, which in turn forwards that mail over a dial-up line to the UUCP host *lady*.

---

*Note that case is not significant in domain names. That is, all of the following are the same: edu, EdU, and EDU.

Machines that have MX records do not necessarily have A records. The host *lady* is such a machine. You tell *nslookup*(1) to look up an A record with the *set* command:

```
> set type=a
> lady.berkeley.edu.

*** No address (A) records available for lady.berkeley.edu.
```

The *nslookup*(1) program is a useful tool for performing all the same lookups done by *sendmail*. Each type of lookup corresponds to a `set type`. The list of some available *nslookup*(1) types is shown in Table 17-1.

Table 17-1: Some nslookup Types

Type	Description
a	IP address
cname	Canonical name for an alias
hinfo	Host CPU and operating system type
mx	Mail exchanger records
ns	Name server record
any	Union of all records

To exit *nslookup*(1), just type `exit`.

Prepare for Disaster

Disasters can take many forms and, by their very nature, are unexpected. If DNS and mail are to continue to work, expecting the unexpected is vital. The kinds of disasters one must anticipate vary from the mundane to the catastrophic:

- A reboot, or scheduled down-time for dumps on the mail or DNS server, should only cause mail to be delayed, not lost.

- A failed component on the mail or DNS server could cause mail delivery to be delayed anywhere from a few hours to a few days. A delay of over three to five days could cause many hosts to bounce queued mail, unless steps are taken to receive that mail elsewhere.

- Natural disasters can disrupt site or network connectivity for weeks. The Loma Priata quake on the West Coast of the United States lasted only a few minutes, but knocked out electric power to many areas for far longer. Fear of gas leaks prevented repowering many buildings for up to two weeks. A hurricane, flood, fire, or even an errant back-hoe could knock out your institution for weeks or even months.

Offsite MX Hosts

When mail can't be received, whether because of a small event or a large disaster, an offsite MX host can save the day. An offsite MX host is simply another machine that can receive mail for your site when your site is unavailable. The "off site" will vary depending on your situation. For a subdomain at one end of a microwave link, a host on the other side of the microwave might be sufficient. For a large site, like a university, a machine at another university (possibly in a different state or country) would be wise.

Before we show how to set up offsite MX hosts, note that offsite MX hosts are not an unmixed blessing. If an offsite MX host does not handle mail reliably, you could lose mail. In many cases it is better not to have an offsite MX host than to have an unreliable one. Without an MX site, mail will normally be queued on the sending host. A reliable MX backup is useful, but an unreliable one is a disaster.

You should not unilaterally select a host to function as an offsite MX host. To set up an offsite MX host, you need to negotiate with the managers of other sites. By mutual agreement, another site's manager will configure that other machine to accept mail bound for your site (possibly queueing weeks worth of mail) and configure that site to forward that mail to yours when your site comes back up.

For example, suppose your site is in the state of Iowa, in the United States. Further suppose that in Northern Japan there is a site with which you are friendly. You could negotiate with them to receive and hold your mail in a disaster. When they are set up to do so, you first add a low preference (high number) MX record for them:

```
mailhost.uiowa.edu.    IN    MX 2      mailhost.uiowa.edu.
mailhost.uiowa.edu.    IN    MX 10     backup.uiowa.edu.
mailhost.uiowa.edu.    IN    MX 900    pacific.north.jp.    ← note
```

To be sure the MX works, send mail to yourself via that new MX site:

```
% mail you%mailhost.uiowa.edu@pacific.north.jp*
```

Here, the `%` in the address causes the message to first be delivered to *pacific.north.jp*. That machine then throws away its own name and converts the remaining `%` to an `@`. The result is then mailed back to you at:

```
you@mailhost.uiowa.edu
```

This verifies that the disaster MX machine can get mail to your site when it returns to service.

During a disaster, the first sign of trouble will be mail for your site suddenly appearing in the queue at *pacific.north.jp*. The manager there should notice and set up a separate queue to hold the incoming mail until your site returns to service (see Chapter 19, *The Queue*). When your site recovers, you can contact that manager and arrange for a queue run to deliver the backlog of mail.

If you are out of service for weeks, the backlog of mail might be partly on tape or some other backup media. You might even want to negotiate an artificially slow feed so that your local spool directory won't overfill.

Even in minor disasters, an MX host can save much grief because delivery will be serialized. Without an MX host, every machine in the world that had mail for your machine would try to send nearly at once when your machine returns to service. That could overload your machine and has been known to crash some machines, causing the problem to repeat over and over.

Offsite Primaries

A disaster MX is only good so long as your DNS services stay alive to advertise it. Most sites have multiple name server machines to balance the load of DNS lookups, and to provide redundancy in case one fails. Unfortunately, few sites have offsite name servers as a hedge against disaster. Consider the disaster MX record developed above:

```
mailhost.uiowa.edu.   IN   MX 900   pacific.north.jp.
```

Ideally, one would want *pacific.north.jp* to queue all mail until the local site is back in service. Unfortunately, all DNS records contain a time to live (TTL) that may or may not be present in the declaration line.

---

*This example presumes that *pacific.north.jp* can handle the `%` "hack"—most places do, so this is probably a safe assumption.

```
mailhost.uiowa.edu.   IN   MX 900   pacific.north.jp.
                      ↑
                      TTL implied

mailhost.uiowa.edu. 86400  IN   MX 900   pacific.north.jp.
                     ↑
                     TTL specified as 24 hours in seconds
```

When other sites look up the local site, they cache this record. They will not look it up again until 24 hours have passed. Thus, if an earthquake strikes, all other sites will forget about this record after 24 hours and will not be able to look it up again.

In general, records set up for disaster purposes should be given TTLs that are over a month:

```
mailhost.uiowa.edu. 3600000  IN   MX 900   pacific.north.jp.
                    ↑
                    TTL specified as 41 days in seconds
```

Note that such long TTLs should only be used for disaster purposes. You should use more appropriate TTLs for all other records so that they will time out in a reasonable amount of time. Otherwise changes will propagate too slowly and ambiguous or wrong information may exist for extended periods.

If many hosts at your site receive mail (as opposed to a central mail server), it is necessary to add this type of disaster record for each. Unfortunately, when the number of such hosts at your site is greater than a hundred or so, individual disaster MX records become difficult to manage simply because of scale.

At such sites, a better method of disaster preparedness is to set up *pacific.north.jp* as another primary DNS server for the local site. There are two advantages to this "authoritative" backup server approach:

- An off-site primary server eliminates the need to set up individual MX disaster records.
- An out-of-country primary server can lower the network impact of DNS lookups of your site.

Unfortunately, setting up an off-site or out-of-country server can be extremely difficult. We won't show you how to do that here. Instead we refer you to the book *DNS and BIND* (O'Reilly & Associates, Inc.)

Pitfalls

- When *sendmail* finds multiple A records for a host (and no MX records), it tries them in the order returned by DNS. DNS usually returns the A record first that is on the same network. The *sendmail* program assumes that DNS returns addresses in a useful order. If the address that *sendmail* always tries first is not the most appropriate, look for problems with DNS, not with *sendmail.*

- There is no way to discover that another site has used yours as a disaster MX site, unless someone at that other site tells you. Instead, you may one day suddenly discover many queued messages from outside your site destined for some host you've never heard of before.

- Under old versions of DNS, an error in the zone file causes the rest of the file to be ignored. The effect is as though many of your hosts suddenly disappeared. This problem has been fixed in 4.8.3 and 4.9.x.

- Sites with a central mail hub should make that hub a primary DNS server. If */etc/resolv.conf* contains `localhost` as its first record, look ups will be faster. Failure to make the mail hub a DNS server runs the risk of mail failing and queueing when the hub is up, but the other DNS servers are down or unreachable.

18

Security

The *sendmail* program can be an open door to abuse. Unless the administrator is careful, the misuse or misconfiguration of *sendmail* can lead to an insecure and possibly compromised system. Since *sendmail* is usually installed to run as an *suid root* process, it is a prime target for intrusion. The "Internet worm," for example, used a flaw in old versions of *sendmail* as one way to gain entry to thousands of machines.* If *sendmail* is not properly installed, external probes over networks can be used to gain information valuable in attempting entry. Once inside, improper file permissions can be used to "trick" *sendmail* into giving away *root* privilege. Even e-mail cannot be trusted, and forged e-mail can cause some users to give away their passwords.

In this chapter, we present several ways to protect your site from intrusion via *sendmail.* Most are just good common sense, and the experienced system administrator may be offended that we state the obvious. But not all system administrators are experienced, and not all who administer systems are system administrators. If you fall into the latter category, you may wish to keep keep a good, general UNIX reference by your side to better appreciate our suggestions.

---

*That flaw has been eliminated—wrongly by some vendors who turned all debugging completely off; correctly by most who simply disabled SMTP debugging.

SMTP Probes

Although SMTP probes can be legitimate uses of the network, they can also pose potential risks. They are sometimes used to see if a bug remains unfixed. Sometimes they are used to try to gather user login names, or to feed a program unexpected input in such a way that it breaks and gives away *root* privilege.

SMTP debug

An "unfixed bug" probe can use the SMTP *debug* and *showq* commands. The SMTP *debug* command allows the local *sendmail* to be placed into debugging mode (as with the −d command-line switch) from any other machine anywhere on the network. The SMTP *showq* command allows outsiders to view the contents of the mail queue.

If the SMTPDEBUG macro is defined when *sendmail* is compiled, the SMTP *debug* and *showq* commands are allowed to work; otherwise they are disabled. SMTPDEBUG should only be defined when modifying the *sendmail* code and testing a new version. It should never be defined in an official release of *sendmail*. To see if it has been defined at your site, run the following command:

```
% telnet localhost 25
Trying 123.45.6.7 ...
Connected to localhost.
Escape character is '^]'.
220 localhost sendmail 8.6 ready at Tue, 22 Sep 1993 04:59:07 +0800
debug
500 Command unrecognized
quit
221 localhost.us.edu closing connection
Connection closed by foreign host.
%
```

When connected, enter the command debug; if you get the answer 500 Command unrecognized, you know that SMTPDEBUG is not enabled. If, on the other hand, you get the answer 200 Debug set, SMTPDEBUG is defined on your system, and you should immediately take steps to correct the situation. Either contact your vendor and request a new version of *sendmail*, or get the *sendmail* source and compile it with SMTPDEBUG undefined (see Chapter 16, *Compile and Install sendmail*).

When SMTPDEBUG is undefined, and an outsider connects to the local machine and attempts to execute the *debug* or *showq* commands, *sendmail* may *syslog*(3) a message like the following:

```
Jul 22 07:09:00 here sendmail[192]: "debug" command from there (1.2.3.4)
```

This message shows the name of the machine attempting the probe (there) and the IP address of that machine. Note that this message is only logged if the L configuration option is nonzero. This message is only available with the IDA and V8 versions of *sendmail.*

SMTP vrfy and expn

You may be dismayed to learn that the login names of ordinary users can be used to break into a system. It is not, for example, all that unusual for a user to select a password that is simply a copy of his or her login name, or first name, or last name, or some combination of initials.

The SMTP *vrfy* and *expn* commands cause *sendmail* to verify that an address is good. If a user's login name is given, the full name and login name are printed:

```
250 George Washington <george>
```

If the user is unknown, *sendmail* prints an error message:

```
550 foo... User unknown
```

A risk of eventual attack can arise from any attempt to *vrfy* or *expn* a mailing list alias. Many sites have aliases which include all or a large segment of users. Such aliases often have easily guessed names, like *all*, or *everyone*, or *staff.* A probe, for example, of *all* might produce something like the following:

```
250-George Washington <george>
250-Thomas Jefferson <tj>
250-Ben Franklin <ben>
250-Betsy Ross <msflag>
250-John Q. Public <jqp>
```

With well-designed passwords, these full and login names can safely be given to the world at large. But, if one user (say jqp) has a poorly-designed password (like *jqpublic*), your site's security can easily be compromised.* Note that not all uses of *vrfy* or *expn* represent probes. Some MUAs, for example, routinely *vrfy* each recipient before sending a message.

---

*The *fingerd*(8) utility can also reveal login IDs.

Some versions of *sendmail* offer the means to monitor the SMTP *vrfy* command. The SunOS version, for example, sends mail to *postmaster* with a message body like the following:

```
    ----- Transcript of session follows -----
<<< vrfy staff
550 staff... User unknown
<<< vrfy all
<<< quit

    ----- No message was collected -----
```

This shows that someone tried to expand the mailing list alias `staff` and failed. Whoever it was then expanded `all` and succeeded. There are two drawbacks to the SunOS approach. First, there is no indication in the mail notification of the name of the host from which the probe came. Second, mail notification is only sent if the SMTP *vrfy* fails and if option P is declared. (If it succeeds, or if option P is undeclared, SunOS *sendmail* remains silent.)

With V8 and the next release of IDA *sendmail*, SMTP *vrfy* commands are individually logged in a form like one of the following:

```
Sep 22 11:40:43 yourhost sendmail[pid]: other.host: vrfy all
Sep 22 11:40:43 yourhost sendmail[pid]: [222.33.44.55]: vrfy all
```

This shows that someone from the outside (`other.host` in the first example) attempted to *vrfy* the mailing list named `all`. In the second example, the probing hostname could not be found, so the IP address is printed instead (in the square brackets). Note that this form of logging is only enabled if the L (logging) option is greater than eight (see Chapter 22, *Logging and Statistics*).

Pre-V8 versions of *sendmail* do not report SMTP *vrfy* attempts at all. Some versions of *sendmail* (such as the HPUX version) appear to verify, but really only echo the address stated.

V8 *sendmail* allows *vrfy* and *expn* services to be selectively accepted or rejected. See Chapter 30, *Options*, for a description of the p (privacy) option.

The Configuration File

There are a number of security holes that can be opened up by commands given carelessly in the configuration file. Such holes can be serious because *sendmail* starts to run as *root*, provided it has not been given any unsafe command-line switches (see Chapter 32, *The Command Line*, for a list of unsafe switches). It continues as *root* until it delivers mail, whereupon it changes its identity to that of an ordinary user. When *sendmail* reads its configuration file, it generally does so while it is still *root*. Consequently, as we will illustrate, it may be able to read and overwrite any file.

The F Command—File Form

The file form of the F (File) configuration command can be used to read sensitive information. That command looks like this in the configuration file:

```
FX/path pat
```

This form is used to read class macro entries from files. It can cause problems through a misunderstanding of the *scanf*(3) pattern *pat*. The */path* is the name of the file, and the optional *pat* is a pattern to be used by *scanf*(3) (see Chapter 28, *Class Macros*).

To illustrate the risk of the *pat*, consider the following configuration file entry:

```
Fw/etc/myhostnames [^#]
```

Normally, the F command reads only the first white space-delimited word from each line of the file. If the optional pattern *pat* is specified, the F command instead reads one or more words from each line based on the nature of the pattern. The pattern is used by *scanf*(3) to extract words, and the specific pattern used here [^#] causes *scanf*(3) to read everything up to the first comment character (the #) from each line. This *pat* allows multiple hostnames to be conveniently listed on each line of the file. Now assume that a new administrator, who is not very familiar with *sendmail*, decides to add an F command to gather a list of UUCP hosts from the */etc/uucp/Systems* file. Being a novice, the new administrator copies the existing entry for use with the new file:

```
FU/etc/uucp/Systems [^#]
```

This is the same pattern that was correctly used for */etc/myhostnames*. Unfortunately, the *Systems* file contains more than just host entries on each line:

```
linda Any ACU 2400 5551212  "" \d\n in:-\r-in: Uourhost word: MublyPeg
hoby Any ACU 2400 5551213  "" \d\n in:-\r-in: Uourhost word: FuMzz3.x
```

A part of each line (the last item in each) contains unencrypted passwords. An unscrupulous user, noticing the mistaken [^#] in the configuration file, could run *sendmail* with a -d36.5 debugging switch and watch each password being processed. For example:

```
% /usr/lib/sendmail -36.5 -bt < /dev/null
← ... some output deleted
STAB: hoby 1 entered
STAB: Any 1 entered
STAB: ACU 1 entered
STAB: 2400 1 entered
STAB: 5551213 1 entered
STAB: "" 1 type 1 val 0 0 200000 0
STAB: \d\n 1 entered
STAB: in:-\r-in: 1 entered
STAB: Uourhost 1 entered
STAB: word: 1 entered
STAB: FuMzz3.x 1 entered                          ← note
STAB: local 3 type 3 val 34d00 0 0 0
STAB: prog 3 type 3 val 34d80 0 0 0
ADDRESS TEST MODE (ruleset 3 NOT automatically invoked)
Enter <ruleset> <address>
```

Note the fifth line from the bottom, where the password for the UUCP login into the host hoby is printed. This example illustrates two rules about handling the configuration file:

- Avoid using the F command to read a file that is not already publicly readable. To do so can reveal sensitive information. Even if the *scanf(3)* option is correct, a core dump* or frozen configuration file can be examined for sensitive information from otherwise secured files.

- Avoid adding a new command to the configuration file by blindly copying and modifying another. Try to learn the rules governing the command first.

---

*Most versions of UNIX disallow core dumps of SUID *root* programs.

The F Command—Program Form

Another form of the F (File) configuration command is the program form, which looks like this:

```
FX| /path
```

Here, the | prefix to the */path* tells *sendmail* that */path* is the name of a program to run. The output produced by the program is appended to the class, here *X*.

To illustrate another potential risk, consider a configuration file that is group writable, perhaps by a few administrators who share the job of *post-master*. All an attacker needs to do is to break into one of those administrator's accounts to become *root*. Consider the following bogus entry added to the configuration file:

```
FX|/tmp/.sh
```

Here the program (actually a shell script) called */tmp/.sh* is run by *sendmail* to fill the class X with new values. But suppose that program does the unexpected:

```
#!/bin/gsh
cp /bin/gsh /tmp/.shell
chmod u+s /tmp/.shell
```

Here the Bourne shell is copied to *tmp/.shell* and the SUID *root* bit is set. Now, any user at all can run *sendmail* and become *root*:

```
% ls -l /tmp/.shell
/tmp/.shell not found
%  /usr/lib/sendmail -bt < /dev/null
ADDRESS TEST MODE
Enter <ruleset> <address>
>
% ls -l /tmp/.shell
-rwsr-xr-x  1 root          122880 Sep 24 13:20 /tmp/.shell
```

The program form of the F configuration command is clearly dangerous (and has been removed from the V8 *sendmail*).

- The *sendmail* configuration file must *never* be writable by anyone other than *root*. It should also live in a directory, every path component of which is owned by and writable only by *root*. (We'll discuss this latter point in greater detail soon.)

The A= of Delivery Agents

Just as the program form of the F command can pose a risk if the configuration file is poorly protected, so can the M delivery agent definition. Specifically, the P= equate for a delivery agent can be modified to run a bogus program that gives away *root* privilege. Consider the following modification to the local delivery agent:

```
Mlocal, P=/bin/mail, F=rlsDFMmnP, S=10, R=20, A=mail -d $u
        ↓
     becomes
        ↓
Mlocal, P=/tmp/mail, F=SrlsDFMmnP, S=10, R=20, A=mail -d $u
```

Here, local mail should be delivered with the */bin/mail* program, but instead it is delivered with a bogus frontend, */tmp/mail*. If */tmp/mail* is carefully crafted, users will never notice that the mail has been diverted. The S flag in the F= equate causes *sendmail* to retain its *root* privilege when executing the bogus */tmp/mail*.

- Delivery agent P= equates must be protected by protecting the configuration file. As an additional precaution, *never* use relative pathnames in the P= equate.

- The F=S delivery agent flag is an especially dangerous one. It should never appear in your configuration file unless you have deliberately placed it there and are 100 percent certain of its effect.

The S Option and the Statistics File

When *sendmail* attempts to record its delivery agent statistics (see Chapter 22, *Logging and Statistics*), it checks for the existence and writability of the file specified in the S configuration file. The *sendmail* program does not care where that file lives or what permissions it has—only that it exists.

A problem can arise if one is tempted to locate the statistics file in a spool or temporary area. Consider the following location, for example:

```
OS/usr/tmp/sendmail.st
```

Here the administrator sets the S option to locate the statistics file in the */usr/tmp* directory. The intention is that the file can be easily created by anyone who wishes to gather statistics for a while, then removed. Unfortunately, the */usr/tmp* directory is usually world-writable.

Thus any unhappy or malicious user can bring the system to its knees:

```
% cd /usr/tmp
% ln -s /vmunix sendmail.st
```

Here, *sendmail* clobbers the disk copy of the kernel. Nothing bad may happen at first,* but the machine will require manual intervention to boot in the future.† Clearly precautions must be taken:

- Any file that *sendmail* writes to (like the S option statistics file, or the *aliases* database files) must be writable only by *root* and live in a directory, every path component of which is only writable by *root*.

Permissions

One technique used to gain *root* privilege is to first become a semi-privileged user like *bin* or *sys*. Such semi-privileged users often own the directories in which *root*-owned files live. By way of example, consider the following:

```
drwxr-sr-x 11 bin      2560 Sep 22 18:18 /etc
-rw-r--r--  1 root     8199 Aug 25 07:54 /etc/sendmail.cf
```

Here, the */etc/sendmail.cf* configuration file is correctly writable only by *root*. But the directory in which that file lives is owned by *bin* and writable by *bin*. Having write permission on that directory means that *bin* can rename and create files. An individual who gains *bin* permission on this machine can create a bogus *sendmail.cf* file by issuing only two simple commands:

```
% mv /etc/sendmail.cf /etc/...
% mv /tmp/sendmail.cf /etc/sendmail.cf
```

The original *sendmail.cf* is renamed . . . (a name that is not likely to be randomly noticed by the real system administrator). The bogus */tmp/sendmail.cf* then replaces the original:

```
drwxr-sr-x 11 bin      2560 Sep 22 18:18 /etc
-rw-r--r--  1 bin      4032 Nov 16 00:32 /etc/sendmail.cf
```

UNIX pays less attention to semi-privileged users than it does *root*. The user *root*, for example, is mapped to *nobody* over NFS, whereas the user *bin*

---

*Programs that need kernel symbols, like *ps*(1), will cease to work, or will produce garbage output.

†The savvy administrator can still boot off the network or from a CD-ROM and quickly install a new kernel.

remains *bin*. Consequently, the following rules must be observed to prevent malicious access to *root*-owned files:

- All directories in the path leading to a *root*-owned file must be owned by *root* and writable only by *root*. This is true for *all* files, not just *sendmail* files.
- Files owned by *root* must be writable only by *root*. Group writability, although at times desirable, should consistently be avoided.

When *sendmail* processes its configuration file, the F configuration command can cause it to read other files or to execute programs. Because *sendmail* is running as *root* when processing the configuration file, care should be taken to insure the safety of system programs as well. Consider the following F configuration command:

```
FU|/usr/bin/gawk '{print $1}' /usr/lib/uuhosts
```

This causes the hostnames in the first column of the file */usr/lib/uuhosts* to be added to the class macro named U. Here we'll assume that the components of the path */usr/lib/uuhosts* have the correct permissions and instead look at a possible problem with the *awk* program:

```
drwxr-sr-x 25 root       1024 Aug 10 08:52 /usr
drwxr-sr-x  3 bin        5120 Aug 18 10:50 /usr/bin
-rwxr-xr-x  1 root      90112 Oct 11  1990 /usr/bin/awk
```

Here the */usr/bin* directory is owned (as it commonly is) by *bin*. Now remember that *sendmail* is running as *root* when it executes *awk*. From the previous discussion about *bin*, you can see what a disaster it would be if the *awk* program were replaced with a bogus copy.

- All system directories and files must live in directories, all of whose path component parts are owned by and writable only by *root*. All system files (except possibly *suid* or *sgid* files) must be owned by *root* and writable only by *root*. If any program "breaks" after securing permissions, complain to your vendor at once!

Permissions for :include:

The *sendmail* program doesn't always run as *root*. When delivering mail, it often changes its identity into that of a nonprivileged user. When delivering to a :include: mailing list, for example, it can change its identity to that of the owner of the list. This too can pose risks if permissions are not appropriate. Consider the following *aliases* file entry:

```
newprogs: :include:/usr/local/lists/proglist
```

Here, notification of new programs are mailed to the alias `newprogs`. The list of recipients is taken from the following file:

```
-rw-rw-r--  2 bin  prog   704 Sep 21 14:46 /usr/local/lists/proglist
```

Because this file is owned by *bin*, *sendmail* changes its identity to *bin* when delivering to the list of recipients. Unfortunately, the file is also writable by the group *prog*. Anyone in the group *prog* can add a recipient to that list, including one of the form:

```
|/tmp/xxx.sh
```

This tells *sendmail* to deliver a copy of the message by running the program (a shell script) */tmp/xxx.sh*. The *sendmail* program (which is still running as *bin*) executes that program as *bin*. Further, suppose the program */tmp/xxx.sh* contains the following:

```
#!/bin/gsh
cp /bin/gsh /tmp/sh
chmod u+s /tmp/sh
cat - > /dev/null
exit 0
```

This causes *bin* to first make a copy of the Bourne shell in */tmp* (a copy which will be owned by *bin*), then to set the SUID bit on that copy (the `u+s`):

```
-rwsr-xr-x  1 bin    64668 Sep 22 07:38 /tmp/sh
```

The script then throws away the incoming mail message and exits with a zero value to keep *sendmail* unsuspecting. Through this process, an ordinary user in the group *prog* has created an *suid* shell that allows anyone to become the semi-privileged user *bin*. From the preceding discussion, you can see the trouble that can cause!

- Mailing lists (`:include:`) must live in a directory, all the components of which are writable only by root. The lists themselves must be writable only by the owner. If the owner is an ordinary user, group writability can be enabled, provided the user is advised of the risks.

- Mailing list (`:include:`) files may safely be owned by *root*. When *sendmail* processes a *root*-owned mailing list, it changes itself to run as the user and group specified by the `u` and `g` options. Those options default to *daemon* for both, but should be set to *nobody* and *nogroup*.

Permissions for ~/.forward Files

The *~/.forward* file can pose a security risk to individual users. There is a higher degree of risk if the user is *root* or one of the semi-privileged users (like *bin*). Because the *~/.forward* file is like an individual mailing list (`:include:`) for the user, risk can be encountered if that file is writable by anyone but the user. Consider, for example:

```
drwxr-xr-x 50 george guest      3072 Sep 27 09:19 /home/george/
-rw-rw-r--  1 george guest        62 Sep 17 09:49 /home/george/.forward
```

Here, the user `george`'s *~/.forward* file is writable by the group `guest`. Anyone in group `guest` can edit `george`'s *~/.forward* file, possibly placing into it something like this:

```
\george
|"cp /bin/gsh /home/george/.x; chmod u+s /home/george/.x"
```

Now all the attacker has to do is send `george` mail to create an SUID `george` shell. Then by executing */home/george/.x*, the attacker becomes `george`.

- The semi-privileged users like *bin*, and *root* in particular, should never have *~/.forward* files. Instead, they should forward their mail by means of the *aliases* file directly.

- User *~/.forward* files must be writable only by the owning user. Similarly, user home directories must live in a directory owned and writable only by *root*, and must themselves be owned and writable only by the user.

Some users, like the pseudo-user *uucp*, have home directories that must be world-writable for software to work properly. If that software is not needed (if a machine, for example, doesn't run UUCP software), that home directory should be removed. If the directory must exist, and must be world-writable, you should create a protected *~/.forward* file there before someone else does. The best protection is to create a nonempty directory called *~/.forward*, owned by *root*, and set its permissions to 000:

```
# cd ~uucp
# rm -f .forward
# mkdir .forward
# touch .forward/uucp
# chown root .forward .forward/uucp
# chmod 000 .forward .forward/uucp
# chmod +t ~uucp
# chown root ~uucp
```

Even though the ˜*uucp* directory is world-writable (so anyone can remove anything from it) no one but *root* can remove the */.forward* directory because it is not empty. The mode of 000 protects the file *.forward/uucp* from being removed. The mode of +t prevents users from renaming files or directories they do not own. Finally, *root* is made to own the ˜*uucp* directory, so that *uucp* will be unable to clear the +t bit. Even with this protection, mail for *uucp* should be routed to a real user with the *aliases*(5) file.

- All critical dot files in a world-writable home directory must be protected from creation by others. Each of *.forward*, *.rhosts*, *.login*, *.cshrc*, *.profile*, and *.logout* should be a non-empty, *root*-owned directory with mode 000. World-writable home directories must be owned by *root* instead of by the user, and they must have the +t (sticky bit) set.

Recommended Permissions

Table 18-1 shows the recommended ownerships and permissions for all the files and directories in the *sendmail* system. The path components will vary depending on the vendor version of *sendmail* you are running. For example, where we show the */usr/lib/sendmail* directory, your site may use */usr/etc/sendmail*, or even */usr/lib/mail/sendmail*.

Table 18-1: Recommended Permissions

Path	Type	Owner	Mode
/	directory	*root*	0755
/usr	directory	*root*	0755
/usr/lib	directory	*root*	0755
/usr/lib/sendmail	file	*root*	06511*
/etc	directory	*root*	0755
/etc/sendmail.cf	file	*root*	0644 or 0640
/etc/sendmail.fc	file	*root*	0644
OS/*etc/sendmail.st*	file	*root*	0644
OH/*etc/sendmail.hf*	file	*root*	0444
OA/*etc/aliases*	file	*root*	0644
/etc/aliases.pag	file	*root*	0644
/etc/aliases.dir	file	*root*	0644
/etc/aliases.db	file	*root*	0644
F/*path*	directory	*root*	0755
F/*path/file*	file	n/a	0444

Table 18.1: Recommended Permissions (continued)

Path	Type	Owner	Mode
/var	directory	*root*	0755
/var/spool	directory	*root*	0755
OQ/*var/spool/mqueue*	directory	*root*	0700†
`:include:`/*path*	directories	*root*	0755
`:include:`/*path/list*	file	any	0644

* The *sendmail* program may need to be SGID *kmem* for the load average to be checked on some systems.

† CERT (the Computing Emergency Response Team) recommends that the *mqueue* directory be mode 0700 to prevent potential security breaches.

The Aliases File

The *aliases* file can easily be used to gain privileged status if it is wrongly or carelessly administered. In addition to proper permissions and ownership, you should be aware of potentially harmful entries you may have inherited from the vendor or previous administrators. For example, many vendors used to ship systems with a decode alias in the *aliases* file. This practice is becoming less common.

```
# you may wish to comment this out for security
decode:    |/usr/bin/guudecode
```

The intention is to provide an easy way for users to transfer binary files using mail. At the sending site, the user uses *uuencode*(1) to convert the binary to ASCII, then mails the result to the decode alias at the receiving site. That alias pipes the mail message through the */usr/bin/uudecode* program, which converts the ASCII back into the original binary file.

The *uudecode*(1) program takes the name of the file to create from the file it is decoding. That information is in the begin line, used by *uudecode*. For example, here's an attempt to use *uudecode*(1) to place a bogus queue file directly into the *sendmail* queue:

```
begin 777 /var/spool/mqueue/qfAA12345
```

Here the begin tells *uudecode* to begin conversion. The 777 is the permissions to give to the file that will be created. That is followed by the full pathname of the file. If the queue directory were wrongly owned by *daemon*, any outsider could create a bogus queued message at your site.

Some versions of *uudecode* (like the one with SunOS) will create SUID files. That is, a `begin` line like the following can be used to create an SUID *daemon* shell in */tmp*:

```
begin 4777 /tmp/sh
```

- The `decode` alias should be removed from all *aliases* files. Similarly, every alias that executes a program—that you did not place there yourself and check completely—should be questioned and probably removed.

The Alias Database Files

The *aliases*(5) file is often stored in *dbm*(3) database format for faster lookups. The database files live in the same directory as the *aliases* file. For all versions of *sendmail*, they are called *aliases.dir* and *aliases.pag* (but for V8 *sendmail* only a single database file might exist and be called *aliases.db*).

It is useless to protect the *aliases*(5) file if you do not protect its corresponding database files. If the database files are not protected, the attacker can create a private *aliases* file, then run:

```
% /usr/lib/sendmail -oA./aliases -bi
```

This causes *sendmail* to build *./aliases* database files in the current directory. The attacker then copies those bogus database files over the unprotected system originals. The *sendmail* program never detects the change, because the database files appear to be newer than the *aliases* file.

- The *aliases* file, and its database files, must be owned by *root* and writable only by *root*. They must live in a directory, every path component of which is owned by and only writable by *root*.

Forged Mail

While aware that paper mail can forged, most users are blissfully unaware that e-mail can be forged. Forged mail can lead to a serious breech of security. Two points of vulnerability particularly deserve your attention: the queue file and the SMTP interface of *sendmail*.

Forging With the Queue Directory

All versions of *sendmail* trust the files in the mail queue. They assume that only *sendmail* has placed files there. As a consequence, a poorly protected queue directory can allow the attacker to create mail that looks 100% authentic. This can be used to send forged mail, or to append to system critical files, or to run arbitrary programs as *root* or other users. Consider the following bogus *qfAA00001* file for sending forged mail (*qf* files are described in Appendix A, *The qf File Internals*):

```
P943442
T717442614
DdfAA00001
S<root@yourhost>
Rgeorge@yourhost
H?P?return-path: <root@yourhost>
Hmessage-id: <9209251736.AA00001@yourhost>
HFrom: root@yourhost
Hdate: Fri, 13 Sep 1992 10:36:53 PDT
HTo: george@yourhost
Hsubject: Change your Password Now!!
```

This qf file causes mail to be sent to *george* that appears in all ways to come from *root*. There is nothing in this qf file to indicate to the recipient or to *sendmail* that the message is not authentic. Now further suppose that the df file (the message body) contains the following text:

```
The system has been compromised. Change your password NOW!
Your new password must be:

                       Fuzz7bal
Thank you,
         --System Administration
```

Unfortunately, in any large organization, there will be more than a few users who will obey a message like this. They will gladly change their password to one assigned to them, thereby providing the attacker with access to their accounts.

- The queue directory must be owned by *root* and writable only by *root*. CERT recommends that the queue directory always be mode 0700.
- The queue files placed into the queue by *sendmail* must be well protected by defining narrow default permissions with the F option. A default of 0600 is best.

Forging with SMTP

We won't illustrate the SMTP interaction here. But note that anyone can connect to your local *sendmail* via *telnet*(1) at port 25, or run *sendmail* with the **-bs** command-line switch. Once connected, *sendmail* must of necessity believe everything it receives. The only exception is the hostname sent in the HELO message.* In that case, the *sendmail* program looks up the real hostname based on the connection. If the stated hostname and the real hostname differ, the false name is used as the name of the sending host with the real name added in parentheses:

```
550 your.host hello false.host (real.host), pleased to meet you
```

The real hostname is then used as the sending hostname in the construction of all headers. The result (the header and body received by the user) might look something like this:

```
From root@false.host Sep 22 14:36:40 1992
Received: from real.host by your.host (5.63/1.42)
        id AA00998; Tue, 22 Sep 92 14:36:38 -0700
Message-Id: <9209222133.AA05059@your.host>
From: root@false.host (System Administration)
To: you@your.host
Subject: Change your password now!
Date: Tue, 22 Sep 92 14:10:43 PDT

To improve security at our location you are requested to immediately
change your password. The password you have been assigned is:

    7Fuzzy1's

Thank you,
    --root
```

Fortunately the `Received:` header above contains the name of the real host (which is not always the case). An attentive user can tell that this is a forged message because the host in that header line differs from the false hostname used in the other header lines.

However, most mail-reading programs allow users to filter out (not see) uninteresting header lines.† Typically, users choose to ignore headers like `Received:` and `Message-Id:`. For such users, the task of detecting

---

*V8 *sendmail* also tries to verify the connection itself with *identd* if possible.

†Old versions of *gnu-emacs*(1) were known to delete those lines irrevocably.

forged mail is much more difficult. Instead of seeing the above message, with real hostnames, they might see the following with only false names:

```
From root@false.host Sep 22 14:36:40 1992
From: root@false.host (System Administration)
To: you@your.host
Subject: Change your password now!
Date: Tue, 22 Sep 92 14:10:43 PDT

To improve security at our location you are requested to immediately
change your password. The password you have been assigned is:

    7Fuzzy1's

Thank you,
        --root
```

Clearly a user seeing only this much of the mail message will be more likely to believe it is real.

- Educate your users that mail can be forged. Teach them what to look for when they receive a message of questionable authenticity.

- Rarely, if ever, send mail as *root*. Always communicate as yourself and always use a distinctive style of writing. If users never see mail from *root*, they will be more likely to question such mail when it arrives.

- Train users to never send (or ask to receive) cleartext passwords or other security-related information by e-mail.

Trusted Users

We now turn our attention from security problems to a security feature: the T configuration command and the concept of the trusted user. This only applies to non-V8 versions of *sendmail*. If you are running V8 *sendmail*, you can safely skip this section.

Trusted users are those who are allowed to use the −f command-line switch to override the sender address with one of their own. Trusted users are necessary for certain kinds of mail to flow properly. By way of example, the *rmail*(8) program of the UUCP suite of programs runs SUID to *uucp*. If *rmail* were not to use the −f command-line switch, all mail from UUCP would wrongly appear to come from the *uucp* user. To circumvent this problem, *rmail* runs *sendmail* as:

```
/usr/lib/sendmail -f reallyfrom
```

This tells *sendmail* to show, in both the header and envelope, the message as being from *reallyfrom*, rather than from *uucp*.

The concept of a trusted user is intended to prevent ordinary users from changing the sender address and thereby forging mail. Although that intention is laudable and good for UUCP, it can cause problems with mailing lists. Consider:

```
list:   "|/usr/lib/sendmail -oi -flist-request -odi list-real"
list-real:    :include:/export/share/mail-lists/list.list
```

The intention here is for all mail sent to the mailing list named list to be dispatched as though it were sent from the address list-request (the -f). This causes errors to be returned to the maintainer of the list (the list-request), but replies still go to the real sender.

Unfortunately, this scheme fails when mail is posted to list from the local machine. Recall that only trusted users can change the identity of the sender with -f. For this reason, V8 *sendmail* eliminated the concept of the trusted user. Other versions of *sendmail* can work around this problem by forwarding all mailing-list mail to another machine, where that other machine uses -f to change the sender address.

Declare Trusted Users (Not V8)

Trusted users are defined by those lines in the *sendmail.cf* file that begin with the upper-case letter T. Only trusted users may use the *sendmail* program's -f command-line switch to specify who sent the message.

The T *sendmail.cf* command must begin a line. One or more space-delimited usernames then follow on that same line. There may be multiple T commands in a *sendmail.cf* file, each *adding* names to the list of trusted users. There may be at most MAXTRUST trusted users, where MAXTRUST is defined in *conf.h* when you compile *sendmail*.

```
T uucp
Troot daemon
```

These two T commands show that there may optionally be white space between the T and the first name in any list of names. They indicate that *uucp*, *root*, and *daemon* are trusted, and have been added to the list of trusted users in that order. If you list more than MAXTRUST trusted users, *sendmail* prints and *syslog*(3)'s a message like this:

```
sendmail: too many T lines, 32 max
```

This message is not fatal. The *sendmail* program issues it for each excess T line (ignoring those trusted users), and continues to run.

If a user who is not trusted attempts to use the -f switch with *sendmail,*
that attempt is silently ignored.

Pitfalls

- The *sendmail* program is only as secure as the system on which it is
  running. Correcting permissions and the like is only useful if such corrections are system-wide and apply to all critical system files and programs.

- Time spent tightening security at your site is best spent before a
  break-in occurs. Never believe that your site is too small or of too little
  consequence. Start out by being wary, and you will be more prepared
  when the inevitable attack happens.

- Get and set up *identd*(8) at your site. When queried about who established a network connection, it returns the login identity of the individual user. If more sites start to adopt user authentication, it will become
  useful to add that authentication to *sendmail* (it is already a compile-
  time option for IDA and V8 *sendmail*).

- Multimedia mail, such as *mime*(5), is more difficult, but not impossible,
  to forge.

- There is no check in the T command that the names listed are names of
  real users. That is, if you mistakenly enter Tuupc when you really
  meant Tuucp, *sendmail* remains silent and UUCP mail begins to mysteriously fail.

- There are many fine books and papers available that can help you
  improve the security at your site. A few are listed in the bibliography of
  this book.

19

The Queue

Mail messages may either be delivered immediately, or held for later delivery. Held messages are referred to as queued. They are placed into a holding directory, usually called *mqueue*, from which they are delivered at a later time. There are many reasons a mail message may be queued:

- If a mail message is temporarily undeliverable, it is queued and delivery is attempted later. If the message is addressed to multiple recipients, it is only queued for those recipients to whom delivery is not immediately possible.

- If the s configuration option is set to true, all mail messages are queued for safety while delivery is attempted. The message is removed from the queue only if delivery succeeds. If delivery fails, the message is left in the queue and another attempt is made to deliver it later. This causes the mail to be saved in the unhappy event of a system crash during processing.

- If *sendmail* is run in queue-only mode, with the −odq command-line switch, then all mail is queued and no immediate delivery attempt is made. A separate queue run is required to attempt delivery.

- If the load (average number of blocked processes) becomes higher than the value given to the x configuration option, *sendmail* queues messages rather than attempting to deliver them. A separate queue run is required later to process the queue.

Overview of the Queue

The *sendmail* queue is implemented by placing held messages into a directory. The queue directory has three uses:

- It is the place where messages are stored prior to delivery.

- It is the place where lock files are created. A lock file prevents two different runs of *sendmail* from processing the same queued message. (V8 *sendmail* uses file locking instead of lock files.)

- It is used as a place to create scratch files (empty temporary files) when creating a unique message identifier. (Obsoleted by V8 *sendmail.*)

The location of that directory and its name (usually *mqueue*) are specified in the configuration file by the Q option:

```
OQ/var/spool/mqueue
```

If the Q option is missing, the name defaults to mqueue. When the location is relative (as mqueue), it is relative to the location where *sendmail* is run. Since the *sendmail* daemon is typically started from an *rc* file at boot time, such relative locations are relative to the *root* (/) directory.

After *sendmail* has processed its configuration file, it does a *chdir*(2) into the queue directory and does all the rest of its work from there. This change into the queue directory has two side effects:

- Should the *sendmail* program fault and produce a core dump, the core image is left in the queue directory.

- Any relative pathnames given to options in the configuration file are interpreted as relative to the queue directory. (This is not true for the F commands. They are processed at the same time as the configuration file, before the *chdir*(2).)

The queue directory should be set to have very narrow permissions. It must be owned by *root*. We recommend a mode of 0711, and CERT recommends a mode of 0700. We recommend that the search bits for group and world be set because *sendmail* often gives up its *root* privilege, yet still needs to be able to find its queued files. Also, when a shell script is run from a user's *.forward* file, that script is run from inside the queue directory with a shell owned by the user. The shell needs to be able to locate .. in order to set up its current working directory.* If it cannot search the queue directory, the user's script will fail. V8 *sendmail* lets you specify alternate

---

* Only the C-shell has this problem.

directories in which to run programs (see Chapter 26, *Delivery Agents*, for a discussion of D=). This allows you to use mode 0700 queue directories, as CERT recommends, without the associated problems.

Parts of a Queued File

When a message is stored in the queue, it is split into pieces. Each of those pieces is stored as a separate file in the queue directory. That is, the header (and other information about the message) are stored in one file, while the body (the data) is stored in another. All told, six different types of files may appear in the queue directory. The type of each is denoted by the first two letters of the filenames. Each filename begins with a single letter followed by an f character. The complete list is shown in Table 19-1.

Table 19-1: Queue File Types

File	Description
df	Data (message body)
lf	Lock file
nf	ID creation file
tf	Temporary qf rewrite image
xf	Transcript file
qf	Queue control file (and header)

The complete form for each filename is:

```
Xfident
```

The X is one of the leading letters shown in Table 19-1. The f is the constant letter f. The *ident* is a unique queue identifier associated with each mail message.

To insure that new filenames are not the same as the names of files that may already be in the queue, *sendmail* uses the following pattern for each new *ident*:

```
AApid            ← all but V8 sendmail
hourAApid        ← V8 sendmail only
```

Here *pid* is the process identification number of the incarnation of *sendmail* that is trying to create the file. Because *sendmail* often *fork*(2)'s to process the queue, that *pid* is likely to be unique, resulting in a unique *ident*. For V8 *sendmail*, an extra letter prefixes the AA. Shown as *hour*, it is an uppercase letter that corresponds to the hour (in a 24-hour clock) that the identifier was created. For example, a file created in hour three of the day will have a D prefixed (the hour is base zero).*

If *sendmail* cannot create an exclusive filename (because a file with that identifier already exists) it clocks the second A of the AA to a B and tries again. It continues this process, clocking the righthand letter from A to Z, and the lefthand letter from A to ~ until it succeeds:

AA	← *start*
AB	← *second try*
AC	← *third try*
... *and so on*	
~W	
~X	
~Y	← *last try*
~Z	← *failure*

If it never succeeds, the `ident` ultimately looks like the following and *sendmail* has failed:

```
~Zpid
↑
```
possible hour prefix for V8 sendmail

This `ident` is unlikely to ever appear, because the clocking provides for over 1600 possibilities.

All the files associated with a given mail message share the same `ident` as a part of their filenames. The individual files associated with a single mail message only differ in the first letter of their names.

In the following sections, we describe each file type in alphabetical order. The internal details of the qf file can vary depending on the version of *sendmail*, so it is discussed separately in Appendix A, *The qf File Internals*.

The Data (Message Body) File: df

All mail messages are composed of a header and a body. When queued, the body is stored in the *df* file.

Traditionally the message body could only contain characters that have the high (most significant) bit turned off (cleared, set to 0). But under the V8 *sendmail*, with a version 2 or higher configuration file (see Chapter 23, *The Configuration File*) the high bit is left as-is. With V8 *sendmail*, the high bit

---

*Programs should not depend on the lead letter actually encoding the hour. It is only intended to ensure that all identifiers be unique within any 24-hour period, and as an aid to scripts that need to extract information from log files.

can be forced off by specifying the 7 option for all mail. Under IDA *send-mail*, the C= delivery agent flag can be used to allow full eight-bit data in the body of selected messages.

Because the message body can contain sensitive or personal information, the df file should be protected from reading by ordinary users. If the queue directory is world-readable, then the F (file-permission) option should specify minimum permissions (such as 0600) for queued files. But, if the queue directory is protected by both narrow permissions and a secure machine, the F option may be relaxed for easier administration.

There is currently no plan to provide for encryption of df files. If you are concerned about the privacy of your message, you should use an end-to-end encryption package (not discussed in this book).

The Lock File: lf

When old versions of *sendmail* process a queued message (attempt to redeliver it) they create an empty lock file. That lock file is necessary to signal to other running *sendmail* processes that the mail message is busy, so they won't try to deliver the message too. New versions simply *flock*(2) or *lockf*(2) the qf file.

The method used by *sendmail* to initially create an exclusive lock when first queueing a file is twofold. First it attempts to *creat*(2) the file with the argument:

```
O_CREAT|O_WRONLY|O_EXCL
```

If that succeeds, it then attempts to lock the file. If LOCKF is defined in *conf.h* when *sendmail* is compiled, *fcntl*(2) is used with an F_SETLK argument. Otherwise, *lockf*(2) or *flock*(2) is used.

When processing an existing queued file for delivery, *sendmail* hard links (with *link*(2)) the qf file to a new lf file to guarantee exclusivity.

When *mailq* is run (or the −bp command-line switch is given to *sendmail*), the contents of the queue are listed. In that listing, an asterisk appearing to the right of the identifier for a mail message indicates that a lock file exists for that message:

```
                        Mail Queue (1 request)
 --QID-- -Size- ----Q-Time----- ------------Sender/Recipient------------
 AA17445*   126 Fri Apr 17 10:17 <gw@wash.dc.gov>
                                 <ben@franklin.edu>
```

It is possible for *sendmail* to be killed in such a way that the lock file is orphaned (wrongly left in existence) even though the queued file is no longer being processed. The system should be set up to handle this situation at boot time with a line like the following in an appropriate *rc* file:

```
if [ -f /usr/lib/sendmail -a -f /etc/sendmail.cf ]; then
        (cd /var/spool/mqueue; rm -f nf* lf*)              ← note
        /usr/lib/sendmail -bd -q1h; echo -n ' sendmail'
    fi
```

The second line above runs a subshell that changes directory to the queue directory and removes all the `lf` and `nf` files it finds there. This is done before the *sendmail* daemon is started, thereby ensuring that any lock files removed are indeed those that were orphaned. The location of the queue directory (here */var/spool/mqueue*) must match the location specified by the Q option in the configuration file. Unfortunately, there is no command-line switch available with *sendmail* that will cause it to print that location for use in *rc* files.

Orphaned lock files may also be removed manually. If the modification time of a lock file is more than a day old (and *sendmail* is not currently processing the queue) that file (and any corresponding `nf` and `xf` files) may safely be removed. The process id part of the identifier portion of the filename is the process id of the *sendmail* program that placed the original mail message into the queue. But it is likely that the process id of the *sendmail* that created the lock file will be different. Unfortunately, *sendmail* does not store that latter process id in the lock file. Instead, a process listing (produced with *ps*(1)) needs to be examined for lines that list queue file identifiers:

```
root      5338 160   -AA01227 To wash.dc.gov (sendmail)
```

This shows that the queued mail message whose identifier is `AA01227` is currently being processed. Because there is a *sendmail* active on this message, the lock file is active, not orphaned.

One indication of an orphaned lock is a series of *syslog* messages about a given identifier:

```
Apr 12 00:33:38 ourhost sendmail[641]: AA00614: locked
Apr 12 01:22:14 ourhost sendmail[976]: AA00614: locked
Apr 12 02:49:23 ourhost sendmail[3251]: AA00976: locked
Apr 12 02:49:51 ourhost sendmail[5977]: AA00614: locked
Apr 12 03:53:05 ourhost sendmail[9839]: AA00614: locked
```

An occasional lock message, like AA00976 in the third line above, is normal. But when an identifier continually reports as locked (like the AA00614 lines), an orphaned lock may exist and should be investigated.

The ID Creation File: nf

Old versions of *sendmail* used an nf file when creating a message identifier to avoid race conditions. But contemporary versions of *sendmail* create the queue identifier when first creating the qf file. The nf file is obsolete.

The Queue Control File: qf

A queued mail message is composed of two primary parts. The df file contains the message body. The qf file contains the message header.

In addition to the header, the qf file also contains all the information necessary to:

- Deliver the message. It contains the sender's address, and a list of recipient addresses.
- Order message processing. It contains a priority that determines the current message's position in a queue run of many messages.
- Expire the message. It contains the date that the message was originally queued. That date is used to time out a message.
- Explain the message. It contains the reason that the message is in the queue, and possibly the error that caused it to be queued.

The qf file is line-oriented, with one item of information per line. Each line begins with a single uppercase character (the code letter), which specifies the contents of the line. Each code letter is then followed by the information appropriate to the letter. The code letters and their meanings are shown in Table 19-2.

Table 19-2: qf File Code Letters

Letter	Meaning
B	Body type (V8 only)
C	Controlling user
D	Data filename
E	Errors to
F	Flag bits (V8 only)
H	Header definition
M	Message (reason queued)

Table 19.2: qf File Code Letters (continued)

Letter	Meaning
P	Priority (current)
R	Recipient address
S	Sender address
T	Time created
$	Restore macro value (IDA and V8 only)

Here is an example of a qf file:

```
P640561
T703531020
DdfAA17445
MDeferred: Host wash.dc.gov is down
S<you@your.domain>
H?P?return-path: <you@your.domain>
Hreceived: by your.domain (6.1/1.12)
        id AA17445; Fri, 17 Apr 92 10:17:00 PDT
H?F?From: you@your.domain (Your Fullname)
H?x?full-name: Your Fullname
Hdate: Fri, 17 Apr 92 10:16:59 PDT
Hmessage-id: <9204171716.AA16912@your.domain>
HTo: george@wash.dc.gov, jefferson
Hsubject: Ben's at it again
R<george@wash.dc.gov>
R<jefferson>
```

This fictional qf file shows the information that will be used to send a mail message from you@your.domain (the S line) to two recipients: george@wash.dc.gov and jefferson (the R lines). It also shows the various headers that appears in that message (the H lines), and the name of the file that contains the message body (the D line). We discuss the individual lines of the qf file in Appendix A.

The Temporary qf Rewrite Image: tf

When processing a queued message, it is often necessary for *sendmail* to modify the contents of the qf file. This usually occurs if delivery has failed, or if delivery for only a part of the recipient list succeeded. In either event, at least the message priority needs to be incremented.

To prevent damage to the original qf file, *sendmail* makes changes to a temporary copy of that file. The temporary copy has the same queue identifier as the original, but its name begins with tf.

After the `tf` file has been successfully written and closed, *sendmail* calls *rename*(2) to replace the original with the copy. If the renaming fails, *sendmail syslog*(3)'s at LOG_CRIT a message like the following:

```
cannot rename(tfAA00000, qfAA00000), df=dfAA00000
```

Failure to rename is an unusual, but serious, problem when it occurs. It means that a queued message has been processed, but its `qf` file contains old and incorrect information. This failure may, for example, indicate a hardware error, a corrupted queue directory, or that the system administrator accidentally removed the queue directory.

The Transcript File: xf

A given mail message may be destined for many recipients, requiring different delivery agents. During the process of delivery, error messages (such as "User unknown" and "Permission denied") can be printed back to *sendmail* by each delivery agent.

While calling the necessary delivery agents, *sendmail* saves all the error messages it receives in a temporary file. The name of that temporary file begins with the letters `xf`. After all delivery agents have been called, *sendmail* returns any collected error messages to the sender and deletes the temporary `xf` file. If there are no errors, the empty `xf` file is silently deleted. The `-d51.4` debugging command-line switch can be used to prevent deletion of the `xf` file.

Printing the Queue

When *sendmail* is run under the name *mailq*, or when it is given the `-bp` command-line switch, it prints the contents of the queue and exits.

Before printing the queue's contents, *sendmail* prereads all the `qf` files in the queue and sorts the mail messages internally. This is done so that the queue's contents are displayed in the same order that the messages will be processed during a queue run.

If there are no messages in the queue (no `qf` files), *sendmail* prints the following message and exits:

```
Mail queue is empty
```

Otherwise, *sendmail* prints the number of messages (number of qf files) in the queue:

```
Mail Queue (# requests)
```

The # is the number of queued messages (requests) in the queue directory. If there are more than the maximum allowed number of messages that may be processed at one time (defined by QUEUESIZE in *conf.h*), *sendmail* instead prints:

```
Mail Queue (# requests, only ## printed)
```

The ## is the value of QUEUESIZE.

Next *sendmail* prints an attractive heading that looks like the following:

```
--QID-- --Size-- -----Q-Time----- ------------Sender/Recipient---------
```

This heading shows the information that is printed about each message in the queue. The items and their meanings are:

QID   The queue identifier for the message—the clocked AA part and the *pid* numeric part (like AA12345). If this item is followed by an asterisk (*), it means the message is locked (an lf file was found or the qf file is locked depending on the kind of locking your version of *sendmail* uses). If this item is followed by an X, then the load average is currently too high to allow delivery of that message.

Size   The size in bytes of the df file. If there is no df file (because *sendmail* is currently receiving this message and hasn't created one yet), this item is absent.

Q-Time   The date and time that the message was first placed into the queue. This is the T line in the qf file converted from an unsigned integer into a more understandable date and time.

Sender   The sender of the message as taken from the S line in the qf file. Only the first 45 characters of the sender address are printed. If there is an M line in the qf file, *sendmail* prints the text of the message on the next line following the sender.

Recipient   After all of the above items have been printed, a list of the recipients (from each R line in the qf file) is printed in the order they are found. If any R line is preceded by a controlling user (C line in the qf file) that controlling user's name is put in parentheses and prepended to the recipient name.

If there are no lines in the qf file, *sendmail* prints the following in place of the Size and continues with the next queued message:

```
(no control file)
```

Printing the Queue in Verbose Mode

The -v command-line switch may be used in combination with the -bp switch to cause *sendmail* to also print the priority of each queued message in the list of queued messages. The usual heading also shows this new item:

```
--QID-- --Size-- -Priority- ---Q-Time--- -----------Sender/Recipient---
```

The Priority is the value from the P line in the qf file. Printing the queue does not change a message's priority, whereas processing the queue does. Also, V8 *sendmail* prints a + after the Q-Time if a warning message has been sent (see Chapter 30, *Options*, for a description of the T (timeout) option).

How the Queue is Processed

Over time, messages may gather in the queue awaiting delivery. They remain there until *sendmail* performs a queue run to process the queue. The *sendmail* program can be told either to process the queue periodically (when run as a daemon) or to process the queue once, then exit. Each time *sendmail* processes the queue, it also performs a series of operations intended to improve the efficiency with which it delivers messages.

First the *queue* directory is opened for reading. If that directory cannot be opened, *sendmail* *syslog*(3)'s the following message at LOG_CRIT and exits:

```
orderq: cannot open "/var/spool/mailq" as "."
```

This error is usually the result of a user running *sendmail* in an unsafe manner, with a -C command-line argument, for example. It can also result from *sendmail* attempting to open an NFS-mounted queue directory, where *root* is mapped to *nobody*.

Next, the qf files are read to gather their priorities and times (the P and T lines). If a qf file cannot be opened, it is quietly ignored unless the −d41.2 debugging command-line switch is specified. That switch causes *sendmail* to print the following error message:

```
orderq: cannot open qfAA12345 (#)
```

Here the # is the error number as specified in */usr/include/errno.h.*

After all the qf files have been gathered, they are sorted in inverse order of priority. Messages with the lowest value of the P line have the highest priority and are processed first.

IDA *sendmail* also sorts the sender and recipient addresses. The idea here is that messages with identical senders and recipients should be processed as a group.

Once all the messages have been sorted, *sendmail* processes each in turn.

Processing a Single Message

A single queued message has a single sender, but may have many recipients. When processing a queued message, *sendmail* attempts to deliver it to all recipients before processing the next queued message.

The first step in processing a queued message is to lock it so that concurrent runs of *sendmail* do not attempt to process it simultaneously. The message is locked by creating an lf file (later versions of *sendmail*, including V8 and IDA, lock the qf file instead of creating an lf file).

After the lf file is created, the qf file is opened and read. The sender and all the recipients are gathered from the corresponding S and R lines.

Then, for each recipient, delivery is attempted. If delivery is successful, that recipient's address is removed from the *sendmail* program's internal list of recipient addresses. If delivery fails, that address either is left in the list or bounced, depending on the nature of the error. If it is bounced, it is either returned to the sender, or, if there are qf file E-line error recipients, sent to those error recipients.

After all recipients have either been delivered, bounced, or left in the list, *sendmail* re-examines that list. If there are no recipients left in it, the message is de-queued (all of the files in the queue directory that compose it are removed). If there are any recipients left, the M line is assigned the error message of the last failed message, and the qf file is rewritten with the list of remaining recipients. Finally, the lf lock file is removed.

Under the V8 *sendmail*, the C option causes checkpointing of this process.* When the C option has a positive value, the qf file is rewritten after that value's number of recipients have been processed. For example, consider a mail message to five recipients. If the C option is set to a value of 2, the qf file is rewritten after the first two recipients have been processed, then again after four, and again after they all have been processed. This keeps the qf file reasonably up-to-date, as protection against *sendmail* being improperly killed or the machine crashing.

Cause the Queue to be Processed

The *sendmail* program offers two different methods for processing the queue. It can be told to process the queue periodically, or to process it once and then exit.

Periodically With –q

The –q command-line switch is used both to cause the queue to be processed and to specify the interval between queue runs.

A typical invocation of the *sendmail* daemon looks like this:

```
/usr/lib/sendmail -bd -q1h
```

Here the *sendmail* program is placed into listening mode with the –bd command-line switch. The –q1h command-line switch tells it to process the queue once each hour. Note that either switch puts *sendmail* into the background as a daemon. The –bd switch just allows *sendmail* to listen for incoming SMTP connections. Consider:

```
/usr/lib/sendmail -bd
/usr/lib/sendmail -q1h
```

This runs two daemons simultaneously. The first listens for incoming SMTP connections. The second processes the queue once per hour.

At small sites, where mail messages are rarely queued, the time interval chosen may be small, to ensure that all mail is delivered promptly. An interval of 15m (15 minutes) may be appropriate.

At many sites, an interval of one hour is probably best. It is short enough to ensure that delays in delivery remain tolerable, yet long enough to ensure that queue processings do not overlap.

---

*Checkpointing will also be in the next major release of IDA *sendmail.*

At large sites with huge amounts of mail, and at sites that send a great deal of international mail, the interval has to be carefully tuned by observing how long it takes *sendmail* to process the queue and what causes that process to take a long time. Points to consider are:

- For all but V8 *sendmail*, the SMTP greeting wait is hardcoded at five minutes. For V8, the greeting wait is set with the r option. Once the SMTP connection has been made, the timeout (for all versions) is set by the r configuration option. That timeout* should be large (like one hour) to ensure that mail to busy sites and to large mailing lists does not time out improperly. In observing the queue processing, you may find that all messages but one process swiftly. That one, you may find, takes over an hour because of a long SMTP timeout. A possible solution to this problem is to make the timeout short, so that most queue runs are processed quickly. Then, for example, the following command could be run a few times each night to specifically flush those long jobs:

  ```
  /usr/lib/sendmail -or2h -q
  ```

- The queue can take a long time to process because too many messages are being queued unnecessarily. Several options affect the placement of mail messages into the queue. The x configuration option tells *sendmail* to queue, rather than deliver, a message if the machine load is too high. Fewer messages will be queued if the value of that option is increased. The s (safety) option tells *sendmail* to queue all messages for safety. If your machine "never" crashes, this may not be necessary. The c option tells *sendmail* to queue messages to "expensive" delivery agents (those with the e flag set in the F= equate) rather then delivering them. If the queue is routinely filled with messages to expensive sites, you should reconsider your reasons for marking those sites as expensive.

- The queue can fill with messages because *sendmail* was run with the -odq command-line switch. At sites that receive a great deal of UUCP mail for forwarding, the *rmail*(8) program is often set up to run *sendmail* in "queue only" mode with the -odq command-line switch. If UUCP mail is clogging your normal mail services, you should consider queueing it to a separate queue directory. You can then process that other directory with a separate queue run of *sendmail*. (Use of separate queue directories is discussed later in this chapter.)

- A slow machine can clog the queue. When a single machine is set up to handle the bulk of a site's mail, that machine should be as swift as

---

*Note that for V8 *sendmail*, the r option may optionally list many individual timeouts.

possible. In general, a dedicated mail server should have a fast CPU with lots of memory. It should never allow users to log into it, and it should run its own name server daemon.

From the Command Line

The -q command-line switch, invoked without a time interval argument, is used to run *sendmail* in queue processing mode. In this mode, *sendmail* processes the queue once and then exits. This mode can be run interactively from the command-line, or in the background via *cron*(8).

Other command-line switches can be combined with -q to refine the way the queue is processed. The -v and -d switches cause *sendmail* to process the queue in the foreground so that you may interrupt it if necessary. The -v (verbose) switch causes *sendmail* to print information about each message it is processing. The -d (debugging) switch may be used to produce additional information about the queue. We'll discuss the -v switch as it applies to the queue later in this chapter. The -d switch is described in Chapter 33.

IDA and SunOS *sendmail* offer three additional command-line switches for processing the queue. The -M switch allows you to specify a specific message for processing. The -R switch allows you to specify specific recipient addresses for processing. The -S switch allows you to specify specific sender addresses for processing. V8 *sendmail* allows -qI, -qR, and -qS switches to achieve similar effects.

Process the queue once: -q

The -q command-line switch, without an interval argument, tells *sendmail* to process the queue once, then exit. As such, this switch is a handy administrative tool. When the queue fills unexpectedly between queue runs of the daemon, for example, the -q command-line switch can be used to force an immediate queue run:

```
# /usr/lib/sendmail -q
```

On machines that do not run the *sendmail* daemon, the -q command-line switch can be used in conjunction with *cron*(8) to periodically process the queue. The following *crontab*(5) file entry, for example, causes *sendmail* to be run once per hour, at five minutes past the hour, to silently process the queue and exit:

```
5 * * * * /usr/lib/sendmail -q >/dev/null 2>&1
```

When used in conjunction with other switches (shown below), the -q switch allows many queue problems to be conveniently handled.

Combine –v with –q

The -q switch without an argument prevents *sendmail* from running in the background and detaching from its controlling terminal. But it also runs silently. To see what is going on, use the -v command-line switch in combination with the -q:

```
% /usr/lib/sendmail -v -q
```

The -v command-line switch causes *sendmail* to print a step-by-step description of what it is doing. To illustrate, consider the following output produced by using both the -v and -q command-line switches:

```
Running AA20989
<adams@dc.gov>... Connecting to dc.gov via ddn...
Trying 123.45.67.8... Connection timed out during user open with DC.GOV
<adams@dc.gov>... Deferred: Host DC.GOV is down

Running AA27002
<help@irs.dc.gov>... Connecting to irs.dc.gov via ddn...
Trying 123.45.67.88... connected.
220 irs.dc.gov Sendmail 5.57/3.0 ready at Mon, 27 Jan 92 09:16:38 -0400
```

Here two queued messages are being processed. The first fails because of a connection timeout and is requeued for a later queue run. The second succeeds (we omit the full SMTP dialogue). After its delivery is complete, it is removed from the queue.

Process by message-ID (IDA and SunOS only): –M

The IDA and SunOS versions of *sendmail* provide the ability to process individual messages in the queue. The -M command-line switch is used in place of the -q switch to specify a particular message and to tell *sendmail* to process it.

The form of the -M command-line switch is:

```
-Mident
```

The *ident* is the identifier for the message. The AA part is optional:

```
-MAA12345        ← AA part included
-M12345          ← pid part only
```

If the AA part is included, it must start with the character A. If the *ident* has clocked to a different starting letter, you may only specify the *pid* part.

This switch is handy for investigating problems in the queue. It allows you to process queued messages individually, in both verbose mode and with full debugging output.

Process by recipient/sender (IDA and SunOS only): −R and −S

Both IDA and SunOS *sendmail* allow you to select queued messages for processing based on the address of the recipient. But only the IDA version of sendmail allows you to select queued messages for processing based on the address of the sender. The recipient is selected with the −R command-line switch, while the sender is selected with the −S switch. These switches are very useful when you need to process the queue for selected sites or users.

The form of the −R and −S command-line switches is:

```
-Raddr
-Saddr
```

For both, the *addr* is an address or part of an address. The *addr* may immediately follow the switch, or there may be space between the two.

When *sendmail* prescans the queue, it looks for a match to the addr specified. For the −R switch, it tries to match the R lines in the qf file. For the −S switch, it tries to match the S lines in the qf file. If any lines match the *addr*, that message is selected to be processed.

The match with the *addr* is a substring match. That is, if the *addr* appears anywhere in an address, a match is made. For example, *george* matches both *george@wash.dc.gov* and *alice@georgetown*.

Process by queueid/recipient/sender (V8 only): −q[ISR]

V8 *sendmail* combines the −M, −R, and −S switches described above into a compact variation of the basic −q switch. The form is one of the following:

```
-qIqueueid
-qRrecipient
-qSsender
```

The -qI variation is followed by a queue identifier like *KAA34556*. The -qR and -qS variations are respectively followed by the address of a recipient or sender. These variations are used to limit the selection of queued files that are processed. For example:

```
% /usr/lib/sendmail -qSroot -qRbiff@here
```

Here, the queue is processed once. Only messages from *root* are processed. Of those, only messages that have *biff@here* as one of the recipients are processed.

In all three variations, a partial specification of `queueid`, `recipient` or `sender` is viewed by V8 *sendmail* as a substring. That is, by way of example:

```
-qSroot
```

matches mail from all of the following:

```
root
ben@groots.edu
ben@GROOTS.EDU
```

The last line further illustrates that the substring match is a case-insensitive one. The substring match is literal. Wildcard characters (like `*`) and regular expressions (like `.*@.*edu`) won't work and may confuse the shell from which you run *sendmail*.

Multiple specifications may be combined on the command line (as shown above), but they all AND together.

```
% /usr/lib/sendmail -qI123 -qSroot -qR@host.edu
```

Here, the queue is only processed for messages with the number 123 anywhere in the message identifier, that are also from *root*, and that are also addressed to anyone at *host.edu*.

Process Alternate Queues

The *sendmail* program provides the ability to use queue directories other than the one listed in the configuration file's Q option. Other queue directories can be used to solve an assortment of problems. One example is that of a site being down for an extended period. When a great deal of mail is sent to such a site, messages collect in the queue and eventually start timing out. By moving those messages to a separate queue directory and processing it at a later time (when that site is back up), unnecessarily bounced mail can be prevented.

The look of the −oQ command-line switch is:

```
-oQdir
```

The −o that begins this switch tells *sendmail* that you are changing the value of an option. The Q says that the option whose value is being changed is the Q configuration file option (the location of the queue directory). The *dir* is the full pathname of the new queue directory. For more details see Chapter 32, *The Command Line.*

The Q option is not safe. If its value is changed by anyone other than *root*, *sendmail* runs as an ordinary user.

Handling a Down Site

If a site is down, messages to that site can collect in the queue. If the site is expected to be down for a protracted period of time, those queued messages will begin to timeout and bounce. To prevent them from bouncing, you can move them to a separate queue directory. Later, when the down site comes back up you can process that separate queue.

To move the affected messages to a separate queue, you may use a Bourne shell script like the following:

```
#!/bin/sh
set -u
QUEUE=/var/spool/mqueue
NEWQ=/var/spool/newqueue

if [ ! -d $QUEUE ]
then
        echo "${QUEUE}: Does not exist or is not a directory"
        exit 1
fi
if [ ! -d $NEWQ ]
then
        mkdir -p $NEWQ
        if [ $? -ne 0 ]
        then
                echo "${NEWQ}: Can't create"
                exit 2
        fi
fi
find ${QUEUE} -type f -name qf* -print |\
while read QF
do
        IDENT=`echo $QF | sed -e "s,^${QUEUE}/qf,,"`
        grep "^R" ${QUEUE}/qf${IDENT}
        echo -n "move ${IDENT}? (y/n) "
        read answer
```

```
        case $answer in
                [nN]*)  continue;;
                *)      ;;
        esac
        # Won't exist for V8
        if [ -f lf${IDENT} ]
        then
                echo "qf${IDENT}: Is currently locked."
        else
                mv ${QUEUE}/*${IDENT} $NEWQ
                if [ $? -ne 0 ]
                then
                        echo "Move failed"
                        exit 3
                else
                        echo "Move succeeded"
                fi
        fi
done
/usr/lib/sendmail -oQ${NEWQ} -bp
```

This script creates a new queue directory, $NEWQ, if it doesn't exist. It then prints the recipient list for each qf file in the queue (the *grep*(1) in $QUEUE) and asks if you want to move that file. If you answer yes, all the files that compose the queued message are moved into $NEWQ. If a lock file (lf) is found, the message is not moved.

After all the messages have been moved, the contents of $NEWQ are printed using the -oQ command-line switch:

```
% /usr/lib/sendmail -oQ${NEWQ} -bp
```

When the down site comes back up at a later time, the messages that have been saved in $NEWQ can be delivered by running the following command by hand.

```
% /usr/lib/sendmail -oQ/var/spool/newqueue -oT99d -v -q
```

The -oT99d causes the T option (time to live in the queue) to be extended to 99 days. This prevents the held mail in ${NEWQ} from wrongly bouncing when you try to deliver it.

Pitfalls

- The queue directory should never be shared among machines. Such sharing can make detection of orphaned locks impossible. Clearing of lock files at boot time can cause one machine to wrongly remove the lock files of another. Bugs in network locking daemons can lead to race conditions where neither of two machines can generate a queue identifier.

- It is possible for an lf file to be left in place even though its corresponding mail message is not being processed by *sendmail*. Such spurious files prevent the message from ever being delivered unless removed by hand. Spurious lock files can be detected by watching the *syslog*(5) file for frequent locked warnings.

- Homespun programs and shell scripts for delivery of local mail can fail and lose mail by exiting with the wrong value. In the case of a recoverable error (a full disk for example), they should exit with EX_OSERR or EX_TEMPFAIL. Both these exit values are defined in *<sysexits.h>* and cause the message to be requeued.

- Because *sendmail* does a *chdir*(2) into its queue directory, you should avoid removing and recreating that directory while the *sendmail* daemon is running. When processing the queue, *sendmail* tries to read the queue directory by doing an *opendir*(3) of the current directory. When the queue directory is removed, *sendmail* fails that open and *syslog*(3)'s the following warning:

```
NOQUEUE: SYSERR: orderq: cannot open "/usr/spool/mqueue" as ".": No
such file or directory
```

- Under a few old versions of *sendmail,* a bug in handling the queue could cause a message to be lost when that message was the last in a queue run to be processed. This, among other reasons, is good cause to always make sure you are running the latest version of *sendmail.*

- The *sendmail* program assumes it is the only one that will place files into the queue directory. Consequently it trusts everything it finds there. The queue directory *must* be protected from other users and programs (see Chapter 18, *Security*).

- If the queue directory is on a disk mounted separately from / and /usr, be certain to mount that disk *before* starting the *sendmail* daemon. If you reverse these steps, the *sendmail* daemon will *chdir*(2) into the queue before the mount. One effect is that incoming mail will use a different directory than outgoing mail. Another effect is that incoming queued mail will be invisible. Yet another effect is that the outgoing queue will never be processed by the daemon.

20

Aliases

Aliasing is the replacing of one recipient address with one or more different recipient addresses. The replacement recipients can be a single user, a list of recipients, a program, a file, or any mixture of these. In this chapter we cover one of the three methods of aliasing available with the *sendmail* program, the *aliases*(5) file. We cover the other two forms, :include: (for including separate files from within the *aliases* file) and ~/.forward (the user's personal :include: file) in the next chapter.

Aliasing can be used to handle several complex delivery problems:

- Delivering mail to a single user under a variety of usernames
- Distributing a mail message to many users by specifying only a single recipient name
- Appending mail to files for archival and other purposes
- Filtering mail through programs and shell scripts

All the information needed to perform these tasks is contained in the *aliases*(5) file (which is often also stored in database format to make lookups faster).

The location of the *aliases*(5) file is specified with the A option in the configuration file. If that option is omitted, *sendmail* silently presumes that it should not do aliasing.

The *aliases*(5) file is composed of lines of text. Any line that begins with a # is a comment and ignored. Empty lines (those that contain only a newline character) are also ignored. Any line that begins with a space or a tab is joined (appended) to the line above it. All other lines of text are viewed as alias lines. The format for an alias line is:

```
local: alias
```

The `local` must begin a line. It is an address in the form of a local recipient address. The colon follows the `local` on the same line, and may be preceded with spaces or tabs. If the colon is missing, *sendmail* prints and *syslog*(3)'s the following error message and skips that alias line:

```
missing colon
```

The `alias` (to the right of the colon) is one or more addresses on the same line. Indented continuation lines are permitted. Each address should be separated from the next by a comma and optional space characters. A typical alias looks like this:

```
root: jim, sysadmin@server,
     gunther
   ↑
   indenting white space
```

Here `root` is the local address to be aliased. When mail is to be locally delivered to `root`, it is looked up in the *aliases*(5) file. If found, `root` is replaced with the three addresses shown above, and mail is instead delivered to those other three addresses.

This process of looking up and possibly aliasing local recipients is repeated for each recipient until no more aliases are found in the *aliases*(5) file. That is, for example, if one of the aliases for `root` is `jim`, and if `jim` also exists to the left of a colon in the *aliases* file, he too is replaced with his alias:

```
jim: jim@otherhost
```

The list of addresses to the right of the colon may be mail addresses (like *gunther* or *jim@otherhost*), the name of a program to run (like */etc/relocated*), the name of a file onto which to append (like */usr/share/archive*), or the name of a file to read for additional addresses (using `:include:`). The `:include:` is used in creating mailing lists and will be covered in the next chapter.

Local Must Be Local

The `local` part of an alias must be in the form of a local recipient. This restriction is enforced each time *sendmail* reads the *aliases*(5) file. For every name to the left of a colon that it finds, *sendmail* performs the following normalization and verification steps.

To begin, *sendmail* normalizes each address by removing everything but the address part. For example, consider the following two alias lines:

```
george (George Washington): gw
George Washington <george>: gw
```

When *sendmail* reads these lines, it normalizes each into its address part:

```
george (George Washington)    becomes →   george
George Washington <george>    becomes →   george
```

After the address part is extracted, it is converted to lowercase, and rewritten by rule sets 3 and 0 to see if it causes the `local` delivery agent to be selected.* Here the address `george` (after processing) selects the `local` delivery agent, and thus these alias lines are legal.

Internally (or in its database) *sendmail* stores the above alias as:

```
george: gw
```

When mail arrives that is addressed for delivery to `george`, *sendmail* rewrites that address with rule sets 3 and 0. Rule set 0 selects the `local` delivery agent. Only if the `local` delivery agent is selected for an address does *sendmail* look up an address in its *aliases* file. The address `george` is looked up and replaced with `gw`. Internally, *sendmail* marks the recipient `george` as defunct, having been replaced with an alias, and adds `gw` to the list of recipients.

The new recipient, `gw`, is then processed for delivery. Rule sets 3 and 0 are called once more and again select the `local` delivery agent. As a consequence, `gw` is also looked up. If it is found to the left of a colon in the *aliases* file, it too is replaced with yet another address (or addresses). This process repeats until no new local addresses are found.

---

*Future releases of V8 *sendmail* may base this decision on a delivery agent flag.

The entry george is marked defunct rather than being deleted in order to detect alias loops. To illustrate, consider the following two mutually referencing aliases:

```
george: gw
gw: george
```

The *sendmail* program first replaces george with gw, marking george as defunct. It then replaces gw with george (which already exists and is ignored), and marks gw as defunct. Aliasing ends because george is defunct and will neither be delivered to, nor processed by, rule sets 3 and 0 again. The result of these self-referencing aliases is that neither george nor gw receives any mail. When aliases cancel out like this, no error message is printed.* But, when *sendmail* receives an EXPN request for a self-referencing loop like the above on an SMTP connection, it prints:

```
Self destructive alias loop
```

Delivery to Users

Any address in the list of addresses to the right of the colon that does not begin with a / character or a | character is considered the address of a user. The address can be local or remote.

If a user address is prefixed† with a backslash character (\), and the address is a local one, all further aliasing is suppressed (including reading the user's ˜/.forward file). The message is delivered with the local delivery agent.

Delivery to Files

In the list of addresses to the right of the colon, *sendmail* considers any local address that begins with the / character to be the name of a file.‡ Whenever the recipient address is a file, *sendmail* attempts to deliver the mail message by appending it to the file. This ability to deliver mail to files is included primarily in *sendmail* so failed mail may be saved to a user's

---

*V8 *sendmail* detects alias looping under most circumstances and tries to correct it. (This is most likely to succeed with a single recipient). If it is unable to correct (likely with multiple recipients), it prints "self destructive alias loop."

†Actually, a backslash anywhere in the name causes the same immediate delivery.

‡Note that an *@host* prevents this interpretation. That is, */a* is a file, but */a@host* is not. This distinction is necessary for X.400 addresses to be handled correctly.

˜/*dead.letter* file. It can also be used (through use of aliases) to deliver mail to other files, but that use is less than optimum, as you will see.

To deliver to a file, *sendmail* first performs a *fork*(2) and gives the child the task of delivery. The *fork* is necessary so that *sendmail* can change its effective *uid* and *gid*, as we will show. The child then performs a *stat*(3) on the file. If the file exists, its file permissions are saved for later use. If it doesn't exist, the saved permissions are defaulted to 0666.

If the saved permissions have any execute bit set, the child exits with EX_CANTCREAT as defined in <*sysexits.h*>. If the file has a controlling user* associated with it, any *suid* and *sgid* bits are stripped from the saved permissions.

Then the queue df file is opened for reading (if it is not already open). If that file cannot be opened, *sendmail* prints the following error message, but continues to attempt delivery.

```
mailfile: Cannot open df for file from sender
```

Here, the df is the name of the queue data file that cannot be opened. The file is the name of the file to which *sendmail* is attempting to deliver the message. The sender is the address of the sender of the mail message.

After the df file is opened (or not), *sendmail* changes its *gid*:

- If the *sgid* bit is set in the file's saved permissions, *sendmail* changes its *gid* to that of the group of the file.
- If the *sgid* bit is not set (or if *sendmail* cannot change its *gid* to that of the group of the file), *sendmail* checks to see if there is a controlling user.
- If there is a controlling user, *sendmail* changes its *gid* to that of the controlling user.†
- If there is no controlling user, *sendmail* changes its *gid* to that specified by the g (group) option.

After this, *sendmail* changes its *uid*, using the same rules it used for the *gid*. Next, the *file* is opened for writing in append mode. If *sendmail* can-

---

*If the file was listed in a ˜/*forward* file, the controlling user is the owner of the ˜/*forward* file. If it was listed in a :include:'d file, the controlling user is the owner of the included file. If it was listed in a qf file's R line, the controlling user is taken from the preceding C line.
†V8 *sendmail* does this first to avoid security problems.

not open the file, it prints the following error message, and the child exits with EX_CANTCREAT:

```
cannot open
```

If an open fails, it is attempted 10 more times (sleeping progressively longer* between each try) on the assumption that on busy systems there may be a temporary lack of resources (such as file descriptors). The open is a simple *fopen*(3). There is no file locking to prevent simultaneous writes.†

Once the file is opened, the header and body of the mail message are written to it. Note that translations are controlled by the F= flags of the `prog` delivery agent for all but V8 *sendmail*. V8 *sendmail* uses the F= flags of the `*file*` delivery agent. For example, F=l marks this as final delivery.

If any write error occurs, *sendmail* prints the following error message and continues:

```
I/O error
```

Finally, the file is closed with *fclose*(3) and its permissions changed to those that were saved above. If the *suid* or *sgid* bits were stripped because there was a controlling user, they are restored here.‡ If the file didn't originally exist, its permissions become 0666.

In general, the file form of an alias is a poor way to save mail messages to a file. For one thing, since there is no file locking, it is easy for the file to become corrupted. Instead, the use of a separate program like *deliver*(8) or *procmail*(8) is recommended (see Chapter 21, *Mailing Lists and ~/.forward*).

Delivery via Programs

When any of the addresses to the right of a colon in the alias list begins with a | character, delivery is made via the `prog` delivery agent. If the address is quoted with full quotation marks, the leading quotation mark is ignored when determining the `prog` delivery agent.

---

*The progression is 0 seconds for the first sleep, then 10 seconds, then 20 seconds, and so on.

†V8 *sendmail* uses *flock*(2) or *fcntl*(2) locking to prevent simultaneous writes.

‡This is because some paranoid systems, like BSD UNIX, turn off the *suid/sgid* bits when a file is written to other than by *root*.

The forms a program address can legally take are:

```
|prg
"|prg args"
|"prg args"
```

Here, `prg` is the full path of the program to be run (the environment variable PATH is not available). If command-line arguments are needed for the program, they must follow `prg`, and the entire expression must be quoted. The leading full quotation mark may either precede or follow the |.

In order to execute the program, *sendmail* executes the command in the A= equate of the `prog` delivery agent. That command is usually:

```
/bin/sh -c
```

This tells *sendmail* to run the Bourne shell in order to execute the program specified by `prg`. The `-c` tells that shell to take any arguments which follow and execute them as though they were commands typed interactively to the shell. These arguments are constructed by removing the leading | from the program address and appending what remains, quotation marks and all, to the P= command. For example, if an alias looked like this:

```
jim: "|/etc/local/relo jim@otherhost"
```

the Bourne shell would be executed with the following command line:

```
/bin/sh -c "/etc/local/relo jim@otherhost"
```

The result of all this is that *sendmail* runs the Bourne shell, and then the Bourne shell runs the */etc/local/relo* program.

Mail is delivered under this scheme by attaching the output of *sendmail* to the standard input of the shell, and the standard output and standard error output of the shell to the input of *sendmail.* The *sendmail* program simply prints the mail message to the shell and reads any errors that the shell prints in return.

Although this process appears to be fairly straightforward, there are many things that can go wrong. Failure usually results in the mail message being bounced.

Possible failures

In order to communicate with the P= program (the Bourne shell) *sendmail* creates two communications channels using *pipe*(2). This can fail because the system is out of file descriptors, or because the system file table is full, and results in one of the following errors:

```
openmailer: pipe (to mailer)
openmailer: pipe (from mailer)
```

Next, *sendmail* executes a *fork*(2). The child later becomes the P= program. This can fail because the system limit on the maximum allowable number of processes has been exceeded, or because virtual memory has been exhausted. Failure causes the following error message to be printed:

```
openmailer: cannot fork
```

In establishing a communications channel, the *sendmail* child process creates a copy of its standard input file descriptor. This can fail because the system limit on available file descriptors has been exceeded. When this happens, the following message is printed. But be aware that not all *dup*(2) failures produce error messages.

```
Cannot dup to zero!
```

The child may change its *uid* and *gid*. If the F=S delivery agent flag is absent (as it should be for the prog delivery agent), the child changes its effective *uid* and *gid*. If a controlling user is present (the sender is local), they are changed to that of the controlling user (as long as that controlling user is not root). Otherwise they are changed to the *uid* and *gid* specified by the corresponding u and g options (usually *daemon* or *nobody*).

Finally, the child transforms itself into the A= program with *execve*(2). If that transformation fails, the following error message is produced, where *program* is argv[0] for the A= program (in this case, usually */bin/sh*):

```
Cannot exec program
```

Failure can be caused by a wide range of problems. If one occurs and the delivery agent is local, the message is queued for a later try. Otherwise, requeueing occurs only if the error return value is one of EIO, EAGAIN, ENOMEM, or EPROCLIM* as defined in *<errno.h>*.

Programs in the *aliases* file are run with the prog delivery agent. As a consequence, that delivery agent should have the F=s (strip quotes) flag set.

---

*Due to a bug in all but the IDA and V8 versions, this requeueing is silently ignored.

Program Behavior

The program driven by the `prog` delivery agent may be a compiled executable binary, a shell script, or even a *perl*(1) script. The limitation on the kind of program that may be run is made by the *sh*(1) shell (if `sh -c` is used in the A=), or by *execve*(2) (if it is launched directly from the A=). You need to read the manuals on your system to determine your limitations. For example, not all versions of *sh*(1) allow constructs like the following in scripts:

```
#!/usr/local/bin/perl
```

When this appears as the first line of a script, the `#!` tells *sh*(1) or *execve*(2) to run the program whose pathname follows, in order to execute the commands in the script.*

When writing a program for mail delivery using the `prog` delivery agent, some unexpected problems can arise. We will illustrate using fragments from a Bourne shell script.

Duplicates discarded

When *sendmail* gathers its list of recipients, it views a program to run as just another recipient. Before performing any delivery, it sorts the list of recipients and discards any duplicates. Ordinarily this is just the behavior desired, but discarding duplicate programs can cause some users to lose mail. To illustrate, consider a program that notifies the system administrator that mail has arrived for a retired user:

```
#!/bin/sh
/usr/ucb/mail -s gone postmaster
```

This script reads everything (the mail message) from its standard input and feeds what it reads to the */usr/ucb/mail* program. The command-line arguments to *mail* are a subject line of `gone` and a recipient of `postmaster`. Now consider two aliases that use this program:

```
george: "|/usr/local/bin/gone"
ben:    "|/usr/local/bin/gone"
```

When mail is sent to both `george` and `ben`, *sendmail* aliases each to the program `|/usr/local/bin/gone`. But since both addresses are identical, *sendmail* discards one.

---

*Not all versions of UNIX support this feature. And on some of those that do support it, only a few shells are supported.

To avoid this problem (which is most common in user `~/.forward` files), design all delivery programs to require at least one unique argument. For example, the above program should be rewritten to require the user's name as an argument:

```
#!/bin/sh
if [ ${#} -ne 2 ]; then
        echo $0 needs a user name.
        exit
fi
/usr/ucb/mail -s "$1 gone" postmaster
```

By requiring a username as an argument, the once-faulty aliases are made unique:

```
george: "|/usr/local/bin/gone george"
ben:    "|/usr/local/bin/gone ben"
```

Although the program paths are still the same, the addresses (name and arguments together) are different, and neither is discarded.*

Correct exit(2) values

The *sendmail* program expects its A= programs to exit with reasonable *exit*(2) values. The values it expects are listed in *<sysexits.h>*. Exiting with unexpected values causes *sendmail* to bounce mail and give an unclear message:

```
554 Unknown status val
```

Here, *val* is the unexpected error value. To illustrate, consider the following rewrite of the previous script:

```
#!/bin/sh
if [ ${#} -ne 2 ]; then
        echo $0 needs a user name.
        exit 64 # EX_USAGE from <sysexits.h>
fi
/usr/ucb/mail -s "$1 gone" postmaster
exit 0  # EX_OK from <sysexits.h>
```

---

*V8 *sendmail* avoids this problem by considering local addresses with different controlling users to be different.

Here, if the argument count is wrong, we exit with the value EX_USAGE thus producing a clearer (two line) error message:

```
/usr/local/bin/gone needs a user name.
/usr/local/bin/gone... Bad usage.
```

If all goes well, we then exit with EX_OK so that *sendmail* knows that the mail was successfully delivered.

Is it really EX_OK?

When *sendmail* sees that the A= program exited with EX_OK, it assumes that the mail message was successfully delivered. It is vital for programs that deliver mail to only exit with EX_OK if delivery was 100% successful. Failure to take precautions to detect every possible error can result in lost mail and angry users. To illustrate, consider the following common C language statement:

```
(void)fclose(fp);
```

If the file being written to is remotely mounted, the written data may be cached locally. All the preceding write statements will have succeeded, but if the remote host crashes after the last write (but before the close) some of the data can be lost. The *fclose*(3) fails, but the (void) prevents detection of that failure.

Even when writing small shell scripts, it is important to include error checking. The following rewrite of our *gone* program includes error checking, but does not handle signals. We leave that as an exercise for the reader:

```
#!/bin/sh
if [ ${#} -ne 2 ]; then
        echo $0 needs a user name.
        exit 64 # EX_USAGE from <sysexits.h>
fi
if `/usr/ucb/mail -s "$1 gone" postmaster 2>&/dev/null`
then
        exit 70 # EX_SOFTWARE from <sysexits.h>
fi
exit 0  # EX_OK from <sysexits.h>
```

Required Aliases

The behavior of the *sendmail* program requires that two specific aliases (*Postmaster* and *MAILER-DAEMON*) be defined in every *aliases* file.

The Postmaster Alias

RFC822 requires every site to accept for delivery mail addressed to a user named *postmaster*. It also requires that mail accepted for *postmaster* always be delivered to a real human being—someone capable of handling mail problems. If *postmaster* is not an alias, or a real user, *sendmail syslog*(3)'s the following error:

```
can't even parse postmaster!
```

Unless a site has a real user account named *postmaster*, an alias is required in every *aliases* file for that name. That alias must be a list of one or more real people, although it may also contain a specification for an archive file or filter program. One such alias might look like this:

```
postmaster: bill, /mail/archives/postmaster,
    "|/usr/local/bin/gnotify root@mailhost"
```

Here, `postmaster` is lowercase. Because all aliases are converted to lowercase for lookup, `Postmaster` or even `POSTMASTER` could have been used for equal effect.

Note that there are three aliases to the right of the colon: a local user named `bill`, the full path of a file onto which mail messages will be appended, and a program to `notify` the user `root` at the machine `mailhost` that `postmaster` mail has arrived on the local machine.

As a convention, the special name *postmaster* can also be that of the user who gets duplicate copies of all bounced mail.* This is enabled by using the P option in the configuration file.

```
OPpostmaster
```

To disable the sending of copies of bounced mail to a special user (perhaps to protect privacy), omit the P option from the configuration file.

Note that some sites define the P-option user as one who is always aliased to a filter program in the *aliases* file. For example, if the P option is declared as:

```
OPmail-errors
```

---

*V8 *sendmail* does not send to the postmaster copies of error mail that include a `Precedence:` header with a value less than zero (like *junk* or *bulk* used by mailing lists).

and the corresponding *aliases* file entry is declared as:

```
mail-errors: "|/etc/mail/filter postmaster"
```

a program `filter` can be designed which discards all common error messages, like mistyped addresses, and forwards what remains to `postmaster`.

Many sites have developed just such filters. One is distributed with the V8 *sendmail* source in the file *contrib/mmuegel.* Written by Michael S. Muegel of Motorola's Corporate Information Office, it is a *shar*(1) file of several useful *perl*(1) scripts. One (*postclip.pl*) is a tool that filters out the body of bounced mail messages to prevent postmasters from potentially violating the privacy of senders. It tries to retain all headers, no matter how deeply they are buried in what appears to be the message body.

The MAILER-DAEMON Alias

When mail is bounced, the notification of failure is always shown as being from the sender whose name is defined by the n macro. Traditionally, that macro is given the value `mailer-daemon`:

```
DnMAILER-DAEMON
```

That tradition is enforced by the fact that if $n is not defined, it defaults to `mailer-daemon`.

There needs to be an alias for whatever name is defined for $n, because users occasionally make the mistake of replying to bounced mail. Two typical aliases are:

```
mailer-daemon: postmaster
mailer-daemon: /dev/null
```

Here, the name to the left of the colon should be whatever was defined for $n in the configuration file, traditionally (and recommended to be) `mailer-daemon`. The first alias forwards all `mailer-daemon` reply mail to the postmaster. Many site administrators prefer the second, which discards such mail by using */dev/null.*

The Aliases Database

Reading the *aliases* file every time *sendmail* begins to run can slow mail delivery and create a lot of unnecessary computational overhead. To improve efficiency, *sendmail* has the ability to store aliases in a separate database format on disk. In this format, *sendmail* rarely needs to read the *aliases* file. Instead, it merely opens the database and performs lookups as necessary.

The *sendmail* program builds its database files by reading the *aliases*(5) file and rewriting that file in *dbm*(5) format. Usually the aliases file is called *aliases*. With that name, the database files are called *aliases.pag* and *aliases.dir*. With the new BSD *db*(5) database format, only one file is created, *aliases.db*.

The *sendmail* program offers several forms of database, one of which is chosen at compile time (see Chapter 16, *Compile and Install sendmail*).

Rebuild the Alias Database

You tell *sendmail* to rebuild its database files by running it in -bi mode. This mode can be executed in two different ways:

```
% newaliases
% /usr/lib/sendmail -bi
```

The first form is shorthand for the second. Either causes *sendmail* to rebuild those files. If the database is successfully built, *sendmail* prints a single line of information:

```
895 aliases, longest 565 bytes, 30444 bytes total
```

This shows that 895 local entries appeared to the left of colons in the *aliases* file. The longest list of addresses to the right of a colon was 565 bytes (excluding the newline). And there were 30,444 total bytes of non-comment information in the file.

V8 *sendmail* supports multiple alias database files (see the A option in Chapter 30, *Options*). Consequently, each line of its output is prefixed with the name of the alias file being rebuilt. For example:

```
/etc/aliases: 895 aliases, longest 565 bytes, 30444 bytes total
```

Check Right Side of Aliases (V8 Only)

When V8 *sendmail* rebuilds the alias database files, it can optionally be told to check the legality of all addresses to the right of the colons. The n option turns on this check:

```
OnTrue    # validate RHS in newaliases
```

Each address is validated by running it through rule set 3, then rule set 0. Rule set 0 must select a delivery agent for the address. If it does, the address is silently validated and accepted. If not, the address is skipped, and the following warning is printed:

> *address*... bad address

Other errors may be printed before the above line that indicate more specific reasons for the failure. For example:

> ... Unbalanced '<'

The -d20.1 debugging switch can be used to gain a better idea why the *address* failed. But be forewarned: the -d20.1 can produce many screens of output.

Prevent Simultaneous Rebuilds

The alias database files can be automatically rebuilt in three ways: by the daemon (if the D option is true), by users sending mail (and thereby indirectly running *sendmail*), and by users intentionally rebuilding the database with *newaliases* (or the -bi command-line switch). To prevent one rebuild from compromising and corrupting another, *sendmail* uses file locking.

The *sendmail* program uses *flock*(2) or *fcntl*(2) with F_SETLK to lock the *aliases* file (depending on how it was compiled). If the *aliases* file is already locked (because the database is currently being rebuilt), *sendmail* prints the following message:

> Alias file is already being rebuilt

If *sendmail* is attempting to rebuild because it was run as *newaliases* or with the -bi command-line switch, the above message is printed, and the program exits. Otherwise, the above message is printed, and *sendmail* waits for the *aliases* file to become unlocked.

Once the *aliases* file is locked, *sendmail* next looks to see if the key @ appears in the database. If that key is missing, *sendmail* knows that the database is still being rebuilt. If the a option has a value, *sendmail* waits that amount of time for the other rebuild to finish. If the a option is missing or has a zero value, *sendmail* plows ahead, trusting the previous lock to prevent simultaneous rebuilds.

The *sendmail* program waits two times the number of seconds specified by the a option for an @ key to appear in the database. If that key doesn't appear within that wait, *sendmail* continues with the rebuild, assuming that some other process died while attempting to rebuild.

Before entering the key (the name to the left of the colon) and contents (everything to the right of the colon) pairs into the database, *sendmail* truncates the database (reduces it to size zero), thereby removing the @ key. After all the key and contents pairs have been written to the database, *sendmail* adds a new @ key to show that it is done.

Finally *sendmail* closes the database and closes the *aliases* file. Closing the *aliases* file releases all locks it has on that file.

No DBM Aliasing

Some versions of UNIX do not provide the libraries needed to compile *sendmail* with database support. When neither the *dbm*(3) nor *ndbm*(3) library is available, *sendmail* keeps aliases in its internal symbol table.

When the symbol table is used, *sendmail* only builds its alias database once. When *sendmail* is run as a daemon, the *aliases* file is only read once. If the file changes, the daemon needs to be killed and restarted. In general, it is not recommended to run *sendmail* in daemon mode without external database files.

Prevent Aliasing With -n

At times, it is desirable to run *sendmail* so that it does not perform aliasing. When aliasing is disabled, *sendmail* uses the recipient address as-is. No addresses are ever looked up in the *aliases* file, even if they are local.

The -n command-line switch tells *sendmail* not to perform aliasing of recipient addresses. This switch is rarely used, but can be handy in a couple of situations.

Is An Alias Bad?

When tracking down delivery problems, it can be difficult to determine where the problem lies. If you suspect a bad alias, you can force aliasing to be skipped and see if that causes the problem to go away:

```
% /usr/lib/sendmail -n user < /dev/null
```

This tells *sendmail* to send an empty mail message (one containing mandatory headers only) to the recipient named user. The -n prevents *sendmail* from looking up user in either the *aliases* database or in ~/.forward. If user resolves to the local delivery agent, the message will be delivered, and you should therefore suspect an aliasing problem.

Other switches can be combined with −n to view the delivery process in more detail, like −v (verbose) and −d (debugging).

Filtering Recipients With a Shell Script

The −n command-line switch can also be used to suppress aliasing when delivering to a list of recipients that has already been aliased. For example, consider the following script, which attempts to restrict delivery to users who have mail delivered locally and to skip users who have mail forwarded off-site:

```
#!/bin/sh
if [ ${#} -ne 2 ]; then
        echo Usage: $0 list-name
        exit 64 # EX_USAGE from <sysexits.h>
fi
trap "exit 70" 1 2 13 15
LIST= "`/usr/lib/sendmail -bv $1 \
        | sed 's/\.\.\..*$//' \
        | grep -v @ 2>&1`"
if [ -z "$LIST" ]
        echo "$1 expanded to an empty list"
        exit 67 # EX_NOUSER
fi
if `/usr/lib/sendmail -n $LIST 2>&/dev/null`
then
        exit 70 # EX_SOFTWARE from <sysexits.h>
fi
exit 0  # EX_OK from <sysexits.h>
```

The *sendmail* program is called twice inside this script. First, it is given the −bv switch, which causes it to expand the list of recipients in $1. That expansion includes aliasing (and *˜/.forward* aliasing) for each name in the list. The output produced looks like this:

```
user1... deliverable
user2@otherhost... deliverable
```

The *sed*(1) program then discards from the . . . to the end of each line, and *grep*(1), with the −v switch, deletes any line that contains an @ character (indicating a remote site). The result, a list of local recipients only, is saved in the shell variable LIST.

The *sendmail* program is called with the −n switch, which prevents it from re-aliasing the list of names in $LIST (they have already been aliased once).

This script should not be used as-is because it does not check for local addresses that are programs or files.

Pitfalls

- The *dbm* and *ndbm* forms of the *aliases*(5) database files contain binary integers. As a consequence, those database files cannot be shared via network-mounted file systems by machines of differing architectures. This is not a problem for 4.4 BSD *db* files.
- The *aliases* file and database files can be used to circumvent system security if they are writable by the wrong users. Proper ownership and permissions are neither checked for nor enforced by *sendmail*.
- Versions of *sendmail* that use the old-style *dbm*(3) libraries can cause overly long alias lines (greater than 1024 bytes) to be silently truncated. With the new databases, like *ndbm*(3), a warning is printed.
- Recursive (circular self-referencing) aliases are only detected when mail is being delivered. The *sendmail* program does not look for such alias loops when rebuilding its database.

21

Mailing Lists and ~/.forward

As shown in the previous chapter, the *sendmail* program is able to obtain its list of recipients from the *aliases* file. It can also obtain lists of recipients from external files. In this chapter, we will examine the two forms those external files take: the `:include:` form (accessed from the *aliases* file) and the individual user's ~/.forward file. Since the chief use of the `:include:` form of alias is to create *mailing lists*, we will first discuss mailing lists in general, their creation and management, then the user's ~/.forward file.

A mailing list is the name of a single recipient that, when expanded by *sendmail* aliasing, becomes a list of many recipients. Mailing lists can be internal (where all recipients are listed in the *aliases* file) or external (where all recipients are listed in external files) or a combination of the two. The list of recipients that forms a mailing list can include users, programs, and files.

Internal Mailing Lists

An internal mailing list is simply an entry in the *aliases* file that has more than one recipient listed on the righthand side. Consider, for example, the following *aliases* file entries:

```
admin:    bob,jim,phil
bob:      \bob,/u/bob/admin/maillog
```

Here, the name `admin` is actually the name of a mailing list, because it expands to more than one recipient. Similarly, the name `bob` is a mailing list, because it expands to two recipients. Since `bob` is also included in the `admin` list, mail sent to that mailing list will be alias-expanded by *sendmail* to produce the following list of recipients:

```
jim, phil, \bob, /u/bob/admin/maillog
```

This causes the mail message to be delivered to the local users `jim` and `phil` in the normal way. That is, each undergoes additional alias process-ing, and the *˜/.forward* file of each is examined to see if either should be forwarded. The recipient `\bob`, on the other hand, is delivered without any further aliasing because of the leading backslash. Finally the message is appended to the file */u/bob/admin/maillog*.

Internal mailing lists can become very complex as they strive to support the needs of large institutions. Examine the simple, but revealing, example below:

```
research:     user1, user2
applications: user3, user4
admin:        user5, user6
advertising:  user7, user8
engineering:  research, applications
frontoffice:  admin, advertising
everyone:     engineering, frontoffice
```

Only the first four aliases above expand to real usernames. The last three form mailing lists out of combinations of those four, the last being a super-set that includes all users.

When the number of mailing lists is small, and they don't change often, they can be effectively managed as part of the *aliases* file. But, as their number and size grow, you should consider moving individual lists to external files.*

---

*Only *root* should be permitted to write to the *aliases* file. If you keep mailing lists inside that file, it may need to be writable by others. This can create a security breach (see Chapter 18, *Security*).

:include: Mailing Lists

The special notation :include: in the righthand side of an alias causes *sendmail* to read its list of recipients from an external file. That notation is used like this:

```
localname:    :include:/path
```

The expression :include: is literal. It must appear exactly as shown, colons and all, with no space between the colons and the "include". As with any righthand side of an alias, there may be space between the alias colon and the lead colon of the :include:.

The /path is the full pathname of a file containing a list of recipients. It follows the :include: with intervening space allowed.

The /path should be a full pathname. If it is a relative name (like *../file*), it is relative to the *sendmail* queue directory. For all but V8 *sendmail*, the /path must not be quoted. If it is quoted, the quotation marks are interpreted as part of the filename. For V8 *sendmail*, the /path may be quoted and the quotation marks are automatically stripped.

If the /path cannot be opened for reading for any reason, *sendmail* prints the following warning and ignores any recipients that might have been in the file:

```
Cannot open /path: reason
```

Here, *reason* is "no such file or directory," or "permission denied," or something similar. If /path exists and can be read, *sendmail* reads it one line at a time. Empty lines are ignored.

Each line in the :include: file is treated as a list of one or more recipient addresses. Where there is more than one, each should be separated from the others by commas.

```
addr1
addr2, addr3, addr4
```

Spaces around the commas are optional. The addresses may themselves be aliases that appear to the left in the *aliases* file. They may also be user addresses, program names, or filenames. A :include: file may also contain additional :include: lists.

```
engineers                          ← to an alias
biff, bill@otherhost               ← to two recipients
|"/etc/local/loglists thislist"    ← to a program alias
/usr/local/archive/thislist.hist   ← to a file
:include:/yet/another/file         ← from another file
```

After *sendmail* opens the */path* for reading, but before it reads the file, it sets the controlling user (if one is not already set) to be the owner of the file. The controlling user provides the *uid* and *gid* identities of the sender when delivering mail from the queue (see Chapter 19, *The Queue*).

Comments In :include: Lists

IDA and V8 *sendmail* allow comments in `:include:` files. Comment lines begin with a # character. If the # doesn't begin the line, it is treated as the beginning of an address, thus allowing valid usernames that begin with a # (like `#1user`) to appear first in a line by prefixing them with a space.

```
# Management          ← a comment
frida
george@wash.dc.gov
# Staff               ← a comment
ben
steve
 #1user               ← an address
```

Note that since comments and empty lines are ignored by *sendmail*, they can be used to create attractive, well-documented mailing lists.

Under older versions of *sendmail*, comments can be emulated through the use of RFC822-style comments.

```
( comment )
```

By surrounding the `comment` in parentheses, you cause *sendmail* to view it and the parentheses as an RFC-style comment and ignore them.

```
( Management )
frida
george@wash.dc.gov
( Staff )
ben
steve
```

This form of comment works with both the old and new *sendmail* programs.

Tradeoffs

As has been noted, the *aliases* file should be writable only by *root* for security reasons. Thus, ordinary users, like nonprivileged department heads, cannot use the *aliases* file to create and manage mailing lists. Fortunately, `:include:` files allow ordinary users (or groups of users) to maintain mailing lists. This offloads a great deal of work from the system administrator, who would otherwise have to manage these lists, and gives users a sense of participation in the system.

The *aliases* database (because it is binary) cannot be shared by hosts of differing architectures.* But `:include:` files can (because they only contain ASCII text). Furthermore, when the list of recipients in a `:include:` file is changed, no separate run of *sendmail* is required to rebuild any database. The change takes effect immediately.

Unfortunately, reading `:include:` lists is slower than reading an entry from the *aliases* database. At busy sites, or sites with numerous mail messages addressed to mailing lists, this difference in speed can become significant. Note that the `-bv` command-line switch can be used with *sendmail* to time and contrast the two different forms of lists.

One possible disadvantage to all types of mailing lists is that they are visible to the outside world. This means that anyone in the world can send mail to a local list intended for internal use. Many lists are intended for both internal and external use. One such list might be one for discussion of the O'Reilly books. Called, say, *nuts@ora.com*, anyone inside *ora.com* and anyone in the outside world can send mail messages to this list, and those messages will be forwarded to everyone on the *nuts* mailing list.

Defining a Mailing List Owner

Notification of an error in delivery to a mailing list is sent to the original sender as bounced mail. Although this behavior is desirable for most mail delivery, it can have undesirable results for mailing lists. Because the list is maintained locally, it does not make sense for an error message to be sent to a remote sender. That sender is likely to be puzzled or upset and unable to fix the problem. A better solution is to force all error messages to be sent to a local user, no matter who sent the original message.

When *sendmail* processes errors during delivery, it looks to see if an "owner" was defined for the mailing list. If one was defined, errors are sent to that owner, rather than to the sender. The owner is defined by prefixing

---

*The *db(3)* database supplied with 4.4BSD UNIX *can* be shared by machines of differing architectures.

the original mailing list alias with the phrase `owner-`, as shown in the following code:

```
nuts:   :include:/home/lists/nuts.list
owner-nuts: george
```

Here, `nuts` is the name of the mailing list. If an error occurs while attempting delivery to the list of recipients in the file `/home/lists/book.list`, *sendmail* looks for an alias called `owner-nuts` (the original name prefixed with `owner-`). If *sendmail* finds an owner (here `george`), it sends error notification to that owner, rather than to the original sender. Generally, it is best to have the `owner-` of a list be the same as the owner of the mailing-list file, since that user is best suited to correct errors as they appear.

To ensure that all errors in mailing lists are handled by someone, an owner of owners should also be defined. That alias usually looks like this:

```
owner-owner:    postmaster
```

If *sendmail* cannot deliver an error message to the `owner-` of a mailing list, it instead delivers it to the `owner-owner`.

Exploder Mailing Lists

When mailing lists get extremely large, they sometimes include the names of other lists at other sites as recipients. Those other lists are called *exploder* lists, because they cause the size of a list (the number of recipients) to *explode.* For example, consider the situation in Figure 21-1.

This figure shows that a message sent to *nuts@ora.com* will, in addition to its list of users, also be forwarded to *allgov@wash.gov* and *ads@uu.uu.net* But each of these recipients is also a mailing list. Like the original *nuts* list, they deliver to ordinary users and forward to other sites' mailing lists.

Unless exploding lists like this are correctly managed, problems that are both mysterious and difficult to solve can arise. A bad address in one of the distant exploding lists, for example, can cause a delivery error at a remote exploder site. If this happens, it is possible that the error notification will be sent to either the original list maintainer, or (worse) the original submitter, although neither is in a position to correct such errors.

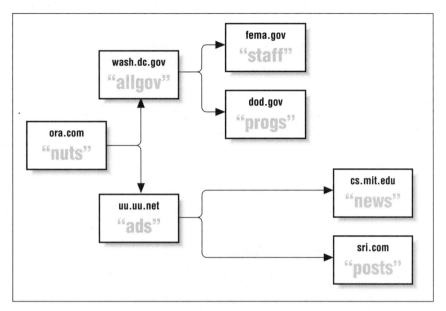

Figure 21-1: Exploding a mailing list

To insure that error notification is sent to the person best able to handle the error, mailing list entries in the *aliases* file should be set up like the following.* It is an approach to setting up a mailing list that is well suited for both exploder and originating sites.

```
list:      "|/usr/lib/sendmail -oi -odq -flist-request list-real"
list-real: :include:/path/to/real/list
list-request:    realperson
owner-list:      list-request
```

Here, the name of the mailing list is `list`. Mail sent to this list, whether from an outside individual or from another list, is handled by passing that mail message to *sendmail* with special command-line arguments.

-oi   Tells *sendmail* that a line containing only a dot (.) is not to be interpreted as the end of the message.

-odq   Tells *sendmail* to queue the message for later delivery. This helps to keep the load down on a machine by serializing mailing list delivery.

-flist-request

Causes *sendmail* to set the envelope sender address to `list-request`. If a remote exploder site is misconfigured, it tries to

---

*The f option *must* be false in your configuration file for this to work.

return error messages to the envelope sender, rather than trying to handle them locally. This argument helps to insure that errors resulting from the local `list` will cause mail notification to go to the local `list-request`, who is a real person.*

`list-real`

> The actual mailing list. For all but V8 *sendmail*, users on the local machine need to submit messages to this name rather than `list` because the `-f` command-line switch can only be used by *trusted users* (see Chapter 18, *Security*).

Note that the `-oQ` command-line switch can be added if mailing lists need to be queued separately from ordinary mail (see Chapter 19, *The Queue*).

Problems With Mailing Lists

At small sites that just use mailing lists internally, the problems are few and can be easily solved locally. But as lists get to be large (over a few hundred recipients), many (over fifty lists), or complex (using exploders), problems become harder to localize and more difficult to solve. In the following discussion, we present the most common problems. It is by no means comprehensive, but it should provide information to solve most problems.

Reply Versus Bounce

The eventual recipient of a mailing-list message should be able to reply to the message and have that reply go to either the original sender or the list as a whole. Which happens is an administrative decision. In general, replies go to the address listed in the `From:` or `Reply-To:` headers. If the intention is to have replies go to the list as a whole, these headers need to be rewritten by a filter at the originating site:

```
list:    "|/etc/local/mailfilter list -oi -odq -flist-request list-real"
```

Here, the name of the filter has replaced *sendmail* in the *aliases* file entry. Writing such a filter is complex (see Chapter 20, *Aliases*). The original addresses needs to be preserved with appropriate headers (see Chapter 31, *Headers*), before they are rewritten by the filter.

---

*The `-flist-request` is not needed with V8 *sendmail*. The `owner-list` is automatically propagated into the envelope.

The converse problem is that not all mail-handling programs handle replies properly. Some programs (like UUCP and certain versions of *emacs-mail*) insist on replying to the envelope sender as conveyed in the five-character "From " header. By setting up lists correctly (as we showed earlier), an administrator can at least guarantee that those replies are sent to the list maintainer, who can then forward them as required.

A more serious problem is the way other sites handle bounced mail. In an ideal world, all sites would correctly bounce mail to the `Errors-To:` address* and (less desirably) to the envelope sender. Unfortunately, not all sites are so well-behaved. If a mailing list is not carefully set up, there is a possibility that bounced mail will be resent to the list as a whole. To minimize such potential catastrophes, follow the guide in Table 21-1.

Table 21-1: Mailing List Header Use

Header	Use
Envelope sender	Should be local list maintainer
From	Same as envelope sender
From:	Original submitter
Reply-To:	The local list maintainer, the list as a whole, or the original submitter
Errors-To:	Local list maintainer

Gateway Lists to News

When gatewaying a mailing list to USENET news, the *inews*(1) program bounces the message if it is for a moderated group and lacks an `Approved:` header. This header can be added by a filter program (see Chapter 20) or by a news gateway delivery agent.

If your site is running (or has access to) USENET news, the *recnews*(1) program included therein may be used to gateway mail to newsgroups. It inserts the `Approved:` header needed by *inews*, and generally handles its

---

*`Errors-To:` was originally a hack to get around the fact that UUCP confused envelope and header.

gateway role well. One minor pitfall to avoid with *recnews* is making separate postings when you intend cross-postings:

```
mail-news: "|/usr/local/recnews comp.mail comp.mail.d"  ← separate postings
mail-news: "|/usr/local/recnews comp.mail,comp.mail.d"  ← cross-posted
                                           ↑
                                      note comma
```

A list-bounced Alias

There are many ways to handle bounced mail when managing a mailing list. One of the best ways for large lists to create a *bounce* alias for a list:

```
list-bounce: :include:/usr/local/lists/list-bounce
```

When an address in the main list begins to bounce, move it from the main list's file to the corresponding `list-bounce` file. Then nightly (via *cron*(8)) send a message to that list advising the users in it that they will soon be dropped. To prevent the bad addresses from deluging you with bounced mail, set up the return address and the envelope to be an alias that delivers to */dev/null*:

```
black-hole:   /dev/null
```

Finally, arrange to include the following header in the outgoing message:

```
Precedence: junk
```

This prevents most sites from returning the message if it cannot be delivered.

There are also programs available that can help manage large and numerous mailing lists. We will cover them later in this chapter.

Users Ignore List-request

It is impossible to cause all users to interact properly with a mailing list. For example, all submissions to a list should (strictly speaking) be mailed to *list*, whereas communications to the list maintainer should be mailed to *list-request*. As a list maintainer, you will find that users mistakenly reverse these roles surprisingly often.

One possible cure is to insert instructions in each mailing at the start of the message. In the header, for example, `Comment:` lines can be used like this:

```
Comment: "listname" INSTRUCTIONS
Comment: To be added to, removed from, or have your address changed
Comment: in this list, send mail to "listname-request".
```

Unfortunately, user inattention usually dooms such schemes to failure. You can put instructions everywhere, but some users will still send their requests to the wrong address.

Precedence: bulk

All mass mailings, such as mailing-list mailings, should have a header `Pre-cedence:` line that gives a priority of `bulk`, `junk`, or `list`. On the local machine, these priorities cause the message to be processed from the queue after higher priority mail. At other sites, these priorities will cause well-designed programs (like the newer *vacation*(1)* program) to skip automatically replying to such messages.

X.400 Addresses

The X.400 telecommunications standard is finding increased acceptance in Europe and by the United States government. Addresses under X.400 always begin with a leading slash, which can cause *sendmail* to think the address is the name of a file when the `local` delivery agent is selected:

```
/PN=MS.USER/O=CORP/PRMD=CORP/ADMD=TELE/C=US/
```

To prevent this misunderstanding, all such addresses should be followed by an *@domain* part to route the message to an appropriate X.400 gateway:

```
/PN=MS.USER/O=CORP/PRMD=CORP/ADMD=TELE/C=US/@X.400.gateway.here
```

Packages That Help

As the number and size of mailing lists at your site become large, you may wish to install a software package that automates list management. All of the following packages are available with anonymous FTP.

---

*The *vacation*(1) program is a wonderful tool for advising others that mail will not be attended to for a while. Unfortunately some older versions of that program still exist that reply to `bulk` mail, thereby causing problems for the mailing-list maintainer.

Majordomo

The *Majordomo* mailing-list management software was written by Brent Chapman using the *perl*(1) language. Its chief features are that it allows users to subscribe to and remove themselves from lists without list manager intervention, and that it allows list managers to manage lists remotely. In addition, users can obtain help and list descriptions with simple mail requests. Note that *Majordomo* aids in managing a list (the list addresses), but does not aid in list moderation (the contents of mail messages). *Majordomo* is available for anonymous FTP from *FTP.GreatCircle.COM,* in the file *pub/majordomo.tar.Z.*

Almanac

The *Almanac* mailing-list management software was written at Oregon State University, Extension Service, in the C language. It also allows users to subscribe to and be removed from mailing lists themselves, without maintainer intervention. In addition, it services requests for file transfers (similar to *ftp*) via e-mail. It is purported to be highly configurable in that the grammar for requests is determined by the site administrator, and any request can be bound to *any* (predefined) Bourne shell program. Thus, for example, *Almanac* sites in France are at liberty to speak French to their *Almanac* server. The *Almanac* software is available for anonymous FTP from *OES.OrSt.EDU,* in the file *pub/almanac-*.tar.Z.*

ListProcessor

The *ListProcessor* system was written by Tasos Kotsikonas. It is an automated system for managing mailing lists that replaces the *aliases* file for that use. According to the author, it includes support for "public and private hierarchical archives, moderated lists, peer lists, peer servers, private lists, address aliasing, news connections and gateways, mail queueing, list ownership, owner preferences, crash recovery, and batch processing." The system also accepts Internet connections for "live" processing of requests at port 372 (as assigned by the IANA*). The *ListProcessor* system is available via anonymous FTP from *cs.bu.edu* in the directory *pub/listserv.*†

---

*IANA stands for Internet Assigned Numbers Authority. It is currently housed in Marina del Rey, California, and staffed by Joyce Reynolds and Jon Postel (iana@isi.edu).

†In July of 1993, the name was changed from *UNIX Listserv* to *ListProcessor* to avoid confusion with the BITNET LISTSERV service. The FTP source distribution directory name kept the old name.

The User's ~/.forward File

The *sendmail* program allows each user to have a `:include:` style list to customize the receipt of personal mail. That file must be located in the user's home directory and must be called *.forward.* We use the C-shell notation ~ to indicate user home directories, so we will compactly refer to this file as ~/.forward.

If a recipient address selects the `local` delivery agent, it is considered the address of a local user. If that address contains a backslash, it disallows further processing, and the message is handed to the `local` delivery agent's P= program for delivery to the mail-spooling directory. If a backslash is absent, *sendmail* tries to read that user's ~/.forward file.

If the ~/.forward file cannot be read, its contents are silently ignored. This is also how *sendmail* behaves when that file doesn't exist. Users often choose not to have ~/.forward files. But problems may arise when user home directories are remotely mounted. Over NFS, for example, *root* is usually mapped to *nobody.* If a user's home is mode 0700, *root* as *nobody* is unable to search that home directory for a *.forward* file. Similarly, if the home is searchable (0711), but the file itself is protected (0600), *root* as *nobody* again lacks permission to read the user's *.forward* file.† Both of these problems cause *sendmail* to silently ignore the ~/.forward file.

If a user has no home directory, *sendmail* *syslog*(3)'s the following error message and skips forwarding.

```
forward: no home
```

If *sendmail* cannot read the ~/.forward file (for any reason), it silently ignores that file. Under V8 *sendmail*, the J option can be used to set up additional *.forward* files (see Chapter 30, *Options*), thereby enabling *sendmail* to have a fallback position should the ~/.forward file be unreadable.

Before reading the ~/.forward file, *sendmail* checks to see if it is a "safe" file—one that is owned by the user or *root* and that has the read permission bit set for the owner. If the ~/.forward file is not safe, *sendmail* silently ignores it.

---

*V8 *sendmail* allows you to create a *search path* of forward files. Conventionally, this path includes a file named `.forward` in the user's home directory.

†This is less of a problem with V8 *sendmail*. Before opening the ~/.forward file, *sendmail* temporarily assumes the identity of the user. However, this is not possible on all operating systems.

If *sendmail* can find and read the ˜/.forward file, and if that file is safe, *sendmail* opens the file for reading and gathers a list of recipients from it. Internally, the ˜/.forward file is exactly the same as a `:include:` file. Each line of text in it may contain one or more recipient addresses. Recipient addresses may be e-mail addresses, the names of files onto which the message should be appended, the names of programs through which to pipe the message, or `:include:` files.

Under V8 *sendmail*, ˜/.forward files may contain comments (lines that begin with a # character). Other versions of *sendmail* treat comment lines as addresses and bounce mail seemingly addressed to #.

Unscrambling Forwards

The traditional use of the ˜/.forward file, as its name implies, is to forward mail to another site. Unfortunately, as users move from machine to machine, they can leave behind a series of ˜/.forward files, each of which points to the next machine in a chain. As machine names change and as old machines are retired, the links in this chain can be broken. One common consequence is a bounced mail message ("host unknown") with a dozen or so `Received:` header lines.

As the mail administrator, you should beware of the ˜/.forward files of users at your site. If any contain offsite addresses, you should periodically use the SMTP *expn* command* to examine them. For example, consider a local user whose ˜/.forward contains the following line:

```
user@remote.domain
```

This causes all local mail for the user to be forwarded to the host `remote.domain` for delivery there. The validity of that address can be checked with *telnet*(1) at port 25† and the SMTP `expn` command:

```
% telnet remote.domain 25
Trying 123.45.123.45 ...
Connected to remote.domain.
Escape character is '^]'.
220 remote.domain Sendmail 4.1/1.42 ready at Wed, 28 Oct 91 05:28:20 PST
expn user
250 Joe User <user@another.site>
quit
```

---

*Under old versions of *sendmail*, the *vrfy* and *expn* commands are interchangeable. Under V8 *sendmail* and other, modern SMTP servers, the two commands differ.

†In place of specifying port 25, you can either use *mail* or *smtp*. These are more mnemonic and easier to remember (although we "oldtimers" tend to still use 25).

```
221 remote.domain closing connection
Connection closed by foreign host.
%
```

This shows that the user is known at `remote.site`, but also shows that mail will be forwarded (yet again) from there to `another.site`. By repeating this process, you will eventually find the site at which the user's mail will be delivered. Depending on your site's policies, you can either correct the user's *˜/.forward* file, or have the user correct it. It should contain the address of the host where that user's mail will ultimately be delivered.

Forwarding loops

Because *˜/.forward* files are under user control, the administrator occasionally needs to break loops caused by improper use of those files. To illustrate, consider a user who wishes to have mail delivered on two different machines (call them machines A and B). On machine A, the user creates a *˜/.forward* file like this:

```
\user, user@B
```

Then on machine B, the user creates this *˜/.forward* file:

```
\user, user@A
```

The intention is that the backslashed name (`\user`) will cause local delivery, and the second address in each will forward a copy of the message to the other machine. Unfortunately, this causes mail to go back and forth between the two machines (delivering and forwarding at each) until the mail is finally bounced with the error message "too many hops."

On the machine the administrator controls, a fix to this looping is to temporarily edit the *aliases* database and insert an alias for the offending user like this:

```
user:  \user
```

This causes mail for `user` to be delivered locally, and for that user's *˜/.forward* file to be ignored. After the user has corrected the offending *˜/.forward* files, this alias can be removed.

Appending to Files

The *˜/.forward* file can contain the names of files onto which mail is to be appended. Such filenames must begin with a slash character that cannot be quoted. For example, a user may wish to maintain a backup copy of incoming mail:

```
\user
/home/user/mail/in.backup
```

The first line (\user) tells *sendmail* to deliver directly to the user's mail spool file using the `local` delivery agent. The second line tells *sendmail* to append a copy of the mail message to the file specified (`in.backup`).

This use of the *˜/.forward* file is not recommended. Because old versions of *sendmail* do no special file locking,* it is possible for the specified file to become trashed. The preferred method for appending to files is to use programs specifically designed for this purpose (which we describe after the next section).

Piping Through Programs

The *˜/.forward* file can contain the names of programs to run. A program name is indicated by a leading pipe (|) character, which may or may not be quoted. For example, a user may be away on a trip and want mail handled by the *vacation*(1) program:

```
\user, "|/usr/ucb/vacation user"
```

Recall that prefixing a local address with a backslash tells *sendmail* to skip additional alias transformations. For \user, this causes *sendmail* to deliver the message (via the `local` delivery agent) directly to the user's spool mail box.

The quotes around the *vacation* program are necessary to prevent the program and its single argument (`user`) from being viewed as two separate addresses. The *vacation* program is run with the command-line argument `user`, and the mail message is given to it via its standard input.

Because *sendmail* sorts all addresses and deletes duplicates before delivering to any of them, it is important that programs in *˜/.forward* files take unique arguments. Consider a program that doesn't take an argument and suppose that two users both specified that program in their *˜/.forward* files:

---

*V8 *sendmail* locks the file during writing.

```
user 1 →   \user1, "|/bin/notify"
user 2 →   \user2, "|/bin/notify"
```

When mail is sent to both `user1` and `user2`, the address `/bin/notify` appears twice in the list of addresses. The *sendmail* program eliminates what seems to be a duplicate,* and one of the two users does not have the program run.

If a program *requires* no arguments (as opposed to ignoring them), the ˜/.*forward* program specifications can be made unique by including a shell comment:

```
user 1 →   \user1, "|/bin/notify #user1"
user 2 →   \user2, "|/bin/notify #user2"
```

Specialty Programs for Use With ˜/.forward

Rather than expecting users to write home-grown programs for use in ˜/.*forward* files, offer them any or all of the publicly available alternatives. The most common are listed below.

The deliver Program

The *deliver*(1) program, by Chip Salzenberg, is specifically designed to handle all types of final delivery for users. It is intended for use in the ˜/.*forward* file, but also functions as a `local` delivery agent. The *deliver* program supports a large number of command-line options and can reliably handle delivery to files and through programs. It is typically used in the ˜/.*forward* file like this:

```
"|/usr/local/bin/deliver user"
```

The *deliver* program is available via anonymous FTP from many archive sites.

The procmail Program

The *procmail*(1) program, by Stephen R. van den Berg, is purported to be the most reliable of the delivery programs. It can sort incoming mail into separate folders and files, run programs, preprocess mail (filtering out unwanted mail), and selectively forward mail elsewhere. It can function as

---

*V8 *sendmail* uses the owner of the ˜/.*forward* file in addition to the program name when comparing.

a substitute for the `local` delivery agent or handle mail delivery for the individual user. The *procmail* program is typically used in the ˜/.*forward* file like this:

```
"|exec /usr/local/bin/procmail #user"
```

Note that *procmail* does not accept a username as a command-line argument. Because of this, a dummy shell comment is needed to make the address unique to *sendmail*. The *procmail* program is available via anonymous FTP from many archive sites.

The slocal Program

The *slocal* program, distributed with the *mh* distribution, is useful for sorting incoming mail into separate files and folders. It can be used with both UNIX-style mail files and with *mh*-style mail directory folders. It is typically used in the ˜/.*forward* file like this:

```
"| /usr/local/lib/mh/slocal -user user"
```

The disposition of mail is controlled using a companion file called ˜/.*maildelivery*.

Force Requeue on Error

Normally, a program in the user's ˜/.*forward* file is executed with the Bourne shell. The precise means used is defined by the `prog` delivery agent.

```
Mprog, P=/bin/sh,   F=lsDFMeuP,   S=10, R=20, A=sh -c $u
                                                 ↑
                                          The Bourne shell
```

One drawback to using the Bourne shell to run programs is that it exits with a value of one when the program cannot be executed. When *sendmail* sees the exit value one, it bounces the mail message.

There will be times when bouncing a mail message because the program could not execute is not desirable. For example, consider the following ˜/.*forward* file:

```
"| /usr/local/lib/slocal -user george"
```

If the directory */usr/local/lib* is unavailable (perhaps because a file server is down or because an automounter failed) the mail message should be queued, rather than bounced. To arrange for requeueing of the message on failure, users should be encouraged to construct their ˜/.forward files like this:

```
"| /usr/local/lib/slocal -user george || exit 75"
```

Here, the || tells the Bourne shell to perform what follows (the exit 75) if the preceding program could not be executed. The exit value 75 is special, in that it tells *sendmail* to queue the message for later delivery, rather than to bounce it.

Pitfalls

- When *sendmail* collects addresses, it discards duplicates. A program entry in a ˜/.forward file must be unique, otherwise an identical entry in another user's ˜/.forward causes one or the other to be ignored. Usually this is solved by requiring the program to take an argument. If the program won't accept an argument, add a shell comment inside the quotes. This is fixed in V8 *sendmail*.

- The database forms of the *aliases*(5) file contain binary integers. As a consequence, those database files cannot be shared via network-mounted file systems by machines of differing architectures. This has been fixed with V8 *sendmail* which can use the 4.4 BSD UNIX *db*(3) form of database.

- As network-mounted file systems become increasingly common, the likelihood that a user's home directory will be *temporarily* unavailable increases. The *sendmail* program does not handle this problem well. Instead of queueing mail until a user's home directory can be accessed, *sendmail* wrongly assumes that the ˜/.forward doesn't exist. This can cause mail to be delivered locally, when it should have been forwarded to another site. This can be fixed by using the J option of V8 *sendmail*.

- There is no way to disable user forwarding via ˜/.forward files. At sites with proprietary or confidential information, there is no simple way to prevent local users from arbitrarily forwarding confidential mail off-site. (But ˜/.forward files can be centrally administered by using the J option of V8 *sendmail*, even to the point of completely disabling forwarding with OJ/dev/null.)

- Programs run from ˜/.forward files should take care to clear or reset all untrusted environment variables. Only V8 and the next release of IDA *sendmail* properly preset the environment.

- If a user's ˜/.forward file evaluates to an empty address, the mail will be silently discarded. This has been fixed in IDA and V8 *sendmail*.

- A program run from a `~/.forward` file is always run on the machine running *sendmail*. That machine is not necessarily the same as the machine housing the `~/.forward` file. When user home directories are network-mounted, it is possible that one machine may support the program (like */usr/ucb/vacation*), while another may lack the program or call it something else (like */usr/bsd/vacation*).

22

Logging and Statistics

The *sendmail* program can keep the system administrator up-to-date about many aspects of mail delivery and forwarding. It does this by logging its activities using the *syslog*(3) facility. It can also gather (or aid in gathering) statistics about what it is doing. Information about things like total message volume and site connectivity, for example, can help the administrator make *sendmail* more efficient.

In this chapter, we cover these two important aspects of *sendmail*. First, we explain the use of the *syslog*(3) facility and illustrate several ways to tune its logging. Second, we show the built-in means that *sendmail* has for recording statistics and how scripts can be used to extend that information.

Logging

Logging is the process of issuing one-line warnings that will either be displayed to a human or archived to a file or both. The mechanism used by *sendmail* to produce these warnings is called *syslog*(3). The *sendmail* program is only concerned with issuing its warnings. Once they are issued, the *syslog* facility takes over and disposes of them in a manner described in the file */etc/syslog.conf*. Statements in this file determine whether a warning is written to a device (like */dev/console*), appended to a file, forwarded to another host, or displayed on a logged-in user's screen.

In the following discussion of *syslog* and *syslog.conf*, we will describe the BSD 4.3 version. Some versions of UNIX, like Ultrix, use the 4.2 version of *syslog*, but, because *syslog* is public domain, we recommend upgrading and will not cover that old version here.

syslog(3)

The *syslog(3)* facility uses two items of information in determining how to handle messages: *log-type* and *level.* The log-type is the category of program issuing a message. The *syslog* facility can handle many types, but only one, `mail`, is used by *sendmail.* The level is the degree of severity of the warnings. The *sendmail* program issues messages with *syslog(3)* at various levels depending on how serious the warning.

When *sendmail* first starts to run, it opens its connection to the *syslog* facility with the following C language line:

```
openlog("sendmail", LOG_PID, LOG_MAIL);
```

This tells *syslog* three things:

- All messages should be printed using `sendmail` as the name of the program doing the logging. This means that no matter what name is used to run *sendmail* (like *newaliases* or *smtpd*) the name logged will always be `sendmail`.

- The `LOG_PID` tells *syslog* that the PID (process identification number) should be included when each message is written. This is necessary because *sendmail* forks often, and each parent and child will have a different PID. Because queue file identifiers are constructed from PIDs, this record helps determine which invocation of *sendmail* created a particular queued file. The PID also allows messages from the daemon form of *sendmail* to be differentiated from others.

- The log-type for *sendmail* (and all mail-handling programs) is `LOG_MAIL`. We'll show why this is important when we discuss the *syslog.conf* file.

Just before *sendmail* issues a warning, it looks at the logging level defined by its L option. If the severity of the warning is greater than the logging level, nothing is output. If the severity of the warning it intends to issue is less than or equal to the logging level (lower is more serious), it issues that warning with a C language call like this:

```
syslog(pri, msg);
```

Here, `pri` is the *syslog* logging priority, and `msg` is the text of the warning message. Note that the option L level is different than the *syslog* priority. The former is used internally by *sendmail* to decide if it should print a warning. The latter is used by *syslog* to determine how it will dispose of the message (if it gets one).

The L configuration option sets a threshold at and below which *sendmail* will issue warnings. When L has a zero value, nothing is ever issued. When L has a low value, only critical warnings are issued. As the value of L becomes higher, less critical messages are also issued.

The syntax of the L option, and the kinds of information issued for each level, are explained in Chapter 30, *Options*. For each level, all the information of lower levels is also issued. That is, setting L to 9 causes messages for levels 1 through 8 to also be issued.

The correspondence between L option logging levels and *syslog* priorities is shown in Table 22-1.

Table 22-1: L Levels Versus syslog Priorities

Level	Priority
1	LOG_CRIT and LOG_ALERT
2-8	LOG_NOTICE
9-10	LOG_INFO
11+	LOG_DEBUG

Tuning syslog.conf

Although all messages are emitted by *sendmail* using a single facility, that of *syslog*, they need not all arrive at the same place. The disposition of messages is tuned by the *syslog.conf* file.

The file *syslog.conf* (usually located in the */etc* directory) contains routing commands for use by *syslog*. That file can be complex, because it is designed to handle messages from many programs other than *sendmail*, even messages from the kernel itself. Under SunOS the *syslog.conf* file is also complex because it is preprocessed by *m4*(1) when it is read by *syslog*.

The file *syslog.conf* is composed of lines of text that each have the form:

```
facility.level          target
```

The `facility` is the type of program that may be producing a message. The complete list is shown in Table 22-2. The `facility` called `mail` is the one used by *sendmail*.

Table 22-2: syslog.conf Facilities

Facility	Messages Generated By
user	User processes
kern	The kernel
mail	The mail system, such as *sendmail*
daemon	System daemons, such as *ftpd*(8)
auth	The authorization system, such as *login*(1)
lpr	The line printer spooling system
news	The USENET news system
uucp	The UUCP system
cron	The *cron*(8) and *at*(8) facilities
local0-7	Eight facilities reserved for local use
*	All of the above
mark	Time stamps produced internally by *syslogd*(8)

The `level` indicates the severity at or above which messages should be handled. These levels correspond to the L option levels shown in Table 22-1. The complete list of *syslog.conf* levels is shown in Table 22-3. Those produced by *sendmail* are marked with an asterisk.

Table 22-3: syslog.conf Levels

Level	Meaning of Severity (Highest to Lowest)
emerg	Panic situations requiring broadcast to all users
alert*	Conditions requiring immediate correction
crit*	Critical conditions for which action may be deferred
err	Other errors
warning	Warning messages
notice*	Nonerrors that may require special handling
info*	Statistical and informational messages
debug*	Messages used only when debugging a program
none	Do not send messages from the indicated facility

The `target` is one of the four possibilities shown in Table 22-4. It is the `target` and the preceding `level` that must be tuned for use by *sendmail*.

Table 22-4: syslog.conf Targets

Target	Description
@*host*	Forward message to named *host*
/*file*	Append message to named *file*
user,user, . . .	Write to users' screens, if logged in
*	Write to all logged-in users' screens

For example, the following *syslog.conf* line causes messages from "mail" (the `facility`), that are at or above severity "info" (the `level`), to be appended to the file */var/log/syslog* (the `target`):

A typical (albeit much simplified) */etc/syslog.conf* file might look like this:

```
*.err;kern.debug;user.none    /dev/console
*.err;kern.debug;user.none    /var/adm/messages
auth.notice                   @authhost
mail.info                     /var/log/syslog
*.emerg;user.none             *
```

Notice that there may be multiple `facility.level` pairs on the left, each separated from the others by semicolons. The first two lines handle messages for all facilities at level `err`, all kernel messages (`kern`) at level `debug` and above, and none of the levels (`none`) for the facility `user`. The first line sends those messages to the file `/dev/console`, the computer's screen. The second appends its messages to the file `/var/adm/messages`.

The third line sends authorization messages (like repeated login failures) to the host named `authhost`.

The fourth line appends all messages printed by *sendmail* at level `info` and above (option L level 10 and below) to the file `/var/log/syslog`.

The last line is an emergency broadcast facility. A message to any facility (the leftmost `*`) at the highest level (`emerg`), except for the facility `user` (the `.none`), will be written to the screen of all currently logged-in users (the target `*`).

Finally, note that facilities may be listed together using a comma:

```
mail,daemon.info
```

This causes the level `info` to be the level for both the facilities `mail` and `daemon`. Only the facility may be listed this way. The level may not and (unfortunately) the target may not.

Using m4 (SunOS only)

When *syslogd*(8) under SunOS reads (or re-reads) *syslog.conf*, it filters that file through *m4*(1). Consequently, *m4* commands can be placed into the *syslog.conf* file to tune it for specific needs. We won't describe *m4* in detail, but we will give one example shortly of its application that may prove illuminating to SunOS users.

Logging to a dedicated host

At sites with many hosts to administer, it is often advantageous to have all mail warning messages routed to a central mail server. That way, only the files on a single host need to be examined to discover potential problems. One way to do this is with the *syslog.conf* file. On all the hosts except for the mail server, mail warnings can be handled by a single line of information:

```
mail.debug      @mailhost
```

This tells *syslog* to send all warning messages produced by the `mail` facility (programs like *sendmail*), at all levels (the `debug`) to the host whose name is `mailhost` (the mail server).

Then a *syslog.conf* file that contains the following lines can be set up on the mail server:

```
mail.debug      /var/log/mail/debuglog
mail.info       /var/log/mail/syslog
mail.crit       /var/log/mail/critlog
```

This says that on the `mailhost` machine, warnings from the `mail` facility are archived by appending them to one of three files, depending on the `level` of the warning.

Although this scheme works well, it can lead to problems if different machines are used to archive messages from different facilities. If one host, for example, is an authentication server, another a mail server, and another a finger server, a different *syslog.conf* would be required for each. A better approach is to design a single *syslog.conf* file that can be used on all machines. This is done by designing a single *syslog.conf* file that uses *m4* commands to perform the correct processing on each machine. For the `mailhost` example, such a file might be:

```
sinclude(/etc/syslog.roles)
ifelse(MAILSERVER, `
mail.debug    /var/log/mail/debuglog
mail.info     /var/log/mail/syslog
mail.crit     /var/log/mail/critlog

'
mail.debug    @mailhost
)
```

Ignore the first line for the moment. The rest of the file tells *m4* to do one thing if `MAILSERVER` is defined, and another if it is not. The general form for such an *m4* statement looks like this:

`ifelse`(*this is defined, do this, else do this*)

When `MAILSERVER` is not defined, all `mail` facility messages are forwarded to `mailhost`.

The first line in the file tells *m4* to open and read the contents of the file specified, as if they were additional parts of the *syslog.conf* file. The `s` that begins the name `sinclude` tells *m4* to be silent if that file doesn't exist.

On machines where the file */etc/syslog.roles* does not exist (all except the mail server) `MAILSERVER` is undefined, so all `mail` facility messages will be sent to the host named `mailhost`. On the mail server, however, where the file */etc/syslog.roles* does exist, that file contains the following single line of information:

```
define(MAILSERVER)
```

When *m4* `sinclude`'s this line from the file */etc/syslog.roles*, it makes it a part of the *syslog.conf* file. In the eyes of *m4*, the *syslog.conf* file on the mail server is then transformed into:

```
define(MAILSERVER)
ifelse(MAILSERVER,
mail.debug    /var/log/mail/debuglog
mail.info     /var/log/mail/syslog
mail.crit     /var/log/mail/critlog

'
mail.debug    @mailhost
)
```

The transformed first line tells *m4* to define the term MAILSERVER. Then, on the mail server machine, the *m4* ifelse command finds that MAIL-SERVER is defined, so the configuration information supplied to *syslog* becomes:

```
mail.debug    /var/log/mail/debuglog
mail.info     /var/log/mail/syslog
mail.crit     /var/log/mail/critlog
```

The *m4* preprocessing language is far more powerful than it would appear from this simple example. It is also used in all source distributions of *sendmail* to build complex configuration files. We highly recommend that you become familiar with the use of *m4*. It can make complex administration chores simpler and more bearable.

Statistics

The *sendmail* program provides two ways of gathering information that can be used to assemble valuable statistics. The S configuration option specifies a file into which delivery agent statistics can be saved. And the L option, via *syslog*, can provide a wealth of information for later summary.

The sendmail.st File

The *sendmail* program can maintain an ongoing record of the total number and total sizes of all outgoing and incoming mail messages handled by each delivery agent. This ability is enabled using the S configuration option:

```
OS/path
```

The */path* is the full pathname of the file into which statistics are saved. Most vendors provide configuration files that specify */path* as:

```
OS/etc/sendmail.st
```

Just declaring the S option is not enough, however, for if the file does not exist (or if it is unwritable), *sendmail* silently ignores the S option and does not save statistics. You must also create the empty file:

```
% touch /etc/sendmail.st
```

Note that the gathering of statistics can later be turned off merely by renaming or removing the file.

If the S option has not already been declared, you need to declare it, then kill and restart the *sendmail* daemon, for that declaration to take effect. If you are using a frozen configuration file, you also need to refreeze it with the -bz option.

Viewing Statistics: mailstats

The *mailstats* program is supplied with *sendmail* to provide a convenient way to print the contents of the *sendmail.st* file. The output of the *mailstats* program varies depending on the version of *sendmail* installed. For SunOS 4.1.1, the output looks like this:

```
Mail statistics from Thu Sep 17 12:19:06 '92 to Fri Sep 18 12:54:36 '92

    Mailer   msgs from  bytes from    msgs to    bytes to
  0 local       475       3861K        1230       5244K
  1 prog                                126       1231K
  2 ether        10         17K         179        430K
  4 ddn         537       3160K         543       3757K
```

This SunOS output, like that of all early versions of *sendmail*, shows both the delivery agent number (under `Mailer`), and the delivery agent's symbolic name. Note that the symbolic names are hardcoded into the program and do not necessarily correspond to those in the configuration file.

Under IDA and older versions of *sendmail*, the output of *mailstats* looks like this:

```
Statistics from Thu Sep 17 12:19:06 1992
M msgsfr bytes_from  msgsto   bytes_to
0   475     3861K     1230      5244K
1     0       0K      126       1231K
2    10      17K      179        430K
3   537     3160K     543       3757K
```

Under V8 *sendmail*, the output of *mailstats* looks like this:

```
Statistics from Thu Sep 17 12:19:06 1992
M msgsfr bytes_from  msgsto   bytes_to  Mailer
0   475     3861K     1230      5244K   local
1     0       0K      126       1231K   prog
2    10      17K      179        430K   ether
3   537     3160K     543       3757K   ddn
```

All three versions of output show the same general information. The first line shows the time the statistics file was begun and the current time (implied in some versions). The next lines show the number of messages, and the total size in kilobytes of those messages, both received (`msgs from` and `msgsfr`) and sent (`msgs to` and `msgsto`) for each delivery agent.

Using cron for Daily and Weekly Statistics

The *mailstats* program prints the contents of the *sendmail.st* file, but it does not zero the counters in that file. To clear (zero) that file, you need to truncate it. One easy way to truncate the *sendmail.st* file is:

```
% cp /dev/null /etc/sendmail.st
```

When *sendmail* discovers an empty *sendmail.st* file, it begins gathering statistics all over again. One use for truncation is to collect daily reports from *mailstats*. Consider the following simple shell script:

```
#!/bin/sh
ST=/etc/sendmail.st
MS=/usr/ucb/mailstats
if [ -s $ST -a -f $MS ]; then
        $MS | mail -s "Daily mail stats" postmaster
        cp /dev/null $ST
fi
exit 0
```

When run, this script checks to see if a non-empty *sendmail.st* file and program *mailstats* exist. If they do, *mailstats* is run, printing the statistics, which are then mailed to `postmaster`. The *sendmail.st* file is then truncated to a size of zero. Such a script could be run once per night using the *cron*(8) facility with a *crontab*(5) entry like this:

```
0 0 * * * sh /usr/ucb/mailstats.script >/dev/null 2>&1
```

Here, `mailstats.script` is the name given to the above shell script, and the 0 0 causes that script to be executed once per day at midnight.

Some versions of *mailstats* allow you to specify a different location for the statistics file. The form of that specification varies with the version of *sendmail* being run (see *mailstats*(8)). Yours may look like one of the following:

```
% mailstats /var/log/statlog
% mailstats -f /var/log/statlog
```

If your version of *mailstats* allows a different location (and name) for the statistics file, you can move that file to the new location by revising the S option in the *sendmail* program's configuration file:

```
OS/var/log/statlog
```

Moving and renaming the statistics file allows one to automatically collect daily copies of that file. Consider the following variation on the previous shell script:

```
#!/bin/sh
DIR=/var/log
ST=statlog
MS=/usr/ucb/mailstats
if [ -d $DIR ]; then
        cd $DIR
        if [ -s $ST -a -f $MS ]; then
                $MS -f $DIR/$ST | mail -s "Daily mail stats" postmaster
                test -f ${ST}.5 && mv ${ST}.5 ${ST}.6
                test -f ${ST}.4 && mv ${ST}.4 ${ST}.5
                test -f ${ST}.3 && mv ${ST}.3 ${ST}.4
                test -f ${ST}.2 && mv ${ST}.2 ${ST}.3
                test -f ${ST}.1 && mv ${ST}.1 ${ST}.2
                test -f ${ST}.0 && mv ${ST}.0 ${ST}.1
                test -f ${ST}    && mv ${ST}    ${ST}.0
                touch ${ST}
        fi
fi
exit 0
```

As before, the statistics are mailed to `postmaster`. But instead of being truncated, the *sendmail.st* file is renamed *sendmail.st.0*. A series of renames (*mv*(1)) are used to maintain a week's worth of copies. These copies allow the ambitious administrator to create a program for gathering weekly summaries from seven archived daily copies.

Gathering Statistics From syslog

The log files created by *syslog* provide a wealth of information that can be used to examine and tune the performance of *sendmail*. To illustrate, we will present a simple shell script for printing daily total message volume, then describe a few *perl*(1) scripts that are publicly available for performing other analyses.

In the following discussion, we will assume that *sendmail* logging is enabled (the `L` configuration option is non-zero) and that all *syslog*(8) messages for the facility `mail` at level `LOG_INFO` are being placed into the file */var/log/syslog*.

message_volume.sh

Each mail message received for delivery by *sendmail* (excluding those processed from the queue), causes *sendmail* to log a message like this:

```
month day time host sendmail[pid]: ident: from=sender, size=bytes, ...
```

That is, for each `sender` (the `from=`) logged, *sendmail* also logs the total size of the message in `bytes` (the `size=`).

By summing all the `size=` lines in a */var/log/syslog* file, we can generate the total volume of all messages for the period represented by that file. One way to generate such a total is shown in the Bourne shell script below:

```
#!/bin/sh
LOG=/var/log/syslog
TOTAL=`(echo 0;
        sed -e '/size=/!d' -e 's/.*size=//' -e 's/,.*/+/' $LOG;
        echo p;
        ) | dc`
echo Total characters sent: $TOTAL
```

The *sed*(1) selects only the lines in */var/log/syslog* that contain the expression `size=`. It then throws away all but the number immediately following each `size=` (the actual number of bytes of each message), and appends a + to each.

The entire sequence of processes is enclosed in parentheses. An *echo* statement first prints a zero. Then the list of +-suffixed sizes is printed. And finally another *echo* prints a character p. The resulting combined output might look like this:

```
0
123+
456+
7890+
p
```

The leading 0, the + suffixes, and the final p are commands for the *dc*(1) program, which adds up all the numbers (the + suffixes) and prints the total (the p). That total is saved in the variable TOTAL for later use in the final *echo* statement. The output of this simple script might look something like this:

```
Total characters sent: 8469
```

More sophisticated scripts are possible, but the Bourne shell's lack of arrays suggest that *perl*(1) would provide a more powerful scripting environment. Indeed, most of the scripts available publicly are written in the *perl* scripting language.

Available perl(1) scripts

We won't describe the *perl* language here. Instead we recommend *Programming Perl*, by Larry Wall and Randal L. Schwartz (O'Reilly & Associates, 1992).

Many scripts are available publicly via anonymous FTP, that can be used to summarize statistics found in the *syslog* file. Many can be located using the *archie*(1) program. Here, we describe two typical *perl* script programs as examples of two possible uses for the *syslog* file.

The ssl script

The *ssl* script by Tom Christiansen is available by anonymous FTP from *convex.com* in the file *pub/perl/scripts/ssl.Z*. It summarizes incoming and outgoing mail by user. The total message traffic (in bytes) and message count for each user is printed, along with the grand total for all users. Its output looks like this:

```
% ssl /var/log/syslog
To: 9
     4 messages     7740 bytes fflo@kbs.kst.ac.kr
     3 messages        0 bytes mang@cc.sic.es
     2 messages     5263 bytes kif@dbserv.aist.ac.kr
From: 7
     1 message      1484 bytes ludwig
     1 message       288 bytes george
     2 messages     4877 bytes bill@inf0.thz.ch
     3 messages     6149 bytes davids
```

The syslog-stat.pl script

The second *perl* script is by Paul Vixie. Called *syslog-stat.pl*, it is distributed with IDA *sendmail*. This script assumes that the */var/log/syslog* file is rotated daily and that the name of each copy ends with a dot and a digit:

```
syslog.0
syslog.1
syslog.2
syslog.3
syslog.4
syslog.5
syslog.6
```

The *syslog-stat.pl* script summarizes each file, printing total incoming and outgoing message statistics and the averages for sizes and delays. An example of its output is shown below:

```
% syslog-stat.pl
 Syslog    Input: (total)       (mail11)      Output Statistics:
 File Date Msgs Kbytes AvgSz  Sndrs Rcips  Sent AvgDelay Dferd Que'd
 .0 Sep 19  422   2656  6446     0     0    449  02:16     10     0
 .1 Sep 18 1362   7196  5410     0     0   1736  05:40     18     0
 .2 Sep 17 1718  11580  6902     0     0   2129  01:40     22     0
 .3 Sep 16 1691  11344  6869     0     0   2309  07:31     22     0
```

.4	Sep 15	1611	15404	9791	0	0	2301	11:52	27	0
.5	Sep 14	1926	15734	8366	0	0	2700	06:26	15	0
.6	Sep 13	900	7906	8996	0	0	1027	02:08	10	0
.7	Sep 12	641	3352	5355	0	0	890	01:18	6	0

Because *perl* scripts are scripts, they can be easily edited (even without a full understanding of *perl*) to customize them for your particular needs. It is trivial, for example, to modify the above *syslog-stat.pl* script to look elsewhere for the *syslog* files, or to use something other than ascending numeric suffixes for those files.

Pitfalls

- The *syslog*(3) library uses datagram sockets for passing information to other hosts. As a consequence, there is no guarantee that all logged information will be received by those other hosts.

- When using *m4*, exercise care to avoid using *m4* keywords in unexpected places. For example, attempting to notify a user named dnl in the *syslog.conf* file causes that name and all the text following on the same line to be lost.

- The *sendmail* program uses no record or file locking with the S option's statistics file. As a consequence, it is not guaranteed to contain 100 percent accurate information. As another consequence, statistics files should *never* be shared among multiple hosts using remote file systems. This is fixed in V8 *sendmail*.

- The location of the *sendmail.st* file is hardcoded into the *mailstats* program. Changing the location of the *sendmail.st* file with the S option may cause the *mailstats* program to thereafter always print old information. This is fixed in V8 *sendmail*.

III

Reference

The third part of this book documents the inner workings of *sendmail* and provides instructional materials and full reference listings for readers of all levels of ability.

23

The Configuration File

The *sendmail* configuration file is usually called *sendmail.cf*. It provides all the central information that controls the *sendmail* program's behavior. Among the key pieces of information provided are:

- The location of all the other files *sendmail* needs to access and the location of all the directories in which *sendmail* needs to create and remove files.

- The definitions *sendmail* uses when rewriting addresses. Some of those definitions can come from files, which are also specified.

- The mail header lines *sendmail* should modify, pass through, and/or augment.

- The rules and sets of rules *sendmail* uses for transforming mail addresses (and aliases for those addresses) into usable information, like which delivery agent to use and the correct form of the address to use with that delivery agent.

The location of the *sendmail.cf* file is compiled into *sendmail*. It is usually found in one of the directories: */etc*, */usr/lib*, or */etc/mail*. If you are compiling *sendmail*, you may specify the location of that file yourself by defining _PATH_SENDMAILCF in *pathnames.h* (or in *sendmail.h* for IDA *sendmail*). We recommend, however, that one of the standard locations be used unless you have a compelling reason to do otherwise. Nonstandard locations may, for example, make operating system upgrades difficult should you need to revert to the vendor's *sendmail*.

The configuration file is read and parsed by *sendmail* every time it starts up. Because *sendmail* is run every time electronic mail is sent, its configuration file is designed to be fast for *sendmail* to parse, rather than easy for humans to read.

Overall Syntax

The *sendmail.cf* file is line-oriented, with one configuration command per line. Each configuration command consists of a single letter* that must begin a line. Each letter is followed by other information as required by the purpose of the particular command.

In addition to commands, the configuration file may also have lines that begin with a # to form a comment line, or with a tab or space character to form a continuation line. A list of all legal characters that may begin a line in the configuration file is shown in Table 23-1.

Table 23-1: sendmail.cf Configuration Commands

Command	Description	Chapter
#	A comment line, ignored	23
space	Continue the previous line	23
tab	Continue the previous line	23
C	Define a class macro	28
D	Define a macro	27
F	Define a class macro from a file or a pipe	28
H	Define a header	31
K	Create a keyed map entry (V8 only)	29
M	Define a mail delivery agent	26
O	Define an option	30
P	Define delivery priorities	31
R	Define a transformation rule	25
S	Declare a rule-set start	24
T	Declare trusted users	18
V	Version of configuration file (V8 only)	23

*A quick bit of history: initially there was almost nothing in the configuration file except R rules (and there was only one rule set). Eric recalls adding M and O fairly quickly. Commands like T and V came quite late.

Most configuration commands are so complex that each requires a chapter or two of its own. A few, however, are simple. In the balance of this chapter, we will describe the simple ones: comments, continuation lines, and the V (version) command.

Comments

Comments provide you with the documentation necessary to maintain the configuration file. Because comments slow down *sendmail* by only a small amount, it is better to over-comment than to under-comment.

Blank lines and lines that begin with a # character are considered comments and are ignored. A blank line is one that contains no characters at all (except for its terminating newline). Indentation characters (spaces and tabs) are invisible and can turn an apparently blank line into an *empty-looking line*, which is not ignored.

```
# text           ← a comment
tabtext          ← a continuation line
                 ← a blank line
tab              ← an "empty-looking line"
```

Except for V8 *sendmail*, and two special cases, comments occupy the entire line. The two special cases are the R and S configuration commands. The R command is composed of three tab-separated fields, with the third field a comment that does not require a leading # character:

```
Rlhs      rhs      comment
```

The S command looks only for a number following it and ignores everything else, so it may also be followed by a comment:

```
S3 this is a comment
```

No other commands allow comments to follow on the same line:

```
CWlocalhost mailhost  # This won't work
```

V8 Comments

Under the new version of *sendmail* (V8), all lines of the configuration file may have optional trailing comments. That is, all text from the first # character to the end of the line is ignored. Any white space (space or tab characters) leading up to the # is also ignored:

```
CWlocalhost mailhost  # This is a comment
                     ↑
```
from here to end of line ignored

To include a # character in a line under V8 *sendmail*, precede it with a backslash:

```
DM16\#megs
```

Note that you do not need to escape the # in the $# operator. The $ has a higher precedence, and $# is interpreted correctly.

Continuation Lines

A line that begins with either a tab or a space character is considered a continuation of the preceding line. Internally, such continuation lines are joined to the preceding line, and the newline character of that preceding line is retained. Thus, for example,

```
DZzoos
        lions and bears
↑
```
line begins with a tab character

is internally joined by *sendmail* to form:

```
DZzoos\n        lions and bears
       ↑
```
newline and tab retained.

Both the newline (\n) and the tab are retained. When such a joined line is later used (as in a header), the joined line is split at the newline and prints as two separate lines again.

The V Configuration Command

The V configuration command was added to V8 *sendmail* to prevent old versions of configuration files from breaking when used with V8 *sendmail*. The syntax for the V configuration command looks like this:

```
Vlevel
```

Here, *level* is a positive integer from 0 through 5. Currently, 3 and 4 are equivalent. If *level* is higher than the maximum allowed for the current version, *sendmail* prints the following warning and accepts the value:

```
Warning: .cf version level (lev) exceeds program functionality (max)
```

If *level* is less then 0, or if the V configuration command is omitted, the default *level* is 0.

The effects of the various version levels are relatively minor. As *sendmail* continues to develop, they may become more pronounced. Currently they are:

0 or 1   A level of 0 or 1 causes *sendmail* to behave like older versions of itself. Specifically, MX records are looked up with all resolver flags set except RES_DEFNAMES and RES_DNSRCH. The high bit is always stripped from the body of every mail message.

2   A level of 2 or higher does three things: The *sendmail* program automatically adds a `-a.` to the "`host  host`" map if that map isn't declared in the configuration file (see Chapter 29, *Database Macros*); RES_DEFNAMES and RES_DNSRCH are not turned off as they were for older versions; and rule set 5 behavior is enabled.

A level of 2 or lower causes the `l` option (see Chapter 30, *Options*) to be set automatically.

3 or 4   A level 3 or higher configuration file may use the new-style comments.

5   A level 5 or higher configuration file automatically sets the `$w` macro to be the short name instead of the fully-qualified local hostname (`$j` still contains the fully-qualified name and `$m` the local domain).

Pitfalls

- Avoid accidentally creating an empty-looking line (one that contains only invisible space and tab characters) in the *sendmail.cf* file, when you really intend to create a blank line (one that contains only the newline character). The empty-looking line is joined by *sendmail* to the line above it and is likely to cause mysterious problems that are difficult to debug.

- The maximum length of any given *sendmail.cf* line of text is defined in *conf.h* as MAXLINE. That maximum length is usually 1024 characters, which includes the end-of-line character and any continuation lines. If *sendmail* reads a line that is longer than MAXLINE, it *silently* truncates that line to MAXLINE-1 and terminates the result with a zero value. Note that *sendmail* reads the entire line, but ignores the excess characters. This allows it to accurately keep track of where the next line starts. Note also that V8 *sendmail* has no limit for line lengths.

- The last line in your *sendmail.cf* file must end with a newline character. Some editors, such as *emacs*(1), are capable of writing a file in which the last line does not end with a newline character. If that trailing newline is missing from the last line, *sendmail* silently ignores it, thus treating that line as though it didn't exist. This has been fixed in V8 *sendmail.*

24

Rule Sets

Rule sets in the configuration file, like subroutines in a program, control the sequence of steps *sendmail* uses to rewrite addresses. Inside each rule set is a series of zero or more individual rules. Rules are used to select the appropriate delivery agent for any particular address, to detect and reject addressing errors, and to transform addresses to meet particular needs.

In this chapter, we will cover all aspects of rule sets, showing that rule sets are called in particular orders, and explaining why. We will illustrate the differences between pre-V8 *sendmail*, IDA, and V8. Finally, we will explain many of the rules that typically appear in rule sets.

But be forewarned: the examples of rules in this chapter are explanatory only. Your *sendmail.cf* file is likely to have rules somewhat different from these examples. Copying or using these examples, without first understanding the underlying principles (see Chapter 25, *Rules*), can cause e-mail to begin to fail.

The S Configuration Command

The S configuration command declares the start of a rule set. It is perhaps the simplest of all configuration commands and looks like this:

```
S#
```

The S, like all configuration commands, must begin the line. The # is the number of the rule set. There may be white space between the S and the #. If the # is missing or non-numeric,* the rule set defaults to 0. If the # is greater then the maximum number of rule sets allowed (MAXRWSETS in *conf.h*), or is negative, *sendmail syslog(3)*'s the following error message at the level LOG_CRIT and defaults the rule set to 0:

```
bad ruleset # (n max)
```

Here, the # is the bad rule-set number from the configuration file, and *n* is the maximum allowable rule-set number (the value of MAXRWSETS).

If # is in the correct range, all rules (R lines) which follow it are added to the rule set of that number:

```
S0
R...              ← rules added to rule set 0
S2
R...              ← rules added to rule set 2
S1
R...              ← rules added to rule set 1
```

Rule sets need not be declared in any particular order. Any order that clarifies the intention of the configuration file as a whole is acceptable. If a rule set appears more than once in a configuration file, all rules after the second declaration overwrite the rules of the first declaration:

```
S0
R...              ← rules added to rule set 0
S2
R...              ← rules added to rule set 2
S0
R...              ← rules overwrite previous rule set 0
```

Other configuration commands may be interspersed among rule definitions without affecting the rule set to which the rules are added:

---

*V8 *sendmail* prints a warning if it finds a non-numeric #.

```
S0
R...              ← rules added to rule set 0
Pjunk 100
DUuucphost.our.domain
R...              ← rules added to rule set 0
```

Any rules that appear before the first S command are added to rule set 0 by default:

```
R...              ← rules added to rule set 0
S1                ← first S command in configuration file
R...              ← rules added to rule set 1
```

Arbitrary text may follow the # in the S command. It is ignored unless it appears to be part of the number:

```
S11 1 more rule set     ← rule set 11
S111 more rule set      ← rule set 111, illegal
```

The # is interpreted internally by the *atoi*(3) C language library routine. Thus, rule-set numbers may be expressed in octal or hexadecimal:

```
S16               ← rule set 16 in decimal
S020              ← rule set 16 in octal
S0xf              ← rule set 16 in hexadecimal
```

Needless to say (unless you intend to create an obscure and unreadable configuration file), the octal and hexadecimal forms should be avoided.

A rule-set declaration that has no rules associated with it is exactly the same as a rule set that is not declared. Both are like "do-nothing" subroutines.

```
                  ← rule set 1 not declared. Same as
S2                ← rule set 2 without rules
S3
R...
```

The Sequence of Rule Sets

When *sendmail* rewrites addresses, it applies its rule sets in a specific sequence. The sequence differs for sender and recipient addresses, with a third branch used to select delivery agents. Figure 24-1 shows a map of the different paths taken by each kind of address. Those paths show how addresses flow through rule sets.

Both sender and recipient addresses are first input into rule set 3. Then each takes a different path through the rule sets based on its type. Recipient addresses take the dashed path, whereas sender addresses take the solid path. But before those paths can be taken, *sendmail* needs to select a delivery agent (the dotted path) to get rule-set numbers for the R= and S= of each path.

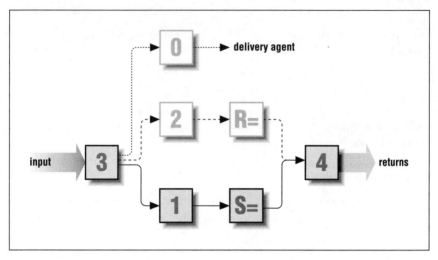

Figure 24-1: The flow of rules through rule sets

To select a delivery agent, *sendmail* rewrites the recipient address with rule sets 3 and 0 (the dotted path in Figure 24-1). Rule set 0 selects a delivery agent appropriate for the recipient. That delivery agent supplies rule set values for the S= and R= in the corresponding sender (solid) and recipient (dashed) paths.

After a delivery agent has been selected, the sender address is processed (Figure 24-2). As mentioned above, it is first input into rule set 3. Then it flows through rule set 1, then the S= rule set as determined by the delivery agent. Finally, it flows through rule set 4, which returns the rewritten address. This rewritten sender address appears in the header and envelope of the mail message.

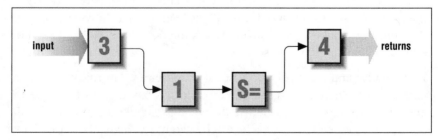

Figure 24-2: The flow of sender addresses through rule sets

Note that all addresses are eventually rewritten by rule set 4. In general, rule set 4 undoes any special rewriting that rule set 3 did.

Lastly, the recipient address also needs to be rewritten for inclusion in the header and envelope of mail messages (Figure 24-3). Recall that it was already used once to select the delivery agent. It is used as input to rule set 3, as are all addresses. It then flows through rule set 2, then the R= rule set selected by the delivery agent, and finally through rule set 4.

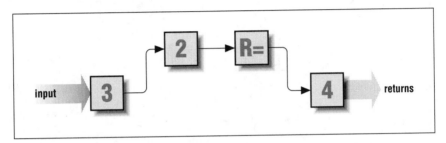

Figure 24-3: The flow of recipient addresses through rule sets

The need for separate paths for the sender and the recipient is best explained with an example. Consider a site that wants the addresses of all local users to appear as though they are "from" the local domain. Such rewriting is appropriate for local users on outgoing mail, but inappropriate for recipients at other sites. Clearly such rewriting should be restricted to the sender path, probably in rule set 1.

The flow of rules through rule sets (as was shown in Figure 24-1) is appropriate for *all* versions of *sendmail*. Some versions, like V8 and IDA, enhance these rules with others, but all those enhancements begin with this basic set.

IDA Enhancements

Header addresses and envelope addresses normally flow through the same sequence of rule sets. Although this treatment is appropriate for Internet-based mail, it is not appropriate for UUCP-based mail. To satisfy the need for UUCP support, IDA *sendmail* can pass header addresses through one series of rules and envelope addresses through another. Figure 24-4 shows that under IDA *sendmail*, header addresses are rewritten by different rules (the dashed sequence) than are envelope addresses (the solid sequence).

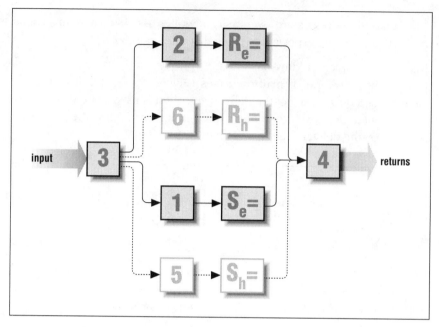

Figure 24-4: IDA splits rewriting: envelope (solid) versus header (dashed)

This splitting of envelope and header paths through the rule sets is not automatic. To enable it, the / option must be declared in the configuration file. Note that you should avoid setting this option to true when using a non-IDA configuration file with the IDA version of *sendmail*. In non-IDA configuration files, rule sets 5 and 6 are likely to be wrong for this use.

In addition to allowing the use of two different paths through rule sets, the S= and R= equates of delivery agents may also allow the use of different rules for rewriting envelope addresses (the e subscript) and header addresses (the h subscript). These equates, and how they differ from non-IDA equates, are described in Chapter 26, *Delivery Agents.*

V8 Enhancements

V8 *sendmail* allows envelope addresses to be rewritten separately from header addresses. This separation takes place in the delivery agent R= and S= specific rule sets as illustrated in Figure 24-5.

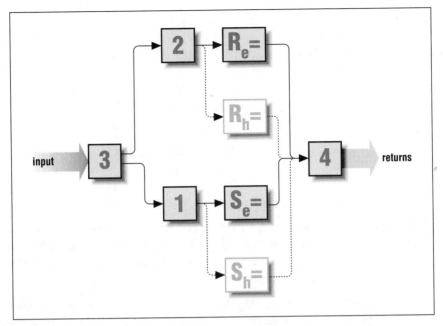

Figure 24-5: V8 splits rewriting: envelope (solid) versus header (dashed)

The method used to split rewriting is described in Chapter 26.

V8 Rule Set 5 Enhancement

For version 2 and higher configuration files (see the V configuration command in Chapter 23, *The Configuration File*), V8 *sendmail* allows local recipients to undergo additional rewriting. Recall that each recipient address is processed by rule sets 3 and 0 to select a delivery agent. If the delivery agent is `local`, that recipient then undergoes aliasing (via the *aliases* and the ˜/.*forward* files) which may result in a local address.

Under V8 *sendmail*, if a local address makes it through aliasing unchanged, it is given to rule set 5, which may select a new delivery agent. A new delivery agent might be needed in the case of a mail *firewall* machine, for example. A firewall machine is one that sits between the local network and the outside world, and protects the local network from intrusion by outsiders. In such an arrangement, it may be desirable for all incoming mail to be delivered to the firewall so that no outsider needs to know the real names of machines on the local network.

Consider mail to the address *john@firewall.* On the firewall machine, rule set 3 recognizes the host part as local and throws away the *@firewall.* Rule set 0 then selects the `local` delivery agent. Because the address *john* is local, it is looked up in the *aliases* file. For this example, it is not found there. The user's */.forward* file would be examined next, but user home directories are not visible to the firewall machine.

Because the address *john* is not aliased, it is passed to rule set 5, which selects another delivery agent to forward the message into the local network:

```
S5
R$-      $#TCP $@hub.internal.net $:$1
```

Here, the *john* matches the `$-` in the LHS, so the `TCP` delivery agent is selected. The mail message is forwarded to the local network with *john* (the `$1`) as the username, and `hub.internal.net` as the name of the receiving machine on the internal network.

For such a scheme to work, all local machines must send off-site mail addressed as though it were from the firewall, and local names must be changed to off-site forms when forwarded off site. For example, the name *john@local.host* needs to be changed to *john@firewall* for all outgoing off-site mail.

For those times when rule set 5 may not be appropriate, V8 *sendmail* offers a technique for bypassing it. In rule set 0, if the first token following the `$:` of a rule that selects the `local` delivery agent is an `@`, *sendmail* removes the `@` and skips calling rule set 5:

```
R$-      $#local $: @ $1
                    ↑
```
removed and rule set 5 skipped

Note that rule set 5 is not limited to use for firewalls. It can also be used as a hook into forwarding to other types of networks, or with special mailing list software, or even as a way to handle retired accounts.

Rule Set 3

Rule set 3 is the first to process every address. It puts each into a form that simplifies the tasks of other rule sets. The most common method is to have rule set 3 *focus* an address (place angle brackets around the host part). Then later rules don't have to search for the host part, because it is already highlighted. For example, consider trying to spot the recipient host in this mess:

```
uuhost!user%host1%host2
```

Here, `user` is eventually intended to receive the mail message on the host `uuhost`. But where should *sendmail* send the message first? As it happens, *sendmail* selects `uuhost`. Focusing on this address therefore results in the following:

```
user%host1%host2<@uuhost.uucp>
```

Note that `uuhost` was moved to the end, the `!` changed to an `@`, and `.uucp` appended. The `@` is there so that all focused parts uniformly contain an `@` just before the targeted host. Later, when we take up post-processing, we'll show how rule set 4 moves the `uuhost` back to the beginning and replaces the `!`.

A Special Case: From:<>

The first rule in a typical rule set 3 handles addresses that are composed of empty angle brackets. These represent the special case of an empty or nonexistent address. Empty addresses should be turned into the address of the pseudo-user who bounces mail, *Mailer-Daemon*.

```
# handle "from:<>" special case
R$*<>$*      @       empty becomes special
```

Here, empty angle brackets, no matter what surrounds them (`$*`), are rewritten to be a lone `@`. Rule set 0 later turns this special token into `$n` (which contains *Mailer-Daemon* as its value).

Basic Textual Canonicalization

Addresses can be legally expressed in only four formats:

```
address
address (full name)
<address>
full name <address>
```

When *sendmail* preprocesses an address that is in the second format, it removes (and saves for later use) the full name from within the parentheses. The last two formats, however, contain additional characters and information that are not discarded during preprocessing. As a consequence, rule set 3 must take on the job of discarding the unwanted information.

```
# basic textual canonicalization
R$*<$*<$*<$*>$*>$*>$*      $4          3-level <> nesting
R$*<$*<$*>$*>$*            $3          2-level <> nesting
R$*<$*>$*                  $2          basic RFC821/822 parsing
```

Here, we discard everything outside of and including the innermost pair of angle brackets. Three rules are required to do this because of the minimal-matching nature of the LHS operators. Consider trying to de-nest a three-level workspace using only a rule like the third:

```
the workspace →   A < B < C < D > C > B > A
$*    matches → A
<     matches → <
$+    matches → B < C < D
>     matches → >
$*    matches → C > B > A
```

Clearly the result B<C<D is not the value between the innermost pair of angle brackets and will result in an address that produces the error message:

```
Unbalanced '<'
```

A clever* alternative to the above rules is offered in the IDA distribution of *sendmail.* In its *Sendmail.mc* master configuration file are the following lines:

```
# The next four rules come from nahaj@cc.utah.edu.  They are intended
# to transform "Name" <mailbox> "Phone number" into just mailbox
# But they must deal with extra level of <brackets> that are sometimes
# incorrectly added.  They must also deal with the fact that sendmail
# processes left to right, and becomes unhappy with anything not having
# <balanced brackets>.
R$*<$*>$*<$*>$*      <$2>$3$4$5        Remove right branches.
R$*<$*<$*>$*>$*      <$3>$5            Trim left branches.
R$*<>$*              $n                default user
R$*<$*>$*            $2                Last level
```

Observe that in each iteration of the second rule, only a single pair of angle brackets is removed, leaving the result properly balanced at each stage. That rule will correctly de-nest a virtually unlimited number of nested angle bracket pairs.

---

*Designed by John Halleck, it is so clever that it is now included in the V8 configuration files.

Handling Routing Addresses

The *sendmail* program must be able to handle addresses that are in *route address* syntax. Such addresses are in the form *@A,@B:user@C* (which means mail should first be sent to *A*, then from *A* to *B*, and finally from *B* to *C*). The commas are converted to colons for easier design of subsequent rules. They must be converted back to commas by rule set 4. Rule set 3 uses a simple rule to convert all commas to colons:

```
# make sure list syntax is easy to parse
R@$+,$+        @$1:$2          change all "," to ":"
```

The recursive nature of rules comes into play here. As long as there is an @ followed by anything ($+), then a comma, then anything, this rule repeats, converting the comma to a colon. The result is then carried down to the next rule which focuses:

```
R@$+:$+        $@<@$1>:$2      focus route-addr
```

Once that host has angle brackets placed around it (is focused), the job of rule set 3 ends, and it exits (the $@ prefix in the RHS).

Handling Specialty Addresses

A whole book is dedicated to the myriad forms of addressing that might face a site administrator: *!%@:: A Directory of Electronic Mail Addressing & Networks* by Donnalyn Frey and Rick Adams (O'Reilly & Associates, 1993). We won't duplicate that work here; rather, we point out that most such addresses are handled nicely by existing configuration files. To illustrate, consider the format of a DECnet address:

```
host::user
```

One approach to handling such an address in rule set 3 is to convert it into the Internet *user@host.domain* form:

```
R$+::$+        $@$2@$1.decnet
```

Here we reverse the host and user and put them into Internet form. The .decnet can later be used by rule set 0 to select an appropriate delivery agent.

This is a simple example of a special address problem from the many that can develop. In addition to DECnet, for example, your site may have to deal with Xerox *Grapevine* addresses, X.400 addresses, or UUCP addresses. The best way to handle such addresses is to copy what others have done. The IDA *Sendmail.mc* prototype file, for example, includes rules for almost any form of address that currently exists.

Focusing for @ Syntax

The last few rules in our illustration of rule set 3 are used to process the Internet-style *user@domain* address:

```
# find focus for @ syntax addresses
R$+@$+              $:$1<@$2>        focus on domain
R$+<$+@$+>          $1$2<@$3>        move gaze right
R$+<@$+>            $@$1<@$2>        already focused
```

For an address like *something@something*, the first rule focuses on all the tokens following the first @ as the name of the host. Recall that the $: prefix to the RHS prevents potentially infinite recursion. Assuming the workspace started with:

```
user@host1@host2
```

This first rewrite results in:

```
user<@host1@host2>
```

The second rule (move gaze right) then attempts to fine-tune the focus by making sure only the rightmost @host is selected. This rule can move the focus right using recursion and can handle addresses that are as extreme as:

```
user<@host1@host2@host3@host4>  becomes → user@host1@host2@host3<@host4>
```

The third rule checks to see if the workspace has been focused. If it has, it returns the focused workspace (the $@ prefix in the RHS), and its job is done.

Any address that has not been handled by rule set 3 is unchanged and probably not focused. Because rule set 0 expects all addresses to be focused so that it can select appropriate delivery agents, such unfocused addresses will probably bounce.

Rule Set 4

Just as all addresses are first rewritten by rule set 3, so are all addresses rewritten last by rule set 4. Its job is to undo any special processing done by rule set 3, such as focusing. In this section, we'll examine some typical rule set 4 rules.

Resolving Numeric Addresses

After an address is processed by the other rules, rule set 4 may need to convert it from an IP number into a fully-qualified domain name. (This conversion often appears in rule set 3 too.) Addresses that are IP numbers are those that are surrounded in square brackets; for example:

```
[123.4.5.6]
```

In the following rule, the $[and $] operators are used to perform the conversion:

```
# resolve numeric addresses to name if possible
R$*<@[$+]>$*    $:$1<@$[[$2]$]>$3        look up numeric internet addr
```

This tries to convert the numeric form of a name, such as *[123.4.5.6]*, into its canonical form, such as *fbi.dc.gov*. Notice that the LHS looks for a focused host part that is surrounded by square brackets. Again, the $: prefix to the RHS prevents recursion should the conversion fail and leave the square brackets in place.

Stripping Trailing Dots

Under some versions of *sendmail*, a successful conversion to a fully-qualified domain name leaves an extra dot trailing the result. The following rule strips that dot.

```
# strip trailing dot off possibly canonical name
R$*<@$+.>$*        $1<@$2>$3
```

Note that this rule recursively removes as many trailing dots as it finds. Also note that the host part remains focused after rewriting.

Restoring Source Routes

Recall that rule set 3 converted the commas of source route addresses into colons. Rule set 4 now needs to restore those commas:

```
R$*:$+:$+<@$+>    $1,$2:$3<@$4>            <route-addr> canonical
```

This rule recursively changes all but one (the rightmost) colon back into a comma.

Removing Focus

Rule set 4 also removes the angle brackets that were inserted by rule set 3 to focus on the host part of the address. This is necessary because mail fails if they are left in place.

```
# externalize local domain info
R$*<$+>$*          $1$2$3                        defocus
```

Correcting Tags

After defocusing, rule set 4 may need to convert some addresses back to their original forms. For example, consider UUCP addresses. They entered rule set 3 in the form *host!host!user*. Rule set 3 rewrote them in the more normal *user@host* form, and added a `.uucp` to the end of the host. The following rule in rule set 4 converts such normalized UUCP addresses back to their original form.

```
# UUCP must always be presented in old form
R$+@$-.uucp          $2!$1                        u@h.UUCP => h!u
```

Rule Set 0

The job of rule set 0 is to select a delivery agent for each recipient. It is called once for each recipient and must rewrite each into a special form called a *triple*. A triple is simply three pieces of information: the symbolic name of the delivery agent, the host part of the address, and the user part of the address. Each part is indicated in the RHS by a special prefix operator, as shown in Table 24-1.

Table 24-1: Rule Set 0 Special RHS Operators

Operator	Description
$#	Delivery agent
$@	Recipient host
$:	Recipient user

The triple is formed by rewriting with the RHS. It looks like this:

```
$#delivery_agent $@host $:user
```

The delivery agent selection must be the first of the three. In addition to specifying the delivery agent, $# also causes rule set 0 to exit. The other two parts of the triple must appear in the order shown ($@ first, then $:).

All three parts of the triple must be present in the RHS. The only exception is the $@*host* part when the delivery agent has the F=l flag set. It *may* be present for IDA and V8 *sendmail*, but must be absent for all other versions of *sendmail*.

Not all rules in rule set 0 are specifically used to select a delivery agent. It may be necessary, for example, to canonicalize an address with $[and $] before being able to decide if the address is local or remote.

If an address passes through rule set 0 without selecting a delivery agent, the following error message is produced, and the mail message bounces:

```
cannot resolve name
```

Thus it is important to design a rule set 0 that selects a delivery agent for every legitimate address.

If a triple is missing the user part, the following error is produced:

```
buildaddr: error: no user
```

If the delivery agent selected is one for which there is no corresponding M configuration file declaration, the error is:

```
buildaddr: unknown mailer bad delivery agent name here
```

Further Processing: $:user

The user part of the triple is intended for use in the command line of the delivery agent and in the RCPT command in an SMTP connection. For either use, that address is rewritten by rule set 2, the R= equate of the delivery agent, and rule set 4, as illustrated in Figure 24-6. This means that the user part can be in focused form, because the focus is later removed by rule set 4. But, the user part *must* be a single username (no host) for the local delivery agent.

The rewritten result is stored for use when a delivery agent's $u command-line argument is expanded. The rewritten result is, for example, the username as it will be given to */bin/mail* for local delivery.

The rewritten result is also given to a remote site during the exchange of mail using the SMTP protocol. The local machine tells the remote machine the name of the recipient by saying RCPT to: followed by the rewritten user portion of the triple.

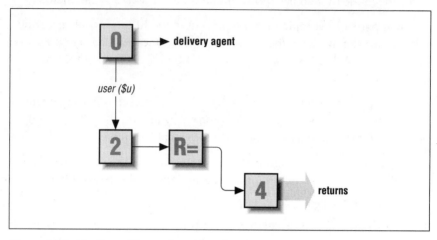

Figure 24-6: The flow of $:user through rule sets

Selecting S= and R=

When it selects a delivery agent, rule set 0 also selects the rules that will be used in rewriting sender and recipient addresses. A sender address is rewritten by the rule set specified by the S= equate. The recipient addresses are rewritten by the rule set specified by the R= equate.

If the R= or S= specifies rule set 0, or if either is undeclared, then that portion of rewriting is skipped.

We won't cover individual R= or S= rule sets here, because they depend on the individual needs of delivery agents. Instead, we recommend that you examine how your configuration file uses them. You'll probably be surprised to find that many R= and S= equates reference nonexistent rules (which means that *sendmail* will do no rewriting).

Delivering to Local Recipient

Typically, the first few rules in rule set 0 are intended to detect addresses that should be delivered locally. A rule that accomplishes that end might look like this:

```
    R$+<@$w>          $#local $:$1                  local address
```

Here the $w macro is the name of the local host. Note that the RHS strips the focused host part from the username.

At some sites, the local host can be known by any of several names. A rule to handle such hosts would begin with a class declaration that adds those names to the class w (like the first line below):

```
Cw font-server fax printer3
R$+<@$=w>          $#local $:$1                      local address
```

The class w is special because it is the one to which *sendmail* automatically appends the alternative name of the local host. The class declaration line above adds names that *sendmail* might not automatically detect. Usually, such a declaration would be near the top of the configuration file, rather than in rule set 0, but technically it can appear anywhere in the file. This rule looks to see if an address contains any of the names in class w. If it does, the $=w in the LHS matches and the RHS selects the local delivery agent.

On central mail server machines, rule set 0 may also have to match from a list of hosts for which the central server is an MX recipient machine.

Forwarding to a Knowledgeable Host

After handling mail destined for the local host, rule set 0 generally looks for addresses that require a knowledgeable host to forward messages on the local host's behalf. In the following rule, $B is the name of a machine that knows how to deliver BITNET mail:

```
R$*<@$+.BITNET>$*    $#smtp $@$B $:$1<@$2.BITNET>$3    user@host.BITNET
```

The tag .BITNET would have been added by users when sending mail. Note that BITNET in the LHS is case-insensitive: a user can specify Bitnet, bitnet, or even BiTNeT, and this rule will still match. A similar scheme can be used for other specialty addresses, like UUCP and DECnet.

Handling UUCP Locally

Hosts sometimes deliver mail to a few UUCP connections locally and forward to other UUCP connections through a knowledgeable host. The rules that handle this situation make use of another class.

```
R$*<@$=U.UUCP>      $#uucp $@$2 $:$1                  user@localuucp
R$*<@$+.UUCP>       $#smtp $@$B $:$1<@$2.UUCP>        kick upstairs
```

Here, the class U contains a list of local UUCP connections. They are matched by the first rule, which selects the uucp delivery agent. All other UUCP addresses are passed to the knowledgeable host in $B (kicked upstairs). The user part ($:) given to the knowledgeable host is the original address as it appeared to the LHS.

Forwarding Over the Network

Next, rule set 0 typically sees if it can send the mail message over the network. In the following example, we assume the local host is connected to an IP network:

```
# deal with other remote names
R$*<@$*>$*        $#smtp $@$2 $:$1<@$2>$3        user@host.domain
```

Remember that we have already screened out and handled delivery to the local host, and therefore the focused host (in the <@$*> of the LHS) is on the network. The smtp delivery agent is selected (to deliver using the SMTP protocol), with connection to be made to $2 (the $* part of the <@$*> in the LHS).

The focus is kept in the user portion of the RHS triple. Remember that the user portion will be rewritten by rule sets 2, R=, and 4. Also remember that rule set 4 will defocus the address. The reason we keep the focus here is because rule set 2 and all R= rules expect the host part of addresses to be focused.

Handling Leftover Local Addresses

Whatever is left after all the preceding rules in rule set 0 have selected delivery agents is probably a local address. Here we check for a username without a host part:

```
R$+       $#local $:$1        regular local names
```

Notice that the user part is not focused; it is unfocused because there is no host part on lone local usernames.

Rule Set 2

All recipient addresses are rewritten by rule set 2 and the R= of delivery agents. But in almost all configuration files, rule set 2 is unused because no processing is needed:

```
# Recipient processing: none needed
S2
```

But note that rule set 2 can be used to debug rules. Consider the following rule in rule set 2:

```
R$#$+$:$+    $:$2    Strip delivery agent and host when debugging
```

Recall that rule set 0 returns a triple. When testing an address, rule set 2 can be called following rule set 0 to simulate the rewriting of the user portion of rule set 0. Here the LHS matches only a triple, so normal recipient addresses are unaffected. The user part returned by the RHS can then be used to test individual R= rules of delivery agents.

Rule Set 1

Rule set 1 is intended to process all sender addresses. It is rarely used, but can find application at sites where all outgoing mail should appear to come from a central mail server. Rules to handle this "host hiding" might look like this:

```
R$-              $@$1<@$R>           user => user@ourdomain
R$*<@$=w>$*      $@$1<@$R>$3         user@localhost => user@ourdomain
```

In the LHS, the $=w matches any name from a list of names by which the local host is known. In the RHS, the $R contains the name of the mail server. If the mail is not from the local host, it is unchanged.

Other uses for rule set 1 might include:

- Normalizing senders; for example, making mail from the users *operator* and *dumper* appear to come from *root*.
- Hiding user login names by mapping them (through an external database) to the form *firstname.lastname*.

Needless to say, great care should be exercised when adding schemes such as these to your configuration file.

Rule Set Testing With −bt

The *sendmail* program offers a mode of operation (called rule-testing mode) that allows you to observe the flow of addresses through rule sets. The −bt command-line switch causes *sendmail* to run in rule-set testing mode. This mode is interactive. You enter rule-set numbers and addresses, and *sendmail* processes them and prints the results. The −bt switch's chief use is in testing changes in the configuration file. It is also useful for learning how rules and rule sets work. The following command runs *sendmail* in rule-testing mode:

```
% /usr/lib/sendmail -bt
```

Other switches may also be used in the command line (like −d; see Chapter 33, *Debugging With −d*), but any addresses on the command line are ignored.

Rule 3 Always Called First With −bt

When *sendmail* starts to run in rule-testing mode, its appearance and initial behavior vary from vendor to vendor and from version to version. When rule-testing mode begins, *sendmail* always prints an introductory banner. SunOS *sendmail* prints the following banner:

```
ADDRESS TEST MODE
Enter <ruleset> <address>
>
```

It is important to note that unless a version of *sendmail* says otherwise, it always calls rule set 3 first. That is, even if you try to test rule set 0, you always first see the effects of rule set 3. Newer versions of *sendmail* do not automatically call rule set 3 first. To ensure that there is no confusion, they announce this fact. IDA *sendmail* prints the following:

```
ADDRESS TEST MODE
Enter <ruleset> <address>
[Note: No initial ruleset 3 call]
>
```

V8 *sendmail* prints this message:

```
ADDRESS TEST MODE (ruleset 3 NOT automatically invoked)
Enter <ruleset> <address>
>
```

Note that in all three versions, the last line is a > prompt. At this prompt, you can specify a rule set and an address. The *sendmail* program shows how it rewrites that address using the specified rule set. An example under IDA *sendmail* (which does not call rule set 3 first) follows:

```
ADDRESS TEST MODE
Enter <ruleset> <address>
[Note: No initial ruleset 3 call]
> 0 bill
rewrite: ruleset  0    input: bill
rewrite: ruleset  0 returns: $# local $: bill
>
```

Here, 0 is specified as the rule set, and bill as the address. IDA *sendmail* then prints the address as it was rewritten by rule set 0, which selected the local delivery agent.

Under old versions of *sendmail*, the same rule set and address are handled differently:

```
ADDRESS TEST MODE
Enter <ruleset> <address>
> 0 bill
rewrite: ruleset  3    input: "bill"  ← note, rule set 3 called 1st
rewrite: ruleset  3 returns: "bill"  ← note
rewrite: ruleset  0    input: "bill"
rewrite: ruleset  0 returns: $# "local" $: "bill"
>
```

Note here that rule set 3 is called first, even though it is not specified at the > prompt. This behavior is a carryover from the original version of *sendmail* (when only a single rule set could be specified at the prompt). Since rule set 3 was always called first in rule-set processing, it made sense to insert it artificially before any other rule set. As *sendmail* evolved, however, it became possible to specify multiple rule sets at the prompt. But the initial rule set 3 call had by then become traditional and, until recently, was retained.

Syntax of –bt

The > prompt expects rule sets and addresses to be specified like this:

```
> num,num,num... address
```

Each *num* is a rule-set number. When there is more than one rule-set number, they must be separated from each other by commas (with no spaces between them). Individual rule-set numbers must be in the range of 0 through the highest number of a rule set in the configuration file. Any that are out of range (less than zero or greater than the number in the configuration file) cause *sendmail* either to produce a core dump or to treat the rule set as one without rules.

If the number of any rule set in the comma-separated list of rule sets is omitted (e.g. *num,,num*), *sendmail* interprets the missing rule as rule set 0. The address is everything following the first white space (space and tab characters) to the end of the line. If white-space characters appear anywhere in the list of rule sets, the rule sets to the right of the white space are interpreted as part of the address.

The Address

Each address that is specified at the > prompt is processed by *sendmail* in the same way that mail addresses are processed when actual mail is being sent. Each is parsed and normalized to throw away everything but the actual address. Each is then tokenized and placed into the workspace for rule-set processing. To illustrate, observe the following rule-testing session:

```
ADDRESS TEST MODE (ruleset 3 NOT automatically invoked)
Enter <ruleset> <address>
> 0 bill (Bill Bix)
rewrite: ruleset  0   input: "bill"
rewrite: ruleset  0 returns: $# "local" $: "bill"
> 0 Bill Bix <bill>
rewrite: ruleset  0   input: "Bill" "Bix" "<" "bill" ">"
rewrite: ruleset  0 returns: $# "local" $: "Bill" "Bix" "<" "bill" ">"
> 3,0 Bill Bix <bill>
rewrite: ruleset  3   input: "Bill" "Bix" "<" "bill" ">"
rewrite: ruleset  3 returns: "bill"
rewrite: ruleset  0   input: "bill"
rewrite: ruleset  0 returns: $# "local" $: "bill"
>
```

The first test illustrates that *sendmail* strips RFC822-style comments from addresses before tokenizing them. This results in the (Bill Bix) being thrown away so that rule set 0 sees only the address bill.

The second test illustrates that *sendmail* does not internally recognize addresses in angle brackets. Instead, rule set 3 must throw away everything but the address in angle brackets, as shown in the third test.

Note that in many actual configuration files, rule set 3 also focuses on the host part of the address.

The Output Produced by −bt

Each line of output produced in rule-testing mode begins with an indication of the rule-set number being processed:

```
rewrite: ruleset  3   input: "Bill" "Bix" "<" "bill" ">"
```

The word `input` precedes each address that is about to be processed by a rule set:

```
rewrite: ruleset  3   input: "Bill" "Bix" "<" "bill" ">"
```

The word `returns` precedes each address that is the result of rewriting by a rule set:

```
rewrite: ruleset  3 returns: "bill"
```

When rule sets call other rule sets as subroutines, those calls are shown in the output with `input` and `returns` pairs. In the following, rule set 11 is called as a subroutine rule set from inside rule set 3:

```
rewrite: ruleset  3   input: "Bill" "Bix" "<" "bill" ">"
rewrite: ruleset  11  input: "bill"
rewrite: ruleset  11 returns: "bill"
rewrite: ruleset  3   returns: "bill"
```

The output can also contain rule-set operators:

```
rewrite: ruleset  0 returns: $# "local" $: "bill"
```

In this output, the operators are printed as they would appear in the configuration file. The `$#` selects a delivery agent, and the `$:` specifies the user. Under old versions of *sendmail*, those operators are printed in the output as control characters:

```
rewrite: ruleset  0 returns: ^V "local" ^X "bill"
```

The correspondence between control characters in the output and *sendmail* configuration file operators is given in Table 24-2.

Table 24-2: Control Characters Versus Operators

Control	Operator	Meaning
^V	$#	Select delivery agent
^W	$@	Specify host for delivery agent
^X	$:	Specify user for delivery agent

Bypassing Rule Set 3 With –bt

Unless you are using IDA or V8 *sendmail*, you may sometimes need to test individual rules without having them automatically preceded by rule set 3. We offer two approaches to satisfy this need.

A permanent $1.testing

Your configuration file can be permanently changed to allow rule set 3 to be bypassed for specially constructed addresses. Using this approach, special addresses can be tested with your production configuration file, while leaving normal mail unaffected. The modification is:

```
S3
R$*.testing    $@$1    bypass rule set 3 for testing
...rest of rule set 3 here
```

This new rule (now the first rule under rule set 3) looks for any address that ends with `.testing`. If such an address is found, it strips off the `.testing` and skips the rest of rule set 3. To illustrate its use, consider the following rule-testing run done with this modification in place. In it, we are trying to find out why rule set 11 is unable to strip the hostname.

```
ADDRESS TEST MODE
Enter <ruleset> <address>
> 11 bill@ourhost
rewrite: ruleset   3    input: "bill" "@" "ourhost"
rewrite: ruleset   3 returns: "bill" "<" "@" "ourhost" ">"
rewrite: ruleset  11    input: "bill" "<" "@" "ourhost" ">"
rewrite: ruleset  11 returns: "bill" "<" "@" "ourhost" ">"
> 11 bill@ourhost.testing
rewrite: ruleset   3    input: "bill" "@" "ourhost" "." "testing"
rewrite: ruleset   3 returns: "bill" "@" "ourhost"
rewrite: ruleset  11    input: "bill" "@" "ourhost"
rewrite: ruleset  11 returns: "bill"
>
```

Here, we first give *sendmail* a normal address. Rule set 3 focuses on the host part by surrounding it with angle brackets. After that, rule set 11 gets the address. It is supposed to remove the host part, but doesn't. Then we give *sendmail* the testing form of an address (the `.testing`). This time, rule set 3 does not focus and rule set 11 succeeds in removing the host part. This shows that rule set 11 is not properly written. It needs to expect the host part to be surrounded in angle brackets.*

---

*It also shows that rule set 3 should always be called first (even with the new *sendmail* programs) unless you are expert at testing rules.

A temporary bypass

An alternative to the permanent patch to rule set 3 is the following temporary one. The advantage to this approach is that it works for all addresses and doesn't require a .testing address. A disadvantage is that you *must* remember to remove it when done. Accidently leaving it in will cause all mail to fail mysteriously.

The temporary patch is a single rule inserted at the start of rule set 3:

```
S3
R$*     $@$1        WARNING!!!!! Remember to remove me!!!!
...remainder of rule set three here
```

This causes rule set 3 to always return the workspace unchanged. It is useful for debugging occasional rule problems, but should probably never be used in your production version of the configuration file, lest it be accidently left in place.

More Detail: −d Combined With −bt

In rule-testing mode, the −d debugging switch (see Chapter 33, *Debugging With −d*) can reveal in great detail how individual rules are being handled. Specifying a debugging category and level of 21.12, for example, causes *sendmail* to print the LHS of each rule as it is tried. To illustrate, consider the following (very simplified) configuration-file rule set:

```
S0
R@                    $#local $:$n                 handle <> form
R$*<@$+>$*            $#$M $@$R $:$1<@$2>$3         user@some.where
R$+                   $#local $:$1                  local names
```

The processing done by the rules in this rule set can be observed by running *sendmail* with the following command:

```
% /usr/lib/sendmail -d21.12 -bt
```

As shown below, the output produced when a rule-set number and address are entered at the > prompt is more verbose than it would be sans the −d switch:

```
Version 8.2
ADDRESS TEST MODE (ruleset 3 NOT automatically invoked)
Enter <ruleset> <address>
> 0 george
rewrite: ruleset  0   input: "george"
-----trying rule: "@"
----- rule fails
-----trying rule: $* "<" "@" $+ ">" $*
----- rule fails
```

```
-----trying rule: $+
-----rule matches: $# "local" $: $1
rewritten as: $# "local" $: "george"
rewrite: ruleset  0 returns: $# "local" $: "george"
>
```

Observe that the first rule in rule set 0 (the lone @) does not match george in the workspace. Thus, that rule fails and is skipped. Then the more complicated rule ($*<@$+>$*) is tried, and it too fails. Finally the $+ operator in the last rule matches george, and the workspace is rewritten.

Note that the extra output produced by −d can potentially run to many lines To capture the output for later examination, consider running *sendmail* in rule-testing mode from within a *script*(1), *emacs*(1), or similar session.

Higher levels of debugging are also available for examining rules and rule sets. The level −d21.15 shows $*digit* operators on the RHS being substituted with values from the LHS. The level −d21.35 causes each comparison, token versus token, to be printed. These and other levels are detailed in Chapter 33, *Debugging With −d*.

A trick

When debugging large configuration files, the output produced by the −d21.15 switch can become too huge to examine conveniently. As an alternative (when modifying or inserting individual rules), a fake subroutine call can be temporarily inserted before and after individual rules to see what they do.

```
R$*      $:$>18 $1      ← fake subroutine call
Rlhs     rhs            ← new rule
R$*      $:$>18 $1      ← fake subroutine call
```

Here, the number 18 is arbitrary. The number of the subroutine chosen must be that of a nonexistent rule set.

With the fake wrapper around the new rule, ordinary rule testing with −bt shows how the address is rewritten by that rule.

```
rewrite: ruleset  3   input: ...
rewrite: ruleset 18   input: ...
rewrite: ruleset 18 returns: ...
                              ← new rule acted here
rewrite: ruleset 18   input: ...
rewrite: ruleset 18 returns: ...
rewrite: ruleset  3 returns: ...
>
```

If you use this technique, remember to remove the fake subroutine calls before putting that configuration file into use.

Batch Rule-set Testing With −bt

The output produced by *sendmail* can become huge, especially when many addresses need testing. To simplify the process (and to help bullet-proof your configuration file), consider using a shell script like the following:

```
#!/bin/sh
/usr/lib/sendmail -bt < $1 | awk '\
      !/^>/ {L = $0} \
      /^>/  {print L; print ""; print substr($0, 3, 256)}' \
   | sed   -e 's/^rewrite: ruleset  //' \
           -e 's/" "//g' \
           -e 's/" //g' \
           -e 's/ "//g' \
           -e 's/"//g'
```

Here, the output is piped through a simple *awk*(1) script. The text following the prompt is printed, then a blank line, then the previous line of *sendmail* output. The *sed*(1) program then throws away the leading `rewrite:` text and any quotes (to detokenize the address).

If this script were to be called *testcf.sh*, it could be invoked with the following command line:

```
% testcf.sh address.list
```

Here, the `address.list` is a file consisting of pairs of rule-set numbers and addresses like the following:

```
0 nobody@ourhost
0 nobody@ourhost.domain
0 nobody@somehost.bitnet
  ... and so on
```

The output produced shows the input to rule set 3* and the delivery agent returned by rule set 0:

```
Enter <ruleset> <address>

3   input: nobody@ourhost
0 returns: $#local$:nobody

3   input: nobody@ourhost.domain
0 returns: $#local$:nobody

3   input: nobody@somehost.bitnet
0 returns: $#ether$@forwarder$:nobody<@somehost.BITNET>
```

---

*The leading 0 will need to be changed to 3 , 0 for IDA and V8 *sendmail* programs.

The `address.list` file should contain every conceivable kind of address. The output from the shell script should be saved. At a later time, after changing the configuration file, *diff*(1) can be used to see if the saved output differs from the new output (to see if anything broke).

Other packages are available for testing the configuration file in rule-testing mode. Some are written in *perl*(1) for better error checking and faster performance. The most notable is a script called *checksendmail*, by Gene Kim, Rob Kolstad, and Jeff Polk. It runs a series of addresses through delivery-agent selection, recipient rewriting, and sender rewriting and is available via anonymous FTP from *boulder.Colorado.EDU* in the file *pub/sendmail/sendmail.test.shar*.

Pitfalls

- Rules that hide hosts in a domain should be applied only to sender addresses. Avoid the temptation to place such substitutions of host for domain names into rule set 3. Rule set 3 applies to all addresses and can wrongly change a nonlocal address.

- Not all configuration files focus with *user<@domain>*. IDA, for example, uses a more complex focus: *<@domain>, ... ,user*. Be sure you understand the style of focusing used in your configuration file before attempting to create new rules.

- Avoid confusing rule sets 1 and 2 when adding rules. Rule set 1 is for the sender; rule set 2 is for the recipient.

- Typos in rule-set declarations can be difficult to locate. For example, S1O (where the last character is the capital letter O) will silently evaluate to rule set 1 when you really meant rule set 10.

- The *sendmail* program always does a *chdir*(2) to its queue directory after reading the configuration file. On protected systems (where the queue is mode 0700), ordinary users need to change the location of the queue with the -oQ*dir* command-line switch for rule testing to work. V8 avoids this problem by not doing a *chdir*(2) in -bt mode.

- All but V8 wrongly call rule set 2 and the recipient R= when processing the envelope sender.

25

Rules

Rules are like little if-then clauses, existing inside rule sets, that test a pattern against an address and change the address if the two match. The process of converting one form of an address into another is called *rewriting*. Most rewriting requires a sequence of many rules, because an individual rule is relatively limited in what it can do. This need for many rules, combined with the *sendmail* program's need for succinct expressions, can make sequences of rules dauntingly cryptic.

In this chapter, we dissect the components of individual rules. In Chapter 24, *Rule Sets,* we showed how groups of rules are combined to perform necessary tasks.

Overview

Like all configuration commands, the R rule configuration command must begin a line. The general form consists of an R command followed by three parts:

```
Rlhs    rhs    comment
     ↑      ↑
   tabs   tabs
```

The lhs stands for *left-hand side* and is most commonly expressed as LHS. The rhs stands for *right-hand side* and is expressed as RHS. The LHS and RHS are mandatory. The third part (the comment) is optional. The three parts must be separated from each other by one or more tab characters (space characters will *not* work).

Space characters between the R and the LHS are optional. If there is a tab between the R and the LHS, *sendmail* silently uses the LHS as the RHS and the RHS becomes the comment.

The tabs leading to the comment, and the comment itself, are optional and may be omitted. If the tabs leading to the RHS are present, but the RHS is absent, the rule has no effect. No error is printed in that case, but if there are no tabs anywhere following the LHS, *sendmail* prints the following warning and ignores that R line:

```
invalid rewrite line "Rline"
```

Here, *Rline* is the full text of the R command from the configuration file. (This warning is usually the result of tabs being converted to spaces when text is copied from one window to another in a windowing system.)

Macros in Rules

Each noncomment part of a rule is expanded as the configuration file is read. Any references to defined macros are replaced with the value that the macro has at that point in the configuration file.

```
DAvalue1
R$A     $B
DAvalue2
R$A     $B
```

Here $A has the value `value1` when the first R line is expanded and `value2` when the second is expanded. A macro that is undefined expands to an empty string.

Rules Are Treated Like Addresses

After each side (LHS and RHS) is expanded, each is then normalized just as though it were an address. A check is made for any tabs that may have been introduced during expansion. If any are found, everything from the first tab to the end of the string is discarded. Then RFC822-style comments are removed. An RFC822 comment is anything between and including an unquoted pair of parentheses:

```
DAroot@my.site (Operator)
R$A    tab RHS
   ↓
Rroot@my.site (Operator)    tab RHS        ← expanded
   ↓
Rroot@my.site    tab RHS                   ← RFC822 comment stripped
```

Finally, a check is made for balanced quotation marks, right parentheses balanced by left, and right angle brackets balanced by left.* If any right-hand character appears without a corresponding left-hand character, *sendmail* prints one of the following errors:

configfile: line #: Unbalanced '>'
configfile: line #: Unbalanced '"'
configfile: line #: Unbalanced ')'

Here, *configfile* is the name of the configuration file that is being read, and line # shows the line number in that file. Note that only an unbalanced right character is checked:†

```
R<A>>   tab RHS          ← Unbalanced '>'
R<<A>   tab RHS          ← Undetected by some versions of sendmail
```

If you get one of the Unbalanced errors, be sure to correct the problem at once. If you leave the faulty rule in place, *sendmail* will continue to run, but is likely to crash and produce a core dump when the rule is referenced.

Backslashes in rules

Backslash characters are used in addresses to protect certain special characters from interpretation (see Chapter 31, *Headers*). For example, the address *blue;jay* would ordinarily be interpreted as having three parts (or tokens, which we'll discuss soon). To prevent *sendmail* from treating this address as three parts, and instead have it viewed as a single item, the special separating nature of the ; can be *escaped* by prefixing it with a backslash:

```
blue\;jay
```

For addresses and rules (which are normalized as addresses), the backslash is removed by *sendmail* and the high bit of the character following the backslash is set (turned on).

```
blue;jay
    ↑
high-bit turned on
```

In the next section, you will see that addresses and rules are split into parts based on special separation characters. The high bit that was set on the previously-escaped character (the ;) prevents this special separation character from creating a split.

---

*The $> operator isn't counted when checking balance.

†That is, for example, there must not be a > before the < character, and they must pair off.

After we talk about tokenizing, we'll show how split-up addresses are later pasted back together. Once the backslash has been removed and the high-bit set, the backslash is not replaced when the address is pasted back together. Even if an address is tokenized (see the following section), then pasted back together, then tokenized again, the high-bit representation of a backslash will be maintained. Thus, backslashed characters in rules will alway work properly for matching addresses, because backslashed characters are handled identically in all addresses.

Backslashes under V8

V8 *sendmail* handles backslashes differently than other versions have in the past. Instead of stripping a backslash and setting a high bit, it leaves backslashes in place. This still causes the backslash to mask the special meaning of characters, because *sendmail* always recognizes the backslash in that role.

The only time that V8 *sendmail* strips backslashes is during local delivery, and then only if they are not inside full quotation marks. Thus, mail to *\user* is delivered to *user* on the local machine (bypassing further aliasing) with the backslash stripped. But for mail to *\user@otherhost*, the backslash is preserved in both the envelope and the header.

Tokenizing Rules

The *sendmail* program views the text that makes up rules and addresses as being composed of individual tokens. Rules are *tokenized*—divided up into individual parts—while the configuration file is being read and while they are being normalized. Addresses are tokenized at another time (as we'll show later), but the process is the same for both.

The text *our.domain*, for example, is composed of three tokens, *our*, a dot, and *domain*. These ten characters are divided into tokens by the list of separation characters defined by the o macro:

```
Do.:%@!^=/[]
```

When any of these separation characters are recognized in text, they are considered individual tokens. Any leftover text is then combined into the remaining tokens.

```
xxx@yyy;zzz      becomes → xxx  @   yyy;zzz
```

@ is defined to be a token, but ; is not. Thus, the text is divided into three tokens. However, in addition to the characters in the o macro, *sendmail* defines ten tokenizing characters internally (in *parseaddr.c*):

```
( )<>,;\"\r\n
```

These two lists are combined into one master list that is used for all tokenizing. The above example, when divided using this master list, becomes five tokens instead of just three:

> xxx@yyy;zzz   *becomes* → xxx @   yyy ;   zzz

In rules, quotation marks can be used to override the meaning of tokenizing characters defined in the master list. For example:

> "xxx@yyy";zzz   *becomes* → "xxx@yyy" ;   zzz

Here, three tokens are produced, because the @ appears inside quotation marks. Note that the quotation marks are retained.

Because the configuration file is read sequentially from start to finish, the o macro should be defined before any rules are declared.

$ Operators Are Tokens

As we progress into the details of rules, you will see that certain characters become operators when prefixed with a $ character. Operators cause *sendmail* to perform actions, like looking for a match ($*) or replacing tokens with others by position ($1).

For tokenizing purposes, operators always divide one token from another, just like the characters in the master list did. For example:

> xxx$*zzz   *becomes* → xxx $* zzz

The Space Character Is Special

The space character is special for two reasons. First, although the space character is not in the master list, it *always* separates one token from another.

> xxx zzz   *becomes* → xxx zzz

Second, although the space character separates tokens, it is not itself a token. That is, in the above example, the seven characters on the left (the seventh is the space in the middle) become two tokens of three letters each, not three tokens. Thus, the space character can be used inside the

LHS or RHS of rules for improved clarity, but does not itself become a token, nor change the meaning of the rule.

Pasting Addresses Back Together

After an address has passed through all the rules (and has been modified by rewriting), the tokens that form it are pasted back together to form a single string. The pasting process is very straightforward in that it mirrors the tokenizing process:

> xxx @ yyy   *becomes* →   xxx@yyy

The only exception to this straightforward pasting process is when two adjoining tokens are both simple text. Simple text is anything other than the separation characters (defined by $o and internally by *sendmail*) or the operators (characters prefixed by a $ character). The **xxx** and **yyy** above are both simple text.

When two tokens of simple text are pasted together, the character defined by option B is inserted between them.* Usually that option is defined as a dot, so two tokens of simple text would have a dot inserted between them when they are joined.

> xxx yyy   *becomes* →   xxx.yyy

Note that the improper use of a space character in the LHS or RHS of rules can lead to addresses which have a dot (or other character) inserted where one was not intended.

The Workspace

As mentioned, rules exist to rewrite addresses. We won't cover the reasons this rewriting needs to be done just yet, but will instead concentrate on the general behavior of rewriting.

Before any rules are called to perform rewriting, a temporary buffer called the workspace is created. The address to be rewritten is then tokenized and placed into that workspace. The process of tokenizing addresses in the

---

*In the old days (RFC733) usernames to the left of the @ could contain spaces. But UNIX also uses spaces as command-line argument separators, so option B was introduced.

workspace is exactly the same as the tokenizing of rules that you saw before.

> gw@wash.dc.gov   *becomes* → gw @ wash . dc . gov

Here the tokenizing characters defined by the o macro (and those defined internally by *sendmail*) caused the address to be broken into seven tokens. The process of rewriting changes the tokens in the workspace:

>   ← workspace is: "gw" "@" "wash" "." "dc" "." "gov"
> R*LHS* RHS
> R*LHS* RHS   ← *rules rewrite the workspace*
> R*LHS* RHS
>   ← workspace is: "gw" "." "LOCAL"

Here the workspace began with seven tokens. The three hypothetical rules recognized that this was a local address (in token form) and rewrote it so that it became three tokens.

The Behavior of a Rule

Each individual rule (R command) in the configuration file can be thought of as a while-do statement. Recall that rules are composed of an LHS (left-hand side) and an RHS (right-hand side), separated from each other by tabs. As long as (while) the LHS matches the workspace, the workspace is rewritten (do) by the RHS. (See Figure 25-1.)

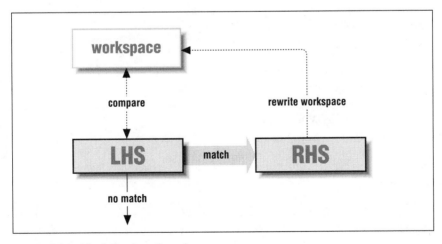

Figure 25-1: The behavior of a rule

Consider a rule in which we want the name tom in the workspace changed into the name fred. One possible rule to do this might look like this:

```
Rtom    fred
```

If the workspace contains the name tom, the LHS of this rule matches exactly. As a consequence, the RHS is given the opportunity to rewrite the workspace. It does so by placing the name fred into that workspace. The new workspace is once again compared to the tom in the LHS, but now there is no match because the workspace contains fred. When the workspace and the LHS do not match, the rule is skipped, and the *current* contents of the workspace are carried down to the next rule. Thus, in our example, the name fred in the workspace is carried down.

Clearly, there is little reason to worry about endless loops in a rule when using names like *tom* and *fred*. But the LHS and RHS can contain pattern-matching and replacement operators, and those operators *can* lead to loops.

The LHS

The LHS of any rule is compared to the current contents of the workspace to see if the two match. The *sendmail* program offers a variety of special operators to make comparisons easier and more versatile. (See Table 25-1).
Table 25-1: LHS Operators

Operator	Description or Use
$*	Match zero or more tokens
$+	Match one or more tokens
$-	Match exactly one tokens
$@	Match exactly zero tokens (V8 only)
$=	Match any in a class*
$~	Match any not in a class

* Class matches either a single token or multiple tokens, depending on the version of *sendmail*. See Chapter 28, *Class Macros*.

The first four operators in Table 25-1 are pattern-matching operators, which can be used to match arbitrary sequences of tokens in the workspace. Consider the following rule, which employs the $- operator (match any single token):

```
R$-     fred.local
```

Here a match is found only if the workspace contains a single token (like *tom*). If the workspace contains multiple tokens (like *tom@host*), the LHS does not match. A match causes the workspace to be rewritten by the RHS to become `fred.local`. The rewritten workspace is then compared again to the $- but this time there is no match because the workspace contains three tokens (`fred`, a dot (`.`), and `local`). Since there is no match, the *current* workspace (`fred.local`) is carried down to the next rule (if there is one).

Note that all comparisons of tokens in the LHS to tokens in the workspace are done in a case-insensitive manner. That is, `tom` in the LHS matches `TOM`, `Tom`, and even `ToM` in the workspace.

Minimum Matching

When a pattern-matching operator can match multiple tokens ($+ and $*), *sendmail* performs *minimum matching*. For example, given a workspace of **xxx.yyy.zzz** and an LHS of:

```
$+.$+
```

the first $+ matches only a single token (**xxx**), but the second $+ matches three (**yyy**, a dot, and **zzz**). This is because the first $+ matches the minimum number of tokens that it can, while still allowing the whole LHS to match the workspace. Shortly, when we discuss the RHS, we'll show why this is important.

Backup and Retry

Multiple token-matching operators, like $*, always try to match the fewest number of tokens that they can. Such a simple-minded approach could lead to problems when matching (or not matching) classes in the LHS. For example, consider the following five tokens in the workspace:

```
"A" "." "B" "." "C"
```

Given the following LHS rule:

```
R$*.$=X$*
```

Because the first $* tries to match the minimum number of tokens, it first matches only the A in the workspace. The $=X then tries to match the B to the class X. If this match fails, *sendmail* backs up and tries again.

The next time through, the lead $* matches the A.B and the $=X tries to match the C in the workspace. If C is not in the class X, the entire LHS fails.

The ability of the *sendmail* program to back up and retry LHS matches eliminates much of the ambiguity from rule design. The multitoken matching operators try to match the minimum, but match more if necessary in order for the whole LHS to match.

The class-matching operators ($= and $~) are explained in Chapter 28, *Class Macros*.

The RHS

The purpose of the RHS in a rule is to rewrite the workspace. To make this rewriting more versatile, *sendmail* offers several special RHS operators. The complete list is shown in Table 25-2.

Table 25-2: RHS Operators

RHS	Description or Use
$*digit*	Copy by position
$:	Rewrite once (prefix)
$@	Rewrite and return (prefix)
$>*set*	Rewrite through another rule set
$#	Specify a delivery agent
$[$]	Canonicalize hostname
$($)	Database lookup (IDA and V8)
${ $}	NIS map lookup (SunOS)

Copy by Position: $digit

The $*digit* operator in the RHS is used to copy tokens from the LHS into the workspace. The *digit* refers to positions of LHS operators in the LHS.

```
R$+@$*    $2!$1
  ↑ ↑
 $1 $2
```

Here, the $1 in the RHS indicates tokens matched by the first operator in the LHS (in this case the $+), and the $2 in the RHS indicates tokens matched by the second operator in the LHS (the $*). In this example, if the workspace contains A@B.C, it will be rewritten by the RHS as follows:

$*	*matches*	B.C	*so* $2 *copies it to workspace*
		!	*explicitly placed into workspace*
$+	*matches*	A	*so* $1 *copies it to workspace*

The $*digit* copies all the tokens matched by its corresponding operator. For the $+ operator, only a single token (A) is matched and copied with $1. The ! is copied as-is. For the $* operator, three tokens are matched (B.C), so $2 copies all three. Thus, the above rule rewrites A@B.C into B.C!A.

Not all LHS operators *need* to be referenced with a $*digit* in the RHS. Consider:

```
R$*<$*>$*    <$2>
```

Here, only the middle LHS operator (the second one) is required to rewrite the workspace. So only the $2 is needed in the RHS ($1 and $3 are not needed and not present in the RHS).

Although macros appear to be operators in the LHS, they are not. Recall that macros are expanded when the configuration file is read. As a consequence, although they appear as $*letter* in the configuration file, they are converted to tokens when that configuration file is read. For example:

```
DAxxx
R$A@$*    $1
```

Here the macro A is defined to have the value xxx. To the unwary, the $1 *appears* to indicate the $A. But, when the configuration file is read, the above rule is expanded into:

```
Rxxx@$*    $1
```

Clearly the $1 refers to the $* (because $*digit* references only operators and $A is a macro, not an operator). The *sendmail* program is unable to detect errors of this sort. If the $1 were instead $2 (in a mistaken attempt to reference the $*), *sendmail* would print the following error:

```
ruleset replacement out of bounds
```

The error of referencing a nonexistent operator is not detected when the configuration file is read.* Instead, this error is printed only when the rule is called during mail processing.†

The *digit* of the $*digit* must be in the range one through nine. A $0 is meaningless and causes *sendmail* to crash and produce a core dump‡ when the rule containing that RHS expression is called. Extra digits are considered tokens, rather than extensions of the $*digit*. That is, $11 is the RHS operator $1 and the token 1, not a reference to the eleventh LHS operator.

Rewrite Once Prefix: $:

Ordinarily, the RHS rewrites the workspace as long as the workspace continues to match the LHS. This looping behavior can be useful. Consider the need to strip extra trailing dots off an address in the workspace:

```
R$*..    $1.
```

Here, the $* matches any address that has two or more trailing dots. The $1. in the RHS then strips one of those two trailing dots when rewriting the workspace. For example:

```
xxx . . . . .      becomes → xxx . . . . .
xxx . . . .        becomes → xxx . . . .
xxx . .            becomes → xxx . .
xxx . .            becomes → xxx .
xxx .              ← match fails
```

Although this looping behavior of rules can be handy, for most rules it can be dangerous. Consider the following example:

```
R$*    <$1>
```

The intention of this rule is to cause whatever is in the workspace to be surrounded with angle brackets. But after the workspace is rewritten, the LHS again checks for a match, and since the $* matches anything, the match succeeds, the RHS rewrites the workspace again, and again the LHS checks for a match.

---

*V8 *sendmail* catches these errors in when the configuration file is read. It prints "replacement $*num* out of bounds" (where *num* is the *digit*) and skips the rule.

†It is also detected in -bt (testing) mode. A good reason to always test new rules before releasing them.

‡V8 *sendmail* simply prints an error message when $0 is used and skips that rule.

```
xxx                   becomes → < xxx >
< xxx >               becomes → < < xxx > >
< < xxx > >           becomes → < < < xxx > > >
     ↓
  and so on, until ...
     ↓
```
sendmail prints: `rewrite: expansion too long`

In this case *sendmail* catches the problem, because the workspace has become too large. It prints the above error message and yields a workspace that looks like the following (really all one line):

```
< < < < < < < < < < < < < < < < < < < < < < < < < < < < < <
< < < < < < < < < < < < < < < < xxx > > > > > > > > > > > > > > >
> > > > > > > > > > > > > > > > > > > > > > > > > > > > > > >
```

But, unfortunately, not all such endless looping produces a visible error message. Consider the following example:

```
R$*     $1
```

Here is an LHS that matches anything, and an RHS that rewrites the workspace in such a way that the workspace never changes. For older versions, this causes *sendmail* to appear to hang (as it processes the same rule over and over and over). Newer versions of *sendmail* will catch such endless looping and print (*syslog*) one of the following errors:

```
address causes rewrite loop: <workspace>
Infinite loop in ruleset ruleset_number
```

The first is printed by IDA *sendmail* and the second by V8 *sendmail.**
Note that neither message prevents *sendmail* from hanging; they just notify you that the looping is happening.

It is not always desirable (or even possible) to write "loop-proof" rules. To prevent looping, *sendmail* offers the `$:` RHS prefix. By starting the RHS of a rule with the `$:` operator, you are telling *sendmail* to rewrite the workspace exactly once.

```
R$*     $:<$1>
```

Again the rule causes the contents of the workspace to be surrounded by a pair of angle brackets. But here the `$:` prefix prevents the LHS from checking for another match after the rewrite.

---

*For V8, the workspace is also printed on the line which follows the error.

Note that the $: prefix must begin the RHS to have any effect. If it instead appears inside the RHS, its special meaning is lost:

foo	*rewritten by*	$:$1	*becomes →*	foo
foo	*rewritten by*	1:	*becomes →*	foo $:

Rewrite-and-return Prefix: $@

The flow of rules is such that each and every rule in a series of rules (a rule set) is given a chance to match the workspace:

```
Rxxx   yyy
Ryyy   zzz
```

The first rule matches **xxx** in the workspace and rewrites the workspace to contain **yyy**. The first rule then tries to match the workspace again, but of course, fails. The second rule then tries to match the workspace. Since the workspace contains **yyy**, a match is found, and the RHS rewrites the workspace to be **zzz**.

There will often be times when one rule in a series performs the appropriate rewrite and no subsequent rules need to be called. In the above example, suppose **xxx** should only become **yyy** and that the second rule should not be called. To solve problems like this, *sendmail* offers the $@ prefix for use in the RHS.

The $@ prefix tells *sendmail* that the current rule is the last one that should be used in the current ruleset. If the LHS of the current rule matches, any rules that follow (in the current rule set) are ignored.

```
Rxxx   $@yyy
Ryyy   zzz
```

If the workspace contains anything other than **xxx**, the first rule does not match, and the second rule is called. But if the workspace contains **xxx**, the first rule matches and rewrites the workspace. The $@ prefix for the RHS of that rule prevents the second rule (and any subsequent rules) from being called.

Note that the $@ also prevents looping. The $@ tells *sendmail* to skip further rules *and* to rewrite only once. The difference between $@ and $: is that both rewrite only once, but $@ *doesn't* proceed to the next rule, whereas $: *does*.

The $@ operator must be used as a prefix because it has special meaning only when it begins the RHS of a rule. If it appears anywhere else inside the RHS it loses its special meaning.

foo	*rewritten by*	$@$1	*becomes* →	foo
foo	*rewritten by*	1@	*becomes* →	foo $@

Rewrite Through Another Rule Set: $>set

Rules are organized in sets that can be thought of as subroutines (see Chapter 24, *Rule Sets*). Occasionally a rule or series of rules can be common to two or more rule sets. To make the configuration file more compact and somewhat clearer, such common series of rules can be made into separate subroutines.

The RHS $>*set* operator tells *sendmail* to perform additional rewriting using a secondary set of rules. The *set* is the rule-set number of that secondary set. If *set* is the number of a nonexistent rule set, the effect is the same as if the subroutine rules were never called (the workspace is unchanged).

If the *set* is greater than the maximum number of allowable rule sets, or less than zero, *sendmail* either acts as though the rule set is nonexistent or crashes and produces a core dump.

The process of calling another set of rules proceeds in five stages:

First   As usual, if the LHS matches the workspace, the RHS gets to rewrite the workspace.

Second The RHS ignores the $>*set* part and rewrites the rest as usual.

Third   The rewritten workspace is then given to the set of rules specified by *set*. They either rewrite the workspace or do not.

Fourth The original RHS (the one with the $>*set*) leaves the possibly rewritten workspace as-is, as though it had performed the subroutine's rewriting itself.

Fifth   The LHS gets a crack at the new workspace as usual, unless prevented by a $: or $@ prefix in the RHS.

For example, consider the following two sets of rules:

```
# first set
S21
R$*..    $:$>22 $1.      strip extra trailing dots
   ...etc.

# second set
```

```
S22
R$*..    $1.              strip trailing dots
```

Here, the first set of rules contains, among other things, a single rule that removes extra dots from the end of an address. But, because other rule sets may also need extra dots stripped, a subroutine (the second set of rules) is created to perform that task.

Note that the first rule strips one trailing dot from the workspace, and then calls rule set 22 (the $>22), which then strips any additional dots. The workspace as rewritten by rule set 22 becomes the workspace yielded by the RHS in the first rule. The $: prevents the LHS of the first rule from looking for a match a second time.

For all but IDA *sendmail*, the subroutine call must begin the RHS (immediately follow any $@ or $: prefix, if any) and only a single subroutine may be called. That is, the following causes rule set 22 to be called, but does not call 23.

   $>22 xxx $>23 yyy

Instead of calling rule set 23, the $> operator and the 23 are copied as-is into the workspace, and that workspace is passed to rule set 22:

   xxx $> 23 yyy   ← *passed to rule set 22*

For IDA *sendmail*, subroutine calls may appear anywhere inside the RHS and there may be multiple subroutine calls. Consider the same RHS as above:

   $>22 xxx $>23 yyy

Under IDA *sendmail*, rule set 23 is called first, and is given the workspace yyy to rewrite. The workspace, as rewritten by rule set 23, is added to the end of the xxx and the combined result passed to rule set 22.

Under IDA *sendmail*, subroutine rule-set calls are performed from right to left. The result (rewritten workspace) of each call is appended to the RHS text to the left.

You should beware of one problem with all subroutine calls. When ordinary text immediately follows the number of the rule set, that text is likely to be ignored. This can be witnessed by using the -d21.3 debugging switch.

Consider the following RHS:

```
$>3uucp.$1
```

Because *sendmail* parses the 3 and the uucp as a single token, the subroutine call succeeds, but the uucp is lost. The -d21.3 switch illustrates this problem.

```
-----callsubr 3uucp         ← atoi(3) sees this
-----callsubr 3             ← but should have seen this
```

The 3uucp is interpreted as the number three by the *atoi*(3) library routine, so it is accepted as a valid number despite the fact that uucp was attached. Since the uucp is a part of the number, it is not available for comparison to the workspace and so is lost. The correct way to write the above RHS is like this:

```
$>3 uucp.$1
```

Note that the space between the 3 and the uucp causes them to be viewed as two separate tokens.

This problem can also arise with macros. Consider:

```
$>3$M
```

Here, the $M is expanded when the configuration file is parsed. If the expanded value lacks a leading space, that value (or the first token in it) is lost.

Note that operators which follow a rule-set number are correctly recognized.

```
$>3$[$1$]
```

Here, the 3 is immediately followed by the $ [operator. Because operators are token separators, the call to rule set 3 will be correctly interpreted as:

```
-----callsubr 3             ← good
```

But as a general rule, and just to be safe, the number of a subroutine call should always be followed by a space.

Specify a Delivery Agent: $#

The $# operator in the RHS is copied as-is into the workspace and functions as a flag advising *sendmail* that a delivery agent has been selected. The $# must be the first token copied into the rewritten workspace for it to have this special meaning. If it occupies any other position in the workspace, it loses its special meaning.

```
$# local          ← selects delivery agent
xxx $# local      ← no special meaning
```

When it occurs first in the rewritten workspace, the $# operator tells *send-mail* that the second token in the workspace is the name of a delivery agent. The $# operator is useful only in rule set 0 (and for BSD *sendmail*, rule set 5).

Note that the $# operator may be prefixed with a $@ or a $: without losing its special meaning, because those prefix operators are not copied to the workspace.

```
$@ $# local      rewritten as → $# local
```

However, those prefix operators are not necessary, because the $# acts just like a $@ prefix. It prevents the LHS from attempting to match again after the RHS rewrite, and it causes any following rules to be skipped. In Chapter 26, *Delivery Agents,* you will see that $@ and $:, when used in non-prefix roles in rule sets, also act like flags, conveying host and user information to *sendmail.*

Canonicalize Hostname: $[and $]

Tokens that appear between a $[and $] pair of operators in the RHS are considered to be the name of a host. That hostname is looked up using DNS and replaced with the full canonical form of that name. If found, it is then copied to the workspace, and the $[and $] are discarded.

For example, consider a rule that looks for a hostname in angle brackets, and (if found) rewrites it in canonical form:

```
R<$*>     $@ <$[ $1 $]>     canonicalize hostname
```

Such canonicalization is useful at sites where users frequently send mail to machines using the short version of a machine's name. The $[tells *send-mail* to view all the tokens which follow (up to the $]) as a single host-name.

If the name cannot be canonicalized (perhaps because there is no such host), the name is copied as-is into the workspace. No indication is given that it could not be canonicalized.

Note that if the $[is omitted and the $] included, the $] loses its special meaning and is copied as-is into the workspace.

The hostname between the $[and $] can also be an IP address. By surrounding the hostname with square brackets ([and]) you are telling *sendmail* that it is really an IP address:

```
wash.dc.gov          ← a hostname
[123.45.67.8]        ← an IP address
```

When the IP address between the square brackets corresponds to a known host, the address and the square brackets are replaced with that host's canonical name.

Under V8 *sendmail*, if the version of the configuration file is 2 or greater (as set with the V configuration command), a successful canonicalization has a dot appended to the result.

```
myhost      becomes →  myhost . domain .    ← success
nohost      becomes →  nohost               ← failure
```

Note that a trailing dot is not legal* in an address specification, so subsequent rules (like rule set 4) *must* remove these added trailing dots.

Also, under V8 *sendmail*, the K configuration command can be used to redefine (or eliminate) the dot as the added character. For example,

```
Khost host -a.found
```

This causes *sendmail* to add the text .found to a successfully canonicalized hostname, instead of the dot. The K option is described in Chapter 29, *Database Macros*.

One final difference between V8 *sendmail* and other versions is in the way it looks up names from between the $[and $] operators. The rules for V8 *sendmail* are:

First   If the name contains at least one dot (.) anywhere within it, it is looked up as-is. For example, *host.CS.*

Second   If that fails, it appends the default domain to the name (as defined in */etc/resolv.conf*) and tries to look up the result. For example, *host.CS.our.Sub.Domain.*

Third   If that fails, the leftmost part of the subdomain (if any) is discarded and the result appended to the original host. For example, *host.CS.Sub.Domain.*

---

*Under DNS, the trailing dot signifies the root (topmost) domain. Thus under DNS, a trailing dot is legal. For mail, however, RFC1123 specifically states that no address is to be propagated which contains a trailing dot.

Fourth   If the original name did not have a dot in it, it is looked up as-is. For example, *host.*

This approach allows names like *host.CS* to first match a site in Czechoslovakia* (if that was intended), rather than to wrongly match a host in your local Computer Science (CS) department.

An example of canonicalization

The following four-line configuration file can be used to observe how *sendmail* canonicalizes hostnames:

```
V3
Mlocal, P=X,A=X
Do.:%@!^=/[]
R$*        $@$[$1$]
```

If this file were called *fourline.cf, sendmail* could be run in rule-testing mode with a command like the following:

```
% /usr/lib/sendmail -oQ. -Cfourline.cf -bt
```

Thereafter, hostname canonicalization can be observed by specifying rule set 0 and a hostname. One such run of tests is shown below (using V8 *sendmail*):

```
ADDRESS TEST MODE (ruleset 3 NOT automatically invoked)
Enter <ruleset> <address>
> 0 wash
rewrite: ruleset  0   input: "wash"
rewrite: ruleset  0 returns: "wash" "." "dc" "." "gov" "."
> 0 nohost
rewrite: ruleset  0   input: "nohost"
rewrite: ruleset  0 returns: "nohost"
>
```

Note that the known host named **wash** is rewritten in canonicalized form with a dot appended. The unknown host named **nohost** is unchanged and has no dot appended.

---

*For example, *uscbt.cs* is the name of a real machine in Czechoslovakia. (Arrg! During the writing of this book it became two countries: the Czech Republic and the Slovak Republic.)

Default in Canonicalization: $:

IDA and V8 *sendmail* both offer an alternative to leaving the hostname unchanged when canonicalization fails with $[and $]. A default can be used instead of the failed hostname by prefixing that default with a $:.

```
$[ host $: default $]
```

The $:*default* must follow the *host* and precede the $]. To illustrate its use, consider the following rule:

```
R$*     $:$[ $1 $: $1.notfound $]
```

If the hostname $1 can be canonicalized, the workspace becomes that canonicalized name. If it cannot, the workspace becomes the original hostname with a .notfound appended to it. If the *default* part of the $:*default* is omitted, a failed canonicalization is rewritten as zero tokens.

Other Operators

Many other operators (depending on your version of *sendmail*) may also be used in rules. Because of their individual complexity, all of the following are detailed in other chapters. We outline them here, however, for completeness.

Class macros   The class macro is described in Chapter 28, *Class Macros*. Class macros may appear only in the LHS. They begin with the prefix $= to match a token in the workspace to one of many tokens in a class. The alternative prefix $~ causes a token in the workspace to match if it does *not* appear in the list of tokens that are the class.

Conditionals   The conditional macro operator $? is rarely used in rules. It is described in Chapter 27, *Defined Macros*. When used in rules, the result is often not what was intended.

Database Operators

There are three major forms of database operators. The IDA version is used to look up tokens in *dbm*(3) files and NIS maps. The SunOS version is used to look up tokens in NIS maps only. The V8 version is used to look up tokens in separate *dbm*(3) or *db*(3) files and NIS maps. All three forms are covered in Chapter 29, *Database Macros*.

Pitfalls

- If, during the processing of the configuration file, either the LHS or the RHS of a rule silently "pre-expands" to NULL, referencing that rule can cause *sendmail* to crash and produce a core dump.

- Referencing a rule set with a $>*set* operator that is out of bounds (less than zero or greater than MAXRWSETS) can cause *sendmail* to crash and produce a core dump at unexpected times.

- Any text following a rule-set number in a $> expression in the RHS should be separated from the expression with a space. If the space is absent, and the text is other than a separating character or an operator, the text is ignored. For example, in $>22xxx, the **xxx** is ignored.

- Because rules are processed like addresses when the configuration file is read, they can silently change from what was intended if they are parenthesized or if other non-address components are used.

- Copying rules between screen windows can cause tabs to invisibly become spaces, leading to rule failure.

- A lone $* in the LHS is especially dangerous. It can lead to endless rule looping and cause all rules which follow it to be ignored (remember the $: and $@ prefixes in the RHS).

- Failure to test new rules can bring a site to its knees. A flood of bounced mail messages can run up the load on a machine and possibly even require a reboot. *Always* test every new rule both with -bt (testing) mode (see Chapter 24, *Rule Sets*), and selected -d (debugging) switches (see Chapter 33, *Debugging With –d*).

Delivery Agents

The *sendmail* program does not perform the actual delivery of mail. Instead, it calls other programs, (called mail delivery agents) to perform that service. Because the mechanics of delivery can vary so widely from delivery agent to delivery agent, *sendmail* needs a great deal of information about each delivery agent. Each *sendmail* M configuration-file command defines a mail delivery agent and provides *sendmail* with that information.

Syntax

Like all *sendmail.cf* commands, the M mail delivery agent command must begin a line. One typical such command looks like this:

```
      delivery program                     command line
            ↓                                   ↓
Mlocal, P=/bin/mail, F=rlsDFMmnP, S=10, R=20, A=mail -d $u
                        ↑                ↑    ↑
                      flags        sender/recipient rules
```

This M configuration command is composed of six parts: a symbolic name followed by five equates, each separated from the others by commas. Spaces between the parts are optional. The specific syntax of the mail delivery agent command is:

```
Msymname, equate, equate, ...
```

The letter M always begins the delivery agent definition, followed by a symbolic name (the *symname*) of your choosing and a comma-separated list of delivery agent equates. Only the P= and A= equates are required. The others are optional.

The comma following the symbolic name is optional. As long as there is a space following the symbolic name, *sendmail* parses it correctly. The comma should, however, always be included for improved clarity.*

In the following, the first includes the comma, and the second omits it. Both are parsed by *sendmail* in exactly the same way:

```
Mlocal, P=/bin/mail, F=rlsDFMmnP, S=10, R=20, A=mail -d $u
Mlocal  P=/bin/mail, F=rlsDFMmnP, S=10, R=20, A=mail -d $u
```

The Symbolic Name

The M that begins the delivery agent definition command is immediately followed, with no intervening white space, by the name of the delivery agent. Note that the name is symbolic, and is only used internally by *sendmail*. The name may contain no white space, and, if quoted, the quotation marks are interpreted as part of its name. In the following, only the first is a good symbolic name:

```
Mlocal          ← name is "local", good
M local         ← name has lead space " local"
Mmy mailer      ← name is wrongly "my"
```

The symbolic name may not contain any of the separation characters defined by the $o macro. Those excluded characters are usually:

```
. : % @ ! ^ = / [ ]
```

Nor may the symbolic name contain any of the separation characters defined internally by *sendmail*. Those additional excluded characters are:

```
( ) < > , ; \ " \r \n
```

In the following, only the first is a good symbolic name:

```
Mprog-mailer    ← name is "prog-mailer", good
Mprog.mailer    ← name contains a dot ".", bad
Mmy\mailer      ← name contains a "\", bad
```

The symbolic name is case-insensitive. That is, local, Local, and LOCAL are all identical.

---

*SunOS 4.1.2's *sendmail* does not properly support freezing if the comma is present.

Required Symbolic Names

Two delivery agent symbolic names *must* be defined in every configuration file:

local   The symbolic name of the program that handles delivery on the local machine (usually */bin/mail*).

prog   The symbolic name of the program that executes other programs for delivery (usually the */bin/sh* shell).

If either definition is missing, *sendmail* prints one of the following warning messages, but continues to run:

```
No prog mailer defined.
No local mailer defined.
```

The Equates

Recall that the form for the M command is:

```
Msymname, equate, equate, equate, ...
```

Each *equate* expression is of the form:

```
field=arg
```

The field is selected from those in Table 26-1. Only the first character of the field is recognized. That is, all of the following are equivalent:

```
S=21
Sender=21
SenderRuleSet=21
```

The field is followed by optional white space, the = character, optional white space, and finally the arg. The form of the arg is specific to each field.

Table 26-1: Delivery Agent Equates

Equate	Name	Meaning
A=	Argv	Delivery agent's command-line arguments
C=	Charset	Default character set (IDA only)
D=	Directory	Paths to directories for execution (V8 only)
E=	EOL	End-of-line string
F=	Flags	Flags describing a delivery agent's behavior
L=	Linelimit	Maximum line length (IDA and V8 only)
M=	Maximum	Maximum message size

Table 26.1: Delivery Agent Equates (continued)

Equate	Name	Meaning
P=	Path	Path to the delivery program
R=	Recipient	Recipient rewriting rule set
S=	Sender	Sender rewriting rule set
X=	Xescape	Default escape character (IDA only)

A full description of each field follows. They are presented in alphabetical order, rather than in the order they would appear in typical delivery agent definitions.

The Argv for This Delivery Agent: A=

The program that is to be run (specified by the P= equate) is given its C language `char **argv` array (list of command-line arguments) by this A= equate. This equate must always be the last one specified, because the `argv` arguments are all those from the = to the end of the line.

```
Mlocal, P=/bin/mail, F=rlsDFMmnP, S=10, R=20, A=mail -d $u
                                                 ↑
                                   argv to end of line →
```

Macros are expanded and may be used in this `argv` array. For example:

```
A=mail -d $u
```

The A= begins the declaration of the argument array. The program specified by the P= equate (`/bin/mail`) will be executed with an `argv` of:

```
argv[0] = "mail"
argv[1] = "-d"        ← switch means perform final delivery
argv[2] = "fred"      ← where macro $u contains "fred"
```

The macro value of $u contains the current recipient name. Another macro that commonly appears in A= fields is $h, the recipient host. You are, of course, free to use any macro you find necessary as a part of this `argv` array. Any arguments in excess of the maximum number defined by MAXPV in *conf.h* (usually 40) are silently ignored.

$h and other arguments in A=[IPC]

For network delivery via the P=[IPC] delivery agent, the A= equate is usually declared like this:

```
A=IPC $h
```

The value in $h is the value returned by rule set 0's $@ operator and is usually the name of the host to which *sendmail* should connect. In V8 *sendmail*, it can be a colon-separated list of hosts. V8 *sendmail* attempts to connect to each in turn, left to right:

```
A=IPC hostA:hostB:hostC
```

Here, V8 *sendmail* tries to connect to *hostA* first. If that fails, it next tries *hostB*, and so on. As usual, trying a host means trying its MX records first, then its A record if there are no MX records.

The host (as $h) is usually the only argument given to IPC. But, strictly speaking, IPC can accept three arguments, like this:

```
A=IPC hostlist port
```

The *port* (third argument) is usually omitted, and so defaults to 25. However, a port number can be included to force *sendmail* to connect on a different port.

To illustrate, consider the need to force mail to a gateway machine to be always delivered on a particular port. First, design a new delivery agent that uses IPC for transport.

```
Mgateway, P=[IPC], ..., A=IPC gateway.domain $h
```

Here, any mail which selects the gateway delivery agent is transported over the network (the [IPC]) to the machine gateway.domain. The port number is carried in $h, which usually carries the hostname.

Next, design a rule in rule set 0 which selects this delivery agent:

```
R$+<@$+.gateway>$*    $#gateway $@ 26 $: $1<@$2.gateway>$3
```

This rule selects the gateway delivery agent for any address that ends in .gateway. The host part returned by the $@ is the port number to use. The $: part (the address) is passed in the envelope. Note that the gateway also has to be listening on the same port for this to work.

$u in A=

The $u macro is special in the A= equate's field. If $u *does not* appear in the array, *sendmail* assumes that the program in P= equate speaks SMTP (the Simple Mail Transfer Protocol). Consequently, you should never use a $u when defining mail delivery agents that must speak SMTP. Typically those are the agents which use [IPC] or [TCP] in their P= equate's field.

If $u *does* appear in the array, *sendmail* assumes that the program in P= does *not* speak SMTP.

If $u appears, and the F=m delivery agent flag is also specified, then the argument containing $u is repeated as many times as there are recipients. For example, a typical uucp delivery agent definition looks like this:

```
Muucp, P=/bin/uux, F=msDFMhuU, S=13, R=23, A=uux - -r $h!rmail ($u)
                   ↑                                          ↑
                 note                                        note
```

In the above, the m flag is set in the F= equate's field, which tells *sendmail* that this delivery agent is able to deliver to multiple recipients simultaneously. The $u macro is also included as one of the arguments specified by the A= command-line array. Thus, if mail is sent with this delivery agent to multiple recipients, say jim, bill, and joe, then the ($u) argument is repeated three times, once for each recipient:

```
uux - -r $h!rmail (jim) (bill) (joe)
```

The Default Character Set (IDA only): C=

The C= field for the IDA version of *sendmail* allows you to use an alternative to ASCII for the character set used by the delivery agent.* The character sets available, their aliases and meanings are documented in the file *ida/charset/CHARSETS* supplied with the IDA distribution. To use alternate character sets, you need to define BIT8 in *conf.h*. (See the IDA installation documents for more details about this feature.)

Although this feature allows you to transmit data using an alternative alphabet, like Arabic, you must first be sure that the receiving site is able to receive this data correctly, and that users at the other end have the necessary software for conversion. Of particular concern is the fact that some character sets require all eight bits for transmission, whereas some sites

---

*Note that the IETF committees are currently developing a standard for multiple character-set support. This IDA implementation is only an interim measure.

only support seven bits at this time. Consequently, both your site and the other site must agree in advance to communicate using eight bits.

Under V8 *sendmail,* 8-bit data is enabled by default, and disabled with the 7 option or the F=7 flag.

Paths of Working Directories (V8 only): D=

Ordinarily, whenever *sendmail* executes a program via the `prog` delivery agent, it does so from within the *sendmail* queue directory. One unfortunate side effect of this behavior is that shell scripts written with the C-shell (and possibly other programs) may fail because they cannot *stat*(2) the current directory. To alleviate this problem, V8 *sendmail* has introduced the D= delivery agent equate. This new equate allows you to specify a series of directories for *sendmail* to attempt to *chdir*(2) into before invoking the delivery program.

The form of the D= equate looks like this:

```
D=path1:path2...
```

The D= is followed by a colon-separated series of directory pathnames. Before running the delivery program, *sendmail* tries to *chdir*(2) into each in turn, leftmost to rightmost, until it succeeds. If it does not succeed with any of the directories (perhaps because none of them exist), *sendmail* remains in its queue directory.

One recommended setting for the D= equate is this:

```
D=$z:/tmp
```

Here, *sendmail* first tries to *chdir*(2) into the directory defined by the $z macro. That macro either contains the full pathname of the recipient's home directory, or is NULL. If it is NULL, or if the home directory is unavailable, the *chdir*(2) fails, so *sendmail* instead does a *chdir*(2) to the */tmp* directory.

The End-of-line String: E=

The E= equate specifies the end-of-line character or characters. Those characters are generated by *sendmail* for outgoing messages and recognized by *sendmail* for incoming messages.

The end-of-line characters are defined with the E= equate as backslash-escaped control characters, such as:

```
E=\r\n
```

The default end-of-line string, if the E= field is missing, is usually the C language newline character, \n. On some NeXT computers (previous to OS version 2.0), the default E= terminator is \r\n. This can cause serious problems when used with some non-TCP delivery agents like UUCP. If you have a system that does this, you can override that improper default with:

```
E=\n
```

In general, delivery agents that speak SMTP (those that *lack* a $u in the A= argument array) should have their end-of-line field set to E=\r\n (for a carriage return/newline pair). Delivery agents that do not speak SMTP (those that *include* a $u in the A= argument array), should have their end-of-line field set to E=\n (for a lone newline character).

Delivery Agent Flags: F=

The F= equate is probably more fraught with peril than the others. The flags specified with F= tell *sendmail* how the delivery agent will behave and what its needs will be. These flags are used in one or more of three ways:

First, if a header definition relies conditionally on a flag:

```
H?P?Return-Path: <$g>
   ↑
   apply if P flag specified in F= equate.
```

and if that flag is listed as a part of the F= equate:

```
Mlocal, P=/bin/mail, F=rlsDFMmnP, S=10, R=20, A=mail -d $u
                         ↑
                    apply in header
```

then that header is included in all mail messages sent via this delivery agent.

Second, if a delivery agent needs a special command-line argument that *sendmail* can produce for it, but only requires that argument under special circumstances, selected F= flags can produce that result. For example, the F=f flag specifies that the delivery agent needs a -f command-line switch when it is forwarding network mail.

Third, the F= flags also tell *sendmail* how this particular delivery agent behaves. For example, it performs final delivery or it requires uppercase preserved for usernames.

Many flags have special meaning to *sendmail*, while others are strictly user-defined. All of the flags are detailed at the end of this chapter.

Maximum Line Length (IDA and V8 only): L=

The L= equate is used to limit the length of text lines in the body of a mail message. If this equate is omitted, *sendmail* defaults to having no limitation on the length of lines. (For compatibility with older versions of *sendmail*, the inclusion of the F=L flag causes the default to be 990 characters.)

Limiting line length causes overly long lines to be split. When an output line is split, first the text up to the split is transmitted, followed by the ! character. Finally the characters defined by the E= equate are transmitted. A line may be split into two or more pieces. For example, consider the following text from the body of a mail message:

```
The maximum line length for SMTP mail is 990 characters.
But that length is only enforced if the F=L flag is included
in a delivery agent definition. A delivery agent speaks
SMTP when the $u macro is omitted from the A= equate.
```

A delivery agent could limit line length to 20 characters with a declaration of:

```
L=20
```

With that limit, the above text would be split during transmission into the following:

```
The maximum line len!
gth for SMTP mail is!
990 characters.
But that length is o!
nly enforced if the !
F=L flag is included
in a delivery agent !
definition. A delive!
ry agent speaks
SMTP when the $u mac!
ro is omitted from t!
he A= equate.
```

Limiting the line length can find application with programs that can't handle long lines. A 40-character braille print-driving program might be one example.

If the L= equate is specified, but given a value of zero or less, then no line-length limiting is done.

Maximum Message Size: M=

The M= equate is used to limit the total size (header and body combined) of messages handled by a delivery agent. The form for the M= equate is:

```
M=nbytes
```

Here, *nbytes* is the ASCII representation of an integer that specifies the largest size in bytes that can be transmitted. If *nbytes* is missing, or if the entire M= equate is missing, *nbytes* becomes zero. If the value is zero, no checking is done for a maximum.

If the size of the message exceeds the limit specified, an error message is returned (bounced) that looks like this:

```
----- Transcript of session follows -----
550 <recipient>... Message is too large; 64000 bytes max
```

This equate is usually used with UUCP agents, where the cost of telephone connections is of concern. It may also find application in mail to files, where disk space is limited.

Care should be used to avoid setting M= to a non-zero value when the delivery agent has the F=e flag set. That flag tells *sendmail* that the delivery agent is *expensive*. If the c option is also set, expensive mail is queued rather than delivered. A problem arises because the size of the message is ignored when it is delivered from the queue, so no queued messages are ever bounced for exceeding the M= limit.*

Path to the Delivery Agent: P=

The P= equate takes as its argument the full pathname of a program that is going to be run. The form of the P= equate is:

```
P=pathname
```

The *pathname* can be either the full pathname of an executable program (like */bin/mail*), or one of two special program names that are defined internally to *sendmail*. Those two internally-defined names are [IPC],

---

*This has been fixed in V8 *sendmail*.

which tells *sendmail* to forward mail over a TCP/IP network, and [LPC] which is used for debugging.

P=path   When the program specified by the P= equate is a full pathname, *sendmail* first forks (creates a copy of itself), then the child process (the copy) execs (replaces itself with) the program. The argument vector (*argv*, or command-line arguments) supplied to the program is specified by the A= equate. The program inherits the environment* of *sendmail*, and has its standard input and output connected to the parent process (the *sendmail* that forked). The message (header and body) are fed to the program through its standard input. The envelope (sender and recipient addresses) may or may not be provided on the command line, depending on the nature of the program as defined by its F= flags. If the A= *does not* include the $u macro, then *sendmail* will speak SMTP with the program.

P=[IPC] The special internal name [IPC] specifies that *sendmail* is to make a network connection to the recipient host, and that it should talk SMTP to that host. Most current versions of *sendmail* allow the name [TCP]† to be a synonym for [IPC], but [IPC] should be used when portability is of concern. The $u macro should *never* be included in the A= for this internal name.

P=[LPC] The special internal name [LPC] (for Local Person Communication) causes *sendmail* to run in a sort of debugging mode. In this mode, the mail message is sent to the *sendmail* program's standard output, and replies are read (in the case of SMTP) from its standard input; you act as the SMTP server.

The [LPC] mode can be very helpful when tracking down mail problems. Consider the mystery of duplicate five-character "From " header lines at the beginning of a mail message when mail is sent with UUCP. To solve the

---

*In most versions of *sendmail* the environment is stripped for security. V8 only passes TZ= and AGENT=.

†Originally, IPC meant "Inter-processor Communications", not "Inter-process Communications" as it does today. Some vendors have made TCP a synonym, thinking that it was more descriptive of the TCP/IP network mechanism. That may be a mistake on their part, because other networks exist, like XNS.

mystery, make a copy of your *sendmail.cf* file and change the P= for the UUCP delivery agent to [LPC] in that copy:

```
Muucp, P=/usr/bin/uux, F=msDFMhuU, S=13, R=23, A=uux - -r $h!rmail ($u)
     ↓
     change to
     ↓
Muucp, P=[LPC], F=msDFMhuU, S=13, R=23, A=uux - -r $h!rmail ($u)
```

Then run *sendmail* by hand to see what it is sending to the *uux* program:

```
% /usr/lib/sendmail -Ccopy.cf uucpaddress < message
```

Here the -C*copy.cf* command-line argument causes *sendmail* to use the copy of the *sendmail.cf* file, rather than the original. The *uucpaddress* is the address of a recipient that would normally be sent via UUCP. The *message* should only contain a Subject: header line and a minimal body:

```
Subject: test   ← one line header
                ← a blank line
This is a test. ← one line body
```

If *sendmail* prints the message with a five-character "From " header line at the top, then you know that *sendmail* is the culprit.

Recipient Rewriting Set: R=

There are two forms for the R= equate. One is the standard form, and the other is an optional alternative for IDA and V8 *sendmail*:

```
R=ruleset               ← legal for all
R=eset/hset             ← legal for IDA and V8 sendmail only
```

The *ruleset* specifies a rule set for processing all envelope and header recipient addresses for a specific delivery agent. If the value specified is zero, or if the entire R= equate is missing, no rule set is called. Figure 26-1 shows how R= fits into the flow of addresses through rule sets.

For IDA and V8 *sendmail*, there may be two rule sets specified. One rule set is specific to the envelope, and the other is specific to the header. The envelope-specific rule is the one to the left of the slash; the header-specific rule is to the right (R=eset/hset). If either value is missing, it defaults to zero for IDA, but defaults to the other specified value for V8.

If a rule-set value is greater than the maximum defined in *conf.h* with MAXRWSETS, the *sendmail* program logs the following error:

```
invalid rewrite set, 32 max
```

and ignores that delivery agent definition.

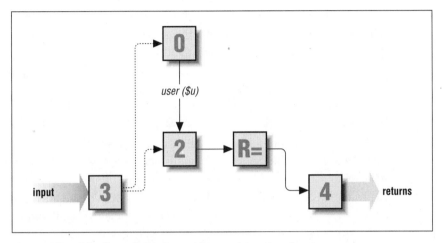

Figure 26-1: The flow of recipient addresses through rule sets

There is always at least one recipient for any given mail message, but there may be more. The addresses of the recipients are either given in the envelope or in the mail message's header. The envelope address is given to *sendmail* in one of three ways: as a command-line argument; as an SMTP RCPT command; or as in header To: lines. Header lines that can list additional recipient addresses are the To:, Cc:, and Bcc: lines.

The envelope recipient address is processed by *sendmail* first. It is rewritten by a fixed sequence of rule sets that includes the R= rule set.

S3   Rule set 3 is always the first to rewrite all addresses.

S0   The envelope recipient address is next processed by rule set 0. Rule set 0 is special because it resolves to the triple that selects the delivery agent.

S2   The username part of the envelope recipient (now in $u) is rewritten by rule set 2.

R=   Next, the envelope recipient address (from rule set 3) is processed by the rule set specified by the selected delivery agent's R= equate.

(For IDA and V8 *sendmail,* when two rule sets are specified, it is the one to the left of the / character.)

S4   Rule set 4 is always last to rewrite all addresses.*

After the envelope recipient address has been processed and the result stored in $u, each of the header recipient addresses is processed. Header lines that can list recipient addresses are the `To:`, `Cc:`, and `Bcc:` lines. Each header recipient address is processed by rule sets as follows:

S3   Rule set 3 is always first to rewrite all addresses.

F=C   If the header recipient address lacks an @ character, and if the sender's delivery agent flag F=C is specified, then the *@domain* part of the envelope sender address is appended to the header recipient address, and the result is reprocessed by rule set 3.

S2   Each header recipient address is then processed by rule set 2. (For IDA *sendmail,* if the option / is set, then process with rule set 6 instead.)

R=   Next, the header recipient address is processed by the rule set specified by the selected delivery agent's R= equate. (For IDA and V8 *sendmail,* when two rule sets are specified, it is the one to the right of the / character.)

S4   Rule set 4 is always last to rewrite all addresses.

Sender Rewriting Set: S=

There are two forms for the `S=` equate. One is the standard form, and the other is an optional alternative for IDA and V8 *sendmail*:

```
S=ruleset            ← legal for all
S=eset/hset          ← legal for IDA and V8 sendmail only
```

The `ruleset` specifies a rule set for processing both envelope and header sender addresses. If the value specified is zero, or if the entire `S=` equate is missing, no rule set is called.

For IDA and V8 *sendmail,* there may be two rule sets specified. One rule set is specific to the envelope and the other is specific to the header. The envelope-specific rule is the one to the left of the slash, the header-specific one to the right (`S=eset/hset`). If either value is missing it defaults to zero for IDA, but defaults to the other value for V8.

---

*If the delivery agent speaks SMTP (if there is no $u in the A= command-line arguments for the delivery agent), the envelope recipient address is processed once again, for use in the SMTP *rcpt* command.

If a rule-set value is greater than the maximum defined in *conf.h* with MAXRWSETS, *sendmail* logs the following error:

```
invalid rewrite set, 32 max
```

and ignores that delivery agent definition. The sender's address is either given in the envelope or in the mail message's header. The envelope address is given to *sendmail* in one of three ways: as a -f command-line argument; as an SMTP RCPT command; or as in header From: or Sender: lines.

Figure 26-2 shows how the S= equate fits into the flow of addresses through rule sets.

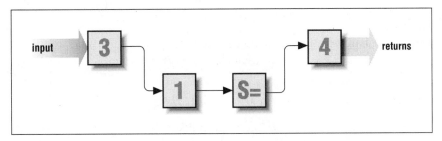

Figure 26-2: The flow of sender addresses through rule sets

Both the envelope and header sender addresses are processed by the same sequence of rule sets:

S3   Rule set 3 is always first to rewrite all addresses.

S1   The sender address is processed by rule set 1. (For IDA *sendmail*, if the option / is set, the envelope is processed with rule set 5 and the header with rule set 1.)

S=   Next, the sender address is processed by the rule set specified by the delivery agent's S= equate. The delivery agent was selected when the recipient envelope address was processed. (For IDA and V8 *sendmail*, when two rule sets are specified, the rule set for the envelope is the one to the left of the / character, and for the header it is the one to the right.)

S4   Rule set 4 is always last for all addresses.

Default Escape Character (IDA only): X=

When using alternate character sets with the IDA version of *sendmail*, it is necessary to have a special escape character that can be inserted into the character stream for toggling between the alternate and ASCII character sets. That character can occupy as many bytes as there are in the C language type `long` (at least four bytes). The X= equate looks like this:

```
X=val
```

Here, `val` is a numeric representation of the character that is converted to a `long` using the *atol*(3) C library routine. If `val` is missing, or if the entire X= equate is missing, the escape character defaults to zero. The character may be multiple characters (up to four) or it may be multibyte characters. Representation as an unsigned `long` may be tricky.

This X= equate only has meaning if the C= equate is also declared. Both may only be used if `BIT8` was defined in *conf.h*.

Special V8 Symbolic Names

The V8 version of *sendmail* internally predefines two delivery agents for the special handling of files. The `*file*` delivery agent (the `*` characters are part of the name) handles delivery to files. The `*include*` delivery agent handles delivery through `:include:` lists. Neither is a real delivery agent, because actual delivery is still handled internally by *sendmail*. Instead, they provide a way to tune delivery-agent behavior for these special delivery needs.

The predefined defaults for the `*file*` delivery agent are:

```
M*file*, P=/dev/null, S=0, R=0, M=0, F=lsDFMPEu, E="\n", A="FILE"
```

The predefined defaults for the `*include*` delivery agent are:

```
M*include*, P=/dev/null, S=0, R=0, M=0, F=su, E="\n", A="INCLUDE"
```

Either may be declared in the configuration file to overwrite these defaults. For example, the following could be used to limit the size of any mail message delivered to files to one megabyte:

```
M*file*, P=/dev/null, M=1000000, F=DElsu, A="FILE"
```

Note that any equate that is not zero in the default (like the P=, F=, and A= equates) needs to be copied to this configuration file declaration, or the original value will be lost.

The following command can be run to see what defaults are predefined with your copy of V8 *sendmail*:

```
% /usr/lib/sendmail -d0.15 -bt < /dev/null | egrep "file|include"
```

Pitfalls

- The F=f and F=r flags are similar in their implementation, but can differ in their result. Consider, for example, the SunOS 4.x version of */bin/mail*. That program expects the -r command-line argument to specify the sender's name. Setting the F=r flag correctly causes mail to be seen as from the sender (-r sender), but mistakenly using the F=f flag invokes */bin/mail* with -f sender instead. This fails, because the SunOS 4.x version of */bin/mail* expects the -f command-line argument to mean that it should interactively *read* mail from the mailbox named *sender*.

- The F=C flag can cause problems when it is specified for delivery agents for which the *@domain* form of address is inappropriate. This flag should be avoided for DECNET and the local delivery agents.

- A common problem with SysV versions of */bin/mail* is its annoying habit of prepending a "From " line to the beginning of each message, even if one is already there. This confuses users, because it makes their mail appear to come from *uucp* or *daemon* instead of the real sender. The problem stems from the fact that the SysV */bin/mail* lacks a -r command-line argument (or its equivalent) to indicate who the sender is. Instead that program assumes that the sender's identity can be taken from the identity of the person who ran the program. This works correctly with local mail, but when mail comes in from the outside world, */bin/mail* is being run by *root, daemon,* or *uucp*. The best fix is to get a newer */bin/mail** from one of the many anonymous FTP sites. A less satisfactory fix is to add the F=n flag for the appropriate (usually local) delivery agent. This leaves two "From " lines, the second prefixed with a > character (the correct line).

- Never use either the F=f or F=r flags with the prog delivery agent. That delivery agent usually runs programs by evoking the Bourne shell, which misinterprets either flag. The -f command-line argument tells */bin/sh* to disable filename-generation. The -r command-line argument

---

*The BSD */bin/mail* requires considerable hacking to get it to work on a SysV machine. Alternatives are *deliver* and the *mh* suite's *slocal*.

is unknown to */bin/sh*. Both command-line arguments produce the wrong result.

Alphabetized Reference

In this section we detail each of the delivery agent flags. The complete list is shown in Table 26-2. They are presented in alphabetical order. Lowercase letters precede uppercase letters for each flag.

Table 26-2: Delivery Agent F= Flags

Flag	Meaning
7	Use 7-bit path (V8 only)
a	Run extended SMTP protocol (V8 only)
A	Set ARPAnet compatible (not V8)
b	Add a blank line after message (V8 only)
B	Don't wait for SMTP response (IDA only)
C	Add *@domain* to recipient
D	Need `Date:` in header
e	Mark expensive delivery agents
E	Change extra `From` to `>From`
f	Delivery agent adds -f to argv
F	Need `From:` in header
g	Suppress `From:<>` (V8 only)
h	Preserve uppercase in hostname
H	Preview header for DECnet sites (IDA only)
I	Use more efficient SMTP exchange
l	Delivery agent is local (final) delivery
L	Limit message length (IDA and V8 only)
m	Multiple recipients possible
M	Need `Message-ID:` in header
n	Don't use UNIX-style `From` in header
N	Accept multiple status returns for DECnet sites (IDA only)
p	Process return path correctly
P	Need `Return-Path:` in header
r	Delivery agent adds -r to argv
R	Use a reserved TCP port (V8 only)
s	Strip quotation marks
S	Don't reset SUID for delivery agent
u	Preserve uppercase for username

Table 26.2: Delivery Agent F= Flags (continued)

Flag	Meaning
U	Use UNIX-style From line
V	Convert header to UUCP form (IDA only)
x	Need Full-Name: in header
X	Delivery agent needs RFC821 hidden dot

F=7
Use 7-bit path (V8 only)

Under old versions of *sendmail*, all lines of text output by *sendmail* (including the header and body of a message) automatically have the high bit cleared (zeroed) for every character. Under V8 *sendmail*, this behavior is unchanged for configuration file versions 2 (the V configuration command) or less. With new (version 3 and above) configuration files, the message body is transmitted with the high bit intact by default. For those delivery agents which should not allow 8-bit data to be transmitted, you may use the F=7 flag to force the old behavior.

F=a
Run extended SMTP protocol (V8 only)

Most versions of *sendmail* only run the SMTP (Simple Mail Transfer Protocol) defined in RFC821. In 1993, that service was extended by RFC1425 to become the Extended SMTP (or ESMTP). Under V8, you can enable a delivery agent to use ESMTP by specifying the F=a flag. This causes *sendmail* to first try to use the extended form of the HELO command, called EHLO. If that fails to be acknowledged as okay, *sendmail* tries again with non-extended SMTP. If the initial inbound greeting includes a line beginning with ESMTP, the F=a flag is assumed.

F=A
Set ARPAnet compatible (not V8)

This flag is obsolete and no longer has any special meaning.

F=b

Add a blank line after message (V8 only)

Some UNIX mailbox formats require a blank line at the end of a message. If your local version of */bin/mail* does not assure one, you may use the F=b flag. If this flag is specified, and if the message being sent to the delivery agent lacks a blank line at the end, *sendmail* adds one. This flag is also appropriate for use with the *file* delivery agent.

F=B

Don't wait for SMTP response (IDA only)

This flag tells *sendmail* to ignore responses (always return SMTPREPLYOK) when transmitting mail using the Simple Mail Transfer Protocol (SMTP). This mode provides a way to design an SMTP debugging delivery agent. It is, for example, easier to write a shell script that ignores SMTP input and never needs to reply, than one that can parse and converse in SMTP.

This flag can be very dangerous, possibly causing undetectable lost mail. Its use is best reserved for the expert who knows what he or she is doing. It should *never* be used with actual delivery agents.

F=C

Add @domain to recipient

The F=C flag causes *sendmail* to append an *@domain* extension to any recipient address which lacks one. The *@domain* that is added is copied from the sender's address.

This F=C flag is not looked for in the delivery agent definition that was selected to send the message. Rather, it is looked for in the delivery agent that would be selected if the sender were the recipient (as in the case of bounced mail). For example, consider the following mail:

```
From: bill@oursite.edu
To: john@remotesite.gov, alice
```

The recipient address `alice` lacks an *@domain* specification. The *sendmail* program processes the envelope sender address `bill@oursite.edu` to decide on a delivery agent definition that can be used should this mail need to be returned. If that sender's return mail delivery agent has the F=C flag set, then the @oursite.edu part of the sender's address is appended to alice.

```
From: bill@oursite.edu
To: john@remotesite.gov, alice@oursite.edu
```

The F=C flag is traditionally used for the IPC (TCP) delivery agent which is supposed to always supply an *@domain* part for all addresses.

A well-designed rule set 3 should convert all addresses to the *@domain* form (such as *@site.uucp* for uucp addresses). When rule set 3 does its job well, this F=C flag may safely be used with all delivery agents. When rule set 3 is not properly designed, care should be taken to avoid using the F=C flag with delivery agents that do not understand the *@domain* form.

F=D

Need Date: in header

The F=D flag is used by *sendmail.cf* header commands to force the inclusion of date information (see page 386):

```
H?D?Resent-Date: $a
H?D?Date: $a
```

The F=D flag has no special internal meaning to *sendmail* and is a convention used only in the assorted Date: header definitions (see page 386).

F=e

Mark expensive delivery agents

The *sendmail.cf* option c tells *sendmail* not to connect to expensive delivery agents. Instead, mail destined for those agents is queued for later delivery. This F=e flag marks a delivery agent as expensive.

For example, consider a site connected to the Internet over a 56k dedicated phone line. Such a site might want all the Internet mail to be queued and would arrange for that queue to be processed only once every other hour.

F=E

Change extra From to >From

All UNIX mail-reading programs, such as */usr/ucb/Mail,* require that each mail message in a file of many mail messages be delimited from the others by a blank line, then a line that begins with the five characters "From ":

```
and thanks again. -- bill          ← one message ends
                                   ← a blank line
From kristin Fri Apr  6 12:03:45 1990    ← next message starts
```

This means that any given mail message may have only one line in it that begins with the five characters "From ". To prevent such lines being improperly fed to such mail delivery agents, *sendmail* offers the F=E flag. This flag tells *sendmail* to insert a > character at the front of all but the first such lines found. Consider:

```
From wc@lady.Berkeley.EDU Mon Nov 25 13:00:03 1991

From now on, let's meet on Saturdays instead of Tuesdays
like we discussed.
```

If the F=E flag is specified for the delivery agent that delivers the above message, *sendmail* converts it to read:

```
From wc@lady.Berkeley.EDU Mon Nov 25 13:00:03 1991

>From now on, let's meet on Saturdays instead of Tuesdays
like we discussed.
```

This F=E flag is rarely needed. Usually the program specified by the local delivery agent definition handles From line conversions. This flag should *only* be used with delivery agents that handle final local delivery.

You may wish to consider omitting this flag from the prog definition. Omitting it allows a user the option of *not* transforming "From " lines, by specifying a program in his or her ~/.forward file.

F=f

Delivery agent adds –f to argv

If *sendmail* is run with a −f command-line argument, and if the F=f flag is specified, the A= for this delivery agent will have the two additional arguments −f and $g inserted between its argv[0] and argv[1]. For example, if *sendmail* is run as:

```
/usr/lib/sendmail -f jim host!bill
```

and if the delivery agent for sending to host is defined as:

```
Muucp, P=/bin/uux, F=fmsDFMhuU, S=13, R=23, A=uux - -r $h!rmail ($u)
```

Then the f in F=fmsDFhuU causes the A= of:

```
A=uux - -r $h@rmail ($u)
```

to be rewritten as:

```
A=uux -f $g - -r $h@rmail ($u)
```

Here $g is jim from the original command line (but rewritten to be a return address relative to the recipient). The original -f argument jim, is first rewritten by rule sets 3, 1, and 4. The result of those rewrites is placed into $f. The $f macro is rewritten by rule sets 3, 1, S=, and 4, and the result is placed into $g.

Note that the F=f and the F=r flags are very similar and easily confused.

F=F
Need From: in header

The F=F flag is used by *sendmail.cf* header commands to force the inclusion of sender (From) information (see page 386):

```
H?F?Resent-From: $q
H?F?From: $q
```

The F=F flag has no special internal meaning to *sendmail*, and is a convention used only in the assorted From: header definitions (see Chapter 31, *Headers*).

F=g
Suppress From:<> (V8 only)

The special address <> is used as the envelope sender when *sendmail* bounces a mail message. This address is intended to prevent bounced messages from themselves bouncing. Unfortunately, not all configuration files properly handle this form of sender address. The stock SunOS configuration files, for example, cause SunOS *sendmail* to enter an endless loop when processing <>.

As an interim measure, until all sites learn to correctly handle the <> address, you may use the F=g flag to suppress that address. If the F=g flag is set for a delivery agent, it uses the value of $g in place of the <> (where $g contains $n with an @ and your domain name appended).

F=h

Preserve uppercase in hostname

Some delivery agents, like those that deal with files, require that the recipient's hostname be left as-is. The hostname portion of the recipient's address is ordinarily converted to all lowercase before being tucked into $h. Specifying the F=h flag tells *sendmail* to not convert that address to lowercase.

The $h is usually used with the A= equate of a delivery agent. For example:

```
Muucp, P=/usr/bin/uux, F=msDFMhuU, A=uux - -r $h!rmail ($u)
```

Here the h in F=msDFMhuU tells *sendmail* to leave the $h alone and *not* to convert the hostname in that defined macro to lowercase.

F=H

Preview headers DECnet (IDA only)

Ordinarily, the names of the recipients and of the sender are sent over an SMTP connection before the message itself. This F=H flag causes *sendmail* to violate that standard specifically so that it can talk to the *mail11* program. The *mail11* program is used in communicating with DECnet sites, and those sites require that the message itself (both header and body) be transmitted before the envelope information (sender and recipient). This flag is only available if you define MAIL11V3 in *conf.h*.

F=I

Use a more efficient SMTP exchange

If you know that one *sendmail* program is going to be talking to another via SMTP, a slight advantage can be gained by using the F=I flag. Ordinarily the receiving *sendmail* program forks once to establish a connection to the sending *sendmail*. The receiving *sendmail* then forks again for each *mail* or *rcpt* SMTP command sent by the sending *sendmail*, to process each received mail message separately.

The F=I flag tells the local *sendmail* to send to the receiving *sendmail* the following two SMTP commands:

```
>>> VERB                       ← ours sends
200 Verbose mode               ← recipient replies
>>> ONEX                       ← ours sends
200 Only one transaction       ← recipient replies
```

The VERB SMTP command causes the receiving *sendmail* to go into verbose mode *and* to set its deliver mode to *interactive*. This has the same effect as if the receiving *sendmail* had been run with the command-line options -ov and -odi set.

The ONEX SMTP command prevents the receiving *sendmail* from *fork*(2)ing a copy of itself for each transaction. The net result of these two commands is that the sending *sendmail* has the dedicated attention of the receiving *sendmail* for a batch of mail messages.

The F=I flag is only appropriate when it is *known for certain* that the receiving host runs *sendmail*. Not all hosts run *sendmail* to receive mail. The efficiency added by this F=I flag is slight, except in unusual circumstances.

One application for the F=I flag is as an aid in debugging a remote receiving site's *sendmail*. The VERB SMTP command causes that remote site to run in verbose mode. By temporarily adding the F=I flag to a delivery agent's definition and then running *sendmail* locally with the -v command-line argument, you can watch both the local and the remote's verbose output.

F=l

Agent performs local (final) delivery

The F=l flag tells *sendmail* that this delivery agent will be performing final delivery (usually on the local machine). This notification affects *sendmail's* behavior in two ways.

First, it enables the return-receipt mechanism. That is, if the message header contains the line:

```
Return-Receipt-To: address
```

then *sendmail* sends back to the original sender an e-mail message acknowledging receipt. This mechanism should be used sparingly, as it is intended for use in debugging mail routes and can cause problems with mailing lists.

Second, it causes *sendmail* to ignore any host part of the triple returned by rule set 0. That is, the $@ operator should not appear in the RHS of rule set 0. If it does, that host information is ignored and is not copied into $h. Note that other actions (such as looking for a ~/.forward file) are keyed off the delivery agent named local.

Under IDA and V8 *sendmail*, the $@ may be included in rule set 0 when resolving a local (final) delivery agent. This permits a uniform format for its MAILERTABLE entries.

F=L
Limit line length (IDA and V8 only)

The RFC821 SMTP definition requires that each line of text be no longer than 990 characters, including the end-of-line characters (\r and \n). The F=L flag causes *sendmail* to split output lines in the message body so that they do not exceed this length. If the L= equate is present and specifies a non-zero value, then that value is taken as the limit, overriding the default SMTP limit.

The F=L flag also causes *sendmail* to ensure that the most significant bit of each character is clear, so that there is no chance of conflict with the *telnet*(1) protocol. Note that 8-bit characters are never allowed in the message header.

When an output line is split, first the text up to the split is transmitted, then the ! character is transmitted, and finally the characters defined by the E= equate are transmitted. A line may be split into multiple pieces. (See L= for an illustration of this process.)

F=m
Allow Delivery to Multiple Recipients

Whenever the *sendmail* program executes the program specified by the P= delivery agent equate, that program is given its *argv* vector as specified by the A= equate. As the last step in building that *argv*, *sendmail* appends one or more recipient addresses.

The decision as to whether it appends one address or many is determined by the F=m flag. If this flag is not specified, the delivery agent is given only one recipient. Otherwise, if it is specified, the delivery agent may be given many recipients. In either case, if there are more recipients than the argv can accept, the delivery agent is rerun as many times as is necessary to handle them all.

F=M
Need Message-ID: in header

The F=M flag is used by *sendmail.cf* header commands to force the inclusion of message identification information (see page 386):

```
H?M?Resent-Message-ID: <$t.$i@$j>
H?M?Message-ID: <$t.$i@$j>
```

The F=M flag has no special internal meaning to *sendmail* and is a convention used only in the assorted Message-ID: header definitions (see Chapter 31).

Note that the Message-ID: header definition should always be included in the *sendmail.cf* file. The presence of that header is expected by many software packages.

F=n
Don't use UNIX-style From in header

The UNIX-style mailbox (a single file into which many mail messages are placed) requires that each message be separated from the others by a blank line followed by a line that begins with the five characters "From ":

```
and thanks again. -- bill                       ← one message ends
                                                ← a blank line
From kristin Fri Apr  6 12:03:45 1990           ← next message starts
```

Ordinarily, *sendmail* adds a five-character "From " line to a message if there isn't one. The F=n flag prevents *sendmail* from doing this when we are not dealing with a UNIX-style mailbox.

If the F=n flag is *not* specified, two other considerations come into play. For IDA only, if the F=p flag is specified, $g is turned into the UUCP ! form of address. For all other versions of *sendmail*, if the F=U flag is specified (but not F=n), then the five-character "From " header line is created, and the words remote from $g are appended to that line.

The F=n flag should *always* be specified for SMTP delivery agents. The five-character "From " line is not a valid RFC822 header (because it lacks a colon) and is not permitted.

Apart from SMTP, the use of the F=n flag is best determined on a case-by-case basis. Some delivery agents always generate a "From " line, so the F=n flag can be used to avoid duplication. Some delivery agents only generate a "From " line if there is not already one there, so the F=n flag is

optional, and perhaps best omitted. Some delivery agents never generate a
"From " line, yet require one (like the *uux* program); for these the F=n flag
should always be omitted.

F=N

Multiple status returns for DECnet (IDA only)

Ordinarily, during SMTP transactions, only a single status line is returned
from the recipient following receipt of the DATA:

```
>>> DATA
354 Enter mail, end with "." on a line by itself
>>> .
250 Mail accepted          ← a single status line returned
>>> QUIT
```

When communicating to DECnet sites with the *mail11* program, it is necessary for *sendmail* to accept multiple status lines. The F=N flag causes
sendmail to issue a nonstandard MULT SMTP command at the start of the
connection to see if the recipient will issue multiple status lines. If the
recipient responds that it will, *sendmail* prepares itself for special handling
of those lines:

```
>>> MULT
250 Ok                      ← yes, multiple lines returned
```

For this flag to take effect, you must define MAIL11V3 in *conf.h* when
compiling IDA *sendmail*.

F=p

Process return path correctly

The SMTP *mail* command normally uses the envelope address for the
sender:

```
MAIL From:<jqp@wash.dc.gov>
```

If the F=p flag is specified, *and* if the F=l flag (for final local delivery) is
also specified, *sendmail* instead sends a transformed version of that
address. The transformation can take one of two forms, depending on the
first character of the envelope address. If that address begins with an @
character, then an @, the local hostname and a comma are prepended to
that address to create a legal return path:

```
<@hub:jqp@wash.dc.gov>
        ↓
becomes
        ↓
<@ourhost,@hub:jqp@wash.dc.gov>
```

If the envelope address for the sender does not start with an @ character, then an @, the local hostname, and a colon are prepended to that address:

```
<jqp@wash.dc.gov> becomes <@ourhost:jqp@wash.dc.gov>
```

The IDA version of *sendmail* has this property and one other for the F=p flag. Consider that the return address for a mail message can take one of two possible forms, a domain-style address such as:

```
jqp@wash.dc.gov
```

or a UUCP-style series of linked machines, such as:

```
hub!washington!jqp
```

The UUCP form of addressing is used by UUCP delivery agents. In general, the F=p flag should be specified for UUCP delivery agents under IDA. For those agents, this flag forces the five-character "From " header line to contain the full return path. That is, it prepends the local hostname and the ! to the front of the sender's address, if they are not already there.

F=P
Need Return-Path: in header

The F=P flag is used by *sendmail.cf* header commands to force the inclusion of return-path information (see page 386):

```
H?P?Return-Path: <$g>
```

The F=P flag has no special internal meaning to *sendmail* and by convention is used only in the assorted `Return-Path:` header definitions (see Chapter 31).

The sender's envelope address (the address that would be used to return mail if it were bounced, for example) is placed into $g for use in the `Return-Path:` header line. This is usually done during final delivery, although it can also be done for delivery agents that lack a clear envelope address. The form of the address in $g depends on the setting of the F=p flag.

F=r

Delivery agent adds –r to argv

If *sendmail* is run with a -f command-line argument, and if the F=r flag is specified, the A= for this delivery agent has the two additional arguments, -r and $g, inserted between its argv[0] and argv[1]. Consider a case where *sendmail* is run as:

```
/usr/lib/sendmail -f jim bill
```

If bill is a local user, and the delivery agent for local is defined as:

```
Mlocal,     P=/bin/mail, F=rlsDFMmnP, S=10, R=20, A=mail -d $u
```

then the r in F=rlsDFmnP will cause the A= of:

```
A=mail -d $u
```

to be rewritten as:

```
A=mail -r $g -d $u
```

The $g is jim from the original command line (but rewritten to be a return address relative to the recipient). The original -f argument jim is first rewritten by rule sets 3, 1, and 4. The result of those rewrites is placed into $f. The $f macro is rewritten by rule sets 3, 1, S=, and 4, and the result is placed into $g.

Note that the F=f and the F=r flags are very similar and easily confused.

F=R

Use a reserved TCP port (V8 only)

The F=R flag causes *sendmail* to connect on a reserved (privileged) TCP port for additional security. Privileged Internet ports are those in the range 0 to 1023. Only *root* is allowed to connect to such ports.

This flag is only suitable for use with the [IPC] and [TCP] delivery agents. Note that *sendmail* is usually SUID *root* when run as a daemon.

F=s

Strip quotation marks

Some delivery agents don't correctly understand quotation marks in addresses.*

---

*Fortunately, quoted addresses are not common. However, as the X.400 protocol becomes more common, quoted addresses will appear more often.

An address that contains quotation marks looks like this:

```
"John.Q.Public"@wash.dc.gov
```

For those delivery agents that do not correctly understand them, the F=s flag causes *sendmail* to strip all quotation marks from the address before handing it to the delivery agent.

```
John.Q.Public@wash.dc.gov
```

The `local` delivery agent should always have the F=s flag specified. The `prog` delivery agent commonly has the F=s flag specified. The uucp delivery agent may or may not require that flag depending on the specifics of the program specified in the P= equate. The [IPC] and [TCP] delivery agents should *never* specify the F=s flag.

F=S

Don't reset SUID for delivery agent

There are two major ways that *sendmail* can be run: as an SUID *root* process (that is, with the permissions of *root* no matter who runs it); or as an ordinary process, run by an ordinary (non-privileged) user (that is, with *root* privilege *only* if it is run by *root*). When *sendmail* is running with *root* privilege, and when the F=S flag is specified for a delivery agent, *sendmail* *always* invokes that delivery agent as *root*. When *sendmail* is run with *root* privilege, it must give up that privilege under certain circumstances in order to remain secure.

When the F=S flag is *not* specified, *sendmail* changes its owner and group identity to that of an ordinary user in the following circumstances:

1. If the mail message is forwarded because of a user's ~/.*forward* file, and delivery is via the `prog` delivery agent or to a file, then *sendmail* changes its owner and group identity to that of the user whose ~/.*forward* was read.

2. Otherwise, if the mail message is being delivered through an *aliases*(5) file's `:include:` mailing-list expansion, and delivery is via the `prog` delivery agent or to a file, then *sendmail* changes its owner and group identity to that of the owner of the file that was specified by the `:include:` line.

3. Otherwise, if the sender of the mail message is local, and delivery is via the `prog` delivery agent or to a file, then *sendmail* changes its owner and group identity to that of the sender. If the sender is *root, sendmail*

changes its owner and group identity to that specified by the g and u options, usually *daemon*.

4. Otherwise, if delivery is via the `prog` delivery agent or to a file, then *sendmail* changes its owner and group identity to that specified by the g and u options, usually *daemon*.

If the F=S flag is set, *sendmail* executes the delivery agent as *root*, no matter what.

F=u

Preserve uppercase for username

The username portion of the recipient's address is ordinarily converted to lowercase before being tucked into $u. The $u is usually used with the A= equate of a delivery agent:

```
Mprog,  P=/bin/sh,   F=lsDFMeuP,  S=10, R=20, A=sh -c $u
```

Some delivery agents, like the `prog` agent, execute programs. They require that the program (user) name be left as-is (otherwise the program name would not be found). Specifying the F=u flag tells *sendmail* to *not* convert that name to lowercase.

F=U

Use UNIX-Style From line

The F=U flag causes *sendmail* to prepend a five-character "From " line to the start of the headers if there is not already one there. Whether one was prepended or not, this flag also tells *sendmail* to add the words `remote from` *host* to the end of that line and also requires that $g be in the form *host!* . . . .

The F=U flag is required when a neighbor UUCP site runs an old (or possibly SysV) version of the *rmail* program. The newer BSD versions of *rmail* do not require this flag.

F=V

Convert header to UUCP form (IDA only)

The F=V flag tells IDA *sendmail* to change headers for UUCP mail such that they are made relative to the receiving host. The traditional way to do this is with rewriting rules. They remove the local hostname from the addresses in the `To:` and `Cc:` header lines, and add the local hostname to the address in the `From:` header line.

Unfortunately, this traditional method does not always work. An address in the `Cc:` header line may be that of the sender, for example, and should be treated the same as the sender's address.

The `F=V` flag moves this processing out of the rule sets and into internal *sendmail* code. The internal rules used are:

1. If any address begins with the name of the receiving host, remove both that receiving host's name and the `!` character that follows it.

2. Otherwise, prepend the local host's name and the `!` character, unless they are already there.

The rule sets distributed with the IDA version of *sendmail* use the `F=V` flag for the `uucp` delivery agent, which uses `!`-style addressing. The `F=V` flag is not used with the `uucp-a` delivery agent, which uses domain-style addressing.

F=x

Need Full-Name: in header

The `F=x` flag is used by *sendmail.cf* header commands to force the inclusion of the user's full name (see page 386):

```
H?x?Full-Name: $x
```

The `F=x` flag has no special internal meaning to *sendmail* and is a convention used only in the assorted `Full-Name:` header definitions (see Chapter 31). The user's full name is available in the `$x` defined macro.

F=X

Need RFC821 hidden dot

Delivery agents that speak SMTP require that any line of the message that begins with a dot signifies the end of the message. Delivery agents speak SMTP when the `$u` is missing from the `A=` equate. For example:

```
Mether, P=[TCP], F=msDFMuCX, S=11, R=21, A=TCP $h
```

An example of a file that contains leading dots is a *troff*(1) source file:

```
.\" Show example
.Ps
Mether, P=[TCP], F=msDFMuCX, S=11, R=21, A=TCP $h
.Ps
```

In the above, three lines begin with a leading dot. Ordinarily, SMTP would interpret the first of those lines as the end of the mail message. To prevent that misinterpretation, it is necessary to double the leading dot in transmission. The F=X flag causes *sendmail* to transmit the above message as:

```
..\" Show example
..Ps
Mether, P=[TCP], F=msDFMuCX, S=11, R=21, A=TCP $h
..Ps
```

The extra leading dot is automatically restored to a single dot at the receiving end.

This F=X flag should only be used with delivery agents that speak SMTP. It should not be used with other delivery agents, because they will not know to strip the extra dots.

27

Defined Macros

The *sendmail* program supports three kinds of macros. Defined macros represent a single value symbolically. Class macros (see Chapter 28, *Class Macros*) represent multiple values. Database macros (see Chapter 29, *Database Macros*) represent values stored in external files or networked NIS maps. In this chapter we discuss defined macros.

Defined macros allow strings of text to be represented symbolically. They are *declared* (given names and assigned the strings of text that will become values) at four different times:

1. When *sendmail* first begins to run, it pre-assigns strings of text to certain macros.

2. When *sendmail* processes the options in its command line, macros that were declared using the −oM command-line switch are assigned their values.

3. When *sendmail* reads its configuration file, macros that were declared using the D configuration-file command are assigned their values.

4. Finally, many macros are assigned values internally by *sendmail* as mail is received and sent.

Macros can be used in any configuration-file command. Generally they are expanded (their value used) when mail is sent or received.

Pre-assigned Macros

When *sendmail* first begins to run, it pre-assigns values to certain macros. The complete list of these macros is shown in Table 27-1. Each is described in detail at the end of this chapter.

Table 27-1: Pre-assigned Macros

Macro	Description
$_	RFC1413-validated user and host (V8 only)
$b	Date in RFC822 format
$k	UUCP node name (IDA and V8 only)
$m	NIS domain name (SunOS only)
$m	DNS domain name (V8 only)
$v	*sendmail* program's version
$w	Canonical hostname

All pre-assigned macros can be redefined in the configuration file or in the command line.

Command-line Definitions

When *sendmail* processes its command line, macros may also be declared and given values. Macros are declared and assigned values in the command line by using the M option. The form for this command-line declaration is:

    -oMXtext

The -o switch tells *sendmail* that this is an option. The M is the name of the option. The M option causes *sendmail* to use the characters that follow the M as a macro definition. The first of those characters (the *X*) is the macro name; the remaining characters (the *text*) are its value.

Because this form of definition is a part of the command line, all special characters are interpreted by the shell. Any *text* that contains shell wild-card or history characters should be quoted (we'll cover this in detail soon).

Command-line macros are defined before the configuration file is read and parsed by *sendmail.* If *sendmail* uses a freeze file, command-line macros override those in the configuration file. Otherwise, configuration-file macros always override command-line macros. Despite this, command-line definitions may still be useful. Pre-assigned macros may be given new values, and user-defined macros may be initialized in the command line.

For security reasons, only the r and s macros* allow *sendmail* to retain its *root* privilege. Overriding the value of any other macro from the command line causes *sendmail* to run as an ordinary user.

Syntax of the Command-line Macro's Text

When a macro is declared on the command line, its text value is taken from the command line as-is:

```
-oMXtext
```

Unlike macros declared in the configuration file (which we describe next), this form of declaration does not strip commas from *text* nor does it handle escape characters.

The whole suite of special operators available to your shell may be used to generate an appropriate *text* value. For example, the following assigns the local NIS domain to the macro N on SunOS systems:

```
-oMN`domainname`
```

The `domainname`, in back quotes, causes the *domainname*(1) program to be run and the output from that program to replace the `domainname` on the command line.

Configuration File Definitions

When *sendmail* reads the configuration file, macros declared in that file are assigned values. The configuration-file command that declares macros begins with the letter D. There may only be a single macro command per line. The form of the D macro configuration command is:

```
DXtext
```

The symbolic name of the macro is a single character (here *X*). This must immediately follow the D with no intervening space. The value given to the macro is the *text*, consisting of all characters beginning with the first

---

*For V8 *sendmail*, r and s should be set with the -p command-line switch.

character following the name (*X*) and including all characters up to the end of the line. Any indented lines that follow the definition are joined to that definition. When joined, the newline and indentation characters are retained. Consider the following three configuration lines:

```
DXsometext
        moretext
        moretext
    ↑
    tabs
```

These are read and joined by *sendmail* to form the following `text` value for the macro named X:

```
sometext\n\tmoretext\n\tmoretext
```

The notation \n represents a newline character, and the notation \t represents a tab character.

If `text` is missing, the value assigned to the macro is that of an empty string; that is, a single byte that has a value of zero.

If both the name (here *X*) and `text` are missing, a macro whose name is the value zero is given arbitrary garbage as a value. This can cause the *sendmail* program to crash.

Required Macros

Table 27-2 shows the macro names that *must* (except under rare circumstances) be given values in the configuration file.

Table 27-2: Required Macros

Macro	Description
e	The SMTP greeting message
j	Our official canonical hostname
l	UNIX From format
n	Name used for error messages
o	Delimiter operator characters
q	Default format of the sender's address

Each of these macros is described at the end of this chapter. Failure to define a required macro can result in unpredictable problems.

Syntax of the Configuration File Macro's Text

The `text` of a macro's value in the configuration file may contain escaped control codes. Control codes are embedded by using a backslash escape notation. The backslash escape notations that are understood by *sendmail* are listed in Table 27-3.

Table 27-3: Special Characters Allowed in Macro Text

Notation	Placed in Text
\b	Backspace character
\f	Formfeed character
\n	Newline character
\r	Carriage-return character
\\	Backslash character

All other escaped characters are taken as-is. That is, the notation \, becomes a ,, whereas the notation \b is converted to a backspace character (usually a CTRL-H). For example:

```
DXO\bc May\, 1992     becomes →   O^Hc May, 1992
```

Here the \b is translated into a backspace (^H) character, and the \, is translated into a lone comma character.

A bug in pre-V8 versions of *sendmail* causes the first comma, and all characters following it, to be stripped from the text, unless it is quoted or escaped. For example:

```
DXO\bc May, 1992     becomes →   O^Hc May
```

Note that under V8 *sendmail*, this bug has been fixed.

Quoted `text` will have the quotation marks stripped. Only double quotation marks are recognized. Multiple parts of `text` may be quoted, or it may be entirely quoted. If a comma appears in `text` (for all but V8 *sendmail*), it must be quoted or escaped. For example:

```
DX"O\bc May, 1992"     becomes →   O^Hc May, 1992
DXO\bc May"," 1992     becomes →   O^Hc May, 1992
```

For V8 *sendmail*, the comma is not special, but may be quoted or escaped without harm.

Leading and trailing space characters are retained in `text`. Spaces are harmless provided the macro is used only in rules (because spaces are token separators), but if the macro is used to define other macros, problems can arise. For example:

```
Dw ourhost
DH nlm.nih.gov
Dj $w.$H
```

Here, the `text` of the w and H macros is used to define the j macro. The j macro is used in the HELO SMTP command and in the `Message-ID:` header line. The value given to `$j` by the above is:

```
  ourhost. nlm.nih.gov
↑             ↑
two         a space
spaces
```

Here the value of j should contain a correctly formed, fully-qualified domain name. The unwanted spaces cause it to become incorrectly formed, which can cause mail to fail.

Characters That May Be Macro Names

The name of a macro must be a single character. Any character may be used. However, *sendmail* uses many characters internally and requires that they serve specific purposes. In general, only uppercase letters should be employed as user-defined macro names. Arbitrary use of other characters can lead to unexpected results.

The character that is the macro's name must be a single-byte character. Multibyte international characters have only the first byte (or last, depending on the machine architecture) used for the macro's name, and what remains is joined to the `text`.

The high (most significant) bit of the character is always cleared (set to zero) by *sendmail*.

Macro Expansion: $, $&, and $!

The value of a macro can be used by putting a $ character in front of the macro's name. For example, consider the following definition:

```
DXtext
```

Here, the macro named *X* is given `text` as its value.

If you later prefix a macro name with a $ character, you may use that value. This is called *expanding* a macro:

```
$X
```

Here, the expression $X tells *sendmail* to use the value stored in X (the *text*) rather than its name (*X*).

Macro expansion is recursive

When *text* contains other macros, those other macros are also expanded. This process is recursive and continues until all macros have been expanded. For example, consider:

```
DAxxx
DByyy
DC$A.$B
DD$C.zzz
```

Here the *text* for the macro D is $C.zzz. When the expression $D appears in a line in the configuration file, it is recursively expanded like this:

```
$D              → becomes →   $C.zzz
$C.zzz          → becomes →   $A.$B.zzz
$A.$B.zzz       → becomes →   xxx.$B.zzz
xxx.$B.zzz      → becomes →   xxx.yyy.zzz
```

Notice that when *sendmail* recursively expands a macro, it does so one macro at a time, always expanding the leftmost macro.

In rules, when *sendmail* expands a macro, it also tokenizes it. For example, placing the above $D in the following rule's LHS:

```
R$+@$D       $1
```

causes the LHS to contain seven tokens, rather than three:

```
R$+@xxx.yyy.zzz       $1
```

When Is a Macro Expanded?

A macro can either be expanded immediately or at runtime, depending on where the expansion takes place in the configuration file. In rule sets, macros are expanded as the configuration file is read and parsed by *sendmail*. In all other configuration lines, expansion is deferred until *sendmail* actually needs to use that value. This is an important distinction to remember.

To illustrate, macros used in header commands are not be expanded until the headers of a mail message are processed:

```
H?x?Full-Name: $x
```

Here, $x may change as *sendmail* is running. It contains as its value the full name of the sender. Clearly, this macro should not be expanded until that full name is known.

On the other hand, macros in rules are always expanded *when the configuration file is read*. Thus, macros like x should never be used in rules, because the configuration file is read long before mail is processed:

```
R$x    ($x)
```

Rules like this won't work, because x lacks a value when the configuration file is read. This rule will be expanded to become a meaningless:

```
R       ( )
```

The $*digit* operator (see Chapter 25, *Rules*) in the RHS may not be used to reference macros in the LHS. Consider this example, where X has the value myhost:

```
R$X      <$1>
```

This is expanded when the configuration file is read and is transformed into this:

```
Rmyhost    <$1>    ← error
```

Here, the $1 has no operator in the LHS to reference.

Use Value As-is (IDA and V8 only): $&

For those times when a macro should not be recursively expanded, but rather used in rules as-is, IDA *sendmail* offers the $& prefix. For example, consider the following RHS of a rule:

```
$w.$&m
```

When *sendmail* encounters this RHS in the configuration file, it recursively expands $w into its final text value (where that text value is your hostname, like *lady*). But, because the m macro is prefixed with $&, it is not expanded.

This could be useful, because it appears to offer a way to delay expansion of macros in rules until after the configuration file is read. Unfortunately such is not the case, because the expanded text returned by the $& prefix is always a single token. That is, because the above is tokenized before each token is evaluated, it appears in the workspace as:

```
"lady" "." "$m"
```

The `$&` prefix is intended to provide a way to access macros that are given values after the configuration file is read. Thus, the failure of `$&` to recursively expand is the result of an implementation designed to meet the limited goal of accessing those runtime macros.

To illustrate one application of `$&`, consider the client/hub setup described in the tutorial. In that setup, all mail sent from a client machine is forwarded to the hub for eventual delivery. If the client were to run a *sendmail* daemon to receive mail for local delivery (and in the absence of an MX record), a mail loop could develop where a message would bounce back and forth between the client and the hub, eventually failing.

To break such a loop, a rule must be devised which recognizes that a received message is from the hub:

```
R$+             $: $&r @ $&s <$1>   Get protocol and host
Rsmtp@$H<$+>    $#local $: $1       Local delivery breaks a loop
R$*<$+>         $#smtp  $@ $H $: $2 Punt to hub
```

These rules appear in rule set 0. By the time they are reached, other rules have forwarded any nonlocal mail to the hub. What is left in the workspace is a lone username. The first rule above matches the workspace and rewrites it to be the sending protocol (`$&r`), an @, the sending host (`$&s`), and the username in angle brackets.

```
user    → becomes →    smtp@hub<user>
```

The second rule checks to make sure the message was received with the SMTP protocol from the hub. If it was, then the `local` delivery agent is used to deliver the message on the local machine. If it was received from any other host, or by any other protocol, the second rule fails and the third forwards the lone user address to the hub.

Quote Special Characters (IDA only): $!

RFC822 defines the format for all legal addresses. IDA *sendmail* offers the `$!` prefix to rewrite the address value of a macro to conform to that standard. For example, consider the following address value:

```
John F. Kennedy <jfk@wash.gov>
```

This address does not conform to the standard, because it contains a dot character in the full name part of the address. If it were stored in the macro named **x** and expanded with the prefix $!, IDA *sendmail* would quote the nonstandard parts:

```
"John F..Kennedy" <jfk@wash.gov>
```

For example, consider the need to give a value to the macro named q (the default form of the sender's address). One common way to define that macro is:

```
Dq$x <$g>
```

Unfortunately, this definition assumes that $x (the full name of the sender) always conforms to the RFC822 standard. To insure that it does, the IDA prefix of $! can be used in place of the usual $ prefix:

```
Dq$!x <$g>
```

Note also that if the $! prefix is used in rules, it is expanded when the configuration file is read.

Note that V8 *sendmail* doesn't offer the $! operator. Instead, V8 *sendmail* contains code to handle the same corrections. Whenever it outputs an address, it detects forms that violate RFC822 or RFC1123 and adaptively corrects them.

Macro Conditionals: $?, $|, and $.

Occasionally it is necessary to test a macro to see if a value has been assigned to it. To perform such a test, a special prefix and two operators are used. The general form is:

```
 if        else        endif
 ↓          ↓           ↓
$?x text1 $| text2 $.
       ↑          ↑
 if x is defined    if x is not defined
```

This expression yields one of two possible values: `text1` if the macro named x has a value, `text2` if it doesn't. The entire above expression, starting with the $? and ending with the $. yields a single value, which may contain multiple tokens.

The following, by way of example, includes the configuration-file version in the SMTP greeting message, but only does so if that version is defined:

```
De$j Sendmail ($v/$?V$V$|generic$.) ready at $b
                       ↑
                      note
```

Here the parenthetical version information is expressed one way if V has a value (like 1.4):

```
($v/$V)
```

but is expressed differently if V lacks a value:

```
($v/generic)
```

The *else* part ($|) of this conditional expression is optional. If it is omitted, the result is the same as if the text2 were omitted.

```
$?xtext1$|$.
$?xtext1$.
```

Both of the above yield the same result. If x has a value, then text1 becomes the value of the entire expression. If x lacks a value, then the entire expression lacks a value (produces no tokens).

Note that it is *not* advisable to use the $? conditional expression in rules. It may not have the intended effect, due to the fact that macro conditionals are expanded when the configuration file is read.

Conditionals May Nest (V8 Only)

V8 *sendmail* allows conditionals to nest. To illustrate, consider the following expression:

```
$?x $?y both $| xonly $. $| $?y yonly $| none $. $.
```

This is just like the example in the previous section:

```
$?x text1 $| text2 $.
```

Except that text1 and text2 are both conditionals:

```
text1 = $?y both $| xonly $.
text2 = $?y yonly $| none $.
```

The grouping when conditionals nest is from the outside in. In the following example, parentheses have been inserted to show the groupings (they are not a part of either expression):

```
($?x (text1) $| (text2) $.)
($?x ($?y both $| xonly $.) $| ($?y yonly $| none $.) $.)
```

Interpretation is from the left to right. The logic of the second line above is therefore this: If both $x and $y have values, the result is both. If $x has a value, but $y lacks one, the result is xonly. If $x lacks a value, but $y has one, the result is yonly. And if both lack values, the result is none.

The *sendmail* program does not enforce or check for balance in nested conditionals. Each $? should have a corresponding $. to balance it. If they do not balance, V8 *sendmail* will not detect the problem. Instead it may interpret the expression in a way that you did not intend.

The only limit to the depth to which conditionals may be nested is one of ease of comprehension. More than two deep is not recommended and more then three deep is vigorously discouraged.

Pitfalls

- Macros that are given values while *sendmail* processes mail may not get the value expected. If that happens, careful hand-tracing of rule sets is required to find the fault. For example, the value in $g is the result of sender address rewriting and rewriting by the rule set specified in the S= equate of the selected delivery agent. Because $g is used to define the From: header line, errors in that line should be traced through errors in the S= equate's rule set.

- Macros can have other macros as their values. The *sendmail* program expands macros recursively. As a consequence, unintentional loops in macro definitions can cause *sendmail* to hang.

Alphabetized Reference

The *sendmail* program reserves for its own use all lowercase letters, punctuation characters, and digits. Table 27-4 lists all the macro names that have special internal meaning to *sendmail*. Although not all of the reserved characters are shown in this table, all should still be considered for the *sendmail* program's exclusive use.

Table 27-4: Reserved Macros

Macro	Description
$_	Validated origin user and host (V8 only)
$a	Origin date in RFC822 format
$b	Current date in RFC822 format
$c	Hop count
$d	Origin date in UNIX *ctime(3)* format (IDA only)
$d	Current date in UNIX *ctime(3)* format (not IDA)
$e	SMTP greeting message
$f	Sender's address

Table 27.4: Reserved Macros (continued)

Macro	Description
$g	Sender's address relative to recipient
$h	Recipient host's name
$i	Queue identifier
$j	Official canonical name
$k	UUCP node name (IDA and V8 only)
$l	UNIX From format
$m	DNS domain name (V8 only)
$m	NIS domain name (SunOS only)
$m	Original user address (IDA only)
$n	Error message sender
$o	Token separation characters
$p	*sendmail* process id
$q	Default format of the sender's address
$r	Protocol used
$s	Sender host's name
$t	Current time in seconds
$u	Recipient's username
$v	Version of *sendmail*
$w	Local hostname
$x	Full name of the sender
$y	Name of the controlling tty
$z	Recipient's home directory

The following pages present a complete reference for each reserved macro. They are presented in alphabetical order for ease of lookup.

$_

The validated origin user and host (V8 only)

RFC1413, *Identification Protocol,* describes a method for identifying the user and host that initiate network connections. It relies on the originating host, which must be running the *identd*(8) daemon.

When the V8 *sendmail* daemon receives a network connection request (and if IDENTPROTO* is defined when *sendmail* is compiled), it attempts to connect to the originating host's *identd*.† If the originating host supports identification, *sendmail* reads the login name of the user who initiated the connection. The *sendmail* program then appends an @ and the name of the originating host. If the name of the originating host is an IP number in square brackets, *sendmail* attempts to convert the number to a hostname. The final result, in the form *user@host,* is assigned to $_.

When *sendmail* is run on the local machine, it sets $_ to be the name of the user corresponding to the *uid* of the process that ran *sendmail.* It gets that name by calling *getpwuid*(3). If the call fails, the name is set to the string:

```
Unknown UID: num
```

Here, *num* is the *uid* for which a login name could not be found.

Next, an @ and the name of the local machine is appended to the name, and the result assigned to $_.

The $_ macro is not used by *sendmail.* Rather it is offered as a means for the administrator to use authentication information. One possibility would be to include it in the `Received:` header:

```
HReceived: $?sfrom $s $.$?_($_) $.by $j ($v/$Z) id $i; $b
```

Another possibility is to customize *checkcompat*() in *conf.c* (see Chapter 16, *Compile and Install sendmail*). One might, for example, wish to reject any mail where the host part of $_ does not match the contents of $s.

---

*Bugs in Ultrix and OSF/1 (and maybe others) break the *ident* protocol. For an explanation, see *conf.h.*

†Don't fear *sendmail* hanging if it tries to use *identd.* V8 *sendmail* includes timeouts as a precaution against a site that accepts connection but never replies.

$a
The origin date in RFC822 format

The $a macro holds the origin date of a mail message (the date and time that the original message was sent). It holds a date in ARPAnet format, defined in RFC822, section 5.1, and amended by RFC1123, section 5.2.14.

The *sendmail* program obtains that date in one of the following four ways:

- When *sendmail* first begins to run, it presets several date-oriented macros internally to the current date and time. Among those are the macros t, d, b, and a. This initialization is done after the configuration file is read, so all but b may be given initial values in that file.

- Each time a new envelope is created, the macros t, d, b, and a are each given a default value that is the current time, unless that macro already has a value.

- Whenever *sendmail* collects information from the stored header of a message (whether after message collection, during processing of the queue, or when saving to the queue) it sets the value of $a. If a Posted-Date: header line exists, the date from that line is used. Otherwise, if a Date: header line exists, that date is used. Note that no check is made by *sendmail* to ensure that the date in $a is indeed in RFC822 format. Of necessity, it must trust that the originating program has adhered to that standard.

- When *sendmail* notifies the user of an error, it takes the origin date from $b (the current date in RFC822 format) and places that value into $a.

$a is chiefly intended for use in configuration file header definitions. It may also be used in delivery agent A= equates (argument vectors), although it is of little value in that case.

$a is transient. If defined in the configuration file or in the command line, that definition may be ignored by *sendmail*.

$b

The current date in RFC822 format

The b macro contains the current date in ARPAnet format, as defined in RFC822, section 5.1, and amended by RFC1123, section 5.2.14.

Because $b holds the current date and time, *sendmail* frequently updates the value in that macro. When *sendmail* first starts to run, it places the current date and time into $b. Thereafter, each time an SMTP connection is made, and each time the queue is processed, the value of the date and time in that macro is updated.

If the system call to *time*(3) should fail, the value stored in $b becomes Wed Dec 31 15:59:59 1969,* and no other indication of an error is given.

$b is chiefly intended for use in configuration-file header definitions that require ARPAnet format (such as `Received:`). It may also be used in delivery agent A= equates (argument vectors), although it is of little value in that case.

$b is transient. If defined in the configuration file or in the command line, that definition may be ignored by *sendmail*.

$c

The hop count

The c macro is used to store the number of times a mail message has been forwarded from site to site. It is a count of the number of `Received:`, `Via:`, and `Mail-From:` header lines in a message.

The value in $c is not used by *sendmail*. Rather it is made available for use in configuration-file header line definitions. When calculating the hop count for comparison to the h option (maximum hop count), *sendmail* uses internal variables.

$c is transient. If defined in the configuration file or in the command line, that definition may be ignored by *sendmail*.

---

*The actual time depends on the local time zone.

$d
The origin date in UNIX ctime(3) format (IDA only)

The d macro holds the origin date of a mail message (the date and time that the original message was sent). $d is given its value at the same time as $a is defined. The only difference between the two is that $a contains the date in RFC822 format, whereas $d contains the same date in UNIX *ctime*(3) format.

The form of a date in *ctime*(3) format is generally:*

```
Sun Sep 16 01:03:52 1973\n\0
```

When *sendmail* stores this form of date into $d, it converts the trailing newline (the \n) into a zero, thus stripping the newline from the date.

$d
The current date in UNIX ctime(3) format (not IDA)

All but the IDA versions of *sendmail* use $d to store the current time, rather than the origin time. Otherwise its contents are the same as described above.

$e
The SMTP greeting message

The e macro is used to hold the SMTP greeting message. When *sendmail* accepts an incoming SMTP connection, this message is the first thing it sends to say it is ready.

The value in $e must begin with the fully-qualified name of the local host. Usually that name is stored in $j. Thus, the minimal definition for $e is:

```
De$j
```

The e macro must be defined in the configuration file. The only exception is on a machine where *sendmail* never listens for SMTP connections.

---

*The format produced by *ctime*(3) varies depending on the area of the world.

Additional information may follow the local hostname in the definition of $e. Any additional information must be separated from the hostname by at least one space:

```
De$j additional information
     ↑
     at least one space
```

Traditionally, that additional information is the name of the listening program (in our case always *sendmail*), the version of that program, and a statement that the program is ready. For example:

```
De$j Sendmail $v ready at $b
```

Although it is not uncommon to see imaginative variations in additional information:

```
De$j Sun's sendmail.mx is set to go (at $b), let 'er rip!
```

The *sendmail* program provides no default value for $e. If *sendmail* listens for incoming SMTP connections, $e must be given a correctly-formed value either in the configuration file or in the command line.

$f
The sender's address

The f macro is used to hold the address of the sender. That address can be obtained by *sendmail* from any of a variety of places:

- During an SMTP conversation, the sending host specifies the address of the sender by issuing a *mail* SMTP command.
- Trusted users are those declared with a T configuration command. Those users, and programs running under the identity of those users, may specify the address of the sender by using the -f command-line switch when running *sendmail*.
- When processing a message from the queue, the sender's address is taken from the qf file's S line.
- When processing bounced mail, the sender becomes the name specified by the value of $n, usually *mailer-daemon*.
- In the absence of the above, *sendmail* tries to use the user identity of the invoking program to determine the sender.

Once *sendmail* has determined the sender (and performed aliasing for a local sender), it rewrites the address found with rule sets 3, 1, and 4. The rewritten address is then made the value of $f.

$f is intended for use in both configuration-file header commands and delivery agent A= equates. $f differs from $g in that $g undergoes additional processing to produce a true return address. When *sendmail* queues a mail message, and when it processes the queue, the values in $f and $g are identical.

$f is transient. If defined in the configuration file or in the command line, that definition may be ignored by *sendmail.*

$g
The sender's address relative to recipient

The g macro is identical to $f except that it undergoes additional rule-set processing to translate it into a full return address. During delivery, the sender's address is processed by rule sets 3, 1, and 4, and then placed into $f. That rewritten address is further processed by 3 and 1 again, then custom rewritten by the rule set specified in the S= equate of the delivery agent. Finally, it is rewritten by rule set 4 and the result placed into $g.

$g holds the official return address for the sender. As such, it should be used in the From: and Return-Path: header definitions, and in $q (the default format of the sender's address).

The S= equate for each delivery agent must perform all necessary translations to produce a value for $g that is correct. Because the form of a correct return address varies depending on the delivery agent, other rule sets should generally not be used for this translation.

$g is transient. If defined in the configuration file or in the command line, that definition may be ignored by *sendmail.*

$h
The recipient host's name

Rule set 0 is used to resolve the recipient address into a triple: the delivery agent (with $#), the host part of the address (with $@), and the recipient user's name (with $:). The host part, from the $@, is made the value of $h. Once $h's value has been set, it undergoes no further rule-set parsing.

$h is intended for use in the A= equate of delivery agent definitions. For local delivery, the value in $h is NULL. Under IDA *sendmail*, $h may contain the name of the local host for local delivery, so that the MAILERTABLE feature can work.

$h is transient. If defined in the configuration file or in the command line, that definition may be ignored by *sendmail*.

$i
The queue identifier

Each queued message is identified by a unique identifier (see Chapter 19, *The Queue*). When a file is first placed into the queue, its identifier is assigned to $i. That is the only time $i has its value changed. Specifically, $i is *not* updated when the queue is processed.

$i is not used by *sendmail* internally. It should be trusted for use only in the Received: and Message-ID: headers.

$j
Our official canonical name

The j macro is used to hold the fully-qualified domain name of the local machine. It *must* be defined in the configuration file*.

A fully-qualified domain name is one that begins with the local hostname, and which is followed by a dot and all the components of the local domain.

The hostname part is the name of the local machine. That name is defined at boot time in ways that vary with the version of UNIX.

The local domain refers to the DNS domain, not the NIS domain. If running DNS, the domain is defined in the */etc/resolv.conf* file, for example:

    domain wash.dc.gov

At many sites, the local hostname is already fully qualified. To tell whether your site just uses the local hostname, run *sendmail* with a -d0.4 switch:

```
% /usr/lib/sendmail -d0.4 -bt < /dev/null
canonical name: wash          ← not fully qualified
canonical name: wash.dc.gov   ← fully qualified
```

The j macro is used in two ways by *sendmail*. Because $j holds the fully-qualified domain name, *sendmail* uses that name to avoid making SMTP connections to itself. It also uses that name in all phases of SMTP conversa-

---

*Except in V8 *sendmail*, where $j is automatically defined to be the fully-qualified canonical name of the local host. However, it is still possible to redefine $j if necessary.

tions that require the local machine's identity. One indication of an improperly formed $j is the following SMTP error:

```
553 wash.dc.gov.dc.gov host name configuration error
```

Here $j was wrongly defined by adding the local domain to a $w that already included that domain:

```
# Our domain
DDdc.gov
# Our fully qualified name
Dj$w.$D
```

One way to tell if $j contains the correct value is to send mail to yourself. Examine the `Received:` headers. The name of the local host must be fully qualified where it appears in them:

```
Received: by wash.dc.gov     ...other text here
             ↑
          must be a fully qualified domain name
```

$j is also used in the `Message-Id:` header definition. (See Chapter 31, *Headers.*)

For all but V8 *sendmail*, $j *must* be defined in the configuration file. For V8, it is automatically defined. It must *never* be defined in the command line. $j must appear at the beginning of the definition of the e macro. When using SunOS *sendmail.mx*, $w must also be the fully-qualified domain name.

$k

Our UUCP node name (IDA and V8 only)

The UUCP suite of software gets the name of the local host from the *uname*(2) system call, whereas *sendmail* gets the name of the local host from the *gethostbyname*(3) system call. In order for *sendmail* to easily handle UUCP addresses, the IDA and V8 versions also make use of the *uname*(2) function.

For IDA, first *gethostbyname*(3) is called and the result saved into $w. Then *uname*(2) is called, and the *nodename* returned is compared to $w. If they are the same, $k is given the same value as $w. If they differ, $k is given the value of the returned *nodename*.

For V8, the host part of the fully-qualified name returned by *gethostbyname*(3) is saved as the first string in the class $=w. Then *uname*(2) is called. If the call succeeds, the macro k and the class k are both given the *nodename* value returned. If the call fails, both are given the same host-name value that was given to the class **w**.

For both versions of *sendmail*, $k is assigned its value when *sendmail* first begins to run. It can be given a new value in either the configuration file or from the command line.

$l

The From format

The l macro has two functions:

- It defines the look of the five character "From " header line needed by UUCP software.
- It defines the format of the line used to separate one message from another in a file of many mail messages.

$l in UUCP software

UUCP software requires all messages to begin with a header line that looks like:

```
From sender  date remote from <host>
```

The *sendmail* program prepends such a line to a mail message's headers if the F=U equate is set for the delivery agent. This behavior is supported only if UGLYUUCP is defined in *conf.h* when *sendmail* is compiled. If the local machine supports UUCP, the l macro must be supplied with "From ", *sender*, and *date*:

```
DlFrom $g $d
```

The rest of the information is supplied by *sendmail*.

$l with mail files

Under UNIX, in a file of many mail messages such as a user's mailbox, lines that begin with the five characters "From " are used to separate one message from another. This is a convention that is not shared by all MUAs. The *sendmail* program appends mail messages to files under only two circumstances: when saving failed mail to the user's *dead-letter* file and when delivering to a local address that begins with the / character. When appending messages to files, it uses $l to define the form of the message separator lines.

For sites that use the Rand MUA (and that do not also use UUCP), $1 can be defined to be four CTRL-A characters:

```
D1^A^A^A^A
```

$1 must be defined in the configuration file.

$m
Domain part of hostname (V8 only)

Under V8 *sendmail*, the m macro is used to store the domain part of the local host's fully-qualified domain name. A fully-qualified domain name begins with the local hostname followed by a dot and all the components of the local DNS domain.

The value in $m is derived from $w. When V8 *sendmail* first starts to run, it calls *gethostname*(3) to get the name of the local machine. If that call fails, it sets that local name to be *localhost*. Then *sendmail* calls *gethostbyname*(3) to find the official name for the local host, which is assigned to $w as that macro's initial value. V8 *sendmail* then looks for the leftmost dot in $w. If it finds one, everything from the first character following that dot to the end of the name becomes the value for $m.

```
host.domain
      ↑→
   domain part made the value of $m
```

V8's $m is initialized before the configuration file is read. Consequently, it may be redefined in the configuration file or as a part of the command line.

Note that the meaning and use of $m differ among the IDA, V8, and Sun versions of *sendmail*.

$m
NIS domain (SunOS only)

Under Sun *sendmail*, the value of the m macro is set to the NIS domain name. The NIS domain name is used by the Network Information Services (like *ypmatch*(1)) to share information among many machines on a local network. The NIS domain is rarely the same as the DNS domain (and, for security reasons, should probably never be the same).

When Sun *sendmail* first starts to run, it calls *getdomainname*(3) to get the NIS domain name. If that call fails, the m macro is left undefined.

If the NIS domain name begins with a + or a dot, the first character is stripped, and the remainder becomes the value of $m.

```
+domain
↑
lead plus or dot stripped
```

Otherwise, Sun *sendmail* looks for the leftmost internal dot, and if it finds one, makes all the characters following that dot the value of $m.

```
host.domain
    ↑→
    domain part made the value of $m
```

Otherwise, if there is no leading plus or dot, and if there is no internal dot, the whole name becomes the value of $m.

Sun's $m is defined before the configuration file is read. Unless the NIS domain is identical to the DNS domain, the value of $w *must* be redefined in the configuration file.

Note that the meaning and use of $m differ among the IDA, V8, and Sun versions of *sendmail.*

$m
Original user address (IDA only)

Under IDA *sendmail,* the m macro contains the recipient's address as it appeared before aliasing*.

As each mail message is processed for delivery, the recipient's address is checked to see if it is the address of a local user. If it is, that address is saved in $m. Local recipient addresses may change as *aliases* are processed, and $m preserves a copy of the original address.

IDA's $m is intended for use in header definitions and in delivery agent A= equates. It is transient. If defined in the configuration file or in the command line, that definition may be ignored by *sendmail.*

Note that the meaning and use of $m differ among the IDA, V8, and Sun versions of *sendmail.*

---

*The original recipient is available in V8 *sendmail,* via the $u macro, while the message is initially being read. This allows you to add that information to the Received: header.

$n

The error message sender

The n macro contains the name of the person from whom failed mail is returned. Traditionally, that value is the name *mailer-daemon*.

When delivery fails, and notification of that failure is being prepared to be sent to the originating sender, *sendmail* "fakes up" a header. That header prepends the original header (and any included error messages). The sender of the error mail message (and the sender in the envelope) is taken from $n.

The n macro must contain either a real user's name or a name that resolves to a real user through aliasing. If *sendmail* cannot resolve $n to a real user, the following message is printed via *syslog*(3) and the returned error mail message is saved in */usr/tmp/dead.letter.*

```
Can't parse myself!
```

When an error mail message is sent, $f is given the value of $n. $n *must* be defined in the configuration file.

$o

Token separation characters

The o macro is intended to store as its value a sequence of characters, any one of which can be used to separate the components of an address into tokens. The traditional declaration for the o macro is:

```
Do.:%@!^=/[]
```

The list of separation characters declared with the o macro is joined by *sendmail* to an internal list of hardcoded separation characters:

```
()<>,;\"\r\n
```

The combined lists are used when tokenizing the workspace for rule-set processing. The order of the characters in the o macro declaration may be arbitrary. The space and tab characters need not be included in that list because they are always used to separate tokens.

Care should be taken when eliminating any given character from this list. The entire configuration file needs to be examined in detail to be sure no rule requires that character. For example, if you wish to eliminate the dot so that usernames of the form "First.Last" may be used, you need to find and rewrite any rules that expect the dot to be a separator:

```
R$+@$=w.$D
```

Such rewrites may require a massive revision of the configuration file and should not be approached lightly.

The use of the individual characters in addresses is beyond the scope of this book. The book *!%@:: A Directory of Electronic Mail Addressing and Networks*, by Donnalyn Frey and Rick Adams (O'Reilly & Associates, 1993) contains the many forms of addressing in great detail.

The o macro must be defined in the configuration file. There may be at most 39 separation characters listed. More than that will overflow the *sendmail* program's internal buffer.

$p

The sendmail process id

The p macro contains the process id of the *sendmail* that executes the delivery agent. Every process (running program) under UNIX has a unique identification number associated with it (a process ID). Process IDs are necessary to differentiate one incantation of a program from another. The *sendmail* program *fork*(2)'s often to perform tasks (like delivery) while performing other tasks (like listening for incoming SMTP connections). All copies share the name *sendmail*; each has a unique process ID number.

$p is intended for use in header definitions, but may also be used in the A= equate of delivery agents.

$p is transient. If defined in the configuration file or in the command line, that definition may be ignored by *sendmail.*

$q

The default format of the sender's address

The q macro is used to specify the form that the sender's address will take in header definitions. It is most often used in the From: and Resent-From: header lines.

The definition of $q must adhere to the standard form of addresses as defined by RFC822. It may contain just an address or an address and a comment. The traditional definitions of $q are:

```
Dq<$g>          ← as <george@wash.dc.gov>
Dq$g            ← as george@wash.dc.gov
Dq$x <$g>       ← as George Washington <george@wash.dc.gov>
Dq$g ($x)       ← as george@wash.dc.gov (George Washington)
```

The full name is not always known, and thus $x can be undefined (empty). As a consequence, when the full name is included in the q macro definition, it is often wrapped in a conditional test:

```
Dq$g$?x ($x)$.
Dq$?x$x $.<$g>
```

Of these, the second form is recommended for clients that forward all mail to a central mail-handling machine. If the full name is unknown locally, the header and envelope are identical and bracketed:

```
From: <user@slave.domain>       ← header
MAIL From: <user@slave.domain>  ← envelope
```

At the central mail-handling machine, both versions of the From: address are recognized as identical (only if the address is bracketed). As a consequence, the central machine deletes and recreates the From: line, adding the full name if known.

$q must be defined in the configuration file.

$r

The protocol used (IDA and V8 only)

The r macro stores the name of the protocol used when a mail message is first received. Currently, only the names SMTP and (ESMTP for V8) are used. If mail was received by means other than SMTP or ESMTP, $r is given a NULL value.

$r is intended for use in the Received: header definition:

```
HReceived: $?sfrom $s $.by $j$?r with $r$. id $i
```

Here the phrase "with SMTP" is included in this header line if $r has the value SMTP, or (with V8) the phrase "with ESMTP" if it has the value ESMTP.

The value in $r is saved to the qf file when the mail message is queued, and it is restored to $r when the queue is later processed. This is automatic with V8 *sendmail*, but needs to be enabled with IDA by defining QUEUE_MACVALUE in *conf.h*.

$r may be used only with the IDA and V8 versions of *sendmail*. $r is transient. It may be defined on the command line, but should not be defined in the configuration file. With V8, the -p switch is the recommended way to assign a value to $r.

$s
The sender host's name (IDA and V8 only)

The s macro contains the name of the sender's machine (host). Currently, $s is given a value by *sendmail* only if the mail message was received via SMTP.

The s macro is intended for use in the Received: header definition:

```
HReceived: $?sfrom $s $.by $j$?r with $r$. id $i
```

The phrase from *host* will be included in this header line if $s has any value. Here, *host* is the name of the sending machine.

The value in $s is saved to the qf file when the mail message is queued and restored to $s when the queue is later processed. This is automatic with V8 *sendmail,* but needs to be enabled with IDA by defining QUEUE_MACVALUE in *conf.h.*

$s may be used only with the IDA and V8 versions of *sendmail.* $s is transient. It may be defined on the command line, but should not be defined in the configuration file. With V8, the -p switch is the recommended way to assign a value to $s.

$t
The current time in seconds

The t macro contains the current date and time represented as an integer. The value of $t is set in two places:

- When *sendmail* first begins to run, it presets several date-oriented macros internally to the date and time it was run. Among those are the macros a, d, b, and t. This initialization is done after the configuration file is read.

- Each time a new envelope is created, the macros a, d, b, and t are initially given a default that is the current time, unless any already has a value.

$t is intended for use in configuration-file header definitions. $t is transient. If defined in the configuration file or in the command line, that definition may be ignored by *sendmail*.

$u

The recipient's username

Rule set 0 is used to resolve the recipient address into a triple: the delivery agent (with $#), the host part of the address (with $@), and the recipient's username (with $:). The recipient's username is then processed by rule set 2 (the generic rule set for all recipient addresses), then the rule set indicated by the R= equate of the delivery agent (the custom recipient address processing), and finally by rule set 4 (post-processing for all addresses).

If the delivery agent is local, that rewritten recipient's username is looked up in the *aliases* file and replaced with its alias if one exists. For V8 only, if not replaced, the address is rewritten by rule set 5 to possibly pick a new delivery agent and repeat this process.

After aliasing, the rewritten recipient's username is then assigned to $u. If the delivery agent is local, the value of $u is then used to look up information about that user with *getpwent*(3). The user's home directory from *pw_dir* is made the value of the $z and used to access that user's ˜/.*forward* and *dead.letter* files.

For all delivery agents, the final value of $u may be used as a component of the delivery agent's A= (argument vector) equate. For example:

```
A=uux - $h!rmail ($u)
```

Note that $u is special in delivery agent A= equates. If absent, *sendmail* speaks SMTP. If present *and* the F=m delivery agent flag is also present, the argument containing $u is repeated as many times as there are recipients.

In V8 *sendmail*, $u is also set to the original recipient (prior to aliasing) while the message headers are initially being read. Thus the original recipient information is available for use in the Received: header line. In this use, V8's $u is similar to IDA's $m.

$u is transient. If defined in the configuration file or in the command line, that definition is ignored by *sendmail*.

$v

The version of sendmail

The v macro contains the current version of the *sendmail* program, taken from the Version variable that is initialized in *version.c* of the *sendmail* source. In general, it is the SCCS revision number of the source. $v is used when defining $e and in Received: header lines.

The value given to v varies with the vendor as shown in Table 27-5.

Table 27-5: Meaning of Various Versions

Version	Vendor
5.65	Old BSD
8.*x*	V8
4.1	SunOS 4.1.*x*, initially based on BSD 3.67
5.65	IDA
5.65c	IDA with BIT8 support
5.65+	IDA with MAIL11 support
5.65	KJS
1.1	NeXT OS 2.1, based on BSD 5.52
911016.SGI	SGI, based on BSD 5.21
920330.SGI	SGI, based on IDA 5.65

There is currently no standard for identifying variations on the *sendmail* program. Clearly, $v may not contain a true picture.

$v is internally defined when *sendmail* starts up. It may be redefined in the configuration file or as part of the command line.

$w

The name of this host

When BSD *sendmail* first starts to run, it calls *gethostname*(3) to get the name of the local machine. If that call fails, it sets that local name to be localhost. Then *gethostbyname*(3) is called to find the official name for the local host. If that call fails, the official name for the local host remains unchanged. The official name for the local host is assigned to $w.

The IDA version of *sendmail* behaves identically to BSD except for three details. First, when calling *gethostbyname*(3), failure is not accepted. Instead, IDA *sendmail* waits a bit, then tries again. It tries as often as necessary until it succeeds. Second, on Sun machines, IDA *sendmail* always sets the initial value of $w to NULL. Third, DNS lookup of the host's official name is skipped unless NAMED_BIND is defined in *conf.h* when *sendmail* is compiled.

The SunOS version of *sendmail* is identical to the BSD version except that the call to *gethostbyname*(3) uses the NIS services.

V8 *sendmail* is identical to BSD, but it also checks the configuration version level (see Chapter 23, *The Configuration File*). If the version is 5 or higher, V8 *sendmail* discards the domain, thereby reducing $w to the first component of the name (the short name):

```
here.us.edu
    ↑
    from here to end of name discarded
```

If the version is 4 or less, $w retains the fully-qualified name (and is identical to $j).

$w is used internally by *sendmail* to screen all MX records found when delivering mail over the network.* Each such record is compared in a case-insensitive fashion to $w. If there is a match, that MX record and all additional MX records of lower priority are skipped. This prevents *sendmail* from mistakenly connecting to itself.

Any of the following errors (or variations on them) indicate that $w may contain a faulty value, most likely given by a bad declaration in the configuration file:

```
553 host config error: mail loops back to myself
553 Local configuration error, host name not recognized as local
553 host host name configuration error
```

Note that if $w is pulled from the name server, and the host is running BIND, and a cache is being down-loaded, $w could be periodically unresolved. Also, on SunOS, $w must be the fully-qualified domain name (see warning under $j). Under Ultrix, $w is always set to the first component of the fully-qualified domain name.

---

*Except for V8, which matches against the class macro $=w.

$w is defined when *sendmail* starts up. It may be redefined in the configuration file or as part of the command line.

$x
The full name of the sender

The x macro holds the full name of the sender. When *sendmail* processes a mail message for delivery, it rewrites the sender's address using rule sets 3 and 0 so that it can determine if the sender is local. If the sender is local, rule set 0 provides the sender's login name with the $: operator. Then *sendmail* calls *getpwent*(3) using that login name as the argument. If the login name is known, *getpwent*(3) returns the sender's full name in its *pw_gecos* field. The *sendmail* program then processes that *pw_gecos* field, throwing away phone numbers and the like, and converting the & character where necessary. The result, usually fairly close to the sender's full name, is the value assigned to the x macro.

Under certain circumstances, *sendmail* places a different value in $x:

- When processing the headers of a message, if *sendmail* finds a Full-Name: header, it assigns the text of that header to the x macro.
- When sending a failed mail message, the login name of the sender is taken from $n, and the full name is set to be:

```
Mail Delivery Subsystem
```

The x macro is intended for use in header definitions. If it used in the From: header definition, the sender's full name also appears in the SMTP envelope *mail* line.

Note that unusual *gecos* fields in the password file can cause mail to fail. The *sendmail* program accepts anything up to the first comma, semicolon, or percent as part of the full name. Consider the following *passwd*(5) entry:

```
happy:123:456:Happy Guy ;-),Ext 789,,:/u/happy:/bin/sh
```

The *gecos* field here will be parsed by all but V8 *sendmail* into a value for $x that can yield a faulty header—one with unbalanced parentheses:

```
From: happy@our.domain (Happy Guy ;-))
```

$x is transient. If defined in the configuration file or the command line, that definition will be ignored by *sendmail*.

$y

The basename(1) of the controlling tty

The y macro holds the name of the controlling terminal device, if there is one. The controlling terminal is determined by first calling *ttyname*(3) with the *sendmail* program's standard error output as an argument. If *ttyname*(3) returns the name of a terminal device (such as /dev/ttya) *sendmail* strips everything up to and including the last / character, and stores the result into $y.

$y is intended for use in debugging *sendmail* problems. It is not used internally by *sendmail*. When determining whether or not it can write to a user's terminal screen, *sendmail* calls *ttyname*(3) separately on its standard input, output, and error output, without updating $y.

Note that the device name in $y depends on the implementation of *ttyname*(3). Under BSD UNIX, all terminals are in */dev*, whereas under other versions of UNIX, they may be in subdirectories like */dev/ttys*.

$y is transient. If defined in the configuration file or the command line, that definition will be ignored by *sendmail*.

$z

The recipient's home directory

The z macro holds the location of the local user's home directory. This macro is only given a value if delivery is by the local delivery agent, and if delivery is to a user (as opposed to a file or a program). The home directory is taken from the *pw_dir* field as returned by *getpwent*(3).

The *sendmail* program uses $z to access a user's `~/.forward` file, and to save failed mail to a user's *dead-letter* file.

$z can be passed in the A= equate to a custom written local delivery agent. One reason to do so would be to deliver mail to a user's home directory, rather than to a central spool directory. $z is also very useful with the V8 J option.

$z is transient. If defined in the configuration file or the command line, that definition will be ignored by *sendmail*.

28

Class Macros

A class is like an array of string values. In the LHS of rules, it is sometimes advantageous to compare individual tokens to multiple strings when determining a match. The configuration class command provides this ability. The class command is similar to the macro definition command, except that instead of assigning a single value to a macro, it assigns many values to a class (similar to an array). Class differs from macros in that it can be used only in the LHS of rules, whereas macros can be used in either the RHS or LHS.

Two different configuration commands can be used to assign values to a class. The C configuration command is used to assign values from within the configuration file. The F configuration command is used in two ways: to assign values by reading them from a disk file, or to assign values by running a program and reading the output. These commands may be intermixed to create a single class or used separately to create multiple classes.

You may wish to review Chapter 12, *Class Macros*, in the tutorial to see a few typical applications of class.

Class Configuration Commands

The three forms for the class configuration command are:

```
CX list        ← values from configuration file
FX file        ← values from a disk file
FX |program    ← values via another program
```

The class configuration command starts with either the letter C or F, which must begin a line. The C says that values will be assigned as a part of the configuration command. The F says that values will be assigned from an external file or program.

The C or F is immediately followed (with no intervening white space) by the name of the class (the X above). A class name is any single ASCII character. Classes are separate from macros, so they may both use the same letter as a name with no conflict.

The *sendmail* program reserves the lowercase letters for its own use as internally defined class names (although currently only w and m are actually used). All uppercase letters are available for your use.

The C Class Command

The C form of the class command causes values to be assigned from within the configuration file. In general, the class command looks like this:

```
CX list          ← values from configuration file
```

Here, a `list` is a list of string elements (delimited by white space) that follows on the same line as the C command. Each word in `list` is appended to the array of values in the class *X*.

Multiple declarations of the same named class may coexist in the configuration file. Each declaration after the first appends its string elements to the preceding list. That is:

```
CX string1 string2
CX string3 string4
```

produces the same class as does:

```
CX string1 string2 string3 string4
```

Both create a class with four strings as array elements.

When an array of values is built, white space is used to separate one value from another. White space is defined by the C language *isspace*(3) routine, and usually includes the space, tab, newline, carriage return, and form feed characters. Each line of text assigned to a class is broken up by *sendmail* into white-space delimited words. When a line is indented with a space or a tab, that line is joined by *sendmail* to the preceding line. Thus the following three declarations also append four words to the class X:

```
CX string1
CX string2
CX string3
      string4
   ↑
   tab
```

Words that are added to a class cannot be removed after *sendmail* has read them. Instead, they must be edited out of whatever file or program produced them, and the *sendmail* daemon must be killed and restarted.

The F Class Command

The F form of the class configuration command allows values to be appended to a class from outside the configuration file. In general, the file command looks like either of the following:

```
FX file                ← values from a disk file
FX |program            ← values via another program (not V8 or old BSD)
```

The F is followed by optional white space, then the name of a file or program. If the file/program begins with the pipe character (|), it is taken to be the name of a program to run.* Otherwise it is taken to be the name of a file to read.

Each line read by *sendmail* from a file or program is parsed by the C language *scanf*(3) library routine. The formatting pattern given to *scanf*(3) is a %s. This causes each line of text read to be assigned to the class as a single *scanf*(3)-style word. The file is opened for reading or the program is executed when the configuration file is processed. If either cannot be opened (for reading or execution), *sendmail* *syslog*(3)'s the following error and ignores that configuration command:

```
can't open what
```

Here, the *what* is the exact text that was given in the configuration file.

The C and F forms of the configuration command may be intermixed for any given class name. For example, consider a file named */etc/local/names* with the following contents:

```
string3
string4
```

---

*This has been removed from V8 *sendmail* because it presents a security risk.

The following two configuration commands add the same four strings to the class X as did the C command alone in the previous section:

```
CX string1 string2
FX /etc/local/names
```

This creates a class with four strings as array elements. White space delimits one string from the others in the C line declaration, and they are stored in the order that they are listed. The file */etc/local/names* is then opened and read, and each of the two words in that file is appended to the two words already in the class.

scanf(3) variations

The file form of the class configuration command allows different formatting patterns to be used with *scanf*(3). But the program form does not allow any variation, and so its *scanf*(3) pattern is always %s, which tells *scanf*(3) to read only the first white-space delimited word from each line of text.

```
FX file pat        ← with scanf(3) pattern
FX |program        ← always "%s"
```

If the optional pat argument to the file form is missing, the pattern given to *scanf*(3) is %s. The optional pat argument is separated from the file argument by one or more spaces or tabs. It should not be quoted, and it consists of everything from its first character to the end of the line. Internally, *scanf*(3) is called with:

```
sscanf(result, pat, input)
```

Here, result is the string array element to be added to the class definition. The pat is the *scanf*(3) pattern, and input is the line of text read from the file.

After each line of text is read from the file and filtered with the *scanf*(3) pattern, it is further subdivided by *sendmail* into individual words. That subdividing uses white space (as defined by the C language *isspace*(3) routine) to separate words. Each separate word is then appended as an individual element to the class array.

Consider the contents of the following file named */etc/local/myhosts*:

```
server1 server2 # my two nets
uuhost          # my uucp alias
#mailhost       # mail server alias (retired 06,23,91)
```

This file contains three hostname aliases to be added to a class, say H. The following configuration command does just that:

```
FH /etc/local/myhosts %[^#]
```

The pattern `%[^#]` causes *scanf*(3) to read all characters in each line up to, but not including, the first `#` character. The first line includes two white-space delimited words that are appended to the class H. The second line contains one word, and the third contains none.

Executing the program (not V8)

In the program form of the class configuration command, the leading `|` character is stripped off and the rest of the line is executed using the *popen*(3) function.

```
FX |program
   ↑→
   entire rest of line becomes shell command
```

Because *popen*(3) always uses the Bourne Shell for command execution, *csh*(1) intrinsics like *pushd* may not be used. The program form reads each line of output produced by the **program**, filtering each with the default *scanf*(3) pattern `%s` (to read only the first "word" in each line). The program itself is really a shell command line, and may contain internal pipes, redirection, shell variables, and command-line sequences. Error messages are printed by both the shell and by all processes executed by the shell, rather than by *sendmail*, which can be confusing.

Generally, the program form of class should be used only if you also use a *sendmail* freeze file. Reading the output of another program is expensive and slows down *sendmail* every time it reads its configuration file. With a freeze file, the program is run only once, during the building of the freeze file (see `-bz` in Chapter 32, *The Command Line*, for a discussion of the freeze file.)

The F form of the class configuration command is processed only once, when the configuration file is first read by *sendmail*. Subsequent changes to the file or program are not detected by *sendmail*. For such changes to become effective, the *sendmail* daemon needs to be killed and restarted.

Access Class in Rules

Class arrays are useful only in the LHS of rules. The *sendmail* program offers two ways to use them:

$=X   The $= prefix causes *sendmail* to seek a match between the workspace and one of the words in a class list.

$~X   The $~ prefix causes *sendmail* to accept only an entry in the workspace that does not match any of the words in a class list.

Matching Any in a Class: $=

The list of words that form a class array are searched by prefixing the class name with the characters $=.

```
R$=X     $@<$1>
```

In this rule, the expression $=X causes *sendmail* to search a class for the word that is in the current workspace. If *sendmail* finds that the word has been defined, and if it finds that the word is associated with the class X, then a match is made.

The matching word is then made available for use in the RHS rewriting. Because the value of $=X is not known ahead of time, the matched word can be referenced in the RHS with the $*digit* positional operator.

Consider the following example. Two classes have been declared elsewhere in the configuration file. The first, w, contains all the possible names for the local host:

```
Cw localhost mailhost server1 server2
```

The second, D, contains the domain names of the two different networks on which this host sits:

```
CD domain1 domain2
```

If the object of a rule is to match any variation on the local hostname at either of the domains, and to rewrite the result as the official hostname at the appropriate domain, the following rule can be used:

```
R$=w.$=D     $@$w.$2     make any variations "official"
```

If the workspace contains the tokenized address *server1.domain2*, *sendmail* first checks to see if the word *server1* has been defined as part of the class w. If it has, the dot in the rule and workspace match each other, and then *sendmail* looks up *domain2*.

If both the host part and the domain part are found to be members of their respective classes, the RHS of the rule is called to rewrite the workspace. The $2 in the workspace corresponds to the $=D in the LHS. The $=D matches the *domain2* from the workspace. So that text is used to rewrite the new workspace.

Note that only words may be in classes. When *sendmail* looks up the workspace to check for a match to a class, it looks up only a single token. That is, if the workspace contained *server1@domain2.edu*, the LHS expression $=D would cause *sendmail* to look up only the *domain2* part. The *.edu* part would not be looked up, and consequently the rule would fail.

The IDA, SunOS, and V8 versions of *sendmail* allow multitoken class matching; they do so, however, at the expense of extra execution time.

Matching Any Not in a Class: $~

The inverse of the $= prefix is the $~ prefix. It is used to match any word in the workspace that is not in a class. It is seldom used in production configuration files, but when the need for its properties arises, it can be very useful.

To illustrate, consider a network with three PC machines on it. The PC machines cannot receive mail, whereas all the other machines on the network can. If the list of PC hostnames is defined in the class P:

```
CP pc1 pc2 pc3
```

Then a rule can be designed that will match any but a PC hostname:

```
R$*<@$~P>      $:$1<@$2>        filter out the PC hosts
```

Here the LHS looks for an address of the form:

```
"user" "<" "@" "not-a-PC" ">"
```

This matches only if the @ token is *not* followed by one of the PC hosts listed in class P. If the part of the workspace tested against the list provided by $~ is found in that list, then the match fails.

The $*digit* positional operator in the RHS (the $2 above) references the part of the workspace that doesn't match. If the workspace contains *ben<@philly>*, the $2 references the *philly*.

Backup and Retry

In Chapter 25, *Rules*, we explained that multitoken matching operators, like $*, always try to match the least that they can. Such a simple-minded approach could lead to problems when matching (or not matching) classes in the LHS. However, the ability of *sendmail* to backup and retry alleviates this problem. For example, consider the following five tokens in the workspace:

```
"A" "." "B" "." "C"
```

And consider the following LHS rule:

```
R$*.$=X$*
```

Because, the initial $* tries to match the minimum, it first matches only the A in the workspace. The $=X then tries to match the B to the class X. If this match fails, *sendmail* backs up and tries again.

The next time through, the lead $* matches the A.B and the $=X tries to match the C in the workspace. If C is not in the class X, the entire LHS fails.

The ability of the *sendmail* program to back up and retry LHS matches eliminates much of the ambiguity from rule design. The multitoken matching operators try to match the minimum, but match more if necessary for the whole LHS to match.

Class Name Hashing Algorithm

When comparing a token in the workspace to a list of words in a class array, *sendmail* tries to be as efficient as possible. Instead of comparing the token to each word in the list, one by one, it simply looks up the token in its internal *string pool.* If the token is in the pool, and if the pool listing is marked as belonging to the class sought, then a match is found.

The comparison of tokens to entries in the string pool is case-insensitive. Each token is converted to lowercase before the comparison, and all strings in the string pool are stored in lowercase.

Because strings are stored in the pool as text with a type, the same string value may be used for different types with no conflict. That is, for example, the symbolic name of a delivery agent and a word in a class may be identical, yet they will still be separate entries in the string pool.

```
CA localhost proghost local prog
Mprog,  P=/bin/sh, F=lsDFMeuP, S=10, R=20, A=sh -c $u
```

In the above, the word **prog** in class A is stored in the string pool as type *class*. The identical word **prog** in the delivery agent definition is stored separately in the string pool as type *mailer*.

The *sendmail* program uses a simple hashing algorithm to ensure that the token is compared to the fewest possible strings in the string pool. In normal circumstances that algorithm performs its job well. At sites with unusually large classes (perhaps a few thousand hosts in a class of host aliases), it may be necessary to tune the hashing algorithm. The code is in the file *stab.c* with the *sendmail* source. The size of the symbol table hash is set by the constant STABSIZE.

As an alternative to large class arrays, IDA and V8 *sendmail* offer external database macros and NIS maps. SunOS offers NIS maps only. (See Chapter 29, *Database Macros.*) There is currently no information available contrasting the efficiency of the various approaches.

Internally Defined Class w

When *sendmail* first starts, it predefines the class macro w. Because you may only append to a class, and not overwrite it, you need to be aware of this predefined class.

Before the *sendmail* program reads its configuration file, it calls *gethostbyname*(3) to find all the known aliases for the local machine. The argument given to *gethostbyname*(3) is the value of the $w macro that was derived from a call to *gethostname*(3).

Depending on the version of *sendmail* you are running, the aliases found will either be those from your */etc/hosts* file or those found as additional A records in a DNS lookup. To see the aliases that *sendmail* found, or to see what it missed and should have found, use the -d0.4 debugging command-line switch. Any aliases found are printed as:

aka: *alias*

Depending on your version of *sendmail*, each *alias* is either a hostname (like *rog.stan.edu*) or an Internet IP number (like *[123.45.67.8]*).

Adding to Class w

Many *sendmail.cf* files use the w class macro to define all the ways users might reference the local machine. This list must contain all names for the local machine as given in the */etc/hosts* file, and all names for the local host as listed in the Domain Naming System (including CNAME and MX records). For example:

```
# All our routing identities
Cw server1 server2
# All our local aliases
Cw localhost mailhost tops-link print-router loghost
# DNS records
Cw serv-link
# We are a bitnet registered node
Cw bitserver
```

If you notice mail failing because users commonly misspell the local machine name (e.g., *ol11l0* when they really mean *o1ll10*); you might want to consider adding that misspelled version to a Cw declaration.

A typical use of the w class macro looks like this:

```
R$*<@$=w>          $:$1<@LOCAL>              force ournames to local
R$*<@$=w.$m>       $:$1<@LOCAL>              force ournames.ourdomain to local
```

Here, $m contains our local domain name. The LOCAL will be used later to decide on the `local` delivery agent program.

Pitfalls

- Although a class macro name may be any ASCII character (any character in the range 0x0 to 0x7f), avoid using any of the nonletter characters. At the very least, they create confusing reading, and at worst, may cause *sendmail* to completely misinterpret your intentions.

- Although strings may traditionally be made to contain white space by quoting them, class macros will misinterpret those quotes. For example, *"vax ds1"* wrongly parses into two class entries: *"vax* and *ds1"*, with the quotes a part of each.

- Duplicate strings are silently ignored. Therefore, typos in a list of strings may cause an accidentally duplicated entry to be silently excluded.

- Avoid creating a new class macro name without first checking to see if it has already been used. That is, don't create a list of UUCP hosts within class u without first checking for *both* pre-existing Cu and Fu definitions and for rule-set uses of $=u and $~u. It is perfectly legal for the $=u and $~u expressions to exist in rule sets, without a corresponding

Cu or Fu definitions. Beware, however, that such empty references still cause *sendmail* to search the string pool.

- Under IDA and V8 *sendmail,* you may watch your class macro definitions being formed by using the -d37.2 debugging switch. Under other versions of *sendmail,* you may only approximate this information by using the -d36.9 command-line switch.

- The class macro expansion prefixes $= and $~ are intended for use only in the LHS of rules. If you use those characters in the RHS of rules, most versions of *sendmail* do not print an error; instead they silently accept those characters as-is. V8 *sendmail,* on the other hand, prints one of the following messages as a warning and ignores the entire rule.

  ```
  Inappropriate use of $=
  Inappropriate use of $~
  ```

- The file form's *scanf(3)* pattern can produce unexpected results. Remember that the pattern is applied to a line, not to a stream.

- There is no error checking performed during reads for the F form of the class configuration command. An error reading from a file silently causes the rest of that file's contents to be ignored. An unreported error from a program (one that silently returns 0 on both success and failure) is also silently ignored by *sendmail.*

- There is no check that the file specified in the F configuration command is indeed a file. If it is instead the name of a directory, device, or named pipe, *sendmail* will behave unpredictably and may hang. This has been fixed in V8 *sendmail.*

- Be careful using defined macros in the C form of class macro definitions. Some versions of *sendmail* store the macro itself, instead of the expanded value of the macro, leading to unexpected results. V8 and IDA *sendmail* store the expanded macro value.

29

Database Macros

Database macros are special forms of defined macros. When used with certain special operators, they can cause rules to access information in external files. We will cover three distinctly different forms of database macros:

SunOS   Since Sun developed the Network Information Service (NIS*), it is natural that they would adapt *sendmail* to use that service. By default, SunOS uses the *hosts.byname* map (an NIS version of the */etc/hosts*(5) file), but it can easily be made to access other maps, including "home-grown" maps.

IDA   The IDA version of *sendmail* allows the easy creation of *dbm*(3)-style files. Special operators allow the information in those files to be accessed from within rules. To maximize portability, IDA *sendmail* supports a wide variety of *dbm* packages and can use NIS maps.

V8   V8 *sendmail* allows the easy creation of both *ndbm*(3) and *db*(3) files. As with IDA, special operators allow those files to be accessed from within rules. V8 *sendmail* can also access the information in NIS maps.

Although the three forms of database macros differ in their implementations, they all share some advantages:

- Database information is external to the configuration file, so information may be easily changed without having to kill and restart *sendmail*.

---

*Formerly called "Yellow Pages."

- Only the location of the information is stored at startup, rather than the information itself, so *sendmail* starts up faster.
- Database information can be used in the RHS side of rules, so rules are more versatile. Class macros are still of use in the LHS.

To fully appreciate *sendmail* databases, consider the only alternative, the F configuration command. For example, mail sent using UUCP is a typical application that requires lists of information:

```
FU /etc/mail/uuhosts
```

Here, the external file */etc/mail/uuhosts* contains a list of UUCP hosts which are connected to the local machine. If the list rarely changes, the F command is appropriate. On the other hand, if the list is volatile and changes often, the F command has drawbacks. The file */etc/mail/uuhosts* is read only when the configuration file is processed. Any change to that file is ignored by a running *sendmail* (like the daemon). To make the change effective, the daemon needs to be killed and restarted, and if there is a freeze file, it also needs to be removed and recreated.

In such volatile situations, storing UUCP information in a database is preferred. A change to a database is immediately available to the running daemon, eliminating the need to kill, restart, and re-freeze.

Sun NIS Databases

The Sun version of database macros is designed for use with the NIS maps. The information in those maps can be accessed using the $% prefix in the LHS, or the ${ and $} operators in the RHS.

Creating an NIS Map

SunOS uses the *makedbm*(8) program to build NIS maps. An NIS map is an *ndbm*(3) database that is read by a server in order to answer requests from networked clients. There may (and should) be multiple NIS servers on each network that share copies of databases kept in sync with *yppush*(8). Three very good sources of information about how to create NIS maps are:

- The online manual for *makedbm*(8) shows its usage and explains its many command-line switches. But be aware of the easily overlooked warning that *makedbm* does not recognize comments in its input. Almost any file fed to *makedbm* needs to be preprocessed by a set of filtering commands.

- The hardcopy manuals for SunOS in the *System and Network Adminis-tration* volume contain large sections which describe how to create new NIS maps in detail. (The printed manuals are currently being replaced by the online *AnswerBook*(1) software.)
- The book *Managing NFS and NIS*, by Hal Stern (O'Reilly & Associates, 1992), contains a wealth of information about NIS in general and covers how to make and manage NIS maps.

An NIS map is just a database whose information is available over the net-work. Like most databases, it has *key* and *data* parts. The *key* is the item looked up, and the *data* is the information returned. For example, in the *aliases* file, the *key* is the name to the left of the colon, and the *data* is everything to the right:

```
george: gw@wash.dc.gov
   ↑       ↑
  key     data
```

Matching From an NIS Map in the LHS

In the LHS of rules, Sun NIS maps may be accessed by using the $% prefix to reference a defined macro's value. To illustrate, the following LHS accesses the NIS map named *uuhosts*:

```
DUuuhosts
R$*<@$%U>$*      rhs
```

Here, the first line defines the macro named U and gives it the value uuhosts. The second line contains the expression $%U, which causes the corresponding token in the workspace to be looked up in the NIS map whose name is the value of $U. Since $U contains the value uuhosts, the token in the workspace is looked up in the NIS map called uuhosts.

If there is no NIS map with that name, the LHS of the rule always silently fails. If the map exists, and if the token in the workspace is found in that map, then the LHS is a match. Any $*digit* in the RHS substitutes with the original token in the workspace, not with anything taken from the map. Essentially, then, the $% prefix merely verifies that the token is present in the map (which is identical to the class matching described in Chapter 28, *Class Macros*).

The $% prefix allows one or more tokens to be looked up. Such multitoken lookups use a *sub-token* match, which can prove tricky. To illustrate, consider the following map:

```
host1.cs.edu
host2.cs.edu
```

This map contains the name of two hosts. If the workspace contains the tokens host1.cs.edu (five tokens), the $% prefix matches the first line in the map as expected. But so does host1.cs and just plain host1. Unfortunately, this willingness to match multiple tokens can lead to mistakes. Because $% matches *any part* of a map entry, the tokens cs.edu, or cs or even edu in the workspace will also wrongly match the first map entry.

The lesson here is to create and use only maps that have single tokens in them. Using multitoken maps can lead to unexpected problems that are difficult to debug.

Name server lookups: $%y

The macro y, when given a $% prefix, is predefined to call *gethostbyname*(3) to look up the token that follows it. If *sendmail.mx* is being used, $%y does a name server lookup, rather than an NIS lookup. But if the non-Mx version of *sendmail* is used, $%y does an NIS lookup with the *hosts.byname* map (or looks in */etc/hosts* if NIS is not running).

To illustrate, consider a workspace that contains the tokens:

```
"george" "<" "@" "foo" ">"
```

The following LHS uses $%y, and, when given the above workspace, causes the hostname foo to be looked up:

```
R$+<@$%y>     rhs
```

The name foo is looked up using the DNS name services if *sendmail.mx* is running; otherwise, it is looked up in the *hosts.byname* NIS map (or */etc/hosts* file).

Note that $%y cannot be redefined or changed. If y is given a different value with a D configuration command, that different value can be used with all *but* the $% prefix.

Rewriting With an NIS Map in the RHS

NIS database maps can be used in the RHS of rules to replace address tokens with new tokens from the database. This replacement is made by using the $\${$ and $\$}$ operators:

```
${X tok $}
```

Here, the $\${$ begins the expression and is a prefix for the macro *X*. The macro *X* must contain the name of an NIS map as its value. The *tok* is the key that will be looked up in the map *X*, and the $\$}$ terminates the expression. If the map *X* exists, and if the key (*tok*) is found in that map, the entire expression is replaced by the *data* from the map. Otherwise, the *tok* becomes the value of the expression. For example, consider a map that contains UUCP routing information:

```
host1    a!b!host1
host2    c!d!host2
```

Here, the left column is the key and the right is the data. If we called this map *uuhosts*, the following rule could be used to perform the appropriate replacement:

```
DUuuhosts
R$*@$%U       $: ${U $2 $} ! $1
```

The LHS uses the $\$%$ prefix we described in the previous section. The $\$%U$ matches a token in the workspace only if it is in the key column of the map *uuhosts*. If the workspace contained the expression user@host1, the LHS would match, and the RHS would be given the opportunity to rewrite.

The RHS begins with a $\$:$ to prevent recursion. The $\${$ operator then causes the $2 (which, by position, is the value of the $\$%U$ in the LHS) to be looked up in the map U (*uuhosts*). Because host1 exists in that map, the entire expression from the leading $\${$ to the terminating $\$}$ is replaced by the data from that map:

```
user @ host1    becomes→   a ! b ! host1 ! user
```

As with $\$%$, the $\${$ performs a multitoken lookup for its key. Because multitoken matching is imprecise, map keys should be restricted to single tokens.

The macro y does not have any special meaning in the RHS. If you use $\$%y$ to look up a host by name in the LHS, you will need to separately define y with the name *hosts.byname* for use in the RHS.

If the terminating $\$\}$ operator is missing, everything following the $\${ *macro* (the remainder of the RHS) is viewed by *sendmail* as the key:

```
${X $1 ...    tab comment
   ↑→
   from here to tab is key
```

Space may exist between the $\${ and the macro letter with no change in effect. If the macro is present and contains a valid map name as its value, and if the key part is missing:

```
${X  $}
   ↑
   key is missing
```

the following error is printed and garbage is placed into the workspace:

```
Can't prescan NIS result
```

Because there is no way to tell if a lookup and replacement failed, it is best to use the $\${ RHS operator in conjunction with its corresponding $\$%$ LHS operator. That way you ensure that the RHS will rewrite only tokens which you are sure exist in the map.

IDA Databases

IDA *sendmail* is designed to operate with a variety of *dbm* implementations (*dbm*(3), *ndbm*(3), *sdbm*(3), *hdbm(3)*, and *mdbm*(3)), as well as with SunOS NIS maps. The database implementation it uses is determined at compile time with declarations in the *Makefile* (see Chapter 16, *Compile and Install sendmail*). For any selected implementations of a database, the K option names the database, and the $\$($ and $\$)$ operators use the database to rewrite the RHS of rules.

Creating the Database Files

The program *dbm*(1) creates database files for use with the IDA version of *sendmail*.* It is supplied in source form with the IDA distribution and supports a wide variety of *dbm*(3) and *ndbm*(3) libraries. The general form for its use looks like this:

```
% dbm switches command
```

All `switches` must precede the `command`. Switches are command-line arguments that begin with a - character. The `switches` modify the

---

*The *dbm* program is designed to be very general-purpose, with many uses beyond those needed by *sendmail*. This explains why it has so many switches and options.

behavior of the *command* and specify the location of the input and output files. (We'll detail the individual *switches* soon.)

dbm commands

The command is a single word (usually followed by additional arguments) that tells the *dbm* program what to do. The possible commands are:

clear   The *clear* command either creates a new and empty database (if one doesn't already exist) or removes all the entries from (truncates to zero size) an existing database.

delete `key`

The *delete* command removes one or more entries from the database. The `key` is a list of one or more keys to be removed.

dump   The *dump* command prints the database to the standard output. In each line of that output, the key is printed first, then a tab character, then the data for the key. The `-o` switch can be used to specify the name of an output file, instead of the standard output.

fetch `key`

The *fetch* command causes one or more keys to be looked up in the database and printed if found. The `key` is a list of one or more keys to look up. Each entry found is printed with the key coming first, then a tab character, then the data for the key. Keys that are not found are printed as [NOT_FOUND]. Output goes to the standard output, unless the `-o` switch directs it to a file.

load `file`

The *load* command adds entries to a database sequentially from one or more input files. The argument `file` is a list of one or more files. If `file` is omitted, input is taken from the standard input. If a filename is `-`, input is taken from the standard input at that point in the sequence of input files. The database is first emptied (truncated to zero size) unless the `-A` (append) switch was specified. The form of the input line is described in *parse* below.

make `file`

The *make* command combines the *parse* and *load* commands into one.

parse `file`

The *parse* command allows each line of input to specify multiple keys for each single data part. The `file` is the same as that for the *load* command above. Each line of input read by *parse* must be in the following form: data, then white space, then a white space delimited list of keys. Each key is output in the form created by *dump* and expected by *load*. Unquoted # characters are used to begin comments. A comment extends to the end of the current line of input. A backslash (\) prefix quotes a single character. Full quotation marks and paired angle brackets allow the white space and the comment character they enclose to appear inside the data part. Any line of input that begins with white space is joined to the end of the preceding line.

store `key data`

> The *store* command adds one or more `key` and `data` pairs to a database file. The `data` must be quoted if it contains internal white space. This command does not automatically clear (truncate) the database.

dbm command-line switches

In the command line of the *dbm* program, all `switches` must precede the `command`:

```
% dbm switches command
```

The uppercase switches take no arguments:

```
-A
```

The lowercase switches take arguments, which must immediately follow them, separated by white space:

```
-d dbm_file
```

Thus, the complete usage for the *dbm* program looks like this:

```
dbm [-AILNRSU] [-d dbm_file] [-m mode] [-o output_file] command
```

The square brackets show that all switches are optional. The `command` is not.

-A   The *load* and *make* commands automatically clear (truncate to zero size) the database. The -A command-line switch prevents truncation, thus allowing new information to be added to an existing database.

-I   Ordinarily, if you attempt to add two keys that are identical, *dbm* inserts only the first and prints a warning for the second. The -I switch prevents *dbm* from printing the warning. (See also -R below.)

-L   Ordinarily, all keys are added to or printed from a database as-is (without case conversion). The -L switch causes all keys to be converted to lowercase before they are added or printed. This switch must be used when creating databases for use with IDA *sendmail.*

-R   Ordinarily, when two identical keys are added to a database, the first is entered and the second skipped. The -R command-line switch inverts this. If two keys are identical, the second replaces the first in the database.

-S   The -S switch prevents simultaneous rebuilds of a database. It causes a key of @@@ to be added to the database after all other keys have been added. Unfortunately, the -S switch doesn't work when keys are being appended (-A), because an existing @@@ is not removed at the start.

-U   The -U switch normalizes all keys to uppercase letters when reading from or writing to a database. It is of questionable value for use with *sendmail.*

-d *dbm_file*

The -d switch specifies the name of the database file to be created or appended to. It must be followed by the name of the database file. The filename suffixes *.pag* and *.dir* (defining the two *dbm*(3) parts) should be omitted from *dbm_file*. If this switch and its argument are missing, the last argument following the *command* is used as the name of the database file.

-m *mode*

The -m switch is used to override the current *umask*(2), and specifies the mode (permissions) given to a newly-created database. The *mode* is interpreted as a decimal value unless it starts with a zero, which causes it to be interpreted as an octal value.

-o *output_file*

Ordinarily, all output from the *dump* and *parse* commands is printed to the standard output. The -o switch causes that output to be written to a file (*output_file*).

Define a Database With Option K

The K option declares the existence of a database file and associates the name of that file with a macro. The general form begins with an O and looks like this:

```
OKXdatabase
```

Here, *X* is the name of the macro which will be referenced in later rules. The *database* is either the pathname of a database file or (if prefixed with a %) the name of a SunOS NIS map.*

---

*NIS maps are usable only if YP is defined in *conf.h* when compiling IDA *sendmail.*

```
OKXdatabase                    ← a file
OKX%database                   ← a NIS map
```

There must be no space between the K and the macro name (here *X*), nor between the macro name and the file or map (here *database*). Space between the K and *X* causes the space to become the macro name and the *X* to be joined to the *database* name. Space between the *X* and *database* causes the space to become part of the *database* name and, because of that, later lookups will fail.

If DBM_AUTOBUILD is not defined in *conf.c* when compiling IDA *sendmail*, then the *database* name is taken as-is. If DBM_AUTOBUILD is defined, *database* may be three separate pieces of information:

```
OKXfile source process|pat
```

The intention here is to cause the database *file* to be automatically rebuilt (from the file *source*, using the process or *scanf*(3) pattern *pat*) whenever the database becomes out-of-date relative to its *source* file. Unfortunately, this feature is not yet fully implemented.

Rewriting in the RHS

Unlike SunOS, the IDA database macros can be used only in the RHS of rules.* This seeming deficiency is more than made up for by their greater versatility. In its simplest form, the IDA approach uses the special operators $(and $) to look up tokens in a database:

```
$(X tok $)
```

This expression in the RHS of a rule causes *sendmail* to look up the token *tok* in the database or NIS map *X*. If *tok* is found, the entire expression, including the $(and $), is replaced with the value from the database or NIS map. If *tok* is not found, the entire expression becomes the unchanged value of *tok*.

If the $) is missing, IDA *sendmail* experiences a segmentation fault and produces a core dump. If the *tok* is missing, the following error message is printed and the rule fails:

```
rewrite: cannot prescan dbm lookup result:
```

---

*Actually, 5.6c IDA *sendmail* does support $% in the LHS of rules. Unfortunately, there are some bugs in $% which make its use unwise. These bugs will be corrected, and $% will be improved in functionality, in the next major release of IDA *sendmail*.

The *tok* may be multiple tokens. When multiple tokens are looked up, matching in the database is a token-by-token match. That is, for example, if the database contains the following entry:

```
host.dept.domain   value
```

Only the tokens `host.dept.domain` match and are replaced by `value`. But `dept.domain`, for example, does not match, and so is left unchanged.

Comparisons between the *tok* and the contents of the database are done by first temporarily converting the tokens in *tok* into lowercase. Therefore, it is essential that the database files be built using only lowercase keys. This can be done by using the `-L` switch with the *dbm* program.

As mentioned, everything between, and including, the `$(` and `$)` is replaced by either the *tok* (if there is no match) or the result of the lookup (if there is). Other text and operators in the RHS are replaced as they normally would be. For example, consider the following rule, which checks to see if a UUCP host is locally connected:

```
R$* <@$+.uucp> $*       $: $1 <@ $(U $2.uucp $) > $3
```

If the database defined by `OKU` were a list of locally connected UUCP hosts:

```
host1.uucp  host1.localuucp
host2.uucp  host2.localuucp
```

Then this rule would perform the following translations:

```
user<@host1.uucp>    becomes →   user<@host1.localuucp>
user<@host3.uucp>    becomes →   user<@host3.uucp>
```

Here, the new *tag* `.localuucp` can later be matched by rule set 0 to select the uucp delivery agent, while the old tag `.uucp` would be forwarded to a more knowledgeable host.

As a final note, be aware that the macro database names defined with the `K` option differ from those defined with the `D` and `C` configuration commands. The letter `U`, for example, can be the name of a database (with option `K`), the name of a forwarding host (with the `D` command), and a list of users (with the `C` and `F` commands), all at the same time! The three different uses of the name `U` do not interfere with each other, but they can make for a confusing configuration file.

A default if the lookup fails

Recall that the following expression in the RHS of a rule causes the entire expression to be replaced with the result from looking up *tok* in the database *X*:

```
$(X tok $)
```

If the lookup fails (because *tok* was not found, or because database or NIS map *X* didn't exist), the entire expression is replaced by the original value of *tok*.

For situations when *tok* is not an appropriate replacement, IDA *sendmail* offers the $: operator:

```
$(X tok $:default $)
```

When the $: operator follows the *tok* in a database lookup expression, it specifies a default value to use instead of *tok*.

The $:*default* must follow the *tok* or the special meaning of $: is lost. If the $: is present, but the *default* missing, a lookup failure results in an empty string (0 tokens), which becomes the value for the entire expression.

To illustrate, consider a scheme whereby users can get information on selected topics by sending mail to *topic.help*. The database to implement this scheme might look like the following. Note that the *tok* tokens are on the left (the key) and the replacement tokens are on the right (the data):

```
x11.help          john
x.help            john
postscript.help   bill
ps.help           bill
troff.help        linda
ditroff.help      linda
```

Further, suppose the above database is stored in the NIS map called *help.map* and declared in the configuration file like this:

```
OKH%help.map
```

The following rule can then be designed to route help requests:

```
R$+.help        $(H $1.help $:root $)
```

If a user sends mail to, for example, `x11.help`, the RHS in this rule will rewrite that address to be `john`. If, on the other hand, the user sends mail for help that isn't listed in the database, such as `ftp.help`, the lookup will fail and the $: will cause the RHS to rewrite the address as `root`.

String replacement with %s

For some kinds of information (like UUCP paths), the replacement value taken from the database needs to be customized. With IDA *sendmail*, the $@ operator can be used in the RHS to customize any %s in the database value:

```
$(X tok $@customize $:default $)
```

As before, if the *tok* is successfully found in the database *X*, the entire expression is rewritten to be the data from the database. But here, the $@ tells *sendmail* to replace any literal %s found in that data with the tokens in *customize*. If the lookup fails, the value of the whole expression becomes *default*. If $:*default* is omitted, the value becomes *tok*. The $@ and $: parts must appear in the order shown. If reversed, the $@ part is silently ignored. If the database value doesn't contain a %s, the effect is the same as if the $@*customize* were ignored. If the database value contains a %s but the RHS lacks a $@*customize*, that %s appears untranslated in the returned value.

To illustrate, consider a database that maps UUCP hostnames to UUCP paths:

```
lady    lambda!snide!lady!%s
bug     leaf!%s@lady.uucp
```

Notice that the data part of each line contains a %s placeholder into which the recipient's username needs to be placed. If this database were called uuhosts, it could be declared in the IDA configuration file like this:

```
OKU/etc/mail/lib/uuhosts
```

Thereafter, rules can be designed that use the information in the database to rewrite UUCP addresses:

```
R$-@$+.uucp     $:$(U $2 $@$1 $:$2.uucp $)
```

Here, any workspace which contains address tokens of the form user@host.uucp will be rewritten by this RHS. The $: prefix prevents recursion. The $(U tells *sendmail* to look up the first $2 (the host part) in the database defined with the OKU line above. If the address was fred@bug.uucp, the bug would be looked up in */etc/mail/lib/uuhosts* and replaced with leaf!%s@lady.uucp.

After the *tok* portion is replaced, *sendmail* scans the replacement text to see if it contains a %s expression. If one is found, the tokens following the $@ replace the %s:

```
fred@bug.uucp
     ↓
  becomes
     ↓
leaf!%s@lady.uucp
     ↓
  becomes
     ↓
leaf!fred@lady.uucp
```

If the data part of the database entry lacks a **%s**, the **$@** part of the RHS is simply ignored. This is because the **$@** causes the **%s** to be replaced using an *sprintf*(3) call like the following:

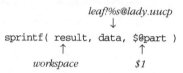

Note that **$:** and **$@** are independent options. You can use either or both or neither.

V8 Databases

V8 *sendmail* is designed to rewrite addresses based on information looked up in external databases or in its internal symbol table. It can use either *ndbm*(3)- or *db*(3)-style database files, or NIS maps. The K configuration command is used to declare the name, location, and other parameters of database files, or to modify use of its symbol table. The **$(** and **$)** operators are used in the RHS of rules to access and utilize that information.

Create the Map With makemap

The *makemap* program is supplied with V8 *sendmail* to create database files for later use. It is run from the command line:

```
% makemap switches class file
```

We'll discuss the *switches* in the next section. The *class* can either be *dbm* (which uses the *ndbm*(3) library routines), *hash*, or *btree* (which both use the *db*(3) library routines). The *file* is the location and name (full path or relative name) for the database file to create. For *dbm* files, the *.pag* and *.dir* suffixes are added automatically. For the *db* files, the *.db* suffix may be added automatically.

The *makemap* program reads from its standard input. That input is line oriented and contains the text from which the database files will be created. Lines that begin with a # are interpreted as comments and ignored. Lines that contain no characters (empty lines) are also ignored. White space (spaces or tabs) separates the *key* on the left from the *data* on the right. An example of one such input file is shown below:

```
lady      relaysite!lady
my.host   relaysite!lady
bug       bug.localuucp
```

The second line above shows that *keys* may be multitokened (my.host is three tokens). When reading from existing files, some conversion may be required to massage the input into a usable form. To make a database of the */etc/hosts* file (for converting hostnames into IP addresses), for example, a command line like the following might be required:

```
% awk '/^[^#]/ {print $2, $1}' | makemap ...
```

Here *awk*(1) needs to eliminate comment lines (the /^[^#]/); otherwise it will move comments to the second column, where *makemap* will not recognize them as comments.

makemap command-line switches

The command-line switches for *makemap* must precede the `class` and the `file`.

```
makemap switches class file
```

Switches are single characters, prefixed with a – character. Switches may be combined:

```
-N -o      ← good
-No        ← also good
```

(See *getopt*(3) for additional information about the way switches are handled.)

-f   Normally, both the key and the data are converted to lowercase before being stored in the database. When the key entries are case sensitive, the –f switch may be used to prevent conversion to lowercase. When tokens in rule sets are later looked up in the database, you may select (with the K command) to either leave those tokens as-is, or convert them to lowercase before the comparison to keys. This switch and the K command should parallel each other.

-N   The –N switch tells *makemap* to include a trailing zero byte with each key that it adds to the database. When V8 *sendmail* looks up a key in the database, it uses a binary comparison. Some databases, like */etc/aliases* under SunOS, append a zero byte to each key. When a trailing zero byte is included with a key, it must also be included with the tokens being looked up, or the lookup will fail. The use of this switch *must* match the K command described below.

-o   The –o switch causes *sendmail* to append to a map, rather than to overwrite it. Ordinarily, *makemap* overwrites any existing map with completely new information. The appended information must be all new information (no duplicate keys), unless the –r switch is also used.

-r   Ordinarily it is an error to specify a key that already exists in a map. That is:

```
john    john@host1
john    john@host2
```

Here, the second john line produces an error, instead of replacing the first with the second. To allow replacement keys, use the –r switch with *makemap*. Generally the –r and –o switches should be combined when updating a database with new information.

-v   To watch your keys and data being added to a database, use the –v switch. This switch causes the following line of output to be produced for each key processed:

```
key=`key', val=`data'
```

Note that the trailing zero added by the –N switch is not displayed with the –v output. Also note that verbose output is printed to the standard output, whereas error messages are printed to the standard error output.

The K Configuration Command

The K configuration command is used to associate a symbolic name with a database file. The symbolic name will later be used in the RHS of rules. The form of the K command looks like this:

```
Kname class args
```

The *name* is the symbolic name. The *class* is the kind of database to use and must be either *host* (which is special), *dbm, btree, hash,* or *nis*. The *args* specifies the location and properties of the database file. The *args* is like a mini-command line, which we will describe after we describe `class`.

The class

The `class` is the type of database and must be either *dbm, btree, hash,* or *nis* for an external database, or *host* for an internal database. The first three correspond directly to the `class` argument given to *makemap* when the database file was created. The *nis* corresponds to NIS maps, the creation of which is documented in the first part of this chapter. We will discuss the *host* class later in this chapter.

The args

The `args` of the K configuration command specify (among other things) the location of the database file or the name of an NIS map. The `args` is like a miniature command line, and its general form looks like this:

```
switches file_or_map
```

The `switches` are letters prefixed with a – character, that modify the use of the database (we'll discuss them in the next section). The `file_or_map` is the location of the database file or the name of an NIS map. The `file_or_map` should exclude the *.pag* and *.dir* suffixes for *dbm* class files, and exclude the *.db* suffix for *hash* or *btree* class files.

A database or map is opened for reading when the configuration file is processed. If the `file` cannot be opened (and the –o is omitted; see below), an appropriate error is printed. The `file_or_map` should be an absolute pathname of a file (like */etc/uuhosts*) or a literal NIS map name (like *hosts.byname*). An NIS map specification can include an NIS domain:

```
map@domain
```

Relative filenames (names that omit a leading /) are interpreted as relative to the current directory of the process that invoked *sendmail,* and so should never be used.

The switches for file_or_map

The `switches` must follow the `class` and precede the `file_or_map`.

```
Kname class switches file_or_map
```

If any `switches` follow `file_or_map`, they are silently ignored. All `switches` begin with a – character. Each is described below.

-a   When a key is looked up in a database (from inside the $ (and $) operators of the RHS of rules), a successfully found key is replaced by its data. If the -a switch is given, the text following that switch, up to the first delimiting white-space character, is appended to the replacement data.

-a	*appends*	*nothing*
-a.	*appends*	.
-a,MAGICTOKEN	*appends*	,MAGICTOKEN

The text to be appended is taken literally. Quotation marks and backslashed characters are included without interpretation, so white space cannot be included in that text. Because the rewritten RHS is normalized as an address, special address expressions (like parentheses) should be avoided. The use of appended text is one of two methods used for recognizing a successful lookup in rules. We'll discuss the other ($:) when we discuss the $ (and $) operators.

-d   Under SunOS NIS it is possible to have multiple NIS servers, each serving a different NIS domain. They need not serve the same maps. When the normal server (see *ypbind*(8)) does not provide the information needed by *sendmail,* the -d switch can be used to force *sendmail* to use a different NIS domain. The -d switch is recognized only by the *nis* class; it is ignored by all other classes.

-f   Ordinarily, *sendmail* will normalize a key to lowercase before looking it up in the database. If the keys in the database are case sensitive ("TEX" is considered different from "tex", for example), the -f switch should be used to prevent this normalization. Note that if the -f switch is omitted (the default), the database must have been created with all lowercase keys.

-m   Ordinarily, a successful lookup in a database or map causes the key to be replaced by its value. When the intention is to merely verify that the key exists (not replace it), the -m switch can be used to suppress replacement. For example, the values returned from the *hosts.byname* NIS map are not generally useful (they contain multiple hostnames). When looking up a key in this map (with $ (and $), described in the next section), the -m switch prevents those multiple names from wrongly replacing the single hostname in the key. Note that the -a can still be used to append text to a successful lookup. Also, the $:*default* (described in the next section) is still used if the lookup fails.

-N   If a database was created with *makemap* and -N, to include the
       terminating zero byte with each key, this -N switch may be speci-
       fied with the corresponding K configuration command to force all
       lookups to include a zero byte. Note that -N is not needed for the
       nis class, and if included, is ignored. See also -O below.

-O   If neither -N nor -O is specified, *sendmail* uses an adaptive algo-
       rithm to decide whether or not to look for the terminating zero
       byte. It starts by trying both. If it finds any key with a zero byte, it
       never tries again without a zero byte, and vice versa. If this -O
       switch is specified, *sendmail* never tries a zero byte, which can
       speed matches (but is never necessary). Note that if both -N and
       -O are specified, *sendmail* will never try to match at all, thus caus-
       ing all lookups to appear to fail.

-o   Ordinarily *sendmail* will complain if a database file cannot be
       opened for reading. If the presence of a database file is optional
       (as it may be on certain machines), the -o switch should be used
       to tell *sendmail* that the database is optional. Note that if a data-
       base is optional and cannot be opened, all lookups will silently fail
       for rules which use that database.

Use the Map with $(and $)

The information in database files is accessed for use in the RHS of rules.
The syntax is:

    $(name key $)

The *key* is looked up in the database whose symbolic name (as declared
with the K configuration command) is name. If the *key* is found, the entire
expression, including the $(and $), is replaced with the data from the
database entry for that *key*. Any *suffix*, as specified with the -a switch
in the K configuration declaration for *name*, is appended to the data. If the
key is not found, the entire expression is replaced with key. If the $) is
omitted, all tokens up to and excluding the tab and comment, or end-of-line
if there is no comment, are taken as the key. To illustrate one use for $(
and $), consider the following rule:

    R$-.uucp $:$(uucp $1.uucp $)

and the following K command:

    Kuucp hash /etc/uucp.db

This associates the symbolic name uucp with a hash class file called /etc/uucp.db. If the *uucp.db* database contained entries like this:

```
lady.uucp      lady.localuucp
sonya.uucp     sonya.localuucp
```

then a workspace of lady.uucp would match the LHS, so the RHS would look up $1.uucp (thus lady.uucp) in the *uucp.db* database. Because lady.uucp is found, the entire $(to $) RHS expression is replaced with lady.localuucp from the database. Any UUCP hosts other than lady or sonya would not be found in the database, so the RHS expression would become the original workspace, unchanged.

Note that the entire RHS is prefixed with a $:. This prevents *sendmail* from re-testing with the LHS after the RHS rewrite. If this prefix were omitted, endless looping would occur.

Also note that the −a switch of the K command can be used to simplify the writing of this rule. For example:

```
Kuucp dbm -a.localuucp /etc/uuhosts
```

The −a switch tells *sendmail* to append the text .localuucp to all successful lookups. Thus the preceding database can be simplified to look like this:

```
lady.uucp      lady
sonya.uucp     sonya
```

But the preceding rule remains the same:

```
R$-.uucp        $:$(uucp $1.uucp $)
```

Specify a default with $:

V8 *sendmail* offers the $: operator as an alternative to the −a switch (or for use in conjunction with it). The $: operator inside the $(and $) specifies a default to use instead of the *key*, should a lookup fail.

```
R$-.uucp        $:$(uucp $1 $:$1.uucp $)
```

Here, the $− part of the LHS is looked up in the uucp database. If it is found, the $(to $) of the RHS expression is replaced by the data from that database. If it is not found, the $: causes the expression to be replaced with the $− LHS part and a .uucp suffix ($1.uucp).

This version of our rule further simplifies the contents of the database file. With this rule, the database file would contain information like the following:

```
lady    lady
sonya   sonya
```

The −a is still used as before to append a .localuucp to each successful match.

```
Kuucp dbm -a.localuucp /etc/uuhosts
```

In the RHS expression, the $: must follow the *key* or it loses its special meaning:

```
$(name key $:default $)
```

If the $:*default* wrongly precedes the *key*, it is used as the key, lookups fail, and replacements are not as expected. If the *default* is missing, the rewriting of the RHS fails and *sendmail* prints the following error message:

```
rewrite: cannot prescan map value:
```

Specify numbered substitution with $@

For more complex database substitutions, V8 *sendmail* offers the $@ operator for use in the RHS with the $(and $) expression. There may be multiple $@ prefixed texts between the *key* and the $: (if present) or the $).

```
$(name key $@text1 $@text2 $:default $)
```

The $@*text* expressions are each numbered by position (from left to right):

```
$(name key $@text1 $@text2 $:default $)
            ↑         ↑
            1         2
```

In this numbering scheme, the *key* is always number 0, even if there are no $@'s listed.

These numbers correspond to literal %*digit* expressions in the data portion of the database.

```
lady    %0!%1@%2
```

When a lookup of the *key* in the RHS of the rule is successful, the data is examined for %*digit* expressions. Each such expression is replaced by its corresponding $@*text* from the rule. In the case of the above database, %0 would be replaced with lady (the *key*), %1 with text1, and %2 with text2.

To illustrate, consider the above database entry and the below rule:

```
R$-@$-.uucp    $:$(uucp $2 $@$1 $@mailhost $:$1.$2.uucp $)
```

If the workspace contains the address *joe@lady.uucp*, the LHS matches. The RHS rewrites only once because it is prefixed with the $: operator. The expression between the $(and $) causes the second $- from the LHS (the $2, the *key*) to be looked up in the database whose symbolic name is uucp. Since $2 references lady from the workspace, lady is found and the data (%0!%1@%2) used to rewrite. The %0 is replaced by lady (the *key* via $2). The *text* for the first $@ ($1 or joe) then replaces the %1. Then the second *text* for the second $@ (mailhost) replaces the %2. Thus the address *joe@lady.uucp* is rewritten to become *lady!joe@mailhost*.

If a different host, other than lady, appeared in the workspace, this RHS would use the $:*default* part. Thus an address like *joe@foo.uucp* would become (via the $:$1.$2.uucp) *joe@foo.uucp*. That is, any address not found in the database would remain unchanged.

If there are more $@*text* expressions in the RHS than there are numbers in the data, the excess $@*text* parts are ignored. If a %*digit* in the data references a nonexistent $@*text*, it is simply removed during the rewrite.

All $@*text* expressions must lie between the *key* and the $:*default* (if present). If any follow the $:*default*, they become part of the default and cease to reference any %*digits*.

$[and $] a special case

The special database class called *host* can be declared to modify name-server lookups with $[and $]. The special symbolic name and class pair, host and host, is declared for use with the $(and $) operators.

```
Khost host -a.
```

The -a switch was discussed earlier in this chapter. Here, it is sufficient to note how it is used when resolving fully-qualified domain names with the $[and $] operators in the RHS of rules. Under V8 *sendmail*, $[and $] are a special case of the following database lookup:

```
$(host foo )$
```

A successful match will ordinarily append a dot to a successfully resolved hostname.

When a *host* class is declared with the K command, any suffix of the −a replaces the dot as the character or characters added. For example:

```
$[ foo $]        found so rewritten as foo.domain.

Khost host -a
$[ foo $]        found so rewritten as foo.domain

Khost host -a.yes
$[ foo $]        found so rewritten as foo.domain.yes
```

The first line above shows the default action of the $[and $] operators in the RHS of rules. If `foo` can be fully qualified, its fully-qualified name becomes the rewritten value of the RHS and has a dot appended. The next two lines show the −a of `host host` with no suffix (note that with no suffix the −a is optional). In this configuration file, the fully-qualified name has nothing (not even a dot) appended. The last two lines show a configuration file with a `.yes` as the suffix. This time, the fully-qualified name has a `.yes` appended instead of the dot.

The dequote class

V8 *sendmail* can remove quotation marks from around tokens by using the special *dequote* class. Because *dequote* is a class, not a map, you need to declare it with a K configuration command before you can use it:

```
Kunquote dequote
```

This declares a map named *unquote* of the class *dequote*. Once a map name has been declared, the *dequote* class can be used in the RHS of rules to remove quotation marks. It is used with $(and $), just like database lookups:

```
$(unquote tokens $)
```

Here, arbitrary *tokens* are looked up in the database named `unquote`. That database is special because it is of the class *dequote*. Instead of being looked up in a database, *tokens* will have any surrounding quotation marks removed.

```
"A.B.C"          becomes   A.B.C
"A"."B"."C"      becomes   A.B.C
"first last"     becomes   "first last"
```

The first example shows that surrounding quotation marks are removed. The second shows that multiple quoted tokens are all dequoted. The last shows that *sendmail* refuses to dequote any tokens that will form an illegal or ambiguous address when dequoted.

A simple way to understand the dequoting process is by running the following three-line configuration file in rule-testing mode:

```
V5
Kunquote dequote
R$*    $:   $(unquote $1 $)
```

In addition to removing quotes, the *dequote* class also tokenizes everything returned. It does this because quotes are ordinarily used to mask the separation characters that delimit tokens. A good way to see how and why this is done is by considering the $& operator. It prevents a macro in a rule from being expanded when the configuration file is read. It also always returns a single token, to matter how many tokens it really contains. Consider this configuration file:

```
V5
DXhost.domain
Kunquote dequote
R$*    $: $&X , $(unquote "" $&X $)
```

Here, the macro X is assigned host.domain as its value. The single rule, when *sendmail* is run in rule-testing mode, prints the expression $&X to show that it is a single token, then prints the result of dequoting that same expression. Note that an empty token needs to be dequoted. Putting quotes around $&X itself won't work. The output produced by rule-testing multimode looks like this:

```
> 0 foo
rewrite: ruleset  0   input: foo
rewrite: ruleset  0 returns: host.domain , host . domain
>
```

Pitfalls

- Multitoken matching with SunOS *sendmail* may not be accurate, so care should be taken with their use.

- When creating databases for use with IDA *sendmail*, avoid using more than one %s in any data entry. If you do, and if that entry is later referenced with a $@ operator inside the $(and $) operators, it causes a segmentation fault and produces a core dump.

- Under IDA *sendmail*, you should avoid clearing or overwriting database files while they are in use. The preferred method is to create a new database with a different name, then *mv*(1) the new one over the original:

```
% dbm make mailertable+ mailertable
% rm -f mailertable.dir
% mv mailertable+.pag mailertable.pag
% mv mailertable+.dir mailertable.dir
```

The second line (the **rm**) is there because IDA *sendmail* sleeps, and tries again, if it finds the `.dir` part of a database missing.

30

Options

Options affect the operation of the *sendmail* program. They can be specified either in the command line with a -o command-line switch or in the *sendmail.cf* file with an O configuration command. Among the many behavioral characteristics that can be *tuned* with options are:

- Locations of all the other files *sendmail* needs to access, such as the *aliases* file.
- Location of the queue directory.
- Time limits that should be applied to the time to live in the queue, the length of the wait with an SMTP connection, and so on.
- Default permissions for files, and the default user and group identities to use when not running as another user.

Most options are preset in your *sendmail.cf* file to be appropriate for your site. Those that need local definitions will usually be indicated by comments. Some sites, especially those that have high mail loads or those connected to many different networks, will need to tune most of the options based on their unique needs.

In this chapter we show how options are declared in both the command line and the configuration file. Then we discuss typical uses and values for groups of options. We conclude with a reference section where we explain each option in greater detail.

Command-line Options

The form of an option declaration on the command line is:

```
-oXargument
```

The `-o` switch is immediately followed (with no intervening space) by the one-letter name of the option (here X). Depending on the option selected, an *argument* may be required. If that *argument* is present, it must immediately follow the option name with no intervening space. Only one option may be specified for each `-o` switch.

Some options are intended for use on the command line, and make little or no sense when used in the configuration file. Those options inappropriate to the configuration file are shown in Table 30-1.

Table 30-1: Options Inappropriate to the Configuration File

Option	Description
d	Set delivery mode*
e	Specify mode of error handling
i	Ignore leading dots in messages
M	Define a macro's value in command line
v	Run in verbose mode

* The db and dq options are reasonable in the configuration file, although they are technically sub-options.

It is common to install *sendmail* so that it runs with *root* privilege. Security considerations require that *sendmail* give up that privilege for most command-line options specified by the ordinary user. But there are a few options the ordinary user can specify that allow *sendmail* to keep its *root* privilege. Those options are called "safe," and are shown in Table 30-2.

Table 30-2: Options that are Safe

Option	Description
7	Force 7-bit input (V8 only)
b	Set maximum blocks free in queue (V8 only)
d	Set delivery mode
C	Checkpoint the queue (V8 only)
e	Specify mode for error handling
E	Set error message header (V8 only)

Table 30.2: Options that are Safe (continued)

Option	Description
i	Ignore leading dots in messages
j	Return MIME format errors (V8 only)
L	Set logging level
m	Send to me too
o	Allow old-style space-delimited recipient lists
p	Tune the privacy of the SMTP daemon (V8 only)
r	Set timeout for SMTP reads
s	For safety, queue everything just in case
v	Run in verbose mode

For example, the A option (location of the *aliases* file) is unsafe (not in Table 30-2). If you were to send mail by specifying a new location with -oA./myaliases, *sendmail* would change its identity from *root* to an ordinary user (you). One side effect is that *sendmail* would be unable to queue the mail message, because the queue directory is usually not writable by ordinary users like you. Your mail would fail, and the error printed would be something like this:

```
/var/spool/mqueue: Permission denied
```

Configuration File Options

The form of an option command in the *sendmail.cf* file is:

```
OXargument
```

Like all configuration commands, the letter O must begin the line. It is immediately followed (with no intervening space) by another single letter, which selects a specific option. Depending on the option selected, an `argument` may be required. Again, there must be no intervening space between the option and its argument.

Table 30-3: The Complete List of Options

Option	Type	Description
7	boolean	Force 7-bit input (V8 only)
a	numeric	Wait for the *aliases* file to be rebuilt
A	string	Define the *aliases* file location
b	numeric	Set minimum blocks free in queue (V8 only)
b	numeric	Set maximum recipients for empty body (SunOS only)
B	character	Set unquoted space replacement character
c	boolean	Don't connect to expensive delivery agents
C	numeric	Checkpoint the queue (V8 only)
d	character	Set delivery mode
D	boolean	Automatically rebuild the *aliases* database
E	string	Set error message header (V8 only)
e	character	Specify mode of error handling
f	boolean	Save UNIX-style From lines
F	octal	Set default file permissions for temporary files
g	numeric	Set default group ID for delivery agents
G	boolean	Match recipient against *gecos* field
h	numeric	Set maximum hop count
H	string	Specify location of the help file
i	boolean	Ignore leading dots in messages
I	boolean	Queue on connection refused
I	string	Use DNS lookups, and tune them (V8 only)
j	boolean	Return MIME-format errors (V8 only)
J	string	Set *.forward* search path (V8 only)
k	numeric	Number of SMTP connections to maintain (V8 only)
K	time	Multiple-SMTP connection time-out (V8 only)
K	string	Associate key with database (IDA only)
l	boolean	Use Errors-To: for errors (V8 only)
L	numeric	Set logging level to level #
m	boolean	Send to me too
M	string	Define a macro's value in command line
n	boolean	Check validity of the right side of aliases (V8 only)
N	n/a	Define the network name (obsolete)
o	boolean	Allow old-style space-delimited recipient lists
O	string	Set network options for the daemon (V8 only)

Table 30.3: The Complete List of Options (continued)

Option	Type	Description
p	string	Tune how private you want the SMTP daemon (V8 only)
p	numeric	Don't connect if too many processes (NeXT only)
P	string	Extra copies of postmaster mail
q	numeric	Multiplier (factor) for high-load queueing
Q	string	Location of queue directory
r	time	Set timeouts for SMTP reads (not V8)
r	string	Set timeouts for SMTP (V8 only)
R	boolean	Don't prune route addresses (V8 only)
R	string	Route on NFS-mounted spool directory (SunOS only)
s	boolean	For safety, queue everything just in case
S	string	Specify statistics file
t	string	Set timezone (SysV only)
T	time	Limit life in queue to days
u	numeric	Set user id of mailer
U	string	Specify user database (V8 only)
v	boolean	Run in verbose mode
V	string	Fall-back MX host (V8 only)
w	boolean	Use A for ambiguous MX (V8 only)
x	numeric	On high load, queue only
X	numeric	Refuse SMTP connections on high load
y	numeric	Penalize large recipient lists
Y	boolean	Process queue files individually (not SunOS)
Y	string	Name of NIS aliases map (SunOS only)
z	numeric	Multiplier for priority increments
Z	numeric	Increment priority per job processed
/	boolean	Split rewriting header/envelope (IDA only)

Option Argument Types

The middle column of Table 30-3 shows the type of the argument for each option. The allowable types are:

Boolean   A boolean-type argument can have only one of two possible values, true or false. If the boolean argument is present, its first letter is compared to the four letters T, t, Y, and y. If that first letter matches any of those four, the option is set to true, otherwise it is set to false. If a boolean argument is absent, the option defaults to true. For example:

```
Oc          ← bool absent, 'c' is set true.
OcTrue      ← bool='T'rue, 'c' is set true.
OcFalse     ← bool='F'alse, 'c' is set false.
```

Character A character type is a single ASCII character. Options that take a single character as an argument may legally be given a whole word or sentence, but only the first character is used.

```
Odb            ← b for background mode
Odbackground   ← same
```

The argument is case-sensitive, that is, the character b is different from the character B.

```
Odb      ← b for background mode
OdB      ← meaningless
```

Numeric A numeric type is an ASCII representation of an integer value. It may be positive, zero, or negative. The base is determined after any leading sign is handled. A leading 0 causes the octal base to be used. A leading 0x or 0X causes the hexadecimal base to be used. Otherwise, a decimal base is used (see *atoi*(3)). Decimal is best to use for options like the hop count (option h).

```
Oh15           ← decimal for hop count
```

String A string type is a line of ASCII text. A string is all text from the option name up to the end of the line. If the following line is a continuation line (one that begins with a tab or a space), it is joined (appended) to the string. If the string is quoted, the quotation marks are not stripped by *sendmail.* The maximum length of a string is defined by MAXLINE in *conf.h.*

```
OA/etc/aliases      ← location of the aliases file
OA"/etc/aliases"    ← bad, quotes are retained
```

Octal An octal type is like the numeric type above, but is always interpreted as an octal (base 8) number even if the leading zero is absent. This type is specially designed for file permissions.

OF0600	← *octal for file permissions*
OF600	← *octal even without the leading zero*

Time   A time type is the expression of a period of time. Time is expressed as a number modified by a trailing letter. The recognized letters (shown in Table 30-4) determine what the number means. For example, 24h means 24 hours, and 15m means 15 minutes. Times may be mixed, for example 1h30m means one hour and 30 minutes. If the letter modifier is missing, the time is in days.

Or2h	← *SMTP timeout is 2 hours*
OT2	← *life in queue is 2 days*

Note that V8 uses different default units depending on the specific option. For consistent results, always include the units.

Table 30-4: Option Time Argument Units

Letter	Units
s	Seconds
m	Minutes
h	Hours
d	Days
w	Weeks

Interrelating Options

At the end of this chapter, we explain each option in detail, and do so in alphabetical order for easy lookup. Because options tend to group by application and use, we present here a summary grouped by classification.

File Locations

The only file that *sendmail* knows the location of is its configuration file. Options in the configuration file tell *sendmail* where all other files are located. The options that specify file locations are summarized in Table 30-5. All file location options are of type *string*.

Table 30-5: File Location Options

Option	File
A	Aliases file and its database files
H	SMTP help file
S	Statistics file
E	Error message file (V8 only)

File locations should be expressed as full pathnames. Use of relative names will cause the location to become relative to the queue directory.

The Queue

Several options combine to determine your site's policy for managing the *sendmail* queue (see Chapter 19, *The Queue*). Among them is one that specifies the location of the queue directory and another that sets the permissions given to files in that directory. The list of all options that affect the queue is shown in Table 30-6.

Table 30-6: Options that Affect the Queue

Option	Description
b	Reserve disk blocks on the queue disk (V8 only)
C	Checkpoint the queue
F	Mode for temporary files
Q	Location of the queue directory
s	For safety, queue everything
T	Time limit for life in the queue
Y	Process queue files individually (not SunOS)
Z	Increment priority for job processed

Managing Aliases

In addition to the location of the *aliases* file, some options determine how that file and its associated database files will be used. There is, for example, an option that tells *sendmail* to automatically rebuild the database files whenever the *aliases* file is changed. The list of all *aliases*-related options is shown in Table 30-7.

Table 30-7: Options for Managing Aliases

Option	Description
A	Define the location of the *aliases* file
D	Automatically rebuild the *aliases* file
a	Wait for the *aliases* file to be rebuilt
Y	Name of NIS aliases map (SunOS only)

Controlling Machine Load

An interaction of several options controls the *sendmail* program's behavior under high machine-load conditions. These are intended to reduce the impact of *sendmail* on machines that provide other services and to help protect *sendmail* from loading down a machine. The list of options that determine and help prevent high load conditions is shown in Table 30-8.

Table 30-8: Options that Determine Load

Option	Description
x	On high load queue only
X	On high load refuse SMTP connections
q	Multiplier (factor) for high load queueing
z	Multiplier for priority increments
p	Don't connect if too many processes (NeXT only)
c	Don't connect for expensive delivery agents
h	Limit the maximum hop count

Connection Caching

V8 *sendmail* has introduced connection caching to improve the performance of SMTP-transported mail. When processing the queue, or when delivering to a long list of recipients, keeping a few SMTP connections open (just in case another message is for one of those same sites) will improve the speed of transfers. Caching is of greatest benefit on busy mail hub machines, but can benefit any machine that sends a great deal of network mail. Table 30-9 lists the options that determine how connections will be cached.

Table 30-9: Options that Determine Connection Caching

Option	Description
k	The number of SMTP connections to maintain
K	Multiple SMTP connection time-out

Problem Solving

All versions of *sendmail* offer three options that will help in locating and solving some mail delivery problems. You are encouraged to enable the first two shown in Table 30-10. The third is of value only if you have many delivery agents (see Chapter 26, *Delivery Agents*).

Table 30-10: Options that Help with Problem Solving

Option	Description
L	Set logging level
P	Extra copies of postmaster mail
S	Specify statistics file

Other Options

As you saw in Table 30-3, *sendmail* supports a vast array of options. Some other options relate to each other more loosely than the ones we've shown above, so we will not carry this discussion of relating options any further. Our recommendation is that you take the time to study all the options (described at the end of this chapter) at least once to get a basic feeling for what they do. Then, as you gain experience with *sendmail*, you'll know just where to look for any particular option that will meet your needs.

Pitfalls

- If the option letter is one that is unknown to *sendmail*, it *silently* accepts the line but doesn't use it. For example, entering O1 when you really mean OI causes the unknown option 1 to be defined, and the intended option I to remain undefined. Because no error message is printed, this kind of mistake is difficult to find.

- Accidentally placing a space character between the O and the option letter does not cause an error. Rather, *sendmail* silently accepts the space character as the option name. For example, the space in "O A/etc/aliases" gives to the option "space" the argument A/etc/aliases.

- Options are parsed from the top of the *sendmail.cf* file down. Later declarations of an option supersede earlier declarations. For example, if you try to change the location of the *aliases* file by placing the line OA/tmp/aliases at the top of your *sendmail.cf* file, that change is masked (ignored) by the existence of OA/etc/aliases later in the file.

- Command-line options always supersede the *sendmail.cf* file options, because the command line is parsed after the *sendmail.cf* file is parsed. One way to change the location of the *aliases* file (perhaps for testing) is with a command-line argument like -oA/tmp/aliases. For security reasons, however, not all command-line options are available to the ordinary user.

Alphabetized Reference

In the following sections, we present all the options currently available for many versions of *sendmail*. If one applies only to a particular version, it is noted in parenthesis, as (V8 only). They are in alphanumeric order. When two options differ by case, the lowercase one is discussed first.

O7

Force 7-bit input (V8 only)

By default, V8 *sendmail* leaves as-is all bytes of every mail message it reads. This differs from other releases of *sendmail* that always clear (zero) the high (most-significant) bit. To make V8 *sendmail* behave like older versions and always clear the high bit on input, the 7 option is available.

The forms of the 7 option are:

```
O7bool      ← configuration file
-o7bool     ← command line
```

The argument *bool* is of type boolean. If *bool* is missing, the default value is true. If this option is omitted entirely, the default is false (the eighth bit is unmodified).

Note that option 7 affects input only. The F=7 delivery agent flag can be used to set 7-bit output on an individual delivery agent basis.

The 7 option is safe. If specified from the command line, *sendmail* will not relinquish its *root* privilege.

Oa

Wait for the aliases database to be rebuilt

When *sendmail* starts, it checks to see if its *aliases* file (see Chapter 20, *Aliases*) is newer than its database versions of that file (*aliases.pag* and *aliases.dir*). If it is, and if both the D (auto-rebuild aliases) and a options are set, *sendmail* attempts to rebuild the database files. If the D option is not set, *sendmail* simply issues a warning:

```
Warning: alias database out of date
```

and uses the information in the old database. If neither is set, *sendmail* remains silent about the need to rebuild.

When *sendmail* rebuilds the *aliases* database, it first clears the old database. It then rebuilds the database, and when done, adds the special entry @:@. Before *sendmail* attempts to automatically rebuild the database, it first looks in that database for the special entry @:@ that should be present. This curious entry is employed because it is one that is always illegal in an *aliases* file. If *sendmail* doesn't find that entry (whether because a user ran *newaliases* or because another invocation of sendmail is currently rebuilding it) it waits 30 seconds for that entry to appear, then checks again. The number of 30-second intervals *sendmail* waits is two times the number of *minutes* specified by this a option. As soon as the @:@ appears, *sendmail* checks to see if the database still needs to be rebuilt, and rebuilds it if it does.

If the special entry @:@ does not appear after the specified time, *sendmail* assumes that some other process died while that other process was rebuilding the database. This assumption paves the way for *sendmail* to go ahead and rebuild the database.

The forms of the a option are:

```
Oamin      ← configuration file
-oamin     ← command line
```

The *min* argument is of type *numeric*, and, if omitted, defaults to five. If the entire a option is omitted, or if *min* is zero or non-numeric, the database is not automatically rebuilt. This option is available only if the D option is also set.

The a option is not safe. If specified from the command line, it may cause *sendmail* to relinquish its *root* privilege.

OA

Define the aliases file location

The A option must be declared for *sendmail* to do aliasing. If you omit this option, *sendmail* silently assumes that you do not want to do aliasing at all.

There is no default compiled into *sendmail* for the location of the *aliases* file. If you specify a file that doesn't exist (like */ect/aliases* if you really meant */etc/aliases*), or one that is unreadable, *sendmail* complains, for example with:

```
Can't open /ect/aliases
```

This is a non-fatal error. The *sendmail* program prints it and continues to run, but assumes that it shouldn't do aliasing.

The forms of the A option are:

```
OAlocation      ← configuration file
-oAlocation     ← command line
```

The *location* is an argument of type string and can be an absolute or a relative pathname. A relative path (such as *../aliases*) can be used for testing, but should *never* be used in the production version of your *sendmail.cf* file. To do so opens a security hole. Such a path is interpreted by *sendmail* as relative to the queue directory.

This option can be used to change the name of the *aliases* file (a possible consideration for security). If you change the location or name of the *aliases* file, be aware that other programs (such as *emacs* and Sun's NIS services) may cease to work properly.

V8 *sendmail* allows you to use several alias databases simultaneously. They are listed with the A option as, for example, this:

```
OA/etc/aliases/users, /etc/aliases/maillists
```

In this case, V8 *sendmail* will look up an alias first in the database */etc/aliases/users*. If it is not found, *sendmail* will then look in */etc/aliases/maillists*. The number of simultaneous alias files is limited to MAXALIASDB as defined in *conf.h* (by default 12). The -bi command-line switch will rebuild all alias databases in the order listed in this A option.

Multiple OA lines may appear in the file, each adding an alias database to the list:

```
OA/etc/aliases/users     # aliases local users first
OA/etc/aliases/maillists # then mailing lists
OA/etc/aliases/retired   # then retired accounts
```

Duplicates are not detected. Thus, the following causes */etc/aliases* to be searched and rebuilt twice each time:

```
OA/etc/aliases
OA/etc/aliases
```

Multiple alias files may similarly be specified on the command line with the −oA switch. But be aware that any −oA switch causes all the configuration file OA lines to be ignored.

In addition to the name of alias databases, V8 *sendmail* also allows you to specify the class of each. The class is the same as the classes available for the K configuration command (see Chapter 29, *Database Macros*). The class prefixes the name and the two are separated by a colon:

```
OAnis:mail.aliases
```

This example tells *sendmail* to look up aliases in the NIS class (the nis) database called mail.aliases. The class can include switches that mean the same thing as those allowed for the K configuration command. For example:

```
OAnis -N:mail.aliases
```

Here, the −N class switch causes lookups to include a trailing null byte with each key.

If a class is not a known one, and if the −d27 command-line switch is specified, *sendmail* prints:

```
Unknown alias class badclass
```

If the class is one that cannot support aliasing (as defined by MCF_ALIASOK in *conf.c*) and if the −d27 command-line switch is specified, *sendmail* prints:

```
setalias: map class badclass can't handle aliases
```

In both cases the *badclass* is the offending class. Both errors cause the A option alias file declaration to be ignored.

The A option is not safe. If specified from the command line, it may cause *sendmail* to relinquish its *root* privilege.

Ob

Set free blocks and maximum message size (V8 only)

The SIZE option to the ESMTP MAIL command tells V8 *sendmail* that an incoming message is SIZE bytes in size. If SIZE is not specified, *sendmail* assumes the size is zero. In either case, it calls the subroutine *enoughspace()* in *conf.c* to see if there is enough space available in the queue to accept the message. Unless *sendmail* is told otherwise, it assumes it can use 100% of the disk space in the queue. If SIZE bytes will overfill the queue disk, *sendmail* prints the following error and rejects the mail message:

```
Insufficient disk space; try again later
```

Note that SIZE (if received) is just an estimate so that oversized mail can be rejected early in the ESMTP dialogue. V8 *sendmail* still properly diagnoses out-of-space conditions when it actually reads the message.

V8 *sendmail* can also reject a message at this point if it is larger than a definable maximum message size:

```
552 Message size exceeds fixed maximum message size (max)
```

Here, *max* is the maximum acceptable size in bytes.

If using 100% of the disk space is unacceptable, you can use the b option to reserve space for other kinds of files. If huge incoming ESMTP messages are unacceptable, you can use the b option to define an upper limit.

The b option is used like this:

```
Obminblocks/maxsize          ← configuration file
-obminblocks/maxsize         ← command line
```

Here, `minblocks` is of type numeric, and is the number of disk blocks you wish to reserve. If `minblocks` is missing or negative, or if the entire option is omitted, no blocks are reserved. The slash is required to separate the `minblocks` from the `maxsize`. If `maxsize` is missing, the slash may be omitted. The `maxsize` is of type numeric and is a number of bytes. If it is less than or equal to zero, non-numeric, or missing, no check is made for maximum size.

Note that `minblocks/maxsize` are reserved only for the ESMTP SIZE option to the MAIL command. No check is made for any other kind of queueing to reserve space. Consequently, you should reserve a sufficient number of blocks to satisfy your normal queueing needs.

The b option is not safe. If specified from the command line, it may cause *sendmail* to relinquish its *root* privilege.

Ob

Set maximum recipients for empty body (SunOS only)

Users occasionally send e-mail, but leave the message body empty. When a user accidently sends such an empty message to a mailing list, the result can be a world-wide distribution of empty mail. The b option offers a simple means of limiting the extent of such accidents. The b option—available only on SunOS—tells *sendmail* to refuse to send empty mail when there are more than a specified number of recipients.

The forms of the b option are:

```
Obnum        ← configuration file
-obnum       ← command line
```

The argument *num* is of type numeric. If *num* is missing, or if the entire b option is missing, or if the value of *num* is zero, this feature is disabled.

The b option is safe. Even if it is specified from the command line, *sendmail* retains its *root* privilege.

OB

Set unquoted space replacement character

Some mailer programs have difficulty handling addresses that contain spaces. For *sendmail*, a space is any of those characters defined by the C language library routine *isspace*(3). By way of example, the address:

```
John Q Public@wash.dc.gov
```

is viewed by some mailer programs as being composed of three separate addresses: `John`, `Q`, and `Public@wash.dc.gov`. To prevent this misinterpretation, such mailers usually either quote the user portion or escape each space with a backslash:

```
"John Q Public"@wash.dc.gov              ← quoted
John\ Q\ Public@wash.dc.gov              ← escaped
```

The B option is intended to handle an address that is *neither* quoted nor escaped.

Most sites use a . (dot or period) or an _ (underscore) character to replace unquoted space characters. That is, they declare the B option as one of the following:

```
OB.
OB_
```

Feeding the address:

```
John Q Public@wash.dc.gov
```

through *sendmail* with the OB. option set, yields:

```
John.Q.Public@wash.dc.gov
```

The forms of the B option are:

```
OBchar      ← configuration file
-oBchar     ← command line
```

The argument *char* is of type character and is a single character. The default, if this option is omitted, or if the *char* argument is omitted, is that an unquoted space character is replaced with a space character (which does nothing to correct the problem at all).

Note that old-style addresses are delimited from each other with spaces rather than commas. Such addresses may be wrongly joined into a single address if the *char* is other than a space. Acceptance of such old-style addresses is determined by the setting of the o (old-style) option.

Also note that the B option may also be used when tokenized addresses are reassembled; see Chapter 25, *Rules*.

The B option is not safe. If specified from the command line, it may cause *sendmail* to relinquish its *root* privilege.

Oc

Don't connect to expensive mailers

An *expensive mailer* is a delivery agent that contains an e flag in its F= equate. Typically, such delivery agents are associated with slow network connections like SL/IP, or with costly networks like those with high per-connect or connection startup rates. Whatever the reason, the c option allows you to queue all such mail for later delivery, rather than connecting on demand. (Queueing is described in Chapter 19, *The Queue*.)

Note that this option affects only the initial delivery attempt, not later attempts when the queue is processed. Essentially, all this option does is to defer delivery until the next time the queue is processed.

The forms of the c option are:

```
Ocbool          ← configuration file
-ocbool         ← command line
-c              ← command-line shorthand (not recommended)
```

The argument *bool* is of type boolean. If the *bool* argument is missing, the default is true. If the entire c option is missing, the default value is false.

The -v (verbose) command-line switch automatically sets option c to false.

The c option is not safe. If specified from the command line, it may cause *sendmail* to relinquish its *root* privilege.

OC

Checkpoint the queue (V8 only)

When sending a single e-mail message to many recipients (those on a mailing list, for example) a single *sendmail* process handles all the recipients. Should that *sendmail* process die or be killed halfway through processing, there is no record that the first half was delivered. As a result, when the queue is later reprocessed, the recipients in that first half will receive the message a second time.

The C option can limit this duplication.* It tells *sendmail* to rewrite (checkpoint) its qf file (the file that contains the list of recipients) after each group of a specified number of recipients has been delivered. Recipients who have already received mail are deleted from the list and that list is rewritten to the qf file.

The forms of the C option are:

```
OCnum       ← configuration file
-oCnum      ← command line
```

The *num* argument is of form numeric and specifies the number of recipients in each group. If *num* is entirely missing, or is zero, or if the entire C option is missing, this feature is disabled. There is a small performance penalty that increases as *num* approaches 1. A good starting value is 4.

---

*The next major release of IDA *sendmail* will also support this option.

The C option is safe. Even if it is specified from the command line, *sendmail* retains its *root* privilege.

Od

Set delivery mode

There are three modes that *sendmail* can use for delivering mail. They are background, interactive, and queue-only.

Background mode—intended for use in the configuration file—allows *sendmail* to run *asynchronously*. This means that once *sendmail* has gathered the entire message, and verified that the recipient is deliverable, it will *fork*(3) a copy of itself and exit. The copy, running in the background (asynchronously), will then handle the delivery. From the user's point of view, this mode allows the mail interface program to act as though it sent the message instantaneously.

Interactive mode—intended for use from the command line—causes *sendmail* to run *synchronously*. This mode is useful primarily for debugging mail problems. Instead of going into the background with *fork*(3), it runs in the foreground (synchronously). In this mode, error messages are printed back to the controlling terminal, rather than being mailed to the user as bounced mail. The -v command-line switch automatically sets the mode to foreground.

Queue-only mode—for use in either the command line or the configuration file—causes *sendmail* to synchronously queue mail. Queue-only mode is useful at sites that have huge amounts of UUCP mail or USENET news batch feeds. Queueing has the beneficial effect of serializing delivery through queue runs, and it reduces the load on a machine that many parallel backgrounded *sendmail* processes can cause. Queue-only mode is typically supplied as a command-line option to sendmail by the *uuxqt*(8) program. When queue-only mode is selected, all mail is queued for delivery and none is actually delivered. A separate run of *sendmail* with its -q command-line switch is needed to actually process the queue.

The forms of the d option are:

```
Odmode     ← configuration file
-odmode    ← command line
```

The *mode* argument is of type character and is selected from one of the letters shown in Table 30-11.

Table 30-11: Delivery Mode Letters for Option d

Letter	Description
b	Background (asynchronous) delivery
i	Interactive (synchronous) delivery
q	Queued (deferred) delivery

If the mode argument is missing, this option defaults to the i or interactive mode. If the entire d option is missing, V8 *sendmail* defaults to background mode, but old *sendmail* behaves unpredictably; consequently, this option should be considered mandatory.

The d option is safe. Even if it is specified from the command line, *sendmail* retains its *root* privilege.

OD

Automatically rebuild the aliases database

The need to rebuild the *aliases* database is determined by comparing the modification time of the *aliases* file to the modification time of the corresponding *aliases.page* and *aliases.dir* database files. If the *aliases* file is newer, and if this D option is set, *sendmail* attempts to rebuild the *aliases* database. If this option is not set, *sendmail* prints the following warning and uses the information in the old database:

```
Warning: alias database out of date
```

If you set this D option, be sure that the a option is also declared and given a non-zero argument. (Locking, to prevent simultaneous rebuilds, is described under the a option.)

The forms of the D option are:

```
ODbool      ← configuration file
-oDbool     ← command line
```

With no argument, D is set to true. If the optional argument *bool* is present, it is of type boolean and is interpreted appropriately.

All versions of the *sendmail* program use *flock*(3) to prevent simultaneous rebuilds (V8 and IDA *sendmail* can also use *lockf*(3)).

The D option is not safe. If specified from the command line, it may cause *sendmail* to relinquish its *root* privilege.

Oe

Specify mode of error handling

The *sendmail* program is flexible in its handling of delivery errors. By selecting from five possible modes with the e option, you can tailor notification of delivery errors to suit many needs.

This option is primarily intended for use from the command line. If included in the configuration file, it should be given only the p argument, for print mode (the default).

The forms of the e option are:

```
Oemode      ← configuration file
-oemode     ← command line
-emode      ← command-line shorthand (not recommended)
```

The type of *mode* is character. If *mode* is missing, the default value is p (for print normally). Under older versions of *sendmail*, if the e option is entirely missing, the default value for *mode* is the C language character constant "\0". Under V8 *sendmail*, the default value in this case is p.

The possible characters for the *mode* argument are:

p   Print error messages (the default). The *sendmail* program simply tries to save a copy of the failed mail in ~/*dead.letter* and prints an error message to its standard output. If the sender is remote, it sends notification of the problem back to that sender via e-mail. If ~/*dead.letter* is not writable, a copy is saved to /*usr/tmp/dead.letter*.*

q   Quiet; remain silent about all delivery errors. If the sender is local, this mode assumes that the normal mail-reading program already gave notification of the error. Mail is not sent, and ~/*dead.letter* is not saved. Error information is provided only in the *sendmail* program's *exit*(2) status. This mode is intended for use from the command line. One possible use might be exploding a junk-mail mailing list with a program that could correctly interpret the exit status.

m   Mail error notification to the sender no matter what. This mode tries to find the most rational way to return mail. All aliasing is disabled to prevent loops. Nothing is ever saved to ~/*dead.letter*. This mode is intended for use from the command line. The m mode is appropriate for mail generated by an application which arises from a login, but for which there is no human present to monitor messages. One example

---

*This latter path is hardcoded into *sendmail*.

might be a data-acquisition system which is manually logged in, but is then left to fend for itself. Similarly, when the user *news* sends articles by mail, error messages should not be placed in ~*news/dead.letter* where they may be overlooked; rather, this mode should be used so that errors are placed in a mail spool file where they can be periodically monitored.

w   Write errors to the sender's terminal screen if logged in (similar to *write*(1)); otherwise, send mail to that user. First tries to write to *stdout*. If that fails, it reverts to mail notification. This mode is intended for use from the command line. The reason for this mode has been lost to history,* and it should be considered obsolete.

e   Like m above, but always exit with a zero exit status. This mode is intended for use from the command line. This e mode is used by the *rmail*(8) program when it invokes *sendmail*. On some systems, if *sendmail* exits with a non-zero value (fails), the *uuxqt*(8) program sends its own error message. This results in two error messages being sent, whereas only one should ever be sent. Worse still, the error message from *uuxqt* may contain a bad address, one that may itself bounce.

Note that the error-handling mode is automatically set to m (for mail errors) in two special circumstances. First, if a mailing list is being processed, and if an owner is found for that list (see Chapter 20, *Aliases*), the mode is set to m, to force mail notification to that owner. Second, if SMTP delivery is to multiple recipients, the mode is set to m, to force mail notification to the sender. This latter assumes that multiple recipients qualify as a mailing list.

The e option is safe. Even if it is specified from the command line, *sendmail* retains its *root* privilege.

OE
Error message header (V8 only)

When a notification of a mail error is sent to the sender, the details of the error are taken from the text saved in the **xf** file (see Chapter 19, *The Queue*). The E option, available only with V8 *sendmail*, allows you to prepend custom text ahead of that error text.

---

*According to Eric Allman: "Dubious, someone bugged me for it; I forget why."

Custom error text is useful for sites that wish to offer help as part of the error message. For example, one common kind of error message is notification of an unknown user:

```
----- Transcript of session follows -----
550 smith@wash.dc.gov... User unknown
----- Unsent message follows -----
```

Here, the user `smith` is one that is unknown. A useful error help message for your site to produce might be:

```
Common problems:
       User unknown: the user or login name is wrong.
       Host unknown: you mistyped the host part of the address.
----- Transcript of session follows -----
550 smith@wash.dc.gov... User unknown
----- Unsent message follows -----
```

The form for the E option is:

```
OEtext        ← configuration file
-oEtext       ← command line
```

The argument *text* is mandatory. If it is missing, this option is ignored. The *text* is either the actual error text that is printed, or the name of a file containing that text. If *text* begins with the / character, it is taken as the absolute pathname of the file (a relative name is not possible). If the file cannot be opened for reading, this option is silently ignored.

Macros may be used in the error text, and they are expanded as they are printed. For example, the text might contain:

```
For help with $u, try "finger $u"
```

which might produce this error message:

```
For help with smith@wash.dc.gov, try "finger smith@wash.dc.gov"
----- Transcript of session follows -----
550 smith@wash.dc.gov... User unknown
----- Unsent message follows -----
```

The E option is not safe. If specified from the command line, it may cause *sendmail* to relinquish its *root* privilege.

Of

Save UNIX-style From lines

Many UNIX MUAs, as well as some transmittal systems like UUCP, require that a mail-message header begin with a line that begins with the five-character sequence "From ". All other header lines must adhere to the RFC822 standard and be delimited with a colon:

```
From jqp@Washington.DC.gov Fri Jul 26 12:35:25 1991
Return-Path: <jqp@Washington.DC.gov>
Date: Fri, 26 Jul 91 12:35:15 PDT
From: jqp@Washington.DC.gov (John Q Public)
```

If you don't set the f option, the first line in the above example is stripped out by *sendmail*. The f option prevents this, because it tells *sendmail* to keep header lines that begin with the five characters "From ".

The forms of the f option are:

```
Ofbool            ← configuration file
-ofbool           ← command line
-s                ← command-line shorthand (not recommended)
```

The optional argument *bool* is of type boolean. If *bool* is missing, this option becomes true.

Be aware that "bad" versions of programs like *rmail*(8) add a "From " line, even if one exists. If you set the f option and start getting duplicate "From " lines, don't blame *sendmail*!

The f option is not safe. If specified from the command line, it may cause *sendmail* to relinquish its *root* privilege.

OF

Set default file permissions for temporary files

The F option tells *sendmail* what mode (file permissions) to give its temporary files and its freeze file.* Because the files in the queue contain private e-mail, this option is usually set to the least permissive level, 0600. On dedicated mail servers (hub machines), where logins are restricted to mail managers, you may wish to loosen permissions for easier problem solving.

---

*V8 *sendmail* no longer supports freeze files.

The forms of the F option are:

```
OFmode    ← configuration file
-oFmode   ← command line
```

The *mode* is of type octal. If the F option is entirely missing, the default permissions are 0644. Beware of omitting just the *mode* argument—if you do, the permissions become 0000, and *sendmail* may not be able to read or write its own files.

The F option is not safe. If specified from the command line, it may cause *sendmail* to relinquish its *root* privilege.

Og and Ou
Set default identity for delivery agents

There are two major ways that *sendmail* can be run. One is as an SUID *root* process (that is, with the permissions of the *root* no matter who runs it). The other is as an ordinary process, run by an ordinary (non-privileged) user (that is, with *root* privilege *only* if it is run by *root*). When *sendmail* is run such that it has *root* privilege, it must give up that privilege under certain circumstances in order to remain secure.* When it can't set its identity to that of a real user, *sendmail* sets its *gid* to that specified by the g option and its *uid* to that specified by the u option.

When *sendmail* is running with *root* privilege, and when the F=S delivery agent flag is *not* specified, *sendmail* changes its owner and group identity to that of an ordinary user in the following circumstances:

1. If the mail message is forwarded because of a user's `~/.forward` file, and if delivery is via the `prog` delivery agent or to a file, then *sendmail* changes its owner and group identity to that of the user whose `~/.forward` file was read.

2. Otherwise, if the mail message is being delivered through an *aliases*(5) file's `:include:` mailing list expansion, and if delivery is via the `prog` delivery agent or to a file, then *sendmail* changes its owner and group identity to that of the owner of the file that was specified by the `:include:` line.

3. Otherwise, if the sender of the mail message is local, and if delivery is via the `prog` delivery agent or to a file, then *sendmail* changes its owner and group identity to that of the sender. If the sender is *root*,

---

*V8 presumes it is still *root* even if it has given up that privilege. It does this to be more security conscious.

> *sendmail* changes its owner and group identity to that specified by the
> u and g options, respectively. (This step is skipped in V8 *sendmail*).

4. Otherwise, *sendmail* changes its owner and group identity to that
   specified by the u and g options.

These options are ignored if the delivery agent's F= equate includes the S
flag, *and* if *sendmail* is running in daemon mode.

The forms of the g and u options are:

```
Ouuid      ← configuration file
-ouuid     ← command line
Oggid      ← configuration file
-oggid     ← command line
```

The arguments *uid* and *gid* are of type numeric.* If an argument is missing, the value 0 is used for the respective user or group id. If an entire u or
g option is missing, the default value becomes 1 (usually *daemon*). In NFS-
mounted environments, safe values for these options are those of the user
nobody and the group *nogroup*.

The g option is not safe. If specified from the command line, it may cause
sendmail to relinquish its *root* privilege.

OG

Match recipient from gecos field (V8 only)

The *gecos* field is the portion of a *passwd*(5) file line that contains a user's
full name. Typical *passwd* file lines are illustrated below with the *gecos* field
of each highlighted:

```
george:Vnn9x34sEVbCN:101:29:George Washington:/usr/george:/bin/csh
bcx:/a88.97eGSx11:102:5:Bill Xavier,,,:/usr/bcx:/bin/csh
tim:Fss9UdQl55cde:103:45:& Plenty (Jr):/usr/tim:/bin/csh
```

When *sendmail* attempts to deliver to a local user, it looks up the recipient's name in the *passwd* file so that it can locate the user's home directory.
That lookup only tries to match the login name, the leftmost field in the
passwd file. But if *sendmail* has been compiled with MATCHGECOS defined
in *conf.h*, and if this G option is true, *sendmail* also tries to match the recipient name to the *gecos* field.

---

*V8 *sendmail* allows user- or groupnames to be used in addition to numbers (for example,
Ognobody).

As the first step, *sendmail* converts any underscore characters into space characters, and if the B option is set, any characters that match that space substitution character into spaces. This makes the recipient name look like a normal full name.

Second, *sendmail* normalizes each *gecos* entry by throwing away everything following and including the first comma, semicolon, and percent characters. Along the way, it converts the & to the login name wherever one is found. If any of the characters:

```
< >( ) ' .
```

are found inside the name, the entire *gecos* name is quoted; otherwise, it is unquoted.

After each *gecos* name is normalized, it is compared in a case-insensitive manner to the recipient. If they match, the *passwd* entry for that user is used.

This feature allows users to receive mail addressed to their full name as given in the *gecos* field of the *passwd* file. The usual form is to replace spaces in the full name with dots or underscores.

```
George_Washington
Bill.Xavier
"Tim_Plenty_(Jr)"
```

Note that full names in *gecos* fields that contain characters with special meaning to *sendmail*, like the last one above, need to be quoted when used as addresses.

As a word of warning, you should not enable this option if your site allows users to edit their own *gecos* fields with the *chfn*(1) program. At a minimum, they can change their name in a way that can cause mail to start failing. Or worse, they can change their full name to match that of another user and begin to capture that other user's mail.

The G option is safe. Even if it is specified from the command line, *sendmail* retains its *root* privilege.

Oh

Set maximum hop count

A *hop* is the transmittal of a mail message from one machine to another.* Many hops may be required to deliver a message. The number of hops is determined by counting the `Received:` and `Via:` lines† in the header of an e-mail message.

The h option tells *sendmail* the maximum number of times a message can be forwarded (the maximum hop count). When *sendmail* receives an e-mail message, it calculates the hop count. If that count is above the maximum allowed it bounces the message back to the sender with the error:

```
sendmail: too many hops (17 max)
```

The 17 is the maximum in this example. Detecting too many hops is useful in stopping *mail loops*—messages endlessly being forwarded back and forth between two machines.

The forms of the h option are:

```
Ohhops      ← configuration file
-ohhops     ← command line
```

The *hops* argument is of type numeric. If *hops* is missing, the value becomes zero, thereby causing all mail to fail with the error:

```
sendmail: too many hops (0 max)
```

If the entire h option is missing, *hops* defaults to the value MAXHOP as defined in *conf.h* (see Chapter 16, *Compile and Install sendmail*). That default varies between 15 for IDA *sendmail* and 30 for SunOS *sendmail*.

In IDA *sendmail*, there is no h option for setting the maximum number of hops. Instead, the number of hops can be limited only by the compile-time definition of MAXHOP in *conf.h*.

A good value for MAXHOP is 15 or more. This allows mail to follow a fairly long route through many machines (as it could with UUCP), but still catch and bounce mail caught in a loop between two machines.

---

*The IP transport protocol also has the concept of hops. A message going from one machine to another has only one mail hop, but may have many IP hops.

†Actually the hop count is the number of headers marked with an H_TRACE flag (see Chapter 16, *Compile and Install sendmail*).

The h options should not be confused with the −h command-line switch. The h option specifies the maximum number of hops allowed, whereas the −h command-line switch presets the base (beginning) hop count for a given e-mail message.

The h option is not safe. If specified from the command line, it may cause *sendmail* to relinquish its *root* privilege.

OH

Specify location of the help file

The *sendmail* program implements the SMTP HELP command by looking up help messages in a text file. The location and name of that text file are specified using the H option. If that name is the C language value NULL, or if *sendmail* cannot open that file for reading, *sendmail* issues the following SMTP message, and continues:

```
502 HELP not implemented
```

The help file is composed of lines of text, separated by tab characters into two fields per line. The leftmost field is an item for which help is offered. The rightmost field (the rest of the line) is the help text to be printed. A few lines in a typical help file might look like this:

```
rset    RSET
rset            Resets the system.
quit    QUIT
quit            Exit sendmail (SMTP).
verb    VERB
verb            Go into verbose mode.  This sends 0xy responses that
verb            are not RFC821 standard (but should be).  They are
verb            recognized by humans and other sendmail implementations.
vrfy    VRFY <recipient>
vrfy            Verify an address.  If you want to see what it aliases
vrfy            to, use EXPN instead.
```

For an SMTP request of help vrfy, *sendmail* might produce:

```
214-VRFY <recipient>
214-    Verify an address.  If you want to see what it aliases
214-    to, use EXPN instead.
214 End of HELP info
```

The forms of the H option are:

```
OHfile     ← configuration file
-oHfile    ← command line
```

The argument *file* is of type string, and may be a full or relative path-name. Relative names are always relative to the queue directory. If *file* is omitted, then the name of the help file defaults to *sendmail.hf.* If the entire H option is omitted, the name of the help file becomes the C language value NULL. The Simple Mail Transfer Protocol (SMTP) is described in RFC821.

The H option is not safe. If specified from the command line, it may cause *sendmail* to relinquish its *root* privilege.

Oi

Ignore leading dots in messages

There are two ways that *sendmail* can detect the end of a mail message: by noting an end-of-file (EOF) condition, or by finding a line composed of a single dot. According to the SMTP protocol (RFC821), the end of the mail data is indicated by sending a line containing only a period. The i option tells *sendmail* to treat any line that contains only a single period as ordinary text, not as an end-of-file indicator.

This option is used from the command line to prevent *sendmail* from wrongly thinking that a message is complete when collecting the message from its standard input. This differs from the correct behavior when *sendmail* is reading from an SMTP connection. Over SMTP, a lone dot must signal the end of the message.

This option is intended for use from the command line. This option should be used in the configuration file only for sites that have no SMTP network connections. But V8 *sendmail* has built-in protection. If this option is specified in the configuration file, it is automatically forced false for all SMTP connections.

The forms of the i option are:

```
Oibool      ← configuration file
-oibool     ← command line
-i          ← command-line shorthand
```

The argument *bool* is of type boolean. If *bool* is missing, the default value is true. If the i option is entirely omitted, the default is false.

The i option is safe. Even if it is specified from the command line, *sendmail* retains its *root* privilege.

OI

Queue on connection refused (all but V8)

The I option forces *sendmail* to use the Domain Naming System (DNS) to convert hostnames to IP addresses. This option causes mail to be requeued if a hostname cannot be found, or a DNS lookup times out, or a DNS connection fails. Those lookups and connections will likely work at a later time.

If your site is not connected to the Internet and not running DNS, you should *not* declare this option. Hostnames will instead be looked up in the file */etc/hosts*. If a name cannot be found in that file, mail will fail rather than be requeued.

The forms of the I option are:

```
OIbool     ← configuration file
-oIbool    ← command line
```

The argument *bool* is of type boolean. If it is missing, the default value is true. If this option is entirely omitted, the default is false. This option is effective only if NAMED_BIND is defined in *conf.h*.

If your site is not currently on the Internet, but plans to be, you should define NAMED_BIND when compiling, but not declare the I option. Later, after you set up DNS and connect to the Internet, you may simply declare this option and those services will become available.

On Sun systems running the Network Information Services (NIS), hostnames are found by querying the *hosts.byname* map. If the NIS */var/yp/Makefile* has the B=-b uncommented, NIS uses DNS when queried for hostname resolution. Unfortunately, NIS is somewhat deficient in this role. When a host is looked up through NIS, there is no way to distinguish between a temporary and a permanent failure. Thus, mail can be rejected as "Host Unknown" when the real problem is a temporary DNS lookup failure. The SunOS non-MX version of *sendmail* should be used only to forward mail over the local network. The MX version of *sendmail* (*/usr/lib/sendmail.mx*) can be used on a central mail server (one that delivers to the world). Serious sites should probably use IDA or V8 *sendmail* instead.

The I option is not safe. If specified from the command line, it may cause *sendmail* to relinquish its *root* privilege.

OI

Use DNS lookups and tune them (V8 only)

The V8 version of the I option operates the same as that for other versions (as shown above), except that it can take string arguments instead of the boolean:

```
OI arg ...
```

The *arg* is one or more arguments that allow you to tune the behavior of the name server. There must be white space between the I and the first *arg*. The *arg* arguments are identical to the flags listed in *resolver*(3), but you omit the RES_ prefix. For example, RES_DNSRCH is expressed DNSRCH. A flag may be preceded by a plus or minus to enable or disable the corresponding name server option. If no pluses or minuses appear, the default is to enable the option. Consider:

```
OI +AAONLY -DNSRCH
```

This turns on the AAONLY name server option (Authoritative Answers Only) and turns off the DNSRCH name server option (search the domain path). The default is for the DNSRCH, DEFNAMES, and RECURSE name server options to be enabled, and all others disabled.

If the I option is entirely omitted, the DNS lookup is not used. Under V8 *sendmail* any boolean argument following the I is silently ignored. Thus, an initial `True` may be included for compatibility with previous versions of *sendmail*.

```
OITrue +AAONLY -DNSRCH
```

Note that a `False` is ignored and cannot be used to disable this I option. Instead, it can be disabled only by omitting or commenting out the entire option.

Version 1 configuration files (see Chapter 23, *The Configuration File*) cause *sendmail* to disable DNSRCH and DEFNAMES when doing delivery lookups, but leave them on at all other times. Version 2 and above configuration files cause *sendmail* to use the resolver options defined by the I option, except that it always enables DNSRCH when doing lookups with the $[and $] operators.

Oj

Return MIME format errors (V8 only)

MIME (Multipurpose Internet Mail Extensions) is documented in RFC1341, with addition details in RFC1344, RFC1426, RFC1428, and RFC1437. MIME is a method of incorporating non-ASCII text in mail messages (like images and sounds).

When *sendmail* composes an error notification of failed (bounced) mail, the j option tells V8 *sendmail* to include MIME format headers in that error notification. The j option affects only returned (bounced) mail.

If the j option is true, and if *sendmail* is composing a returned mail message, the following two headers are added to the header portion of that message:

```
MIME-Version: 1.0
Content-Type: multipart/mixed; boundary=magic
```

The version (1.0) of `MIME-Version:` is hardcoded into V8 *sendmail*, so it cannot be changed. The *magic* of `Content-Type:` is a string that is used to separate the various parts of the message body. The string is formed from the queue id, the time, and the hostname, as for example:

```
Content-Type: multipart/mixed; boundary=AA26662.9306241634/hostname
```

Then *sendmail* prefixes the body of the returned message (if there is one), a line of notification, and this boundary:

```
This is a MIME-encapsulated message

--AA26662.9306241634/hostname
                - message body begins here
```

Newer MUAs are aware of MIME and can send and receive MIME messages. Such MUAs understand `MIME-Version:` header in a mail message. Older (non-MIME aware) MUAs ignore that header.

At sites that want to encourage the use of MIME, option j can comfortably be set in the configuration file. Setting option j won't break existing MUAs; it simply causes bounced mail messages to be displayed in a somewhat unattractive manner. The j option is safe. Even if it is specified from the command line, *sendmail* retains its *root* privilege.

OJ

Set ˜/.forward search path (V8 only)

When mail is being delivered to a local user, *sendmail* attempts to open and read a file in the user's home directory called *.forward*. If that file exists and is readable, the aliases in that file replace the local username for delivery.

Under V8 *sendmail*, the J option is used to define alternative locations for the user's *.forward* file. The form for the J option looks like this:

```
OJpath
```

The *path* is a colon-separated list of files. An attempt is made to open and read each in turn, from left to right, until one is successfully read.

```
OJ/var/forward/$u:$z/.forward
```

Macros may, and should, be used in the *path* file locations. In the above example, *sendmail* first looks in the file */var/forward/$u* (where the macro $u contains the user's login name). If that file can't be opened for reading, *sendmail* tries reading *$z/.forward* (where the $z macro contains the user's home directory). Other macros of interest are $w (the local hostname), $f (the user's full name), $r (the sending protocol), and $s (the sending host).

If the *path* or the entire option is omitted, the default is *$z/.forward*. Thus, omitting option J causes V8 *sendmail* to emulate older versions by looking only in the ˜/.forward file for user forwarding information.

Ok

Number of SMTP connections to maintain (V8 only)

Usually, *sendmail* uses a single autonomous SMTP session to transmit one e-mail message to another host. It connects to the other host, transmits the message, and closes the connection. Although this approach is sufficient for most mail, there are times when sending multiple messages during a single connection is preferable.

The k option of V8 *sendmail* specifies that open connections to other hosts should be maintained and the maximum number of those connections. This is called *caching* connections. When *sendmail* caches a connection, it connects to the other host and transmits the mail message as usual. But instead of closing the connection, it keeps the connection open so that it can transmit additional mail messages without the additional overhead of opening and closing the connection each time.

The form of the k option is:

```
Oknum
```

There may be optional white space between the k and the *num*. The *num* is an integer which specifies the maximum number of simultaneous connections to keep open. If *num* is zero, this caching feature is turned off. A value of 1 is good for workstations that forward all mail to a central mail server and is the default used if this option is entirely missing. A value of 4 appears good for most machines which forward mail directly over the Internet.

Caching is of greatest benefit when processing the queue. V8 *sendmail* automatically adapts to conditions to avoid caching connections for each invocation of *sendmail.* Maintenance of an open connection can delay return to the user's program, for example, and too many open connections to a common target host can create a high load on that host.

When caching is enabled with this k option, the K option (see below) should also be declared to set the connection timeout. The k option is not safe. If specified from the command line, it may cause *sendmail* to relinquish its *root* privilege.

OK
Multiple SMTP connection time out (V8 only)

Maintaining a cached connection to another host (see option k above) imposes a penalty on that other host. Each connection means the other host is running a forked *sendmail* process that is doing nothing but waiting for an SMTP QUIT message to close the connection, or for more mail to arrive.

To limit the impact on other hosts, V8 *sendmail* offers the K option. This option tells *sendmail* how long to wait for another mail message before closing the connection.

The form of the K option is:

```
OKwait
```

There may be optional white space between the K and the *wait*. The *wait* is of type time and specifies the period to wait before timing out a cached connection. If the K option is entirely missing, the default is 300 seconds (five minutes). When specifying the `wait`, be sure to include a trailing s character. If you don't, the number you specify is interpreted as a number of minutes. The `wait` should never be longer than five minutes. A value of 0 essentially turns off caching.

This K option has an effect only if the k option is also declared. The K option is not safe. If specified from the command line, it may cause *send-mail* to relinquish its *root* privilege.

OK
Associate key with database (IDA only)

The *aliases* file is usually stored in a *dbm*(3) database format to make the lookup of aliases faster. The K option for IDA *sendmail* allows you to store other useful information in fast-lookup database form as well. Examples are a list of known UUCP neighbors, or a list of workstations that are not running the *sendmail* daemon.

The forms of the K option are:

```
OKdatabase      ← configuration file
-oKdatabase     ← command line
```

The `database` argument is a combination of two types. A character first gives a name to the database, then a string gives the location of the database. The two forms of the K option's `database` argument are:

```
Xpath        ← dbm file
X%nis_map    ← NIS map
```

The arguments `path` and `nis_map` are of type string. If either is missing, the database name X is undefined and ignored. The `path` form declares that the macro named X is associated with the *dbm*(3) file whose full path-name is `path`. The `nis_map` form declares that the macro named X is associated with the NIS (Network Information Services) map named *nis_map*. The % in front of the `nis_map` is what differentiates the two forms.

The K option form of the IDA database macros is covered more fully in Chapter 29, *Database Macros*. That chapter also illustrates how the database macros are used in rules, and cautions about their misuse.

The K option is not safe. If specified from the command line, it may cause *sendmail* to relinquish its *root* privilege.

O1

Use Errors-To: for error notification (V8 only)

Ordinarily, V8 *sendmail* sends notification of failed mail to the envelope sender. It specifically does not send notification to the addresses listed in the `Errors-To:` header. It does this because the `Errors-To:` header violates RFC1123. For additional information about `Errors-To:`, see Chapter 31, *Headers*.

The 1 option is available to prevent older versions of software from failing. When set, it allows error notification to be sent to the address listed in the `Errors-To:` header, in addition to that sent to the envelope sender.

The forms of the 1 option are:

```
O1bool    ← configuration file
-o1bool   ← command line
```

The optional argument *bool*, when missing, defaults to true. If this option is entirely missing, it defaults to false.

The 1 option is safe. Even if it is specified from the command line, *sendmail* retains its *root* privilege.

OL

Set logging level

The *sendmail* program is able to log (record for later use) a wide variety of information about what it is doing. There is no default file for recording this information. Instead, *sendmail* sends all such information by means of the UNIX *syslog*(3) mechanism. The disposition of messages by *syslog* is determined by information in the file */etc/syslog.conf* (see Chapter 22, *Logging and Statistics*). One common scheme places non-critical messages into the file */var/log/syslog*, but routes important messages to */dev/console* or */var/adm/messages*.

Unfortunately, there is not a tight correspondence between *sendmail*'s logging levels and *syslog*'s priorities. Nor is there a continuous range of logging levels. The meaningful values for the logging level, with their corresponding *syslog* priorities, are outlined below. Note that higher logging levels include the lower logging levels. For example, logging level 2 also causes level 1 messages to be logged. Also note that the V8 organization differs, and we cover that next.

The *sendmail* (all but V8) program's logging levels are defined as follows:

0   No logging at all. The *sendmail* program is completely silent, so far as logging is concerned. Normal error messages are still printed.

1   Log major problems only, like the unexpected loss of an SMTP connection, or the inability to allocate needed memory. These are logged at the *syslog* priorities of LOG_CRIT or LOG_ALERT.

2   Record message collections and notify about failed deliveries. Deliveries can fail for a variety of reasons, such as unknown user, unknown host, and bad permissions on a file or program. These are logged at the *syslog* priority of LOG_NOTICE.

3   Record successful deliveries. All this really means is that the program called to do the actual delivery exited with a zero value. Note that homegrown shell scripts for delivery can fool *sendmail* by failing, yet returning a zero by mistake. These are logged at the *syslog* priority of LOG_NOTICE.

4   Record all abnormally deferred deliveries. Mail is deferred by being left in the queue, for example, because some resource is temporarily absent (the destination host might be down). These are logged at the *syslog* priority of LOG_NOTICE.

5   Record all normal queue activity. Mail can be intentionally queued because a mailer is expensive (the c option), for safety (s option), or because the load average (or number of processes) is too high. These are logged at the *syslog* priority of LOG_NOTICE.

6   Record any errors that are really harmless, for example, trying to process a message that is already locked. These are logged at the *syslog* priority of LOG_NOTICE.

7-8   Unused.

9   Record mappings of message identification numbers. Messages can each have two different identifiers: a queue id number, and a **Message-id**. This logging level causes *sendmail* to record the mapping between these two forms of identifier. This mapping is useful for tracing a message as it travels from host to host. These are logged at the *syslog* priority of LOG_INFO.

10   Unused

11-22   Record debugging information. The higher the logging level, the more debugging information is emitted. Such information ranges from: the deallocation of an envelope (LogLevel> 10) to the failure to *unlink*(2) a temporary file (LogLevel> 21). The mid-range logging level of 16 produces a great deal of information about how *sendmail* is handling the queue. Debugging information is logged at the *syslog* priority of LOG_DEBUG.

The V8 organization of logging levels is the following:

0   No logging.

1   Only serious system failures and security problems. These are logged at LOG_CRIT or LOG_ALERT.

2   Communication failures, like lost connections, or protocol failures. These are logged at LOG_CRIT.

3   Malformed addresses. These are logged at LOG_NOTICE.

4   Malformed qf filenames and similar minor errors. These are logged at LOG_NOTICE.

5   A record of each message received. These are logged at LOG_INFO.

6   SMTP VRFY attempts and messages returned to the original sender. These are logged at LOG_INFO.

7   Delivery failures, excluding mail deferred because of a temporary lack of a needed resource. These are logged at LOG_INFO.

8   Successful deliveries. These are logged at LOG_INFO.

9   Mail deferred because of a temporary lack of a needed resource. These are logged at LOG_INFO.

10   Each key as it is looked up in a database, and the result of each database lookup. These are logged at LOG_INFO.

11-98   Debugging information. You'll need the source to understand this logging. These are logged at LOG_DEBUG.

The forms of the L option are:

```
OLlev     ← configuration file
-oLlev    ← command line
```

The type for lev is *numeric,* and defaults to 0. Negative values are legal and are equivalent to a logging level of 0.

The L option is safe. Even if it is specified from the command line, *sendmail* retains its *root* privilege. For V8 *sendmail*, the logging level can be increased only from the command line.

Om

Send to me too

When you send mail to a mailing list that includes your name as a part of that list, *sendmail* normally excludes you from that mailing. There are two good reasons for that behavior:

- Since you sent the mail, it is assumed that you already have a copy of the letter. Most mailing programs have options that allow you to automatically retain copies of your outgoing mail. The BSD *Mail* program, for example, has the *outfolder* option.

- When mail passes through a site that is acting as an exploder for an outside mailing list, mail loops could be caused by sending a copy of the message back to the original sender.

Option m overrides this behavior, but it is usually best to keep it turned off. If individual users want to be included in mailings to lists that they belong to, they can set this behavior from their mail-sending programs. BSD *Mail*, for example, allows you to set `metoo` in your `~/.mailrc` file. This use of `metoo` simply causes *Mail* to invoke *sendmail* with the -om switch, thereby setting the m option.

The forms of the m option are:

```
Ombool      ← configuration file
-ombool     ← command line
-m          ← command-line shorthand
```

The optional argument *bool*, when missing, defaults to true. If this option is entirely missing, it defaults to false.

The m option is safe. Even if it is specified from the command line, *sendmail* retains its *root* privilege.

OM

Define a macro's value on the command line

The M option is used to set or change a defined macro's value. Although this option is allowed in the *sendmail.cf* file, it is exclusively intended for use from the command line. When a macro value is set from the command line, that new value overrides any value given in the configuration file.

The forms of the M option are:

```
OMXvalue    ← configuration file
-oMXvalue   ← command line
DXvalue     ← both are equivalent of this in the configuration file
```

In all three cases, the argument *value* is of type string. The *value* is assigned to the macro named X. Macro names are always a single character.

One example of the usefulness of this option concerns the *rmail*(8) program. Suppose a machine is used for networked mail. Ordinarily, the r macro is given the value "smtp" to signify that mail is received over the network. But for UUCP mail, the r macro should be given the value "UUCP". One way to effect such an change is to arrange for *rmail*(8) to invoke *sendmail* with a command-line argument of:

```
-oMrUUCP
```

In this command line, the −o switch tells *sendmail* to define a macro (the M) whose name is r to have the text UUCP as its new value.* This new value overrides whatever value r may have been given in the configuration file. The M option should be approached with caution. If you later upgrade your *sendmail* program and install a new configuration file, you may find that the names of macros aren't what you expect. Previous command-line assumptions about names may suddenly break.

The M option is safe only when assigning values to the r and s macros. For all other macros it is unsafe, and if specified from the command line, may cause *sendmail* to relinquish its *root* privilege. SunOS *sendmail* is an exception, in that it considers this option safe for all macros.

On
Check validity of the right-hand side of aliases (V8 only)

Ordinarily, when *sendmail* processes the *aliases*(5) file, it checks only the addresses to the left of the colon to make sure they all resolve to the local delivery agent. With V8 *sendmail*, it is possible to also have addresses to the right of the colon checked for validity by setting option n to true.

---

*Under V8 *sendmail*, the $s and $r macros should be assigned values with −p command-line switch (see Chapter 32, *The Command Line*).

```
OnTrue                          ← configuration file
-onTrue                         ← command line
```

Addresses to the right of the colon are checked only to be sure they are good addresses. They do not need to select the `local` delivery agent. They merely need to successfully select any delivery agent. V8 *sendmail* prints the following warning and skips any address that fails to select a delivery agent:

address... bad address

The n option is safe. Even if it is specified from the command line, *sendmail* retains its *root* privilege.

ON

Define the network name (obsolete)

The N option tells *sendmail* the name of the local network. This option was long ago made obsolete by adoption of the Domain Naming System (DNS). Do not set the option—it is likely to be reused and have a different meaning in future releases of *sendmail*.

Oo

Allow old-style space-delimited recipient lists

In pre-RFC821 days, lists of recipients were commonly space-delimited. That is:

hans christian anderson

was considered a list of three mail recipients, rather than a single, three-part name. Currently, individual recipient names must be delimited with commas, and internal spaces must be quoted. That is:

```
hans,christian,anderson          ← three recipients
"hans christian anderson"        ← a single three-part name
hans christian anderson          ← illegal
```

Since some users and some old programs still delimit recipient lists with spaces, the o option can be used to tell *sendmail* to internally convert those spaces to commas.

The forms of the o option are:

```
Oobool      ← configuration file
-oobool     ← command line
```

The argument *bool* is of type boolean. If that argument is missing, the default value is true. If the entire o option is missing, it defaults to false.

The *sendmail* program is somewhat adaptive about commas. When first examining a list of addresses, it looks to see if one of the following four characters appears in that list:

```
,  ;  <  (
```

If it finds any of these characters in an address list, it turns off the o option for the remainder of the list. You always want to enable this option in your configuration file. The only exception might be the unusual situation where all addresses are normally comma-separated, but some legal addresses contain spaces.

Note that comma delimiting allows spaces around recipient names for clarity. That is, both of the following are equivalent:

```
hans,christian,anderson
hans, christian, anderson
```

The o option is safe. Even if it is specified from the command line, *sendmail* retains its *root* privilege.

OO
Set network options for the daemon (V8 only)

The O option under V8 *sendmail* is used to customize the daemon's SMTP service. The form for the O option looks like this:

```
OOpair,pair,pair      ← configuration file
-oOpair,pair,pair     ← command line
```

The O is followed by a comma-separated list of pairs, where each *pair* is of the form:

```
key=value
```

There are only five keys available and they are case sensitive.

Port   The Port key is used to specify the service port on which the daemon should listen. This is normally the port called smtp, as defined in the */etc/services* file. The value may be either a services string (like smtp) or a number (like 25). This key is useful inside domains that are protected by a firewall. By specifying a non-standard port, the firewall can communicate in a more secure manner with the internal network, while still accepting mail on the normal port from the outside world. If this pair is missing, the port defaults to smtp.

Addr   The Addr key is used to specify the network to use. The value is either the name of a network (from */etc/networks*) or the IP address of a network. If the Addr pair is omitted, the default network becomes INADDR_ANY (the first network reported by *netstat –i*).

Family

The Family key is used to specify the network family. The legal possible values are "inet" for AF_INET, "iso" for AF_ISO, "ns" for AF_NS, or "x.25" for AF_CCITT. Note that only "inet" and "iso" are currently supported. The default is "inet."

SendSize and ReceiveSize

The SendSize key is used to specify the size of the TCP/IP send buffer. The ReceiveSize key is used to specify the size of the TCP/IP receive buffer. The value for each is a size in bytes. These should not be set unless you are having performance problems. Slow links (such as 9.6K SL/IP lines) might profit from a setting of 256 for each. The default values are set by the system (see *setsockopt*(2)).

Only the first character in each *key* is recognized, so a succinct declaration like the following can be used to change the port used by the daemon:

```
OOP=26,A=our-net      # Only listen for local mail
```

The O option is not safe. If specified from the command line, it may cause *sendmail* to relinquish its *root* privilege.

Op

Tune privacy of the SMTP daemon (V8 only)

The p option is used in two ways. It is primarily intended as a way to force other sites to adhere to SMTP conventions. It can also be used to improve security.

The form of the p option looks like this:

```
Opwhat,what,what,...        ← configuration file
-opwhat,what,what,...       ← command line
```

The *what* arguments must be separated from one another by commas. The known list of *what* arguments and the meaning of each is:

public

> The default for the p option is `public`. This means that there is no checking for valid SMTP syntax, and no checking for the security matters described below.

needmailhelo

> The SMTP protocol specifies that the sending site should issue the HELO or ELHO command to identify itself, before specifying the name of the sender with the MAIL command. By listing need-mailhelo with the p option, you cause the following error to be returned to the sending site in this situation:

> ```
> 503 Polite people say HELO first
> ```

> If needmailhelo is not specified, but authwarnings is specified, then the following header is added to the message describing the problem:

> ```
> X-Authentication-Warning: us: Host them didn't use HELO
> protocol
> ```

needexpnhelo

> The SMTP EXPN command causes *sendmail* to print what a local address "expands" to. If the address is an alias, it shows all the addresses that result from the alias expansion. If the address is local, it shows the result of aliasing through a user's ~/.forward file. If needexpnhelo is specified, *sendmail* requires that the requesting site first introduce itself with an SMTP HELO or ELHO command. If the requesting site has not done so, *sendmail* responds with the following message rather than providing the requested expansion information:

> ```
> 503 I demand that you introduce yourself first
> ```

needvrfyhelo

> The SMTP VRFY command causes *sendmail* to verify that an address is that of a local user or local alias. Unlike EXPN above, VRFY does not cause mailing list contents, the result of aliasing, or the contents of ~/.forward files to be displayed. If needvrfyhelo is specified, *sendmail* requires that the requesting site first introduce itself with an SMTP HELO or ELHO command. If the requesting site has not done so, *sendmail* responds with the same message as for

needexpnhelo above, rather than providing the requested verification information.

noexpn

Setting noexpn causes *sendmail* to disallow all SMTP EXPN commands. In place of information, *sendmail* sends the following reply to the requesting host:

```
502 That's none of your business
```

novrfy

Setting novrfy causes *sendmail* to disallow all SMTP VRFY commands. In place of verification, *sendmail* sends the following reply to the requesting host:

```
252 Who's to say?
```

authwarnings

Setting authwarnings causes *sendmail* to insert special headers into the mail message which advise the recipient of reasons to suspect that the message may not be authentic. The general form of this special header is shown below. The possible reasons are listed in Chapter 31, *Headers*.

```
X-Authentication-Warning: ourhost: reason
```

goaway

A shorthand way to set all of the above (except for public) is with goaway.

restrictmailq

Ordinarily, anyone may examine the mail queue's contents by using the *mailq*(1) command. To restrict who may examine the queue's contents, specify restrictmailq. If restricted, *sendmail* allows only users who are in the same group as the group ownership of the queue directory to examine the contents. This allows the queue directory to be fully protected with mode 0700, yet for selected users to still be able to see its contents.

restrictqrun

Ordinarily, anyone may process the queue with the -q switch. To limit queue processing to *root* and the owner of the queue directory, specify restrictqrun.

If *what* is not one of the words listed above, *sendmail* prints the following message and ignores the unknown word:

```
readcf: Op line: unknown_word unrecognized
```

The p option is safe. If specified from the command line, it does not cause *sendmail* to relinquish its *root* privilege. Because it is really a mask, specifications in the configuration file or on the command line can only make it more restrictive.

Op
Don't connect if too many processes (NeXT only)

To insure that the load on a machine is kept reasonably low, it is sometimes necessary to have *sendmail* refuse SMTP network connections. The *sendmail.cf* file has several options to tune this behavior. On the NeXT computer, the p option can be used to cut off connections based on the total number of user processes currently running.

The forms of the p option are:

```
Opnum      ← configuration file
-opnum     ← command line
```

The argument *num* is of type numeric, and must be greater than zero to have any effect. If either *num* or this option is missing, the test and cutoff are disabled. The NeXT documentation contains no recommendation of a good value and fails to reveal the default value.

The p option is useful only in daemon mode and is available only on a NeXT machine running OS 2.0 or later.

The p option is not safe. If specified from the command line, it may cause *sendmail* to relinquish its *root* privilege.

OP
Extra copies of postmaster mail

The RFC822 *Standard for the Format of ARPA Internet Text Messages* requires that all sites be set up in such a way that mail addressed to the special name *Postmaster** always be successfully delivered. This requirement ensures that notification of mail problems can always be sent and

---

*The name *Postmaster* is case insensitive. That is, *POSTMASTER, Postmaster, postmaster,* and even *PoStMaStEr* are all equivalent.

successfully delivered to the offending site.* At most sites the name *Post-master* is an alias to a real person's name in the *aliases* file.

Ordinarily, notification of locally bounced mail and other mail problems is sent back (bounced) to the sender of the message. The local person in the role of *Postmaster* does not get a copy of local failed mail.

The P option tells *sendmail* to send a copy of all failed mail to another person, often *Postmaster.* Under V8 and SunOS, that copy contains only the failed message's header. Under other versions of *sendmail,* that copy includes both the header and the body.

The forms of the P option are:

```
OPuser      ← configuration file
-oPuser     ← command line
```

The argument `user` is of type string. If the argument is missing, or if the P option is entirely missing, no extra copy is sent.

While debugging a new *sendmail.cf* file, it is wise to define the P option so that you receive a copy of all failed mail. Once the configuration file is stable, the P option may either be removed or the name replaced with an alias to a program. Such a program could filter the copies of error mail so that only serious problems would be seen.

Macros used in the `user` argument will be correctly expanded before use. For example:

```
DHmailhost
OPPostmaster@$H
```

The P option is not safe. If specified from the command line, it may cause *sendmail* to relinquish its *root* privilege.

Oq

Multiplier (factor) for high-load queueing

When the load average on a machine (the average number of processes in the run queue over the last minute) becomes too high, *sendmail* can compensate by queueing all mail, rather than delivering it. The q option is used

---

*This is not true for hosts addressed as *user@host.domain* that are really X.400 sites masquerading as Internet sites. They may bounce *postmaster* mail, and may require that you instead use names like *system* or *helpdesk.* This problem is currently being debated around the Internet draft *draft-ietf-x400ops-postmaster-00.txt.*

in combination with the x option to calculate the point at which *sendmail* stops delivering. If the current load average is greater than or equal to the value given to the x option, then the following formula is evaluated:

```
msgpri > q / (la - x + 1)
```

Here q is the value set by this option, la is the current load average, and x is the cutoff load specified by the x option. If the value yielded by this calculation is less than or equal to the priority of the current mail message (msgpri), the message is queued rather than delivered. Priorities are initialized with the P *sendmail.cf* command and tuned with the y and z options.

Note that under V8 *sendmail*, this queue-only mode also becomes true if the current load average is greater than the value of the X option.

The forms of q option are:

```
Oqfact      ← configuration file
-oqfact     ← command line
```

The argument *fact* is of type numeric. It may be positive, negative, or zero. If *fact* is missing, the value defaults to zero. If the entire q option is missing, the default value given to *fact* is 10,000.

The q option is not safe. If specified from the command line, it may cause *sendmail* to relinquish its *root* privilege.

OQ

Location of queue directory

Mail messages that have not yet been delivered are stored in the *sendmail* program's queue directory.

The location of the queue directory is defined by the Q option. That location may be a relative pathname (for testing) or an absolute pathname. If the specified location does not exist, *sendmail* prints something like:

```
cannot chdir(/var/spool/mqueue): No such file or directory
```

If the location exists, but is not a directory, sendmail prints something like:

```
cannot chdir(/var/spool/mqueue): Not a directory
```

In both cases, *sendmail* also logs an error message via *syslog*(8) if the logging level of the L option permits. In both cases, *sendmail* aborts immediately.

The forms of the Q option are:

```
OQpath     ← configuration file
-oQpath    ← command line
```

The *path* argument is of type string. If it is missing, the value for *path* defaults to "mqueue". Relative names for the queue are always relative to the directory in which *sendmail* was invoked. If the entire Q option is missing, the value for *path* defaults to the C language value of NULL, and *sendmail* complains with:

```
cannot chdir((null)): Bad file number
```

The Q option is not safe. If specified from the command line, it may cause *sendmail* to relinquish its *root* privilege.

Or

Set timeout for SMTP reads (not V8)

When *sendmail* speaks SMTP and connects via TCP over the network to another host, it is possible that the connection may hang. A common cause of a hung connection is a temporary failure in a network link (one long enough to cause packets to be lost and the retry limit to be exceeded). Rather than having *sendmail* wait forever for a reply that never arrives, it is possible to have *sendmail* time out instead. The amount of time it should wait before timing out is specified by the r option. When a connection is timed out, the mail message is placed into the queue to be retransmitted at a later time.

The forms of the r option are:

```
Ortimeout     ← configuration file
-ortimeout    ← command line
```

The argument *timeout* is of type time. That is, one minute can be expressed as 1m, or 60s or simply 60. If *timeout* is missing, or if the entire r option is missing, timeouts are disabled.

Note that this timeout is different from the timeout that is set internally by *sendmail* for the initial greeting. The SMTP conversation with the other site always begins by the local *sendmail* waiting for a HELO message. The wait for that message is internally limited to 300 seconds (five minutes).

In practice, the value given to the r option should be high, like two hours (2h). A heavily-loaded site, when expanding a huge mailing list, can legitimately take a very long time to respond. Don't be tempted to make the timeout short just because your machine is fast. The other sites you connect to may not be so fortunate.

The r option is safe. Even if it is specified from the command line, *send-mail* retains its *root* privilege.

Or

Set timeouts for SMTP (V8 only)

When reading commands or data from a remote SMTP connection, it is possible for the other side to take so long that it becomes necessary for the local *sendmail* to time out and break the connection. Similarly, when reading from its standard input, *sendmail* may find that the program feeding it information is taking too long. In the absence of timeouts, *sendmail* can hang forever.

The V8 version of the *sendmail* program has introduced defaults for the amount of time it waits under various circumstances. The V8 r option has been improved to allow you to tune those timeouts to meet your local needs. The form of the r option is:

```
Orkeyword=value,keyword=value,...      ← configuration file
-orkeyword=value,keyword=value,...     ← command line
```

The recognized keyword words, and the default and minimum value for each, is shown below. The minimums are not enforced, but are rather the minimums recommended by RFC1123, section 5.3.2.* The value is of type time.

initial

> The amount of time to wait for the initial greeting message. This messages is printed by the remote site when it first makes its connection. The greeting message always starts with 220 and looks something like this:

> ```
> 220 there.dc.gov Sendmail 8.1/3x ready at ...
> ```

> The default for the greeting wait and the recommended minimum are both five minutes.

---

*Note that these minimums are, in all likelihood, too short for any real-world applications.

helo   After the greeting, the local *sendmail* sends a HELO message to identify itself. That message looks something like this:

```
HELO here.us.edu
```

The other site then replies with acknowledgment of the local HELO:

```
250 there.dc.gov  Hello here.us.edu, pleased to meet you
```

The amount of time the local *sendmail* waits for the other site to acknowledge the local HELO is set with the `helo` keyword. The default value is five minutes. There is no specified minimum, but we recommend no less than five minutes.

mail   The local *sendmail* next sends the address of the sender (the envelope sender address) with an SMTP MAIL command:

```
MAIL From:<you@here.us.edu>
```

The local *sendmail* then waits for acknowledgment, which looks like this:

```
250 <you@here.us.edu>... Sender ok
```

The amount of time that the local *sendmail* waits for acknowledgment of its MAIL command is set with the `mail` keyword. The default value is ten minutes and the specified minimum is five minutes.

rcpt   Next, the local *sendmail* issues one RCPT command to specify each envelope recipient. One such RCPT line might look like this:

```
RCPT To:<them@there.dc.gov>
```

The local *sendmail* then waits for acknowledgment which looks like this:

```
250 <them@there.dc.gov>... Recipient ok
```

The amount of time that the local *sendmail* waits for acknowledgment of each RCPT command is set with the `rcpt` keyword. The default value is one hour, and the specified minimum is five minutes. This time out should be generously long because a recipient may be the name of a mailing list and the other side may take a long time to expand all the names in that list before replying.

datainit

> After all the recipients have been specified, the local *sendmail* declares that it is ready to send the mail message itself. It issues the SMTP DATA command to the other site:
>
>   DATA
>
> The local *sendmail* then waits for acknowledgment, which looks like this:
>
>   354 Enter mail, end with "." on a line by itself
>
> The amount of time that the local *sendmail* waits for acknowledgment of its DATA command is set with the `datainit` keyword. The default value is five minutes and the specified minimum is two minutes.

datablock

> The local *sendmail* then sends the mail message to the receiving site one line at a time. The amount of time that the local *sendmail* waits for acknowledgment of receipt of each line is set with the `datablock` keyword. The default value is one hour and the specified minimum is three minutes. This value assigned to `datablock` should be long, because it also applies to programs piping input to *sendmail* (which have no guarantee of promptness).

datafinal

> After the entire mail message has been transmitted, the local *sendmail* then sends a lone dot to say that it is done, and it waits for the receiving *sendmail* to acknowledge acceptance of that dot:
>
>   250 Mail accepted
>
> The amount of time that the local *sendmail* waits for acknowledgment that the mail message was received is set with the `datafinal` keyword. The default value is one hour and the specified minimum is ten minutes. If the value is shorter than the time actually needed for the receiving site to deliver the message, the local *sendmail* times out before seeing the "Mail accepted" message when, in fact, the mail was accepted. This can lead to the local *sendmail* wrongly attempting to deliver the message later for a second time.

rset If connection caching is enabled (see option k), the local *sendmail* sends an SMTP RSET command to reset the other side. Some other sites require this to force the mail to really be delivered when the connection is kept open. The time the local *sendmail* waits for acknowledgment of the RSET command is defined with the `rset` keyword. The default is five minutes, and there is no minimum specified.

quit   When the local *sendmail* is finished and wishes to break the connection, it sends the SMTP QUIT command.

        QUIT

The other side acknowledges and the connection is terminated:

        221 there.dc.gov delivering mail

The time the local *sendmail* waits for acknowledgment of the QUIT command is defined with the `quit` keyword. The default is two minutes and there is no minimum specified.

misc   During the course of mail transfer, the local *sendmail* may issue short miscellaneous commands. Examples are NOOP (which stands for no operation) and VERB (which tells the other side to enter verbose mode). The time that the local *sendmail* waits for acknowledgment of these miscellaneous commands is defined with the `misc` keyword. The default is two minutes and there is no minimum specified.

command

When roles are reversed (another site contacts the local site for transfer of mail), the other site issues the SMTP commands and waits for the local *sendmail* to acknowledge them. The amount of time the local *sendmail* waits for commands is defined with the `command` keyword. The default is one hour, and the minimum is specified as five minutes.

ident   When *sendmail* tries to check the identification of the mail sender using the RFC1314 (IDENT) protocol, it waits only 30 seconds for a response. The `ident` keyword is used to change this timeout.

For compatibility with old configuration files, if no *keyword=* is specified, timeouts for the `mail`, `rcpt`, `datainit`, `datablock`, `datafinal`, and `command` keywords are set to the defaults listed above.

    Or   ← *use defaults*

An example of the r option with "keyword=" pairs looks like this:

    Orrcpt=25m,datablock=3h

Here, the timeout for acknowledgment of the the SMTP RCPT command (list a recipient) is 25 minutes and the timeout for acknowledgment of receipt of each line of the mail message is three hours; all the others not specified assume the default values.

The r option is not safe. If specified from the command line, it may cause *sendmail* to relinquish its *root* privilege.

OR
Don't prune route addresses (V8 only)

One form of address is called a *route address*, because it specifies a route (sequence of hosts) through which the message should be delivered. For example:

```
@hostA,@hostB:user@hostC
```

This address specifies that the message should first go to hostA, then from hostA to hostB, and finally from hostB to hostC for delivery to user.

RFC1123, in Section 5.3.3, specifies that delivery agents should always try to eliminate source routing when they are able. V8 *sendmail* takes an address like the above and checks to see if it can connect to hostC directly. If it can, it rewrites the address like this:

```
user@hostC
```

This is called pruning route addresses. There may be times when such pruning is inappropriate. Internal networks, for example, may be set up to encourage manual specification of a route through a high-speed network. If left to its own, *sendmail* always tosses the route and tries to connect directly.

The R option causes *sendmail* to never prune route addresses. The forms of the R option are:

```
ORbool      ← configuration file
-oR         ← command line
```

The argument *bool* is of type boolean. If it is missing, the default value is true. If the entire R option is missing, the default becomes false.

The R option is safe. Even if it is specified from the command line, *sendmail* retains its *root* privilege.

OR

Route on NFS mounted spool directory (SunOS only)

One approach to handling mail at large sites is that of having a central machine that is the master mail-handling machine (the hub). In this scheme, all other machines send their mail to the hub for handling. Sun Microsystems introduced an option intended to make the implementation of this scheme easy. The R option tells *sendmail* to route all mail to a machine named *mailhost* if the spool directory (*/var/spool/mail*) is NFS-mounted. Unfortunately, as of SunOS Release 4.1.3, the R option creates more problems than it solves. For example:

- If an SMTP connection is broken during the DATA transfer phase, and the R option is enabled, a mail message can be lost, rather than saved in the queue.

- The -t command-line switch can cause *sendmail* to hang forever, and continue to use cpu time, if the *mailhost* is down and the R option is used.

- This R option can cause the message header and body to be joined (the blank line between them removed). This can cause part of the message's body to wrongly appear as header information.

A better approach is to use a *sendmail.cf* file that is custom written for clients. A boiler-plate version of such a *sendmail.cf* file is developed in the tutorial part of this book.

The forms of the R option are:

```
ORhost      ← configuration file
-oRhost     ← command line
```

The optional argument *host* is of type string. If *host* is present, it gives the name of the host to which all mail should be forwarded. If *host* is missing, and */var/spool/mail* is NFS-mounted, mail is forwarded to the host from which that directory is mounted. If */var/spool/mail* is not NFS-mounted, or if it is a symbolic link, this option is ignored.

The R option is safe. Even if it is specified from the command line, *sendmail* retains its *root* privilege.

Os

For safety, queue everything

At times, such as when calling */bin/mail* to deliver local mail, *sendmail* holds an entire message internally while waiting for that delivery to complete. Clearly, this runs the risk of the message being lost should the system crash at the wrong time.

As a safeguard against such rare catastrophes, the s option can be used to force *sendmail* to queue every message. The queued copy is left in place until *sendmail* is sure that delivery was successful.

The forms of the s option are:

```
Osbool      ← configuration file
-os         ← command line
```

The argument *bool* is of type boolean. If it is missing, the default value is true. If the entire s option is missing, the default becomes false.

The s option is safe. Even if it is specified from the command line, *sendmail* retains its *root* privilege.

OS

Specify statistics file

At busy and complex mail sites, many different delivery agents are active. For example, one kind of mail might be routed over the Internet using the TCP delivery agent, while another might be routed via the UUCP suite of programs, and yet another over a DS3 link to a group of research machines. In such circumstances, it is useful to gather statistical information about the total use to date of each delivery agent.

The S option tells *sendmail* the name of the file into which it should save those statistics. This option does *not* cause statistics to be gathered. It merely specifies the name of the file where they may be saved. When *sendmail* runs, it checks for the existence of such a file. If the file exists, it opens and updates the statistics in the file. If the file doesn't exist, *sendmail* quietly ignores statistics. The statistics can be viewed using the *mailstats*(8) program. The statistics file is covered in detail in Chapter 22, *Logging and Statistics*.

The forms of the S option are:

```
OSpath      ← configuration file
-oSpath     ← command line
```

The optional argument *path* is of type string. It may be a relative or a full pathname. The default value for *path* is *sendmail.st*. Relative names are always relative to the queue directory. If the entire option is missing, the value for path becomes the C language value NULL.

The S option is not safe. If specified from the command line, it may cause *sendmail* to relinquish its *root* privilege.

Ot

Set time zone (SysV only)

Under System V UNIX, processes must look for the local time zone in the environment variable TZ. Because *sendmail* is often run as an SUID *root* program, it cannot (and should not) trust its environment variables. Consequently, on System V machines, it is necessary to use the t option to give *sendmail* the correct time zone information.

The forms of the t option are:

```
OtS#D       ← configuration file
-otS#D      ← command line
```

Here, the argument S#D is really three arguments in one. Each is of type string. The first is the local abbreviation for standard time (S). The second is the number of hours the local time differs from GMT (#). And the third is the local abbreviation for daylight savings time (D). For example, on the west coast of the United States, you might declare:

```
OtPST8PDT
```

The default, if the *S#D* argument is omitted, or if the entire t option is omitted, is the east coast of the United States, EST5EDT.

Under V8 *sendmail*, if the entire t option is missing, the environment variable TZ is used. If S#D is missing, TZ is set to the system default. If S#D is present, TZ is set to the zones specified.

The t option is not safe. If specified from the command line, it may cause *sendmail* to relinquish its *root* privilege.

OT

Limit life of a message in the queue

When mail cannot be delivered promptly, it is left in the queue. At intervals specified by *sendmail's* -q command-line switch, redelivery of that queued mail is attempted. The maximum time a mail message can remain in the queue before being bounced as undeliverable is defined by the T option.

The forms of the T option are:

```
OTqtime      ← configuration file
-oTqtime     ← command line
```

The argument *qtime* is of type time. If this argument is missing, or if the entire T option is missing, the value given to *qtime* is zero, and no mail is ever queued. The *qtime* is generally specified as a number of days, 5d for example. (Coincidently, RFC1123 recommends five days as a minimum.)

All queued mail is timed out based on its creation time compared to the timeout period specified by the T option. Each queued message has its creation time stored in its qf file. When *sendmail* is run (either as a daemon or by hand) to process the queue, it gets its timeout period from the value of the T option. As the queue is processed, each message's creation time is checked to see if it has timed out based on the *current* value of option T. Since the configuration file is read only once (when *sendmail* first starts), the timeout period cannot be subsequently changed. There are only two ways to lengthen the timeout period. First, by modifying the configuration file's T option (which could involve recreating the freeze file) and killing and restarting *sendmail*. Second, by running *sendmail* by hand with the -q command-line switch and setting a new timeout using the -oT*timeo* command-line switch.

Since the creation time is stored in a queued file's qf file, messages can theoretically be rejuvenated (made to appear young again) by simply modifying that entry. The details of the qf queue file are presented in Appendix A, *The qf File Internals*.

The first time delivery fails and the mail message is queued, the sender is sent mail notification that the message could not be immediately delivered. Under V8 *sendmail*, such notification need not be sent immediately. For V8, a second argument can follow the *qtime* in the T option declaration:

```
OTqtime/notify     ← configuration file
-oTqtime/notify    ← command line
```

If the second argument is present, it must be separated from the first by a
/. The `notify` specifies the amount of time *sendmail* should wait, after
the message is first queued, before sending notification. If *notify* is missing, the old behavior is used. If *notify* is longer than *qtime*, no notification is ever sent.

The T option is not safe. If specified from the command line, it may cause
sendmail to relinquish its *root* privilege.

Ou

Set user id of mailer

The u option is covered jointly with the g option on page 509.

OU

Specify user database (V8 only)

BSD 4.4 UNIX includes UDB, a *user database* which holds a variety of information about each user on the system, including an entry for each user
which specifies where that user's mail is to be delivered.*

When the user database is available, the U option can be used to cause
sendmail to access the information in that database. Address information in
the database supersedes conflicting information in the `˜/.forward` file, but
does not supersede information in the *aliases* file.

The forms of the U option are:

```
OUpath,...      ← configuration file
-oUpath,...     ← command line
```

The argument *path, . . .* is of type string. The *path, . . .* is a comma-
separated list of full or relative database pathnames. Relative names are
always relative to the queue directory. If *path, . . .* is missing, or if the
entire U option is missing, the user database is not used. Otherwise, the
user database is used, and each database is accessed in turn, leftmost to
rightmost, in *path, ...*

The user database can only be used if USERDB is defined in *conf.h* when
you compile *sendmail.* You should define USERDB only if you are running
BSD 4.4 UNIX or are set up to use the user database.

---

*UDB is available from *ftp.cs.berkeley.edu.* It can easily be ported to many systems.

Ov

Run in verbose mode

The *sendmail* program offers a verbose mode of operation. In this "blow-by-blow" mode, a description of all the *sendmail* program's actions is printed to the standard output. This mode is valuable when running *sendmail* interactively, but useless when running in daemon mode. Consequently, you should never set this option in the *sendmail.cf* file. Instead, you should set it from the command line using the −v switch.

After the *sendmail.cf* file is parsed, and after the command-line arguments have been processed, *sendmail* checks to see if it is in verbose mode. If it is, it sets the c option (don't connect to expensive mailers) to false, and sets the d option (deliver mode) to interactive.

The forms of the v option are:

```
Ovbool       ← configuration file
-ovbool      ← command line
-v           ← command-line shorthand
```

The argument *bool* is of type boolean. If it is missing, the default value is true. If the entire option is missing, the default value is false.

The v option is safe. Even if it is specified from the command line, *sendmail* retains its *root* privilege.

OV

Fall-back MX host (V8 only)

At sites with poor (connect on demand, or unreliable) network connections, SMTP connections may often fail. In such situations, it may not be desirable for each workstation to queue the mail locally for a later attempt. Under V8 *sendmail*, it is possible to specify a *fallback* host to which the mail should instead be forwarded. One such host might be a central mail hub machine.

The V option specifies the name of a mail exchanger machine (MX record) of last resort. It is given an artificially low priority (high preference number) so that *sendmail* tries to connect to it only if all other connection attempts for the target host have failed.

Note that this fallback MX host is used only for connection failures. It is not used if the name server lookup failed.

The form of the V option looks like this:

```
OVhost              ← configuration file
-oVhost             ← command line
```

Here, *host* is of type string and is the fully-qualified domain name of the fallback host. If *host* or the entire option is missing, no fallback MX record is used.

The V option is not safe. If specified from the command line, it may cause *sendmail* to relinquish its *root* privilege.

Ow

Use A record if no best MX record (V8 only)

RFC974 says that when mail is being sent from a host that is an MX record for the receiving host, all MX records of a preference equal to or greater than the sending host must be discarded. In some circumstances, this can leave no usable MX records. In this absence, V8 *sendmail* bases its action on the setting of its w option.

If option w is false, *sendmail* bounces the mail message. If true, *sendmail* looks to see if the receiving host has an A record. If it does, *sendmail* tries to deliver the mail message directly to that host. If the host doesn't have an A record, *sendmail* bounces the message. See Chapter 17, *DNS and sendmail*, for a discussion of why one setting may be preferable over the other.

The w option is safe. If specified from the command line, *sendmail* will not relinquish its *root* privilege.

Ox

On high load, queue only

The x option specifies the load above which *sendmail* queues messages rather than delivering them. The x and q options interact to determine this cutoff; they are both covered under option q on page 533.

The forms of the x option are:

```
Oxload     ← configuration file
-oxload    ← command line
```

The optional argument *load*, of type numeric, defaults to zero if it is missing. If the entire x option is missing, the default value given to *load* is eight. On newer, faster machines, a higher setting may be more appropriate.

The **x** option is not safe. If specified from the command line, it may cause *sendmail* to relinquish its *root* privilege.

OX
Refuse SMTP connect on high load

When the load average on a machine (the average number of jobs in the run queue over the last minute) becomes too high, *sendmail* can compensate by refusing to accept SMTP connections. This is more serious than the queueing caused by the **x** option, and so the load specified for **X** should be higher than that specified for **x**.

The forms of the **X** option are:

```
OXload      ← configuration file
-oXload     ← command line
```

The argument *load* is of type numeric. If *load* is missing, the value becomes zero, causing SMTP connections to be refused. If the entire **X** option is missing, the value for the load cutoff defaults to 12.

Note that under V8 a load greater than the value of the **X** option causes *sendmail* to revert to queue-only mode until the load drops. Under queue-only mode, *sendmail* queues all messages, rather than delivering them.

The **X** option is not safe. If specified from the command line, it may cause *sendmail* to relinquish its *root* privilege.

Oy
Penalize large recipient lists

Not all messages need to be treated equally. When sendmail processes the messages in its queue, it sorts them by priority. The priority given to a message is calculated once, when it is first created, and adjusted (incremented or decremented) each time it is processed in the queue. Mail with the *lowest* priority number is handled first. The formula for the initial calculation is:

```
priority = nbytes - (class * z) + (recipients * y)
```

The items in this calculation are:

priority
> Priority of the message when it was first created.

nbytes
> Number of bytes in the total message, including the header and body of the message.

class Value given to a message by the Precedence: line in the header of the message. The string following the Precedence: is usually either first-class, special-delivery, junk, or bulk. That string is converted to a numeric value determined by the P command in the *sendmail.cf* file.

z Value given the z option and a weighting factor to adjust the relative importance of the class.

recipients
> Number of recipients to whom the message is addressed. This number is counted *after* all alias expansion.

y Value given this y option, and weighting factor to adjust the relative importance of the number of recipients.

The forms of the y option are:

```
Oyfactor      ← configuration file
-oyfactor     ← command line
```

The argument **factor** is of type numeric. If that argument is missing, the default value is zero. If the entire y option is missing, the default value is 1000 (30000 for V8).

The y option is not safe. If specified from the command line, it may cause *sendmail* to relinquish its *root* privilege.

OY

Process queue files individually (not SunOS)

On machines with a small amount of memory (like 3B1s and old Sun 3s) it is best to limit the size of running processes. One way to do this is to have the *sendmail* program *fork*(2) a copy of itself to handle each individual queued message. The Y option can be used to allow those *fork*(2)'s.

The forms of the Y option are:

```
OYbool      ← configuration file
-oYbool     ← command line
```

The argument **bool** is of type boolean. If **bool** is missing, the default is true (fork). If the entire Y option is missing, the default is false (don't fork).

If option Y is set (true), there is a *fork*(2) to start processing of the queue, then another *fork*(2) to process each message in the queue. If option Y is not set (false), only the initial *fork*(2) takes place, greatly improving the efficiency of a queue run. For example, a single process (as with Y false) retains information about down hosts, and so does not waste time trying to connect again for subsequent mail to the same host during the current queue run. For all modern machines, the Y option should be false.

The Y option is not safe. If specified from the command line, it may cause *sendmail* to relinquish its *root* privilege.

OY

Name of NIS aliases map (SunOS only)

At large sites, it can be advantageous to have a single *aliases*(5) file that is shared by many workstations. Under Sun's Network Information Services (NIS) you can create an NIS database of such *aliases* file information. The Y option specifies the name of that database, usually *mail.aliases*.

The forms of the SunOS version of the Y option are:

```
OYXmap      ← configuration file
-oYXImap    ← command line
```

The argument *map* is of type string. If *map* is missing, the default NIS database is *mail.aliases*. If the entire option is missing, the value is the C language value NULL. The *X* is a single-character name that is used in rule sets to reference the NIS database.

Information in the *map* is accessed from rule sets with expressions like this:

```
${X name $: default $}
```

This causes the token *name* to be looked up in the NIS database whose name is defined by the Y option, and referenced by the macro name X. If *name* is found in that database, the result of the lookup is used as a replacement for the entire expression. If it is not found, then `default` becomes the value.

This Y option is similar to the IDA K option. It can be used to set up and use other NIS databases, but unlike the K option, it cannot be used to access *dbm*(3) disk-based databases. NIS databases are more fully covered in Chapter 29, *Database Macros*.

The SunOS Y option is wrongly safe. Even if it is specified from the command line, *sendmail* retains its *root* privilege.

Oz

Multiplier for priority increments

The z option specifies a multiplying weight for a message's precedence when determining a message's priority. Option z interacts with option y, and both options are described under option y on page 547.

The forms of the y option are:

```
Ozfactor      ← configuration file
-ozfactor     ← command line
```

The argument *factor* is of type numeric. If that argument is missing, the default value is zero. If the entire z option is missing, the default value is 1000 (1800 under V8).

The z option is not safe. If specified from the command line, it may cause *sendmail* to relinquish its *root* privilege.

OZ

Increment priority per job processed

When sendmail processes the messages in its queue, it sorts them by priority and handles those with the *lowest* (least positive) priority first.

The priority of a message is calculated once, using the y and z options, when the message is first created, and it is adjusted, using the Z option, each time the message is processed in the queue.

Each time a message from the queue fails to be delivered and needs to be requeued, its priority is adjusted. That adjustment is made by adding the value of the Z option.

The forms of the Z option are:

```
OZinc      ← configuration file
-oZinc     ← command line
```

The argument *inc* is of type numeric. If *inc* is missing, the default value is zero. If the entire Z option is missing, the value for *inc* defaults to 9000 (90000 for V8). The increment is performed by adding the value of *inc* to the previously-stored message priority each time that message is queued.

The Z option is not safe. If specified from the command line, it may cause *sendmail* to relinquish its *root* privilege.

O/

Split rewriting header/envelope (IDA only)

When handling UUCP mail, it is often advantageous to leave header addresses in the domain form (you@here.us.edu), but rewrite the envelope addresses to satisfy the UUCP protocols (here!you). The IDA / option allows you to process envelope addresses separately from header addresses.

The forms of the IDA / option are:

```
O/     ← configuration file
-o/    ← command line
```

The / option ignores any arguments. If the entire / option is missing, the default is false.

Ordinarily, sender addresses are processed by rule set 1 and recipient addresses are processed by rule set 2. No distinction is made between header and envelope addresses. When the IDA / option is declared, envelope addresses are processed in the usual way: rule set 1 for the sender and rule set 2 for the recipient. However the header addresses are processed by different rules; rule set 5 for header sender addresses and rule set 6 for header recipient addresses (see Chapter 24, *Rule Sets*). Note that this is similar to the IDA and V8 use of a / in the delivery agent S= and R= equates (see Chapter 26, *Delivery Agents*).

The IDA / option is not safe. If specified from the command line, it may cause *sendmail* to relinquish its *root* privilege.

31

Headers

All mail messages are composed of two distinct parts: the header (containing information such as who the message is from) and the body (the actual text of the message). The two parts are separated from each other by a single blank line (although there are exceptions which we will cover). The header part used by *sendmail* is mainly defined by RFC822 with some minor clarification contained in RFC1123. These two documents detail the required syntax and contents of most header lines in mail messages. Many other RFCs define other headers, but in this chapter we will discuss header lines as they relate specifically to *sendmail*.

When *sendmail* receives a mail message, it gathers all the header lines from that message and saves them internally. Then, during queueing and delivery, it recreates them and and augments them with any new ones that may be required either by the configuration file or by *sendmail*'s internal logic.

The H Configuration Command

The H header configuration file command tells *sendmail* which headers are required for inclusion in the header portion of mail messages. Some headers, like Date:, are added only if one is not already present. Others, like Received:, are added even if one or more are already present.

The form for the header command is:

```
H?flags?name:field
```

The H must begin the line. The optional ?*flags*? (the question marks are literal), if present, must immediately follow the H with no intervening space. We will discuss header ?*flags*? after the *name* and *field* are explained.

The *name* is the name of the header, like From. The *name* must immediately follow the ?*flags*?, if present, or the H if there are no flags.

A colon then follows, which may be surrounded by optional space characters. The *field* is last, and constitutes everything from the first non-space character following the colon to the end of the line.

```
Hname   :   field
            ↑
            from here to end of line is the field
```

The colon must be present. If it is absent, *sendmail* prints the following error message and ignores that H command:

```
chompheader: syntax error, line "offending H command here"
```

The "*offending H command here*" is the full text of the H command in the configuration file that caused the error.

As with all configuration commands, a line that begins with a space or a tab is joined to the line above. In this way, header commands can be split over one or more lines:

```
HReceived: $?sfrom $s $.by $j ($v/$V)
    id $i; $b
  ↑
  tab
```

When these two lines are read from the configuration file by *sendmail*, they are internally joined to form the single line:

```
HReceived: $?sfrom $s $.by $j ($v/$V) \n       id $i; $b
                                      ↑
                                     tab
```

The \n above illustrates that, when lines are joined, the newline and tab character are retained. This results in the header looking the same as it did in the configuration file (sans the H) when it is later emitted by *sendmail*.

Header Names

The *name* portion of the H configuration command may only be one of the names shown below. Other names do not produce an error, but may confuse other programs that need to process those illegal names. Those marked with an asterisk are defined by RFC822.

apparently-to	full-name	reply-to*	return-receipt-to
bcc*	in-reply-to*	resent-bcc*	sender*
cc*	keywords*	resent-cc*	subject*
comments*	mail-from	resent-date*	text*
content-length	message*	resent-from*	to*
content-type	message-id*	resent-message-id*	via
date*	posted-date	resent-reply-to*	x400-received
encrypted*	precedence	resent-sender*	
errors-to	received*	resent-to*	
from*	references*	return-path*	

These are discussed individually in the reference at the end of this chapter.

The RFC822 standard allows a special form to be used for creating custom header names. All mail programs, including *sendmail*, are required to accept and pass through as-is any header name that begins with the special characters x-. The following header definition, for example, can be used to introduce information that your site is running an experimental version of *sendmail*:

```
HX-Beware: This message used an experimental version of sendmail
```

The *name* part of header definitions is case-insensitive. That is, X-Beware, x-beware, and X-BEWARE are all the same. Internally, *sendmail* converts all header names to lowercase, then "capitalizes" them when the message is delivered.*

---

*V8 *sendmail* leaves the capitalization of headers alone. It passes them through without case conversion of any kind. Previous assumptions about capitalization are no longer valid in light of new headers generated and expected by programs.

The capitalization used is similar to that of proper names, where the first letter of each word is capitalized. For example:

REPLY-TO *becomes* →reply-to *then* → Reply-To

The *name* part of header definitions may contain only printable characters. It may not contain control characters, space characters (like space and tab), or the colon character.

Note that the *sendmail* program does *not* detect control or space characters in the *name*. If an illegal *name* like the following is declared in the configuration file, it is silently accepted and propagated.*

HFull Name: $x

Header Field Contents

The *field* of the H configuration command may contain any ASCII characters, including white space and newlines that result from joining. For most headers, however, those characters must obey the following rules for grouping:†

Atom   In the header *field*, space characters separate one item
                from another. Each space-delimited item is further subdi-
                vided by the specials (see below), into atoms. That is:

                    smtp   ← *an atom*
                    foo@host   ← *atom special atom*
                    Babe Ruth   ← *atom atom*

                An atom is the smallest unit in a header and may not contain
                any control characters. When the *field* is an address, an
                atom is the same thing as a token (see Chapter 25, *Rules*).

Specials   The special characters are those used to separate one com-
                ponent of an address from another. They are internally
                defined as:

                    ( ) < > @ , ; : \ " . [ ]

                A special character can be made nonspecial by preceding it
                with a backslash character, for example:

---

*This has been fixed in V8 *sendmail*.
†This discussion is adapted from RFC822.

```
foo;fum        ← atom special atom
foo\;fum       ← one atom
```

The space and tab characters are also used to separate atoms and can be thought of as specials.

Quoted text   Quotation marks can be used to force multiple items to be treated as a single atom. For example:

```
Babe Ruth      ← atom atom
"Babe Ruth"    ← a single atom
```

Quoted text may contain any characters except the quotation mark (") and the backslash character (\).

Any text   Some headers, like Subject:, impose no rules on the text in the header *field*. For such headers, atoms, specials, and quotes have no significance, and the entire field is taken as arbitrary text.

The detailed requirements of each header name are covered at the end of this chapter.

Macros in the Header Field

Macros may appear in any position in the *field* of a header definition line. Such macros are not expanded (their values tested or used) until mail is queued or delivered. For the meaning of each macro name, and a description of when each is given a value, see Chapter 27, *Defined Macros*.

Only two macro prefixes may be used in the *field* of header definitions:

$ The $ prefix tells *sendmail* to replace the macro's name with its value at that place in the *field* definition.

$?   The $? prefix tells *sendmail* to perform conditional replacement of a macro's value.

For example, the following header definition uses the $ prefix to insert the value of the macro x into the header field:

```
HFull-Name: $x
```

The macro $x contains as its value the full name of the sender.

When the possibility exists that a macro will not have a value at the time the header line is processed, the $? conditional prefix may be used:

```
HReceived: $?sfrom $s $.by $j ($v/$V)
```

Here, the $? prefix and $. operator cause the text:

```
from $s
```

to be inserted into the header field *only* if the macro s has a value. The macro $s may contain as its value the name of the sending site.

Escape Character in the Header Field

Recall that the backslash escape character (\) is used to deprive the special characters of their special meaning. In the field of header definitions the escape character may be used only inside quoted strings (see next item), domain literals (addresses enclosed in square bracket pairs), or in comments (see below). Specifically, this means that the escape character may *not* be used within atoms. Thus, the following is not legal:

```
Full\ Name@domain       ← not legal
```

Instead, the atom to the left of the @ must be isolated with quotation marks:

```
"Full Name"@domain      ← legal
```

Quoted Strings in the Header Field

Recall that quotation marks (") force arbitrary text to be viewed as a single atom. Arbitrary text is everything (including joined lines) that begins with the first quotation mark and ends with the final quotation mark. The following example illustrates two quoted strings:

```
"Full Name"
"One long string carried over
        two lines by indenting the second"
   ↑
   white space
```

The quotation mark character may appear inside a quoted string only if it is escaped using a backslash.*

```
"George Herman \"Babe\" Ruth"
```

---

*Note that the backslash itself may not appear within full quotation marks.

Internally, *sendmail* does not check for balanced quotation marks. If it finds the first, but not the second, it takes everything up to the end of the line as the quoted string.

When quotation marks are used in an H configuration command, they must be balanced. Although *sendmail* remains silent, unbalanced quotation marks can cause serious problems when they are propagated to other programs.

Comments in the Header Field

Comments consist of text inside a header `field` that is intended to give humans additional information. Comments are saved internally by *sendmail* when processing headers, then restored, but otherwise not used. A comment begins with a left parenthesis and ends with a right parenthesis. Comments may nest. The following lines illustrate a non-nested comment and a comment nested inside another:

```
(this is a comment)
(text(this is a comment nested inside another)text)
```

Comments may be split over multiple lines by indenting:

```
(this is a comment
      split into two lines)
   ↑
   white space
```

A comment (even if nested) separates one atom from another just like a space or a tab does. Thus, the following produces two atoms rather than one:

```
Bill(postmaster)Johnson
```

However, comments inside quoted strings are not special, so the following produces a single atom:

```
"Bill(postmaster)Johnson"
```

Parentheses may exist inside of comments only if they are escaped with a backslash:

```
<root@host.domain> (The happy administrator ;-\))
                                              ↑
                                            note
```

Balancing special characters

Many of the special characters used in the header *field* and in addresses need to appear in balanced pairs. Table 31-1 shows these characters and the characters needed to balance them. The *sendmail* program does not attempt to balance unbalanced characters.* Failure to maintain balance can lead to failed mail. Note that only parentheses may be nested. None of the other balanced pairs may nest.

Table 31-1: Balancing Characters

Begin	End
"	"
(	)
[	]
<	>

You have already seen the quoted string and comments. The angle brackets (< and >) are used to specify a machine-readable address, like <gw@wash.dc.gov>. The square brackets ([and]) are used to specify a direct internet address (one that bypasses normal DNS name lookups) like [123.45.67.89].

The *sendmail* program gives warnings about unbalanced characters only when it is attempting to extract an address from a header definition, from the header line of a mail message, or from the envelope. When it finds an unbalanced condition, it prints one of the following error messages and bounces that address:

```
Unbalanced ')'
Unbalanced '>'
Unbalanced '('
Unbalanced '<'
Unbalanced '"'
```

---

*V8 *sendmail* tries to balance these characters as rationally as possible.

?flags? in Header Definitions

The *name* part of a header configuration command can be prefixed with a list of flags. This list, if present, must be surrounded by ? characters:

```
H?flags?name:field
```

The ? characters must immediately follow the H and immediately precede the *name* with no intervening spaces. If a space precedes the first ?, that ? is misinterpreted as part of the header *name*, rather than as the start of a list of flags.

If the first ? is present, but the second is absent, *sendmail* prints the following error message and skips that H configuration command:

```
chompheader: syntax error, line "offending H line here"
```

The flags listed between the ? characters correspond to flags listed with delivery agent F= equates. When processing a mail message for forwarding or delivery, *sendmail* adds a header line if a flag is common to both the H definition list of flags and the delivery agent's list of flags. For example:

```
H?P?Return-Path: <$g>
```

The above H definition begins with a P flag. This tells *sendmail* to add this header line to the mail message only if a selected delivery agent also contains that flag. Since the `Return-Path:` header should be added only during final delivery, the P flag appears only in the `prog` and `local` delivery agent definitions:

```
Mprog,  P=/bin/sh,   F=lsDFMeuP,  S=10, R=20, A=sh -c $u
Mlocal, P=/bin/mail, F=rlsDFMmnP, S=10, R=20, A=mail -d $u
                                       ↑
                                     note
```

There is no check made to ensure that the H flags correspond to existing delivery agent flags. Beware that if a corresponding F= flag does not exist in some delivery agent definition, a header may never be added to any mail message.

Care should be used to avoid selecting flags that have other meanings for delivery agents. Chapter 26, *Delivery Agents*, lists all the delivery agent flags that have predefined meanings, including those traditionally used with header definitions.

Headers by Category

The *sendmail* program contains an internal list of header *names* that are organized conceptually into categories. The names and categories are defined in *conf.c* (see Chapter 16, *Compile and Install sendmail*). Each category is defined by one or more H_ flags in that file, the names of which are listed under the **Flags** column of all the tables that follow.

Recommended Headers

Every *sendmail.cf* file should have a minimal complement of header definitions. Below we present a recommendation. Don't use this recommendation as-is. The details are not generic to all versions of *sendmail*, nor are they appropriate for all sites.

```
H?P?Return-Path: <$g>
HReceived: $?sfrom $s $.by $j ($v/$V) id $i; $b      ← mandatory
H?D?Date: $a                                          ← mandatory
H?F?From: $q                                          ← mandatory
H?x?Full-Name: $x
HSubject:
H?M?Message-Id: <$t.$i@$j>                            ← mandatory
H?D?Resent-Date: $a                                   ← mandatory
H?F?Resent-From: $q                                   ← mandatory
H?M?Resent-Message-Id: <$t.$i@$j>                     ← mandatory
```

Each of these is described individually at the end of this chapter. Except for `Received:`, none is added to any mail message that already has that particular header present.

The `Return-Path:` is added only if not already present, and if the delivery agent for the recipient has the `F=P` flag present. Similarly, the `Date:` relies on `F=D`, the `From:` relies on `F=F`, the `Full-Name:` relies on `F=x`, and the `Message=Id:` relies on `F=M`.

Of those shown, only the seven indicated are truly mandatory, and must be declared in *every* configuration file. The others are highly recommended.

Sender Headers

Certain header *names* are assumed by *sendmail* to contain information about the various possible senders of a mail message. They are listed in Table 31-2, in descending order of significance. Addresses with the H_FROM flag are rewritten as sender addresses. The H_ flags are covered in Chapter 16, *Compile and Install sendmail*.

Table 31-2: Sender Headers (Most to Least Significant)

Header	Flags	Defined By
`Resent-Sender:`	H_FROM, H_RESENT	RFC822
`Resent-From:`	H_FROM, H_RESENT	RFC822
`Resent-Reply-To:`	H_FROM, H_RESENT	RFC822
`Sender:`	H_FROM	RFC822
`From:`	H_FROM	RFC822
`Apparently-From:`	n/a	Smail 3.0
`Reply-To:`	H_FROM	RFC822
`Full-Name:`	H_ACHECK	All sendmails
`Return-Receipt-To:`	H_FROM	All sendmails
`Errors-To:`	H_FROM	BSD and IDA
`Errors-To:`	H_FROM, H_ERRSTO	SunOS and V8 only

When returning bounced mail, *sendmail* always uses the envelope sender's address. If the special header `Errors-To:` appears in the message, a copy of the bounced mail is also sent to the address in that header. This is hardcoded into all but SunOS and V8 *sendmail*, which use the H_ERRSTO header flag instead. (V8 also requires the 1 (use errors-to) option.)

Recipient Headers

Recipient headers are those from which one or more recipients can be parsed. Addresses in headers with the H_RCPT flag are rewritten as recipient addresses. When invoked with the -t command-line switch, *sendmail* gathers a list of recipients from all the headers marked with an H_RCPT flag, and delivers a copy of the message to each.

The list of recipient headers used by *sendmail* is shown in Table 31-3.

Table 31-3: Recipient Headers

Header	Flags	Defined By
`To:`	H_RCPT	RFC822
`Resent-To:`	H_RCPT, H_RESENT	RFC822
`Cc`	H_RCPT:	RFC822
`Resent-Cc:`	H_RCPT, H_RESENT	RFC822
`Bcc:`	H_RCPT, H_ACHECK	RFC822

Table 31.3: Recipient Headers (continued)

Header	Flags	Defined By
`Resent-Bcc:`	H_RCPT, H_ACHECK, H_RESENT	RFC822
`Apparently-To:`	H_RCPT	IDA, V8, and SunOS

Identification and Control Headers

Some headers serve to uniquely identify a mail message. Others affect the way *sendmail* processes a mail message. The complete list of all such identification and control headers is shown in Table 31-4.

Table 31-4: Identification and Control Headers

Header	Flags	Defined By
`Message-Id:`	n/a	RFC822
`Resent-message-Id:`	H_RESENT	RFC822
`Message:`	H_EOH	All sendmails
`Text:`	H_EOH	All sendmails
`Precedence:`	n/a	All sendmails
`Posted-Date:`	n/a	All sendmails

Note that the `Precedence:` and `Posted-Date:` headers are hardcoded into *sendmail*, rather than being declared in *conf.c*.

Date and Trace Headers

Date headers are used to document the date and time that the mail message was sent or forwarded. Trace headers (those with an H_TRACE header flag) are used to determine the hop count of a mail message, and to document the message's travel from machine to machine.

Table 31-5: Date and Trace Headers

Header	Flags	Defined By
Date:	n/a	RFC822
Resent-Date:	H_RESENT	RFC822
Received:	H_TRACE, H_FORCE	RFC822
Via:	H_TRACE, H_FORCE	All sendmails
Mail-From:	H_TRACE, H_FORCE	All sendmails
X400-Received:	H_TRACE	IDA and V8 only

Other RFC822 Headers

Other headers that you will see in mail messages are defined by the RFC822 standard, but are not otherwise internally defined by *sendmail*. A few of them, like Return-Path: and Subject:, should be declared in the configuration file. The others are usually inserted by MUAs.

Table 31-6: Other RFC822 Headers

Header	Flags	Defined By
Return-Path:	n/a	RFC822
In-Reply-To:	n/a	RFC822
References:	n/a	RFC822
Keywords:	n/a	RFC822
Subject:	n/a	RFC822
Comments:	n/a	RFC822
Encrypted:	n/a	RFC822
X-*user-defined*:	n/a	RFC822

Forwarding with Resent- Headers

Some mail reading programs (MUAs) allow users to forward messages to other users. For example, the *mush*(1) MUA forwards the current message to the user named fred with the following command:

```
message 1 of 3> m -f fred
```

Messages can also be forwarded with *dist*(1) from *mh*(1) and from within other MUAs.

When messages are forwarded, header lines that describe the forwarding user must begin with the `Resent-` prefix. When `fred` receives this message, he sees two similar header lines:

```
From: original-sender
Resent-From: forwarding-sender
```

When both the original `From:` and the forwarded `Resent-From:` appear in the same header, the `Resent-` form is always considered the most recent.

The *sendmail* program examines only a few header names to see if a mail message has been forwarded. Those that it knows are listed in Table 31-7.

Table 31-7: Known Resent- Headers

Resent—Form of	Header
`Resent-Bcc:`	`Bcc:`
`Resent-Cc:`	`Cc:`
`Resent-Date:`	`Date:`
`Resent-From:`	`From:`
`Resent-Message-Id:`	`Message-Id:`
`Resent-Reply-To:`	`Reply-To:`
`Resent-Sender:`	`Sender:`
`Resent-To:`	`To:`

If *sendmail* finds any of its known `Resent-` header names in a mail message, it marks that message as one that is being forwarded, preserves all `Resent-` headers, and creates any needed ones.

Then, whether the message is forwarded or not, *sendmail* compares the sender envelope address to the address in the `From:` header (or `Resent-From:`, if present). If they are the same, *sendmail* deletes the `From:` (or `Resent-From:`). The purpose of this deletion is to add the sender's full name (the $x macro) to the address. If the envelope and sender addresses are the same, it is safe to delete and regenerate those header lines. If the message is being forwarded, *sendmail* recreates the `Resent-From:` header; otherwise, it recreates the `From:` header.

This recreation is useful because some old versions of *mh*(1) added a `From:` header without the full name ($x). It is also useful in mail client/server arrangements where all mail is sent to the server. Because that mail is sent with the TCP delivery agent, no $x full name is added. On the server, the `From:` is discarded and there is a second chance to add the $x. This can happen, however, only if the address in the envelope and the address in the `From:` are identical. Since the address in the envelope is surrounded with angle brackets, so must be the address in the `From:` header. One way to ensure that they are the same is by defining the `From:` header with $g in angle brackets, as `<$g>` in the client's configuration file.

Precedence: Configuration and Header

The priority of a mail message determines its ability to be sent despite a high machine load, and its position in the queue when the queue is processed. Each mail message has two forms of priority: its *class* and its *priority*. The initial class of a mail message is defined by the optional presence of a `Precedence:` header line inside the message with a symbol corresponding to a value defined by this P command.

For example, if your *sendmail.cf* file contained this line:

```
Pspecial-delivery=100
```

and your mail message header contained this line:

```
Precedence: special-delivery
```

then your mail message would begin its life with a class of 100. We'll cover how this is done soon.

After the message's initial class value is set, that value is never changed. As soon as the class is determined, the initial priority value is calculated. This priority is the value that is used to determine if a message will be sent despite a high machine load (defined by the X and x options), and to determine its order in queue processing. The formula for the initial calculation is the following:

```
priority = nbytes - (class * z) + (recipients * y)
```

Where `nbytes` is the total size in bytes of the message, `recipients` is the number of recipients specified in the `To:`, `Cc:`, and `Bcc:` header lines (after alias expansion), and z and y are the values of those *sendmail.cf* options.

Syntax

The P *sendmail.cf* command must begin a line. This command is composed of four parts:

```
Pstring=value
```

The *string* is text, like `special-delivery`. Everything between the P and the = (*including* any white space) is taken as-is for *string*. The *value* is evaluated as a signed integer, and may be decimal, octal (with a leading 0), or hexadecimal (with a leading 0x).

Although you may define any *string* you choose, only four have any universal meaning. Those four usually appear in *sendmail.cf* files like this:

```
Pspecial-delivery=100
Pfirst-class=0
Pjunk=-100
Pbulk=-200
```

You may, of course, define your own priority strings for internal mail, but they will be ignored (evaluate to 0) by all outside *sendmail* programs.

The classes `junk` and `bulk` are also recognized by many other programs. Newer versions of the *vacation*(1) program, for example, silently skip replying to messages which have a `Precedence:` header line of `junk` or `bulk`.

As a general rule, `special-delivery` is rarely used. Most mail has a class of `first-class`. Mailing lists and other bulk mailings should always have a class of `bulk`.

Because your local *sendmail.cf* file is where values are given to these classnames, you are free to modify those values locally. The values affect only the delivery at your site. If, for example, yours is a specialty mailing-list machine, you might wish to make `bulk` more positive than `first-class`. That way, mailing-list messages will tend to be processed first from the queue.

Old versions of *sendmail* didn't return errors on messages with a negative priority. V8 *sendmail* does, but omits the message body. V8 also defines:

```
Plist=-50
```

You can use `list` with the `Precedence:` header if you want to send mail to a mailing list and get errors returned.

The `Precedence:` header should rarely be declared in the configuration file. Instead, it is added to messages by MUAs and by mailing-list software. If it is declared in the configuration file, it should be prefixed with an appropriate ?*flag*? so that it is inserted only for an appropriate delivery agent.

Pitfalls

- Not all MTAs are as RFC822-compliant as *sendmail*. Occasionally headers appear that were legal under the defunct RFC733. The `In-Reply-To:` header, for example, used to be a comma-separated list of addresses under RFC733 and may cause problems. Note also that RFC733 date and time syntax differs from that of RFC822 and RFC1123.

- If the *name* part of a header definition is missing (the H is followed by a colon), a header whose name is the character value zero is silently accepted and wrongly propagated. This has been fixed in V8.

- Long header lines in messages (such as `To:` with many recipients listed) can cause the internal buffer used by *sendmail* to overflow. Currently, the size of that buffer is defined in *conf.h* as MAXLINE and is 1024 characters. The IDA version, however, is defined as 2048 characters. V8 *sendmail* dynamically allocates memory and so can handle headers of any size.

- When generating an `Apparently-To` header, *sendmail* checks for the absence of only the `To:`, `Cc:`, `Bcc:`, and `Apparently-To:` headers. The H_RCPT flag in *conf.c* is ignored.

- The *sendmail* program's handling of unbalanced special characters can lead to an explosion of error mail. Instead of simply bouncing the offending mail message, it both returns an error message and forwards the message to the recipient. If the message is being exploded through a series of mailing lists, the error messages continue to increase, possibly drowning the original site with mail.

- Priority values are stored in integer variables, so care should be exercised on two-byte integer machines to avoid having priorities wrap unexpectedly.

- Macros are not expanded in the P command. That is, expressions like $U do not have the desired effect. The literal text $U is wrongly listed as the name or the value.

Alphabetized Reference

Some header lines need to be declared in the configuration file using the H command. Others are created internally by *sendmail*. Still others are created by mail MUAs. These differences are described individually with each header-line *name*. The following discussion of header names is in alphabetical order.

Apparently-From:
The unknown sender

The *Smail 3.x* program (a UUCP-oriented replacement for *sendmail*) produces an Apparently-From: header when it is unable to find any of the official sender headers in a mail message. The address it provides to this nonstandard header is taken from the envelope of the message.

The *sendmail* program, on the other hand, places the envelope sender into a From: header in this situation. If there is no envelope sender, and if the sender was not specified in the command line, *sendmail* sets the sender to be postmaster.

The Apparently-From: header is mentioned here only because it may appear in messages received at sites that run *sendmail*. It shouldn't cause problems, because a good sender address still appears in the SMTP envelope.

The Apparently-From: header should never be declared in the configuration file, and should not be added to *conf.c.*

Apparently-To:
The unknown recipient

If the header of a mail message lacks recipient information (lacks all of the To:, Cc:, and Bcc: header lines), *sendmail* adds an Apparently-To: header line and puts the recipient's address from the envelope into the field of that line. This behavior is hardcoded into *sendmail.*

The Apparently-To header name is not defined in RFC822. It is added by *sendmail* because RFC822 *requires* at least one To: or Cc: header, and neither is present.

Note that Bcc: by itself can lead to problems. The *mh*(1) program, for example, can produce mail messages that list only the recipient in a Bcc: header. If there is a Bcc: header, *sendmail* does not add an Apparently-To: even though it discards the Bcc:. A problem arises when the mail message is forwarded to another machine. That next machine's *sendmail* sees no recipient headers (because the Bcc: was discarded) and so adds an Apparently-To: header. If there is only one recipient in the envelope, no privacy is violated. But if there are more, all are listed in the Apparently-To: header, violating the presumed privacy of the original Bcc: header.

One workaround for this problem is to ensure that all mail messages, including those produced by *mh*(1), always include a minimal To: line. If a message has a To: header line with only an RFC822 comment, then *sendmail* does not add an Apparently-To: header. The following, for example, although of questionable RFC822 validity, prevents the Bcc: problem:

```
To: (names withheld)
```

An Apparently-To: header should *never* be defined in the configuration file.

Bcc:
Blind carbon copy

A blind carbon copy is a copy of the mail message that is sent to one or more recipients without the knowledge of the primary recipients. Primary recipients are listed in the To: and Cc: lines. When there are multiple blind carbon copy recipients, knowledge of each other is also hidden.

When run with a -t command-line switch (to gather recipients from the headers), the *sendmail* program achieves this end by saving a list of all the blind carbon copy recipients, deleting the Bcc: header line, and then delivering to each blind carbon copy recipient. See Apparently-To: above.

The Bcc: header may be declared in the configuration file to force its inclusion in messages. If it is declared, it *must* include ?*flags*? as part of its definition. If ?*flags*? is omitted, the declaration is silently ignored.

The field for the Bcc: header must contain one or more properly formed addresses. Where there is more than one, each should be separated from the others by commas.

CC:
Carbon copy

The Cc: header is one of a few that specify the list of primary recipients. The *sendmail* program treats the Cc: header no differently than it treats the To: header. From the user's point of view, the Cc: header implies that there are recipients to whom an informational copy of the message was supplied.

The Cc: header should *never* be declared in the configuration file.

The field for the Cc: header must contain one or more properly formed addresses.

Comments:
Header commentary

The Comments: header is used to place explanatory text into the header portion of a mail message. The field portion of the Comments: header may contain arbitrary text.

One possible use for a Comments: header would be to notify recipients that one person is replying to mail for another:

```
Comments: Ben is in France for the next month or
          so gathering information for the meeting.
          I am handling his mail while he is away.
     ↑
     white space
```

The Comments: header should *rarely* be declared in the configuration file. If it is, it should be prefixed with appropriate ?*flags*?. For example:

```
H?B?Comments: Local delivery is experimentally being handled
          by a new program. Complaints to root.
```

This comment is included only in headers delivered via the local delivery agent, because that delivery agent is the only one to include the F=B flag as shown below:

```
Mlocal, P=/bin/mail, F=rlsDFMmnPB, S=10, R=20, A=mail -d $u
```

For all versions of *sendmail* except V8, if there is already a Comments: header in the message, this configuration-file declaration is ignored. For V8 *sendmail*, this declaration always causes the new Comment: header to be *added* to the mail message.

Content-Length:

The size of the body of the message

The `Content-Length:` header describes the approximate size of the body of a message. The size is always a decimal expression of the number of bytes occupied by the body.

```
Content-Length: 5678
```

It is used by some MUAs to find a message faster in a large file of many messages. It is always created or added by MUAs and never by MTAs. It should never be declared in the configuration file.

Content-Type:

The nature of the body of the message

The `Content-Type:` header describes the nature of the body of a mail message. In the absence of such a header, the body is presumed to be ASCII characters all with the high (most significant) bits turned off.

```
Content-Type: postscript
```

This header says that the body is in the PostScript typesetting language. The field of this header is described in RFC1049.

This header is usually created by the originating MUA. It should never be declared in the configuration file.

Date:

The origin date

The `Date:` header specifies the date and time that the mail message was originally sent. All mail messages must include this header line. Consequently, the `Date:` header must be declared in the configuration file like this:

```
H?D?Date: $a
```

The macro $a is mandatory in the field for this header. The value in $a is the current time in RFC822 format. (See Section 5.1 in RFC822 and Section 5.2.14 in RFC1123.) Only the $a macro should be used with the `Date:` header, because it is the only one that is guaranteed to contain the current date and time in RFC822 (and RFC1123) format.

The ?D? flag is always included with the `Date:` declaration in the configuration file. All the standard delivery agents always include a `F=D` flag. The ?D? allows custom delivery agents to be designed that do not need a `Date:` header.

Encrypted:
Message is transformed

The `Encrypted:` header is used to describe a translation that has been performed on the body of the mail message. Although encryption is implied, other forms of translation, like compression and *uuencode*(1), are perfectly legal.

The *sendmail* program ignores the `Encrypted:` header. This header is intended for use by MUAs. Unfortunately, most (if not all) UNIX MUAs also ignore this header. The form for the `Encrypted:` header is:

```
Encrypted: prog key
```

The field contains one mandatory item, the `prog`, and one optional item, the `key`. The `prog` is the name of the program that was used to transform the message body. The optional `key` is a decryption key.

When translating the message body into a different form, be aware that many versions of *sendmail* strip the eighth bit from all bytes of the body during transmission.

The `Encrypted:` header should never be declared in the configuration file.

Errors-To:
Error notification redirect

Ordinarily, errors are bounced to the envelope sender. The `Errors-To:` header specifies the address, or addresses, to which *sendmail* should send additional notification of delivery errors.

The `Errors-To:` header is intended for use by mailing lists, in order to prevent errors in a list from being rebroadcast to the list as a whole. For example, consider the mailing list *allusers*. Mail sent to this list should contain the following header lines:

```
To: allusers
From: allusers-submit
Errors-To: allusers-errors
```

The From: header allows reply mail to be submitted for distribution to the list. The Errors-To: header causes error notification to be sent to allusers-errors so that the maintainer can fix any errors in the list. The original sender also gets error notification, unless the mailing list software represents the maintainer in the envelope (see Chapter 21, *Mailing Lists and ˜/.forward*).

Under SunOS and V8 *sendmail*, the Errors-To: is flagged in *conf.c* with the H_ERRSTO header flag. This allows other headers to be declared in that file as error redirect headers. Under SunOS, the Errors-To: header is ignored if the error mode set by the e option is set to m.

Under V8 *sendmail*, the Errors-To: header is ignored unless the l option is true. It does this because the Errors-To: header violates RFC 1123. Errors-To: was needed only to take the place of the envelope sender in the days when most UNIX delivery agents couldn't differentiate between header and envelope.

The Errors-To: header should never be declared in the configuration file.

From:
The sender

The From: header lists the address of the sender. There are only four legal forms that the field of this header can take:

```
From: address
From: <address>
From: Full Name <address>
From: address (comment)
```

The From: must be declared in the configuration file, and its field is composed of the $q macro (which in turn is built from the $x and $g macros). For example:

```
Dq$g
Dq<$g>
Dq$?x$x $.<$g>
Dq$g $?x($x)$.
```

The $g macro contains the official return address of the sender. The $x macro contains the full name for the sender. The $x macro may be undefined for some addresses, so it should be wrapped in the $? and $. conditional operators.

The From: header is then declared with $q:

```
H?F?From: $q
```

The From: header must be prefixed by the ?F? flag because all the traditional delivery agents use the F=F flag to force inclusion of that header. Use of the ?F? flag allows new delivery agents to be written that don't require the From: header.

The resent- form of the From: header must also be declared in the configuration file:

```
H?F?Resent-From: $q
```

This ensures that every mail message has a sender, even if the mail message has been forwarded.

Note that *sendmail* does not add the From: header, nor its resent- form, if one already exists in the header portion of the mail message. A possible exception is the From: header. If the address of the envelope sender is identical to the address in the From: header, the From: header is discarded and a new one created.

Full-Name:
The sender's full name

The Full-Name: header is used to list the sender's full name if it is known. The field for this header may be arbitrary text, but is usually the value in the $x macro.

```
H?x?Full-Name: $x
H?x?Full-Name: (User names hidden for security)
```

The Full-Name: header should be prefixed with the ?x? flag so that selected delivery agents may require inclusion of that header. This header definition is usually meaningless, because all traditional delivery agents omit the F=x flag. It can be useful, however, for mailing through sites that strip or destroy From: headers.

The Full-Name: header may be specified in the configuration file. If this header is already in the mail message, *sendmail* does not replace it.

In-Reply-To:

Identify previous correspondence

The `In-Reply-To:` header is used to identify previous correspondence that the current message is in reply to. This header is generated by MUAs, not by *sendmail*. The field for this header is arbitrary text with one restriction. If that text includes the message identifier, that identifier must be enclosed in angle brackets (< and >) and must adhere to the format for all message identifiers (see `Message-Id:` below). Note that the message identifier *should* be included, but is not required.

A typical use of the `In-Reply-To:` header might look like the following:

```
In-Reply-To: Your message of Mon, Jul 12, 1992 10:52:23 PST
        The subject of which was: "Which came first?"
    ↑
    white space
```

The `In-Reply-To:` header should never be declared in the configuration file.

Keywords:

Index to contents

The `Keywords:` header is used to list significant words from the body of the mail message that aid in the indexing of its contents. This header is never added by *sendmail*. Although some user mail-reading programs can create this header, it is usually created by USENET news-posting programs.

The field for the `Keywords:` header is arbitrary text. This header should never be declared in the *sendmail* configuration file.

Mail-From:

Synonym for received: (obsolete)

The `Mail-From:` header is not defined by any of the RFCs and is rarely seen in message headers. The *sendmail* program defines it internally as a synonym for the `Received:` header. The `Mail-From:` header is obsolete.

Message-Id:

Unique identifier for message

The `Message-Id:` header is used to uniquely identify each mail message. This header must be declared in the configuration file. The field for this header must be an expression in the form of a legal address enclosed in angle brackets (< and >). The address must be composed of elements that create an identifier that is truly unique worldwide. The `Message-Id:` header is declared in the configuration file like this:

```
?M?Message-Id: <$t.$i@$j>
```

Here, the field is an address of the form *user@domain*, which is enclosed in angle brackets. The `$t` macro is an integer representation of the current time to the nearest second. The `$i` macro is the unique queue identifier used to identify this message locally. The `$j` is the fully-qualified domain name of the local host. The `Message-Id:` header as it might appear in an actual mail message would look like this:

```
Message-Id: <9207100411.AA14505@nic.cerf.net>
```

The `Message-Id:` header should be prefixed with a `?M?` flag so that it is inserted only into headers of messages whose delivery agents have the `F=M` flag set. The standard delivery agents include this flag.

The `resent-` form of the `Message-Id:` header must also be declared in the configuration file:

```
?M?Resent-Message-Id: <$t.$i@$j>
```

This ensures that every mail message has a message identifier even if the message is forwarded.

Note that *sendmail* does not add a `Message-Id:` header nor its `Resent-` form if it already exists in the header portion of a mail message. Nor is the `Resent-` form added unless *sendmail* determines that the message is a resent message.

Message:

Marks end of headers

The `Message:` header is used to mark an early end to a mail message's headers. When *sendmail* finds this header, it immediately stops gathering the message's header lines and treats the rest of the header as the start of the message body. This header is useful for including non-Internet headers in the header portion of a mail message. For example:

```
To: george@wash.dc.gov (George Washington)
Subject: Re: More text
Date: Tue, 04 Aug 92 14:14:56 -0400
Message-Id: <31842.AA01513@wash.dc.gov>
Received: by wash.dc.gov (4.1/1.12 $)
        id AA01513; Tue, 4 Aug 92 12:15:01 PDT
From: Ben Franklin <ben@philly.dc.gov>
Message:
ROUTED BY BITNET\/CO=US/ROUTE=INTERNET/
FORMAT OF MESSAGE /LANG=USENGLISH/FORM=PLAINTEXT/
```

Here, the last two header lines are non-Internet headers that may confuse some programs. But the `Message:` header that precedes them tells *sendmail* to treat them as message body, and problems are avoided.

The `Message:` header should never be declared in the configuration file.

MIME-Version:

Notify that error return contains MIME support (V8 only)

If the `j` option is set, V8 *sendmail* includes the following header in all returned (bounced) mail:

```
MIME-Version: 1.0
```

This is hardcoded into *sendmail.* See option `j` for further details about this header. MIME is documented in RFC1341, with additional details in RFC1344, RFC1426, RFC1428, and RFC1437.

The `MIME-Version:` header should never be declared in the configuration file.

Posted-Date:

Date submitted

The `Posted-Date:` header is used by some old USENET news software and some mailing list software to indicate the date and time that a mail message was posted (submitted for distribution). The `Date:` header, on the other hand, shows when the message was mailed. In actual practice, the two usually show the same date and time.

The `Posted-Date:` header is not a part of the RFC822 standard, so it should not be declared in the *sendmail* configuration file.

Precedence:

Set ordering in queue

The Precedence: header is used internally by *sendmail* to order the processing of messages in its queue. A full description of the possible field values for this header are given on page 568. The effect of those values on ordering the queue is described in Chapter 19, *The Queue.*

The Precedence: header should never be declared as an H line in the configuration file. However, P precedence lines should be declared in that file.

Received:

Trace routing of mail

The Received: header is used to record information about each and every site a mail message passes through on its way to ultimate delivery. This header is first inserted by the original sending site, then another is added by each site that the message passes through, including the site performing final delivery. Each new header is added to the end of the list of Received: headers, forming a chronological record (reading bottom up through the headers) of how the mail message was handled.

The contents of the Received: header's field is narrowly defined by RFC822. Its defined form looks like this:

```
Received: ["from" host] "by" host ["via" atom] ["with" atom]
      "id" string ["for" addr] ";" date
   ↑
   white space
```

The field is composed of six items which may be split over multiple lines by using white space to indent the second. Those items that are optional are enclosed in square brackets. Each item is composed of two parts, a word (shown in quotation marks) and a value. All, or only the few required items, need be present. When present they must be in the order shown below:

from	Full canonical name of the sending host (if available)
by	Full canonical name of the receiving host (required)
via	Physical network that was used to transmit the message, like INTERNET, JANET, or XNS (optional)
with	Protocol used to receive the message, like SMTP (optional)
id	Unique queue identifier assigned by the local host (required)

for   Initial, untranslated address of the recipient (seldom used)

;date   Date this message was received (required)

The `Received:` header must be declared in the configuration file. It is a mandatory header, so it should never be prefixed with `?`*flags*`?`. A typical declaration of this header would look like this:

```
HReceived: $?sfrom $s $.by $j ($v/$V) id $i ; $b
```

Here, four items are included in the field:

`$?from $s $.`

    If the macro `$s` contains a value, the word `from` and that value are inserted into the header. The `$s` macro contains the full canonical name of the sender's host.

`by $j ($v/$V)`

    The `$j` macro contains the full canonical name of the local host. The parentheses surround a comment that is formed from `$v`, the version of the *sendmail* program, and `$V`, traditionally the version of the configuration file.

`id $i`   The `$i` macro contains the identifier created by *sendmail* to uniquely identify this mail message at this host.

`; $b`   The `$b` macro contains the current date and time in RFC822 format.

The `Received:` declaration shown above is the one typically used by most sites. It may contain more items, but should never contain fewer.

References:
Reference to original message

The `References:` header is used by mail-reading programs to include a reference to the original message in replies. Although this header may legally contain arbitrary text as its field, it usually contains a copy of the original `Message-Id:` header field.

The `References:` header typically looks something like this:

```
References: <9205041920.AA27932@wash.dc.gov>
```

Notice that the message identifier is wrapped in angle brackets, which cause it to look like an address.

The `References:` header should never be declared in the configuration file.

Reply-To:
Alternative reply address

The `Reply-To:` header forces replies to messages to go to an address that is different than that of the original sender. This header is usually inserted by mailing-list software, where the `From:` is the address of the mailing list, and the `Reply-To:` is the address of the list's maintainer.

The field for the `Reply-To:` header must obey the same rules as those for the `From:` header's field. One example of the use of this header might look like this:

```
From: mailinglist@list.server.com
Reply-To: mailinglist-request@list.server.com
```

The `-request` suffix is used by many mailing lists to specify the list maintainer (see Chapter 20, *Aliases*).

The `Reply-To:` header should never be declared in the configuration file.

Return-Path:
Return address of sender

The `Return-Path:` header is intended to show the envelope address of the real sender as opposed to the sender used for replying (the `From:` and `Reply-To:` headers). When posting USENET news, for example, the `Return-Path:` shows "news" and the `From:` shows the address of the posting user. But in general, `Return-Path:` should never be used for replying to mail. It is solely intended to be used for notification of delivery errors.

There must be only one `Return-Path:` header in any mail message, and it should be placed there by the site performing final delivery. This header should be declared in the configuration file like this:

```
H?P?Return-Path: <$g>
```

The `?P?` flag ensures that only delivery agents which perform final delivery insert this header. Those delivery agents are usually `prog` and `local` which usually contain an `F=P` delivery agent flag.

The `$g` macro contains as its value the address of the sender relative to the recipient (see Chapter 27, *Defined Macros*).

Unfortunately, two circumstances can cause the `Return-Path:` header to contain incorrect information. First, the message may arrive at your site with that header already there. If this happens, there is usually no way to get rid of it, because most versions of *sendmail* lack a *conf.c* H_ flag that means to replace an existing header. However, with V8 *sendmail*, defining H_ACHECK in *conf.c* causes a header to be replaced even if one is already in the message.

The second problem stems from the fact that final delivery may not really be final. The `local` delivery agent program may be something like *procmail*(8), which allows mail to appear to be locally delivered, while also allowing users to run shell scripts that may forward their mail to another site.

To minimize these problems, always declare the `Return-Path:` header with the proper `?flags?` in the configuration file. Doing this ensures that it will be inserted when legal and that the address your site places in it is usually correct.

Return-Receipt-To:

Verify delivery

The `Return-Receipt-To:` header causes *sendmail* to send a mail message back to the specified recipient confirming final delivery. If *sendmail* finds this header when it is processing mail for delivery, and if the selected delivery agent has the F=l flag set, *sendmail* creates a bounced mail message. The recipient is set to the person specified in the `Return-Receipt-To:` header, and the following subject header line is included:

```
Subject: Returned Mail: Return Receipt
```

The message appears to originate from the user defined by the $n macro, and contains a copy of the original header as its body.

The `Return-Receipt-To:` header should never be declared in the configuration file, and, in fact, should rarely be used at all. It is not intended as a routine delivery-verification mechanism, but rather is intended for occasional use in debugging delivery problems. It is especially dangerous when used in outgoing mailing-list mail, because it can cause an avalanche of returned mail, and can possibly bring a host to its knees.

Sender:

The real sender

The Sender: header is like the From: header. But whereas the From: header shows the address of one sender, the Sender: header shows the address of the *real* sender. For example, an assistant can mail a letter for the boss using the boss's account. The boss's address is in the From: header, the assistant's address is in the Sender: header. The syntax for the two is identical.

Newer MUAs allow the user to create a custom Sender: header. The Sender: header should never be declared in the configuration file.

Subject:

Topic of the message

The Subject: header can be included in mail messages to give the topic of the message. Most user mail-reading programs display the arbitrary text that forms the field of this header when listing received messages. Although such text can legally extend over multiple indented lines, most mail-reading programs recognize only the first such line:

```
Subject: About yesterday's meeting, I had some second
         thoughts about why the shape of the bonnet should
         remain so sharply curved at the ends.
    ↑
    white space
```

This would be displayed by the *mailx*(1) program in truncated form as:

```
14    gw@wash.dc.gov Fri Aug  7 12:57  22/770 "About yesterday's meeting"
```

The Subject: header is not used by *sendmail,* but it is often included in the configuration file to ensure that every mail message has at least an empty Subject: line:

```
HSubject:
```

Text:

A synonym for message:

The Text: header is the same as the Message: header. Both cause all lines that follow in the header portion of a mail message to be treated as message body.

The Text: header should never be declared in the configuration file.

To:
The primary recipients

The `To:` header lists one or more of the recipients of the mail message. Other headers, like `Cc:`, also list recipients.

The *sendmail* program attempts to deliver a copy of the mail message to every recipient address that it can find in all the recipient headers, and in the envelope. If the header of a mail message lacks recipient information (`To:`, `Cc:`, and `Bcc:` header lines), *sendmail* adds an `Apparently-To:` header line and puts the recipient's address from the envelope into the field of that header.

Via:
An unofficial trace header

The `Via:` header is not defined by RFC822, but occasionally appears in mail messages that *sendmail* needs to process. It is used by a few other networks to mark a mail message's transit through a forwarding host. It is an early, and now obsolete, version of the `Received:` header. The *sendmail* program counts the `Via:` header when determining the hop count, but has no other use for it.

The `Via:` header should never be declared in the configuration file.

X-
Official custom headers

The `X-` prefix is used to create custom headers that are legal under RFC822. Except for the IDA version of *sendmail*, such headers are passed through as-is by *sendmail*. Those that have special meaning for IDA *sendmail* are:

`X-Charset:`
> This header corresponds to the IDA C= delivery agent equate. Its presence causes IDA *sendmail* to select an alternative to the ASCII character set for use in delivering the message body.

`X-Char-Esc:`
> This header corresponds to the IDA X= delivery agent equate. Its presence causes IDA *sendmail* to use a character other than the one-byte decimal value 29 as a signal to switch between character sets.

These two special headers have special meaning for IDA *sendmail* only if BIT8 was declared in *conf.h* when that program was compiled.

X-Authentication-Warning:
Notification of security matters (V8 only)

If the p (privacy) option is declared with authwarnings, V8 *sendmail* inserts a special header line for possible security concerns. That header line looks like this:

```
X-Authentication-Warning: host: message
```

Here, *host* is the canonical name of the host that inserted this header. The *message* is one of the following:

Processed by *user* with -C *file*

> An attempt was made by a *user* other than *root* to run *sendmail* with the -C command-line switch. That switch caused *sendmail* to read *file* in place of the system *sendmail.cf* file.

user set sender to *other* using -f

> A *user* or program's *user* identity used the -f command-line switch to change the identity of the sender to *other*. This can be legitimate when the *user* is *uucp* or *daemon*. It can also be legitimate when the *user* is sending to some mailing lists. Such a warning can also indicate someone trying to forge mail.

user-owned process doing -bs

> A *user* or program's *user* identity used the -bs command-line switch to make *sendmail* receive a mail message via its standard input/output using the SMTP protocol. This parallels network notification set up by defining IDENTPROTO when compiling *sendmail* and by use of the $_ macro in Received: headers.

Processed from queue *dir*

> A user other than *root* used the -oQ switch to process mail from a queue directory (*dir*) that was different from the one specified with the Q option in the configuration file. The *sendmail* program can run as an ordinary user because this or some other command-line switch caused it to give up *root* privilege.

Host *name1* claimed to be *name2*

> In the HELO message of an SMTP conversation, the remote host *name1* specified its canonical name as *name2* and the two didn't match. This always indicates a problem. Either the remote host is

misconfigured (a bad value in $j), or the DNS maps for that host are wrong, or someone is trying to spoof the local *sendmail*.

Host *name* didn't use HELO protocol

Every SMTP conversation for transfer of mail must start with the HELO (or EHLO) greeting. If, instead, a MAIL command was first, and if needhello was listed with the p option, this header is inserted in the incoming message. The most likely cause of a missing HELO is the mistake of someone attempting to carry on an SMTP conversation by hand.

X400-Received:
Received via X400 (IDA and V8 only)

The X400-Received: header is added by IDA *sendmail* to document receipt of a mail message from an X400 network. This header is used by both IDA and V8 to count the number of forwarding sites when computing the hop count of a mail message.

The X400-Received: should never be declared in the configuration file.

32

The Command Line

The initial behavior of *sendmail* is largely determined by the command line used to invoke it. The command line can, for example, cause *sendmail* to use a different configuration file, or to rebuild the *aliases* file rather than deliver mail. The command line can be typed at your keyboard, executed from a boot-time script, or even executed by an MUA when sending mail.

The format of the *sendmail* command line is:

```
argv[0] switches recipients
```

Here, `argv[0]` is the name used to run *sendmail*. The `switches`, if any are present, must always precede the list of recipients. The `recipients` is a list of zero or more recipient address expressions.

Alternative argv[0] Names

The *sendmail* program may exist in any of several places, depending on your version of operating system. Usually, it is located in the */usr/lib* directory and is called *sendmail,** but it can alternatively be located in the */etc, /usr/sbin,* or */usr/etc* directory. The location of the *sendmail* program can be found by examining the */etc/rc* files for BSD UNIX, or the */etc/init.d* files for Sys V UNIX (see Chapter 3, *The Roles of sendmail*).

---

*On Sun systems, you will find */usr/lib/sendmail.mx* for use with the Domain Naming System.

In addition to the name *sendmail,* other names (in other directories) can exist which alter the behavior of *sendmail.* Those alternate names are usually symbolic links to */usr/lib/sendmail.* On some systems they may be hard links, and in rare cases you may actually find them to be copies. The complete list of other names is shown in Table 32-1.

Table 32-1: Alternative Names for sendmail

Name	Mode of Operation
newaliases	Rebuild the *aliases* file
mailq	Print the queue contents
smtpd	Run in daemon mode
bsmtp	Run in batched SMTP mode (IDA only)

When *sendmail* looks for the name under which it is running, it strips any leading directory components from *argv[0]* and compares the result (in a case-sensitive fashion) to its internal list of alternative names (Table 32-1). If a match is found, its mode of operation is changed to conform to that of the alternative name. If no match is found (if, say, a link is named *Mailq*), *sendmail* does not change its mode.

The name found is used to build an argument list for use with process listings. For example, if the name was *sendmail.mx* (from SunOS), a process listing produced with *ps*(3) would look something like this:

```
root  1247  620 p0 S  07:22 0:00 -AA15186 (sendmail.mx)
```

Here, the (`sendmail.mx`) shows that *sendmail* was run under the name *sendmail.mx.*

Note that *sendmail* uses the hardcoded name *"sendmail"* for logging purposes with *syslog*(3) (see Chapter 22, *Logging and Statistics*). Thus, logged errors and warnings always appear to come from *sendmail,* no matter what name was used to run it.

As a final note, be aware that command-line switches are processed immediately *after* the name. The use of particular switches can completely cancel any special meaning given a name.

newaliases

The name *newaliases* is a synonym for the −bi and −I (obsolete) command-line switches. It causes *sendmail* to rebuild the *aliases* database files, print summary information, and then immediately exit. In this mode, the −v switch is automatically implied, and *sendmail* runs in verbose mode.

The location of the *aliases* file is given in the configuration file with the A option. That location can be overridden from the command line with the −oA switch, but if it is, *sendmail* gives up its *root* privilege (unless it was run by *root*).

A description of the process of rebuilding the *aliases* database is given in Chapter 20, *Aliases*.

mailq

The name *mailq* is a synonym for the −bp command-line switch. It causes *sendmail* to print the contents of the mail queue and then exit. The output produced is described in Chapter 19, *The Queue*.

Note that the location of the queue can be changed by using the −oQ command-line switch. Changing the location of the queue causes *sendmail* to give up its *root* privilege (unless it was run by *root*).

smtpd

The name *smtpd* is a synonym for the −bd command-line switch. It causes *sendmail* to run in the background as a daemon, listening for incoming SMTP mail. This mode of operating is usually combined with the −q switch, which causes *sendmail* to periodically process the queue.

bsmtp (IDA only)

The IDA name *bsmtp* is a synonym for the IDA −bb command-line switch. It is like the usual −bs command-line switch, in that it causes *sendmail* to process SMTP mail on its standard input and output. But here the IDA b stands for batch. In batch mode, *sendmail* uses unbuffered I/O and doesn't wait for SMTP replies. This mode is intended for use with the *bsmtp* program for sending UUCP mail.

Batched SMTP should be used only with programs designed for that purpose. It uses a non-RFC821 SMTP TICK command, and does not wait for replies that can indicate errors.

Command-line Switches

Command-line switches are command-line arguments that begin with a –
character, and precede the list of recipients (if any). The forms for command-line switches, where *X* is a single letter, are:

```
-X              ← boolean switch
-Xarg           ← switch with argument
```

All switches are single letters. A complete list of switches is presented at
the end of this chapter.

Some switches are called boolean because they are either present or absent
(true or false). The –v switch, for example, is boolean because it puts *sendmail* into verbose mode if it is present. If absent, *sendmail* does not run in
verbose mode.

Some switches take arguments. The –C switch, for example, tells *sendmail*
where to find its configuration file. When most switches take an argument,
the argument must immediately follow the letter with no intervening space.

```
-Ctest.cf       ← good
-C test.cf      ← bad
```

But some switches, like –f (set the sender's address), can have an optional
space between the letter and the `arg`. For the syntax of individual switches
see the end of this chapter.

Some switches, like –d (run in debugging mode), can either be boolean or
take an argument:

```
-d              ← boolean
-d27.12         ← with argument
```

The position of switches in the command line is critical. If any follow the
list of recipients, they are wrongly taken as mail addresses and lead to
bounced mail. But the order in which switches appear is not important.
That is, they may appear in any order without changing the behavior of
sendmail.

An undefined switch letter is silently ignored.

V8 uses getopt(3)

V8 *sendmail* uses the *getopt*(3) library routine to process command-line
switches. Consequently, any switch may have optional space between the
letter and the `arg`.

```
-Ctest.cf        ← good
-C test.cf       ← also good
```

Another advantage of *getopt*(3) is that undefined switches produce an error message rather than being ignored. For example:

```
% /usr/lib/sendmail -X
sendmail: illegal option -- X
```

Another advantage of *getopt*(3) is that the special switch – can be used to delimit the switches from the list of recipients:

```
% /usr/lib/sendmail -- -jim
```

Here, the recipient is -jim. To prevent the – of -jim from being wrongly interpreted as indicating a switch, the special switch – is used to mark the end of all switches.

List of Recipient Addresses

All command-line arguments that follow the switches (if any) are taken to be the addresses of recipients. The addresses in the list may be separated by spaces, or by commas or by both:

```
addr1 addr2 addr3
addr1,addr2,addr3
addr1, addr2, addr3
```

Certain modes specified by the -b command-line switch, like -bp (for print the queue's contents), cause *sendmail* to ignore any list of recipients.

Be sure to escape any characters in addresses that have special meaning to your shell. For example, because the ! character has special meaning to the C-shell,* it should be escaped by preceding it with a backslash character:

```
host\!user
```

If *sendmail* expects a list of recipients and finds none, it prints the following message and exits:

```
Recipient names must be specified
```

Under pre-V8 *sendmail*, recipient names should never begin with a -C, -b, -d, -q, or -Z. If any do, they are wrongly interpreted as switches during preprocessing (described below).

---

*And its derivatives like *tcsh*(1).

Processing the Command Line

The *sendmail* program's ability to perform different tasks necessitate its processing the command line in steps. It needs to prescan for the −C switch, for example, because that switch tells *sendmail* where to find its configuration file. The steps *sendmail* uses to processes its command line are:

First The command line is prescanned to see, for example, if a different configuration file should be used. This is done before internal macros are given values. If a freeze file (see −bz) exists, it is thawed next.

Second After internal macros are given values (and a possible freeze file thawed), the command line's *argv[0]* (the name used to run *sendmail*) is processed. That name can determine the *sendmail* program's mode of operation.

Third The command-line switches are processed. If there was no freeze file, the configuration file is read next.*

Fourth After the configuration file is read, if *sendmail* is running in a mode which allows it to verify or deliver to recipients, the remainder of the command line is processed to extract the recipient list.

Prescanning the Command Line

When *sendmail* begins to run, it performs a preliminary scan of its command-line arguments. It does this because some actions need to be performed before its configuration (or frozen configuration) file is read. The list of switches that it prescans for is shown in Table 32-2.

The −C, −d, and −Z switches are processed only during this prescanning phase. The −bz switch is processed during the prescan to prevent "thawing" the frozen configuration file. The −bd and −q switches (both in IDA only) are noted during the prescan to prevent setting the user's full name from the environment variable NAME. After that they are processed as usual.

---

*Although the configuration file is read after the command line is processed, options in the command line still supersede those in the configuration file.

Table 32-2: Prescanned Switches

Switch	Description
-C	Location of configuration file
-bz	Freeze the configuration file (not V8)
-d	Enter debugging mode
-bd	Run in daemon mode (IDA only)
-q	Process the queue once (IDA only)
-Z	Location of frozen configuration file (IDA only)

Processing Prior to the Switches

After the command-line switches are prescanned, but before they are processed in full, *sendmail* performs six important internal tasks.

Thaw the frozen configuration file

A frozen configuration file is simply a copy of the memory variables used by *sendmail* that have been placed into a disk file. That file contains the same information as the configuration file, but is faster to read because it doesn't need to be parsed and interpreted. If the frozen configuration file (see -bz) exists, it is thawed (read instead of the configuration file).

Initialize the environment

The environment variables given to *sendmail* when it is first run are saved in an internal array. That array is later passed to each executed delivery agent program as environmental variables. Note that the next release of IDA *sendmail* will only pass through environment variables like NAME and HOME, and will specifically set a safe PATH, and eliminate IFS and LD_*. Also note that V8 *sendmail* is very security conscious and will only ever pass AGENT=sendmail and possibly TZ=.

Initialize macros

Certain macros are next declared and assigned values. The $w macro (see Chapter 27, *Defined Macros*) and the w class macro (see Chapter 28, *Class Macros*) are given values that identify the current host. The $v macro is assigned a value that is the current version of the *sendmail* program. The $b macro is given the current date and time as its value.

If a frozen configuration file is read, only the $b macro is given a value. The others inherit their values from those saved in the frozen configuration file.

Process switches

Command-line switches are processed by *sendmail* as they appear in the command line, from left to right. Processing of switches ends when an argument is found that lacks a leading – character.

Read the configuration file

The fact that the configuration file is read *after* the command-line switches are processed can lead to some confusion. Some, but not all, command-line switches can overwrite some configuration file commands. There is no general rule. Instead, the behavior of each item (like macros and options) is described in a chapter dedicated to each.

Collect recipients

The final step *sendmail* undertakes in processing its command line is gathering the list of recipients. Each recipient (or list of recipients if more than one is contained in a single command-line argument) is fully processed for delivery, and any error messages are printed before delivery is actually undertaken.

If sendmail is running in a mode that doesn't require recipients, any list of recipients in the command line is silently ignored.

Pitfalls

- If the list of recipients contains an address that begins with any of the prescanned switches, *sendmail* wrongly views that recipient as a switch during its prescan phase. For example, mail to `joe, bill, -Cool` causes *sendmail* to try to use a file named `ool` as its configuration file.
- The first command-line argument without a leading – ends switch processing (except during the prescan phase). Consequently, switches mixed in with recipient names are treated as recipient addresses.
- Most versions of *sendmail* (including IDA and some versions of BSD, but excluding SunOS and V8) *syslog*(3) a warning if the frozen configuration file doesn't exist. This can be annoying at sites which intentionally choose not to use a frozen configuration file.
- Under pre-V8 *sendmail*, unknown command-line switches are silently ignored. Thus, sending mail from a shell script can fail for reasons that

are difficult to find. For example, specifying the preliminary hop count wrongly with -j, instead of correctly with -h, causes your presetting of the hop count to be silently ignored.

- BSD and SunOS versions of sendmail set the default sender's full name from the environmental variable NAME even when running as a daemon or when processing the queue. This can lead to the superuser's full name occasionally showing up wrongly as a sender's full name. IDA and V8 *sendmail* clear the full name in -bd and -q modes, but use different methods. To prevent this problem under other versions of *sendmail*, the *env*(1) program can be used to clean up the environment passed to *sendmail*:

```
% env - /usr/lib/sendmail -bd -q1h
```

Alphabetized Reference

Command-line switches are those command-line arguments which precede the list of recipients and which begin with a – character. The complete list of currently implemented command-line switches is shown in Table 32-3.

Table 32-3: Command-line Switches

Switch	Description
-B	Specify message body type (V8 only)
-b	Operating mode
-C	Location of configuration file
-c	Set option c, expensive delivery agents (obsolete)
-d	Enter debugging mode
-e	Set option e, error mode (obsolete)
-F	Sender's full name
-f	Sender address
-h	Initial hop count
-I	Synonym for -bi
-i	Set option i, leading dots (obsolete)
-M	Process the queue by ID (IDA and SunOS only)
-m	Set option m, me too
-n	Don't do aliasing
-o	Set an option from the command line
-p	Set protocol and host (V8 only)
-q	Process the queue

Table 32.3: Command-line Switches (continued)

Switch	Description
-R	Process the queue by recipient (IDA only)
-r	Synonym for -f
-S	Process the queue by sender (IDA only)
-s	Set option f, UNIX from (obsolete)
-T	Set option T, queue timeout (obsolete)
-t	Get recipients from message header
-v	Run in verbose mode
-x	Ignored
-Z	Location of freeze file (IDA only)

In this section we present a full description of each switch in alphabetical order. Where two switches differ by case, the uppercase switch precedes the lowercase switch.

–B

Set body type (V8 only)

MIME (Multi-media) support in V8 *sendmail* has been coupled to ESMTP (Extended SMTP) of the new BODY parameter for the MAIL command. The BODY parameter is passed through as-is to the delivery agent. Two special parameters are internally recognized by *sendmail*. They tell *sendmail* that the message body is either 7bit or 8bitmime. 7bit forces the high bit off. 8bitmime causes *sendmail* to leave the high bit unchanged. Both override any setting of the 7 option or F=7 flag.

When *sendmail* connects to another site for incoming mail, it has no way to determine from context whether or not it is dealing with MIME mail. To override any configured assumptions, you may use the –B command-line switch.

```
-B 7BIT
-B 8BITMIME
```

Case is unimportant (7BIT and 7bit both work). The 7bit causes the local *sendmail* to tell the remote *sendmail* (in ESMTP mode) that the message body should have the high bit stripped from every byte. Conversely, the 8bitmime tells the remote *sendmail* to preserve the high bit of each byte.

The −B command-line switch has an effect only if the remote *sendmail* supports both ESMTP and MIME. The local *sendmail* ignores incoming MIME support unless MIME is defined in *Makefile* when *sendmail* is compiled. Note, however, that MIME support in V8 *sendmail* is actually pretty minimal.

−b

Operating mode

The −b switch tells *sendmail* in what mode to operate. For example, *sendmail* can "become" a daemon listening for incoming SMTP connections, or it can run in a mode that tells it to simply print the contents of the queue and exit. The form of the −b switch is:

```
-bmode
```

There must be no space between the −b and the *mode*. The *mode* must be one of the letters listed in table Table 32-4. If *mode* is more than a single letter, all but the first letter is silently ignored. If the *mode* is missing, or not one of those in the table, *sendmail* prints the following error message and exits:

```
Invalid operation mode bad
```

Here, *bad* is the offending letter. If the −b command-line switch is omitted altogether, the default mode becomes −bm (deliver mail and exit).

Table 32-4: The -b Modes

Mode	Description
−ba	Use old-style Arpanet protocols (obsolete)
−bb	Use batched SMTP mode (IDA only)
−bd	Run as a daemon
−bi	Initialize alias database
−bm	Be a mail sender
−bp	Print the queue
−bs	Run SMTP on standard input
−bt	Test mode: resolve addresses only
−bv	Verify: don't collect or deliver
−bz	Freeze the configuration file (not V8)

−ba Use old-style ARPAnet protocols (obsolete)

In the the distant past, mail messages on ARPAnet were sent using the *ftp*(1) protocol. Because that protocol was never intended for use with e-mail, many different departures were designed ("patched in") to solve particular problems. That growing anarchy caused Jonathan B. Postel to design the Simple Mail Transfer Protocol (SMTP) in 1982, and to document that protocol in RFC821. Since then, SMTP has gradually phased out FTP as the default standard.

Now that sufficient time has passed for all sites to adopt SMTP, the −ba mode can be considered obsolete. In fact, it has been completely removed from the V8 *sendmail*.

−bb Use batched SMTP (IDA Only)

The −bb switch is a synonym for running IDA *sendmail* under the name *bsmtp*. It is like the usual −bs command-line switch, but causes *sendmail* to process SMTP mail on its standard input and output in batch mode. In batch mode, *sendmail* uses unbuffered I/O and doesn't wait for SMTP replies. This mode is intended for use with the *bsmtp* program for sending UUCP mail.

−bd Run as a daemon

The −bd command-line switch causes *sendmail* to become a daemon, running in the background, listening for and handling incoming SMTP connections.

To become a daemon, *sendmail* first performs a *fork*(2). The parent then exits, and the child becomes the daemon by disconnecting itself from its controlling terminal. The −d debugging switch can be used to prevent the *fork*(2) and the detachment, and allows the *sendmail* program's behavior to be observed while it runs in daemon mode.

As a daemon, *sendmail* does a *listen*(2) on TCP port 25 for incoming SMTP messages. When another site connects to the listening daemon, the daemon performs a *fork*(2) and the child handles receipt of the incoming mail message.

Daemon mode is available only if DAEMON is defined when compiling *sendmail*. Sites which do not run a *sendmail* daemon may wish to leave it undefined in order to produce a smaller executable program.

–bi   Initialize alias database

The -bi command-line switch causes *sendmail* to rebuild its *aliases*(5) database, and exit. This switch is described in Chapter 20, *Aliases*. The name *newaliases* and the (obsolete) -I command-line switch are synonyms for this mode.

–bm Be a mail sender

The -bm command-line switch (the default) causes *sendmail* to run once in the foreground. A list of recipients is taken from the command line (unless the -t switch is used), and the message is read from the standard input and delivered.

This is the mode used by MUAs when they invoke *sendmail* on the user's behalf. The *sendmail* program processes the recipients first, then the message header, then the message body. Usually, the envelope recipients are those on the command line. But if the -t command-line switch is also used, the recipients are taken from the message header. The envelope sender is more difficult to determine:

- Trusted users, and programs running under the identity of those users, may specify the address of the sender by using either the -f or the -r command-line switch when running *sendmail*. Trusted users are those declared with a T configuration command (see Chapter 18, *Security*).

- When processing a message from the queue, the sender's address is taken from the qf file's S line (see Appendix A, *The qf File Internals*).

- In the absence of all the above, *sendmail* tries to use the user identity of the invoking program to determine the sender.

- When processing bounced mail, the sender becomes the name specified by the value of the $n macro, usually *mailer-daemon*.

–bp   Print the queue

The -bp command-line switch is a synonym for *mailq*(3). That mode and the output produced is described in Chapter 20, *Aliases*.

–bs   Run SMTP on standard input

The -bs command-line switch causes *sendmail* to run one time in the foreground, collect an SMTP message over its standard input and output, deliver the message, and exit.

This mode is intended for use at sites that wish to run *sendmail* with the *inetd*(3) daemon. To implement this, place an entry like the following in your *inetd.conf*(5) file, then restart *inetd*(3) by killing it with a -HUP signal.

```
smtp   stream  tcp    nowait   root /usr/lib/sendmail sendmail -bs
```

With this scheme, it is important to use *cron*(3) to run *sendmail* periodically to process its queue:

```
0 * * * * /usr/lib/sendmail -q
```

The look of these lines varies depending on the version of UNIX you are running.

There are advantages and disadvantages in using *inetd*(3) instead of the –bd daemon mode to listen for and process incoming SMTP messages. The advantages are:

- At security-conscious sites, *sendmail* can be hidden behind a *tcpd*(3) or *miscd*(3) wrapper that can selectively accept or reject connections.
- At hosts that receive few incoming mail messages, this mode avoids the need to run a daemon.

The disadvantages are:

- At sites that receive many incoming mail messages, this mode causes a new *sendmail* process to be started for each connection. Compared to daemon mode, this can adversely impact system performance.
- At highly-loaded sites, this mode circumvents the *sendmail* program options intended to avoid overloading the system with too many concurrent *sendmail* processes.

In general, the *inetd*(3) approach should be used only on lightly-loaded machines that receive few SMTP connections.

The –bs switch is also useful for user mail-sending programs that prefer to use SMTP rather than a pipe to transfer a mail message to *sendmail*. Depending on how it is configured, *mh*(1) can use this feature.

–bt   Test mode: resolve addresses only

The bt command-line switch causes *sendmail* to run in rule-testing mode. This mode is covered in detail in Chapter 24, *Rule Sets*.

−bv Verify: don't collect or deliver

The −bv command-line switch causes *sendmail* to verify the list of recipients. Each recipient in the list of recipients is fully processed up to the point of delivery, without actually being delivered. If mail can be successfully delivered to a recipient, *sendmail* prints a line like the following:

```
name ...deliverable
```

Here, the *name* is the original recipient address after it has undergone aliasing and rule-set rewriting. A local user's name expands to the contents of that user's *.forward* file. A mailing list expands to many names (and produces many lines of output).

If the recipient cannot be delivered to, *sendmail* instead prints the following:

```
name ...reason recipient is undeliverable
```

The *reason* can be any of many possible error messages (like "No such user") that would prevent successful delivery.

The −bv switch also prevents *sendmail* from collecting any mail message from its standard input unless −t is also given.

−bz Freeze the configuration file (not V8)

The −bz command-line switch causes *sendmail* to build (or rebuild) its frozen configuration file. The frozen configuration file is just a simple image of *sendmail*'s variables after it has read and parsed the configuration file. The purpose of the frozen file is to enable *sendmail* to start up more swiftly than it can when parsing the configuration file from scratch.*

The frozen file is usually located in the same directory as the configuration file and ends with the characters fc.

```
/etc/sendmail.cf     ← configuration file
/etc/sendmail.fc     ← frozen configuration file
```

Under IDA *sendmail*, the location can be changed with the −Z command-line switch.

---

*In practice, freeze files help you only on systems with very fast I/O systems relative to their CPU speeds. Although this was true in the day of the VAX 11/750, improvements in processor technology have reversed this tradeoff. In fact, V8 *sendmail* has removed frozen configuration files completely.

There are some problems associated with the use of frozen configuration files that you should be aware of:

- If you compile or install a different version of *sendmail* than was used to create the freeze file, you *must* create a new freeze file. Failure to make a new frozen file causes the new *sendmail* to fail and to produce a core dump or deliver mail in bizarre ways.

- If you change the *sendmail.cf* configuration file, changes in that file do not take effect until you either remove or recreate the freeze file. This is a common mistake. If you are using a freeze file, place a comment to that effect into the configuration file so you will remember.

- Some systems handle memory in a way that is incompatible with freeze files. Under SunOS, for example, freeze files won't work if *sendmail* is compiled with dynamic libraries.

On modern, fast machines, the freeze file is unnecessary.

If the frozen configuration file exists, it is thawed, and read in place of reading the configuration file when *sendmail* starts up. If no frozen file is found, *sendmail* *syslog*(3)'s at LOG_WARNING the following warning and uses the configuration file instead:

```
Cannot read frozen config file
```

V8 *sendmail* remains silent if the configuration file doesn't exist.

Then, *sendmail* reads the header of the frozen configuration file to see if it appears current and correct. If it is wrong (created by a different version of *sendmail*, for example), *sendmail* *syslog*(3)'s at LOG_WARNING the following message and reads the configuration file instead:

```
Wrong version of frozen config file
```

The header of the frozen configuration file also tells *sendmail* how much memory it needs. It attempts to get that memory with *sbrk*(2)* and, if it can't, prints the following error and reads the configuration file instead:

```
Cannot break to addr
```

Here, the `addr` is the amount of memory, in hexadecimal, that *sendmail* could not get.

---

*The *Mach* operating system on the NeXT machine lacks an *sbrk*(2) library call, so freezing won't work on that machine.

Finally, *sendmail* reads the frozen configuration file with a single *read*(2) instruction. If this read fails, *sendmail* panics and exits. It panics because an incomplete read trashed its memory. It *syslog*(3)'s and writes the following error message to its stderr:

```
Cannot read frozen config file
```

If the frozen configuration file is successfully read, *sendmail* skips reading the configuration file. (See -d0.1 in Chapter 33, *Debugging With –d*, for additional information about freeze-file error messages.)

Note that frozen configuration files may not be shared among machines. Defined macros (specifically $w) and all classes (even those read from files with the F configuration command) take their values from the frozen file. Minimally, this can cause *sendmail* to think it is running on the wrong machine.

–C

Location of the configuration file

The -C command-line switch tells *sendmail* where to find its configuration file. The form of the -C switch is:

```
-Cpath
```

There must be no space between the -C and the *path* (except for V8, where space is permitted). If there is a space, the location of the configuration file becomes *sendmail.cf* in the current directory, and the *path* is incorrectly treated as the name of a mail recipient. If no space exists, the *path* correctly becomes the location of the configuration file. That location may be either a relative or a full pathname. If *path* is missing, the location becomes the file *sendmail.cf* in the current directory.

The -C command-line switch is intended as an aid in testing new configuration files. Thus, it causes *sendmail* to change its *uid* and *gid* to that of the user that ran it. If used by someone other than the superuser, the -oQ switch should also be used to set the location of the queue directory. If that location is not changed, *sendmail* fails because it cannot *chdir*(2) into its queue directory.

The -C command-line switch prevents *sendmail* from "thawing" its frozen configuration file.

Under V8 *sendmail*, the −C command-line switch also causes *sendmail* to internally mark the configuration file as unsafe. An unsafe configuration file is prohibited from reading files with the F configuration command. It also prevents all but *root* from setting certain options.

−c

Set option c, expensive delivery agent

The −c command-line switch is a synonym for the c option (-oc). See Chapter 30, *Options*. As of V8 *sendmail*, this switch is obsolete.

−d

Enter debugging mode

The −d command-line switch causes *sendmail* to run in debugging mode. This switch is described Chapter 33, *Debugging With −d*.

−e

Set option e, set error mode

The −e command-line switch is a synonym for the e option (-oe). See Chapter 30. As of V8 *sendmail*, this switch is obsolete.

−F

Set sender's full name

The −F command-line switch specifies the full name for the sender, which is used in mail headers and the envelope. The form of the −F switch is:

```
-Ffullname
-F fullname
```

Space between the −F and the *fullname* is optional. If *fullname* is missing, *sendmail* prints the following error and exits:

```
Bad -F flag
```

When specifying the sender's full name, be sure to quote any internal spaces or shell special characters. For example, for the C shell, the following would be needed to specify the full name Happy Guy!:

```
"Happy Guy\!"
```

In the absence of this switch, sendmail finds the sender's full name in any of several places. These are described in Chapter 27, *Defined Macros*, in the section discussing the $x macro.

-f and -r
Set sender's address

The -f and -r command-line switches are interchangeable. Either causes *sendmail* to take the address of the sender from the command line, rather than from the envelope or message header. The -r switch is obsolete, so we restrict our discussion to the -f switch. The form of the -f switch is:

```
-faddr
-f addr
```

Space between the -f and the *addr* is optional. If *addr* is missing, *sendmail* prints the following error message and ignores the -f switch:

```
No "from" person
```

Multiple -f switches cause *sendmail* to print the following error message and exit:

```
More than one from person
```

The *uid* of the user running *sendmail* and specifying the -f switch must match one of the usernames given in the T configuration command. If they do not match, non-V8 *sendmail* silently converts the sender's address that was specified to the C language value NULL, and determines the sender's address in the usual ways. The -f switch is used by UUCP software (the trusted user *uucp*) and by mailing list software (the trusted user *daemon*).

Under V8 *sendmail*, the T configuration command has been eliminated. If the -f or -r switch is used, and if the p (privacy) option was given "authwarnings," V8 *sendmail* includes an X-Authentication-Warning: header in the mail message. That header warns that the identity of the sender was changed.

-h
Initial hop count

A hop is the transmittal of a mail message from one machine to another. Many such hops may be required to deliver a message. The number of hops (the hop count) is determined by counting the number of Received:*

---

*Actually, all headers marked with the H_TRACE flag in *conf.c* (see Chapter 16, *Compile and Install sendmail*) are counted.

header lines in the header portion of an e-mail message. The maximum number of allowable hops is compiled-in for most versions of *sendmail,* but set by the h option with V8. When the hop count for a message exceeds the limit set by the h option, the message is bounced. Ordinarily, the count begins at zero. The -h command-line switch is used to specify a different beginning hop count for a mail message, thus reducing the total number of allowable hops. The forms for the -h switch are:

```
-hnum
-h num
```

Space between the -h and *num* is optional. If *num* is missing, *sendmail* prints the following error message and ignores that switch:

```
Bad hop count (<NULL>)
```

If *num* begins with a character other than a digit, the offending text is printed in place of <NULL>:

```
Bad hop count (-5)
```

The failure above illustrates that the beginning hop count must be positive, and may be used only to decrease the relative maximum hop count.

The -h switch is primarily used by mailing-list software to limit the possible propagation of errors.

-I

Synonym for –bi

The -I command-line switch is a synonym for the -bi command-line switch and the *newaliases* name. It is obsolete, but retained for compatibility with the *delivermail*(1) program.

-i

Set option i, leading dots

The -i command-line switch is a synonym for the i option (-oi). See Chapter 30.

–M

Process the queue by ID (IDA and SunOS only)

The –M command-line switch causes *sendmail* to process its queue, but limits that processing to a message whose identifier is specified by this switch. The –M switch is explained in Chapter 19, *The Queue*. Under V8 *sendmail*, you can use –qI instead.

–m

Set option m, me too

The –m command-line switch is a synonym for the m option (–om). See Chapter 30.

–n

Don't do aliasing

The –n command-line switch prevents *sendmail* from changing local recipient addresses with aliases. The –n switch is described in Chapter 20, *Aliases*.

–o

Set an option from the command line

The –o command-line switch is used to set a configuration option from the command line. The –o switch is described in Chapter 30.

–p

Set protocol and host (V8 only)

The $r macro holds as its value the protocol used when receiving a mail message (usually SMTP or UUCP). The $s macro holds as its value the name of the sending host. Some programs, like UUCP, need to be able to set the values of these macros from the command line. The old way to set them looked like this:

```
-oMrUUCP -oMslady
```

Here, the M option sets $r to be UUCP and $s to be lady.

Under V8 *sendmail*, the setting of $r and $s has been simplified. A single switch, –p, can be used to set them both:

```
-prval:sval
```

Here the *rval* is the value assigned to $r and the *sval* the value assigned to $s. The two are separated by a colon. If the *sval* is omitted, the colon must also be omitted.

–q

Process the queue

The –q command-line switch causes *sendmail* to process its queue. The –q switch is described in Chapter 19.

–R

Process queue by recipient (IDA only)

The –R command-line switch of IDA *sendmail* causes it to process the queue, but limits that processing to any messages whose recipient address contains the argument given to this switch. The –R switch is explained in Chapter 19. Under V8 *sendmail*, you can use –qR instead.

–S

Process queue by sender (IDA only)

The –S command-line switch of IDA *sendmail* causes it to process the queue, but limits that processing to any message whose sender address contains the argument given to this switch. The –S switch is explained in Chapter 19. Under V8 *sendmail*, you can use –qS instead.

–s

Set option f, UNIX from

The –s command-line switch is a synonym for the f option (–of). See Chapter 30. As of V8 *sendmail*, this switch is obsolete.

–T

Set option T, queue timeout

The –T command-line switch is a synonym for the T option (–oT). See Chapter 30. As of V8 *sendmail*, this switch is obsolete.

–t

Get recipients from message header

The –t command-line switch causes *sendmail* to gather its list of recipients from the message's header, in addition to gathering them from its command line. The –t switch takes no arguments.

When this switch is specified, *sendmail* gathers recipient names from the To:, Cc:, and Bcc: header lines. It also gathers recipient names from its command line, if any were listed there. Duplicates are discarded, and the message is delivered to all that remain.

The –t switch is intended for use by user mail-sending programs. It should never be specified when running *sendmail* in daemon mode.

–v

Run in verbose mode

The –v command-line switch tells *sendmail* to run in verbose mode. In that mode, *sendmail* prints a blow-by-blow description of all the steps it takes in delivering a mail message.

After the *sendmail.cf* file is parsed, and after the command-line arguments have been processed, *sendmail* checks to see if it is in verbose mode. If it is, it resets the c option (don't connect to expensive mailers) to false, and sets the d option (deliver mode) to interactive.

The –v switch is most useful for watching SMTP mail being sent and for producing expanded output when viewing the queue.

–x

Ignored (V8 only)

V8 *sendmail* prints an error if an illegal switch is specified (whereas other versions of *sendmail* silently ignore them). The *mailx* program supplied with OSF/1 from DEC and AIX from IBM issues an illegal –x switch. To keep *sendmail* from uselessly complaining under OSF/1 and AIX, that switch is specifically ignored for V8.2 and above *sendmail.* To get the same behavior with AIX under V8.1 *sendmail,* look for *_osf_* in *main.c* and uncomment the code necessary to ignore that switch.

-Z

Location of the freeze file (IDA only)

Under all but the IDA version of *sendmail,* the location of the freeze file is hardcoded. Under IDA *sendmail,* the -Z command-line switch can be used to specify an alternative location (and name) for the frozen configuration file. The form for the -Z switch is:

```
-Zpath
```

No space is allowed between the -Z and the *path.* If the *path* is missing, the default relative name *sendmail.fc* is used.

The -Z switch causes *sendmail* to change its *uid* and *gid* to that of the user who ran it. But if IDA *sendmail* has been compiled without _PATH_SEND-MAILFC defined, and this switch is used, the following error message is printed and the -Z switch ignored:

```
Frozen configuration files not available
```

33

Debugging With –d

The *sendmail* program offers a command-line switch for investigating and solving mail problems. The debugging –d switch allows you to observe the detailed inner workings of the *sendmail* program.

Syntax of –d

The form for the –d command-line switch is:

```
-dcategory.level,category.level,....
```

The –d may appear alone, or it may be followed by one or more *category.level* pairs separated by commas. The *category* limits debugging to an aspect of *sendmail* (such as queueing or aliasing). The *level* limits the verbosity of *sendmail* (with low levels producing the least output).

The *category* is either a positive integer, or a range of integer values specified as:

```
first-last
```

When *category* is a range, *first* is a positive integer which specifies the first category in the range. It is followed by a hyphen character (–) and then *last*, a positive integer that specifies the last category in the range. The value of *first* must be less than the value of *last*, or the range will be ignored.

The level is a positive integer between 0 and 127. A level of 0 causes *sendmail* to produce *no* output for the category.

When the -d is specified without *category* and *level*, an internal *sendmail* default is used:

    0-99.1

This default causes *sendmail* to set all the categories, from zero through 99 inclusive, to a level of 1.

When *category* is included but *level* is omitted, the value for *level* defaults to 1. When a dot (.) and *level* are included, but *category* is omitted, the value for *category* defaults to 0.

The maximum value that may be specified for a single *category* is 127. The maximum value for *level* is also 127. Any value specified above the maximum is reduced to the maximum. Non-digits for the *category* or range evaluate to zero. Non-digits for the *level* evaluate to 1.

The *level* specifies the maximum amount of verbose output to produce. All levels below the *level* specified also produce output.

The expression that produces the maximum debugging output is:

    -d0-99.127

Debugging Behavior

When *sendmail* is given the -d debugging command-line switch, it internally performs three distinct actions. First, if the *category.level* is omitted, *sendmail* presets all the categories 0 through 99 inclusively to a level of 1. It then sets the categories in the command line (if any) to the corresponding levels specified (or to 1 if no level is specified). Finally it calls *setbuf*(3) to place the standard output in unbuffered mode.

Presetting categories 0 through 99 to a level of 1 has two side effects:

- If *sendmail* is run in daemon mode (with -bd or as *smtpd*), or if it was given a queue processing interval with -q, it normally places itself in the background and disconnects from its controlling terminal. But setting category 0 to a level of 1 keeps *sendmail* in the foreground and allows your terminal to control (interrupt) it.

- Usually, certain errors are not reported because they are tolerable, but a level of 1 generally causes those otherwise missing error messages to be printed. For example, if the *aliases* file is missing, *sendmail* does not perform aliasing, but is silent about it. A category 27 level of 1, on the other hand, causes *sendmail* to print the reason it could not open the *aliases* file.

Interpreting the Output

Unfortunately, there is no clear differentiation between debugging output that is intended for a programmer (who is writing or modifying the *sendmail* program) and output intended for a user (who is trying to solve a mail problem). The *sendmail* program is so complex and sophisticated that there is no easy way to determine what output will be of use to which user.

Some debugging output references C language structures that are internal to *sendmail*. For those, it will help if you have access to *sendmail* source. One subroutine, called *printaddr()*, is used to dump complete details about all the recipients for a given mail message. This subroutine is used by many categories of debugging output, but rather than describe it repeatedly, we describe it once here and reference this description as needed.

The Output Produced by printaddr( )

In many debugging categories, the *sendmail* subroutine *printaddr()* is used to print details about each recipient of a given mail message. Its output looks like this:

```
ra=addr: mailer mnum (mname), host hname, user uname, ruser rname
        next=link, flags=octal, alias aname
        home=home, fullname=fname
```

First, *sendmail* prints the address in memory, `ra`, of the C language *struct* that contains the information necessary to deliver a mail message. It then prints the information in that structure:

`addr`	The mail address
`mnum`	Number of the delivery agent to be used (an index into the array of delivery agents)
`mname`	Symbolic name of that delivery agent (from rule set 0, $#)
`hname`	Name of the recipient's host machine (from rule set 0, $@)
`uname`	Recipient's mail name (from rule set 0, $:)
`rname`	Recipient's login name, if known; otherwise, it is <null>
`next`	Address in memory of the next C language structure of information about the next recipient in the list of recipients
`octal`	Octal representation of the possible status flags that can apply to the current message (see Table 33-1 below)
`aname`	Alias (if there was one) that originally expanded to the current recipient

dir	Home directory of the recipient (for local mail only)
fname	Full name of the recipient if it is known

Table 33-1: Octal Envelope Flags

Name	Octal	Description
QDONTSEND	0001	Don't send to this address
QBADADDR	0002	This address is verified bad
QGOODUID	0004	The uid and gid fields are good
QPRIMARY	0010	Status was set from argv
QQUEUEUP	0020	Queue for later transmission
QSENT	0040	Message has been successfully delivered
QNOTREMOTE	0100	Not an address for remote forwarding
QSELFREF	0200	Address is part of a loop (V8 only)

Pitfalls

- It is best to debug *sendmail* in a window environment, within *script*(1), with *emacs*(1), or something similar. Debugging output can run to many screens.

- Activities of the daemon can be observed only if the −d0.1 switch is combined with the others selected. This switch prevents the daemon from disconnecting from the controlling terminal. Without this switch, *sendmail* silently discards its debugging output.

Reference in Numerical Order

The *sendmail* debugging command-line switches vary from vendor to vendor and from version to version. This section is specific to the IDA 5.65c, BSD 8.6, and Sun 4.1 versions of *sendmail*. Other versions (including more recent versions of IDA and BSD) may have more or fewer switches, and the meanings of many may vary. These switches are perhaps best used with a copy of the *sendmail* source by your side. Be further advised that many of the internal details shown here will change as *sendmail* continues to evolve and improve.

In this section we provide a detailed description of each combination of debugging category and level. They are presented in ascending numeric order, first by category, then by level within each category.

Note that for all categories, a −d*category* and a −d*category*.1 are always equivalent.

You may notice that the category numbers don't always make sense. Logical functions, for example, are not always grouped in adjacent categories. This is an artifact of the way *sendmail* was developed. Over time, new debugging categories were added and old ones changed in response to specific needs. There was never a "grand plan" for all debugging switches. One consequence of this is that some debugging switches are more helpful in resolving problems than others.

Finally, note that several new debugging switches in V8 *sendmail* did not make it into this chapter by press time. They are indicated in Table 33-2 by asterisks. Included with the V8 source is a file called *src/TRACEFLAGS*, which serves as a guide equating category to source filename.

Table 33-2: Debugging Switches by Category

Category	Description
−d0	General debugging
−d1	Show sender information
−d2	End with *finis*( )
−d3	Print the load average (IDA only)
−d3	Print the load average (V8 only)
−d4	Show forks (IDA only)
−d4	Enough disk space (V8 only)
−d5	Show events
−d6	Show failed mail
−d7	The queue filename
−d8	DNS name resolution
−d9	Make hostname canonical (IDA and V8 only)
−d9	Trace RFC1413 queries (V8 only)
−d10	Show recipient delivery
−d11	Show selected delivery agents' argv (not V8)
−d11	Trace delivery (V8 only)
−d12	Show mapping of relative host
−d13	Show delivery
−d14	Show header field commas
−d15	Show network get request activity
−d16	Outgoing connections
−d17	List MX hosts (V8 only)

Table 33.2: Debugging Switches by Category (continued)

Category	Description
-d18	Show SMTP replies
-d19	Show ESMTP MAIL parameters (V8 only)
-d20	Show resolving delivery agent: *parseaddr*( )
-d21	Trace rewriting rules
-d22	Trace tokenizing an address: *prescan*( )
-d24*	Show local allocation of addresses (V8 only)
-d25	Trace "sendtolist"
-d26	Trace recipient queueing
-d27	Trace aliasing
-d28	Trace user database transactions (V8 only)
-d29	Special rewrite of local recipient (V8 only)
-d29	Watch fuzzy match (BSD only)
-d30	Trace processing of header
-d31	Show entry into *chompheader*( )
-d32	Show received headers
-d33	Watch *crackaddr*( )
-d34*	Watch header assembly for output (V8 only)
-d35	Show macro definition/expansion
-d36	Show processing of the symbol table
-d37	Trace setting of options
-d38*	Watch K command-map initializations (v8 only)
-d39	Display %*digit* database mapping (V8 only)
-d40	Trace processing of the queue
-d41	Show reason queue failed
-d42	Trace caching (V8 only)
-d45	Show envelope sender
-d49*	An example in *checkcompat*( ) (V8 only)
-d50	Show envelope being dropped
-d51	Trace unlocking and unlinking
-d52	Disconnect from controlling TTY
-d53	Show file closing (V8 only)
-d54*	Watch error messages being output (V8 only)
-d55*	Trace attempts at file locking (V8 only)
-d59	XLA from contrib (V8 only)
-d60	Trace use of *dbm*(3) *files (IDA only)*

–d0

General debugging

The –d0 command-line switch tells *sendmail* to print its version number, not run in the background, and (for IDA only) show why the freeze file version is wrong.

When *sendmail* is run with the –bd command-line switch, it places itself into daemon mode. It becomes a daemon by forking a copy of itself. The original exits, and the copy (the child) continues to run. The child then detaches itself from its controlling tty device (possibly your keyboard).

The –d0.1 command-line switch prevents *sendmail* from forking and detaching itself, even if it is run with –bd. This is necessary to see the output produced by other debugging switches when running *sendmail* as a daemon. See –d52.5 to allow the fork, but prevent the detach.

–d0.1   Freeze-file version (IDA only)

When *sendmail* starts, it first checks to see if a freeze file (*sendmail.fc*) exists. If one does, *sendmail* reads that file instead of the *sendmail.cf* file. (See –bz in Chapter 32, *The Command Line*, for a discussion of the freeze file.) The freeze file is compared to an internal idea of what that file should look like. If the freeze file appears to be wrong (most likely because the *sendmail.cf* file was changed and not refrozen), *sendmail* syslog(3)'s an error and uses the *sendmail.cf* file instead. (See Chapter 22, *Logging and Statistics* for more information about *syslog*(3).)

With IDA *sendmail*, the reason the freeze file looks wrong is also printed:

```
Wrong version of frozen config file (reason mismatch)
```

Here the *reason* is one of the following: Edata (position of the envelope data was wrong), End (position of the top of memory was wrong), Version (mismatched version of *sendmail*), or Datecompiled (mismatch of date *sendmail* was compiled). Note that BSD *sendmail* syslogs only errors, and checks only Edata, End, and Version. Also note V8 *sendmail* doesn't support freeze files.

–d0.4   Our name and aliases

When *sendmail* starts, it calls *gethostname*(3) to determine the name of the host on which it is running. The name found is placed into the defined macro $w. (If *gethostname*(3) fails, the name *localhost* is used.) The

-d0.4 debugging command-line switch tells *sendmail* to print the found hostname as:

```
canonical name: hostname
```

If the *hostname* is not a fully-qualified domain name (not canonical), then you may be running the wrong *sendmail* (such as the */usr/lib/sendmail* rather than */usr/lib/sendmail.mx* under SunOS). If that is not the problem, you may have to tune the definition of $w in *sendmail.cf*.

If the canonical name contains a dot, *sendmail* saves the part of the name to the right of the leftmost dot as the domain name in the defined macro $m. It also appends the part of the name to the left of the leftmost dot to the class w. If the canonical name doesn't contain a dot, the $m macro is undefined, and the whole name is appended to the class w.

In addition, IDA and V8 *sendmail* also set the defined macro $k to be the correct UUCP name for the machine. For IDA *sendmail*, if HASUNAME is defined in *conf.h*, it uses *uname*(3) to find that name; otherwise, it uses the same strategy as for class w above. The -d0.4 debugging switch causes *sendmail* to print the name found:

```
UUCP nodename: name
```

After *gethostname*(3) has finished its work, *sendmail* calls *gethostbyname*(3) to gather any aliases for the host. If it finds any, it appends each to the class macro w. The -d0.4 debugging command-line switch tells *sendmail* to also print each alias found as:

```
aka: alias
```

Each *alias* prints as either a hostname (like *wash.dc.gov*) or as an Internet number (like [*128.23.45.3*]), depending on the vendor of the *sendmail* you are using.

−d0.15   Dump rule sets and delivery agents

The -d0.15 debugging command-line switch causes *sendmail* to display its internal interpretations of the rewriting rules and delivery agent definitions it took from the configuration file. The rule sets look like this:

```
----Rule Set 9:
LHS: "@"
RHS: $@ "Mailer-Daemon"

LHS: $* "<" $* "LOCAL" ">" $*
RHS: $1 "<" $2 "Podunk" "." "EDU" ">" $3
```

```
LHS: "<" "@" $+ ">" $* ":" $+ ":" $+
RHS: "<" "@" $1 ">" $2 "," $3 ":" $4
```

The rule sets are printed in numeric order, rather than in the order that they appeared in the configuration file. The rewriting rules are printed under each rule set (but these *are* in the order that they appeared in the configuration file). Rule sets that are declared, but lack rewriting rules, are not printed. Note that defined macros in the RHS are expanded (the value used) when the configuration file is parsed. Also note that expressions like $+ may be printed as control characters (e.g., ^A) under older versions of *sendmail*.

The delivery agent configuration-file definitions are displayed after the rule sets. The clarity and completeness of the delivery agent information varies with the version of *sendmail* you use. The following (the most complete) was generated with V8 *sendmail*:

```
mailer 0 (prog): P=/bin/sh S=0/0 R=0/0 M=0 F=DFMPelsu E= A=sh -c $u
mailer 1 (*file*): P=/dev/null S=0/0 R=0/0 M=0 F=DEFMPlsu E= A=FILE
mailer 2 (*include*): P=/dev/null S=0/0 R=0/0 M=0 F=su E= A=INCLUDE
mailer 3 (local): P=/bin/mail S=0/0 R=0/0 M=0 F=DFMPlmnrs E= A=mail
-d $u
mailer 4 (ether): P=[TCP] S=11/11 R=0/0 M=0 F=CDFMXmsu E= A=TCP $h
mailer 5 (uucp): P=/usr/bin/uux S=13/13 R=23/23 M=0 F=DFMUhmsu E= A
=uux - -r $h!rmail ($u)
```

The delivery agents are printed in the same order that they appear in the configuration file.

−d0.44   *Print addresses of strings*

The −d0.44 debugging switch causes *sendmail* to print the address in memory of each string that it prints. With this debugging level, part of the previous listing of rule sets would look like this:

```
LHS:
        00037b88="@"
RHS:
        00037bb0=$@
        00037bc0="Mailer-Daemon"
```

This debugging level can be useful to the programmer who wishes to modify the *sendmail* source. It might, for example, be helpful in designing more efficient string storage.

–d1

Show sender information

Although there are many kinds of information one might like to trace about the sender of an e-mail message, *sendmail* provides only the means to trace one. The -d1.1 debugging switch causes *sendmail* to print its interpretation of whom the message is from (the name of the sender as it was used in the envelope).

```
From person = "sender"
```

Here, *sender* is the user portion of the mail address of the sender. This output is most useful when combined with the -f command-line switch (which sets the name of the sender from the command line).

–d1.5   Dump sender envelope (V8 only)

Under V8 *sendmail,* the -d1.5 debugging switch causes additional information about the sender to be printed. That output looks like this:

```
main: QDONTSEND output of printaddr() here
```

The QDONTSEND means that the sender is not a recipient, so should not get a copy of the message. That is followed by the output of the *printaddr()* routine (see page 615).

–d2

End with finis( )

Ordinarily, *sendmail* exits silently when it is done (unless an error causes an error message to be printed). The -d2.1 debugging command-line switch causes *sendmail* to print two useful values when it exits. The message it prints looks like this:

```
====finis: stat num e_flags octal
```

The *num* is the final value of the *sendmail* program's global ExitStat variable. It is usually updated to contain the latest value of the C library variable errno whenever there is a system error.

The *octal* is an octal representation of the possible envelope flags that were in effect with the current envelope when *sendmail* exited. Those possible values are shown in Table 33-3. For example, if the message was too old, no longer required a copy, and also needed a return receipt, the *octal* value would print as 034.

Table 33-3: Octal Envelope Flags

Octal	Description
00001	Use spaces (not commas) in headers
00002	This message is fully queued
00004	This message is too old
00010	Disk copy is no longer needed
00020	Send a return receipt
00040	Fatal errors occurred
00100	Keep queue files always
00200	This is an error or return receipt
00400	This message is being forwarded
01000	Verify only, don't expand aliases (V8 only)
02000	Warning message has been sent (V8 only)
04000	Envelope is from the queue (V8 only)

–d3

Print the load average (IDA only)

The *sendmail* program is often run on machines that are used for other purposes. As a consequence, it is designed to change its behavior whenever the load average on such a machine becomes too high. The load average is the average number of blocked processes (processes that are runnable, but not able to run because of a lack of resources) over the last minute. The x option sets the maximum load average under which *sendmail* runs normally. If the load average grows beyond that limit, *sendmail* queues mail, rather than delivering it.

With the –d3.1 debugging command-line switch, IDA *sendmail* prints the following whenever it checks the load average:

    Load average: *la*

Here, *la* is the current load average printed as a floating-point value (just like the floating-point values printed by the *uptime*(1) command).

If IDA *sendmail* cannot get the load average, it *syslog*(3)'s a warning, and prints:

    Load average: getloadavg() returned –1

–d3

Print the load average (V8 only)

V8 *sendmail* queues mail, rather than delivering it, if the load average (number of processes in the run queue) exceeds the value set by the x option. Exceeding that value also prevents messages already in the queue from being delivered (prevents a queue run). If the load average becomes higher than the value of the X option, *sendmail* rejects incoming SMTP connections until the load average drops.

The –d3.1 debugging switch causes V8 *sendmail* to print the load average found by its internal *getla()* routine each time that routine is called:

```
getla: la
```

Here, *la* is the current load average printed as an integer. The –d3.1 switch also causes *sendmail* to print any errors it encounters while obtaining the load average.

```
getla: open(/dev/kmem): error
```

Here, /dev/kmem is the device used to access kernel memory. The *error* is the system error that caused the failure, like "Permission denied" if *sendmail* is not properly *sgid* to the group *kmem*.

```
getla: nlist(unix): error
```

The *nlist*(3) function extracts a list of symbols from an executable binary (among them, the symbol for the load average). The binary it extracts is the kernel whose pathname is *unix* (such as */vmunix* for SunOS 4.x). Here, the *error* is the reason *nlist*(3) failed. One possibility is that you booted from a nonstandard kernel name (like */vmunix.new*) and the expected file didn't exist.

```
getla: nlist(unix, la) ==> 0
```

If the expected kernel exists (*unix*), but the machine was booted from a different kernel, the symbol representing the load average may not be found. In that instance, *la* is the value of the load average before the failure.

–d3.5   Print three load averages

The load average used by *sendmail* is averaged over the last minute. Internally, the kernel keeps track of three load averages. In addition to the last minute, it also tracks the last five and fifteen minutes.

The -d3.5 debugging switch causes V8 *sendmail* to print all three load averages:

```
getla: averun = la1, la5, la15
```

Here, the three load averages are printed either in integer or in floating point, depending on the setting of LA_TYPE in *conf.h*.

–d3.20   Show offset for load average

The *nlist*(3) routine (described above) provides the offset into the kernel file where the value of the load average is found. The -d3.20 debugging switch causes that offset to be displayed:

```
getla: symbol table address = offset
```

Here, the *offset* is printed in hexadecimal. The load average is read by seeking in the kernel file and reading it. If the seek or read fails, the -d3.1 debugging switch causes *sendmail* to print:

```
getla: seek or read: error
```

This can indicate a wrong or corrupted kernel image.

–d4

Show forks (IDA only)

When a process forks, it makes a copy of itself. The copy (child) can then perform one task while the original (parent) either waits or performs another task. The *sendmail* program *fork*(2)'s for many reasons. When listening for a TCP/IP connection, it forks once to connect, and then again to deliver each message. When processing the queue, it may fork once for each queued message. When running a delivery agent, it forks so that it may later *exec*(2) each agent.

There is no -d4.1 information.

–d4.2   Show forks (IDA only)

Under IDA *sendmail*, the -d4.2 debugging command-line switch causes information to be printed about each *fork*(2) that *sendmail* makes. It also causes IDA *sendmail* to print related information (like waiting for a child to exit). That output looks like this:

subroutine: *what* (pid = *pid*)

Here, *pid* is the process identification number of the child process. The *what* is one of the two strings `forking` or `wait`. The *subroutine* is the name of the subroutine within the *sendmail* program that executed the *fork*(2) or *wait*(2) instruction. Those subroutines are shown in Table 33-4.

Table 33-4: IDA Subroutines That fork(2) or wait(2)

Subroutine	What It Does
dowork	Forks to process a single queued message
getrequests	Forks to handle an IPC connection
mailfile	Forks to deliver to a file
openmailer	Forks to *exec*(2) a delivery agent
reapchild	Waits for child to prevent zombies
runinchild	Forks to handle SMTP batch command
runqueue	Forks to process the queued messages
sendall	Forks to send all messages
waitfor	Waits for a child to finish

–d4

Enough disk space (V8 only)

The `b` option under V8 *sendmail* defines the minimum number of disk blocks that must be reserved on the queue disk. If an incoming SMTP message will fill the disk beyond this minimum, the message is rejected. (See Chapter 30, *Options*, for additional information.)

There is no `-d4.1` information available.

–d4.80   *Trace enoughspace ( )*

The `-d4.80` debugging switch traces the *enoughspace()* routine in *conf.c*. That routine examines the disk space and allows or disallows incoming mail.

```
enoughspace: no threshold
```

This debugging output says that no limit was defined with the b option.

```
enoughspace: bavail=haveblocks need=needblocks
```

This debugging output shows that the number of blocks free (available) on the disk is *haveblocks*, and that the number of blocks required by incoming mail is *needblocks*.

```
enoughspace failure: min=boption need=needblocks
```

If the required number of blocks (*needblocks*) exceeds the minimum reserved as defined by the b option (*boption*), use of the disk is disallowed.

−d5

Show events

The *sendmail* program frequently creates a copy of itself by calling *fork*(2). It does so for many reasons. For example, a copy (child) can process the queue while the original (parent) continues to listen for IPC connections. Each child can then *fork*(2) again, so that its child can handle the delivery of each individual message.

Throughout these many possible levels of forks and children, *sendmail* must keep track of timeouts—the maximum amount of time it should wait for an event to occur. For example, a child must not wait forever for an SMTP greeting message, because the program at the other end may never provide that message (because it died or is just too busy).

In order to keep track of which child should be notified at which time, *sendmail* maintains an internal queue of events. The various levels of the −d5 debugging command-line switch cause *sendmail* to print information about the various aspects of its queued events.

There is no −d5.1 information.

−d5.4   Tick for queued events

The *sendmail* program uses the SIGALARM signal and the *alarm*(2) system call to set the interval it waits to next check its queue of events for timeouts. That interval (called a *tick*) is either the period of the timeout itself, or a default of 3 seconds. The −d5.4 debugging command-line switch causes *sendmail* to print the current time whenever the queue of events is examined.

```
tick: now=time
```

Here, *time* is the current time in seconds.

−d5.5 Events set and cleared

Events are set by the process (child or parent) that needs a timeout. The −d5.5 command-line switch causes *sendmail* to print the information that is used to set up for that timeout:

```
setevent: intvl=secs, for=timeo, func=addr, arg=pass, ev=env
```

The information is the timeout in seconds (*secs*), the time in seconds that the timeout will occur (*timeo*), the address in memory of the subroutine that will be called if a timeout occurs (*addr*), the argument to be passed to that subroutine (*pass*), and the address in memory of the C language structure that contains this information (*env*).

When an event is cleared because a timeout was no longer needed, *sendmail* prints:

```
clrevent: ev=env
```

Here, *env* is the address in memory of the C language *struct* that stored the event information. This is the same as the last item printed by `setevent` above.

−d5.6 Show events triggered

The −d5.6 debugging command-line switch tells *sendmail* to print the following information when a timeout occurs:

```
tick: ev=env, func=addr, arg=pass, pid=pid
```

This shows that the event stored in the C language structure, whose address in memory is *env*, has timed out. The subroutine whose address in memory is *addr* will be called with an argument of *pass*. The process identification number of the parent process that asked for the timeout is shown as *pid*.

–d6

Show failed mail

Mail can fail for a wide variety of reasons. The way that *sendmail* handles errors is determined by the setting of the e option in the configuration file. The –d6.1 debugging command-line switch causes *sendmail* to print the error handling mode that is in effect at the time it first begins to handle failed mail:

```
savemail, ErrorMode = char
```

Here, *char* is either: p for print errors; m for mail back errors; w for write back errors; e for special BERKnet processing; or q for "don't print anything."

If the error processing mode is m (for mail back), and if the –d6.1 switch is in effect, *sendmail* prints details about how the message is being returned to the sender.

```
Return To Sender: msg=reason, depth=num, CurEnv=addr
← output of printaddr() here
```

Here, *reason* is a quoted string of text that explains why the mail failed. This may be an SMTP reply string. The *num* is the number of hops (number of times the message has been received by different machines). If this number is too high (see option h in the configuration file), the *reason* is "too many hops." The *addr* is the location in memory of the information about the current envelope. Finally, *sendmail* calls *printaddr()* (see page 615) to print the details of each recipient for the current message.

–d6.5   *The current error state*

The –d6.5 debugging command-line switch tells *sendmail* to print the error state it was in when it finished processing the error that caused the message to fail.

```
state num
```

If *num* is 7 (successful delivery) then nothing is printed. Otherwise the above message is printed and the value of *num* represents one of the states shown in Table 33-5.

Table 33-5: Error Handling States

State	Description
0	Report to sender's terminal
1	Mail back to sender
2	Messages have already been returned
3	Save in `~/dead.letter`
4	Return to postmaster
5	Save in */usr/tmp/dead.letter*
6	Leave the locked queue/transcript files
7	The message has been successfully delivered

–d7

The Queue filename

The *sendmail* program stores mail messages in its queue for a variety of reasons. For example, the s option causes it to queue all messages just to be safe. Also, messages that cannot be delivered because of a temporary lack of resources (or for any correctable reason) are queued for later delivery.

Mail messages are stored in the queue in two parts. A data part contains the body of the message. An information part stores headers and other information about the message. The filenames of the two parts are identical but for the first two letters. A df begins the name of the data part, and a qf begins the name of the information part. A third type of queue file begins with the letters xf, and is a "transcript" file which holds error messages produced during delivery.

To ensure that these filenames do not conflict with the names of files that may already be in the queue, *sendmail* uses the following pattern to create new names:

    qfAA*pid*

Here, *pid* is the process identification number of the incarnation of *sendmail* that is trying to create the file. Because *sendmail* often *fork*(2)'s to process the queue, the *pid* is likely unique, and therefore creates a unique name.

If *sendmail* cannot create a file with that name (because a file with that name already exists) it increments the rightmost A to a B and tries again. It continues this process, incrementing the right from A to ~, and the left from A to Z until it succeeds. If a unique name cannot be found, *sendmail* has failed in its attempt to queue the message. The last filename tried is:

qf~Z*pid*

This name is unlikely to ever appear, because the clocking provides for over 1600 possible unique names. With some versions of *sendmail*, however, it may appear if the queue directory is not writable. For example, with SunOS *sendmail*, the –C command-line switch, when used by a normal user, causes *sendmail* to give up its *root* privilege, thus causing this message to be printed.

Under V8 *sendmail*, the AA that begins the queue identifier is instead three characters. A letter that represents the current hour of the day (using a 24 hour clock) prefixes the AA producing a more unique identifier. That prefix is constructed by adding the current hour to the letter A (thus 00:23 would produce A+0=A, while 15:45 would produce A+15=P). Although it is not recommended, the prefix can be useful when viewing the queue (with the –bp switch) to observe the particular hours, if any, that messages tend to queue. The hour prefix does not increment. The AA increments as described above.

The –d7.1 debugging command-line switch causes *sendmail* to print the portion of the queue name that is common to all the files that constitute a single queued message.

queuename: assigned id AA*pid*, env=*addr*

Here, *sendmail* prints the identifier portion of the filename (the AA, or whatever letters succeeded, and the *pid*) that is common to the df, qf, and xf files. The *addr* is the address in memory of the C language structure that describes the envelope for the mail message that is queued.

–d7.2   *Show assigned queue file name*

The –d7.2 debugging command-line switch tells *sendmail* to print the full filename of the file it just created in the queue directory:

queuename: *letter*fAA*pid*

The first *letter* of the name is either *d*, *q*, or *x*. The *pid* is the process identification number of the *sendmail* process that created the file.

–d7.20   Show queue names being tried

The -d7.20 debugging command-line switch causes *sendmail* to print each filename that it is attempting to try as it clocks the *AA* in the name from *AA* to ~Z.

```
queuename: trying qfAA16391
queuename: trying qfAB16391
queuename: trying qfAC16391
queuename: trying qfAD16391
← and so on
```

–d8

DNS name resolution

Name resolution is the process of determining a machine's IP address based on its fully qualified domain name. This is done using the Domain Naming System (DNS). Here we show the debugging switches used to monitor that service. The process used by *sendmail* to resolve a name is described in Chapter 17, *DNS and sendmail*.

The following categories and levels are for most versions of *sendmail*. For IDA and V8 *sendmail* all are level 1, except the one indicated in the next paragraph which is level 8.

–d8.1   Result of MX search (low level)

Calls to the DNS resolving library routines (*libresolv.a*) ordinarily produce no output of their own. If that library is compiled with DEBUG defined, then calls that include the RES_DEBUG flag causes those routines to print debugging messages to the standard output. The -d8.1 switch causes *sendmail* to include RES_DEBUG with all its calls. Under IDA and V8 *sendmail*, RES_DEBUG is only included when the -d8.8 debugging level (or higher) is specified.

When *sendmail* finds that a hostname is really an MX (mail exchanger) record, it attempts to look up the A record for the host that handles mail receipt. Two problems can manifest themselves with this request. First, the request itself may fail for a variety of reasons, producing the following message:

```
getmxrr: res_search(host) failed (errno=err, h_errno=herr)
```

Here, *host* is the hostname that was being looked up, *err* is the system error number (if any) from *<errno.h>*, and *herr* is the resolver specific error from *<netdb.h>* as shown in Table 33-6.

Table 33-6: Resolver Errors from netdb.h

Value	Mnemonic	Description
1	HOST_NOT_FOUND	Authoritative server not found
2	TRY_AGAIN	Non-authoritative server not found, or server failure
3	NO_RECOVERY	Non recoverable errors, and refusals
4	NO_DATA	Valid name, but no record of requested type

The second problem is that the request may succeed, but return the wrong (not MX) type of information. When this happens, the following message is printed

```
unexpected answer type wrongtype, size bytes
```

The *wrongtype* is an integer which can be found in *<arpa/nameser.h>*.

–d8.2   Call to getcanonname(3)

The routine *getcanonname*(3) in *domain.c* of the *sendmail* source uses the C library routine *gethostbyname*(3) to convert a hostname to a fully qualified domain name. The -d8.2 debugging switch shows the hostname before it is fully qualified with this call.

```
getcanonname(host)
```

–d8.3   Result from getcanonname(3)

Whether the *getcanonname*(3) of -d8.2 above succeeds or fails, the -d8.3 switch causes *sendmail* to print a summary of the result.

```
rcode = status, ancount=howmany, qdcount=questions
```

Here, *status* is one of the exit codes defined in *sysexits.h*. The *howmany* is a count of how many answers were received to the *gethostbyname*(3) call. The *questions* is the number of queries posed in that call.

−d8.5   *Hostname being tried in getcanonname(3)*

The −d8.5 switch causes the *getcanonname(3)* routine to print the hostname it is trying to fully qualify. It shows the name with the local domain appended, without the local domain appended, and at each step in between. Each try is printed as:

```
getcanonname: trying host (type)
                        ↑
                   for V8 only
```

Here, the *type* (for V8 only) is the type of look up, and is either ANY, A, or MX.

−d8.8 (−d8.7 for V8)   *Yes/no response to −d8.5*

The −d8.8 (−d8.7 for V8) switch causes *sendmail* to print a "Yes" or "No" response to each of the "trying" lines printed by −8.5. "Yes" means that the *host* could successfully be fully qualified, "No" means it couldn't.

−d8.20   *Inconsistency in returned information*

Internally, the resolver library (*libresolv.a*) stores host domain names in compressed form (for transmission efficiency). We won't cover the nature of that compression. For our purposes it is sufficient to know that the *sendmail* program calls *dn_skipname(3)* from that library to skip past the compressed part of a host domain name. That call should never fail, but if it does, the −d8.20 switch causes *sendmail* to print:

```
qdcount failure (questions)
```

The *questions* is a count of the number of queries made.

−d9

Make Hostname canonical (IDA and V8 only)

Under IDA and V8 *sendmail*, the −d9.1 switch can be used to watch the calls to *getcanonname(3)* described above. These calls are made from within *daemon.c*. The output looks like:

```
maphostname(host, size) => result
```

Here, *host* is the hostname that is being looked up as *sendmail* attempts to fully qualify that host's name. The *size* is the maximum size in bytes of the buffer intended to hold that name. The *result* is either the fully qualified name (truncated if it exceeds *size*) or the string "NOT_FOUND".

Under V8 *sendmail*, the -d9.1 shows additional information about the hostname canonicalization process. V8 *sendmail* caches hostname information internally to minimize the number of DNS lookups required.

```
host_map_lookup(host) => CACHE canonical
```

Here, *host* is the hostname that is being canonicalized. And *canonical* is that name in canonicalized form that was cached from a prior DNS lookup. If the *host* was not previously cached, *getcanonname*(3), as above, is called and the result (if successful) is cached.

–d9

Trace RFC1413 queries (V8 only)

Under V8 only, the -d9 switch is also used to display *identd*(8) queries. When a network connection is made from a remote host to the local host, the local *sendmail* uses the RFC1413 identification protocol to query the remote host for the name of the user who instantiated the connection. The result of that query is printed as:

```
getauthinfo: result
```

Here, *result* is two pieces of information: an address composed of the username, an @, and the real name of the remote host; and the IP address of that host. For example:

```
getauthinfo: george@fbi.dc.gov [123.45.67.8]
```

If the query fails, nothing is printed.

–d9.3   Show raw RFC1413 reply (V8 only)

The above information is not provided by the remote host in that clear form. Instead, *sendmail* needs to parse the needed information from a raw reply. The -d9.3 debugging switch causes the raw reply to be printed:

```
getauthinfo:  got raw_reply
```

–d9.10   Show RFC1413 query being sent (V8 only)

The -d9.10 debugging switch causes *sendmail* to display its outgoing RFC1413 query:

```
getauthinfo: sent rport, lport
```

Here, the outgoing query is composed of two numbers. The rport is the TCP port on the remote machine where its RFC1413 server is running. The *lport* is the local port number for the original connection.

–d10

Show recipient delivery

When *sendmail* is about to deliver a mail message, it has already resolved three pieces of information: which delivery agent to use, the name of the host that receives the message, and the name of one or more recipients for that message. The –d10.1 debugging command-line switch tells *sendmail* to display information about the recipient to whom it is about to deliver.

```
--deliver, mailer=num, host=`hname', first user=`uname'
```

Here, *num* is the number of the delivery agent selected. Delivery agent numbers can be displayed using the –d0.15 switch. The *hnname* is the name of the host that receives delivery. The *uname* is the name of the first of possibly many users who receive the mail message. The *uname* can either be a single name like *joe* or a full forwarding address like *joe@jokes.are.us.*

When *sendmail* attempts delivery, it may be delivering to multiple recipients. It stores its list of recipients internally as a linked list of C language structures, each of which holds information specific to each recipient. The –d10.1 command-line switch causes *sendmail* to print that information using the *printaddr()* routine (see page 615).

–d11

Show selected deliver agents' Argv (not V8)

Delivery agents are defined by the M configuration file command. Within each such definition there is a list of command-line arguments that are provided to the delivery agent when it is invoked. That list (defined with A= and standing for the C language "argv") is an array of strings, each of which may contain defined macros.

The –d11.1 debugging command-line switch tells *sendmail* to print the argv for the currently selected delivery agent. Any macros in that argument array are expanded before they are printed. If the original `argv` in the delivery agent definition was, for example:

```
A=uux - -r $h!rmail ($u)
```

and if `$h` was the target hostname *otherhost* and if `$u` was a user named *joe*, then the `-d11.1` debugging output would be:

```
openmailer: "uux" "-" "-r" "otherhost!rmail" "(joe)"
```

–d11
Trace delivery (V8 only)

Under V8 *sendmail*, the `-d11.1` debugging switch is used to trace message delivery. For each delivery agent, the following is printed:

```
openmailer: output of printaddr() here
```

The output of *printaddr()* (see page 615) describes the current recipient.

V8 *sendmail* caches the status of remote hosts internally. Before connecting to a remote host, *sendmail* checks its cache to see if that host is down. If it is, it skips connecting to that host. If the `-d11.1` switch is also specified, the status of the down host is printed as:

```
openmailer: output of mci_dump() here
```

See *mci.c* and *sendmail.h* in the source distribution for an explanation of the *mci_dump()* output.

Next, *sendmail* attempts to connect to the remote host for network SMTP mail. If that connect fails, the `-d11.1` debugging switch causes the following to be printed:

```
openmailer: makeconnection => stat=exitstatus, errno=errno
```

Here, *exitstatus* is a numeric representation of the reason for the failure as documented in *<sysexits.h>*, and *errno* is the system-level reason for the error, as documented in *<errno.h>*.

Other errors, such as an attempt to deliver network mail with DAEMON undefined in *conf.h*, or failure to establish a *pipe*(2), or failure to *fork*(2), causes the following to be printed:

```
openmailer: NULL
```

This message (although it contains no information) signals that a more descriptive error message was logged with *syslog*(3) (see Chapter 22, *Logging and Statistics*).

−d11.20   Show tried D= directories (V8 only)

Ordinarily, delivery through a program is done by executing the program from within the queue directory. Under V8 *sendmail,* execution can be from any of a sequence of directories as defined by the D= delivery agent equate. The −d11.20 debugging switch causes each directory to be printed as it is tried:

```
openmailer: trydir dir
```

Here, *dir* is the name of the directory that *sendmail* is about to *chdir*(2) into.

−d12

Show mapping of relative host

In the SMTP RCPT command, *sendmail* is required to express the recipient's address relative to the local host. For domain addresses, this simply means that the address should be RFC822-compliant.

The −d12.1 debugging command-line switch causes *sendmail* to print the address as it appeared before it was made relative.

```
remotename(address)
```

If the *address* is for the sender or recipient and is being processed from a queue file, then nothing more is printed and the *address* is processed by rule set 3. If the delivery agent for the recipient has the F=C flag set and the recipient *address* lacks a domain part, then the domain of the sender is appended and the result processed by rule set 3 again. Sender/recipient-specific rule sets are then applied (1 and S= for the sender, or 2 and R= for the recipient). Next, rule set 4 is applied, and any macros in the result are expanded. Finally, the fully-qualified and relative address is printed as:

```
remotename => `address'
```

−d13

Show delivery

The −d13 debugging command-line switch causes *sendmail* to display information about the recipients of each mail message as it is being delivered. The –d13.1 command-line switch tells *sendmail* to print the mode of delivery (without a trailing newline) before printing the recipient information:

```
SENDALL: mode dmode, sendqueue:
```

Here, *dmode* is one of those shown in Table 33-7. Modes are detailed in Chapter 32, *The Command Line*. Information about all the recipients is then printed using the *printaddr()* routine (see page 615).

Table 33-7: Delivery Modes

Mode	Description
i	Interactive delivery
j	Deliver w/o queueing
b	Deliver in background
q	Queue, don't deliver
v	Verify only (used internally)

Note that V8 *sendmail* provides additional information with the –d13.1 switch.

–d13.3   Check for errors

The –d13.3 debugging command-line switch tells *sendmail* to show each recipient as it is about to be checked for errors. It prints the word Checking, then dumps the information using the *printaddr()* routine (see page 615).

–d13.4   Show who gets error notification (not V8)

If a recipient address is checked and found to have an error (such as an unknown host or an unknown user), the –d13.4 debugging command-line switch causes *sendmail* to print the address of the user who gets notification of the error:

```
Errors to whom
```

Here, *whom* is normally the address of the sender. For a mailing list, it is the owner of the list (if one is defined).

–d14

Show header field commas

Some programs require that addresses in a list of recipients be separated from each other by space characters. This is called an old-style address. RFC822 requires that addressees be separated from each other with comma characters.

There is no –d14.1 information.

–d14.2   *Show header with need for commas*

The –d14.2 debugging command-line switch tells *sendmail* to show each header line that may need spaces converted to commas.

    commaize(*header*: *list*)

Here, *header* is the caption part of a header line, like From:. The *list* is a sequence of one or more addresses. If the o option is specified in the configuration file to allow old-style addresses, then commas are *not* inserted to separate addresses. Otherwise, commas are used to separate the addresses of the *list*.

–d15

Show network get request activity

When *sendmail* runs in daemon mode, it opens a socket on a port, then listens on that socket for incoming SMTP connections. The –d15.1 debugging switch prints information about both of those steps. Note that –d15.1 should usually be combined with –d0.1 or some output may be lost.

Before the socket is opened, *sendmail* prints the following:

    getrequests: port *portno*

This shows that the port numbered *portno* (printed in hexadecimal notation) is used to open the socket. If that open fails, *sendmail* *syslog*(3)'s one of the following messages at LOG_CRIT and exits:

    getrequests: problem creating SMTP socket   ← *V8 sendmail*
    getrequests: can't create socket   ← *all others*

If the open succeeds, *sendmail* attempts to bind to that socket. If it cannot bind, it *syslogs* the following message at LOG_CRIT and exits:

```
getrequests: can't bind socket
```

After it binds, *sendmail* goes into a loop where it listens for and handles incoming SMTP requests. If the listen fails, *sendmail syslog*(3)'s the following message at LOG_CRIT and exits:

```
getrequests: can't listen
```

If *sendmail* starts to listen successfully, the –d15 debugging command-line switch causes it to print the number of the socket on which it is listening:

```
getrequests: sockno
```

This shows that *sendmail* is listening on the socket whose file descriptor is *sockno*.

–d15.2   Incoming connections

In daemon mode, *sendmail* waits for an incoming SMTP connection. When that connection is made, *sendmail* forks, and the child processes the connection from that point on. The –d15.2 switch causes *sendmail* to print a message that confirms it is performing this fork. Note that –d15.2 should usually be combined with –d0.1 or some output may be lost: •

```
getrequests: forking (fd = sock)
```

Here, *sock* is the value of the socket being used for the connection. The –d15.2 switch also causes a message to be printed when the child process exits:

```
getreq: returning
```

–d15.15 (–d15.101 for V8)   Kernel TCP debugging

On kernels that support this feature, the –d15.15 debugging switch (-d15.101 for V8) turns on kernel debugging for the socket opened to handle an incoming SMTP connection. Debugging is turned off when the socked is closed at the end of receipt of the message. The debugging information gathered can be viewed with the *trpt*(8) program.

–d16

Outgoing Connections

When sending mail messages to a site that can be reached via a TCP/IP connection, the `-d16.1` switch causes *sendmail* to print the following message when it is about to make the connection:

```
makeconnection: (host [ipnum])
```

Here, *host* is the name of the host to which the connection is made. The *ipnum* is the IP number (address) of that host. If the connection can be successfully made, the `-d16.1` switch then causes *sendmail* to print:

```
makeconnection: sock
```

Here, *sock* is the socket descriptor that was issued for use with the socket connection.

Note that the `-d16` switch should usually be combined with the `-d0.1` switch, or some output may be lost.

–d16.15 (–d16.101 for V8)   Kernel TCP debugging

See `-d15.15`. The only difference here is that debugging is turned on for the outgoing socket.

–d17

List MX hosts (V8 only)

When *sendmail* readies to deliver mail to a remote host, it looks up that host using DNS to find Mail Exchanger (MX) records. The `-d17.1` debugging switch causes V8 *sendmail* to print the following:

```
hostsignature(host) = records
```

Here, *host* is the host that was looked up with DNS. The *records* is a colon-delimited list of MX records for that host. It might be only the original hostname if no MX records were found.

–d17.9   Show randomizing MX records (V8 only)

MX records have preferences. Delivery is to the record with the lowest preference first, then to each higher preference, in turn, until a delivery succeeds. When two or more preferences are equal, V8 *sendmail* randomizes them so that they are tried in a different order. The order is the same each time, so this is really a pseudo-randomization (actually a hash function).

The −d17.9 debugging switch causes *sendmail* to print the following each time it randomizes:

```
mxrand(host) = hash
```

This shows that the MX records for *host* have been given a hash value of *hash.*

−d18
Show SMTP replies

The process of transmitting (or receiving) a mail message using the SMTP protocol requires *sendmail* to send replies as its side of the dialog. The −d18 debugging switch causes *sendmail* to print each reply that it sends. It prefixes what it prints with three right angle brackets.

```
>>> RCPT To: gw@wash.dc.gov
```

Note that this is the same output as produced with the −v switch.

−d18.100 Pause on SMTP read error

The −d18.100 debugging switch causes *sendmail* to *pause*(2) after a read error when processing the SMTP dialog. The administrator can then use *ps*(8) or *gcore*(8) to examine the *sendmail* binary and attempt to determine the reason for the read error.

−d19
Show ESMTP MAIL parameters (V8 only)

Under Extended SMTP (ESMTP), the MAIL command can be followed by other optional parameters. V8 *sendmail* recognizes two parameters: *size,* which specifies the size in bytes of the incoming message; and *body,* which specifies the nature of the message body (7bit or 8bitmime).

The −d19 debugging switch causes *sendmail* to print the parameters it received:

```
MAIL: got arg param=value
```

The *param* is the parameter (either *size* or *body*). The *value* for *size* is an integer. The *value* for *body* is the text 7BIT (for a message body that has the high bit turned off for all characters) or 8BITMIME for a message body with all eight bits of every character intact.

If the *size* lacks a *value*, the following warning is issued:

```
SIZE requires a value
```

If the *body* lacks a *value*, the following warning is issued:

```
BODY requires a value
```

Any unknown body type causes the following warning:

```
Unknown BODY type value
```

If the parameter is neither *size* nor *body*, the following warning is issued:

```
501 param parameter unrecognized
```

Note that future releases of V8 *sendmail* may use -d19 to trace additional information in *srvrsmtp.c.*

-d20

Show resolving delivery agent: parseaddr()

The -d20.1 debugging switch causes *sendmail* to print each recipient address before it is rewritten by rule sets 3 and 0:

```
--parseaddr(addr)
```

Here, *addr* is the recipient address before it is rewritten, and before any aliasing has been performed on it.

The -d20.1 switch also causes *sendmail* to print information about problems that may exist in recipient addresses. If an address contains any control character that is not an *isspace*(3) character, *sendmail* prints the following message and skips that address:

```
parseaddr-->bad address
```

If an address is empty (that is, composed entirely of an RFC822-style comment), *sendmail* prints the following and skips that address:

```
parseaddr-->NULL
```

After the recipient address has been rewritten by rule sets 3 and 0, and if a delivery agent was successfully selected, *sendmail* prints the result using the *printaddr()* routine (see page 615).

–d21

Trace rewriting rules

The –d21 debugging switch causes *sendmail* to print each step that it takes in rewriting addresses with rules.

There is no –d21.1 information.

–d21.2   Entry to and return from rule sets

The –d21.2 debugging switch causes output to be produced that is identical to the output produced by the –bt rule-testing switch (see Chapter 24, *Rule Sets*):

```
rewrite: rule set num    input: addr
rewrite: rule set num returns: addr
```

Here, *num* is the rule-set number, and *addr* is first, the address (workspace) before rewriting and second, the address after rewriting.

–d21.3   Show subroutine calls

The –d21.3 debugging switch causes *sendmail* to print the rule-set number of each rule set called as a subroutine. Rule sets are called as subroutines using the $> operator in the RHS of rules (see Chapter 25, *Rules*). The output produced looks like this:

```
-----callsubr rset
```

Here, *rset* is the text that was interpreted as the number of the rule set, rather than the numeric value. If the number in the configuration file was, for example, hexadecimal, it prints as 0xf rather than as 15.

–d21.4   Result after rewriting by a rule

If the LHS of a rule matches the workspace, the workspace is rewritten by the RHS of that rule. The –d21.4 debugging switch causes *sendmail* to print the result of a successful rewrite:

```
rewritten as: addr
```

Note that the rewritten address (*addr*) may be the result of rewriting by a subroutine call.

−d21.10   Announce failure

If the LHS of a rule fails to match the workspace, the −d21.10 debugging switch causes *sendmail* to print:

```
----- rule fails
```

−d21.12   Announce success and show LHS

If the LHS of a rule matches the workspace, the −d21.12 debugging switch causes *sendmail* to print:

```
----- rule matches
```

The −d21.12 debugging switch also causes the LHS of each rule to be printed before it is tried:

```
-----trying rule: lhs
```

Remember that rules are pre-expanded when the configuration file is read. As a consequence, defined macros appear as their values in the *lhs*, rather than in their $*letter* form.

−d21.15   Show $digit replacement

The −d21.15 debugging switch causes *sendmail* to print each replacement that is the result of a $*digit* operator in the RHS.

```
$digit: hex=token ...
```

Here, $*digit* is followed by one or more *hex=token* pairs. The *hex* is the address in memory of the *token*, and the *token* is the token from the LHS that is being copied into the workspace. This output can run to many screens.

−d21.35   Show token by token LHS matching

In addition to the rewriting information shown by the switches mentioned above, the −d21.35 switch also shows each and every attempt by the LHS to match the workspace. Each comparison is printed like this:

```
ap=workspace rp=operator
```

Here, ap (for *address part*) indicates the token in the *workspace* that the rule is currently trying to match. The rp (for *rule part*) is the *operator* or token at this point in the LHS that is trying to match the workspace. Note that the *workspace* is a single token from the workspace, and the *operator* is a single operator or token from the LHS of the current rule. A complete comparison of the LHS to the workspace can produce several lines of output for each rule.

This output can be useful for understanding how the pattern-matching algorithm works.

–d22

Trace tokenizing an address: prescan()

Processing of rules requires that all addresses be divided into tokens. The –d22 debugging switch causes *sendmail* to print the various steps it takes when tokenizing an address.

In addition to tokenizing, the *prescan()* routine normalizes addresses. That is, it removes RFC822-style comments, and recognizes quoted strings. Be aware that rules are also viewed as addresses and processed by *prescan()* when the configuration file is being read.

There is no –d22.1 information.

–d22.11   Show address before prescan

The –d22.11 switch causes the address to be printed as it appears before any tokenizing or normalization:

    prescan: *addr*

–d22.12   Show address after prescan

The –d22.11 switch causes the address to be printed as it appears after all tokenizing and normalization:

    prescan==> *addr*

–d22.36   Show each token

The –d22.36 debugging switch causes each token to be printed when found:

    tok=*token*

−d22.101 Trace low-level state machine

For the purpose of tokenizing, an address is viewed as a stream of characters. The process of tokenizing and normalizing is driven by a *state* machine that handles the stream one character at a time. For example, if the current character is @, *sendmail* sees that it has found both the start and end of a token, and so resets its state to begin looking for a new token. But, if the current character is a, and *sendmail* is currently gathering a token, it knows that it should continue to gather. The use of a state machine enables *sendmail* to easily keep track of things like the nesting level of angle brackets, and whether or not a quoted string is present.

The −d22.101 debugging switch causes *sendmail* to output two lines of information. The first shows entry into a state (or continuation of a state):

    c=*char*, s=*state*

Here, *char* is the current character in the stream of characters that makes up the original address. The *state* is a decimal representation of the current state. The list of states and their meanings is shown in Table 33-8.

Table 33-8: States Used by parseaddr( ) to Tokenize Addresses

Decimal	Octal	Name	Description
0	00	OPR	An operator (like $*)
1	01	ATM	An atom (text token)
2	02	QST	Inside a quoted string
3	03	SPC	Chewing up spaces
4	04	ONE	Pick up one character

The second line of output produced by the −d22.101 switch shows the state changing to a new state:

    ns=*nstate*

Here, *nstate* is the new state number, printed in octal with a leading zero.

Note that the level 101 in −d22.101 means that this debugging output is for true experts only.

–d25

Trace "sendtolist"

Each recipient address for a mail message is added one-by-one to an internal list of recipients. The –d25.1 debugging switch causes *sendmail* to print each address as it is added to this list:

```
sendto: list
ctladdr=output of printaddr() here
```

After each is added, those that have selected the local delivery agent are further processed by aliasing and by reading the user's ~/.forward file. Each new address that results from this processing is added to the list, and any duplicates are discarded. (See page 615 for a description of *printaddr()*'s output.)

–d26

Trace recipient queueing

The –d26 debugging switch causes all versions of *sendmail* to print the addresses of recipients as they are added to the *send queue* —an internal list of addresses used by *sendmail* to sort and remove duplicates from the recipient addresses for a mail message. (Note that IDA *sendmail* uses an additional level of –d26.6 to trace *fuzzy* name matching, which we discuss in the next section.)

On entry to the *recipient()* routine, the –d26.1 debugging switch causes *sendmail* to print the raw address (as it appears before adding it to the send queue):

```
recipient: output of printaddr() here
```

Here, *printaddr()* displays the recipient information (see page 615).

Next, after screening for possible errors, *sendmail* compares the new address to others already in the send queue. If it finds a duplicate, it prints the following message and skips the new address:

```
addr in sendq: output of printaddr() here
```

Here, *addr* is the duplicate address. Information about that address is produced with the *printaddr()* routine (see page 615).

−d26.6   Trace fuzzy matching (IDA only)

Before a local address is added to the send queue, IDA *sendmail* checks to see if it exists in the *passwd*(5) file. If it does not, *sendmail* tries to match it from the *gecos* field of that file using *fuzzy* matching.* The −d26.6 debugging switch first causes IDA *sendmail* to print whether or not the local address (username) was found in the *passwd*(5) file:

```
found password entry for "name"
can't find password entry for "name"
```

If the *name* could not be found, and if FUZZY was defined in *conf.c* when compiling IDA *sendmail*, a fuzzy match is next sought.

```
looking for partial match to "name"
```

A fuzzy match is made by comparing *name* to all the *gecos* fields in the *passwd*(5) file. The comparison is word-by-word, with the highest number of exactly matched words considered the best match. When comparing, non-alphanumeric characters separate words, and all letters are normalized to lowercase.

```
Joe.Able      <=>   Ace Wiggins    match == 0
Joe.Able      <=>   Joe Bobbs      match == 1
Joe.Able      <=>   Joe Able       match == 2 best match
```

Each possible match is printed as:

```
matched on level num with "gecos"
```

The *num* is the number (level) of words matched in the current *gecos* field. After all *gecos* fields have been examined, *sendmail* prints its decision (one of the three following):

```
no match, failing...
ambiguous match, failing...
succeeding on level num...
```

−d27

Trace aliasing

The −d27 debugging switch causes *sendmail* to print each step it takes when processing local addresses through aliasing and the `~/.forward` file. Two levels are used. −d27.1 (−d27.3 under IDA *sendmail*) traces basic aliasing. −d27.3 (V8 *sendmail* only) traces the attempts to locate a

---

*V8 *sendmail* also performs fuzzy matching, but uses a different algorithm than that used by IDA. V8 uses −d29 to trace that matching.

˜/.forward file with the forwarding path mechanism defined by the J option.

The -d27.1 (-d27.3 under IDA *sendmail*) switch first causes *sendmail* to print the addresses being aliased:

    alias(*addr*)

Here, *addr* is the address about to be aliased. Note that it may already be the result of previous aliasing. If the *addr* can be aliased, its transformation is printed as:

    addr (*host, user*) aliased to *newaddr*

Here, *addr* is the address before aliasing and the *newaddr* is the new address that resulted from successful aliasing. The *host* and *user* are the host- and username from the recipient part of the envelope.

If the *addr* cannot be aliased, nothing is printed. If the *aliases* database cannot be opened, *sendmail* prints:

    Can't open *aliasfile*

Here, *aliasfile* is the full pathname of the *aliases*(5) file, as declared by the A option.

The -d27.1 (-d27.3 for IDA *sendmail*) debugging switch also causes *sendmail* to print the following message when it is attempting to read the user's *˜/.forward* file:

    forward(*user*)

If the *user* has no home directory listed in the *passwd*(5) file, *sendmail* issues the following message with a *syslog*(3) level of LOG_CRIT:

    forward: no home

–d27.2   Include file (V8 only)

The -d27.2 debugging switch causes each :include: and *˜/.forward* filename to be printed before each is opened for reading.

    include (*file*)

–d27.3   Forwarding path (V8 only)

Under V8 *sendmail*, the –d27.3 debugging switch causes each path for a possible *.forward* file to be printed before it is tried:

```
forward: trying file
```

Here, *file* is each file in the path of files declared by the J option.

–d27.4   Print not safe (V8 only)

A ~/.forward file must be owned by the user or by root. If it is not, it is considered unsafe and *sendmail* ignores it. The –d27.4 switch causes *sendmail* to print a message describing any such file it finds unsafe:

```
include: not safe (uid=uid)
```

Note that a file is considered unsafe if it lacks all read permissions.

–d28
Trace user database transactions (V8 only)

The BSD 4.4 distribution of UNIX includes programs and library routines for managing information about user accounts. (Note that these are experimental and still in development.) The *udb*(3) library contains routines for accessing that user information. V8 *sendmail* can be compiled to use the *udb*(3) database by defining USERDB in *conf.h*.

If an address is selected by rule set 0 for delivery with the `local` delivery agent and remains local after aliasing, it is looked up in the user database. The –d28.1 debugging switch is used to watch the interaction between *sendmail* and *udb*(3):

```
expand(addr)
```

Here, *addr* is the output of the *printaddr()* routine (see page 615). Similarly, the sender is looked up to correct information like the return address:

```
udbsender(login)
```

Here, *login* is the login name of the sender. If the sender is found in the database, *sendmail* prints:

```
udbsender ==> login@defaulthost
```

Here, *login* may be a new login name. The *defaulthost* is either the site-wide host for all reply mail as defined in the user database, or the default destination host for a particular user.

–d28.2   Show no match (V8 only)

The –d28.2 debugging switch causes *sendmail* to print any failures in lookups:

```
expand: no match on login
udbsender: no match on login
```

The first line above shows that the local recipient was not found in the user database. The second shows that the sender was not found.

–d28.4   Show result of look up (V8 only)

The –d28.4 debugging switch causes *sendmail* to print the result of its attempt to open (initialize) each database. There are four possible results:

1. If the database is on another machine, and if that machine is not currently available, *sendmail* prints:

    ```
    REMOTE: addr host, timeo timeout
    ```

    Here, *host* is the canonical name of the host that was unreachable, and *timeout* is the time-out (in seconds) that may have expired.

2. If a file on the local machine contains the information sought, *sendmail* prints:

    ```
    FETCH: file fname
    ```

    Here, *fname* is the name of the local file.

3. If a mail message should be sent to another host for delivery, *sendmail* prints:

    ```
    FORWARD: host hostname
    ```

    Here, *hostname* is the full canonical name of the host that takes delivery.

4. An unknown result causes the address to remain unchanged and the following message to be printed:

    ```
    UNKNOWN
    ```

–d28.16   MX records for forward host (V8 only)

If a lookup is for a forwarding host (FORWARD above), and the forwarding host has MX records, the –d28.16 debugging switch causes those records to be printed.

```
getmxrr(host): number
    first MX record here
    second MX record here
    ... etc
```

Here, *host* is the name of the host to which the lookup is forwarded. The *number* is the number of MX records found. That line is then followed by *number* MX records for that host.

-d29
Special rewrite of local recipient (V8 only)

With a level 2 or greater configuration file (see the V configuration command), V8 *sendmail* passes the user part ($u) of local recipient addresses through rule set 5 as a hook to select a new delivery agent. Rule set 5 is called if the address is unchanged after all aliasing (including the `~/.forward` file). The -d29.1 debugging switch causes the address to be printed as it appears before the rule set 5 rewrite:

```
maplocaluser: output of printaddr() here
```

Information about the address is printed with the *printaddr()* routine (see page 615). The output of *maplocaluser()* becomes the input to *recipient()*, so the result of rewriting can be seen by using the -d26.1 debugging switch in combination with this one.

Note that if rule set 5 is undeclared in the configuration file, this secondary processing is skipped.

-d29
Watch fuzzy match (V8 only)

The -d29 debugging switch (described for rule set 5 above) is also used by V8 *sendmail* to trace *fuzzy* matching. Fuzzy matching is the attempt to match a local recipient name to one of the names in the *gecos* field of the *passwd*(5) file (or NIS map).

There is no -d29.1 information.

–d29.4   Trace fuzzy matching (V8 only)

The –d29.4 debugging switch causes the process of fuzzy matching to be traced.

```
finduser(name)
```

Here, *name* is an address in the form of a local user address, without the host part. The *name* is first looked up in the *passwd*(5) file on the assumption that it is a login name. If it is found, *sendmail* prints:

```
found (non-fuzzy)
```

If it is not found, the entire *passwd*(5) is searched, to see if *name* appears in any of the *gecos* fields. This search is done only if MATCHGECOS was defined when *sendmail* was compiled, and if the G option is true. If MATCHGECOS was undefined, the search ends and the not-found *name* causes the mail to bounce. If the G option is false, *sendmail* bounces the message and prints the following:

```
not found (fuzzy disabled)
```

If the G option is true, the *gecos* fields are searched. But before the search starts, any underscore characters (and the character defined by the B option) that appear in *name* are converted to spaces. Then, in turn, each *gecos* field has the full name extracted (and & converted to the login name). The two are then compared in a case-insensitive fashion. If they are identical, *sendmail* prints:

```
fuzzy matches gecos
```

If all *gecos* fields are compared and no match is found, *sendmail* bounces the message and prints the following:

```
no fuzzy match found
```

–d30

Trace processing of header

When *sendmail* reads a mail message, it first collects (reads) the header portions of that message (everything up to the first blank line), and places the result into a temporary file in the queue directory. While processing the header, if the f option (save "From ") is not set, the UNIX-style "From " header is removed, and the important information in it is saved for later use.

The -d30.1 debugging switch causes *sendmail* to print the following succinct message when it finds the end of the header portion of a mail message:

    EOH

If end-of-headers was caused by a `Message:` or `Text:` header, then the
rest of the header portion of the message is ignored.

–d30.2   Eat from

When *sendmail* strips (eats) the UNIX-style, five-character "`From `" header
from a mail message, it tries to extract (and save) the date from the header.
The -d30.2 debugging switch causes *sendmail* to print the *field* portion
of the header as it appears before the date is extracted:

    eatfrom(*field*)

–d30.3   Add Apparently-To:

If the header of a mail message lacks recipient information (lacks all of the
`To:`, `Cc:`, and `Bcc:` header lines), then *sendmail* adds an `Appar-
ently-To:` header line and puts the recipient's address from the envelope
into the field of that line. The -d30.3 debugging switch causes *sendmail*
to print that it is adding an `Apparently-To:` header:

    Adding Apparently-To: *recipient*

Here, *recipient* is the address of the recipient as taken from the envelope of
the message.

-d31

Show entry into chompheader()

Header lines from the configuration file and from mail messages are processed by the *chompheader()* routine before they are included in any mail
message. Headers and *chompheader()* are discussed in Chapter 31,
Headers.

There is no -d31.1 information.

–d31.6   Entering chompheader ( )

The -d31.6 debugging switch shows each header as it appears when it enters the *chompheader*( ) routine:

```
chompheader: line
```

Here, *line* is the exact text of the original header before processing.

Unfortunately, there is no debugging switch that allows the result of this processing to be viewed.

–d32

Show received headers

The -d32.1 debugging switch causes *sendmail* to print the header lines that it collected from a received mail message:

```
----- collected header -----
  ← header lines here
---------------------------
```

Each header line is printed as the header name on the left (capitalized to appear attractive), a colon, and the value for that header on the right. This provides a way to see how the capitalization algorithm works. Note that V8 *sendmail* preserves the original capitalization.

–d33

Watch crackaddr( )

The *crackaddr*( ) routine's job is to find an e-mail address amidst other non-address text. For example:

```
gw@wash.dc.gov (George Washington)  → crackaddr( ) → gw@wash.dc.gov
```

The -d33.1 debugging switch causes *sendmail* to print the potential address prior to cracking and, after that, the address it found:

```
crackaddr (potential)
crackaddr=>`addr'
```

Chapter 31, *Headers*, describes the legal ways that addresses can be placed within other text.

-d35

Show macro definition/expansion

The reasons particular values are assigned to macros can be mysterious. The -d35.9 command-line switch causes macro value assignments to be displayed as they happen. The -d35.24 command-line switch also causes the use of macro values (macro expansion) to be displayed.

There is no -d35.1 information.

-d35.9   Macro values defined

The -d35.9 debugging command-line switch causes *sendmail* to print each macro as it is defined. The output looks like this:

    define(X as "value")

Here, the *X* is the macro's name (a single character), and the *value* is the value (text) assigned to the macro.

Although all macro names have the most significant bit cleared (set to 0), that clearing happens after the above output is displayed. As a consequence, 8-bit macro names may be displayed in unexpected ways, even though they are stored properly internally.

-d35.24   Macro expansion

Macros included in text must be translated into values (expanded), so that the values may be used. The -d35.24 command-line switch tells *sendmail* to display such text both before and after the macros in it have been expanded. The "before" looks like this:

    expand("text")

For example:

    expand("$w.$D")

The *text* (here $w.$D) may be any ASCII string. In it, special characters like the newline character are printed in C language, backslash-escaped notation (like \n). Macros are printed either with the $ prefix (like $w above with V8 *sendmail*), or some other prefix (IDA uses ^Aw.^AD, SunOS uses /w./D, others use the archaic \001w.\001D notation).

Expansion is performed only on defined macros (using the $ prefix), and on macro conditionals (where one of two values is used, depending on whether a macro has a value or not, like $?x$x$|nobody$.). Under IDA and V8 *sendmail*, the $& prefix (deferred expansion) is also expanded.

After the first (leftmost) macro or conditional is expanded in *text, sendmail* prints the transformed text as shown below:

```
expanded ==>  "text"
```

For example:

```
expanded ==>  "wash.$D"
```

If there are any unexpanded macros or conditionals remaining in *text*, this expanded process is *recursively* repeated, until everything that can be expanded has been expanded. This process of recursion allows macros to have other macros as their values.

–d36

Show processing of the symbol table

The symbol table is a block of memory that contains information about all the symbolic names used by *sendmail*. Symbolic names are: delivery agent names (like `local`), aliases, and macros. Under V8 *sendmail,* database classes and hostnames are also symbolic names.

There is no `–d36.1` information.

–d36.5   Trace processing by stab( )

Symbols are placed into the symbol table with the *stab( )* routine. That routine is also used to see if a symbol has already been inserted, and if so, to obtain its value. The `–d36.5` debugging switch causes *sendmail* to print the following upon its entry into the *stab( )* routine:

```
STAB: name type
```

Here, *name* is the symbolic name to be inserted. The *type* is one of the values listed in Table 33-9.

Table 33-9: Types of Symbols Recognized by stab( )

Type	Mnemonic	Description
0	ST_UNDEF	Undefined type
1	ST_CLASS	Class (from C and F configuration commands)
2	ST_ADDRESS	An address in parsed format
3	ST_MAILER	A delivery agent (from M configuration command)

Table 33.9: Types of Symbols Recognized by stab ( ) (continued)

Type	Mnemonic	Description
4	ST_ALIAS	An alias
5	ST_MAPCLASS	A database class (V8 K command)
6	ST_MAP	Function that handles a class
7	ST_HOSTSIG	Host MX signature (V8 only)
8	ST_NAMECANON	Cached canonical name (V8 only)
16	ST_MCI	SMTP connection status (V8 only)*

* This is the base (offset) of types 16 through 16+n, where n is the maximum number of connections as defined with the k option.

If *stab( )* is being used to insert a symbol, the above output is concluded with:

```
entered
```

If *stab( )* is being used to look up a symbol, one of the two following messages is printed:

```
not found
type type val hex hex hex hex
```

If found, four hexadecimal digits are printed, which show the first four bytes of the value.

–d36.9   Show hash bucket

A hashing algorithm is used to make the symbol table more efficient. The –d36.9 debugging switch is used to see the hash value selected for any given symbol:

```
(hfunc=hash)
```

The number of hash-table buckets possible is limited by STABSIZE, as defined in *stab.c.**

---

*You can experiment with different hashing algorithms by modifying the code in *stab.c.*

–d37

Trace setting of options

Options can be set on the command line or in the configuration file. The –d37.1 debugging switch allows you to watch each option being defined. As each is processed, the following message is first printed, without a trailing newline:

```
setoption: opt=val
```

Here, *opt* is the option name (a single character) and *val* is the value being given to that option. If the option has already been set from the command line and is thus prohibited from being set in the configuration file, *sendmail* prints:

```
(ignored)
```

A newline is then printed, and the job is done. If defining the option is permitted, *sendmail* next checks to see if it is *safe*. If it is not, *sendmail* prints:

```
(unsafe)
```

If it is unsafe, *sendmail* checks to see if it should relinquish its *root* privilege. If so, it prints:

```
(Resetting uid)
```

A newline is then printed and the option has been defined. Options are covered in Chapter 30.

–d37.2 (–d37.8 for V8)   Trace adding of words to a class

The adding of words to a class (C or F configuration commands) can be traced with the –d37.2 (for IDA, or 37.8 for V8) debugging switch. Each word is printed like this:

```
word added to class num
```

The *word* is the word added. The *num* is the class name (a letter) represented as an integer.

–d39

Display %digit database mapping (V8 only)

When the RHS of a rule matches an entry in a database map with $(and $), that entry replaces the key. If the entry contains %*digit* literals, they are replaced by corresponding $@ values in the RHS (see Chapter 29, *Database Macros*).

The −d39.1 debugging switch causes V8 *sendmail* to print the entry and any replacement values:

```
map_rewrite(entry), av = value1
        value2
...etc
```

After the RHS is rewritten (after all the $@ values have replaced all the %*digit* literals), *sendmail* prints the result:

```
map_rewrite => rewritten RHS here
```

−d40
Trace processing of the queue

There are two aspects of the queue that are traced using the −d40.1 debugging command-line switch: the placing of a mail message into the queue and the processing of queued files.

When a mail message is placed into the queue, its qf file is written as a tf temporary file; then, that temporary file is closed and renamed to be the qf file. The −d40.1 debugging command-line switch causes *sendmail* to announce that it is beginning that process by printing the queued message's identifier:

```
queueing AA123245
← for each recipient, output of printaddr() here
```

Next, *sendmail* prints complete information about each recipient for the message using the *printaddr( )* routine (see page 615).

When *sendmail* processes files in the queue, it first pre-reads all the qf files and sorts the jobs by priority. After the list has been sorted, the −d40.1 debugging command-line switch causes *sendmail* to print that list, one message per line, in the following format:

```
qfident: pri=priority
```

Each line in the list begins with the name of the qf file. The *ident* is the unique identifier shared by all the files that compose a queued message. The *priority* is the value of the qf file's P line.

After the sorted list of messages has been processed, and if there are any messages in that list, *sendmail* then attempts to deliver each of the messages in the order that it appears in the list. The −d40.1 debugging switch causes *sendmail* to print the following line of information for each message processed.

```
dowork: qfident pri priority
```

Here, *ident* is the unique identifier, and *priority* is the value of the qf file's P line.

–d40.4   Show qf file lines as they are read

The qf file is composed of individual lines of information (see Chapter 19, *The Queue*). The –d40.4 debugging switch cause *sendmail* to print each of those lines as it is read:

```
+++++ Xtext
```

Each line begins with five plus characters. The qf file's *key* letter (here *X*) follows, then the rest of the *text* that made up that line. In the qf file, indented lines (lines that begin with a space or tab character) that immediately follow the key line are appended to that key line. Those joined lines are printed after they are joined. Note that the lines of the qf file are printed before they are processed by *sendmail*. An error in a line is printed after the line is printed.

–d40.5   Show controlling user

To ensure secure handling of delivery, recipient addresses that are either a file or a program require that *sendmail* perform delivery as the owner of the file or program rather than as *root*. A file address is one that begins with a / character. A program address is one that begins with a | character. Both characters are detected after quotation marks have been stripped from the address.

The –d40.5 debugging command-line switch causes *sendmail* to print one line of information when the controlling user is set and another when the controlling user is reset (see Appendix A, *The qf File Internals*). When the controlling user is set, *sendmail* prints the following:

```
Set controlling user for `item' to `user'
```

Here, *item* is the name of the file or the name of the program. If an attempt was made to set the controlling user from an empty address, *item* prints as <null>. The *user* is the login name of the owner. If that login name cannot be found, *user* becomes the name of the user specified by the u option in the configuration file.

After the file or program has been delivered, *sendmail* needs to reset its identity back to what it was previously. The -d40.5 debugging command-line switch causes *sendmail* to show that resetting has taken place:

```
Restored controlling user for `addr' to `user'
```

Here, *addr* is the recipient address for which the controlling user is being reset. The *user* is the login name of the user to which *sendmail* is resetting its identity.

-d41

Show reason queue failed

The *sendmail* program is silent if it cannot open a queued message's qf file. The -d41 switch allows it to complain.

There is no -d41.1 information.

-d41.2   Cannot open qf

The -d41.2 debugging switch causes *sendmail* to print the reason the open failed:

```
orderq: cannot open qfname (err)
```

Here, *qfname* is the name of the qf file that could not be opened. The *err* is the number of the error (as defined in *<errno.h>*) that caused the open to fail.

-d42

Trace caching (V8 only)

V8 *sendmail* can be configured (with the k option) to maintain open SMTP connections to a few other hosts. The -d42 debugging switch causes *sendmail* to print information about the status of those connections.

Note that there is no -d42.1 information.

–d42.2   Show connection checking

Before making a new SMTP connection, *sendmail* checks to see if it already has one established. The –d42.2 debugging switch causes *sendmail* to print the result of that check.

```
mci_get(host mailer): mci_state=state, _flags=flag, _exitstat=
stat, _errno=err
```

Here, the *host* is the name of the host to which the connection is to be made, and the *mailer* is the name of the delivery agent. The *state* is the status of the current SMTP connection (if there is one); it is one of the values shown in Table 33-10.

Table 33-10: mci_get() Connection States

State	Mnemonic	Description
0	MCIS_CLOSED	No traffic on this connection
1	MCIS_OPENING	Sending initial protocol
2	MCIS_OPEN	Connection is open
3	MCIS_ACTIVE	Message (DATA) being sent
4	MCIS_QUITING	Running SMTP quit protocol
5	MCIS_SSD	SMTP service shutting down
6	MCIS_ERROR	I/O error on connection

The *flag* describes the overall status of the connection. It can have one or more values from those shown in Table 33-11. where those values are ORd together.

Table 33-11: mci_get() Status Flags

Flag	Mnemonic	Description
001	MCIF_VALID	If set, this entry is valid
002	MCIF_TEMP	If set, don't cache this connection
004	MCIF_CACHED	If set, connection is currently in open cache

The *stat* is the exit status of the last delivered mail message to this connection. It is one of the values defined in *<sysexits.h>*. The *err* is the value of the last system error (if any), as defined in *<errno.h>*.

–d45

Show envelope sender

The –d45.1 debugging switch causes *sendmail* to print the current form of the envelope sender address, before it has fully rewritten that address into its final form:

```
setsender(addr)
```

If the *addr* is empty (as would be the case if the sender were being gathered from the header), *sendmail* prints NULL. The final envelope sender address is placed into the defined macro $f. See Chapter 27, *Defined Macros*, for a description of that macro and the process used by *sendmail* to set the sender's address.

–d50

Show envelope being dropped

Deallocating an envelope frees that envelope's C language structure for future reuse. Deallocation also causes all the queued files for that mail message to be removed (except as possibly prevented by the –d51 switch described in the next section). An envelope is deallocated after its mail message has been delivered to all recipients (including any failed deliveries).

The –d50.1 debugging switch causes *sendmail* to print information about each envelope that is being deallocated.

```
dropenvelope loc id=ident flags=e_flags
```

This output shows the address in memory for the envelope's C language structure (*loc*), the queue identifier (*ident*, as used to name queued files), and an octal representation of the envelope flags (see page 622).

Note that if a Return-Receipt: header was in the message, and delivery was to at least one local recipient, the process of deallocation also causes acknowledgment of delivery to be returned to the sender and triggers error returns.

–d51

Trace unlocking and unlinking

The **xf** file (one of the files that form a queued mail message) holds error messages generated by a delivery agent. The last line of text in this file is made the value of the **E** line in the **qf** file (see Appendix A, *The qf File Internals*). Ordinarily, the **xf** file is removed after that error line is saved.

Note that there is no **–d51.1** information.

–d51.4 (–d51.104 for V8)   Prevent unlink of xf file

The **–d51.4** (**-d51.104** for V8) debugging switch prevents *sendmail* from removing the **xf** file. If mail continually fails, this switch can be used to save all error messages instead of just the one that is usually saved in the **qf** file.

–d51.4   Show queue entries being unlocked (V8 only)

The **–d51.4** debugging switch causes V8 *sendmail* to print the following each time an envelope is unlocked in the queue:

```
unlockqueue(ident)
```

Here, *ident* is the queue identifier.

–d52

Disconnect from controlling TTY

When *sendmail* runs as a daemon, it must disconnect itself from the terminal device used to run it. This prevents arbitrary signals from killing it, and prevents it from hanging (on a dial-in line waiting for carrier detect, for example).

The **–d52.1** debugging switch shows *sendmail* disconnecting from the controlling terminal device:

```
disconnect: In fd Out fd
```

For both its input and output connections, the *fd* is a decimal representation of the file descriptor number. If the **L** logging level option is greater than 11, *sendmail syslog*(3)'s the following message to show that it has disconnected:

```
in background, pid=pid
```

Here, *pid* is the process identification number of the child process (the daemon).

−d52.5   *Prevent disconnect from controlling tty*

The −d52.5 debugging switch prevents *sendmail* from disconnecting from its controlling terminal device. To show that it is skipping the disconnect, it prints:

```
don't
```

This debugging switch is useful for debugging the daemon. Note that −d52.5 prevents the detach, but allows the daemon to *fork*(2). This differs from the behavior of the −d0.1 switch.

−d53

Show file closing (V8 only)

Ordinarily, files are closed silently. The −d53 debugging switch causes V8 *sendmail* to announce each close attempt.

There is no −d53.1 information.

−d53.99   *Trace xclose()*

Under V8 *sendmail*, the −d53.99 debugging switch can be used to observe file closings. Just before the file is closed, *sendmail* prints:

```
xfclose(fp)  what file
```

Here, *fp* is the file pointer for the open file, printed in hexadecimal. The *what* is an indication of the internal function that requires the close (like savemail or mci_uncache). The *file* is the name of the file to be closed.

If the close fails, the following is also printed:

```
xfclose FAILURE: why
```

Here, *why* is the text corresponding to the error value returned by *fclose*(3) (see *sys_errlist*(3)).

XLA from contrib (V8 only)

See the XLA package in the *contrib/xla* directory as distributed with the V8 *sendmail* source.

Trace use of dbm(3) files (IDA only)

The IDA form of database files is described in Chapter 29, *Database Macros*. The –d60 debugging switch is used to watch IDA *sendmail* interact with its database files.

The –d60.1 debugging switch causes IDA *sendmail* to show its attempt to open a database file. If the file cannot be opened (perhaps because it doesn't exist or because *sendmail* lacks permission), the following message is printed:

```
mapinit(macro) => CAN'T OPEN
```

Here, *macro* is the one-character name of the database macro associated with the file. Database macros are defined with the K option. The database file is opened when the K option is defined. At that time its status (modification time) is saved. Later, when the file is used, a check is made to be sure it hasn't been removed. If it has, *sendmail* prints:

```
mapinit(macro) => FILE_REMOVED
```

If the file still exists, IDA *sendmail* compares the file's modification time to the modification time it saved above. If they differ, *sendmail* prints the following message, closes, and re-opens the database:

```
database 'macro' [path] has changed; reopening it
```

Here, *path* is the pathname of the database file as defined by the K option. Note that IDA *sendmail* tries twice to re-open (or open) a database file, sleeping 30 seconds between each try. The intention is to provide a window of time during which a user can rebuild the database.

If the database is the *aliases*(5) database, IDA *sendmail* also checks to see if the file is locked. If it is, the following message is printed, and *sendmail* waits for the lock to be released:

```
path is locked, waiting...
```

Here, *path* is the full pathname of the *aliases* file, as defined with the A option.

If the database is open and not locked, a lookup is done. First, what is being looked up is printed (with no trailing newline):

```
mapkey('macro', "key", "arg") =>
```

The *key* is looked up in the database defined by the *macro* one-character name. If a $@ replacement argument is present in the rule causing the lookup, its value is printed as *arg*. If it is not present, `---` is printed. If the *key* is not found, *sendmail* prints:

```
NOT FOUND
```

Otherwise, it prints the value associated with the key from the database:

```
value
```

In either case, a newline is then printed. If the original rule included a $@ argument, and if the value included a %s literal, then the argument will have replaced the %s in the above *value*.

–d60.2   Trace $@ argument (IDA only)

The **–d60.2** debugging switch causes IDA *sendmail* to show the process of replacing a $@ argument from a rule with a %s in the database value. If a $@ appeared in a rule, but had no argument (is NULL), an empty string is used in place of the missing argument. If no $@ appears, and one is required, *sendmail* prints the following and skips replacement:

```
[ no arg ] value
```

Here, the *value* from the database is displayed with an unconverted %s in it. If the $@ has a valid (non-NULL) argument, but the *value* doesn't contain a %*character* expression, *sendmail* prints the following message and skips replacement:

```
[ no arg expected ] value
```

If the rule had a non-NULL argument, and if the *value* contained a %s, then the replacement is made using *sprintf*(3). The result of the replacement is printed as:

```
[fmt]  arg => value
```

Here, *fmt* is the %s (or any other % formatter, like %d) that appeared in the value. The *arg* is the argument for $@ from the rule and the *value* is the result of the *sprintf*(3).

IV

Appendices

A

The qf File Internals

The `qf` file holds all information about a queued mail message that is needed to perform later delivery of that message. The information in and the look of that file changes from release to release of *sendmail*. We document here the Version 5 contents of the `qf` file, with notations showing IDA and V8 changes.

This appendix must be taken with a proverbial grain of salt. The internals of the `qf` file are essentially an internal interface to *sendmail*, and as such are subject to change without notice. The information offered here is intended only to help debug *sendmail* problems. It is *not* intended (and we strongly discourage its use) as a guide for writing files directly to the queue.

The `qf` file is line-oriented, containing one item of information per line. Each line begins with a single uppercase character (the *code letter*) which specifies the contents of the line. Each code letter is followed, with no intervening space, by the information appropriate to the letter. The complete list of code letters is shown in Table A-1.

Table A-1: qf File Code Letters

Letter	Meaning	How Many
B	Body type (V8 only)	At most one
C	Controlling user	At most one per recipient
D	Data filename	Exactly one
E	Errors to	Many
F	Flag bits (V8 only)	Many

Table A.1: qf File Code Letters (continued)

Letter	Meaning	How Many
H	Header definition	Many
M	Message (reason queued)	At most one
P	Priority (current)	At most one
R	Recipient address	Many
S	Sender address	Exactly one
T	Time created	Exactly one
$	Restore macro value (IDA and V8 only)	At most one each

Some code letters may appear only once in a qf file while others may appear many times. Any line that begins with a tab or space character is joined to the line above it. Empty lines are ignored. The order that these lines appear in the qf file is important for the *mailq* command to work properly.

We discuss the individual lines in the qf file by code letters. Each letter is presented in alphabetical order.

B line
Message body type (V8 only)

The message body type is described under the -B command-line switch. The B line in the qf file stores whatever the body type was set to, either from the command line or by the SMTP MAIL command. The two usual body types are 8BITMIME or 7BIT.

The form of the B line is:

```
Btype
```

There must be no space between the B and the *type*. If the *type* is missing, the body type becomes the character value zero. If the entire B line is missing, the default is 7BIT.

C line
Set controlling user

The *sendmail* program usually runs with *root* privilege. To prevent potential security violations, it must take special precautions when addresses in the qf file result from reading a ˜/.*forward* or :include: file. When such an address is to be placed into the qf file (whether as a recipient's address in an R line or as an error recipient's address in an E line), *sendmail* first places a C line (for Controlling user) into the file, and then the recipient's address. The C line specifies the owner of the ˜/.*forward* or :include: file.

```
Cgeorge
R/u/users/george/mail/archive
Cben
R|/u/users/ben/bin/mailfilter
```

Here, when *sendmail* later delivers to the recipients in this qf file, it first converts its user identity to that of the user george, then resets itself back to being *root* again. The same process repeats with the next recipient, except that *sendmail* changes from *root* to ben and back again.

The form of the C line in the qf file is:

```
Cuser:alias
      ↑
      V8 only
```

The C must begin the line and be immediately followed by *user*, with no intervening space. The *user* is the login name of the owner of the ˜/.*forward* or :include: file that yielded the address in the next following R or E line. If *user* is missing, or the name is of a user unknown to the system, the identity used is that specified by the u option in the configuration file. Under V8 *sendmail*, an optional : and *alias* may follow. If present, the *alias* gives the address to use for error messages.

There may be only one C line immediately preceding each R and E line. Two C lines in a row have the effect of the second superseding the first.

D line
Data filename

The D line in the qf file contains the name of the file that contains the message body. If the D line is missing, there is no message body. It is possible and legal to send mail that has no message body. Users may elect, for example, to place all message information into the `Subject:` header line, and leave the message body empty.

The form of the `qf` file D line is:

```
Dfile
```

The D must begin the line. The *file* must immediately follow with no intervening space. All text, from the first character following the D to the end of the line, is taken as the name of the file. There is no default for *file*; it must either be present, or the entire D line must be absent.

Immediately after reading the D line, *sendmail* opens the *file* for reading. If that open fails, *sendmail* *syslog*(3)'s the following error message at LOG_CRIT and continues to process the `qf` file:

```
readqf: cannot open dfAA12345
```

There may be only one D line in any `qf` file. Multiple D lines cause *sendmail* to use the last one and to (wrongly) leave the preceding files open.

The *file* may be a relative or an absolute pathname. There is no requirement that it have the same *ident* as the `qf` file, nor that it start with the letters `df`. For example, any of the following three is legal (although only the first is typical):

```
DdfAA12345
D../bodydir/dfAA12345
D/n/ftp/pub/docs/dict.shar.1of9
```

Be aware that *sendmail* attempts to remove the *file* after it has been delivered to all recipients. If *sendmail* is unable to remove the *file*, and if the L (logging) option is greater than 21, *sendmail* *syslog*(3)'s the following warning at LOG_DEBUG:

```
file: unlink-fail #
```

The *file* is the name of the file that could not be removed. The `#` is the error number, as defined in */usr/include/errno.h*.

The D line is ignored when printing the queue. That is, the `df` file is opened only when processing the queue file, not when printing it.

E line

Send errors to

Notification of errors often requires special handling by *sendmail*. When mail to a mailing list fails, for example, *sendmail* looks for the owner of that list. If it finds one, the owner, not the sender, receives notification of the error. To differentiate error notification addresses from ordinary sender and recipient addresses, *sendmail* stores error addresses separately in the qf file, one per E line.

The form of the E line in the qf file looks like this:

```
Eaddr
```

The E must begin the line. One or more addresses may be entered on that same line. White space and commas may surround the individual addresses. Note, however, that *sendmail* places only a single address on each E line. There may be multiple E lines. Each is processed in turn.

Each line is fully processed as it is read. That is, the line is scanned for multiple addresses. Each address found is alias-expanded. Each resulting new address is processed by rule sets 3 and 0 to resolve a delivery agent for each.

If an alias expands to a program or a file (text that begins with a / or | character), that text is sent out in the delivered message's Errors-To: line in that form. This can cause confusion when the message is later processed and bounced at the receiving site.

F line
Saved flag bits (V8 only)

Under V8 *sendmail*, the T option can specify an interval to wait before notifying the sender that a message could not immediately be delivered. To keep track of whether such a notification has been sent, *sendmail* stores the state of its EF_WARNING envelope flag in the qf file. If that flag is set, notification has already been sent.

Error mail messages sent by *sendmail* may occasionally be queued, rather than immediately delivered. The T option notification (above) should not be sent for such mail. If such mail remains in the queue too long, it should be canceled, rather than bounced. V8 *sendmail* saves the state of the EF_RESPONSE envelope flag in the qf file. If that flag is set, the message is an error notification.

The F line is used to save envelope flags for later restoration. Its form looks like this:

```
Fflags
```

Here, the *flags* are both w, which restores (sets) the EF_WARNING flag, and r, which restores the EF_RESPONSE flag. Only those two letters are recognized. Any other letters are silently ignored. These flags may go away at a later date, or new flags may be added without notice.

H line
Header line

The lines of text that form the message header are saved to the qf file, one per H line. Any header lines added by *sendmail* are also saved to H lines in the qf file.

The form of the H line is:

```
Hdefinition
```

The H must begin the line and the *definition* must immediately follow with no intervening space. The *definition* is exactly the same as, and obeys the same rules as, the H commands in the configuration file (see Chapter 31, *Headers*).

When *sendmail* writes header lines to the qf file, it pre-expands macros (replaces expressions like $x with their values) and pre-resolves conditionals ($?, $!, and $.).

The order in which H lines appear in the qf file is exactly the same as the order in which they appear in the delivered message.

M line
The reason message was queued

When a mail message is placed into the queue because of an error during the delivery attempt, the nature of that error is stored in the M line of the qf file. The error is usually prefixed with Deferred:

```
Deferred: reason
```

Delivery can be deferred until a later queue run because of a temporary lack of services. For example, the *reason* may be "remote host is down."

The form of the qf file M line is:

```
Mmsg
```

The M must begin the line. It is immediately followed by the *msg* with no intervening space. The text of *msg* is everything up to the end of the line. The *msg* created by *sendmail* may include the word Deferred:, followed by a reason. The M line must appear before the S line.

If the *msg* is missing, *sendmail* simply prints a blank line rather than a reason when showing the queue with *mailq* or the -bp command-line switch. If the M line is entirely missing, *sendmail* prints nothing.

The maximum number of characters in *msg* is defined by MAXLINE in *conf.h*. It is 1024 for all but IDA *sendmail*, where it is 2048. If *msg* exceeds that number of characters, *sendmail* faults and produces a core dump when printing the queue. (This bug has been fixed in V8 *sendmail*.)

There should be only one M line in a qf file. If there are multiple M lines, only the last is used.

P line
Priority when processed from queue

Not all messages need to be treated equally. Messages that have failed often, for example, tend to continue to fail. When sendmail processes the messages in its queue, it sorts them by priority and attempts to deliver those most likely to succeed first.

When a mail message is first placed into the queue, it is given an initial priority by the number in the P line.

```
P640561
```

The *lower* this number, the more preferentially the message is treated by *sendmail*. Each time *sendmail* attempts to deliver this message and fails, it increments that number.

The initial priority number given to a message is calculated when that message is first created. The formula for the initial calculation is:

```
priority = nbytes - (class * z) + (recipients * y)
```

Where the items in this calculation are:

priority

> Priority number of the message when it is first created. This is the value first stored in the P line of the qf file.

nbytes

> Number of bytes in the total message. That includes the header and the body of the message.

class Value given to this message by the Precedence: line in the header of the message (see Chapter 31).

z   Value of the configuration file z option, which gives a weighting factor to adjust the relative importance of the class.

recipients

Number of recipients to which this message is addressed. This number is counted *after* all alias expansion.

y   Value of the configuration file y option, which gives a weighting factor to adjust the relative importance of the number of recipients.

Each time the qf file is read, the number in the P line is incremented. The size of that increment is set by the value of the Z option. If that option is negative, the logic of "what fails will continue to fail" is inverted.

The form of the qf file P line is:

    Ppri

The P must begin the line. The *pri* is a text representation of an integer value. The *pri* must immediately follow the D with no intervening space. The text in *pri* is converted to an integer using the C library routine *atol*(3). That routine allows *pri* to be represented in text as a signed decimal number, an octal number, or a hexadecimal number.

If *pri* is absent, the priority value used is that of the configuration file Z option. If the entire P line is absent, the priority value is zero.

There should be only one P line in any qf file. Multiple P lines cause all but the last to be ignored.

R line

Recipient's address

The qf file lists all the recipients for a mail message. There may be one recipient or many. When *sendmail* creates the qf file, it lists each recipient address on an individual R line.

The form of the R line in the qf file looks like this:

    Raddr

The R must begin the line. One or more addresses may then be entered on that same line. White space and commas may surround the individual addresses. Note, however, that *sendmail* places only a single address on each R line. There may be multiple R lines. Each is processed in turn.

Each line is fully processed as it is read. That is, the line is scanned for multiple addresses. Each address found is alias-expanded. Each resulting new address is processed by rule sets 3 and 0 to resolve a delivery agent for each.

S line
Sender's address

Each mail message must have a sender. The *sendmail* program can determine the sender in four ways:

- If the sender is specified in the envelope of an SMTP connection, that sender's address is used.

- If the -f command-line argument is used to run *sendmail* and the user running *sendmail* is listed as trusted in the configuration file T command, then the sender's address is the address following the -f.

- If the sender is not specified in the envelope, the address used is that of the user who ran the *sendmail* program. If that user is unknown, the sender is made to be *postmaster*.

- When processing the queue, the sender's address is specified in the S line of the qf file.

The form of the S line in the qf file looks like this:

```
Saddr
```

The S must begin the line. Exactly one address must follow on that same line. White space may surround that address. There may be only one S line in the qf file.

If the *addr* is missing, *sendmail* sets the sender to be the user who ran *sendmail*. If that user is not known in the *passwd* file (or database), *sendmail syslog(3)*'s the following message and sets the sender to be *postmaster*.

```
Who are you?
```

The resulting address is then processed to extract the user's full name into $x. Finally, the sender's address is rewritten by rule sets 3, 1, and then 4.

T line

Creation time

In order to limit the amount of time a message can remain in the queue before being bounced, *sendmail* needs to know when that message was first placed in the queue. That time of first placement is stored in the T line in the qf file. For example:

```
T703531020
```

This number represents the date and time in seconds.

Each time *sendmail* attempts to deliver a message from the queue, it first checks to see if too much time has passed. It adds the T line value to the value specified in the T (timeout) option of the configuration file. If that sum is less than the current time, the message is bounced.

Messages are occasionally left in the queue for longer than the normal time-out period. This might happen, for example, if a remote machine is down, but you know it will eventually be brought back up. There are two ways to lengthen the amount of time a message may remain in the queue.

The preferred way is to create a temporary separate queue directory and move the necessary queued file to that temporary holding place. When the remote site comes back up, you can later process the files in that other queue by running:

```
% /usr/lib/sendmail -oQotherdir -oT30d -v -q
```

Here, the -oQ command-line switch tells *sendmail* to process the queued files in the directory named otherdir instead of the normal queue directory. The -oT command-line switch tells *sendmail* to time-out queued files after thirty days (30d) instead of using its normal time-out period. The -v allows you to watch what is happening, and the -q causes *sendmail* to process the queue.

A second way to extend the life of messages in the queue is to edit the qf file and change the value stored in the T line. Just add 86400 to that value for each day you want to extend. Care is required to avoid editing a file that is currently being processed by *sendmail*.

There is currently no plan to give *sendmail* the ability to rejuvenate queued messages (make old messages appear young).

The form of the T line in the qf file is:

    Tsecs

The T begins the line and the *secs* must immediately follow with no intervening space. The numeric text that forms *secs* is converted to an integer using the C library routine *atol*(3). That routine allows *secs* to be represented in text as a signed decimal number, an octal number, or a hexadecimal number.

If *secs* is absent, or the entire T line is absent, the time value is zero. A zero value causes the mail message to time out immediately.

There should be only one T line in any qf file. Multiple T lines cause all but the last to be ignored.

$ line

Restore macro value (IDA and V8 only)

The *sendmail* program uses the r macro to store the protocol used when *sendmail* first received a mail message. If the message was received using SMTP, that protocol is smtp. Otherwise it is NULL.

The *sendmail* program uses the s macro to store the full canonical name of the sender's machine.

When IDA or V8 *sendmail* creates a qf file, it saves the values of the $r and $s macros in lines that begin with $.

The form of the $ line in the IDA and V8 qf file looks like:

    $Xvalue

The $ must begin the line and the macro's name (the X) must immediately follow with no intervening space. The X is followed (again with no intervening space) by the value of the macro.

If *value* is missing, the value given to the macro is NULL. If the X and *value* are missing, the macro \0 is given a value of NULL. If both are present, the macro specified (X) is given the value specified (*value*).

There may be multiple $ lines. Only the $r and $s macros are considered safe in the qf file. Any other macro causes *sendmail* to give up its *root* privilege.

B

Obscure
Error Messages

A full compendium of all the possible error messages that *sendmail* is capable of producing is beyond the scope of this book. Many error messages are clear and require no further amplification. For example, consider:

```
Cannot fstat filename!: reason
```

Here, *sendmail* has called *fstat*(2) to get information about an open file. The name of the file is *filename*. The *reason* is one of the text messages listed in *<errno.h>*. For *fstat*(2) the only possible reasons are an unlikely mistake made by *sendmail* or a problem with your disk hardware (I/O error). Note that messages prefixed with SYSERR are system errors that are not normally caused by users.

In this appendix, we focus on the more arcane error messages produced by *sendmail*. Specifically, we limit our discussion to those for which the meaning is (sadly) less than obvious.

address overflow

In all but V8 *sendmail*, addresses in the command line are (still) allowed to be of the form:

```
user at host.domain
```

Here the at is literal. The *sendmail* program replaces the at with the @ character and joins the three pieces to form *user@host.domain*. If the result exceeds MAXNAME+2 as defined in *conf.h*, *sendmail* prints the following message and skips that address:

```
address overflow
```

address too long

The process of normalizing an address (removing RFC-style comments, and checking for balanced special characters) requires buffer space to store intermediate results. The size of that buffer is MAXLINE+MAXATOM as defined in *conf.h*. The buffer can overflow because an address is absurdly long. If the buffer overflows, *sendmail* prints the following error and skips that address:

```
Address too long
```

To see the address as it appeared before normalization began, use the -d22.11 debugging switch.

alias too long

The text to the right of the colon in the *aliases* file is processed as a single line of text. When subsequent lines are indented, they are joined to the end of the first preceding non-indented line. The total length of that joined line is limited to BUFSIZ-1 characters, as defined in *<stdio.h>*. If that limit is exceeded, *sendmail* prints the following error and skips processing of the overflow:

```
alias too long
```

Under BSD UNIX and derived systems, BUFSIZ is commonly 1024. Under SysV systems, BUFSIZ is 8196. This limit applies only to *alias* databases built using *dbm*(3) or *ndbm*(3). Databases that use *db*(3) have no imposed limit. Note that these limits are set by the *dbm* and *ndbm* libraries, not by *sendmail*.

bad address

When *sendmail* finds that the right-hand side of an alias in the *aliases* file is improperly formed, it prints the following message and skips that address:

```
address... bad address
```

This message is usually associated with the "Unbalanced" message (see below), although it may simply indicate an address that contains illegal characters. The -d20.1 debugging switch can be used to watch addresses being checked.

buildaddr

Rule set 0 must return the triple of a delivery agent, a host, and a user. If any of the three is missing (other than for the error delivery agent), one of the following errors is printed:

```
buildaddr: no net      ← missing $# part
buildaddr: no host     ← missing $@ part
buildaddr: no user     ← missing $: part
```

This error is printed only when mail is being processed, not when the configuration file is read. It is a serious error requiring immediate repair of a defective rule or rules in rule set 0. Specifically, look for misspelled delivery agents, mis-defined macros, and the misuse of $u.

Also, the error message:

```
buildaddr: unknown mailer agent
```

means that rule set 0 selected a delivery agent named agent with a $#agent, but no corresponding M configuration line exists. For example, Mlocal might be misspelled in rule set 0 as $#local.

cannot alias

The name to the left of the colon in the *aliases*(5) file *must* select the local delivery agent. If any does not, the following error is printed and that alias line is ignored:

```
cannot alias non-local names
```

cannot dup

As part of the process of *fork*ing and *exec*ing a delivery agent, *sendmail* must duplicate file descriptors for the later creation of a pipe. If duplication fails, *sendmail* prints the following message and queues the message for a later delivery attempt.

```
Cannot dup to zero!
```

Duplication can fail because too many file descriptors are already open. If you see this message frequently, consider increasing the maximum number of open file descriptors allowed per process on your system.

cannot exec

The way *sendmail* runs a delivery program is to *fork*(2) and *exec*(2) that program. If the *exec*(2) fails, *sendmail* prints the following message:

Cannot exec *delivery agent*

The *delivery agent* is the name of the program it could not *exec*(2). If the failure was for the `local` delivery agent, the mail message is queued for another attempt at a later time. For all other delivery agents, if the reason for failure was an I/O error, insufficient memory, a process limit having been reached, or too many processes, then the mail message is queued for a later try. Any other reason causes the mail message to be bounced.

cannot open

If no *aliases* file is defined for the `A` option, or if the defined file cannot be accessed, *sendmail* prints the following error and doesn't perform any aliasing.

Cannot open *aliasfile*

If *aliasfile* is `<null>`, then option `A` was undefined. Otherwise *aliasfile* is the full pathname of the *aliases* file that could not be accessed. This check is made only once. If the *aliases* file could not be opened, *sendmail* thereafter presumes it is not to perform aliasing. Consequently, you can't rectify the problem while the daemon is running. Instead you need to kill and restart it for the fix to be recognized.

cannot parse postmaster

When bouncing mail, the user of last resort to receive notification of the failure is *postmaster*. If handling the bounce gets this far and if *postmaster* doesn't select a delivery agent with rule set 0, *sendmail* prints the following error and no notification is sent:

cannot parse postmaster!

cannot parse root

If a mail message has no return address (lacks a sender), *sendmail* uses *root* as the sender's name (*postmaster* under V8 *sendmail*). The sender's address is processed with rule sets 3 then 0 to select a delivery agent for use with bounced mail and the `F=C` of the recipient's agent. If rule set 0 can't select a delivery agent for *root*, *sendmail* prints the following message and tries to deliver the mail message anyway:

```
Cannot parse root!
```

This error indicates either that *root* has an unusual alias, or that your rule set 0 is somehow defective.

cannot resolve

The result of processing by rule set 0 must be a triple that begins with the selection of a delivery agent. A delivery agent is indicated with the $# operator. If anything other than $# is returned by rule set 0, the following message is printed:

```
cannot resolve name
```

The consequences of this message vary depending on what *sendmail* is doing when the error occurs. When rebuilding the *aliases* database, for example, that alias is skipped.

can't parse

When mail is being bounced, *sendmail* uses the value of the macro $n as the address of the sender. That address is usually *mailer-daemon*. If $n is given another value, one that is an unparsable address, the following message is printed:

```
Can't parse myself!
```

An unparsable address is one which, when rewritten by rule sets 3 and 0, fails to select a delivery agent. A null value for $n also produces this error.

Under V8 *sendmail*, with a configuration file level (V command) of 3 or greater, the sender is set to be the special address <>; otherwise, it is set to be the value of $n as above.

deliver: pv overflow

Delivery agent M definitions which use $u in the A= equate should never have any arguments following the $u. Such trailing arguments can cause this message to be printed:

```
deliver: pv overflow after $u for address
```

Here, *address* is the mail recipient address that could not be delivered. The message is bounced. If you see this error, examine all the delivery agent definitions in your configuration file, and look for one that has arguments following the $u.

disk space

When *sendmail* creates a qf queue file, it does so by first creating a copy, writing to that copy, then renaming the copy to be the qf file. The copy is a *tf* queue file. If the disk fills to capacity while writing the *tf* file, *sendmail* prints the following error:

```
452 Out of disk space for temp file
```

The mail message is deleted and bounced. This is a very serious error because it means your queue directory is filling the disk to capacity. Look for large queued mail files (df files), numerous queued messages, and possibly even core dumps of *sendmail.*

Under V8 *sendmail,* the b option can be used to specify a minimum amount of space that should be reserved in the queue for the SIZE parameter of the ESMTP MAIL command. If the space available is less than or equal to that minimum, *sendmail* prints the following message:

```
452 Insufficient disk space; try again later
```

The message is rejected in such a way that the sending agent backs off and waits to deliver later. The same causes should be investigated as for the previous message.

dropenvelope: queueup

For queueing to work, QUEUE needs to be defined in *conf.h.* If it is undefined, and if *sendmail* needs to queue a message, the following error is printed and the mail message is lost:

```
dropenvelope: queueup
```

endmailer wait

At times, *sendmail* calls *wait*(2) to wait for delivery agent to finish execution. If the *wait*(2) call fails, *sendmail* prints the following error and queues the mail message for a later attempt at delivery:

```
endmailer name: wait
```

Here, *name* is the symbolic name of the delivery agent. This error is most likely due to a delivery agent dying before *sendmail* was able to wait, possibly due to a lack of system resources.

errbody

For failed mail, *sendmail* returns the body of the original message to the sender. Any error during the copying of the body to the return mail message produces the following output:

```
errbody: reason
```

The specific *reason* for the error follows on the same line.

expected

If you mistakenly leave the = out of one of your delivery agent equates, *sendmail* complains and skips that delivery agent definition. For example:

```
Mlocal, P/bin/mail, F=rlsDFMmnP, S=10, R=20, A=mail -d $u
        ↑
        = is missing
```

The missing = character above produces one of two possible warnings, depending on the version of *sendmail* you are running:

```
sendmail.cf: line 49: = expected                 ← most sendmails
sendmail.cf: line 49: Mlocal, = expected, not found   ← V8 sendmail
```

from person

The -f command-line switch is used to specify the identity of the sender as part of the command line. Any given mail message may have only one sender specified. Any attempt to specify multiple senders with multiple -f switches yields the following message:

```
More than one "from" person
```

If the identity of the sender is missing from the -f switch, IDA and SunOS *sendmail* prints the following error:

```
No "from" person
```

V8 *sendmail* uses *getopt*(3) to process the command line, so it prints a differing message for the same error:

```
sendmail: option requires an argument -- f
```

getrequests

The *sendmail* daemon needs to establish new TCP/IP connections in order to receive mail over the network. If it is unable to connect, it prints one of the following error messages:

```
getrequests: cannot bind
getrequests: cannot listen
```

These are serious errors, which indicate a misconfigured network or that a second *sendmail* daemon is running.

hostname configuration error

When the remote machine sends its hostname to the local machine in the SMTP HELO command, the local machine compares its name to the remote name to make sure it is not talking to itself. If the two are the same, the local machine issues the following error and closes the connection:

```
host name configuration error
```

The name given in the HELO command is the value of the $j macro. That value *must* be a fully-qualified domain name.

illegal alias

Each local part to the left of the colon in the *aliases*(5) file is processed as though it is an address. Various things can go wrong at this point, each causing a specific error message to be printed. For example, parentheses may be unbalanced, or the address (when tokenized) may produce too many tokens. Each address is processed by rule sets 3 and 0. If any fails to resolve to a delivery agent, the following error is printed:

```
illegal alias name
```

Each such bad address causes the alias to be ignored.

invalid rewrite set

When *sendmail* is compiled, the maximum number of rule sets that can be used is defined in *conf.h* as MAXRWSETS (usually 30, but 100 for V8). If you specify a rule set in the R= or S= equate for a delivery agent that is MAXRWSETS or greater in value, *sendmail* prints the following error message:

```
sendmail.cf: line 53: invalid rewrite set, 30 max
```

The line number and maximum rule set may vary. This error is not fatal. The *sendmail* program prints it, ignores the current delivery agent definition, and continues to run.

invalid numeric domain

When *sendmail* establishes a connection to another machine, it does so by using either a host's name or its IP number. IP numbers are four dot-separated integers surrounded by square brackets, for example:

```
[123.45.67.89]
```

If the closing (rightmost) square bracket is missing, *sendmail* prints the following error and bounces the message as "Host Unknown":

```
Invalid numeric domain spec host
```

This error is most likely a bad address specification by a user, although it can also indicate a defective configuration rule.

I refuse to talk to myself

See "hostname configuration error" above.

local name configuration error

See "hostname configuration error" above.

lost child

During SMTP dialogues *sendmail* may need to *fork*(2) and *wait*(2) for the child process to complete. If the *wait*(2) fails, the following error is printed:

```
task: lost child
```

Here, *task* is one of: SMTP-MAIL, SMTP-VRFY, or SMTP-EXPN.

lost lock

If *sendmail* is compiled with LOCKF defined in *conf.h* (which means to use *lockf*(2) instead of BSD *flock*(2)), it is possible to lose a lock on a file. This can happen because *lockf*(2) requires *sendmail* to briefly relinquish the lock and another process (another *sendmail*) can get the lock during that brief window of time.

```
lost lock
```

This is a warning, not an error. The *sendmail* program recovers gracefully, and no mail is lost.

mail loops back to self

See "hostname configuration error" above.

main: reentered!

The *main*() subroutine of a C language program, like *sendmail*, should execute from the top only once. It is, however, possible for faulty code (like an indirect branch through zero) to cause *main*() to be called a second time.

```
main: reentered!
```

This is a *very serious* error. It most likely is the result of modifying the *sendmail* source without first fully understanding the underlying principles of the program.

makeconnection: funny failure

When making a TCP/IP connection, it is possible (but odd and rare) to get a "Permission denied" error. When V8 *sendmail* gets this error, it prints the following error message:

```
makeconnection: funny failure: addr=address port=port
```

Here, *address* is the IP address of the host to which the connection failed. And *port* is the number of the IP port used. This error is usually associated with *sendmail* trying to connect to a host that is in the process of rebooting.

missing colon

While rebuilding the *aliases* database, *sendmail* checks to see that each line it reads is correctly formed. One check is intended to ensure that the required colon is present:

```
name: alias
```

If the colon is missing, *sendmail* prints the following message and continues to run:

```
missing colon
```

net hang

During the receipt of data SMTP phase (DATA), the message-terminating dot on a line by itself may never arrive. The *sendmail* program times out and prints:

```
net hang reading from host
```

If this happens only for a particular user, suspect that the user's mail does not contain a terminating newline character. If it happens at seemingly random times, suspect network problems, and investigate the success (or lack of success) of other network-based programs like *telnet*(1). This can also indicate a SL/IP connection with a misconfigured MTA.

non-continuation line

While reading the *aliases* file, *sendmail* encountered a line that began with a space or a tab, and which was not preceded by an alias line. This error:

```
non-continuation line starts with space
```

is usually the result of an "empty-looking" line (one that contains only spaces or tabs), that was intended to be an empty line.

openmailer: cannot fork

The way *sendmail* runs a delivery program is to *fork*(2) (make a copy of itself) and *exec*(2) that program. If the *fork*(2) fails, *sendmail* prints the following and continues to run:

```
openmailer: cannot fork
```

The mail message that was being sent is queued, and another attempt to send it is tried later. This usually is caused by a temporary lack of some system resource (like running out of file descriptors, or a full process table).

openmailer: no IPC

If *sendmail* has been compiled without the option to run as a daemon, an attempt to deliver mail through the [IPC] delivery agent fails. That ability is enabled by defining DAEMON in *conf.h* (NETINET or NETISO for V8 *sendmail*). If that ability is not supported, *sendmail* prints the following:

```
openmailer: no IPC
```

This error is not fatal. The *sendmail* program prints this message and continues to run. The mail message is bounced back to the sender. To fix it, either recompile *sendmail* with DAEMON (NETINET or NETISO) defined, or replace the IPC (or TCP) in the P= of the offending delivery agent with a correct symbolic name.

openmailer: pipe

The *sendmail* program sends messages to programs by way of the *pipe*(2) system call. The *sendmail* program then *fork*(2)'s and *exec*(2)'s the delivery program. The *sendmail* program (parent process) then writes to the input side of the pipe and the delivery program (child process) reads from the output side of the pipe. Only a few system problems can cause the establishment of the initial pipe to fail. If those errors occur, *sendmail* prints one of the following warnings and continues to run:

```
openmailer: pipe (to mailer)
openmailer: pipe (from mailer)
```

The mail message that was being sent is queued, and another attempt to send it is tried later. This error is usually caused by a temporary lack of some system resource.

out of memory

As *sendmail* runs, it is continually requesting more memory from the operating system, and giving it back when done. If a request for memory is denied, *sendmail* prints the following error and quits running:

```
Out of memory!!
```

This is a very serious problem. It may indicate that too many processes are running and using up all of the available memory. On Sun systems with *tmpfs*, it may indicate that a swap-mounted file system (like */tmp*) is 100 percent full. In general, a central mail server should have lots of memory, a huge swap space, and supply only mail services.

permission denied

The *sendmail* program tries to prevent unauthorized use of itself or its queue. If you are not *root* and you try to run *sendmail* in daemon mode with **-bd**, *sendmail* prints the following message and refuses to run:

```
Permission denied
```

Another way to see this same message is by attempting to process the queue with **-q**. Only *root* may process the queue. Note, however, that SunOS *sendmail* allows anyone to process the queue. Also note that V8 *sendmail* allows the owner of the queue directory (if other than *root*) to process the queue.

prescan: too many tokens

When evaluating addresses against rules, *sendmail* divides each into its component parts called tokens (or atoms). The parts are stored in an array the size of which is limited to MAXATOM as defined in *conf.h*. If an address or rule contains more than MAXATOM parts, *sendmail* prints the following error message and skips that address or rule.

```
prescan: too many tokens
```

The -d22.36 command-line debugging switch can be used to watch addresses and rules being tokenized.

queuename: cannot create

The *sendmail* program usually runs as *root* or *daemon* when it needs to queue a mail message. Mail wrongly sent with a command line like:

```
mail user -s subject
```

can cause the */usr/ucb/mail* program to think the -s is a recipient rather than a command-line argument. It sorts the recipient list and gives the recipients to *sendmail* like this:

```
-s user subject
```

The *sendmail* program sees the -s as an insecure switch and changes its identity to that of the sender. If the queue directory has narrow permissions, the sender is likely to lack write permission, so an attempt to queue the message fails. The *sendmail* program prints the following error and bounces the mail message:

```
queuename: Cannot create "file" in "directory"
```

Here, *file* is the queue file that could not be created and *directory* is the queue directory. Other bad command-line switches (like -C for testing, without a -oQ/tmp) also cause this error.

readaliases: db put

When adding a new entry to the *aliases*(5) database, the local part to the left of the colon is the key, and the list of addresses to the right of the colon is the contents. Failure to write the key and contents, when using NDBM, produces the following nonfatal error:

```
readaliases: db put (key)
```

If *sendmail* was compiled with DBM, failure is silently ignored. Failure is most likely caused by the total size of key and contents together exceeding 1024 bytes for DBM, or 4096 bytes for NDBM.

recipient names

When *sendmail* is run in a mode that requires recipient addresses to be listed on the command line (see Chapter 32, *The Command Line*), and it finds they are missing, it prints the following error and exits:

```
Recipient names must be specified
```

returntosender: infinite recursion

When *sendmail* bounces a mail message, it tries to return that message to the sender. If the sender address is bad, resulting in a bounce back to itself, infinite recursion becomes possible. The *sendmail* program detects such recursion and prints this error message:

```
returntosender: infinite recursion on address
```

Here, *address* is the bad address that led to the problem. If *address* looks okay, suspect your rule sets. If it looks odd, determine if it is a legal address, and if so, design new rules to correctly handle it. If it is simply garbage, complain (politely) to the *postmaster* at the originating site.

rewrite: expansion too long

Unless the $@ or $: prefix is used to prevent recursion, the RHS of rules continues to rewrite so long as the LHS matches the workspace. A poorly designed rule, like:

```
R$+        $U!$1
```

can recursively rewrite until the result becomes too large for *sendmail* to handle. When this happens, *sendmail* prints the following message and aborts the rewriting:

```
rewrite: expansion too long
```

Always test new rules with the –bt rule-testing switch. If in doubt, use the $: prefix.

rewrite: ruleset out of bounds

A $*digit* operator in the RHS of a rule references operators in the LHS by position. Unfortunately, the mere presence of a $ prefix does not necessarily indicate an operator. Defined macros are expanded when the configuration file is read, so do not count when specifying position. For example:

```
R$A.$B.$c.$-        $1
```

Here, the `$1` in the RHS specifies the `$-` in the LHS because `$A`, `$B`, and `$c` are expanded when the configuration file is read and becomes ordinary text. Referencing an operator that doesn't exist (such as wrongly using `$4` in place of `$1` above) causes *sendmail* to print the following error message and ignore the offending rule:

```
rewrite: ruleset set: replacement out of bounds
```

Here, *set* is the number of the rule set that contained the offending rule. V8 *sendmail* also prints the offending `$digit`:

```
rewrite ruleset set: replacement $digit out of bounds
```

V8 *sendmail* also tries to detect this kind of error when reading the configuration file, and if it does it prints:

```
replacement $digit out of bounds
```

savemail: HELP!!!!

The *sendmail* program tries its best to return failed mail. It first tries to return it to the sender. If that fails, it tries to send it to *postmaster*. If that fails (for V8 *sendmail*) it tries to save it to */usr/tmp/dead.letter*. Other versions may take additional steps to save the message. If all attempts fail, *sendmail* prints the following error and the mail message is lost:

```
savemail: HELP!!!!
```

Something is seriously wrong.

sender already specified

During an SMTP exchange of mail, the sending site uses the "MAIL from:" command to specify the address of the sender. Only a single sender is allowed for any given mail message. If a second "MAIL from:" is issued before the current mail message is complete, *sendmail* prints the following error message and ignores the second sender specification:

```
5.xx Sender already specified
```

setsender: can't even parse

The *sendmail* program rewrites the envelope sender's address with rule sets 3 and 0 to select a delivery agent for bounced mail. If the sender address does not select a delivery agent, *sendmail* changes that address to be *postmaster* and tries again. If that fails, *sendmail* prints the following error message:

```
setsender: can't even parse postmaster!
```

This indicates an error in the rewriting rules.

syntax error

If a header definition contains `?flags?` and the rightmost `?` is missing, or if the colon is missing from the definition, *sendmail* prints the following error and skips that definition.

```
chompheader: syntax error, line "line"    ← all but
header syntax error, line "line"          ← V8 sendmail
```

Here, the *line* is the header definition from the configuration file that caused the problem.

time out

When *sendmail* reads from anything that may time out, such as an SMTP connection, it sets a timeout to the value of the `r` option before beginning the read. If the read doesn't complete before the timeout expires, the following message is printed and the read fails:

```
timeout waiting for input
```

If this error appears too often, consider increasing the size of the `r` option. If that option is already large, suspect hardware problems (like poor network connections).

When processing a `~/.forward` or `:include:` file, *sendmail* can time out if the directory containing the file cannot be accessed. The following message is printed with *file*, the full path of the file:

```
451 open timeout on file
```

The mail message is queued for a later delivery attempt.

too many lines

When reading the configuration file, too many of certain types of lines may be found. When the limit is exceeded, *sendmail* prints:

```
too many ident lines, max max
```

Here, *ident* is the name of the item of which there were too many, and *max* is the maximum number allowed. Examples are too many priority configuration commands or too many trusted users listed. If a larger number is required, change the limit in the source and recompile.

too many mailers

When *sendmail* is compiled, the maximum number of delivery agents is defined in *conf.h* as MAXMAILERS (usually 25). If you define too many delivery agents, you see one or more messages like the following:

```
sendmail.cf: line 53: too many mailers defined (25 max)
```

The line number and maximum delivery agent limit may vary. This error is not fatal. The *sendmail* program prints it, ignores the current delivery agent definition, and continues to run, but has a high probability of failing in odd ways later.

too many parameters

The M delivery agent's A= equate has room only for a limited number of command-line arguments. The number available is defined by MAXPV in *conf.h*. If MAXPV-3 arguments appear before the $u, *sendmail* prints the following error and bounces that mail message:

```
Too many parameters to argv[0] before $u
```

Here, *argv*[0] is the first argument following the A= in the offending delivery agent definition.

unbalanced

Certain characters in addresses must be balanced (see Chapter 25, *Rules*). For example, each < character requires a corresponding > character. The *sendmail* program checks every address that it processes to be sure that all such characters are balanced. If it finds an unbalanced pair, it prints the following error and bounces that address:

```
Unbalanced character
```

Here, *character* is the one that was missing its partner. Unfortunately, prior to V8 *sendmail* legal unbalanced characters were also rejected. Consider the following address:

```
george@wash.dc.gov  (George < Washington)
```

Here, the lone < character causes the address to be rejected, despite the fact that it occurs inside an RFC comment. V8 *sendmail* handles unbalanced characters more intelligently. It ignores any that are not a part of the RFC address, and attempts to balance any that it finds unbalanced in that address. Only truly ambiguous addresses yield the "Unbalanced" error message.

unparsable

All recipient addresses (including the names to the left of the colon in the *aliases* file) must successfully select a delivery agent when rewritten by rule sets 3 and 0. Failure to select a delivery agent causes the following error message to be printed and the faulty address to be skipped:

```
Unparsable user
```

A properly designed rule set 0 selects a delivery agent for every possible address. This error means that one address is making it past all the rules in rule set 0.

who are you?

When *sendmail* is processing a mail message (other than one that is from the queue or one that is coming over an SMTP channel), it attempts to look up the real login name of the user who is running it. If that user does not exist in the *passwd*(5) file and is not logged in, *sendmail* prints the following message and sets the real login name to be *postmaster.*

```
Who are you?
```

This message indicates that a legitimate user made a mistake, or that a "cracker" is attempting to use *sendmail,* or that there is a configuration problem.

you cannot use

The -f command-line switch (set the sender name) is reserved for use by the users who are listed in the T (trusted user) configuration command. Anyone else who attempts to use that switch gets the following error message and *sendmail* sets the sender to be the envelope sender.

```
you cannot use the -f flag
```

Note that because it made a poor Maginot line, V8 *sendmail* has removed the concept of trusted user altogether.

C

#define Macros in conf.h

In this appendix, we present each #define (or group of them) in alphabetical order, rather than in the order in which they appear in *conf.h*. Any macros that apply to IDA *sendmail* alone are marked with the notation (IDA only). Similarly, for version 8 *sendmail*, (V8 only) appears.

Although we detail only the IDA and V8 versions of *sendmail* in this appendix, the information here is still of value should you desire to compile a different version of *sendmail*, like KJS or a *sendmail* supplied in vendor source.

Note that the Tune column of Table C-1 recommends whether or not you should adjust (tune) the values for any particular #define. Those marked with yes/no may be adjusted to port *sendmail* to a new operating system, but should otherwise not be adjusted.

Table C-1: All the #define Macros in conf.h

#define	Tune	Version	Description
BIT8	yes	IDA	Support for 8-bit data in message body
*DBM	yes	IDA	Database support
*DB	yes	V8	Database support
DAEMON	yes	IDA	Include Internet support
*_FILENO	no	V8	POSIX-compliant definitions
FORK	no	V8	The type of *fork*(5) to use

Table C.1: All the #define Macros in conf.h (continued)

#define	Tune	Version	Description
FUZZY	yes	IDA	Include support for fuzzy name matching
HASINITGROUPS	yes/no	V8	Supports *initgroups*(3) system call
HASSTATFS	yes/no	V8	Supports *statfs*(2) system call
HASUSTAT	yes/no	V8	Supports *ustat*(2) system call
HASUNAME	yes/no	V8	Support for SysV *uname*(2) function
LOCKF	yes/no	V8	Use SysV *lockf*(3)
LOG	yes	both	Perform logging
MAIL11V3	yes	IDA	Support for the *mail11* program
MATCHGECOS	yes	V8	Support for fuzzy name matching
MAXATOM	no	both	Maximum atoms in an address
MAXFIELD	no	IDA	Maximum length of a header
MAXHOP	no	IDA	Maximum hop count
MAXHOSTNAMELEN	no	V8	Maximum length of a hostname
MAXIPADDR	no	V8	Most IP addresses for local host
MAXKEY	no	V8	Maximum length of a database key
MAXLINE	no	both	Maximum length of an input line
MAXMAILERS	no	both	Maximum number of delivery agents
MAXMXHOSTS	no	both	Maximum number of per host MX records
MAXNAME	no	both	Maximum length of a name
MAXPRIORITIES	no	both	Maximum number of Priority lines

Table C.1: All the #define Macros in conf.h (continued)

#define	Tune	Version	Description
MAXPV	no	both	Maximum arguments to a delivery agent
MAXRWSETS	no	both	Maximum number of rule sets
MAXTRUST	no	IDA	Maximum number of Trusted users
MAXUSERENVIRON	no	both	Limit environment to delivery agent
MEMCHUNKSIZE	no	V8	Optimum memory allocation size
NAMED_BIND	yes	both	Support for DNS name resolution
NET*	yes	V8	Select network type
NIS	yes	V8	Enable support for NIS
NOTUNIX	yes	both	Define if messages lack From line
PSBUFSIZE	no	both	Size of *prescan*() buffer
QUEUE	yes	both	Enable queueing
QUEUESIZE	no	both	Maximum number of messages per queue run
QUEUE_MACVALUE	yes	IDA	Enable saving of `$r` and `$s` in `qf` file
SETPROCTITLE	yes/no	both	Include support for `argv[0]` updates
SMTP	yes	both	Enable SMTP
SMTPDEBUG	yes	both	Enable remote debugging
SMTPLINELIM	no	V8	Maximum length of an SMTP line
SYSTEM5	yes/no	V8	Support for SysV derived machines
TOBUFSIZE	no	V8	Tune for *syslog*(3) limits
TTYNAME	no	both	Set $y as base name of controlling tty
UGLYUUCP	yes	both	Output ugly "`From `" UUCP lines

Table C.1: All the #define Macros in conf.h (continued)

#define	Tune	Version	Description
YP	yes	IDA	Enable support for Yellow Pages (NIS)
config/*.h	yes	IDA	CPU/OS-specific configurations

BIT8
Support for 8-bit data in message body (IDA only)

If BIT8 is defined, IDA *sendmail* includes code to handle extended character sets. The choice of which character set to use is handled by the C= and X= equates of IDA delivery agents.

If you need to exchange non-ASCII character sets with other sites, read the information in *sendmail/ida/charset*. If the approach described there appears workable to you, define BIT8 in *conf.h* and install the appropriate character set support before running the resulting *sendmail* binary.

config/*.h
Select CPU/OS type (IDA only)

With IDA *sendmail*, support for your particular computer brand and version of the UNIX operating system is found in a subdirectory under *sendmail/src* called *config*. Table C-2 lists each of the filenames found in that directory and provides a brief description of each. If yours is not present, the file *proto.h* provides some guidance to help you port IDA *sendmail* to your particular needs.

Table C-2: CPU/OS config/ Support for IDA

config/	Targeted CPU/OS support
config/3b1.h	AT&T 3B1 platforms with WIN/3B TCP/IP
config/aix3.h	IBM AIX 3.0 platforms
config/aixrt.h	IBM RT machines with AIX
config/bsd43.h	BSD Release 4.3 platforms
config/bsd44.h	BSD Release 4.3 (tahoe and reno) and 4.4 platforms

Table C.2: CPU/OS config/ Support for IDA (continued)

config/	Targeted CPU/OS support
config/convex.h	Convex platforms
config/domainos.h	Apollo Domain/OS platforms
config/dynix.h	Dynix platforms
config/hpux.h	HP (not Apollo) platforms running HPUX
config/irix.h	SGI IRIX platforms
config/isc.h	Interactive Systems System V UNIX platforms
config/next.h	NeXT Computers
config/osx.h	Pyramid OSx platforms
config/proto.h	Prototype for other platforms
config/ptx.h	Sequent platforms running ptx
config/riscos.h	MIPS/RISC OS platforms
config/sunos4.h	Sun OS Release 4.x (Solaris 1)
config/ultrix3.h	Pre-4.0 Ultrix platforms
config/ultrix4.h	4.0 Ultrix platforms
config/umax.h	Encore MultiMax platforms
config/usg.h	USG platforms

After you have selected the appropriate *config/* file, edit it and make any selections indicated therein. Then indicate your choice in *conf.h* by changing the `#include` line:

```
# include "config/bsd44.h"
```

Replace the `bsd44.h` with the filename appropriate to your needs.

DAEMON
Include Internet support (not V8)

For all but V8 *sendmail,* you need to define DAEMON to connect to a TCP/IP network and receive SMTP mail. DAEMON should be defined if you intend to run *sendmail* as a daemon, or if you intend to run *sendmail* once per connection with *inetd*(8).

On a workstation that *never* receives mail, it may be safe to comment out the DAEMON definition. On a main mail-handling machine, DAEMON must be defined.

*DB
Database support (V8 approach)

V8 *sendmail* supports two distinctly different types of database files. The *ndbm*(3) form of database utilizes two files (a *.pag* and *.dir*) for each database and cannot be shared by different architectures across a network. The completely new *db*(3) form of database utilizes a single file and can be shared by different architectures. If you intend to support aliasing in an efficient manner, you should define at least one or the other.

Defining NDBM causes the *ndbm*(3) approach to databases to be used. Defining NEWDB causes the *db*(3) approach to be used. Also, defining NIS causes the Network Information Services approach to be used. These definitions are found in *Makefile* rather than in *conf.h*. Defining all forms of database in *Makefile* would look like this:

```
DBMDEF= -DNEWDB -DNDBM -DNIS
```

The default is to use no database package at all.

*DBM
Database support (IDA approach)

In the IDA *conf.h* file, you are offered two choices:

```
# define DBM          1   /* use DBM library (may require -ldbm) */
# define NO_PADDING   1   /* don't pad dbm strings with ASCII NULL */
```

The first, DBM, needs to be defined if you intend to use database support at all. None of the other choices means a thing if DBM is undefined.

The NO_PADDING definition is most useful at sites which run NIS aliases maps, like SunOS. The NIS maps won't work unless the keys are inserted with a trailing NULL-byte at the end of each. To make the NIS maps work, you need to undefine NO_PADDING, thus enabling NULL byte padding.

The exact flavor of database is then offered. There are five to choose from:

```
# define NDBM     1   /* new DBM library available (requires DBM) */
/*# define GDBM    1   /* gnu DBM library available (requires DBM) */
/*# define SDBM    1   /* Ozan Yigit's PD ndbm (requires DBM) */
/*# define MDBM    1   /* UMaryland's ndbm variant (requires DBM) */
/*# define HDBM    1   /* Berkeley's hashing package (requires DBM) */
```

Here, we chose NDBM. Which you select depends on your experience and their availability.

FORK
The type of fork to use (V8 only)

The *sendmail* program forks often to do its job in the most efficient way possible. To minimize system impact, *sendmail* uses *vfork*(2) whenever possible. Unfortunately, not all systems support *vfork*(2). The SGI IRIX version of UNIX, for example, lacks *vfork*(2). For such machines you need to change the definition of FORK (for V8) and `vfork` (for IDA).

```
#define FORK     fork        ← V8
#define vfork    fork        ← IDA
```

Note that for IDA, this definition is located in *config/irix.h*.

FUZZY
Include support for fuzzy name matching (IDA only)

Fuzzy name matching is the ability to resolve a local recipient by looking at the *gecos* field of the *passwd*(5) file (see the G option for a discussion of fuzzy matching). We recommend that you not define FUZZY unless your site prohibits users changing their own *gecos* field entries. This feature under V8 *sendmail* is called MATCHGECOS.

LOG
Perform logging

If defined, LOG enables *sendmail* to use the *syslog*(3) facility to log error messages and other useful information. Logging and *syslog*(3) are described in Chapter 22, *Logging and Statistics*.

```
# define LOG         1       /* enable logging */
```

LOG should be defined only if your system supports *syslog*(3). If you lack *syslog*(3), consider porting it to your system.

MAIL11V3
Include support for the mail11 program (IDA only)

The *mail11*(8) program is used to route mail to and from DECnet sites. It requires special SMTP protocols not normally supported by *sendmail*, like sending the DATA before the envelope information. The MAIL11V3 definition causes *sendmail* to compile with that nonstandard support included.

MATCHGECOS

Include support for fuzzy name matching (V8 only)

See FUZZY above.

MAXATOM

Maximum atoms in an address

Addresses are broken up into tokens (or atoms) so that they can be processed by rules. The MAXATOM definition determines the maximum number of tokens allowed in any given address. If the maximum is exceeded, the following message is printed and *syslog*(3)'d:

```
prescan: too many tokens
```

The default is 200, a value that is probably far larger than you will likely ever need.

MAXFIELD

Maximum length of a header (not V8)

IDA *sendmail* uses a different buffer to hold header text than it uses for most other lines of text (MAXLINE above). Called MAXFIELD, this buffer is larger than MAXLINE because large headers can arrive from the outside world, and are completely beyond your control. Some mailing lists, for example, have a `To:` header which contains all the recipient addresses (instead of the name of the list, as it should). It is important to not lose any recipient addresses in such a circumstance, even if they are many.

The default value for MAXFIELD is 4096 characters, a generous value and a size that is unlikely to be exceeded. However, after you have had IDA *sendmail* running for a while, take note of how often it splits oversize headers. You can tell from the appearance of headers moved to the end of the mail message. For example, an `Apparently-To:` header with 1000 recipients listed could end up like this:

```
%%% overflow headers %%%
Apparently-To: address1, address2, address3, address4, address5,
        address6, address7, address8, address9, address10,
        ... and so on until
        address612, addre
%%% end overflow headers %%%
```

Here, IDA *sendmail* found more recipients in the `Apparently-To:` header than would fit in a MAXFIELD-sized buffer. It discarded the excess characters (`addre` above) and moved the result to the end of the message. If your site starts producing many messages with such overflow headers, you may need to increase the size of MAXFIELD and recompile.

Note that V8 *sendmail* dynamically sizes memory to accept headers of any arbitrary length.

MAXHOP

Maximum hop count (IDA only)

The hop count for a mail message is the number of times it has been transferred from one machine to another, or from one MTA to another on the same machine. It is calculated by counting the number of `Received:` (and related) header lines in the header portion of the mail message. When that count exceeds a preset maximum, the mail message is bounced. IDA *sendmail* uses the MAXHOP definition in *conf.h* to specify the maximum. V8 *sendmail* uses the h option.

The default set by IDA for MAXHOP is 15. You are encouraged to increase this limit only if either of the following applies:

- If mail out of your site is expected to begin with multiple hops (such as UUCP connections to the Internet, or routing mail out of a local network to a well-connected machine), you should increase MAXHOP by the number of expected unavoidable hops.

- If yours is a redistribution site for mailing lists, you should expect to be forwarding mail that already begins with many hops. In this circumstance, it is important that your site be robust and not bounce any such mail because of too many hops. A hop count of 30 may be appropriate.

Note that the V8 h (hop count) option does the same thing.

MAXHOSTNAMELEN

Maximum length of a hostname (V8 only)

V8 *sendmail* uses a separate definition to set the size of buffers that holds hostnames. The recommended value for this definition is 256. This should be enough for the next few years. There is always the risk, considering the explosion of networks and subnets, that even this size buffer will someday overrun, but you shouldn't concern yourself with that. Technically, this is normally set by system include files and should be considered unchangeable.

MAXIPADDR
Most IP addresses for local host (V8 only)

When V8 *sendmail* generates a list of the names by which the local host is known, it also generates a list of the IP addresses assigned to the local host. These addresses are used by the daemon to determine if the local *sendmail* has connected to itself. These addresses are not made a part of any class and are not available to rule sets.

MAXIPADDR defines the maximum number of IP addresses that are detected as belonging to the local host. The default, 16, is generous and rarely needs to be increased (16 is an awful lot of network connections). Nor should it be reduced, because it uses only a tiny amount of memory.

MAXKEY
Maximum length of a database key (V8 only)

Although this appears to be a global declaration, it really affects only the use of the DB form of database described above. It determines the size of the buffer that holds the key in *db*(3) lookups, and is otherwise unused. Specifically, it is not used to detect the presence of oversized keys, and it is completely ignored if NEWDB is undefined. If you use *db*(3) and have extremely long keys, you may want to double the default of 128.

MAXLINE
Maximum length of an input line

MAXLINE limits the size of certain lines of text that *sendmail* reads. The most important are configuration file lines, the text to the right of the colon in alias file lines, lines of text read with the F (file) class configuration command, and incoming mail received as lines of SMTP text. Joined lines, where a line is extended by starting subsequent lines with indent characters (spaces or tabs), count as a single line for this definition. MAXLINE defines the maximum number of characters that are accepted as part of a line and includes the indentation characters of joined lines. Exceeding this maximum can cause the trailing part of the line to be lost. For critical input (like SMTP data), overflow lines are gracefully handled by *sendmail*, without loss of information.

The default value given to MAXLINE (2048) is a good choice for most sites. This value should never be decreased. Reasons to increase it might include:

- If, for security reasons, you maintain mailing lists in the *aliases* file (rather than using :include: files), you may need to accommodate larger-than-usual address lists to the right of the colon. A value of 4096 may prove beneficial.

- If you need to parse extremely long lines from a file using the F class configuration command, you should either modify that file or (if it is an unmodifiable system file) increase the size of MAXLINE.

Note that MAXLINE does not affect the reading of headers. For that purpose, IDA uses a different definition (MAXFIELD), and V8 dynamically sizes memory. See MEMCHUNKSIZ for a description of how V8 handles reading configuration file and qf file lines. Note that V8 dynamic sizing affects only the total size of continued (indented) headers. Each individual line still has its length limited by MAXLINE.

MAXMAILERS
Maximum number of delivery agents

The fewest possible number of delivery agents allowed is three for IDA and five for V8 *sendmail*. For a client workstation that never runs the *sendmail* daemon, the minimum may be appropriate. For hub machines, the default of 25 (for both) is more than adequate. The memory required to reserve space for a delivery agent is tiny, so there is little need to change MAXMAILERS from its default.

MAXMXHOSTS
Maximum number of per-host MX records

Large central mail handling machines often have many MX (Mail eXchanger) records (see Chapter 17, *DNS and sendmail*). The *sendmail* program uses MX records to sequentially try delivery to each in order of preference. As more sites become better connected and more familiar with DNS, the likelihood of a machine with a large number of MX records increases. The default for MAXMXHOSTS is 20, the current recommended value. IDA's default is 10 and should probably be increased to 20.

MAXNAME

Maximum length of a name

MAXNAME is the maximum length in bytes of a wide variety of buffers inside *sendmail.* Those buffers are, among other things, used to hold:

- Each argument in the array of arguments given to a delivery agent

- The addresses of the owners of mailing lists

- The key to be looked up in databases

- Hostnames, usually fully-qualified domain names (IDA only)

- Assorted temporary strings, like the IP address of a host or the full name of a user

Both IDA and V8 *sendmail* recommend the default value of 256 for MAX-NAME.

MAXPRIORITIES

Maximum number of Priority lines

The configuration file's Priority command is used to assign values to strings for later recognition in mail `Precedence:` headers (see Chapter 31, *Headers*). There appears to be a sudden growth in the number of such defined strings. In fact, they increased from three to five during the writing of this book. The default limit of 25 should not be changed.

MAXPV

Maximum arguments to a delivery agent

A delivery agent that has the `F=m` flag present is able to accept multiple recipient addresses each time it is executed. The maximum number of recipient addresses is the value of MAXPV minus a count of any other arguments. For example:

```
Mlocal, P=/bin/mail, F=rlsDFMmnP, S=10, R=20, A=mail -d $u
```

Here there are two other arguments, besides the $u, which represent the recipient's address. If MAXPV is defined as 40, then at most 38 recipient addresses are added to the argument array. Note that if there are more recipients than the *argv* can accept, the delivery agent is rerun as many times as is necessary to handle them all.

MAXPV should not be increased from its default of 40 without first checking each delivery agent that has the F=m flag set. You may need to examine the source for each to be sure none contain hardcoded assumptions about the maximum to expect.

MAXRWSETS
Maximum number of rule sets

Rule sets are declared and numbered with the S configuration command. MAXRWSETS defines the upper limit, at or above which rule set numbers may not be declared. This limit is purely a matter of taste and style. IDA *sendmail* uses a default of 40, which means its rule set number can range from S0 to S39. In the IDA *Sendmail.mc* default configuration file, 28 rule sets are declared, so you have 11 extra for your own use. V8 *sendmail* declares MAXRWSETS as 100. Because unused rule sets only consume the size of a pointer in memory, there is little cost to increasing MAXRWSETS. Indeed, if you intend to design a *huge* configuration file, a value of 1000 may be appropriate.

MAXTRUST
Maximum number of trusted users (not V8)

Trusted users are those who are allowed to change the identity of the sender by using the −f command-line switch. Trusted users are declared in the configuration file using the T command:

```
T uucp root
```

MAXTRUST defines the maximum number of users who can be declared with the T configuration command. The default, 8, is probably more than enough for most sites.

Note that V8 *sendmail* has eliminated the T configuration command and this MAXTRUST definition.

MAXUSERENVIRON
Limit environment variables to delivery agent

Every program under UNIX is provided with a list of environment variables when it starts. The *sendmail* program saves those variables so that it can restore them when executing delivery agents. MAXUSERENVIRON defines the upper limit of how many environment variables *sendmail* saves.

The default for both IDA and V8 *sendmail* is 40. Under no circumstance should you make that value less than 3. If you do, you may cause *sendmail* to fail, and certainly cause some delivery agents to fail. If you are concerned about passing dangerous environment variables (like FS= or LD_*=), you should use V8 *sendmail*: it specifically eliminates dangerous variables, and passes only one (safe) variable to delivery agents—AGENT=sendmail.

If you need to use IDA or some other non-V8 *sendmail* and are concerned about dangerous environment variables, you can modify the code in *deliver.c* to eliminate them. Just insert your new code here:

```
            ← insert new code here
      /* try to execute the mailer */
      execve(m->m_mailer, pvp, environ);
```

But beware: don't replace `environ` with `NULL`, and don't make `*environ` equal to `NULL`. If you do, you'll cause delivery agents to produce core dumps and fail.

MEMCHUNKSIZE

Optimum memory allocation size (V8 only)

When V8 *sendmail* reads lines of text from the configuration file or from `qf` queue files, it calls a routine named *fgetfolded()*. That routine is initially passed a buffer of size MAXLINE into which to fit the read line. If the line is longer than MAXLINE, V8 *sendmail* dynamically increases the space required to hold the line by MEMCHUNKSIZE.

The default value assigned to MEMCHUNKSIZE is 1024 bytes. A useful alternative size might be:

```
      #define MAXCHUNKSIZE (MAXLINE * 2)
```

This way, MAXCHUNKSIZE automatically scales to twice the maximum line length, should you later need to change that length.

NAMED_BIND
Include support for DNS name resolution

The *sendmail* program does not automatically take advantage of DNS look-ups or MX records to resolve addresses and canonical hostnames. To include that support you need to define NAMED_BIND:

```
#define NAMED_BIND 1
```

If your site is a UUCP-only site, and does not run *named*(8) locally, you may undefine NAMED_BIND. If you are not currently running *named*(8) but plan to connect to the Internet, you should define NAMED_BIND but set option I to false in the configuration file. Later, when you connect to the Internet, you can then simply change option I to true.

NET*
Define network support (V8 only)

V8 *sendmail* is designed to support four different kinds of networks. They are:

NETINET   TCP/IP-based network

NETISO   ISO 8022 network

NETNS   Xerox NS protocol network (tentative)

NETX25   CCITT* X.25 network (tentative)

Currently, only NETINET and NETISO are supported. Stubs are included in the source code for any programmer interested in implementing NETNS or NETX25.

Defining network support only causes the code for that network to be included in *sendmail*. The network serviced by a particular invocation of *sendmail* is selected with the p option. In the absence of a p option declaration, NETINET is used as the default.

---

*International Telephone and Telegraph Consultative Committee.

NIS

Enable NIS (Yellow Pages) code (V8 only)

If you intend to have V8 *sendmail* support NIS (formerly Yellow Pages) maps, you need to define NIS in *conf.h* or the *Makefile*. If defined, *sendmail* augments the *aliases* database with two special entries needed by NIS:

```
YP_LAST_MODIFIED
YP_MASTER_NAME
```

If NIS is defined, the A (alias location) option can be specified as:

```
OAnis:mail.aliases
```

NOTUNIX

Define if messages lack From lines

Under UNIX, a file of many mail messages normally has one message separated from another by a blank line and then a line that begins with the five characters "From " (four letters and a space). On such systems, *sendmail* saves important information from such lines for later use.

On non-UNIX machines (like VMS or MS-DOS), the conversions are different, so you won't want *sendmail* to treat such lines as special. Similarly, if your UNIX site has converted entirely away from this convention (with *mhs* or the like), you may not want this special treatment.

To disable special treatment of "From " lines, define the NOTUNIX macro in *conf.h*:

```
#define NOTUNIX 1
```

This macro is present in IDA *conf.h*, but commented out. It is not present in V8, and needs to be added if you require it.

PSBUFSIZ

Size of prescan() buffer

Whenever an address (including rules) is tokenized, it is stored in a single buffer, one token following the next with a zero-value byte separating them. The size of this buffer is defined by PSBUFSIZ. The default size for IDA is (MAXATOM + MAXATOM) and is defined in *sendmail.h*. The default size for V8 is (MAXNAME*4) and is defined in *conf.h*.

Either default is acceptable. If you later start getting warning messages like:

```
Address too long
```

you need to increase the size of PSBUFSIZ and recompile *sendmail.*

QUEUE
Enable queueing

If *sendmail* cannot immediately deliver a mail message, it places that message in a queue to await another try. The QUEUE definition causes queue-handling code to to be included in *sendmail.* If queueing is not enabled, and the need to queue arises, *sendmail* prints the following message and either bounces or discards the message:

```
dropenvelope: queueup
```

A word to the wise—*always* define QUEUE.

QUEUESIZE
Maximum number of messages per queue run

Whenever *sendmail* processes the queue, it handles only QUEUESIZE number of qf files at once. If there are more, they are not processed until the next queue run (providing part of the first queue run succeeded).

During a queue run, *sendmail* holds information in memory about all the files being processed. It does this so that it can sort them by priority for delivery. If your site handles thousands of mail messages hourly, and if each queue run adversely effects system performance, you may wish to reduce QUEUESIZE, and process the queue more often. On the other hand, if your hub machine has plenty of memory (as it should), it may be more efficient to increase QUEUESIZE.

The default for IDA is 600, and for V8 is 1000.

QUEUE_MACVALUE
Enable $r and $s saving in qf file (IDA only)

The $r macro holds as its value the protocol used when receiving the message (like UUCP or SMTP). The $s macro holds the canonical name of the sending site. These macros are used to create a Received: header.

To ensure that these values are available even if a message is delivered from the queue, you need to define QUEUE_MACVALUE.

```
#define QUEUE_MACVALUE '$'
```

Here, QUEUE_MACVALUE is defined as the character constant $. You *must not* change that character. It is compiled into *sendmail* and used as a qf file command. If you change the character, you run the risk of creating duplicate *case* statements in the code and preventing a successful compile.

Defining QUEUE_MACVALUE tells IDA *sendmail* to save the $r and $s macro values to the queue's qf file, and to restore them when the qf file is later processed.

Note that V8 *sendmail* always saves the $s, $r, and $_ macros, without needing to enable this behavior in *conf.h*.

SETPROCTITLE
Include support for argv[0] updates

Whenever a program first begins to run, UNIX provides it with two arrays of information: its command-line arguments, and the environment under which it was run. When you run *ps*(1) to see what processes are doing, *ps* prints the command line that was used to run each program.

To provide more useful information (like current status, or host connected to) *sendmail* saves its command line and environment, then periodically uses that system space to display its status. This ability provides a valuable tool for monitoring what each invocation of *sendmail* is doing. To ensure that *sendmail* is always found in the list, no matter how it was run (i.e., *newaliases*), it always sets *argv[0]* (the first word printed by *ps*) to be "sendmail:".

The SETPROCTITLE macro in *conf.h* enables this updating of status. It should be disabled only for systems derived from SysV UNIX. On some systems, such as Apollo, enabling it causes *sendmail* to produce a core dump and crash.

SMTP
Enable SMTP

If you are running *sendmail* as a daemon, you need to define SMTP to enable mail transfers. If you don't intend to run *sendmail* as a daemon, SMTP may not need to be defined. Only a few programs try to talk to *sendmail* using an SMTP pipe connection (like the *mh*(1) suite). If none of the programs at your site needs this capability, you may safely undefine SMTP.

SMTPDEBUG
Enable remote debugging

The *sendmail* program allows the developer to turn on debugging and to print the queue from any remote site. This capability is useful for solving the occasional problem with *sendmail*, but opens a potentially wide security hole.

In general, SMTPDEBUG should always be undefined. Later, when you become more expert with *sendmail*, you may want to have a standby version of *sendmail* ready (one with SMTPDEBUG defined), just in case you need it.

SMTPLINELIM
Maximum length of an SMTP line (V8 only)

Each delivery agent that is defined in the configuration file may or may not have an L= (Line length) equate. If that equate is missing, or if the value assigned to it is less than or equal to zero, the default value used becomes the value of SMTPLINELIM.

The default for SMTPLINELIM is 990 (defined in RFC821) and that value should not be changed. Rather, if you need a different line-length limit for a particular delivery agent, you should use the L= equate when defining it (see Chapter 26, *Delivery Agents*).

SYSTEM5
Support for SysV-derived machines (V8 only)

If you are compiling *sendmail* on a SysV-derived machine, you should define SYSTEM5. This automatically causes the following SysV support to be included:

```
/* general System V defines */
# ifdef SYSTEM5
# define HASUNAME       1       /* use System V uname(2) system call */
# define HASUSTAT       1       /* use System V ustat(2) syscall */
# ifndef LA_TYPE
#  define LA_TYPE       LA_INT
```

```
# endif
# define bcopy(s, d, l)          (memmove((d), (s), (l)))
# define bzero(d, l)             (memset((d), ' ', (l)))
# define bcmp(s, d, l)           (memcmp((s), (d), (l)))
# endif
```

If you are compiling under Hewlett Packard's HPUX operating system, SYS-TEM5 is automatically defined in *conf.h*.

TOBUFSIZ
Tune for syslog(3) limits (V8 only)

For each delivery of one or more recipients to a single delivery agent, *sendmail* issues a summary of delivery through *syslog*(3) (see Chapter 22, *Logging and Statistics*). A message like the following is always logged, regardless of the setting of the L (Logging) option:

> *id*: to=*recipients*, *relay*, stat=*status*

Here, *recipients* is a comma-separated list of recipients. The maximum number of characters in this list of *recipients* is determined by TOBUFSIZ. That limit is intended to prevent the internal *syslog*(3) buffer from overflowing. On machines with older versions of *syslog*(3), you may need to reduce the size of TOBUFSIZ.

TTYNAME
Set $y as base name of controlling tty (obsolete)

The $y macro is intended to hold as its value the base name of the controlling *tty* device (if there is one). On BSD-derived systems, this is a name like the following, but with the /dev/ prefix removed:

> /dev/tty04

Defining TTYNAME enables *sendmail* to put this information into $y.

UGLYUUCP
Output ugly From UUCP lines

The F=U delivery agent flag (see Chapter 26, *Delivery Agents*) specifies that *sendmail* should modify the five character "From " header for UUCP. To enable the code that recognizes the F=U flag, you need to define UGLYUUCP. If you do not intend to support UUCP and expect never to need that support, you should undefine UGLYUUCP.

YP
Enable Yellow Pages (NIS) code (IDA only)

If you wish to have *sendmail* create an aliases database that is directly usable by NIS, you needs to define YP. When YP is defined, IDA *sendmail* prefixes the database with two special keys needed by NIS:

```
YP_MASTER_NAME
YP_LAST_MODIFIED
```

If YP is defined, the OA (alias location) can be specified as:

```
OA%
```

This causes IDA *sendmail* to use the NIS aliases map in place of the normal *aliases*(5) file.

D

The client.cf File

In Part One of this book, a configuration file is partly developed. This appendix presents the finished file. The *client.cf* file is available via anonymous FTP from *ftp.uu.net* in the directory */published/oreilly/nutshell/sendmail*.

```
# Other names for the local host
Cwlocalhost

# This is the name of the mail hub
DHhub.your.domain
# This is the name of the mail relay
DRmailhost

# Our official canonical hostname.
Dj$w

## Standard macros
# name used for error messages
DnMailer-Daemon
# UNIX header format
DlFrom $g  $d
# separator (operator) characters
Do.:%@!^=/[]
# format of a total name
Dq<$g>
# SMTP login message (unused because no daemon)
De$j Sendmail $v ready at $b

###    Options
# No OA, we don't do aliasing.
# No OD, we don't do aliasing.
# No OH, we don't run as a daemon.
# Process messages in the background.
```

```
Odbackground
# Default permissions for files
OF0600
# Default user and group (daemon/daemon)
Og1
Ou1
# The logging level
OL9
# Accept oldstyle addresses
Oo
# Send a copy of bounced messages to postmaster
OPPostmaster
# SMTP read timeout
Or15m
# Location of the statistics file
OS/etc/sendmail.st
# Note, we do queue, in case hub and MX's are all down.
OQ/var/spool/mqueue
# queue everything for safety
Os
# Time to live in the queue
OT5d


###    Message precedences (all of equal weight. let hub decide.)
Pfirst-class=0
Pspecial-delivery=0
Pjunk=0


###    Trusted users
T root daemon

## Required headers
HReceived: $?sfrom $s $.by $j ($v) id $i; $b
H?D?Date: $a
H?F?From: $q
H?M?Message-Id: <$t.$i@$j>
H?D?Resent-Date: $a
H?F?Resent-From: $q
H?M?Resent-Message-Id: <$t.$i@$j>
H?x?Full-Name: $x


S0 # Punt to hub
R$*                     $#ether $@$R $:$1

S3 # local users made to look like they are from the hub
R$*<$*<$*>$*>$*  $3              de-nest
R$*<$+>$*        $2              basic RFC822 parsing
R$*<>$*          $n              RFC1123 <>
R$-             $@ $1 @ $H       user => user@hub
R$+@$+          $: $1 @ $[$2$]   canonify the hostname
R$+@$=w         $@ $1 @ $H       user@thishost => user@hub
R$=w!$+         $@ $2 @ $H       thishost!user => user@hub
R$+%$=w         $@ $>3 $1 @ $2   handle % hack thishost
R$*             $@ $1            default, unchanged
```

```
Mether, P=[IPC], F=msDFMuCX, S=0, R=0, A=IPC $h
Mlocal, P=xxx, A=Required by sendmail but unused
Mprog,  P=xxx, A=Required by sendmail but unused
```

V8 m4 Configuration

V8 *sendmail* provides an easy way to create a custom configuration file for your site. In the *cf* subdirectory of the source distribution, you will find a file named *README*. It contains easy-to-understand, step-by-step instructions.

In this appendix, we describe many of the m4 macros available for use in creating your configuration file. This appendix is incomplete because V8 *sendmail* continues to be developed. All current m4 macros are documented in the *cf/README* file.

The m4 macros are listed in alphabetical order, with lowercase preceding uppercase for each letter. Care must be taken to quote values exactly as shown in each example:

```
define(`ALIAS_FILE',`/etc/mail/aliases')
```

Each item in the comma-separated list of definitions must begin with a reverse half-quote and must end with a forward half-quote.

ALIAS_FILE
Location of the aliases file

The location of the *aliases*(5) file is defined by the A option. The default for that location is */etc/aliases*. If you wish to change that location, you may do so by defining the ALIAS_FILE m4 macro:

```
define(`ALIAS_FILE', `/etc/mail/aliases')
```

This causes the location of the *aliases*(5) file to be changed from the default of */etc/aliases* to */etc/mail/aliases*. The *aliases*(5) file is described in Chapter 20, *Aliases*, and the A option in Chapter 30, *Options*.

BITNET_RELAY
The machine that will relay BITnet mail

See DOMAIN.

conf*
Redefine defaults for specific macros/options

For those who wish to get their hands dirty (albeit at the m4 level rather than the configuration file level), many m4 options are available for tuning individual defined macros, classes, and options. They all begin with the characters "conf", and may appear anywhere in the *.mc* file.

Each is used with the define m4 keyword. For example:

```
define(`confALIAS_WAIT', `5m')
```

This changes the amount of time to wait for the *aliases*(5) file to be rebuilt, from the default of ten minutes to five minutes.

Table E-1 shows the defined macros that can be redefined in this way. These macros are described individually in Chapter 27, *Defined Macros*.

Table E-1: m4 Names for Defined Macros

Macro	m4 Variable Name	Default
De	confSTMP_LOGIN_MSG	$j Sendmail $v/$Z ready at $b
Dj	confDOMAIN_NAME	(undefined)
Dl	confFROM_LINE	From $g $d
Dn	confMAILER_NAME	MAILER-DAEMON
Do	confOPERATORS	.:%@!^/[]

Table E.1: m4 Names for Defined Macros (continued)

Macro	m4 Variable Name	Default
Dq	confFROM_HEADER	$?x$x <$g>$ I g.

Only one file class can be appended-to in your m4 with a `conf*` definition. The class `w` is used to hold all the names by which the local machine is known. Those names may be listed separately in a file and the location of that file declared with the `confCW_FILE` m4 macro.

m4 Names for File Class

A large number of options can be individually tuned in the *.mc* file by using an appropriate `conf*` macro, as listed in Table E-2. For a more complete explanation of each option, see Chapter 30, *Options*.

Table E-2: m4 Names for Options

Option	m4 Variable Name	Default
O7	confSEVEN_BIT_INPUT	False
Oa	confALIAS_WAIT	10m
Oa	See *ALIAS_FILE*	n/a
Ob	confMIN_FREE_BLOCKS	4
OB	confBLANK_SUB	.
Oc	confCON_EXPENSIVE	False
OC	confCHECKPOINT_INTERVAL	10
Od	confDELIVERY_MODE	background
OD	confAUTO_REBUILD	False
Oe	confERROR_MODE	(undefined)
OE	confERROR_MESSAGE	(undefined)
Of	confSAVE_FROM_LINES	False
OF	confTEMP_FILE_MODE	0600
Og	confDEF_GROUP_ID	1
OG	confMATCH_GECOS	True
Oh	confMAX_HOP	17
OH	See *HELP_FILE*	n/a
Oi	confIGNORE_DOTS	False
OI	confBIND_OPTS	(empty)
Oj	confMIME_FORMAT_ERRORS	(empty)
OJ	confFORWARD_PATH	$z/.forward

Table E.2: m4 Names for Options (continued)

Option	m4 Variable Name	Default
Ok	conf MCI_CACHE_SIZE	2
OK	conf MCI_CACHE_TIMEOUT	5m
Ol	conf USE_ERRORS_TO	True
OL	conf LOG_LEVEL	9
Om	conf ME_TOO	False
On	conf CHECK_ALIASES	True
Oo	conf OLD_STYLE_HEADERS	True
OO	conf DAEMON_OPTIONS	(undefined)
Op	conf PRIVACY_FLAGS	authwarnings
OP	conf COPY_ERRORS_TO	(undefined)
Oq	conf QUEUE_FACTOR	(undefined)
OQ	See *QUEUE_DIR*	n/a
Or	conf READ_TIMEOUT	(undefined)
Os	conf SAFE_QUEUE	True
OS	See *STATUS_FILE*	n/a
Ot	conf TIME_ZONE	USE_SYSTEM
OT	conf MESSAGE_TIMEOUT	5d/4h
Ou	conf DEF_USER_ID	1
OU	conf USERDB_SPEC	(undefined)
OV	conf FALLBACK_MX	(undefined)
Ow	conf TRY_NULL_MX_LIST	True
Ox	conf QUEUE_LA	8
OX	conf REFUSE_LA	12
Oy	conf WORK_RECIPIENT_FACTOR	(undefined)
OY	conf SEPARATE_PROC	False
Oz	conf WORK_CLASS_FACTOR	(undefined)
OZ	conf WORK_TIME_FACTOR	(undefined)

CSNET_RELAY

The machine that will relay CSNet mail

See DOMAIN.

DOL
Include a $ character in a define

Ordinarily, the $ character is interpreted by m4 inside its `define` expressions. But for ambitious undertakings, such as designing your own DOMAIN, FEATURE, or HACK files, you may need to include reference to a macro or operator (and hence a $) inside an m4 `define` expression. The way you do this is with the DOL m4 macro. For example:

```
define(`DOWN', `R DOL(*) < @ $1 > DOL(*)     DOL(1) < @ $2 > DOL(2)')
```

Here, we define the m4 macro named DOWN, which takes two arguments ($1 and $2). When used in one of your `.m4` files:

```
DOWN(badhost, outhost)
```

it creates a rule by substituting the above arguments for the corresponding $1 and $2 in its original definition:

```
R $* < @ badhost > $*        $1 < @ outhost > $2
```

The DOL m4 macro in the original definition allowed the insertion of $ characters (like $*), while protecting those characters from being wrongly interpreted by m4.

Needless to say, you should *never* redefine the DOL macro.

DOMAIN
Access domain-wide information from one file

For large sites, it can be advantageous to gather all configuration decisions common to the entire domain into a single file. The directory to hold domain information files is called *cf/domain*. The configuration information in those files is accessed using the DOMAIN m4 macro, for example:

```
DOMAIN(cs)
```

This line in any of your *.mc* files causes the file *cf/domain/cs.m4* to be included at that point. Examples that come with the distribution illustrate subdomains under *Berkeley.EDU*. If all hosts at your site masquerade behind one e-mail name, you might want to put the MASQUERADE_AS m4 macro in your domain file.

Domain files form a natural location for the definition of site-specific relays. Four types of relay are supported: BITnet, CSNet, UUCP, and local. The declaration for each is identical. For example:

```
define(`LOCAL_RELAY', `agent: host')
```

Here, *agent* is the name of a delivery agent to use, and *host* is the name of the machine to which all such mail will be relayed. If *agent*: is missing, it defaults to a literal `relay:`. The LOCAL_RELAY above can be any of the four relays shown below:

BITNET_RELAY

The host that will forward BITnet-addressed e-mail. If not defined, the .BITNET pseudo-domain won't work.

CSNET_RELAY

The host that will forward CSNet-addressed e-mail. If not defined, the .CSNET pseudo-domain won't work.

LOCAL_RELAY

Unless you specify otherwise, any address that is a username, without any *@host* part, is delivered using the `local` delivery agent. If you prefer to have all such mail handled by a different machine, you may define that other machine with the LOCAL_RELAY m4 macro:

```
define(`LOCAL_RELAY', `agent: host')
```

Note that a relay is different from the knowledgeable hub defined with MAIL_HUB. Also note that you need to include support for any delivery agent specified by using the MAILER m4 macro. See MAIL_HUB for an illustration of how MAIL_HUB and LOCAL_RELAY interact.

UUCP_RELAY

The host that forwards UUCP-addressed e-mail. If not defined, the UUCP pseudo-domain won't work.

EXPOSED_USER
Who should not masquerade

Class macro E is used by the V8 configuration file to hold a list of user-names which should never be masqueraded (even if masquerade is enabled with the MASQUERADE_AS m4 macro). By default, the user *root* is always in that class. There are two ways to add usernames to the class E. They can be added individually with the EXPOSED_USER m4 macro:

```
EXPOSED_USER(user)
```

Here, we cause the name *user* to be appended to the class E. This is identical to the following use of LOCAL_CONFIG to add to the class directly:

```
LOCAL_CONFIG
CEuser
```

If you wish to store the list of non-masqueradable users in an external file, you can cause that file to be read with an F configuration command:

```
LOCAL_CONFIG
FE/usr/local/mail/visible.users
```

The F configuration command and the internal form of such files are described in Chapter 28, *Class Macros*.

FEATURE
Enable special features

V8 *sendmail* offers a number of *features* that you may find very useful. To include a feature, include an m4 command like the following in your *.mc* file:

```
FEATURE(keyword)
```

This declaration causes a file of the name *../feature/keyword.m4* to be read at that place in your *.mc* file. Those *keyword* files are:

use_cw_file   The *use_cw_file* feature causes the file */etc/sendmail.cw* to be read to obtain alternate names for the local host. One use for such a file might be to declare a list of hosts for which the local host is acting as the MX recipient. The *use_cw_file* feature causes the following to appear in the configuration file:

```
Fw/etc/sendmail.cw
```

The actual filename can be changed from */etc/sendmail.cw* by redefining confCW_FILE, described below.

If the local host is known by only a few names, an alternative is to instead include the following line in place of the feature:

```
Cwname1 name2
```

Here, *name1* and *name2* are alternative names for the local host. See Chapter 28, *Class Macros*, for a description of the F and C configuration commands.

redirect

The redirect feature causes all mail addressed to an address of the form:

```
newaddress.REDIRECT
```

to be bounced with a message like this:

```
551 User not local; please try <newaddress>
```

The redirect feature allows aliases to be set up for retired accounts which bounce, with an indication of the new forwarding address. A few lines of such an *aliases*(5) file might look like this:

```
george:    george@new.site.edu.REDIRECT
william:   wc@lady.berkeley.edu.REDIRECT
```

nouucp

If your site wants nothing to do with UUCP addresses, you can enable the *nouucp* feature. Among the changes this causes are: the ! character is not recognized as a separator between hostnames; all the other macros in this appendix that relate to UUCP are ignored. This feature truly means *no* UUCP.

nocanonify

Ordinarily, *sendmail* tries to canonify (add a domain to) any hostname that lacks a domain part. The *nocanonify* feature prevents *sendmail* from passing addresses to $ [and $] for canonicalization. This is generally suitable for use by sites that act only as mail gateways or that have MUAs that do full canonicalization themselves. You may also want to use:

```
define(`confBIND_OPTS',`-DNSRCH -DEFNAMES')
```

to turn off the usual resolver options that do a similar thing.

notsticky

By default, mail addressed to a local user that includes the name of the local host as part of the address (i.e., *user@local.host*) is delivered locally. If MAIL_HUB is *not* defined, lookups in the user database (UDB) and the additional processing of rule set 5 are skipped. Addresses with just the *user* part are always processed by UDB and rule set 5. The *notsticky* feature changes this logic. If this feature is chosen, only users defined by LOCAL_USER are looked up in the user database and the additional processing of rule set 5 is skipped.

mailertable A *mailertable* is a database that maps *host.domain* names to special delivery agent and new domain name pairs. For example, one mapping could be:

```
compuserve      smtp:compuserve.com
```

In the data portion of the database, the delivery agent must be separated from the domain by a colon. The *mailertable* feature causes rules to be included in your configuration file that look up *host.domain* names in the *mailertable* database.

```
FEATURE(mailertable)
```

This declaration also causes the following database declaration to be included in the configuration file:

```
Kmailertable hash -o /etc/mailertable.db
```

(See Chapter 29, *Database Macros*, for more details about the K configuration command.) If you wish to use a different form of database (like *dbm*), the *mailertable* feature accepts an argument:

```
FEATURE(mailertable,`dbm -o /etc/mailertable')
```

The argument corresponds to the arguments given to the K configuration command and must be correctly quoted as shown.

bitdomain Many Internet hosts have BITNET addresses which are separate from their Internet addresses. For example, the host *icsi.berkeley.edu* has the registered BITNET name *ucbicsi*. If a user tried to reply to an address like:

```
user@ucbicsi
```

that mail would fail. To help with translations from registered BITNET names to Internet addresses, John Gardiner

Myers has supplied the *bitdomain* program in the *contrib* subdirectory. It produces a output in the form:

```
ucbicsi    icsi.berkeley.edu
```

that can be put into database form for use with the K configuration command. The *bitdomain* feature causes rules to be included in the configuration file that perform the necessary translation:

```
FEATURE(bitdomain)
```

This also causes the following K configuration command to be included:

```
Kbitdomain hash -o /etc/bitdomain.db
```

As with *mailertable* above, this feature can take an argument to specify a different form of database, like *dbm*.

uucpdomain   The *uucpdomain* feature is similar to *bitdomain* above, but is used to translate addresses of the form:

```
user@host.UUCP
```

into the ! path form or routing used by UUCP. The database for this would contain, for example, key and data pairs like this:

```
host    a!b!c!host
```

Unfortunately software is not supplied to create this database, and the rule produced by this feature is not designed to work with the *pathalias* software's output.

always_add_domain

Normally, addresses that select the `local` delivery agent are left as-is. If the *always_add_domain* feature is defined, local addresses which lack a host part have an @ and the MASQUERADE_AS host appended (if it is defined). If MASQUERADE_AS is not defined, an @ and the value of $j are appended.

allmasquerade   Ordinarily, the MASQUERADE_AS host (if defined) is appended to sender addresses that lack a host part. The *allmasquerade* feature causes the recipient address to also have that host part appended. This is extremely dangerous and should be used only if the MASQUERADE_AS host has an *aliases* file that is a superset of all *aliases* files, and a *passwd* file that is a superset of all *passwd* files at your site.

nodns　　　　The V8 *sendmail* configuration files usually assume that you are using DNS to get host information. If you do not have DNS available (for example, if you are on a remote UUCP node), you must declare that fact:

```
FEATURE(nodns)
```

This tells *sendmail* to assume that DNS is not available.

nullclient　　Some sites have a number of workstations that never receive mail directly. They are usually clustered around a single mail server. Normally, all clients in a cluster like this send their mail as though the mail is from the server, and they relay all mail through that server rather than sending directly. If you have such a configuration, use:

```
FEATURE(nullclient, server)
```

Many of the other m4 options are disabled when this feature is used. It creates a minimal configuration file that does no aliasing and just forwards all mail to the server.

As a final word from Eric, "Other features should be defined, but I was trying to keep these config files fairly lean and mean."

HACK
Site-dependent, transient features

Some things just can't be called features. To make this clear, they go in the *cf/hack* directory and are referenced using the HACK macro. They tend to be site-dependent.

```
HACK(cssubdomain)
```

This illustrates use of the Berkeley-dependent `cssubdomain` hack (that makes sendmail accept local names in either Berkeley.EDU or CS.Berkeley.EDU).

Another way to think of a hack is as a transient feature. Create and use HACK as a temporary solution to a temporary problem. If a solution becomes permanent, move it to the FEATURE directory and reference it there.

HELP_FILE
Location of the SMTP help file

The location of the SMTP *help* file defaults to */usr/lib/sendmail.hf.* To change the location of that file, redefine the HELP_FILE m4 macro:

```
define(`HELP_FILE', `/usr/share/lib/sendmail.hf')
```

This changes the value that is eventually assigned to the H option. Also note that HELP_FILE is usually defined in the OSTYPE file.

LOCAL_CONFIG
Insert custom configuration lines

The LOCAL_CONFIG macro allows custom configuration lines to be inserted via the *.mc* file. The inserted lines are literal and appear in the resulting configuration file just before the rules.

```
LOCAL_CONFIG
FE/usr/local/mail/visible.users
Khostmap hash /etc/hostmap.db
```

In this example, the class E has additional names read from the file *visible.users.* And the *hostmap* database is declared.

LOCAL_MAILER_FLAGS
Add to F= flags for local delivery agent

The F= flags for the `local` delivery agent are `lsDFM`. This is the minimum list of flags for this delivery agent. If you wish to *add* flags, and if they have not already been added as part of OSTYPE, you may define the additional flags like this:

```
define(`LOCAL_MAILER_FLAGS',`E')
```

This adds the new flag E to the original F=lsDFM to form F=lsDFME. All the delivery agent flags are described in Chapter 26, *Delivery Agents.*

Note that LOCAL_MAILER_FLAGS is normally defined in the OSTYPE file.

LOCAL_MAILER_PATH

Give the local delivery agent's P= a different location

The `P=` equate for the `local` delivery agent defaults to */bin/mail*. If your site requires a different program for delivery of local mail, and if the correct definition is not already part of OSTYPE, you may redefine it like this:

```
define(`LOCAL_MAILER_PATH', `/usr/sbin/mail.local')
```

Here, the new path is */usr/sbin/mail.local*.

LOCAL_NET_CONFIG

Forward non-local network stuff to SMART_HOST

One possible setup for mail is to allow hosts on the local network to deliver directly to each other, but for all other mail to be sent to a "smart host" which forwards it offsite. Commonly, such arrangements are used by sites with inhouse networks, but that have access to the outside world only through a UUCP link. For such sites you can use LOCAL_NET_CONFIG.

```
define(`SMART_HOST', suucp:uunet)
LOCAL_NET_CONFIG
R$* < @ $* .$m > $*        $#smtp $@ $2.$m $: $1 < @ $2.$m > $3
```

Here, SMART_HOST is first defined as `suucp:uunet` (send to the host *uunet* with the `suucp` delivery agent). The LOCAL_NET_CONFIG then introduces a rule which causes all names that end in your domain name ($m) to be delivered via the `smtp` delivery agent. Any other addresses fall through to be handled by the SMART_HOST rules.

SMART_HOST can be a network-connected gateway too. Just use `smtp` in place of `suucp` in the SMART_HOST definition, and the name of the gateway.

Note that LOCAL_NET_CONFIG fits into rule set 0 like this:

- Basic canonicalization (list syntax, delete local host, etc.)
- LOCAL_RULE_0
- UUCP, BITNET, etc.
- LOCAL_NET_CONFIG
- SMART_HOST
- SMTP, local, etc. delivery agents

LOCAL_RELAY

How to deliver lone user address

See DOMAIN.

LOCAL_RULE_0

Add custom rules to rule set 0

In rule set 0, after the `local` delivery agent has been selected, and before the `uucp`, `smtp`, and the like have been selected, you can insert custom delivery agents of your own. To do this, use the LOCAL_RULE_0 macro:

```
LOCAL_RULE_0
# We service lady via an mx record.
R$+ < @ lady.Berkeley.EDU >          $#uucp $@ lady $: $1
```

Here, we introduce a new delivery agent selection. The host *lady* is a UUCP host for which we accept mail via an MX record.

Note that LOCAL_RULE_0 fits into rule set 0 like this:

- Basic canonicalization (list syntax, delete local host, etc.)
- LOCAL_RULE_0
- UUCP, BITNET, etc.
- LOCAL_NET_CONFIG
- SMART_HOST
- SMTP, local, etc. delivery agents

LOCAL_RULE_1 and LOCAL_RULE_2

Create rule sets 1 and 2

Rule sets 1 and 2 are normally empty and not included in the configuration file created from your *.m4* file. Rule set 1 processes all sender addresses, and rule set 2 processes all recipient addresses. These m4 macros are used just like LOCAL_RULE_0 above, but they introduce rules that would otherwise be omitted, rather than adding rules to an existing rule set.

LOCAL_RULE_3
Customize rule set 3

All addresses are first rewritten by rule set 3. For complex configuration needs, you can define special rules and cause them to be added to rule set 3. New rules are added to the end of rule set 3 by way of rule set 6. That is, each final decision in rule set 3 (denoted by a $@ in the RHS) calls rule set 6 (with $>6) before returning.

The m4 macro LOCAL_RULE_3 is used to introduce new rules that can be used in canonicalizing the hostnames. Note that any modifications made here are reflected in the header.

One suggested use for LOCAL_RULE_3 is to convert old UUCP hostnames into domain addresses using the UUCPSMTP macro. For example:

```
LOCAL_RULE_3
UUCPSMTP(decvax,    decvax.dec.com)
UUCPSMTP(research, research.att.com)
```

This causes the following address transformations:

| decvax!user | *becomes* → | user@decvax.dec.com |
| research!user | *becomes* → | user@research.att.com |

Another suggested use for LOCAL_RULE_3 is to introduce a new rule to look up hostnames in a locally-customized database:

```
LOCAL_RULE_3
R$*<@$+>$*       $:$1<@ $(hostmap $2 $) >$3
```

The declaration and definition of local database maps should appear in the LOCAL_CONFIG section described above.

LOCAL_USER
Don't forward off local machine

Some unqualified (without an *@host* part) usernames need to be delivered on the local machine even if LOCAL_RELAY (see above) is defined. The user *root* is one such example. By remaining local, aliasing is allowed to take place.

The LOCAL_USER m4 macro is used to add additional usernames to the list of local users. Note that *root* is always a member of that list.

```
LOCAL_USER(operator)
```

This causes the name *operator* to be appended to the list of local users. That list is stored in the class $=L. The disposition of local usernames that include the name of the local host is determined by the *notsticky* feature described under FEATURE, above.

MAILER
Support for a delivery agent

Delivery agents are not automatically declared. Instead, you need to specify which ones you want support included for, and which ones to ignore. Support is included by using the MAILER m4 macro:

```
MAILER(`local')
```

This causes support for both the `local` and `prog` delivery agents to be included. Other delivery agents that are recognized are: `fax`, `smtp` (which includes `esmtp` and `relay`), `usenet`, and `uucp` (which includes `suucp` and `uucp_dom` if `smtp` is defined).

New delivery agents can be created by devising a new m4 file in *cf/mailers*. The MAILER m4 macro performs its inclusion by reading a file with the delivery agent name *.m4* from that directory.

MAIL_HUB
All local delivery on a central server

One scheme for handling mail is to maintain one mail spool directory centrally and to mount that directory remotely on all clients. To avoid file locking problems, delivery to such a spool should be performed only on the central server. The MAIL_HUB macro allows you to specify that all local mail be forwarded to the central server for delivery. The point is to let unqualified names be forwarded through a machine with a large *aliases* file.

It is defined like this:

```
define(`MAIL_HUB', agent:server)
```

The *agent:* is optional. If absent, it defaults to the `smtp` delivery agent. If present, the delivery agent (*agent*) and the colon are required. The *server* is the name of the host on which the spool directory is locally mounted.

If you define both LOCAL_RELAY and MAIL_HUB, unqualified names and names in class L are sent to the LOCAL_RELAY and other local names are sent to MAIL_HUB. To illustrate, consider the result of various combinations for the user *you* on the machine *here.our.site*.

If LOCAL_RELAY is defined as *relay.our.site* and MAIL_HUB is not defined, mail addressed to *you* is forwarded to *relay.our.site*, but mail addressed to *you@here.our.site* is delivered locally.

If MAIL_HUB is defined as *hub.our.site* and LOCAL_RELAY is not defined, mail addressed to *you* and mail addressed to *you@here.our.site* is forwarded to *hub.our.site* for delivery.

If both LOCAL_RELAY and MAIL_HUB are defined as above, mail addressed to *you* is sent to *hub.our.site* for delivery, and mail addressed to *you@here.our.site* is forwarded to *relay.our.site*.

MASQUERADE_AS
Workstation to masquerade as server

At sites with one central mail server (see MAIL_HUB), it can be advantageous for mail from the clients to appear as though it is from the hub. This simplifies mail administration in that all users have the same machine address no matter which workstations they use. You can cause a workstation to masquerade as the server (or as another host) by using the MASQUERADE_AS m4 macro:

```
MASQUERADE_AS(server)
```

This causes outgoing mail to be labelled as coming from the *server* (rather than from the value in $j). The new label is in all but the `Received:` and `Message-ID:` headers.

Some users (such as *root*) should never be masqueraded because one always needs to know their machine of origin. Such users are declared using the EXPOSED_USER m4 macro. Note that *root* is always exposed.

OLDSENDMAIL
Make a cf file for a pre-V8 version of sendmail

The m4 macros included here can be used to create a configuration file that may work with an earlier version of *sendmail*. As of this writing, such configuration files remain untested and may not work.

OSTYPE
Include operating system-specific support

Support for various operating systems is supplied with the OSTYPE m4 macro. The available support is supplied by files in the *bsd/cf/ostype* directory. A listing of those files looks something like this:

```
aix3.m4        hpux.m4      nextstep.m4    solaris2.m4   svr4.m4
bsd4.3.m4      irix.m4      osf1.m4        sunos3.5.m4   ultrix4.1.m4
bsd4.4.m4      linux.m4     riscos4.5.m4   sunos4.1.m4
```

To include support, select the file that best describes your operating system, delete the *.m4* suffix from its name, and include the resulting name in an OSTYPE declaration:

```
OSTYPE(ultrix4.1)
```

Here, support for the DEC Ultrix operating system is defined. Note that some of these are not entirely accurate. For example, `ultrix4.1.m4` includes support for Ultrix versions 4.2 and 4.3, and `sunos4.1.m4` includes support for SunOS versions 4.1.2 and 4.1.3.

QUEUE_DIR
Location of the queue directory

The location of the *sendmail* queue directory defaults to */var/spool/mqueue*. To change the location of that directory, redefine the QUEUE_DIR m4 macro:

```
define(`QUEUE_DIR', `/usr/spool/mqueue')
```

This changes the value that is eventually assigned to the Q option. Also note that QUEUE_DIR is normally declared in the OSTYPE file.

SITECONFIG
Maintain lists of local UUCP connections

The SITECONFIG macro is useful for maintaining lists of UUCP connections. There are two types of connections: those connected to the local host and those connected to another host. The first type is declared with SITECON-FIG like this:

```
SITECONFIG(`file', `host', `class')
```

Here, *file* is the name of a file (without the *.m4* suffix) that is in the directory *bsd/cf/siteconfig*. That file contains a list of SITE declarations (described soon). The *host* is the UUCP node name of the local host. The *class* is the name (one letter) of a class that holds the list of UUCP connections. For example:

```
SITECONFIG(`uucp.arpa',`arpa',`U')
```

Here, the file *bsd/cf/siteconfig/uucp.arpa.m4* contains a list of UUCP hosts directly connected to the machine `arpa`. This declaration would be used only for the machine `arpa`. The list of UUCP hosts is added to the class macro U.

A second form of the SITECONFIG m4 macro is the one used by hosts other than the one with the direct uucp connections. It is just like the above one, but with the full canonical name of the *host*:

```
SITECONFIG(`uucp.arpa',`arpa.Berkeley.EDU',`U')
```

This also reads the file *uucp.arpa.m4*, but instead of causing UUCP connections to be made locally, it forwards them to the host *arpa.Berkeley.EDU*. In all forms of SITECONFIG, the U is literal. Other macros that may be appropriate are V, W, X, and Y.

UUCP connections are declared inside the SITECONFIG file with the SITE macro. That macro just takes a list of one or more names.

```
SITE(lady)
SITE(sonya grimble)
```

Note that SITECONFIG won't work if you disable UUCP with the *nouucp* feature.

SMART_HOST
Where to send non-locally deliverable mail

Some sites can deliver local mail to the local network, but cannot look up hosts on the Internet with DNS. Usually such sites are connected to the outside world with UUCP. To ensure delivery of all mail, such sites need to forward all non-local mail over the UUCP link to a *smart* (or well-connected) host.

You can enable this behavior by defining SMART_HOST. The definition of SMART_HOST looks like this:

```
define(`SMART_HOST', agent:host)
```

Here, *agent* is the name of the delivery agent to use to send the mail to the smart host. And *host* is the host to send the mail to. If *agent* is omitted, it defaults to `uucp`.

Note that SMART_HOST fits into rule set 0 like this:

- Basic canonicalization (list syntax, delete local host, etc.)
- LOCAL_RULE_0
- UUCP, BITNET, etc.
- LOCAL_NET_CONFIG
- SMART_HOST
- SMTP, local, etc. delivery agents

STATUS_FILE
Define location of the status file

The location of the status file is defined by the S option. The STATUS_FILE m4 macro provides a convenient way to change that location from its default of */etc/sendmail.st* to a location of your choosing:

```
define(`STATUS_FILE',`/etc/mail/sendmail.st')
```

Note that STATUS_FILE is usually defined in the OSTYPE file.

USENET_
Include support for USENET news via mail

V8 *sendmail* includes configuration support that allows users to submit USENET news articles via e-mail. Submitted articles are addressed to:

news.group.USENET

Here, *news.group* is the USENET news group name (like *comp.mail.send-mail*) and .USENET is literal.

Support for news posting is enabled by first declaring the location of the program that performs the posting (if it differs from the default of */usr/lib/news/inews*:

```
define(`USENET_MAILER_PATH',`/usr/local/lib/news/inews')
```

Second, either accept or change the delivery agent flags. The default is F=rlsDFMmn:

```
define(`USENET_MAILER_FLAGS',`rlsDFMmnb')
```

Note that the new list of flags replaces the old list.

Then, specify the command-line arguments that are given to the USENET_MAILER_PATH program. The default arguments are: -m -h -n:

```
define(`USENET_MAILER_ARGS', `-o "Ajax Corp" -m -h -n')
```

Note that the new list of command-line switches replaces the old list.

Finally, you can include support for the usenet delivery agent:

```
MAILER(`usenet')
```

This needs to be done last, because the previous USENET_ definitions are used at the moment the MAILER m4 macro for usenet is executed.

Note that USENET is normally declared in the OSTYPE file.

UUCP_RELAY
Deliver versus forward UUCP mail

See DOMAIN.

UUCPSMTP
Individual host UUCP to network address translations

If your site has hosts which used to be UUCP sites, but which are now on the network, you may intercept and rewrite the old address into the new network address. For example, mail to the machine *wash* used to be addressed as *wash!user*. Now, however, *wash* is on the network and the mail should be addressed as *user@wash.dc.gov*.

The UUCPSMTP m4 macro provides the means to specify a UUCP to network translation for specific hosts. The above example would be declared like this:

```
UUCPSMTP(`wash', `wash.dc.gov')
```

The UUCPSMTP m4 macro should be used only under LOCAL_RULE_3 described earlier.

VERSIONID
Identification in the resulting cf file

The VERSIONID m4 macro is used to insert an identifier into each *.mc* and *.m4* file that becomes a part of your final *.cf* file. Each of the files supplied with *sendmail* already has such an identifier. You should include a similar identifier in each of your *.mc* files.

    VERSIONID(` $Revision: 1.15 $')

Here, the VERSIONID macro is being used to insert an RCS-style revision number. The *$Revision: 1.15 $* becomes an actual version number when the file is checked in with *ci*(1). Any arbitrary text may appear between the half quote pairs. You may use RCS, or SCCS, or any other kind of revision identification system. The text may not contain a newline because the text appears in the *.cf* file as a comment:

    ##### $Revision: 1.15 $ #####

Use of VERSIONID and revision control in general is recommended.

IDA m4
Configuration

IDA *sendmail* includes a process that allows you to easily create a custom *sendmail.cf* configuration file that is perfect for your site. In the directory *ida/cf* you will find the following:

Sendmail.mc

> This is the master file from which your custom configuration file is built. You should not edit this file. Instead, you should create your own *m4* file (see below) and *make*(1) it. The *Sendmail.mc* file contains many comments, and should be examined to better understand the options we explain in this appendix.

Makefile

> This file is used to create your configuration file. The one in *ida/cf* should not be edited. The information in it is configured by the top level *Makefile*.

M4   This directory contains an assortment of pre-configured *m4* files. You may either copy one of those, or create your own from scratch.

First, copy one of the preconfigured *m4* files from the *M4* directory, and call it something like *yoursite.m4*. The *yoursite* is the name of your site, or your machine. The *.m4* is literal and the filename must end in those characters.

Second, edit that file and modify it to suit your needs. The balance of this appendix describes the options you need and how best to tune them. You then type the following:

```
% make yoursite.cf
```

The yoursite is the same as the *yoursite* you used for the *m4* file above. This command creates a file named *yoursite.cf* from *yoursite.m4*, which can be installed as your configuration file. See the IDA documentation for further information about this process, and how to automate installation of the new configuration file.

LIBDIR

In the directory above the *cf* directory is the master *Makefile* for building IDA *sendmail*. In that file is the definition for LIBDIR. As distributed, the value for LIBDIR is */usr/lib/mail.* This value is carried into the *yoursite.m4* when your configuration file is made. LIBDIR is the default directory for the aliases database, and for several other sendmail files.

Database Files

Chapter 29, *Database Macros*, describes how to create and manage IDA database files. Here we limit our discussion to the roles of the predefined databases you can use in your *m4* file.

MAILERTABLE

The MAILERTABLE defines a *dbm* database file which contains special treatment information for a specific domain or a specific family of domains. Most users of IDA sendmail quickly find a use for MAILERTABLE. MAILERTABLE is particularly useful for hosts which provide MX-gateway service for UUCP neighbors not directly on Internet. At the more mundane level, it helps avoid the need to write specialized rules for each new addressing problem that arises.

The key is a fully- (or partially-) qualified domain. (A partially-qualified domain is one that begins with a dot.) The value is a delivery agent name, a comma, and a hostname.

For example, the following key/value pair from MAILERTABLE causes all mail for the domain *foo.bar.com* to be delivered via the UUCP delivery agent to the neighbor host *foobar.*

```
foo.bar.com      UUCP-A,foobar
     ↑                ↑
   key             value
```

Whereas the following causes any mail message intended for *any* host in the domain *.bar.com* to be delivered via the UUXP-A delivery agent to the host *foobar.*

```
.bar.com         UUCP-A,foobar
     ↑                ↑
   key             value
```

As a final example, the following key/value pair causes mail to any address that ends in *.bitnet* to be delivered using the TCP delivery agent to the host *cunyvm.cuny.edu* (note that hostnames are case-insensitive).

```
.bitnet          TCP,CUNYVM.CUNY.EDU
     ↑                ↑
   key             value
```

The declaration of MAILERTABLE in your *m4* file looks like this:

```
define(MAILERTABLE, LIBDIR/mailertable)
```

Here, LIBDIR is is literal and is the macro defined in *../Makefile* (see above). The `mailertable` is the name of the MAILERTABLE file in that directory. Other directories and filenames may be used.

PATHTABLE

PATHTABLE defines a file that allows mail to be addressed to any UUCP host listed in the UUCP maps. It can also be used to provide special routing to handle unusual problems. It is usually built with the *pathalias*(1) program (not included in the IDA distribution, but available from many FTP archives).

The declaration of PATHTABLE in your *m4* file looks like this:

```
define(PATHTABLE, LIBDIR/pathtable)
```

This option is particularly useful for major gateway hosts and for hosts which wish to be able to reply to addresses of the form *user@node.uucp* often seen in USENET news postings.

DOMAINTABLE

The domain table deals mostly with special domain qualification problems. It is consulted after a DNS lookup. When the canonical hostname of an address is found, it is looked up in the file defined by DOMAINTABLE, and if found, the hostname is replaced by the corresponding value from that file. For example, if DOMAINTABLE were defined like this:

```
define(DOMAINTABLE, LIBDIR/domaintable
```

and if the file *domaintable* contained this line (with the value on the left and the key on the right):

```
math.niu.edu     math
      ↑            ↑
    value         key
```

this would allow the shorthand address *math* to be specified by users in place of the address *math.niu.edu.*

Most IDA users don't need DOMAINTABLE, but it can provide convenience when a few shorthand names are used locally. It is also useful if your domain name changes. For example:

```
foo.bar.com     bar.com
     ↑             ↑
   value          key
```

This would cause the former domain name of *bar.com* to be rewritten into the new domain name of *foo.bar.com.*

GENERICFROM

This map allows rewriting of local addresses. For example the entry:

```
John.Q.Citizen@company.com    jqc
         ↑                     ↑
       value                  key
```

ensures that the local user *jqc* has his address on outbound mail rewritten to *John.Q.Citizen@company.com*. This map is often generated from an *xaliases* file, so that generic names and aliases can be combined in a single database. A corresponding *xaliases* entry would be:

```
John.Q.Citizen@company.com:    <>jqc
         ↑                       ↑
       value                    key
```

which indicates that on incoming mail, *John.Q.Citizen@company.com* is to be aliased to local user *jqc*, while on outbound mail, the return address is listed as *John.Q.Citizen@company.com.*

The GENERICFROM map is particularly useful when it is desired that all mail be addressed from the main organization name, rather than individual computers within that domain. For example, the *xaliases* entry:

```
John.Q.Citizen@company.com:    <>jqc@foo.company.com,
                               <jqc@bar.company.com
          ↑                              ↑
        value                          keys
```

would result in outbound mail from either *bar.company.com* or *foo.company.com* to be rewritten in the generic format, and incoming mail for *John.Q.Citizen@company.com* to be forwarded to *jqc@foo.company.com*.

UUCPXTABLE

This map can be used for a UUCP host with an Internet hostname. Mail sent by the UUCP mailer has the hostname mapped back to the UUCP name. It is mainly for UUCP neighbors which are incapable of properly handling internet hostnames.

Miscellaneous

The remainder of the *m4* definitions are presented in alphabetical order.

ALIASES

Define the location of the *aliases* file and its database files.

```
define(ALIASES, /etc/aliases)
```

The default location is LIBDIR.

ALWAYSADDDOMAIN

Ordinarily, local usernames without a domain part are left as-is in headers. If you prefer to have the local domain appended to all such addresses, you may define ALWAYSADDDOMAIN:

```
define(ALWAYSADDDOMAIN)
```

This affects only the `local` delivery agent.

BANGIMPLIESUUCP

BANGIMPLIESUUCP is intended for those rare times when a single hostname exists in both your local domain (such as *host.your.domain*) and as a UUCP connection (*host.UUCP*).

Ordinarily, for an address of the form *host!user*, the *host* is looked up with DNS and assumed to be a UUCP node only if that lookup fails. (This latter assumption happens only if you support UUCP.)

By defining BANGIMPLIESUUCP, you are telling *sendmail* to assume instead that, in the expression *host!user*, the *host* is a UUCP node. This means that *host* is not looked up with DNS, but is instead converted to *host.UUCP*. This is done in a manner which internally remembers that the ! was originally in the address.

BANGONLYUUCP

Without BANGONLYUUCP, when mail arrives with an address of the form *user@host* (where *host* is not a fully-qualified domain name), there is always an attempt to fully qualify it locally as *host.your.domain*. If that fails, and if you have a method of sending to an address of the form *user@node.UUCP* (where *host* is either a local UUCP connection or there is a MAILERTABLE or PATHTABLE entry for it), the address is changed to *user@host.UUCP*. But if BANGONLYUUCP is defined, the address is not changed.

Note that mail received via SMTP instead has the address *user@host* changed to *user%host@sending.domain* in the message header. This is independent of any setting of BANGONLYUUCP.

DECNETNAME

DECNETNAME defines the DECNET name of the local host if MAIL11V3 is also defined.

```
define(DECNETNAME, vax4)
```

DEFAULT_HOST

Ordinarily, the value assigned to $w is the result of a call to *gethostname*(2). On some systems, the name returned is not correct or not canonical. To specify a canonical name for $w, you may define DEFAULT_HOST:

```
define(DEFAULT_HOST, here.us.edu)
```

FORCE_NAMED

If defined, sets the I option to enable DNS lookups.

```
define(FORCE_NAMED)
```

HIDDENNET and HIDDENNETHOST

These are used to hide the hostnames of local hosts. For example:

```
define(HIDDENNET, donald.bar.com mickey.foo.bar.com)
define(HIDDENNETHOST, mail.bar.com)
```

These cause an address such as *user@donald.bar.com* to be rewritten as *user@mail.bar.com*. If not defined, HIDDENNETHOST defaults to the hostname of the current host (running sendmail).

To deal with a common special case where, for example, *user@anyhost.math.edu* should be written as *user@math.edu*, you can define:

```
define(HIDDENDOMAIN, math.edu)
```

These hiding options affect only the sender and recipient address in headers. They do not change the actual recipient address on the envelope. Thus it is still possible to alias a specific user address to an address on one of the hidden machines.

ISOLATED_DOMAINS

ISOLATED_DOMAINS is mostly for domains where all outbound mail must go through a gateway host. Thus, for example:

```
define(ISOLATED_DOMAINS, foobar.com)
```

would inform the *sendmail* program that addresses of the form *user@anyhost.foobar.com* can be delivered directly and all other mail must be forwarded to a relay machine (see RELAY_HOST below).

MAILNAME

Ordinarily, outgoing mail is addressed as coming from the local machine. MAILNAME allows you to replace the local machine name with another:

```
define(MAILNAME, us.edu)
```

This causes outgoing mail addressed with just a lone hostname, like *user@here*, to have the host part replaced with *us.edu*. If you wish to hide hostnames that are explicitly specified (have a domain part), you should also use HIDDENNET. When MAILNAME is defined, it becomes the default value for HIDDENNETHOST.

MAILSERVER

This option is used when all local mail should be sent to a central server. It is useful when the mail spool is shared over NFS. External mail is still sent out directly, but local mail is forwarded to the MAILSERVER host for local delivery.

PSEUDODOMAINS

Top-level pseudodomain names such as BITNET and UUCP should be defined by PSEUDODOMAINS to reduce spurious DNS lookups. It is a short-hand way of declaring class P. A typical declaration would look like this:

```
define(PSEUDODOMAINS, `BITNET CSNET UUCP')
```

PSEUDONYMS

PSEUDONYMS is used to add names to the class $=w. That class contains a list of all hostnames which should be considered equivalent to the local hostname. For example:

```
define(PSEUDONYMS, `printer1-server gopher-host mailhost')
```

RELAY_HOST and RELAY_MAILER

These define the host and delivery agent to use for mail which cannot otherwise be delivered. For example:

```
define(RELAY_HOST, foobar.com)
define(RELAY_MAILER, TCP)
```

These are not normally used on hosts directly connected to Internet hosts. They are useful for a domain which is behind a UUCP link, or behind a firewall.

UUCPNAME

UUCPNAME is used to set your host's UUCP nodename in the event that *sendmail* couldn't figure it out for itself (or to override that name).

```
define(UUCPNAME, foo)
```

This causes the name *foo* to be appended to the classes $=k and $=U, and the name *foo.UUCP* to be appended to the class $=w.

UUCPNODES

UUCPNODES is used to list the hostnames of all directly connected UUCP neighbors. Normally, this information is gathered from the output of the *uuname*(1) program.

```
define(UUCPNODES, `|/usr/bin/uuname')
```

The names are appended to the class $=U and used to determine the UUCP delivery agent.

VALIDATION_DOMAINS

VALIDATION_DOMAINS is used to reduce the number of DNS lookups. For hosts with considerable traffic, it can speed processing.

It is essential that all local addresses be looked up with $ [and $], to ensure that any aliases (CNAMES) are properly handled. By defining VALIDATION_DOMAINS to be the major local domain, you can eliminate the $ [$] lookup of non-local addresses. This m4 definition may cause mail to go out with CNAME aliases if your users specify such names in their addresses. Strictly speaking, this violates RFC1123, but it usually does no harm.

Bibliography

Requests for Comments

We have listed the RFCs that pertain to *sendmail* in reverse numeric order with the most recent documents cited first. To learn more about obtaining RFCs, see *The Whole Internet User's Guide & Catalog* from O'Reilly & Associates, Inc.

> Requests for Comments (RFCs) are the documents that define the Internet. They talk about how it works, how to use it, and where it is going. There are over 1200 RFCs. An index is in file *rfc-index.txt*. Some RFCs are distributed in text, and some in postscript. The text documents have names of the form *rfcnnnn.txt*. Postscript RFCs are in files named *rfcnnnn.ps*. In either case *nnnn* is the number of the RFC you want. Many computers only archive partial sets.
>
> -----
>
> Ed Krol, *The Whole Internet User's Guide & Catalog*,
> O'Reilly & Associates, Inc.

RFC1345   *Character mnemonics and character sets*
           K. Simonsen, June 1992, 103 pp.

RFC1344   *Implications of MIME for Internet mail gateways*
           N. Borenstein, June 1992, 8 pp.

RFC1343   *User agent configuration mechanism for multimedia mail format information*
           N. Borenstein, June 1992, 10 pp.

RFC1342   *Representation of non-ASCII text in Internet message headers*
K. Moore, June 1992, 7 pp.

RFC1341   *MIME (Multipurpose Internet Mail Extensions): Mechanisms for specifying and describing the format of Internet message bodies*
N. Borenstein and N. Freed, June 1992, 69 pp.

RFC1328   *X.400 1988 to 1984 downgrading*
S.E. Hardcastle-Kille, May 1992, 5 pp.

RFC1327   *Mapping between X.400(1988)/ISO 10021 and RFC 822*
S.E. Hardcastle-Kille, May 1992, 113 pp. (Obsoletes RFC1148, RFC1138, RFC1026, RFC987; Updates RF C822)

RFC1321   *MD5 Message-Digest algorithm*
R.L. Rivest, April 1992, 21 pp.

RFC1320   *MD4 Message-Digest algorithm*
R.L. Rivest, April 1992, 20 pp. (Obsoletes RFC 1186)

RFC1319   *MD2 Message-Digest algorithm*
B.S. Kaliski, April 1992, 17 pp. (Updates RFC1115)

RFC1186   *MD4 message digest algorithm*
R.L. Rivest, October 1990, 18 pp. (Obsoleted by RFC 1320)

RFC1176   *Interactive Mail Access Protocol: Version 2*
M.R. Crispin, August 1990, 30 pp. (Obsoletes RFC 1064)

RFC1154   *Encoding header field for internet messages*
D. Robinson, R. Ullmann, April 1990, 7 pp.

RFC1153   *Digest message format*
F.J. Wancho, April 1990, 4pp.

RFC1148   *Mapping between X.400(1988)/ISO 10021 and RFC 822*
S.E. Kille, March 1990, 94 pp. (Obsoleted by RFC1327; updates RFC1138)

RFC1138   *Mapping between X.400(1988)/ISO 10021 and RFC 822*
S.E. Kille, December 1989, 92 pp. (Obsoleted by RFC1327; updates RFC1026; Updated by RFC1148)

RFC1137   *Mapping between full RFC 822 and RFC 822 with restricted encoding*
S.E. Kille, December 1989, 3 pp. (Updates RFC976)

RFC1123   *Requirements for Internet hosts—application and support*
R.T. Braden, ed., October 1989, 98 pp.

RFC1122   *Requirements for Internet hosts—communication layers*
R.T. Braden, ed; October 1989; 116 pp.

RFC1115   *Privacy enhancement for Internet electronic mail: Part III—
algorithms, modes, and identifiers [Draft]*
J. Linn, August 1989, 8pp. (Updated by RFC1319)

RFC1114   *Privacy enhancement for Internet electronic mail: Part I: Message encipherment and authentication procedures*
J. Linn, January 1988, 29 pp. (Obsoletes RFC989; Obsoleted
by RFC1113)

RFC1114   *Privacy enhancement for Internet electronic mail: Part
II—certificate-based key management [Draft]*
S.T. Kent and J. Linn, August 1989, 25 pp.

RFC1113   *Privacy enhancement for Internet electronic mail: Part I -
message encipherment and authentication procedures [Draft]*
J. Linn, August 1989, 34 pp. (Obsoletes RFC989, RFC1040)

RFC1036   *Standard for interchange of USENET messages*
M.R. Horton and R. Adams, December 1987, 19 pp. (Obsoletes RFC850)

RFC989   *Privacy enhancement for Internet electronic mail: Part I:
Message encipherment and authentication procedures*
J. Linn, February 1987, 23 pp. (Obsoleted by RFC1040 and
RFC1113)

RFC976   *UUCP mail interchange format standard*
M.R. Horton, February 1986, 12 pp.

RFC850   *Standard for interchange of USENET messages*
M.R. Horton, June 1983, 18 pp. (Obsoleted by RFC1036)

RFC822   *Standard for the format of ARPA Internet text messages*
D. Crocker; August 13, 1982; 47 pp. (Obsoletes RFC733;
updated by RFC1327.)

RFC821   *Simple Mail Transfer Protocol*
J.B. Postel, August 1982, 58 pp. (Obsoletes RFC788)

RFC805   *Computer mail meeting notes*
J.B. Postel; February 8, 1982; 6pp.

RFC773   *Comments on NCP/TCP mail service transition strategy*
V.G. Cerf, October 1980, 11 pp.

RFC771   *Mail transition plan*
V.G. Cerf and J.B. Postel, September 1980, 9 pp.

RFC733   *Standard for the format of ARPA network text messages*
D. Crocker, J. Vittal, K.T. Pogran, and D.A. Henderson;
November 21, 1977; 38 pp. (Obsoletes RFC724; obsoleted by
RFC822)

RFC724   *Proposed official standard for the format of ARPA Network messages*
D. Crocker, K.T. Pogran, J. Vittal, and D.A. Henderson; May 12, 1977; 33 pp. (Obsoleted by RFC733)

RFC720   *Address specification syntax for network mail*
D. Crocker; August 5, 1976; 4 pp.

J.B. Postel; February 8, 1982; 6 pp.

RFC751   *Survey of FTP mail and MLFL*
P.D. Lebling; December 10,1978; 5 pp.

RFC706   *On the junk mail problem*
J.B. Postel; November 8; 1975; 1 p.

RFC788   *Simple Mail Transfer Protocol*
J.B. Postel, November 1981, 62 pp. (Obsoletes RFC780; obsoleted by RFC821)

RFC934   *Proposed standard for message encapsulation*
M.T. Rose and E.A. Stefferud, January 1985, 10 pp.

RFC786   *Mail Transfer Protocol: ISI TOPS20 MTP-NIMAIL interface*
S. Sluizer and J.B. Postel, July 1981, 2 pp.

RFC785   *Mail Transfer Protocol: ISI TOPS20 file definitions*
S. Sluizer and J.B. Postel, July 1981, 3 pp.

RFC784   *Mail Transfer Protocol: ISI TOPS20 implementation*
S. Sluizer and J.B. Postel, July 1981, 3 pp.

RFC772   *Mail Transfer Protocol*
S. Sluizer and J.B. Postel, September 1980, 31 pp. (Obsoleted by RFC780)

RFC780   *Mail Transfer Protocol*
S. Sluizer and J.B. Postel, May 1981, 43 pp. (Obsoletes RFC772; Obsoleted by RFC788)

Publications and Postings

Albitz, Paul, and Cricket Liu. *DNS and BIND*. Sebastopol, CA: O'Reilly & Associates, Inc., 1992.

Allman, Eric. *Sendmail: An Internetwork Mail Router* in the BSD UNIX Documentation Set, Berkeley, CA: University of California, 1986-1993.

Allman, Eric and Miriam Amos. *Sendmail Revisited.* Portland, OR: USENIX Proceedings, Summer 1985.

Anderson, Bart, Bryan Costales, and Harry Henderson. *Unix Communications.* Carmel, Indiana: Howard W. Sams, a division of Macmillan Computer Publishing, 1991.

Cuccia, Nichlos H. *The Design and Implementation of a Multihub Electronic Mail Environment.* San Diego, CA: USENIX Proceedings—LISA V; October 3, 1991.

Darmohray, Tina M. *A sendmail.cf Scheme for a Large Network.* San Diego, CA: USENIX Proceedings—LISA V; October 3, 1991.

Frey, Donnalyn and Rick Adams. *!%@:: A Directory of Electronic Mail Addressing and Networks.* Sebastopol, CA: O'Reilly & Associates, Inc;1993.

Harrison, Helen E. *A Domain Mail System on Dissimilar Computers: Trials and Tribulations of SMTP.* Colorado Springs, CO: USENIX Proceedings—LISA IV; October 19, 1990.

Hedrick, Dr. Charles. *A brief tutorial on sendmail rules.* (A posting to the old USENET groups net.unix-wizards and net.mail. Reposted to *comp.mail.sendmail* August 7th 1992.) Rutgers University, 1985.

Hunt, Craig. *TCP/IP Network Administration.* Sebastopol, CA: O'Reilly & Associates, Inc.; 1993.

Kamens, Jonathan I. *FAQ: How to find people's E-mail addresses.* (A monthly posting to the USENET groups *comp.mail.misc,* and *news. newusers.questions.*) Cambridge, MA: Massachusetts Institute of Technology, Periodic.

Nemeth, Evi, Garth Snyder, and Scott Seebass. Chapter 15, "Mail and Berkeley Sendmail," in *Unix System Administration Handbook.* Englewood Cliffs, NJ: Prentice Hall, 1989.

Quarterman, John S. *The Matrix: Computer Networks and Conferencing Systems Worldwide.* Bedford, MA: Digital Press, 1990.

Rickert, Neil. *Address Rewriting In Sendmail.* (Posted to the USENET group *comp.mail.sendmail.*) DeKalb, IL: Northern Illinois University; Apr 29, 1991.

Stern, Hal. *Managing NFS and NIS.* Sebastopol, CA: O'Reilly & Associates, Inc.; 1991.

Index

About the Authors

Bryan Costales is System Manager at the International Computer Science Institute in Berkeley, California. He has been writing articles and books about computer software for over ten years, most notably *C from A to Z* (Prentice Hall), and *UNIX Communications* (Howard Sams). In his free time he sails San Francisco Bay in his 26-foot sloop, goes camping with his Land Rover, and walks his dog Zypher. He is an avid movie viewer, reads tons of science fiction, and plays chess and volleyball.

Eric Allman is the Lead Programmer on the Mammoth Project at the University of California at Berkeley. Originally, he was the Chief Programmer on the INGRES database management project at Berkeley and was involved early on in the UNIX effort there. He has written a number of utilities that appeared with various releases of BSD, including the *-me* macros, *tset*, *trek*, *syslog*, *vacation*, and of course, *sendmail*. Between his two stays at Berkeley, he designed database user and application interfaces at Britton Lee (later Sharebase), and contributed to the Ring Array Processor project for neural-net-based speech recognition at the International Computer Science Institute. He has co-authored the "C Advisor" column for *UNIX Review* for several years and is a member of the Board of Directors of USENIX Association. Eric has been accused of working incessantly, enjoys writing with fountain pens, and collects wines which he stashes in the cellar of the house that he shares with Kirk McKusick, his partner of 14-and-some-odd years.

Neil Rickert earned his Ph.D. at Yale in Mathematics. Currently a Professor of Computer Science at Northern Illinois University, he likes to keep contact with the practical side of computing by spending part of his time in UNIX system adminstration. He has been involved with the IDA*sendmail* project and is largely responsible for the current version of the IDA configuration.

Colophon

Our look is the result of reader comments, our own experimentation, and feedback from distribution channels.

Distinctive covers complement our distinctive approach to technical topics, breathing personality and life into potentially dry subjects. UNIX and its attendant programs can be unruly beasts. Nutshell Handbooks help you tame them.

The animal featured on the cover of *sendmail* is the flying fox, a species of fruit bat found chiefly on the islands of the Malay-Indonesia archipelago. Of about four thousand species of mammals, nearly one-quarter are bats; and of these, 160 are fruit bats. Sixty of the larger fruit bats make up the flying foxes, the largest having a wingspan of five feet. While smaller insect-eating bats navigate by echolocation, fruit bats depend on a keen sense of sight and smell to perceive their environment. They roost in trees by day, sometimes in extremely large numbers called "camps." They hang from branches by one or both feet, wrap themselves in their wings, and sleep the day away. On hot days, these bats keep cool by fanning themselves with their wings.

Greatly elongated fingers form the main support for the web of skin that has allowed these mammals, alone, to master true flight. At sunset they awaken from their slumber and begin their nocturnal ramblings. A flying fox must flap its wings until it becomes horizontal to the ground before it can let go and fly away. Once airborne, they use their sensitive sense of smell to detect where flowers are blooming or fruits have ripened. Unlike most animals, fruit bats cannot generate vitamin C (a limitation shared by humans and guinea pigs); thus, it is supplied by fruit in the diet. Flying foxes can range up to forty miles for food. Once a target is located, they are faced with a difficult landing. Sometimes they will simply crash into foliage and grab at what they can; other times they may attempt to catch a branch with their hindfeet as they fly over it and then swing upside-down; some will even attempt a difficult half-roll under a branch in order to grip it in the preferred position. Once attached and hanging, they will draw the flower or fruit to their mouths with a single hind-foot, or the clawed thumbs at the top of each wing. These awkward landings often cause fights among flying foxes, especially upon their return to camp at dawn. A single bad landing can cause an entire bat-laden tree to become highly agitated, full of fighting and screaming residents.

People have eaten flying foxes for ages. Samoans, who call the flying fox *manu lagi* (animal of the heavens) use branches bound to the end of long poles to swat the winged delicacy from the sky. Aborigines in Australia build fires beneath flying fox camps—the smoke stupefies the prey—and use boomerangs to knock the creatures to the ground.

Edie Freedman designed this cover and the entire UNIX bestiary that appears on other Nutshell Handbooks. The beasts themselves are adapted from 19th-century engravings from the Dover Pictorial Archive. The cover layout was produced with Quark XPress 3.1 using the ITC Garamond font.

The inside layout was designed by Edie Freedman and implemented by Lenny Muellner in sqtroff using ITC Garamond Light and ITC Garamond Book fonts. The figures were created in Aldus Freehand 3.1 by Chris Reilley. The colophon was written by Michael Kalantarian.

SYSTEM ADMINISTRATION

Books from O'Reilly & Associates, Inc.

Summer 1995

"Good reference books make a system administrator's job much easier. However, finding useful books about system administration is a challenge, and I'm constantly on the lookout. In general, I have found that almost anything published by O'Reilly & Associates is worth having if you are interested in the topic."

—*Dinah McNutt,* UNIX Review

TCP/IP Network Administration

By Craig Hunt
1st Edition August 1992
502 pages, ISBN 0-937175-82-X

TCP/IP Network Administration is a complete guide to setting up and running a TCP/IP network for administrators of networks of systems or lone home systems that access the Internet. It starts with the fundamentals: what the protocols do and how they work, how to request a network address and a name (the forms needed are included in an appendix), and how to set up your network. Beyond basic setup, the book discusses how to configure important network applications, including sendmail, the r* commands, and some simple setups for NIS and NFS. There are also chapters on troubleshooting and security. In addition, this book covers several important packages that are available from the Net (such as *gated*).
Covers BSD and System V TCP/IP implementations.

"Whether you're putting a network together, trying to figure out why an existing one doesn't work, or wanting to understand the one you've got a little better, *TCP/IP Network Administration* is the definitive volume on the subject."
—Tom Yager, *Byte*

Networking Personal Computers with TCP/IP

By Craig Hunt
1st Edition July 1995 (est.)
450 pages (est.), ISBN 1-56592-123-2

If you're like most network administrators, you probably have several networking "islands": a TCP/IP-based network of UNIX systems (possibly connected to the Internet), plus a separate Netware or NetBIOS network for your PCs. Perhaps even separate Netware and NetBIOS networks in different departments, or at different sites. And you've probably dreaded the task of integrating those networks into one.

If that's your situation, you need this book! When done properly, integrating PCs onto a TCP/IP-based Internet is less threatening than it seems; long term, it gives you a much more flexible and extensible network. Craig Hunt, author of the classic *TCP/IP Network Administration*, tells you how to build a maintainable network that includes your PCs. Don't delay; as Craig points out, if you don't provide a network solution for your PC users, someone else will.

Covers: DOS, Windows, Windows for Workgroups, Windows NT, and Novell Netware; Chameleon (NetManage), PC/TCP (FTP Software), LAN WorkPlace (Novell), and Super TCP; and Basic Network setup and configuration, with special attention given to email, network printing, and file sharing.

Computer Crime

By David Icove, Karl Seger & William VonStorch
1st Edition July 1995 (est.)
400 pages (est.), ISBN 1-56592-086-4

Computer crime is a growing threat. Attacks on computers, networks, and data range from terrorist threats to financial crimes to pranks. *Computer Crime: A Crimefighters Handbook* is aimed at those who need to understand, investigate, and prosecute computer crimes of all kinds.

This book discusses computer crimes, criminals, and laws, and profiles the computer criminal (using techniques developed for the FBI and other law enforcement agencies). It outlines the risks to computer systems and personnel, operational, physical, and communications measures that can be taken to prevent computer crimes. It also discusses how to plan for, investigate, and prosecute computer crimes, ranging from the supplies needed for criminal investigation, to the detection and audit tools used in investigation, to the presentation of evidence to a jury.

Contains a compendium of computer-related federal statutes, all statutes of individual states, a resource summary, and detailed papers on computer crime.

Computer Security Basics

By Deborah Russell & G.T. Gangemi Sr.
1st Edition July 1991
464 pages, ISBN 0-937175-71-4

There's a lot more consciousness of security today, but not a lot of understanding of what it means and how far it should go. This handbook describes complicated concepts, such as trusted systems, encryption, and mandatory access control, in simple terms. For example, most U.S. government equipment acquisitions now require "Orange Book" (Trusted Computer System Evaluation Criteria) certification. A lot of people have a vague feeling that they ought to know about the Orange Book, but few make the effort to track it down and read it. *Computer Security Basics* contains a more readable introduction to the Orange Book—why it exists, what it contains, and what the different security levels are all about—than any other book or government publication.

PGP: Pretty Good Privacy

By Simson Garfinkel
1st Edition December 1994
430 pages, ISBN 1-56592-098-8

PGP is a freely available encryption program that protects the privacy of files and electronic mail. It uses powerful public key cryptography and works on virtually every platform. This book is both a readable technical user's guide and a fascinating behind-the-scenes look at cryptography and privacy. It describes how to use PGP and provides background on cryptography, PGP's history, battles over public key cryptography patents and U.S. government export restrictions, and public debates about privacy and free speech.

"I even learned a few things about PGP from Simson's informative book."—Phil Zimmermann, Author of PGP

"Since the release of PGP 2.0 from Europe in the fall of 1992, PGP's popularity and usage has grown to make it the de-facto standard for email encryption. Simson's book is an excellent overview of PGP and the history of cryptography in general. It should prove a useful addition to the resource library for any computer user, from the UNIX wizard to the PC novice."
—Derek Atkins, PGP Development Team, MIT

Practical UNIX Security

By Simson Garfinkel & Gene Spafford
1st Edition June 1991
512 pages, ISBN 0-937175-72-2

Tells system administrators how to make their UNIX system—either System V or BSD—as secure as it possibly can be without going to trusted system technology. The book describes UNIX concepts and how they enforce security, tells how to defend against and handle security breaches, and explains network security (including UUCP, NFS, Kerberos, and firewall machines) in detail. If you are a UNIX system administrator or user who deals with security, you need this book.

It contains an excellent checklist of security procedures and dangerous UNIX system files, a detailed resource summary, and chapters on detecting security attacks, legal options, and viruses and worms.

Building Internet Firewalls

By D. Brent Chapman and Elizabeth D. Zwicky
1st Edition September 1995 (est.)
350 pages (est.), ISBN 1-56592-124-0

Everyone is jumping on the Internet bandwagon, despite the fact that the security risks associated with connecting to the Net have never been greater. This book is a practical guide to building firewalls on the Internet. It describes a variety of firewall approaches and architectures and discusses how you can build packet filtering and proxying solutions at your site. It also contains a full discussion of how to configure Internet services (e.g., FTP, SMTP, Telnet) to work with a firewall, as well as a complete list of resources, including the location of many publicly available firewall construction tools.

SYSTEM ADMINISTRATORS' TOOLS

Essential System Administration

By Æleen Frisch
1st Edition October 1991
466 pages, ISBN 0-937175-80-3

Like any other multi-user system, UNIX requires some care and feeding. *Essential System Administration* tells you how. This book strips away the myth and confusion surrounding this important topic and provides a compact, manageable introduction to the tasks faced by anyone responsible for a UNIX system.

If you use a stand-alone UNIX system, whether it's a PC or a workstation, you know how much you need this book: on these systems the fine line between a user and an administrator has vanished. Either you're both or you're in trouble. If you routinely provide administrative support for a larger shared system or a network of workstations, you will find this book indispensable. Even if you aren't directly responsible for system administration, you will find that understanding basic administrative functions greatly increases your ability to use UNIX effectively.

Managing Internet Information Services

By Cricket Liu, Jerry Peek, Russ Jones,
Bryan Buus & Adrian Nye
1st Edition December 1994
668 pages, ISBN 1-56592-062-7

This comprehensive guide describes how to set up information services and make them available over the Internet. It discusses why a company would want to offer Internet services, provides complete coverage of all popular services, and tells how to select which ones to provide. Most of the book describes how to set up Gopher, World Wide Web, FTP, and WAIS servers and email services.

"*Managing Internet Information Services* has long been needed in the Internet community, as well as in many organizations with IP-based networks. Although many on the Internet are quite savvy when it comes to administering these types of tools, *MIIS* will allow a much larger community to join in and perhaps provide more diverse information. This book will be a welcome addition to my Internet shelf."
—Robert H'obbes' Zakon, MITRE Corporation

sendmail

By Bryan Costales, with Eric Allman & Neil Rickert
1st Edition November 1993
830 pages, ISBN 1-56592-056-2

This Nutshell Handbook® is far and away the most comprehensive book ever written on sendmail, the program that acts like a traffic cop in routing and delivering mail on UNIX-based networks. Although sendmail is used on almost every UNIX system, it's one of the last great uncharted territories—and most difficult utilities to learn—in UNIX system administration. This book provides a complete sendmail tutorial, plus extensive reference material on every aspect of the program. It covers IDA sendmail, the latest version (V8) from Berkeley, and the standard versions available on most systems.

"The program and its rule description file, sendmail.cf, have long been regarded as the pit of coals that separated the mild UNIX system administrators from the real fire walkers. Now, sendmail syntax, testing, hidden rules, and other mysteries are revealed. Costales, Allman, and Rickert are the indisputable authorities to do the text." —Ben Smith, *Byte Magazine*

DNS and BIND

By Paul Albitz & Cricket Liu
1st Edition October 1992
418 pages, ISBN 1-56592-010-4

DNS and BIND contains all you need to know about the Internet's Domain Name System (DNS) and the Berkeley Internet Name Domain (BIND), its UNIX implementation. The Domain Name System is the Internet's "phone book"; it's a database that tracks important information (in particular, names and addresses) for every computer on the Internet. If you're a system administrator, this book will show you how to set up and maintain the DNS software on your network.

"*DNS and BIND* contains a lot of useful information that you'll never find written down anywhere else. And since it's written in a crisp style, you can pretty much use the book as your primary BIND reference."
—Marshall Rose, *ConneXions*

Managing NFS and NIS

By Hal Stern
1st Edition June 1991
436 pages, ISBN 0-937175-75-7

Managing NFS and NIS is for system administrators who need to set up or manage a network filesystem installation. NFS (Network Filesystem) is probably running at any site that has two or more UNIX systems. NIS (Network Information System) is a distributed database used to manage a network of computers. The only practical book devoted entirely to these subjects, this guide is a "must-have" for anyone interested in UNIX networking.

System Performance Tuning

By Mike Loukides
1st Edition November 1990
336 pages, ISBN 0-937175-60-9

System Performance Tuning answers the fundamental question: How can I get my computer to do more work without buying more hardware? Some performance problems do require you to buy a bigger or faster computer, but many can be solved simply by making better use of the resources you already have.

Linux Network Administrator's Guide

By Olaf Kirch
1st Edition January 1995
370 pages, ISBN 1-56592-087-2

A UNIX-compatible operating system that runs on personal computers, Linux is a pinnacle within the free software movement. It is based on a kernel developed by Finnish student Linus Torvalds and is distributed on the Net or on low-cost disks, along with a complete set of UNIX libraries, popular free software utilities, and traditional layered products like NFS and the X Window System.

Networking is a fundamental part of Linux. Whether you want a simple UUCP connection or a full LAN with NFS and NIS, you are going to have to build a network.

Linux Network Administrator's Guide by Olaf Kirch is one of the most successful books to come from the Linux Documentation Project. It touches on all the essential networking software included with Linux, plus some hardware considerations. Topics include serial connections, UUCP, routing and DNS, mail and News, SLIP and PPP, NFS, and NIS.

Managing UUCP and Usenet

By Grace Todino & Tim O'Reilly
10th Edition January 1992
368 pages, ISBN 0-937175-93-5

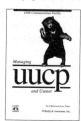

For all its widespread use, UUCP is one of the most difficult UNIX utilities to master. This book is for system administrators who want to install and manage UUCP and Usenet software.

"Don't even TRY to install UUCP without it!"—Usenet message 456@nitrex.UUCP

termcap & terminfo

By John Strang, Linda Mui & Tim O'Reilly
3rd Edition April 1988
270 pages, ISBN 0-937175-22-6

For UNIX system administrators and programmers. This handbook provides information on writing and debugging terminal descriptions, as well as terminal initialization, for the two UNIX terminal databases.

Volume 8: X Window System Administrator's Guide

By Linda Mui & Eric Pearce
1st Edition October 1992
372, pages, ISBN 0-937175-83-8

As X moves out of the hacker's domain and into the "real world," users can't be expected to master all the ins and outs of setting up and administering their own X software. That will increasingly become the domain of system administrators. Even for experienced system administrators, X raises many issues, both because of subtle changes in the standard UNIX way of doing things and because X blurs the boundaries between different platforms. Under X, users can run applications across the network on systems with different resources (including fonts, colors, and screen size.) Many of these issues are poorly understood, and the technology for dealing with them is in rapid flux.

This book is the first and only book devoted to the issues of system administration for X and X-based networks, written not just for UNIX system administrators, but for anyone faced with the job of administering X (including those running X on stand-alone workstations).

Note: The CD that used to be offered with this book is now sold separately, allowing system administrators to purchase the book and the CD-ROM in quantities they choose.

The X Companion CD for R6

By O'Reilly & Associates
1st Edition January 1995
(Includes CD-ROM plus 80-page guide)
ISBN 1-56592-084-8

The X CD-ROM contains precompiled binaries for X11, Release 6 (X11 R6) for Sun4, Solaris, HP-UX on the HP700, DEC Alpha, DEC ULTRIX, and IBM RS6000. It includes X11 R6 source code from the "core" and "contrib" directory and X11 R5 source code from the "core" directories. The CD also provides examples from O'Reilly and Associates X Window System series books and *The X Resource* journal.

The package includes a 126-page book describing the contents of the CD-ROM, how to install the R6 binaries, and how to build X11 for other platforms. The book also contains the X Consortium release notes for Release 6.

AUDIOTAPES

O'Reilly offers audiotapes based on interviews with people who are making a profound impact in the world of the Internet. Here we give you a quick overview of what's available. For details on our audiotape collection, send email to **audio@ora.com**.

"Ever listen to one of those five-minute-long news pieces being broadcast on National Public Radio's 'All Things Considered' and wish they were doing an in-depth story on new technology? Well, your wishes are answered." —BYTE, February '94

Global Network Operations

Carl Malamud interviews Brian Carpenter,
Bernhard Stockman, Mike O'Dell, & Geoff Huston
Released Spring 1994
Duration: 2 hours, ISBN 1-56592-993-4

What does it take to actually run a network? In these four interviews, Carl Malamud explores some of the technical and operational issues faced by Internet service providers around the world.

Brian Carpenter is the director for networking at CERN, the high-energy physics laboratory in Geneva, Switzerland. Physicists are some of the world's most active Internet users, and its global user base makes CERN one of the world's most network-intensive sites. Carpenter discusses how he deals with issues such as the OSI and DECnet Phase V protocols and his views on the future of the Internet.

Bernhard Stockman is one of the founders and the technical manager of the European Backbone (EBONE). EBONE has proven to be the first effective transit backbone for Europe and has been a leader in the deployment of CIDR, BGP-4, and other key technologies.

Mike O'Dell is vice president of research at UUNET Technologies. O'Dell has a long record of involvement in data communications, ranging from his service as a telco lab employee, an engineer on several key projects, and a member of the USENIX board, to now helping define new services for one of the largest commercial IP service providers.

Geoff Huston is the director of the Australian Academic Research Network (AARNET). AARNET is known as one of the most progressive regional networks, rapidly adopting new services for its users. Huston talks about how networking in Australia has flourished despite astronomically high rates for long-distance lines.

The Future of the Internet Protocol

Carl Malamud interviews Steve Deering, Bob Braden,
Christian Huitema, Bob Hinden, Peter Ford, Steve Casner,
Bernhard Stockman, & Noel Chiappa
Released Spring 1994
Duration: 4 hours, ISBN 1-56592-996-9

The explosion of interest in the Internet is stressing what was originally designed as a research and education network. The sheer number of users is requiring new strategies for Internet address allocation; multimedia applications are requiring greater bandwidth and strategies such as "resource reservation" to provide synchronous end-to-end service.

In this series of eight interviews, Carl Malamud talks to some of the researchers who are working to define how the underlying technology of the Internet will need to evolve in order to meet the demands of the next five to ten years.

Give these tapes a try if you're intrigued by such topics as Internet "multicasting" of audio and video, or think your job might one day depend on understanding some of the following buzzwords:

- IPNG (Internet Protocol Next Generation)
- SIP (Simple Internet Protocol)
- TUBA (TCP and UDP with Big Addresses)
- CLNP (Connectionless Network Protocol)
- CIDR (Classless Inter-Domain Routing)

or if you are just interested in getting to know more about the people who are shaping the future.

Mobile IP Networking

Carl Malamud interviews Phil Karn & Jun Murai
Released Spring 1994
Duration: 1 hour, ISBN 1-56592-994-2

Phil Karn is the father of the KA9Q publicly available implementation of TCP/IP for DOS (which has also been used as the basis for the software in many commercial Internet routers). KA9Q was originally developed to allow "packet radio," that is, TCP/IP over ham radio bands. Phil's current research focus is on commercial applications of wireless data communications.

Jun Murai is one of the most distinguished researchers in the Internet community. Murai is a professor at Keio University and the founder of the Japanese WIDE Internet. Murai talks about his research projects, which range from satellite-based IP multicasting to a massive testbed for mobile computing at the Fujisawa campus of Keio University.

Networked Information and Online Libraries

Carl Malamud interviews Peter Deutsch & Cliff Lynch
Released September 1993
Duration: 1 hour, ISBN 1-56592-998-5

Peter Deutsch, president of Bunyip Information Services, was one of the co-developers of Archie. In this interview Peter talks about his philosophy for services and compares Archie to X.500. He also talks about what kind of standards we need for networked information retrieval.

Cliff Lynch is currently the director of library automation for the University of California. He discusses issues behind online publishing, such as SGML and the democratization of publishing on the Internet.

European Networking

Carl Malamud interviews Glenn Kowack & Rob Blokzijl
Released September 1993
Duration: 1 hour, ISBN 1-56592-999-3

Glenn Kowack is chief executive of EUnet, the network that's bringing the Internet to the people of Europe. Glenn talks about EUnet's populist business model and the politics of European networking.

Rob Blokzijl is the network manager for NIKHEF, the Dutch Institute of High Energy Physics. Rob talks about RIPE, the IP user's group for Europe, and the nuts and bolts of European network coordination.

Security and Networks

Carl Malamud interviews Jeff Schiller & John Romkey
Released September 1993
Duration: 1 hour, ISBN 1-56592-997-7

Jeff Schiller is the manager of MIT's campus network and is one of the Internet's leading security experts. Here, he talks about Privacy Enhanced Mail (PEM), the difficulty of policing the Internet, and whether horses or computers are more useful to criminals.

John Romkey has been a long-time TCP/IP developer and was recently named to the Internet Architecture Board. In this wide-ranging interview, John talks about the famous "ToasterNet" demo at InterOp, what kind of Internet security he'd like to see put in place, and what Internet applications of the future might look like.

John Perry Barlow
Notable Speeches of the Information Age

USENIX Conference Keynote Address
San Francisco, CA; January 17, 1994
Duration: 1.5 hours, ISBN 1-56592-992-6

John Perry Barlow—retired Wyoming cattle rancher, lyricist for the Grateful Dead—holds a degree in comparative religion from Wesleyan University. He also happens to be a recognized authority on computer security, virtual reality, digitized intellectual property, and the social and legal conditions arising in the global network of computers.

In 1990, Barlow co-founded the Electronic Frontier Foundation with Mitch Kapor and currently serves as chair of its executive committee. He writes and lectures on subjects relating to digital technology and society, and is a contributing editor to *Communications of the ACM, NeXTWorld, Microtimes, Mondo 2000, Wired*, and other publications.

In his keynote address to the Winter 1994 USENIX Conference, Barlow talks of recent developments in the national information infrastructure, telecommunications regulation, cryptography, globalization of the Internet, intellectual property, and the settlement of Cyberspace. The talk explores the premise that "architecture is politics": that the technology adopted for the coming "information superhighway" will help to determine what is carried on it and that if the electronic frontier of the Internet is not to be replaced by electronic strip malls, we need to make sure that our technological choices favor bi-directional communication and open platforms.

Side A contains the keynote;
Side B contains a question and answer period.

O'Reilly & Associates—

GLOBAL NETWORK NAVIGATOR™

The Global Network Navigator (GNN)™ is a unique kind of information service that makes the Internet easy and enjoyable to use. We organize access to the vast information resources of the Internet so that you can find what you want. We also help you understand the Internet and the many ways you can explore it.

GNN HOME PAGE

Global Network Navigator
Charting the Internet

What you'll find in GNN

There are three main sections to GNN: Navigating the Net, Special GNN Publications, and Marketplace. Here's a look at just some of what's contained in GNN:

Navigating the Net

- The **WHOLE INTERNET USER'S GUIDE & CATALOG**, based on O'Reilly's bestselling book, is a collection of constantly updated links to 1000 of the best resources on the Internet, divided by subject areas.

- The **NCSA MOSAIC "WHAT'S NEW"** page is your best source for the latest Web listings.

Special GNN Publications

- **BOOK STORY**—The first Internet platform to provide an interactive forum for authors and readers to meet. Serializes books, features author interviews and chats, and allows readers to contact authors with the ease of email.

- **TRAVELERS' CENTER**—The center takes advantage of information that's been on the Internet but hasn't been distilled and compiled in an easy-to-use format—until now. You'll also read feature stories and dispatches from fellow travelers.

- **PERSONAL FINANCE CENTER**—The money management and investment forum on the Net. There are original features and columns on personal finance, too.

- **GNN SPORTS**—Net coverage of your favorite professional and college teams with interviews, schedules, and game wrap-ups.

- **EDUCATION**—Tapping into the vast educational resources available on the Net.

- **NETNEWS**—Keep up with events, trends, and developments on the Net.

- **THE DIGITAL DRIVE-IN**—Read this GNN special edition to find out what folks are doing with multimedia resources on the Net.

Marketplace

- **BUSINESS PAGES**—Here's where we've organized commercial resources on the Internet. Choose from a variety of categories like "Business Services," "Entertainment," and "Legal Financial Services."

- **GNN DIRECT**—This is the place to go to read about quality products and services in GNN's collection of catalogs. You can also order online using GNN Direct. Simply browse through product literature, do key word and text searches, and place an order at any time.

Marketing Your Company on GNN

GNN is known as the premier interactive magazine and navigational guide on the Internet. With over 170,000 total subscribers and 8 million document hits every month, GNN attracts a large, dynamic, and growing audience. Because of this, GNN offers exciting opportunities for companies interested in creating a presence on the Internet. We currently offer two programs:

- **TRAFFIC LINKS**—We can link reader traffic from GNN to your Web site. Think of this option as an online form of direct response advertising. GNN staff will work with you to tailor a program to fit your needs. For details about this program, send email to **traffic-links@gnn.com** or call 1-510-883-7220 and ask for our Traffic Link sales representative.

- **BUSINESS PAGES**—Choose from a basic listing (up to 50 words), extended listing (up to 350 words), links from your listing in GNN to your server, or a FAQ (Frequently Asked Questions) document of up to 350 words that's coupled with either a basic or extended listing. For more information, send email to **market@gnn.com** or call 1-510-883-7220.

Get Your Free Subscription to GNN Today

Come and browse GNN! A free subscription is available to anyone with access to the World Wide Web. To get complete information about subscribing, send email to **info@gnn.com** If you have access to a World Wide Web browser such as Mosaic, Lynx, or NetScape, use the following URL to register online: http://gnn.com/

If you use a browser that does not support online forms, you can retrieve an email version of the registration form automatically by sending email to **form@gnn.com** Fill this form out and send it back to us by email and we will confirm your registration.

O'Reilly on the Net—
ONLINE PROGRAM GUIDE

O'Reilly & Associates offers extensive information through various online resources. We invite you to come and explore our little neck-of-the-woods.

Online Resource Center

Most comprehensive among our online offerings is the O'Reilly Resource Center. Here, you'll find detailed information on all O'Reilly products: titles, prices, tables of contents, indexes, author bios, software contents, reviews...you can even view images of the products themselves. With GNN Direct you can now order our products directly off the Net (GNN Direct is available on the Web site only; Gopher users can still use **order@ora.com**). We supply contact information along with a list of distributors and bookstores available worldwide. In addition, we provide informative literature in the field: articles, interviews, excerpts, and bibliographies that help you stay informed and abreast.

To access ORA's Online Resource Center:

Point your Web browser (e.g., `mosaic` or `lynx`) to:

`http://www.ora.com/`

For the plaintext version, `telnet` or `gopher` to:

`gopher.ora.com`
(telnet login: `gopher`)

FTP

The example files and programs in many of our books are available electronically via FTP.

To obtain example files and programs from O'Reilly texts:

`ftp` to:
`ftp.ora.com`

or `ftp.uu.net`
`cd published/oreilly`

Ora-news

An easy way to stay informed of the latest projects and products from O'Reilly & Associates is to subscribe to "ora-news," our electronic news service. Subscribers receive email as soon as the information breaks.

To subscribe to "ora-news":

Send email to:
listproc@online.ora.com

and put the following information on the first line of your message (not in "Subject"):
subscribe ora-news "your name" **of** "your company"

For example enter:
```
mail listproc@online.ora.com
subscribe ora-news Kris Webber of
    Mighty Fine Enterprises
```

Email

Many customer services are provided via email. Here are a few of the most popular and useful.

nuts@ora.com
For general questions and information.

bookquestions@ora.com
For technical questions, or corrections, concerning book contents.

order@ora.com
To order books online and for ordering questions.

catalog@ora.com
To receive a free copy of our magazine/catalog, *ora.com.* Please include a postal address.

Snailmail and Phones

O'Reilly & Associates, Inc.
103A Morris Street, Sebastopol, CA 95472
Inquiries: **707-829-0515**, **800-998-9938**
Credit card orders: **800-889-8969**
(Weekdays 6 A.M.- 5 P.M. PST)
FAX: **707-829-0104**

O'Reilly & Associates—
LISTING OF TITLES

INTERNET

!%@:: A Directory of Electronic Mail Addressing & Networks

Connecting to the Internet: An O'Reilly Buyer's Guide

The Mosaic Handbook for Microsoft Windows

The Mosaic Handbook for the Macintosh

The Mosaic Handbook for the X Window System

Smileys

The Whole Internet User's Guide & Catalog

SOFTWARE

Internet In A Box™

WebSite™

WHAT YOU NEED TO KNOW SERIES

Using Email Effectively

Marketing on the Internet (Fall '95 est.)

When You Can't Find Your System Administrator

HEALTH, CAREER & BUSINESS

Building a Successful Software Business

The Computer User's Survival Guide (Fall '95 est.)

The Future Does Not Compute

Love Your Job!

TWI Day Calendar - 1996

AUDIOTAPES

INTERNET TALK RADIO'S "GEEK OF THE WEEK" INTERVIEWS

The Future of the Internet Protocol

Global Network Operations

Mobile IP Networking

Networked Information and Online Libraries

Security and Networks

European Networking

NOTABLE SPEECHES OF THE INFORMATION AGE

John Perry Barlow

USING UNIX

BASICS

Learning GNU Emacs

Learning the Korn Shell

Learning the UNIX Operating System

Learning the vi Editor

MH & xmh: Email for Users & Programmers

SCO UNIX in a Nutshell

The USENET Handbook

Using UUCP and Usenet

UNIX in a Nutshell: System V Edition

ADVANCED

Exploring Expect

The Frame Handbook

Learning Perl

Making TeX Work

Programming perl

Running LINUX

sed & awk

UNIX Power Tools (with CD-ROM)

SYSTEM ADMINISTRATION

Building Internet Firewalls (Fall '95 est.)

Computer Crime: A Crimefighter's Handbook (Summer '95 est.)

Computer Security Basics

DNS and BIND

Essential System Administration

Linux Network Administrator's Guide

Managing Internet Information Services

Managing NFS and NIS

Managing UUCP and Usenet

Networking Personal Computers with TCP/IP (Summer '95 est.)

Practical UNIX Security

PGP: Pretty Good Privacy

sendmail

System Performance Tuning

TCP/IP Network Administration

termcap & terminfo

Volume 8 : X Window System Administrator's Guide

The X Companion CD for R6

PROGRAMMING

Applying RCS and SCCS (Summer '95 est.)

Checking C Programs with lint

DCE Security Programming (Summer '95 est.)

Distributing Applications Across DCE and Windows NT

Encyclopedia of Graphics File Formats

Guide to Writing DCE Applications

High Performance Computing

Learning the Bash Shell (Summer '95 est.)

lex & yacc

Managing Projects with make

Microsoft RPC Programming Guide

Migrating to Fortran 90

Multi-Platform Code Management

ORACLE Performance Tuning

ORACLE PL/SQL Programming (Fall '95 est.)

Porting UNIX Software (Fall '95 est.)

POSIX Programmer's Guide

POSIX.4: Programming for the Real World

Power Programming with RPC

Practical C Programming

Practical C++ Programming (Summer '95 est.)

Programming with curses

Programming with GNU Software (Fall '95 est.)

Software Portability with imake

Understanding and Using COFF

Understanding DCE

Understanding Japanese Information Processing

UNIX for FORTRAN Programmers

Using C on the UNIX System

Using csh and tcsh (Summer '95 est.)

BERKELEY 4.4 SOFTWARE DISTRIBUTION

4.4BSD System Manager's Manual

4.4BSD User's Reference Manual

4.4BSD User's Supp. Documents

4.4BSD Programmer's Reference Manual

4.4BSD Programmer's Supplementary Documents

4.4BSD-Lite CD Companion

4.4BSD-Lite CD Companion: International Version

X WINDOW SYSTEM

Volume 0: X Protocol Reference Manual

Volume 1: Xlib Programming Manual

Volume 2: Xlib Reference Manual:

Volume 3: X Window System User's Guide

Volume. 3M: X Window System User's Guide, Motif Ed

Volume. 4: X Toolkit Intrinsics Programming Manual

Volume 4M: X Toolkit Intrinsics Programming Manual, Motif Ed.

Volume 5: X Toolkit Intrinsics Reference Manual

Volume 6A: Motif Programming Manual

Volume 6B: Motif Reference Manual

Volume 7A: XView Programming Manual

Volume 7B: XView Reference Manual

Volume 8 : X Window System Administrator's Guide

Motif Tools

PEXlib Programming Manual

PEXlib Reference Manual

PHIGS Programming Manual

PHIGS Reference Manual

Programmer's Supplement for Release 6 (Fall '95 est.)

The X Companion CD for R6

The X Window System in a Nutshell

X User Tools (with CD-ROM)

THE X RESOURCE

A QUARTERLY WORKING JOURNAL FOR X PROGRAMMERS

The X Resource: Issues 0 through 15 (Issue 15 available 7/95)

TRAVEL

Travelers' Tales France

Travelers' Tales Hong Kong (10/95 est.)

Travelers' Tales India

Travelers' Tales Mexico

Travelers' Tales Spain (11/95 est.)

Travelers' Tales Thailand

Travelers' Tales: A Woman's World

O'Reilly & Associates—
INTERNATIONAL DISTRIBUTORS

Customers outside North America can now order O'Reilly & Associates books through the following distributors. They offer our international customers faster order processing, more bookstores, increased representation at tradeshows worldwide, and the high-quality, responsive service our customers have come to expect.

EUROPE, MIDDLE EAST, AND AFRICA
(except Germany, Switzerland, and Austria)

INQUIRIES
International Thomson Publishing Europe
Berkshire House
168-173 High Holborn
London WC1V 7AA, United Kingdom
Telephone: 44-71-497-1422
Fax: 44-71-497-1426
Email: itpint@itps.co.uk

ORDERS
International Thomson Publishing Services, Ltd.
Cheriton House, North Way
Andover, Hampshire SP10 5BE, United Kingdom
Telephone: 44-264-342-832 (UK orders)
Telephone: 44-264-342-806 (outside UK)
Fax: 44-264-364418 (UK orders)
Fax: 44-264-342761 (outside UK)

GERMANY, SWITZERLAND, AND AUSTRIA
International Thomson Publishing GmbH
O'Reilly-International Thomson Verlag
Königswinterer Straße 418
53227 Bonn, Germany
Telephone: 49-228-97024 0
Fax: 49-228-441342
Email: anfragen@ora.de

ASIA *(except Japan)*
INQUIRIES
International Thomson Publishing Asia
221 Henderson Road
#08-03 Henderson Industrial Park
Singapore 0315
Telephone: 65-272-6496
Fax: 65-272-6498

ORDERS
Telephone: 65-268-7867
Fax: 65-268-6727

JAPAN
International Thomson Publishing Japan
Hirakawa-cho Kyowa Building 3F
2-2-1 Hirakawa-cho, Chiyoda-Ku
Tokyo, 102 Japan
Telephone: 81-3-3221-1428
Fax: 81-3-3237-1459

Toppan Publishing
Froebel Kan Bldg. 3-1, Kanda Ogawamachi Chiyoda-Ku
Tokyo 101 Japan
Telex: J 27317
Cable: Toppanbook, Tokyo
Telephone: 03-3295-3461
Fax: 03-3293-5963

AUSTRALIA
WoodsLane Pty. Ltd.
7/5 Vuko Place, Warriewood NSW 2102
P.O. Box 935, Mona Vale NSW 2103
Australia
Telephone: 02-970-5111
Fax: 02-970-5002
Email: woods@tmx.mhs.oz.au

NEW ZEALAND
WoodsLane New Zealand Ltd.
21 Cooks Street (P.O. Box 575)
Wanganui, New Zealand
Telephone: 64-6-347-6543
Fax: 64-6-345-4840
Email: woods@tmx.mhs.oz.au

THE AMERICAS
O'Reilly & Associates, Inc.
103A Morris Street
Sebastopol, CA 95472 U.S.A.
Telephone: 707-829-0515
Telephone: 800-998-9938 (U.S. & Canada)
Fax: 707-829-0104
Email: order@ora.com